Moosewood Restaurant Favorites

The Moosewood Restaurant Cookbook Library

Moosewood Restaurant Favorites

The 250 Most-Requested Naturally Delicious Recipes
from One of America's Best-Loved Restaurants

The Moosewood Collective

Food Photography by Jim Scherer

St. Martin's Griffin
New York

"Southern Nut Pie Eudora," on page 355, has been excerpted from *New Recipes from Moosewood Restaurant*, copyright © 1987 by Moosewood, Inc., with permission from Ten Speed Press, 999 Harrison Street, Berkeley, CA 94707.

Photographs of Moosewood Restaurant and The Moosewood Collective by Justin Zoll

www.stmartins.com

Design by Phil Mazzone

ISBN 978-1-250-00625-7 (paper over board)
ISBN 978-1-4668-3466-8 (e-book)

St. Martin's Griffin books may be purchased for educational, business, or promotional use. For information on bulk purchases, please contact Macmillan Corporate and Premium Sales Department at 1-800-221-7945 extension 5442 or write specialmarkets @macmillan.com.

First Edition: September 2013

10   9   8   7   6   5   4   3   2   1

This book is dedicated to all Moosewood cooks.

Contents

Soups 47

Sandwiches 71

Burgers 85

Main Dish Salads 95

Wraps, Rolls, and Strudels 185

Tofu 199

Pasta 211

Fish 229

Acknowledgments

The food that fills this book has been influenced by all of the people who have cooked in the Moosewood kitchen and everyone who has influenced each of them—family, friends, neighbors, cookbook authors, strangers on airplanes, cooks in other restaurants. We continue to learn from each other in a wonderfully organic way. We're grateful to all those who use our cookbooks and take the time to tell us how important our books are to them, to thank us for a particular recipe, or to tell us their favorite way to make one of our dishes.

Having Arnold and Elise Goodman as our literary agents has been wonderful for us. From our first foray into the cookbook world and straight through to today, they have been excellent advocates and constant and generous friends. With affection and gratitude we say, "Thank you, Arnold and Elise."

Michael Aman, in our first cookbook we thanked you for helping us prepare the manuscript, for your careful, discerning eye as you typed our handwritten recipes on a Smith Corona Electric Selectric, and we thank you again now for the hours you spent checking this book's recipes. You're a true friend. Sam Adler, thank you for your sense of humor and for both okaying and tempering ours. Kip Wilcox, you're a wonderful cook and you stepped up just when we really needed you. Emilio Del Plato, as our technical abilities very slowly improve, we need to call on you less, but you know we're happy you're there. Thank you all.

St. Martin's Press. On the day we first walked into the St. Martin's offices, we were anticipant, eager to see if we were a good fit for each other. At first, we were mainly excited to be in the Flatiron Building, but soon, it wouldn't have mattered where we were. What a lovely group of talented and dedicated people.

Michael Flamini, our gem of an editor. In a previous life, Michael must have been a shepherd, one who loved and cared well for each of his sheep, one with good instincts for the greenest pastures. Michael is boundless in his energy and enthusiasm, not only for our book and the path he forges for it, but best of all he is passionate about good food wherever he finds it. Bon appetit, Michael.

And thank you, Vicki Lame. You always come through for us.

For their generous support of our project, we're

grateful to Sally Richardson, Matthew Shear, and George Witte. And then there is our copyeditor, Leah Stewart, and the production people, Adriana Coada, Elizabeth Curione, Phil Mazzone, James Sinclair, Amelie Littell, Susan Joseph, and Karen Gillis. And Olga Grlic, who designed the cover. Lisa Senz and Sarah Goldstein and Nadea Mina, who are taking this book out into the marketplace.

For the beautiful, lush photographs of food, we thank photographer Jim Scherer and food stylist Catrine Kelty. They are artists . . . and such a pleasure to work with. The glowing photo of the restaurant on the inside cover and the photo of the Moosewood Collective were taken by someone dear to us, Justin Zoll, who, while working at Moosewood, has become an amazing photographer, lucky us.

Introduction

Moosewood Restaurant has been serving delicious food for forty years now, with a menu that changes at every meal. We have written a dozen cookbooks that all together contain about 3,000 recipes. Sometimes at book signing events, Moosewood fans say, "Another one? How can you come up with more?" Well, for us, there's truth in that old Italian saying, *"A tavola non s'in vecchia,"* which translates as "You never grow old at the table" or "It never grows old, being at the table." After spending most of our adult lives cooking, searching for food ideas, experimenting, learning, evolving, and cooking some more, we're still eager to taste something new and to think about how we might improve something old and beloved.

During Moosewood's forty years, the culinary landscape all around us has changed dramatically. In 1973 when Moosewood began, yogurt was advertised as a newly discovered secret-of-longevity food from Russian Siberia where the majority of elderly people were reported to be centenarians. Many of our customers tried it for the first time at the restaurant. In the mid-1980s, when we were putting together *New Recipes from Moosewood Restaurant*, coconut milk was unusual and unavailable enough that we included a recipe for how to make it from fresh coconut . . . so that any reader could try our recipes that included it. Now you can easily find low-fat and full-fat and organic coconut milk, and even coconut water. And now, many supermarkets have a whole aisle of soy, almond, and rice milks.

In our first few cookbooks, we hesitated to call for fresh herbs exclusively in a recipe, because in many areas of the country you could only find dried herbs in little cans, and fresh herbs, when you could find them, were very expensive. Many of us remember vividly the first time we tasted cilantro. It was so emphatically a brand new flavor, often tasting at first like either soap or aluminum, and then after the third or fourth exposure, like something we never wanted to do without again.

The Maine Organic Farmers and Gardeners Association, the oldest and largest state organic organization in the country formed in 1971, and in 1973, fifty-four farmers in California got together, agreed upon standards for producing organically grown produce, and mutually certified each other as organic growers. Awareness of the benefits of organic farming was ground-breaking, even revolutionary, then. Today, most supermarkets have a space that is devoted to organic produce, and farmers' markets and CSAs, with their organic, local, and heirloom fruits and vegetables, are wildly popular.

You could always find cabbage at the store forty years ago, but today you can expect to find four different kinds of cabbage plus bok choy, mizuna, kale, collards, broccoli rabe, turnip and beet greens, escarole, endive, and maybe fresh cactus paddles. Now, you might even stand in the produce aisle and use your smartphone to find shopping information about cardoons or a recipe for tatsoi. Who could have guessed?

When Moosewood opened, every night we served a simple sauté of fresh vegetables, maybe with tofu, over brown rice. Our parents worried about our vegetarian diets because "surely you aren't getting enough protein!" The first USDA dietary guidelines for Americans didn't come out until 1980, and at that time animal protein dominated the picture. The USDA guideline in 2010 recommends filling the majority of your plate with plant foods. At last, a diet of grains, vegetables, fruits, and beans is "officially" recognized as the most healthful.

Most of us at Moosewood grew up in cities or suburbs, and as young adults many of us identified in some way with what was called the "back-to-the-land movement." We built handcrafted houses and learned to garden organically, preserve food, and bake bread. We supported ourselves in small alternative businesses, like Moosewood, interested in fostering community spirit, supporting local farming and environmental consciousness, and offering food made from the freshest, most wholesome ingredients. This sounds like the plan for many new restaurants today, but it wasn't the norm back then.

Some things about Moosewood food haven't changed at all in forty years. When we first started out, we were searching for the authentic rather than the "plastic," so our primary inspiration was ethnic grain-based cuisines with food made from scratch. We felt a new appreciation and pride in our grandmothers' Old World recipes. Transforming traditional dishes while retaining their essential character has been our forte and our passion, and still is today. We want our food to be home-style with fresh ingredients and plenty of seasonings and bright flavors.

Among ourselves, we call this process of experimenting with a traditional dish "Moosewood-izing." It usually means we've simplified ingredients or cooking techniques to make the dish quicker, easier, more healthful, or just plain tastier. It might mean leaving out the meat or lard and adding chickpeas or olive oil or more colorful vegetables, while keeping the same herb and spice profile or bumping up the flavor by toasting the spices or using fresh herbs.

The Moosewood name has become aligned with the burgeoning national awareness that our health and well-being can be directly improved by supporting the growth of organic farming and local farmers' markets and food systems. We've had a part in moving whole grains, vegetables, and beans to the center of the plate, and we're proud of it. We're delighted about the expanding mindfulness of the need to maintain a healthier planet, the widespread work that is being done to preserve the diversity of food plants and the purity of water and to encourage buying local. It feels like we've come into the golden age of foods with an enormous variety available to us and nearly universal interest in the adventure of eating well.

We do understand that not everyone is as focused on food as we are. A request we hear frequently goes something like, "You have so many cookbooks that I get lost trying to decide what to cook. I wish you'd do a cookbook of only your best, your favorite recipes." Well, the more we thought about writing such a book, the more we realized it's not a simple thing to just choose our "best," our "favorites." Our cookbooks have reflected our eclectic and wide-ranging tastes from soups to desserts. One of our books is about the world of ethnic cuisines, and another is about cooking from your own kitchen garden. We've covered quick-and-easy dishes and also elaborate meals for celebrations. Many of our beloved early recipes are loaded with cheese, but we've also done whole books about low-fat fare and cooking for health. We love them all, and each of us has different criteria for choosing the favorites.

But after forty years of daily menu planning at Moosewood, we know what our customers like best. Sometimes a new dish gets great comments and becomes a regular on our menu. As cooks, we know which recipes are foolproof: consistently good and easy to make. We're in a continuous dialogue with cookbook fans on our website, at book signings, and when cookbook users make a pilgrimage to the restaurant. People are eager to tell us which recipes they grew up on in their parents' kitchens and which ones they use regularly now.

We've done surveys online and at the restaurant. Certainly the restaurant staff, our children, friends, and, occasionally, strangers on a plane let us know their favorites. Each of us knows which dishes we ourselves have favored over the years—the ones we never take out of rotation in our homes. So for this book, we got together in meetings, each of us bringing our own lists and our own powers of persuasion, and we argued it out, with only occasional eye-rolling or gasps of incredulity at others' choices. There was consensus about most of the recipes in this book.

Cooking is a collaborative process at Moosewood, so many of us have had a hand in adjusting the way we make a particular dish. Almost all of these 250 or so of our best recipes have gone through the usual "Moosewood-izing" process, both in the restaurant kitchen and in our home kitchens. Some recipes have never been published, but most are gathered from our cookbook history and we've updated and revised them for this book to reflect our current favorite way of preparing them.

There is a broad variety of recipes here. Some are hearty and filling, some are light and low-fat, many are quick and easy, some are elegant enough for a dinner party, plenty are vegan, and some we know to be kids' favorites . . . but our emphasis is on everyday meals. Most of the recipes are the kind we think you'll use again and again. We want them to be useful for both the beginner cook and for the longtime Moosewood fan.

The recipes are reliable and easy to follow because we've developed, tested, and retested them in our own home kitchens, which we think are fairly typical. And, we've cooked them in quantity at Moosewood, which is a different kind of test, a trial by fire. We believe that our instructions will direct you toward maximum efficiencies and minimum clean up. Once in a while we even suggest different cooking methods for hot days or cold days.

You'll find variations on many recipes because we just can't help messing around with them and we can't resist trying to tell you everything! Often the variations give substitutions for ingredients that are seasonal or may be hard to find. We hope you'll keep making changes in our recipes, too.

For extra advice and information, look at the Guide to Ingredients and Basic Cooking (page 371). It has practical information to help a novice cook get started, or to remind an experienced cook about the proportion of water and quinoa to use, for instance. We give baking pan equivalents to help you use the pans you have on hand (page 369), and the Environmental Working Group's "Dirty Dozen" and "Clean Fifteen" lists (page 13) to help you decide which produce is most important to buy organic.

Juxtaposing one dish with another to create a meal is one of the delights of cooking. Resourceful mixing and matching enhances each dish and provides variety and interest. So at the bottom of most recipes you'll find some serving and menu ideas, but the possibilities are almost endless.

We celebrate our many years of delicious cooking at Moosewood and we hope this book distills the best of that. Nourishing and beautiful food has immediate rewards, of course, but we also recognize the long-term pleasures of the kitchen. Cooking can be a lifelong interest and occupation, a satisfying and empowering craft that enhances your life every day. Cooking at home offers opportunities for learning and teaching. A basis for sharing culture and good times, it brings people closer together.

We've come a long way at Moosewood, and it's been a fascinating journey. Is it possible to feel both old and young at the same time? Oh yes. But at the table? Always young. Here's the best of the last forty years, but we trust that the best is also yet to come.

Moosewood Turns Forty

The Collective: Communication, Connection, and Collaboration

A couple of years ago, librarians at Cornell University's Olin Library asked us to participate in their archive that houses historical materials of alternative businesses and projects. We got excited about the idea and gathered photos, magazine and newspaper articles, and other memorabilia from our files at the restaurant and at our homes. After talking with the archivists and seeing the responses to the collection during various presentations about it, we began to realize that our story is of interest not just to us, but also to many others. While the story of Moosewood is unique in many ways, it also reflects what was happening at the time in many places in the United States.

We are frequently asked about how the restaurant got started, about the genesis of the Moosewood Collective, and how we've managed to still be here after all these years. We consider ourselves lucky to have been able to participate in this experiment, to run a restaurant where we could try out new ways of working, encourage each other's creativity, and nurture our interest in food and cooking. The essence of all of that is this: we created a work environment that we wanted to work in, and we managed to keep the food we cooked and ate interesting, tasty, and good for us. And, the years and years of knowing each other and working hard together hasn't hurt.

Our vegetarian cuisine has developed over the restaurant's forty years of business. Adapting ethnic food, our interest in a healthier diet, and our love of tasting new things and new combinations of flavors have all played a part. Except for an occasional intern wanting to learn to cook our cuisine, Moosewood cooks have not been trained in culinary schools. We are self-taught, adventurous people gifted with really good appetites and palates. We're foodies more than we are gourmets.

We've had the freedom to work with good, fresh ingredients, give and take feedback to perfect our ideas, and watch and learn from one another.

Moosewood's roots are in the counterculture of the '70s. The values of at least a good part of our generation included belief in a nonhierarchical structure, shared responsibility, mutual support, and a flexible work schedule in a relaxed, informal, irreverent climate, with a commitment to health and an authentic, earth-friendly lifestyle. Many of us were "moving back to the land," participating in local food coops, learning about organic gardening, and developing a growing respect for natural, unprocessed ingredients.

How did Moosewood start? In 1972 a group of seven friends decided to open a restaurant. They got together and renovated a sunny section of the Dewitt Mall, a group of small shops on the ground floor of a former public school building. Moosewood Restaurant opened in January 1973. There was a tiny, narrow kitchen, fifteen simple wooden tables built by a friend, and wainscoting made from old barn boards. The décor could be described as funk-chic . . . or maybe just funky. The menu was on a chalkboard so that we could change it with every meal. There was a gray metal mechanical cash register that sat on an old Victorian stand, where sales popped up on numbered cards at the top. The highest denomination you could ring up was $5, so the waitrons (that's what we called ourselves when we waited on tables) would press the noisy $5 key over and over for a bill of $10, $15, $20, or more. The stand is still there, but now it holds a touch screen.

Table 13, a round table in the corner beneath the stairs, was our favorite place to eat together and unwind at the end of a shift. Table 14 was where each night after closing, we'd count the cash and personal checks (no credit cards back then) and do the books.

New people began to work at Moosewood and some of the original seven friends moved away. In 1978, twelve employees bought the restaurant from the original owners and formed the Moosewood Collective, and Moosewood became a worker-managed/worker-owned business. We learned to handle everything that comes up when running a business, all the while holding on to an alternative ownership and staffing structure and what it meant to work "organically," i.e., staying alert to the entire flow, seeing what has to be done, and pitching in. We developed an innovative management structure, trained all workers on most of the restaurant's operations, and rotated jobs from washing pots and waiting on tables to cooking, creating menus, and ordering ingredients.

Fast-forward to 1993 when the restaurant was renovated, doubling in size, seating 75 instead of 35. We can't say we miss those nights when customers were queued up all the way down the hallway waiting for tables, tired of standing, blood sugar plummeting, hungry and cranky. Some changes are very good. We expanded the collective to nineteen members.

Forward again to 1997 and another renovation and expansion, a beautiful café space with a full bar. Seating exceeded 100 including the patio, and that's where we are now.

Over the years, we've cooked—for kooky Halloween parties, for benefits, for country spreads at Nancy and Rick's in Danby, Jenny and Penny's in Lansing, or at Lavender Hill. We hosted a wedding in the restaurant for two of our Tibetan employees and cooked for other weddings and commitment ceremonies and for birth and adoption celebrations and memorial services. We've picked strawberries together and danced together to reggae, salsa, Chicago blues, and rockabilly. We have partnered with community volunteers and activists to host scores of benefit brunches at the restaurant, raising many thousands of dollars and a lot of good will for great organizations and causes.

At a recent all-staff meeting at the beginning of our busy summer season, one after another new and old worker alike said that Moosewood is the best place they've ever worked. There's a sense of belonging to something larger than any individual. Feeding people well and treating people well is not just right, it's satisfying. It's good to know that the "collective" spirit of Moosewood has staying power.

Over the years, we've brought our parents in for lunch and published their recipes and their families' recipes and some of their stories in our cookbooks. We watched them get old and have done what we could to support each other as lives changed. Some of our kids grew up in the restaurant. They would walk in after school, hungry, and get a bowl of soup, a huge slice of whole wheat bread with butter and honey, and a cup of fruit salad or a brownie à la mode and hot spiced cider. As they grew up, many of them got their first jobs washing dishes at Moosewood. Now some of us bring our grandchildren in for the same bread and butter and brownie snacks.

We've recycled, used energy-saving lighting and hot water heaters, searched out compostable plastic bags and take-out containers, and bought fair-trade coffee and chocolate. We've offered local wine, beer, and honey, and cooked with locally produced tofu, flours, beans, cheeses, and fresh vegetables. We've composted our nice clean vegetable waste for decades, and it's easier now than ever to find takers for it. From the beginning, local growers have brought their bounty to Moosewood, occasionally even leaving boxes of squash and root veggies too plentiful to sell at the market outside our door overnight.

As we've watched "conventional" restaurants, markets, and businesses adopt the principle of green sustainable practices and buying locally grown foods and products, we're thrilled by the national movement toward a socially just and ecologically sustainable economy. We are so fortunate to be in a region where the earth is good to us, and there are so many hard-working farmers and gardeners using state-of-the-art earth-friendly methods. Now we can offer a lot of locally-grown and organic produce, and list many local producers who are our regular vendors. Even the smallest steps that individuals, families, and small businesses can take to reduce that big old carbon footprint make an enormous difference, and Moosewood is glad to do our part.

Right alongside the national movement for food justice, addressing concerns about obesity, diabetes, people's food safety and security, and the crying need to be able to reliably access fresh, healthful, affordable food, over the forty years, we've seen a rather alarming rise in the number of people with food sensitivities who are looking for a restaurant that can accommodate their health and diet constraints. In the past, just offering natural vegetarian and vegan food made us a valuable alternative; now people contact us in advance to make sure we can offer alternatives to people who want food that is without soy, wheat, gluten, sugar, lactose, nuts, seeds, eggs, fats, or oils. It's a noticeable and dramatic shift in the awareness of how food itself has changed, and how careful people are becoming about what they consume.

We're always trying new things that keep us interested and engaged. We develop new recipes and write cookbooks and magazine articles. We've developed a website, a blog, and a Facebook page, and we post our menus online (although we still have blackboards in the restaurant). We support a significant number of organizations, programs, and causes that are working to help people through better nutrition, healthcare, education, the arts, and protecting the environment, food security, and the civil and human rights of people, especially in our own community.

Most of all, we want people to try our food and to love it enough to cook it at home. Our cookbooks have been a powerful way to influence how people eat today. We've heard from people all over Europe, Asia, Latin America, Australia and New Zealand, the United States, and Canada. People tell us that our food has changed the way they and their families eat and live, and they feel a special connection to us through our books.

By the end of the '90s Moosewood Restaurant had become an iconic brand. Five of our cookbooks were nominated for James Beard Awards, and two won. Moosewood Restaurant received the 1996 James Beard/Bertolli Olive Oil Regional Classics Award. In its Millennium issue, *Bon Appetit* magazine named us "one of the thirteen most influential and revolutionary restaurants of the twentieth century."

Moosewood Restaurant Favorites is the thirteenth cookbook written by the Moosewood Collective. We like to think that our recipes have helped novice cooks become great cooks. We love it that we can share our recipes and culinary tips with people around the world. Fans have written to us from many, many countries and our friends and customers report that in their travels, they see our cookbooks in homes from Costa Rica to Germany, Greece to China, Newfoundland to New Zealand. We are so pleased to know that our books, like our restaurant, have helped inspire cooks, wherever they live, to make flavorful, healthy, interesting food.

What's it like having our fortieth anniversary? It's definitely a case of "Where did the time go?" It's been a wonderful adventure that none of us ever could have predicted in our wildest dreams. The story goes on.

But what's mostly on our minds is this: "What's for dinner?"

A Taste of Moosewood

A hodgepodge of memories, glimpses, snapshots that jump back and forth in time throughout our forty-year history. Picture this:

WEEKDAYS AT MOOSEWOOD

8:30 A.M.: On Seneca Street in Ithaca, a pretty Southern Tier New York town, the perfume of sautéing garlic and onions is coming out of the Moosewood kitchen. The Dewitt Mall's ground floor is waking up. Sara, who was a lunch cook yesterday, starts her menu planning week. She's already discussed with the morning cooks what they will be making for lunch and has checked the basement walk-in cooler to make sure that the local farmer-ground polenta she has asked them to use has been delivered. The menu is set, and she packs up some leftovers from yesterday (the last four piroshkis, zesty red cabbage slaw, and some applesauce) for Dan, our produce delivery guy who's been up and working since 3:30 A.M.

9:00 A.M.: A pot of chocolate melts on a burner of the stove. Its aroma combined with the scent of onions and garlic is absolutely intoxicating, the soul of comfort. One of the cooks is sharing her latest "Moosewood nightmare" and the crew is howling. "I come into the restaurant on a Sunday afternoon. The place is deserted, silent except for giant vats of water boiling on the stove. So I figure I'd better start cooking! Customers start coming in and seating themselves in an unfamiliar, cavernous dining room. So I rush from table to table, filling water glasses. Suddenly, I realize that I have no pants on under my apron. I wonder if any of the customers have noticed. I'm utterly alone, disoriented, and naked, but customers are waiting."

Out in the "old section" of the restaurant, David is burying his nose in a spray of fragrant white blossoms from his garden and putting the final touches on the plan for one of his cooking classes.

10:00 A.M.: Someone answers the old rotary-dial pay phone on the wall (now there are phones all over the restaurant but for years our only phone was this relic) and calls out, "Anyone know anything about our donation of brownies and minestrone for pick up today at 5?"

Lisa walks into the kitchen with a jar full of lime juice. "What's that burning?" she asks. She's always the first to detect even a hint of scorch with her bionic olfactory sense. She transfers the soup to a clean pot and lowers the heat: crisis averted. Now she's pulverizing toasted cumin and coriander seeds in a spice-grinder with one hand, while folding minced jalapeños and lime juice into a big bowl of diced avocadoes with the other.

Maureen is in the wait station, drawn by the enticing aroma of fresh, warm, whole wheat bread just delivered from Oasis Bakery down the hall. She slices a piece of bread, covers it with a slab of butter almost as thick, and pops it into the toaster oven. Someone says, "Whatcha been doing?" She replies, "The disbursements are finally up to date." "You're up and at it early." "Actually, it's late . . . it's been a long night."

Around 11:00: Susan bursts into the wait station with a pan full of white china cups glazed with baked-on blueberry drips and crowned with shiny berries poking through the golden cornmeal crust. Her short skirt swings as she stows the crumbles on the dessert shelf and turns to trade her kitchen apron for a waiter's apron. She jams a "dupe pad" and a pen into her pocket and dashes back to the kitchen to check the brownies in the oven before the restaurant opens for lunch at 11:30.

12:00 noon: Nana is at the serving window reviewing dupes. Looking like Sophia Loren in her magnifiers and counting in her native Spanish the number of casseroles needed, she turns around and ladles *pebre*, a Chilean onion and cilantro salsa, over a plate of corn and cheese casserole, and then returns to eating a whole lemon, tears and mischief in her eyes . . . this Saturday there's a Latin band from Rochester in town. She's gonna dance all night!

At the bar, Neil is brewing a hot ginger tea and a fair trade double cappuccino, maintaining his inscrutable deadpan expression. The bar stools are occupied by a group of guys who call themselves the Counter Culture. Loyal lunchtime pundits, they debate the world's problems each day over a salad du jour and tofu burger. By 1:15 they've got it all figured out.

5:00 P.M.: It's Tuesday, and after a good day selling their Tibetan dumplings and Chilean empandas at the downtown farmers' market, Tashi and Jano are ready for more action. There's still a half-hour until opening, and Jano, a self-described "Moosewood kid" (he's the grown-up son of Nana) who's now a kitchen manager, is already finished making his entrée, as usual. "Need any help, buddy?" he asks his fellow cook. In the dish-room, Tashi is running pots through the machine, warbling Tibetan folk songs, or cranking up a Bollywood CD. Just before opening, Kip walks in with a bag full of ingredients for testing cookbook recipes, and Tashi grins. He teases, "Hi, Kip, you off again today?"

WEEKENDS AT MOOSEWOOD RESTAURANT

4:00 P.M.: It's Friday, and on this particular day there's a rare all-male crew in the kitchen. The cooks are humming along now. John is rocking under his earbuds in time to a tune from his eclectic music collection while grating huge chunks of cheddar and Jarlsberg with R-2, our trusty food processor. In the other corner, half hidden behind bus-trays piled high with eggplants, yellow peppers, red potatoes, carrots, and a log of mozzarella as big as his upper arm, Dave is singing an Elizabethan ballad. Jason, his one red and one black Converse high tops firmly planted in front of the stove, is toasting a spice mix. Just back from a trip to India, he's the current curry enthusiast. Meanwhile, tall Tim, who is tending a stew in the "Bolivian army pot" (taller than a tall stew pot, big enough to hold a toddler), pours white wine into sautéed mushrooms, bay leaves, and fresh thyme. Tim gets a rush of pleasure when he's making soup in the Moosewood kitchen and thinks back to when he was in college. Tired of dining hall food, he often bought a carton of Moosewood soup at the campus minimart . . . and now he knows how to turn it out by the big potful, and he's one of our kitchen managers. It's going to be a busy night.

It's a frosty Saturday in February and folks are swarming up and down the Ithaca Commons. Back at Moosewood, the chili pepper twinkle lights are plugged in and Jenny tends six deep, long pans of her special red and black bean chili with chipotles, enough for a big crowd. Yep, it's the annual Ithaca Chili Fest and we're aiming to win the cook-off again this year. Ned is setting up a table for samples. Our resident fashionista, today she's wearing a vintage cowgirl shirt, miniskirt, and one six-gun earring. Susan and Joan are signing stacks of cookbooks in the café and offering samples of olivada on crackers to customers, when in the midst of it all, Tony, our most persistent activist, rushes in with a petition against GMOs that he wants to post for signatures.

It's a tranquil Sunday afternoon and Linda is conjuring up culinary delights of the Caribbean for ethnic night at Moosewood. She sprinkles diced chilies into a pan of popping black mustard seeds and freshly grated ginger, pokes cinnamon sticks into yellow rice, and removes a tray of perfectly toasted coconut from the oven. The air is filled with wonderful aromas. The restaurant is a place of calm and peace until Linda returns to the moment. She roars, "Alright, which one of you ate my cheese toast! And who stole my towel?"

6:00 P.M.: One of the teenaged Moosewood kids, newly promoted from breaking down boxes for recycling to his first "real" job at the restaurant—dishwasher—announces that the pots are all washed. Linda asks him to put a pan of lasagna into the oven. At serving time an hour later, it's discovered that he baked a pan full of grated Parmesan. Back to the pots.

7:30 P.M.: Penny's the dining room host tonight; she walks into the kitchen and says, "Okay, this customer can't eat onions, garlic, soy, wheat, nuts, nightshades, fats, or oil of any kind, and she's not that into vegetables—what can we feed her? And here: Will everyone sign this cookbook for her? Oh, and also, does anyone know of a good bed and breakfast over on Seneca Lake?" The cooks groan, then the brighten up when they remember that tomorrow is one of Penny and Jenny's sumptuous Sunday brunches; Jenny's making fresh scones, and Penny's baking Regina's Bobka!

ON THE ROAD WITH WYNNIE AND LAURA AND NANCY AND JOAN AND PENNY AND JENNY AND . . .

Washington, D.C.: Ah, the exuberance of youth. Sometime in the late 1980s, Wynnie and Laura rented a van and drove down to D.C. to be food vendors and sell our cookbooks at the SisterFire women's music festival. Over a typically hot and humid Washington weekend, they sold an astonishing number of antipasto pitas to womanists—carpenters and nursing moms, sound engineers and songwriters, activists and topless volley-ball players. Aaron, Wynnie's eight-year-old son, and Dan, Laura's ten-year-old, "manned" the cookbook end of the booth that was piled high with copies of *New Recipes from Moosewood Restaurant*. Onstage, Cris Williamson sang out, and Sweet Honey in the Rock harmonized with Alice Walker. Back at the booth, Wynnie's dad, Milt, took orders at the counter, barking Philly-style, "Wyn! Two pitas and a gazpacho! Hurry it up already!" The presence of an older man ordering women about in the midst of a music festival devoted to the power of womyn . . . well . . . many liberated sisters were heard to say "Patriarchy at Moosewood? What's next—a cheese steak? Who put him in charge?" By late Sunday, all that the Moosewood stand had left to offer the thirsty womyn were orange wedges, lettuce leaves, and ice water. Laura bought a new keyboard amp with her share of the profits. For weeks after (actually, for years), Wynnie reduced us to gasping laughter with stories of the experiences and her observations about that weekend.

New York City: Joan, Nancy, Jenny, and Penny have just returned from a trip to New York City where they cooked a benefit luncheon for the James Beard Foundation. After unloading Moosewood's pots and pans from the back of an old pick-up truck that, surprisingly, had made it there and back, they regale us with tales from the city. They tell us all about the amazing garden behind the James Beard House and what a good time they had eating lunch with the waiters and dishwashers they worked with. They collapse in laughter recounting their stand-off with a stylish, stiletto-wearing woman who asked for our chicken satay recipe. "We're happy to give you that recipe," said Nancy, "but that was tofu, not chicken." "Oh no," said the guest, "I don't do tofu." "That was not chicken on a stick," replied Nancy calmly, "it was tofu." "I know what I've eaten," insisted the woman, "and I don't eat tofu." Nancy stood her ground: "We know what we cooked, and that was tofu!" Finally convinced, she said it would be amusing to serve it at one of her soirees and that she wanted the tofu satay recipe. To this day, we wonder whether tofu sales on the upper east side of Manhattan saw a slight uptick at the end of the last century.

Hundreds of people have been part of Moosewood as workers, customers, vendors, friends. When we get together, there are stories to tell! The reminiscing is fun and funny, sometimes sad, and sometimes contradictory, but always a joy. If you could put it all together, it still wouldn't add up to the whole story.

Organic Food, the Dirty Dozen, and Buying Local

Some of the environmental benefits of eating organic food are right on the farm. When no pesticides and chemical fertilizers are used, workers and farm neighbors aren't exposed to potentially harmful chemicals, less fossil fuel is converted into fertilizers, the soil is richer and healthier, and biodiversity that will help sustain crops for generations to come is supported. For individual health, eating organic means avoiding the pesticide residue left on conventionally grown crops and avoiding growth hormones and antibiotics in dairy and eggs.

Keep in mind that there is often local food that is grown organically but isn't labeled organic. The process for organic certification can be prohibitively complicated and expensive for small farmers. So get to know your local food sources, and in addition to the environmental, economic, and social benefits of buying local, you may also find cleaner food to put into your body.

There are plenty of reasons to buy local eggs from cage-free chickens: no antibiotics or hormones, unadulterated feed, and access to sunlight, fresh air, and bugs and grasses means healthier chickens, better eggs, and a cleaner environment. And pretty much the same for dairy products. An organic label tells you some things (cleaner feed, no growth hormones, and limited use of antibiotics), but it doesn't tell you much about the living conditions of the cows.

About genetically modified crops, there are so many issues, controversies, and unknowns. More than half of all genetically modified foods are produced in the United States, and most of them come from large, industrial farms. By shopping at farmers' markets, a local Community Supported Agriculture (CSA) farm, or a local co-op, you may be able to avoid genetically modified produce and products. Shopping locally may give you the opportunity to talk with farmers and find out what they think about GMOs and whether or not they use them in their operations.

Because of availability and cost, many of us can't buy organic produce all of the time. The "Dirty Dozen" list helps us decide which fruits and vegetables it's most important to search out and buy organic. Each year, the Environmental Working Group (www.ewg.org) releases its guide to the most- and least-contaminated fruit and vegetable crops. The group analyzes U.S. Department of Agriculture data about pesticide residue on conventionally grown produce, and ranks fruits and vegetables based on how much or little pesticide residue they retain after washing. The Environmental Working Group (EWG) estimates that individuals can reduce their exposure to pesticide residue on fresh produce by 80 percent by switching to organic when buying the twelve foods on the "Dirty Dozen" list.

The Department of Agriculture testing is conducted on fruits and vegetables that have been washed and/or peeled—the typical precautions taken by American consumers. The U.S. Federal Food and Drug Administration says that you can remove pesticide residue on the surface of produce by removing outer leaves and rinsing the food under cold running water (no soap or bleach necessary) for 10 seconds.

"The health benefits of a diet rich in fruits and vegetables outweigh the risks of pesticide exposure," the EWG says. They recommend that consumers purchase organic when and where available, and choose items from the "Clean Fifteen" list when buying conventionally grown produce.

THE 2012 DIRTY DOZEN

- apples
- celery
- sweet bell peppers
- peaches
- strawberries
- imported nectarines
- grapes
- spinach
- lettuce
- cucumbers
- domestic blueberries
- potatoes

+ Plus green beans, kale, collards, and leafy greens (often contaminated with organophosphate insecticides)

THE 2012 CLEAN FIFTEEN

- onions
- sweet corn
- pineapples
- avocado
- cabbage
- sweet peas
- asparagus
- mangoes
- eggplant
- kiwi
- domestic cantaloupe
- sweet potatoes
- grapefruit
- watermelon
- mushrooms

Conventionally grown items on the "Clean Fifteen" list are generally low in pesticides. "More than 90 percent of cabbage, asparagus, sweet peas, eggplant, and sweet potato samples had one or fewer pesticides detected," the EWG report says. "Of the 'Clean Fifteen' vegetables, no single sample had more than five different chemicals, and no single fruit sample from the Clean Fifteen had more than five types of pesticides detected."

About the Recipes

We want our recipes to work for you. We try for that delicate balance of telling you all you need to know while still keeping the recipes uncluttered and easy to follow. We're always playing around with the dishes we cook, and we're not very good at following recipes ourselves, except when we're testing and retesting recipes for a cookbook. We want cooking to be enjoyable, so here's a little extra hand-holding in case you need it.

On each recipe, we give the time we think it will take an average cook to finish the dish, and we hope it will be a useful guide for you. We assume in calculating the time that you'll be able to readily put your hands on the various ingredients, that you won't have to wash your soup pot before you can use it, and that a neighbor won't knock on your door and insist on explaining the leash law in detail while you frantically call your dog (who must have slipped out when you came in with a big bag of groceries). We also assume that you'll prep as you go, chopping the carrots while the onions cook, but if you're more comfortable getting everything ready before you turn on the burner, just realize that the recipe will take a little longer. If one recipe takes you a longer or shorter time than our estimate, another one probably will, too. At least, that's what we are striving for: consistency.

Have you stood at the supermarket with a butternut squash in each hand, trying to visualize them peeled and cut into chunks or roasted and mashed: which one will come closest to 4 cups? In the recipe ingredient lists, usually we give you a cup measure and in parentheses the weight of a whole butternut that should yield about the right amount, or sometimes, it made sense to us to do it the other way around and call for a 3-pound squash, but then we give the approximate cup measure, too. When there's really some leeway, we may call for 1 bell pepper, and unless it's tiny or a giant, the amount of chopped will be fine.

That's also what the weights for spinach and mushrooms are about: how much you should buy to have about the amount called for after it's prepped. Of course, 10 ounces of mushrooms or spinach doesn't always yield the same cup measure of sliced or chopped. If there are large stems to trim off, after prepping there may be a little less than called for, but it probably won't be so different that the dish suffers for it. If we suggest 10 ounces of mushrooms and the package at your market is 12 ounces, get it and use them all.

Beans, artichoke hearts, and tomatoes are the canned vegetables we call for in these recipes, and the cans of different brands vary a bit in weight. When we call for a can, we list the median number of ounces among the various size cans we've come across. Take beans, for example. When we say 15-ounce can, we mean a 14-, 14.5-, 15-, or 16-ounce can—all should give you about 1½ cups of drained beans. Cans of tomatoes are usually 14 or 15 ounces and 28 or 32 ounces; if the can you have is a little different, don't worry. See page 371 for a discussion of artichoke hearts in brine.

And also, in general, please take the amounts we call for as guidelines. Say you're making a soup or a salsa, and when you've chopped up that beautiful big Spanish onion and filled your 2-cup measuring cup, there's still a little pile of onion pieces on the cutting board. What do you do? Compost the leftovers? Put them in a little plastic bag and stick them in the fridge to languish until you throw them out? No, neither. Put them all in the pot. And if your measuring cup isn't quite full, that's ok, too. A little more, a little less—there's nothing about a cup that makes it the perfect and only right amount.

We can't tell you exactly how much of some ingredients to use because there's variation in the intensity or flavor, or because how dominant the flavor should be in the dish is a matter of individual taste. Take garlic: personal taste and tolerances aside, some garlic is very strong and other garlic is mild. And what's one clove, anyway? One big clove may equal three small cloves. Same for hot peppers. We usually use jalapeños—some are barely hot, others might as well be habaneros. Some are 5 inches long, some you could easily hold six of on the palm of your hand. You decide whether or not to remove the seeds for a milder "hot" and you decide whether you want the dish to be mildly or intensely hot. The amounts of garlic, hot peppers, and spices called for in these recipes are pretty middle of the road, but you can move your dish to one side or the other.

Examples of other ingredients you'll use that may be inconsistent in some way, or that may just be different from ours, are bulghur and couscous (yours may do better with more or less water), pita bread (many different sizes), vinegar (we use apple cider, red wine, or rice, and occasionally white or balsamic), mustard (we usually specify Dijon, but whatever mustard you like will be fine). Oh, and tofu. We have a lot to say about that. See pages 387–388 for the full discourse.

We usually don't specify how sharp cheddar should be or whether to use whole, reduced fat, or skim milk. Use what's in your refrigerator or what you prefer.

Baking is a different story. Precision has its place in baking. More is not better. And less is also not better. If your cup of flour is a heaping cup of flour, it *can* make a difference. If you throw too many extra blueberries into the pound cake, it may come out of the oven a sodden mass.

Various flours of the same type behave a little differently. In the restaurant, we use flours grown and milled locally that we love, and we've adjusted the recipes we use in the Moosewood kitchen to work with them. For this book, we used King Arthur unbleached white flour for our all-purpose flour because we think it's good and it's widely available. But we hope you'll try your local flours and play around with the recipe if needed: too dry or tough, try a little less flour; texture too coarse, look for a finer grind of flour; too dense or wet, your flour may have a higher moisture content so try reducing the liquid a little.

Some of us prefer pastry flour for some sorts of baking, but we understand that pastry flour isn't available in some parts of the country, so in these recipes, we tried to do without it. The pound cake recipe is the only one that calls for pastry flour, but it works with all-purpose; the crumb will just be less fine. On some recipes, we tell what the difference will be with pastry versus all-purpose.

When we call for a can of diced tomatoes, we mean for you to use the whole can, juice and all; don't drain. We don't instruct you to salt and rinse eggplant before cooking it, because we think that's an unnecessary step. We've done blind taste tests and found no difference.

Most of our fish recipes simply call for firm fish fillets. When you shop for fish, instead of looking for a particular kind, look for the best choice that day. The important considerations are that the fish is fresh, reasonably priced, and not on the don't-buy list: fish that have been so overfished that they're becoming endangered, those caught by methods that endanger other sea life, and fish with high levels of toxins. The species of fish to avoid for environmental or health reasons changes, so if you look online, be aware of the date the list was generated. Sometimes, the most reasonably priced fish at the market is also the freshest (because there's been an abundant catch). Ask to sniff, and if the odor makes you think of anything besides the ocean, turn it down and sniff your second choice.

It's hard to describe, especially to beginning cooks, how to cut vegetables, that is, what size and shape to make the pieces. When we call for cubed potatoes in a stew for example, try to picture what you would like see in a bowl or on a bed of grain and what size you would want to put on your fork or spoon and into your mouth . . . and make them that size. Then cut most of the other vegetables in a complementary shape and size. When cutting vegetables for soup, you probably want to make them smaller. And keep in mind that the cooking time will vary a little depending on the size.

Here's our standard order by size of pieces: mince, finely chop, dice, chop, coarsely chop, cut into chunks. Minced means small, irregularly shaped pieces, ⅛ inch or less. Diced means generally uniform ¼- to ½-inch cubes: a fine dice is smaller, a coarse dice is larger. That said, diced can also simply mean larger than minced and smaller than chopped: diced onions, for example, aren't really little cubes. Chopped means smallish pieces, up to ½ inch, not uniform in shape. Chunks are larger irregular pieces—those stew-size pieces that at the table you'll need to cut to make bite-size.

The terms "grate" and "shred" are often used interchangeably. In our book, grated means small strips or fragments, and shredded means larger, longer strips. Both grating and shredding can be done with a hand grater or a food processor, and also, in the case of cabbage, with a knife. When we say shredded cabbage, we mean for you to shred it with a knife: slice down through the layered leaves into very thin slices, and then across the long slices to make shorter strips. If your knife is sharp, you can make smooth long cuts without "sawing" back and forth.

To shred or grate cheese, we use the same food processor blade, one with medium-large holes. The amount of pressure you put on the block of cheese as it's pushed against the whirling blade is what produces a coarser or finer shred. Cheese that's still cold from the refrigerator grates best. We coarsely shred cheese when we're going to mix it in, and we finely grate it when it will be sprinkled on top.

In soup recipes, we give you a yield only, and that's because, especially with soup, who can say how much soup makes a serving? Some soups are rich and filling, and others are brothy and light. Is soup the whole meal, or just a starter? We could say "eight 1-cup servings or four 2-cup servings," but you can easily figure that out for yourself.

In the Moosewood kitchen, we have both conventional and convection ovens, and we use them both. No recipe in this book requires a convection oven, but when a dish (such as baked tofu) really benefits from one, we mention that. We expect that if you have a convection oven, you know when and how to use it, so we decided to not clutter the recipes with that information. Ditto for immersion blenders, mandolines, Microplane graters, and other kitchen tools—if you've got them, use them.

While we were testing each other's recipes in our home kitchens for this book, we were often mystified when the tester found that a recipe made "too much filling for the pan size specified" or "not enough filling for a 9-inch pie plate." At first, we doubted our co-cooks ability to measure ingredients, but before we got too immersed in accusations and battles, we brought together our baking pans and pie plates and measured their volumes in cups of water. That solved the mystery. Pans that were marked the same size, or appeared to be the same size, held different quantities. So, the pan sizes we recommend are only a guideline. If when you're making a pie with your favorite pie plate, you regularly have extra filling, either adjust the amount of filling you make or be prepared to make a little tartlet in addition to the pie. See page 369 for standard pan volumes and substitutions.

We've tried to anticipate the extra information that you might find helpful. If you have questions, please check the Guide (page 371). Clarification may be there. For example, we've noticed when traveling to some parts of the country that when we ask the server for half-and-half with our coffee, she says, "Half and what?" and then goes on to say, "Oh, you mean creamer" . . . or light cream or single cream, coffee cream, or lightener. In the guide, we tell you what half-and-half is and what to substitute for it if it isn't marketed in your area. We let you know things like that it's fine to use either full-fat or low-fat cream cheese and coconut milk in these recipes. There you can find some basic cooking directions for beans, rice, and pasta, toasting directions for nuts and spices, and pressing and shredding directions for tofu.

We think that cooking is fun and creative, and we hope that for you, too. But even at those times when you're tired and hungry and just need to get some food into your belly, or someone else's, we hope that you'll have a good time both in the kitchen and at the table. And feel satisfied. *Bon appetit!*

APPETIZERS

Spiced Nuts

Peppercorn and Lemon Marinated Feta

Black Bean Ful

Tofalafels

Spanakopita Bites

Greek Spinach Rice Balls

Roasted White and Sweet Potatoes with Chipotle Aioli

Southeast Asian Rolls

Stuffed Tomatoes

Tofukabobs with Peanut Sauce

Spiced Nuts

They glisten, they crunch, they're easy to make and even easier to eat. Indeed, we believe Spiced Nuts are *the* democratic snack, delicious with uptown cocktails and with downtown brews. Take a stash on bike tours or camping for quick energy and great snacking. Serve with a nice ripe cheese and fresh fruit when entertaining. Include in gift bags at holiday time. Sprinkle on salads. Just say YES to these nuts!

We think our recipe strikes a nice balance between sweet and spicy, but the black pepper and cayenne can always be increased for a spicier nut, as can the salt for a more striking salty-sweet sensation.

Yields 3 cups
Prep time: 15 minutes
Baking time: 15 minutes

⅓ cup sugar or pure maple syrup
½ teaspoon ground cardamom
½ teaspoon ground cinnamon
pinch of cayenne (optional)
1 teaspoon finely grated orange zest (optional)
½ teaspoon salt
½ teaspoon ground black pepper
3 cups nuts (walnuts, almonds, cashews, pecans, peanuts)

Preheat the oven to 350°F. Generously oil a rimmed baking sheet.

If you're using sugar, combine it with the cardamom, cinnamon, cayenne, orange zest, if using, salt, and black pepper, and ¼ cup of water in a saucepan. Stirring constantly, bring the mixture to a boil and then reduce to a simmer and cook for a minute or two until the sugar has dissolved. Remove from the heat.

If you're using maple syrup, simply whisk together the syrup and the spices and seasonings until uniform—no need to cook. Because maple syrup has its own flavor, we suggest that you add a bit more salt, cayenne, and black pepper to balance the sweet with more spice and salt.

Stir the nuts into the spiced syrup until evenly coated. Using a slotted spoon, transfer the nuts to the prepared baking sheet and spread them out as much as you can so they don't clump together.

Bake for 5 minutes and then stir. Return to the oven and bake for another 10 minutes, or until browned. Stir well. Cool before serving.

NOTE

The baking sheet may look as if you're going to have a tedious cleanup, but if you rinse it with hot water as soon as you remove the nuts and soak it for a few minutes, it will clean easily.

Peppercorn and Lemon Marinated Feta

This is a simple, quick, and piquant dish to serve as an appetizer for a Mediterranean-style meal. Serve it with a few fresh vegetables or fruits, and you'll have a tasty small meal—or at least a good excuse to open a bottle of wine.

Serves 6 to 8 as an appetizer
Time: 10 minutes

one 8-ounce block feta cheese
1 lemon
2 tablespoons extra-virgin olive oil
cracked or coarsely ground black peppercorns
fresh thyme leaves (optional)

Slice the block of feta into ¼-inch slabs and then into wide strips. Arrange on a plate. Finely grate the zest of the lemon and then juice the lemon. Stir together the lemon juice and olive oil and drizzle over the feta. Sprinkle the lemon zest over the feta. Sprinkle with black pepper and thyme, if you like.

This is best when allowed to marinate at room temperature for 30 minutes or more. It will keep, covered and refrigerated, for several days.

SERVING AND MENU IDEAS
Serve with crackers, pita wedges, or bread. To make a bit more of a meal, serve with olives, tomato slices, cucumber slices, and/or strips of roasted red peppers, or with fresh fruit, such as grapes, cherries, or pears. The feta is great as an accompaniment for Armenian Roasted Eggplant Salad (page 115) and Mediterranean Lentil Salad (page 118), or as a topping for a tossed green salad.

Black Bean Ful

This recipe is a variation of a fava beans side dish called *ful*. Ful is common throughout the Middle East and North Africa and each region, maybe even each family, boasts of its own version. Our favorite black bean ful is still just the way our partner Laura Branca taught us to make it years ago—lemony and garlicky with beautiful, shiny black beans and lots of bright green parsley, served with ripe tomatoes and wedges of warm pita bread for scooping up the beans and soaking up the intoxicatingly delicious juices. It makes a striking, good-looking appetizer or side dish.

Inspired by some of the fuls we've sampled, we sometimes add cumin or cayenne or mint, and we've made it with fresh fava beans when we can get them.

Yields 3 cups
Serves 6
Time: 20 minutes

2 garlic cloves, finely minced or pressed
3 tablespoons olive oil
two 15-ounce cans black beans, rinsed and
    drained (or 3 cups cooked beans)
3 tablespoons fresh lemon juice
½ teaspoon salt
ground black pepper
½ cup chopped fresh parsley

tomato wedges
lemon wedges
pita bread

In a saucepan on medium heat, cook the garlic in the oil just until sizzling and golden, then immediately stir in the beans, and warm through. Transfer the warm beans to a bowl and stir in the lemon juice and salt. Season with black pepper to taste. Stir in the parsley, reserving some to use as a garnish, if you like. Add another tablespoon of olive oil if you think it needs it.

Serve Black Bean Ful warm, at room temperature, or chilled. Garnish with wedges of ripe fresh tomatoes and lemon wedges and serve with pita bread.

VARIATION

- We love ful and, in the way we have of thinking about food, we thought, why not in a pita sandwich? The problem was that all those little beans kept falling out of the pocket. So, when we want to use it as a pita filling (or a spread), we purée about half of it in a food processor and stir that back in with the whole beans and then it all hangs together nicely.
- We also like to stir in diced fresh tomatoes.

SERVING AND MENU IDEAS

Serve with warm pita bread and wedges or slices of hard-boiled eggs. This is also good topped with grated feta or with Peppercorn and Lemon Marinated Feta (page 23).

Tofalafels

These tasty little nuggets, Moosewood's answer to fried falafels, have been a favorite for many years. We serve them in pita sandwiches, on combo plates, as an appetizer, and on green salads. Tofalafels and Lemon-Tahini Dressing (page 304) are made for each other. Tofalafels are great for picnics, parties, or just snacking.

Yields about 30 tofalafels
Tofu pressing time: 30 minutes
Prep time: 30 to 40 minutes
Baking time: 30 to 40 minutes

two 14- to 16-ounce blocks firm or
    extra-firm tofu (see page 387)
2 tablespoons olive oil
1½ cups chopped onions
2 garlic cloves, minced or pressed
½ teaspoon salt
1 tablespoon ground turmeric
1½ teaspoons ground cumin seeds
1 teaspoon ground coriander seeds
¼ teaspoon cayenne, or red pepper flakes
    (optional)
3 tablespoons soy sauce
2 tablespoons dark sesame oil
⅓ cup tahini
⅓ cup finely chopped parsley
¾ cup bread crumbs (optional)
¼ cup fresh lemon juice
¼ cup toasted sesame seeds

First, press the tofu for at least 30 minutes (see page 388).

Preheat the oven to 350°F. Lightly oil a baking sheet.

Warm the oil in a covered skillet on low heat, add the onions, garlic, and salt and cook until the onions are soft and translucent, about 10 minutes. Add the turmeric, cumin, coriander, and cayenne and continue to cook, stirring frequently, for 3 or 4 minutes.

Shred the tofu by hand or in a food processor and put it in a large bowl. Add the cooked onions and spices to the bowl with the tofu. Stir in the soy sauce, sesame oil, tahini, parsley, bread crumbs, if using, lemon juice, and sesame seeds and mix well. Season with more salt to taste.

Form the mixture into walnut-size balls and place them on the prepared baking sheet, spacing them at least an inch apart. Bake for about 30 minutes, or until golden and firm to the touch.

VARIATION

If gluten is a problem for you, keep in mind that there are gluten-free bread crumbs that you can use, or omit the bread crumbs. Tofalafels are more delicate without the bread crumbs.

SERVING AND MENU IDEAS

Serve with Lemon-Tahini Dressing (page 304). Tuck tofalafels into toasted pita bread with lettuce and diced tomatoes and cucumbers . . . and Lemon-Tahini Dressing, of course. Make a combo plate with Tofalafels and Tabouli Salad (page 106), Classic Hummus (page 37), and Peppercorn and Lemon Marinated Feta (page 23). Or serve as an appetizer, on a bed of greens with pita wedges.

Spanakopita Bites

It was a busy Saturday night at Moosewood, and we were fast running out of appetizers. Luckily, Jenny Wang, one our most competent, confident, and innovative cooks, threw this together. The response that night put Spanakopita Bites immediately on our greatest hits list.

Foolproof and delicious, serve this fresh out of the oven, while the filo is crisp and delicate. The filling is so simple, yet so tasty. These bites are great for entertaining: you can make and bake them ahead of time, and then when you're ready, pop them into the oven for a few minutes and voila! We're divided on whether these little bites taste better brushed with butter or olive oil or both—our customers love them any way we do them.

Yields 36 pieces
Prep time: 30 minutes
Baking time: 20 to 30 minutes

10 cups packed fresh baby spinach
   (about 1 pound)
½ cup sliced scallions
4 ounces feta cheese (1 cup crumbled, not packed)
a sprinkling of ground black pepper
six 12 x 17-inch sheets filo dough
about ⅓ cup olive oil and/or melted butter

Rinse the spinach in a colander and drain it a bit. In a covered saucepan on medium-high heat, steam the wet spinach, stirring a couple of times, until wilted, 3 or 4 minutes. Drain the steamed spinach in the colander, pressing out the water. Turn the spinach out onto a cutting board and, when cool enough to handle, squeeze out more liquid. Chop lightly.

In a medium bowl, combine the spinach, scallions, feta, and black pepper.

Preheat the oven to 375°F. Oil or butter a 18 × 12-inch rimmed baking sheet or two smaller ones.

Place the filo sheets in a stack on a flat, clean, dry surface. Working quickly so the filo won't dry out and crack, brush the top sheet with melted butter or olive oil. Spread ¼ cup of the filling in a line (a little bigger than a fat pencil) a couple of inches above the bottom edge. Lift the bottom edge of the top sheet of filo up and over the filling and roll it into a tube. Don't worry if there are small rips at the start—after you've rolled it a couple of turns, it will roll beautifully. Place the roll, seam side down, on the prepared baking sheet and brush the top and sides with butter or oil. Repeat with the remaining filling and filo. Arrange the rolls on the baking sheet so that they don't touch. Using a sharp knife, cut each roll into 6 pieces, about 2 inches long.

Bake for 20 to 30 minutes until the filo is crisp and golden brown.

Using a spatula, transfer the Spanakopita Bites to a serving platter and serve right away—as they cool, the filo becomes less crisp. If you make them ahead of time or have leftovers, reheat in a 350°F oven or toaster oven for a few minutes; the filo re-crisps very nicely.

NOTE

While baking, some liquid flows onto the baking sheet, and when you take it from the oven you think it's going to be difficult to clean, but not so. As soon as you've removed the pastries, and while the baking sheet is still hot, rinse it and then come back in 5 minutes and scrape with the spatula. Everything comes off easily.

SERVING AND MENU IDEAS

Especially nice as an element of a tapas-style meal with any or all of Armenian Roasted Eggplant Salad (page 115), Mediterranean Lentil Salad (page 118), Tabouli Salad (page 106), Classic Hummus (page 37), Black Bean Ful (page 24), Moroccan Couscous Salad (page 107).

Greek Spinach Rice Balls

Rice balls have their place in many cultures, often as street food. This version was inspired by *arancini*, Italian rice balls introduced to us by our partner and Moosewood cook, Tony Del Plato, who grew up in Brooklyn, gobbling down his Italian mama's rice balls. Always on the lookout to exploit a great idea, we expanded our rice ball repertoire to include the ones we give you here.

With just enough rice to hold together the tasty spinach and herb mixture, these are crisp on the outside and appealingly bright green and moist on the inside. They are a wonderful finger food at parties, and they work well as an appetizer or side dish. And, kids like them as snacks!

Yields 24
Prep time: 40 minutes
Baking time: 20 to 30 minutes

14 cups fresh baby spinach (20 to 24 ounces)
1½ cups chopped scallions
3 garlic cloves, minced (optional)
1 tablespoon olive oil
2 cups cooked brown rice
1 cup crumbled feta cheese
3 tablespoons finely chopped fresh dill
2 to 3 tablespoons fresh lemon juice
½ teaspoon salt
¼ teaspoon ground black pepper
1 cup bread crumbs or finely chopped toasted
   walnuts

Rinse the spinach in a colander. In a large covered pot or working in batches, steam the spinach in only the water that clings to the leaves, stirring frequently, just until wilted, 5 to 10 minutes. Drain the steamed spinach in the colander, pressing out the excess water. Turn the spinach out onto a cutting board and, when cool enough to handle, squeeze out more liquid. Chop finely.

In a small skillet on medium heat, cook the scallions and garlic in the oil until softened.

In a large mixing bowl, combine the spinach, scallions, rice, feta, dill, 2 tablespoons of lemon juice, and salt. Stir in the black pepper. Taste and add more salt, pepper, and lemon juice, if you like.

Preheat the oven to 350°F. Lightly oil a baking sheet.

Form the spinach mixture into firm, round balls 2 to 3 inches in diameter. Gently roll each ball in the bread crumbs or walnuts and place on the prepared baking sheet, spacing them about 1 inch apart.

Bake until heated through and crisp on the outside, 20 to 30 minutes.

SERVING AND MENU IDEAS

Greek Spinach Rice Balls pair well with Cream of Asparagus Soup (page 51), Ratatouille (page 133), or Greek Lemon-Mint Beans and Vegetables (page 145). Make a combo plate with Classic Hummus (page 37), Russian Eggplant Spread (page 41), crudités, and olives.

Roasted White and Sweet Potatoes with Chipotle Aioli

Most of us love chipotle aioli with its spicy, smoky flavor, and nothing could be simpler to make. Roasted potato wedges are one of our favorite "platforms" for it.

Yields about ⅔ cup
Serves 4 to 6
Time: 30 minutes

ROASTED POTATOES
2 large white potatoes
1 large sweet potato
2 tablespoons olive oil
1 teaspoon salt
½ teaspoon ground black pepper

CHIPOTLE AIOLI
1 or 2 garlic cloves, minced or pressed
1 tablespoon olive oil
½ cup mayonnaise
1 tablespoon chipotles in adobo sauce
1 tablespoon fresh lime or lemon juice

Preheat a convection oven to 425°F or a conventional oven to 450°F. Oil a rimmed baking sheet.

Scrub the white potatoes and cut them lengthwise in 6 to 8 wedges. Peel the sweet potato and cut it lengthwise into 6 to 8 wedges. If the potatoes are very large, cut the wedges in half. Toss the potatoes with the olive oil, salt, and pepper. Place the potatoes on the prepared baking sheet in a single layer and roast for about 20 minutes, or until tender and browned. Turn the wedges over with a spatula after about 10 minutes of roasting.

While the potatoes roast, make the chipotle aioli. Cook the garlic in the olive oil in a microwave oven or on the stovetop, just until it sizzles. In a food processor, whirl the garlic and oil with the mayonnaise, chipotles in adobo sauce, and lime juice until well combined. Add more chipotles to taste.

Serve the potatoes hot, with chipotle aioli.

VARIATIONS
- You can make this with only one kind of potato or change the proportion of white and sweet; just have 7 to 8 cups total.
- Before roasting, toss the potatoes with garlic and minced fresh rosemary or thyme.

SERVING AND MENU IDEAS
In addition to serving Chipotle Aioli with roasted potatoes, an all-time Moosewood favorite appetizer and side dish, we drizzle it on steamed vegetables, such as broccoli, carrots, and asparagus. We mix it into in egg salad (Mexican Egg Salad, page 78) and potato salad (Sweet Potato Salad with Chipotle Aioli, page 259); and spread it on sandwiches and Fish Cakes (page 237).

Southeast Asian Rolls

Southeast Asian Rolls are a simple yet impressive appetizer. If you've never worked with rice flour wrappers, follow our easy directions and you'll walk away with a swagger. Prepare all of your ingredients ahead of time, as you would for a stir-fry, because the cooking goes quickly.

The wrappers, or rice flour spring roll skins or disks as they are sometimes called, are delicate, so expect to break a few; there are plenty in each package for do-overs. You will find rice paper wrappers on the shelf in Asian markets and well-stocked supermarkets.

Yields 12 rolls; about 1 cup sauce
Time: about 1 hour

FILLING
2 tablespoons peanut, canola, or other vegetable oil
2 cups shredded cabbage
salt
2 cups shredded carrots
1 tablespoon peeled and grated fresh ginger
3 cups sliced mushrooms (12 ounces)
½ cup chopped scallions
3 tablespoons chopped fresh basil or 1 tablespoon chopped fresh tarragon
3 tablespoons chopped fresh cilantro or mint
1 package 8-inch rice paper wrappers

HOISIN DIPPING SAUCE
¾ cup hoisin sauce
2 tablespoons rice vinegar or fresh lime juice
½ teaspoon Chinese Chili Paste with Garlic (see page 374) or hot pepper sauce
1 tablespoon hot water
¼ cup peanut butter or 1 teaspoon dark sesame oil

Prepare the filling ingredients before beginning to stir-fry. You can use a hand grater, food processor, or mandoline.

Heat the oil in a wok or large skillet on medium-high heat and stir-fry the cabbage with a sprinkling of salt until it brightens, about 2 minutes. Add the carrots and stir-fry for another 2 minutes. Stir in the ginger and mushrooms and cook on medium heat until the mushrooms soften, about 3 minutes. Add the scallions and fresh herbs and remove the pan from the heat.

Assemble the rolls on a dry, smooth work surface, working in batches of 3 or 4 if you have the room. Moisten each wrapper by immersing it in a large, shallow bowl of warm water. Lay the moistened wrappers flat, side by side but not touching (or they'll stick together). Let them soften for a couple of minutes.

Place about ⅓ cup of filling on the bottom half of a softened wrapper. Fold the sides up and over the filling, and roll up from the bottom as gently and snugly as possible. Place seam side down on a platter, not touching. Repeat the process, moistening, filling, and rolling the remaining wrappers.

Whisk together the ingredients for the dipping sauce.

Serve the rolls at room temperature with the dipping sauce.

You can make these rolls ahead of time. Store in the refrigerator, covered with damp paper towels and plastic wrap to prevent the wrappers from drying out and becoming hard.

SERVING AND MENU IDEAS
These flavorful rolls are great as a starter for Thai Noodle Salad (page 100), Mushroom Mapo Tofu (page 207), or Malaysian Fish (page 242). Some of us would have them with Thai Butternut Squash Soup (page 58) or Sesame Jeweled Rice (page 290) and call it a perfect dinner.

Stuffed Tomatoes

This is one easy little appetizer. The filling is a snap to make, and it can also double as stuffing for mushrooms or miniature, multicolored sweet peppers.

Yields 12 stuffed tomato halves
Prep time: 30 minutes
Baking time: 30 minutes

1 tablespoon olive oil
3 garlic cloves, finely minced or pressed
¾ cup unseasoned bread crumbs (see page 373)
2 tablespoons finely chopped scallions
1 tablespoon chopped fresh basil or tarragon
1 cup shredded or crumbled cheese, such as
    Gorgonzola, chèvre, sharp cheddar, Fontina,
    or Parmesan

6 plum tomatoes

Warm the oil in a small, heavy skillet on medium heat, and sauté the garlic briefly, just until golden and aromatic, but not browned. Add the bread crumbs and stir to coat evenly with the oil. Remove from the heat and stir in the scallions, basil or tarragon, and the cheese. Most cheeses provide enough salt, but sample a pinch and add salt to taste.

Preheat the oven to 350°F. Lightly oil an 11 × 7-inch baking pan.

Cut the tomatoes in half from pointy top to stem end. Scoop out the seeds. Arrange the tomato halves in the prepared baking pan and sprinkle them lightly with salt. Fill each half with about 2 tablespoons of the filling.

Cover the baking pan with aluminum foil and bake until the tomatoes have softened but still hold their shape and the cheese has melted, about 30 minutes.

VARIATIONS
- Fill mushroom caps with the bread-crumb mixture and bake them with a little sherry in the bottom of the baking pan, and maybe a few sprigs of fresh thyme.
- Roast pepper halves before filling them. Then bake until the bread-crumb–cheese mixture is hot and lightly browned.

Tofukabobs with Peanut Sauce

Tofu cubes baked on a skewer come out nice and chewy, a perfect vehicle for the delicious peanut sauce.

We can't tell you how many people this recipe—twelve tofukabobs—will serve. Is it going to be a snack, appetizer, central on the dinner plate, or part of a buffet? Then there is a bigger consideration: who will be eating them? Some people are happy with one skewer. Others force themselves to stop after four or five. Tofukabob enthusiasts are often people who said when they were first offered one, "Oh. OK, but I'm not too fond of tofu." All it takes is a couple of people who go gaga over them to wipe out a platterful in no time.

All tofu is not the same—the consistency varies. Be sure to get fresh tofu if you can (see page 387). And, if you have a convection oven, use it for this recipe.

Yields 12 skewers; about 1 cup sauce
Prep time: 20 minutes
Baking time: 20 to 25 minutes

TOFU SKEWERS
two 14- to 16-ounce blocks firm or extra-firm tofu (see page 387)
twelve 10-inch bamboo skewers
¼ cup vegetable oil
¼ cup soy sauce

PEANUT SAUCE
⅓ cup smooth peanut butter
2 tablespoons soy sauce
1 tablespoon apple cider vinegar or white vinegar
⅓ cup water
2 teaspoons dark sesame oil
2 teaspoons Tabasco or other hot sauce (optional)
1 tablespoon brown sugar or honey

First, press the tofu for at least 10 minutes (see page 388). Soak the skewers in water.

Preheat the oven to 450°F, or a convection oven to 425°F. Generously oil a large baking sheet.

Cut the blocks of tofu into 1-inch cubes; you should get 24 cubes from each block. Transfer the tofu cubes to a bowl. In a separate bowl, whisk together the oil and soy sauce and pour over the tofu. Using a rubber spatula, gently turn the tofu cubes to coat all sides.

Thread 4 cubes onto each soaked skewer, leaving about ½ inch of space between them, and place on the prepared baking sheet, leaving space between the tofukabobs. Bake until sizzling and golden brown, 20 to 25 minutes; less if using a convection oven.

While the tofu bakes, stir together all of the peanut sauce ingredients until smooth.

Serve warm or at room temperature. Arrange the tofukabobs on a serving platter and drizzle them with peanut sauce. Put the rest of the peanut sauce in a little pitcher, so the peanut sauce lovers can drench their tofukabobs, if they like.

Simple Smooth Guacamole

Vegan Spinach–Artichoke Heart Dip

Classic Hummus

Olivada

White Bean and Basil Spread

Russian Eggplant Spread

Edamame-Wasabi Spread

Herbed Chèvre Spread

Dilled Havarti Spread

Red Bean and Walnut Spread

Simple Smooth Guacamole

A ripe avocado is a thing of beauty, as any Moosewood cook will tell you. Because we love guacamole and it's the perfect thing to serve with so many dishes, we regularly turn a case of avocados into a mound of guacamole. When the avocados are ripe, the guacamole is scrumptious. If the avocados are underripe or overripe, the guacamole will suffer. This simplest of guacamoles is for when your avocados are perfect.

For chunky guacamole, see California Pita (page 76) and Avocado Salsa (page 314). Sure, you can buy guacamole ready to dip out of its plastic container, but it's so easy to make your own: no worries about what may have been added to it—and it tastes better, too.

Yields 1 generous cup
Time: 10 minutes

2 ripe Hass avocados
1 garlic clove, minced or pressed
2 to 3 tablespoons fresh lime or lemon juice
¼ teaspoon salt
splash of Tabasco or other hot sauce (optional)

Slice around each avocado lengthwise down to the pit. Twist the halves apart. Pop out the pit with the tip of the knife. Scoop out the flesh with a spoon.

Mash the avocado flesh, garlic, lime juice, and salt with a fork. Add Tabasco to taste. If you want *really* smooth guacamole, use a food processor.

Serve immediately. Or, if you will serve it later or have leftovers, to prevent discoloration, press plastic wrap directly onto the surface of the guacamole, leaving no air bubbles, and refrigerate.

SERVING AND MENU IDEAS

Of course, serve as dip for tortilla chips, crackers, little rounds of baguette, or crudités. Serve as a topping for beans, burritos, Mexican Corn and Cheese Casserole (page 162), Chilaquiles Casserole (page 161), Mexican Salad Plate (page 113), Black Bean–Sweet Potato Burritos (page 195), and other Mexican, Southwest, and Latin American dishes.

Vegan Spinach–Artichoke Heart Dip

Love this popular appetizer, but wish it were dairy-free? Here's a version that will make you happy. We joke about Flora Marranca, one of Moosewood's earliest and most adventurous cooks, that she is multicultural: part Italian-American and part Vegan. Before vegan fusion food was a twinkle in anyone else's eye, Flora was mass-producing delicious spinach- and tofu-stuffed ravioli in her home kitchen, and the goal of this recipe is the same.

This is a tasty dip that's packed with vitamins, minerals, and phytonutrients from the key ingredients: spinach, basil, and white beans. You can serve it as soon as it's ready, but the flavors develop if it is refrigerated for an hour or more.

Yields 3 cups
Time: 20 minutes

6 cups fresh baby spinach (about 10 ounces)
one 15-ounce can white beans, rinsed and drained
⅓ cup chopped scallions
½ cup chopped fresh basil
2 tablespoons extra-virgin olive oil
1 garlic clove, pressed or minced
3 tablespoons fresh lemon juice
¼ teaspoon salt
⅛ teaspoon ground black pepper
one 15-ounce can artichoke hearts in brine,
    drained and finely chopped

Rinse the spinach leaves and steam them in a saucepan with just the water that clings to the leaves for about 3 minutes, until wilted and still bright green. Drain in a colander, press some liquid out with the back of a large spoon, and turn out into a bowl to cool while you prep the other ingredients.

In a food processor, purée the beans, scallions, basil, olive oil, garlic, lemon juice, salt, and pepper until fairly smooth. When the spinach is cool enough to handle, using your hands, squeeze out more liquid and add the spinach to the food processor. Purée until the spinach is minced and evenly distributed. If the dip is too thick, add a little water. Scrape the dip into a bowl and stir in the chopped artichoke hearts. Add more salt and black pepper to taste.

Serve at room temperature or chilled.

SERVING AND MENU IDEAS
This dip is great with crackers, pita chips, or crudités. Makes a great open-faced sandwich on sliced ciabatta or baguette with tender greens, tomatoes, and fresh mozzarella.

Classic Hummus

Hummus is an easy-to-make and popular dish. It comes to us from the Middle East and Mediterranean, particularly the Levant: Lebanon, Syria, Jordan, Israel, Palestine, and parts of Cyprus, Turkey, and Iraq. The Arabic word for chickpeas is *himmis*. The earliest record of hummus is from thirteenth-century Egypt.

Yields a generous 1½ cups
Time: 10 to 15 minutes

1½ cups cooked chickpeas (or one 15-ounce can), drained
¼ cup water
1 garlic clove, chopped
2 tablespoons fresh lemon juice
¼ cup tahini
¼ teaspoon salt
pinch of cayenne (optional)
½ teaspoon ground cumin seeds (optional)

Place the chickpeas, water, garlic, and lemon juice in a food processor and purée until quite smooth. Add the tahini and salt, and cayenne and cumin, if using, and process until creamy. Add more lemon juice and/or salt to taste. Chill the hummus until ready to serve.

VARIATIONS
- Stir in:
  - finely chopped fresh herbs, such as dill, parsley, or scallions
  - chopped kalamata olives
  - caramelized onions
  - a tablespoon or two of Thai curry paste

- **Spicy Chipotle Hummus**—Omit the garlic, cayenne, and cumin and add about 1 tablespoon of chipotles in adobo sauce. Keep in mind that the chipotle peppers are the spicy part and the adobo sauce adds a rich, smoky flavor. You may want to start with less and add more to taste. Add a tablespoon or two of chopped fresh cilantro, if you like.

- **Roasted Red Pepper Hummus**—Omit the cayenne and cumin. Add a roasted red pepper (from a jar or roasted by you) and 1 tablespoon of extra-virgin olive oil. Omit the water, because the pepper adds enough juiciness for smooth processing. Add 1 or 2 tablespoons of chopped fresh basil at the end. The roasted red pepper makes for a lovely sunset orange–colored hummus. Season with black pepper to taste.

SERVING AND MENU IDEAS
Hummus is often presented drizzled with olive oil and sprinkled with toasted cumin or paprika. Serve it as an appetizer with crackers, pita wedges, or raw vegetable sticks, spread it on toast, or stuff it in a pita. It is good on a tossed green salad or as part of a combo plate with Tabouli Salad (page 106) and Peppercorn and Lemon Marinated Feta (page 23).

Chipotle Hummus is good with tortilla chips, while Roasted Red Pepper Hummus has a more Mediterranean feel and is great with fresh mozzarella and rosemary crackers.

Olivada

Olivada is a glossy and dramatic-looking Italian olive spread akin to tapenade, a glistening deep purple with black and ivory flecks. You can't make a quicker, more foolproof gourmet appetizer.

When we first published a recipe for it, we couldn't find pitted kalamata olives in our markets and we recommended pitting them by hand. Today, many supermarkets have olive bars with a generous selection of Italian, Greek, French, and Spanish olives of many sizes, colors, and pungencies, and so this recipe is now even faster and easier—and potentially, more delicious.

Kalamatas alone in this recipe are too salty for most of us, so we usually use about a fourth or even up to a third kalamatas and the rest a milder black olive, such as the large black Cerignola or little French Niçoise or even canned California black olives. And if you like green olives, go ahead and use some.

Yields 1½ cups
Time: 10 minutes

2½ cups pitted black olives (see headnote)
1 garlic clove, pressed or minced
2 tablespoons pine nuts, lightly toasted
1 or 2 tablespoons extra-virgin olive oil

In a food processor, pulse the olives, garlic, pine nuts, and 1 tablespoon of the olive oil until just smooth enough to spread, but stop before it becomes a paste. It's OK if some of the pine nuts remain whole and some of the chunks of olives are bigger. If the mixture is too stiff, add a second tablespoon of olive oil.

Covered and refrigerated, Olivada will keep for at least a week. It is best served at room temperature.

SERVING AND MENU IDEAS

For an appetizer buffet or fabulous party fare, serve Olivada along with a couple of other dips, such as Edamame-Wasabi Spread (page 42) and Red Bean and Walnut Spread (page 45), and with crudites and crisp toasted bread or crackers. It is also good as a pasta topping and on pizza. Or try it as a stuffing in deviled eggs, in omelets, as a topping for baked potatoes, or as a dip for crackers.

White Bean and Basil Spread

Here is a simple recipe for puréed beans seasoned with olive oil, garlic, lemon juice, and fresh basil. A classic Italian dish, it is a great spread or dip with big flavors and a rich, smooth, satisfying texture. We've been serving it as a pita filling and as an appetizer with crackers or bread for years, but we've never published the recipe.

We also give you our favorite variation, with fennel and sun-dried tomatoes.

Yields 3 cups
Time: 20 minutes

3 cups cooked white beans (or two 15-ounce cans)
3 tablespoons extra-virgin olive oil
2 garlic cloves, minced or pressed
½ teaspoon salt
¼ teaspoon ground black pepper
3 tablespoons fresh lemon juice
¼ cup minced fresh basil

Drain the beans, reserving some of their liquid.

If you prefer a milder garlic flavor, cook the garlic in the oil in a microwave oven or on the stovetop, just until it sizzles.

In a food processor, whirl together the olive oil and garlic until the garlic is pulverized. Add the white beans, salt, pepper, and lemon juice and purée until the beans are smooth. If the mixture is too stiff, add a tablespoon of the reserved bean liquid to make a thick but smooth spread.

Put the spread in a bowl and fold in the fresh basil. Serve at room temperature or chilled.

VARIATION

* Add fennel and sun-dried tomatoes. Before you make the spread, place 5 or 6 sun-dried tomato halves (dry, not oil-cured) in a bowl and cover them with 1½ cups of boiling water. Set aside to rehydrate for about 15 minutes. Make the bean spread. When the tomatoes have absorbed water and are pliable, discard the water, and mince the tomatoes. Fold the tomatoes and 1 teaspoon of ground fennel into the spread with the basil. Add more ground fennel to taste, but only after you've let the spread sit for a bit, because the fennel flavor intensifies over time.

SERVING AND MENU IDEAS

Serve as an appetizer with crusty bread, fresh mozzarella, and roasted plum tomatoes (see page 84), or as a sandwich in a pita or on sliced bread.

Russian Eggplant Spread

This creamy, beige spread looks good served in a colorful bowl, topped with sliced scallions and garnished with cherry tomatoes. The creaminess of the mayonnaise mellows out the "bite" that eggplant often has.

The recipe gives two ways to cook the eggplant. When we make this spread in the restaurant kitchen, we char the eggplant over stovetop flames and call it "smoky eggplant spread," and it does have a lovely smoke flavor. The charring process is messy (our stovetops are designed to be easily cleaned) and very smoky (we have a powerful exhaust fan). It can be fun to char eggplant in your home kitchen, but those of us who have done it advise this: disable the smoke alarm, put the exhaust fan on high speed, open the windows, wear a mask. If you live in an apartment building, think twice about doing it.

Just oven-roast it. Made with oven-roasted eggplant, the lemon, dill, and garlic flavors shine.

The eggplants can be cooked a day or two ahead of time and then refrigerated. The spread will keep for about a week in the refrigerator.

Yields about 3 cups
Eggplant cooking time: about 15 minutes if charring, 30 to 45 minutes if roasting in the oven
Prep time after eggplant is cooked: 15 minutes

2 small eggplants (about 1 pound each)
2 garlic cloves, minced or pressed
2 tablespoons olive oil
2 tablespoons fresh lemon juice
⅓ cup mayonnaise
2 tablespoons chopped fresh dill
salt
ground black pepper

Cook the eggplants directly over a gas flame or on a grill, turning carefully with tongs until all sides are charred and the inside is soft throughout. Or, place the eggplants on a baking sheet, prick several times with a fork, and bake in a 450°F oven until soft, 30 to 45 minutes.

When the eggplants are cool enough to handle, peel off the skin and place the pulp in the bowl of a food processor. For a mellower garlic flavor, heat the garlic in the oil in a microwave oven or in a small skillet just until the garlic sizzles, taking care not to scorch. Add the olive oil and garlic, lemon juice, mayonnaise, and dill to the food processor and process until smooth and creamy. Season with salt and pepper to taste.

The spread can be served at once, but it's best when chilled and given some time for the flavors to meld.

VARIATIONS
- Omit the dill and add chopped scallions or chopped fresh chives or parsley.
- Use vegan mayonnaise.

SERVING AND MENU IDEAS
Serve with pita wedges, crudités, or crackers. Make sandwiches with pita or dark rye bread and Havarti cheese. Russian Eggplant Spread also works well with Greek and Middle Eastern dishes as well as Eastern European ones. Put it on a combo plate with Tabouli Salad (page 106) or Greek Spinach Rice Balls (page 27) and Tomato, Cucumber, and Artichoke Salad (page 256) or Beet Salad (page 258).

Edamame-Wasabi Spread

This is a lovely green spread with a little kick from the wasabi. Bored with hummus? Give this silky spread a try.

Edamame are soybeans, sometimes available fresh, but widely found in the frozen food section of natural food stores and supermarkets. For this recipe, make sure you buy shelled edamame, which may be called mukimame or muki edamame.

Yields 1⅔ cups
Time: 20 minutes

2 cups fresh or frozen shelled edamame
2 teaspoons wasabi powder
2 tablespoons vegetable oil
1 tablespoon light miso
2 teaspoons peeled and grated fresh ginger
1 tablespoon plus 1 teaspoon rice vinegar
⅓ cup water
salt
1 tablespoon chopped scallions (optional)

Cook the edamame in salted water to cover until tender, 5 or 6 minutes for fresh beans or according to package directions if using frozen ones. In a colander or sieve, run cold water over the edamame until cool and then transfer to the bowl of a food processor.

Combine the wasabi powder with an equal amount of water to form a smooth paste. Add it to the bowl of the processor along with the oil, miso, ginger, rice vinegar, and water. Process until smooth, stopping to scrape down the sides if needed. Add a little more water, if necessary, for a smooth spread. Add salt and more vinegar and wasabi paste to taste. If adding the scallions, either pulse them at the end, or sprinkle them on as a garnish. Chill the spread before serving.

VARIATION
- Substitute fresh lemon juice for the rice vinegar.

SERVING AND MENU IDEAS
Edamame-Wasabi Spread is especially good with rice crackers and crudités. It also makes a fine pita sandwich with tomato slices and greens.

Herbed Chèvre Spread

There are several nice goat farms near Ithaca that produce good cheeses, so at Moosewood we often make an herbed chèvre spread to go on crackers for an appetizer, or to use in a sandwich, or to spread on bread to go with a salad. Here's our favorite basic recipe, but notice all the variations. We make them all.

Yields 1½ cups
Time: 15 minutes

4 ounces chèvre, at room temperature
4 ounces cream cheese, at room temperature
1 teaspoon minced fresh thyme
2 teaspoons minced scallions or fresh chives
½ teaspoon lemon zest
⅛ teaspoon ground black pepper

In a small bowl, mash everything together with a fork. Cover and refrigerate for a couple of hours to allow the flavors to permeate the cheeses. Herbed Chèvre Spread will keep for several days.

VARIATIONS
- Try some dried fruit: currants, apricots, pineapple . . .
- Stir in chopped, softened, sun-dried tomatoes and chopped fresh basil.
- Add your favorite herbs: parsley, dill, marjoram, basil, oregano, tarragon . . .

Fig and Chèvre Spread—To the basic recipe, add ¼ cup stemmed and chopped dried figs. Add ¼ cup chopped toasted walnuts, if you like.

SERVING AND MENU IDEAS
As a snack or appetizer, serve any of the chèvre spreads on crackers or small toasts. Try the basic spread on crackers, topped with a little dollop of fruit jam: quince, currant, cherry, whatever you like. This spread complements Armenian, Greek, Turkish, Middle Eastern, and North African meals.

Dilled Havarti Spread

David Hirsch, a longtime Moosewood menu planner, has had some brilliant ideas over the years, and this is one of them. When we write it on our menu, it carries his name. It's a simple spread that is quick and easy to prepare. Originally, it was pretty much just cheese, dill, scallions, and mayonnaise. Now, we toss some colorful, crunchy, diced vegetables into the mix, adding a lighter, fresher taste and a more interesting texture.

Yields almost 2 cups
Time: 15 minutes

1 cup shredded dilled Havarti cheese, packed
   (4 ounces)
1 tablespoon minced scallions
2 tablespoons chopped fresh dill
½ cup diced celery
½ cup seeded and finely diced bell peppers
   (any color)
⅓ cup mayonnaise
½ teaspoon fresh lemon juice or apple cider
   vinegar (optional)
ground black pepper

In a bowl, stir together all of the ingredients except for the lemon juice. Taste, and if you want more tang, add lemon juice or vinegar and black pepper to taste. This spread will keep well for a couple of days in the refrigerator.

SERVING AND MENU IDEAS

For a snack or an appetizer, serve on crackers or toasted baguette rounds. It also makes a great sandwich with lettuce and tomato slices.

Red Bean and Walnut Spread

Since early on, every Sunday night at Moosewood has been "ethnic night." Ethnic night entices our customers with a special menu featuring the foods of a particular culture, region, or theme, and it also sustains our enthusiasm as cooks because we try new things. We adapted this classic Georgian spread known as *lobio* for an Eastern European ethnic night. It is rich, smooth, and satisfying.

Yields 1½ cups
Time: 15 minutes

¾ cup walnuts, toasted (see page 380)
one 15-ounce can red kidney beans, rinsed and
    drained about (1½ cups beans)
1 garlic clove, minced or pressed
½ cup chopped scallions
2 tablespoons olive oil
2 tablespoons apple cider vinegar or red wine
    vinegar
1 tablespoon chopped fresh dill
½ teaspoon salt
⅛ teaspoon ground black pepper
1 tablespoon chopped fresh cilantro (optional)

In a food processor, whirl the toasted walnuts until finely ground. Add the beans, garlic, scallions, olive oil, vinegar, dill, salt, and black pepper and cilantro, if using. Puree until very smooth. If it's too thick, add a little water.

Serve at room temperature or chilled. This spread will keep in the refrigerator for 2 or 3 days, but you may need to add a little more vinegar before serving, to brighten the flavor.

VARIATION
- Sometimes we make this spread with almonds instead of walnuts.

SERVING AND MENU IDEAS
As an appetizer or snack, mound the spread in a brightly colored dish, garnish with some sprigs of dill or cilantro, and serve with wedges of pita, whole-grain crackers, or carrot and celery sticks. For a sandwich, serve with lettuce in whole wheat pita pockets or on rye or pumpernickel toast.

SOUPS

Creamy Herbed Potato Soup and Four Variations

Creamy potato soups abound at Moosewood; we serve some sort of creamy potato soup at least once a week. Here is our best basic version, plus our favorite variations. Use whatever variety of potatoes you like and looks good at the market. Fresh coarsely ground black pepper makes a big difference. These soups freeze well.

Yields 9 cups
Serves 6 to 8
Time: 45 minutes

2 tablespoons olive oil or vegetable oil
2 cups chopped onions
1 cup chopped celery
1 teaspoon salt
5 cups coarsely chopped potatoes, peeled, or if smooth and thin-skinned, unpeeled
5 cups water
2 tablespoons chopped fresh dill
4 ounces cream cheese
⅛ teaspoon black pepper
chopped fresh chives (optional)
chopped fresh parsley (optional)

Warm the oil in a covered soup pot on medium-low heat, add the onions, celery, and salt and cook until very soft but not browned, about 10 minutes. Add the potatoes and water, stir well, and bring to a boil. Reduce the heat and simmer until the potatoes are tender, about 10 minutes.

Add the dill and cream cheese. Working in batches in a blender, purée the soup until smooth. Season with the black pepper and more salt to taste. Gently reheat.

Top each bowl of soup with chives and parsley, if you like.

VARIATIONS

Potato-Cheese Soup
Yields 10 cups

Add some minced or pressed garlic with the onions and celery. After 5 minutes, add 1 cup of finely chopped carrots and cook for 10 minutes, or until the carrots have softened. Then add the potatoes and water. Include the dill, or don't. Stir in 1 packed cup of shredded sharp cheddar cheese along with the cream cheese. Purée the soup.

Potato Florentine Soup
Yields 10 cups

Add 2 teaspoons of finely chopped fresh rosemary with the onions and celery and omit the dill. Add 1 packed cup of shredded Fontina cheese or ½ cup of shredded Parmesan cheese with the cream cheese. Purée the soup, return to the pot, and reheat until hot. Stir in 10 to 12 ounces of rinsed, stemmed, and finely chopped fresh spinach (about 7 cups chopped), and cook for a couple of minutes until the spinach has wilted but is still bright green.

Potato-Cabbage Soup
Yields 10 cups

After the onions and celery have cooked for 8 minutes, stir in 1 teaspoon of ground caraway seeds and 4 cups of chopped cabbage. Cook, stirring frequently, for about 15 minutes, or until the cabbage is soft. Continue with the basic recipe. If you like, add about a cup of shredded cheddar. Serve chunky or puréed.

Vichyssoise
Yields 8 cups

Reduce the onions to 1 cup and add about 4 cups of chopped leeks (see page 379). Reduce the quantity of potatoes to 3 cups, and peel them for a pristine soup and to allow the flavor of the leeks to shine. Replace the dill with 1 tablespoon of chopped fresh tarragon. Replace the cream cheese with 1 cup of half-and-half. Continue with the basic recipe.

Potage Jacqueline
(Creamy Sweet Potato Soup)

Potage Jacqueline is so easy that you can come home from work and whip it up pronto! When your sweet potatoes are that deeply sweet and velvety variety that shows up in the market once in a while, this soup is positively ambrosia—with run-of-the-mill sweet potatoes, it's still a food that's fit and delicious for anyone's dinner. It's velvety, velvety.

Moosewood cook Lisa Wichman created this soup back in the 1980s. We dubbed it Potage Jacqueline after her (Jacqueline is the name her mother gave her), and the soup has been a favorite at the restaurant all these years. For a long time, we added grated fresh ginger, but lately, we like the sweet potato flavor unfettered.

Yields 7 cups
Time: 40 minutes

2 tablespoons vegetable oil
2 cups chopped onions
1 teaspoon salt
1 cup diced celery
4 cups peeled and chopped sweet potatoes
    (about 1½ pounds whole)
3 cups water
1 bay leaf
¼ cup sherry (optional)
1 cup half-and-half or light cream
ground black pepper

In a covered soup pot, warm the oil on medium heat. Add the onions and salt and cook until translucent, about 10 minutes. Add the celery and cook for about 5 minutes. Add the sweet potatoes, water, bay leaf, and sherry, if using. Cover and bring to a boil, and then reduce the heat and simmer for 15 to 18 minutes until the sweet potatoes are tender.

Remove and discard the bay leaf. Add the half-and-half or light cream and purée in a blender or food processor. Season with pepper and more salt to taste. Reheat carefully; do not boil.

VARIATION
Add a teaspoon or two of peeled and grated fresh ginger with the celery.

SERVING AND MENU IDEAS
A bowl of this soup is a great counterpoint to a salad of bitter greens or peppery arugula. Garnish with a sprinkling of chopped fresh herbs, if you like: parsley, dill, tarragon, chives, or scallions.

Cream of Asparagus Soup

Here's a luscious soup, made even better with the addition of butter and cream. We unapologetically add a bit of those bad boys to our asparagus soup because the taste is so divine. Don't worry though, we give you some ideas for a lighter version.

Yields about 7 cups
Time: 50 minutes

2 tablespoons butter
1½ cups chopped onions
½ cup chopped celery
1 bay leaf
1½ teaspoons salt
2 teaspoons dried thyme
2 pounds asparagus
1 cup peeled and diced potatoes
2 cups water
1¼ cups half-and-half
1 tablespoon chopped fresh tarragon

Melt the butter in a covered soup pot on medium-low heat, add the onions, celery, bay leaf, salt, and thyme and cook for about 10 minutes.

While the onions cook, prepare the asparagus. Snap off and discard the tough stem ends. Rinse the spears. Slice off the tips and set aside. Chop the stalks.

Add the chopped asparagus stalks, potatoes, and water to the soup pot. Cover and bring to a boil, then reduce the heat and simmer for about 15 minutes, or until the potatoes and asparagus are tender.

Meanwhile, slice the asparagus tips in ½-inch pieces and steam them for 3 or 4 minutes until tender but still bright green. Set aside.

Remove and discard the bay leaf. In a blender or food processor, purée the soup mixture with the half-and-half and tarragon until smooth. A blender will make it the smoothest.

Reheat gently, add the steamed asparagus tips, and season with more salt to taste.

VARIATIONS
- For a lighter version, use vegetable oil and milk instead of butter and half-and-half.
- For a thicker soup, add 2 to 4 tablespoons of cream cheese while puréeing.

SERVING AND MENU IDEAS
This is a good soup to serve with Rice Salad with Herbs and Vegetables (page 101) or with Roasted, Toasted Ciabatta (page 84).

Portuguese White Bean and Kale Soup

Portuguese white bean and kale soup is such a classic. It is traditionally made with linguica sausage, so it might be hard to convince purists that a vegetarian version could be just as good. (Or better!)

But we did just that while in Provincetown, Massachusetts, where our version was cooked by Wynnie Stein while she was guest chef during Women's Week at the elegant Chester Restaurant. Chester's chefs were skeptical, and she had to ignore their affectionate but mocking comments while chopping mounds of veggies for the soup. But she was really sweating that the customers might also scoff at the changes in this town's signature soup.

Happily, the ingredients won the day. The sun-dried tomatoes and ground fennel add some of the traditional flavor and at the same time enhance the natural sweetness of the kale. Folks (including the chefs—whew!) were swooning about how newly fresh-tasting was their beloved classic.

Yields 10 cups
Time: 1 hour

½ cup sun-dried tomatoes
2 tablespoons olive oil
1½ cups chopped onions
2 garlic cloves, coarsely chopped
2 teaspoons salt
2 teaspoons ground fennel seeds
1 small fennel bulb, diced (about 2 cups)
1 cup diced carrots
1½ cups diced potatoes
2 teaspoons dried thyme or 1 tablespoon fresh
¼ teaspoon ground black pepper
3 cups chopped fresh tomatoes or one 15-ounce can diced tomatoes
3 cups cooked white beans (two 15-ounce cans), drained
4 cups water or vegetable stock
5 or 6 cups loosely packed chopped kale
3 tablespoons fresh lemon juice

If you don't chop the fennel and carrots beforehand, you will probably have trouble keeping up with this cooking schedule. On the other hand, it doesn't hurt to cook a little longer at each stage.

In a small bowl, soak the sun-dried tomatoes in boiling water to cover.

In a covered soup pot on medium-low heat, warm the olive oil. Add the onions, garlic, and salt and cook for about 5 minutes. Add the ground fennel and diced fennel bulb and cook for about 3 minutes. Stir in the carrots, potatoes, thyme, and black pepper and cook for 3 minutes.

Add the tomatoes, beans, and water or stock and bring to a boil. Reduce the heat and simmer, covered, until the potatoes are just tender. If the soup is too thick, add another cup of water.

Meanwhile, remove the sun-dried tomatoes from the soaking liquid and coarsely chop.

Add the kale and sun-dried tomatoes to the pot. Simmer for about 10 minutes, until the kale is tender. Stir in the lemon juice. Season with more salt and black pepper to taste.

SERVING AND MENU IDEAS

Serve with bread and cheese. Fresh fruit would be good, or try Low-fat Lemon Pudding Cake (page 363) for dessert.

Cream of Spinach Soup

A vivid bright green soup, smooth and with plenty of body, simply flavored with spinach, potatoes, and onion. This is one of the soups for which Moosewood is famous and appreciated. You can't buy anything like this commercially prepared. Barely cooked spinach is the key. Adding it at the end to just wilt it and then puréeing everything creates a gorgeous, green soup.

Yields 9 cups
Time: 40 minutes

3 tablespoons vegetable oil
2 cups chopped onions
1 teaspoon salt
3 cups peeled and chopped potatoes
2½ cups water
8 cups fresh baby spinach (12 ounces), rinsed
1 cup milk
½ cup half-and-half
¼ teaspoon freshly grated nutmeg
¼ cup dry sherry (optional)

In a covered soup pot on low heat, warm the oil, add the onions, sprinkle with the salt, and cook for about 10 minutes, or until the onions are translucent and golden, but not browned.

Add the potatoes and water, cover, and bring to a boil. Lower the heat and simmer for about 10 minutes, or until the potatoes are tender. Remove from the heat.

Add the spinach and stir it down into the soup until it has wilted. Stir in the milk, half-and-half, and nutmeg.

Working in batches, purée the soup in a blender until it is completely smooth and evenly bright green. Return the soup to the pot, stir in the sherry, if using, cover, and reheat on very low heat, stirring frequently.

SERVING AND MENU IDEAS
Serve the soup as it is, or top with croutons or sautéed mushrooms. This is excellent served with Spring Egg Salad (page 79) on whole wheat toast, or Antipasto Pita (page 77).

Creamy Hungarian Mushroom Soup

A delicious and attractive golden brown soup, this is very smooth with a succulent mushroom slice in almost every spoonful. We've revised this recipe over the years to achieve a gluten-free velvety smoothness without heavy cream, and to improve on the unappetizing gray that puréed mushroom soups tend toward. Carrots and paprika solve the color problem. Potatoes, cream cheese, and the mushrooms themselves, and thorough puréeing give a nice mouthfeel.

Yields 9 cups
Time: about 1 hour

1½ pounds white mushrooms
    (about 7 cups prepped)
2 tablespoons butter
2 cups chopped onions
1 teaspoon salt
1 cup diced celery
1 cup chopped carrots
1 teaspoon dried thyme or 2 teaspoons
    minced fresh thyme
2 tablespoons soy sauce
1 teaspoon sweet paprika
¼ cup dry sherry (optional)
2 cups peeled and diced potatoes
2½ cups water
2 tablespoons butter
2 cups milk
3 ounces cream cheese
1 tablespoon chopped fresh dill

Coarsely chop half of the mushrooms and set aside. Slice the remaining mushrooms and set aside.

Melt the butter in a covered soup pot on low heat, add the onions and salt, and cook until soft, about 10 minutes. Add the celery, carrots, and thyme, if using dried, and cook, covered, for 5 minutes. Stir in the chopped mushrooms, soy sauce, and paprika, and sherry, if using. Increase the heat to medium and continue to cook, covered, stirring frequently, for about 5 minutes. Add the potatoes and water and bring to a simmer. Simmer until the potatoes are tender, about 10 minutes.

Meanwhile, in a separate pan, sauté the sliced mushrooms and thyme, if using fresh, in butter until tender and lightly browned, usually about 10 minutes. Set aside.

In a blender, working in batches, thoroughly purée the soup with the milk, cream cheese, and fresh dill until very smooth. Return the puréed soup to a soup pot, stir in the sautéed mushrooms, and reheat gently.

VARIATIONS
- For a pleasant, mildly flavored cream of mushroom soup, omit the paprika and dill.
- Sherry isn't essential, but it rounds out the flavor nicely.

SERVING AND MENU IDEAS
Serve with almost any salad; we especially like this soup with Autumn Salad Plate (page 109) or Beet Salad (page 258) on a bed of greens.

Southwestern Sweet Potato–Corn Soup

This soup has a beautiful color like we imagine sunset in the southwestern United States—orange sweet potatoes, red bell peppers, and golden corn. The texture is smooth and creamy and the soup is rich tasting without butter or cream, or *any* dairy in fact. The aroma is fragrant with lime, hot peppers, cumin, and fresh cilantro. We often serve it at as a starter at our benefit brunches because it is satisfying, but not so filling that it spoils anyone's appetite for the other delicious foods to come.

Yields about 7 cups
Serves 6
Time: 50 minutes

2 tablespoons vegetable oil
2 cups finely chopped onions
2 garlic cloves, minced or pressed
1 fresh hot pepper, minced
1 teaspoon salt
1 tablespoon ground cumin seeds
2½ cups peeled and diced sweet potatoes
2 cups seeded and diced red bell peppers
3 cups frozen or fresh corn kernels
2½ cups water
3 tablespoons fresh lime juice
2 tablespoons finely chopped fresh cilantro
1 teaspoon sugar (optional)
ground black pepper

Warm the oil in a soup pot on low heat. Add the onions, garlic, hot peppers, and salt, cover, and cook until the onions are soft, about 10 minutes. Add the cumin and sweet potatoes and cook, covered, on low heat for 4 minutes, stirring occasionally. Stir in the bell peppers, cover, and cook on low heat for 4 minutes, stirring occasionally. Add the corn with the water and bring to a boil. Reduce the heat and simmer, covered, until all of the vegetables are tender, about 8 minutes.

In a blender, purée about half of the soup and stir back into the pot. If the soup is too thick, add another ½ cup of water. Stir in the lime juice and cilantro, and sugar to taste, if using. Season with salt and black pepper.

SERVING AND MENU IDEAS

Serve with Mexican Salad Plate (page 113) or one of our composed seasonal salad plates (page 96 to 118). And it would sure be good with Spanish-style Tortilla (page 152) or Southwestern Bean Burgers (page 93).

Sopa de Lima

This spicy, brothy, tangy Mexican tomato-lime-chile-cilantro soup has been a favorite at Moosewood since Lisa Wichman developed it for *Sundays at Moosewood Restaurant* back in the 1980s, and the Sopa de Lima we serve today is pretty much the same as three decades ago. This is one recipe that we haven't revised much over the years. We've learned that in the winter, when fresh tomatoes aren't so flavorful, you can make a good pot of it with canned tomatoes. It definitely qualifies as comfort food for many of us.

Every day at the restaurant, we make a big pot of vegetable stock, and we always make Sopa de Lima with stock. But at home, many of us usually don't go to that trouble, and when ripe, full-flavored summer tomatoes are available, the soup is fine made with water. With wintertime fresh tomatoes, you really need stock.

Yields about 8 cups
Time: 55 minutes with fresh tomatoes;
    45 minutes with canned tomatoes

2 tablespoons olive oil or vegetable oil
2 cups diced onions
2 garlic cloves, minced or pressed
1 teaspoon salt
1 or 2 fresh hot peppers, minced
2 teaspoons ground cumin seeds
1 teaspoon ground coriander seeds
½ teaspoon dried oregano
4 cups diced fresh tomatoes and 4 cups water or
    stock, or one 28-ounce can diced tomatoes
    and 3 cups water or stock.

⅓ cup fresh lime juice
⅓ cup chopped fresh cilantro

crumbled corn tortilla chips
grated cheddar or Monterey Jack cheese (optional)

Warm the oil in a covered soup pot on medium-low heat. Add the onions, garlic, and salt and cook, stirring occasionally, until the onions have softened, about 10 minutes. Stir in the hot peppers (decide on the quantity and whether or not to seed them to suit your taste), cumin, coriander, and oregano and cook, covered, for 3 or 4 minutes, stirring frequently.

If using fresh tomatoes, stir in the tomatoes and another teaspoon of salt, increase the heat to medium-high, and cook until the tomatoes soften and begin to release juice. Add the water or stock and stir well. Add canned tomatoes, if using, with the water. Bring to a simmer. Simmer, covered, for about 10 minutes.

Stir in the lime juice and cilantro, bring back to a simmer, and cook for a couple of minutes. Add more salt to taste.

To serve, place tortilla chips in large, shallow soup bowls and ladle soup over them. Top with grated cheese, if you like.

SERVING AND MENU IDEAS
What could be better than Sopa de Lima and Mexican Salad Plate (page 113)? Well, let's see . . . Spanish-style Tortilla (page 152), Spinach-Cheese Burritos (page 198), Southwestern Bean Burgers (page 93).

Thai Butternut Squash Soup

This is a velvety smooth soup, vibrant orange and flecked with bright green. The flavor is vibrant as well—spicy, sweet, and tangy all at the same time.

Yields 9 cups
Time: 55 minutes

2 tablespoons vegetable oil
2 cups chopped onions
2 garlic cloves, chopped
1 teaspoon salt
1 tablespoon peeled and grated fresh ginger
1 teaspoon Thai curry paste, or more later to taste
1 butternut squash (about 2½ pounds), peeled, seeded, and chopped (6 cups)
3 cups water
1 lime
one 14-ounce can unsweetened coconut milk
2 cups baby spinach, cut into chiffonade (see page 374)
sugar as needed
¼ cup chopped fresh cilantro (optional)

Warm the oil in a covered soup pot on medium-low heat. Add the onions, garlic, and salt and cook until the onions have softened, about 10 minutes. Stir in the ginger and curry paste and cook for a minute or two more. Add the squash and water and bring to a boil. Reduce the heat and simmer until the squash is tender, 15 to 20 minutes.

While the squash is cooking, zest and juice the lime. Add about a teaspoon of zest and 1 tablespoon of the juice to the pot. When the squash is tender, stir in half of the coconut milk. In a blender or food processor, purée the soup. Be careful, hot soup can erupt!

Return the puréed soup to the pot and reheat. Taste for sweetness, spice, salt, and tang. Depending on the sweetness of your squash, a spoonful of sugar may bring the soup to life. Add more lime juice and/or curry paste to taste.

Stir in the chiffonade of spinach and the cilantro, if using, and cook just until the spinach has wilted.

VARIATIONS

- Add 1 or 2 keiffir lime leaves to the pot while the squash is simmering. Remove and discard before puréeing.
- Substitute lemon zest and juice for the lime.
- Although butternut is the easiest winter squash to peel, other winter squashes can be used. Or, to save time, substitute three 12-ounce packages of frozen winter squash for the fresh, or use the pre-cut fresh squash cubes that many supermarkets offer.
- Replace the squash with sweet potatoes.

SERVING AND MENU IDEAS

Serve the soup topped with chopped scallions and pan-fried tofu cubes (page 202), or cubed Thai Baked Tofu (page 205). Some finely chopped Thai basil would be lovely and tasty. Of course Thai Noodle Salad (page 100) would be good with this soup.

French Onion Soup

French onion soup is one of the world's most evocative and romantic dishes. The soup takes an hour to make—just long enough to listen to an album of Django Reinhardt. You can have a good cry while you cut the onions, and then be rewarded with a most satisfying meal. Remember, we'll always have Paris.

We wish we could report that you can make a good vegetarian version with just water, but you can't. You need a flavorful stock or broth to give this soup depth. At Moosewood, we make big pots of stock every day with lots of vegetables, herbs, and apples. At home, sometimes we make our own and sometimes we buy it (see page 388).

Sherry is another important flavor element. Red or white wine work also, but sherry best enhances the rich sweetness of caramelized onions.

Yields 11 cups
Time: 1 hour

3 tablespoons olive oil
8 cups onions, cut lengthwise into thin slices
1 teaspoon salt
½ teaspoon dried thyme (see Notes)
1 cup sherry
8 cups vegetable stock or broth (see page 388)
2 to 3 tablespoons Dijon mustard
2 to 3 tablespoons soy sauce
1 bunch fresh thyme (see Notes) (optional)
ground black pepper
grated Gruyère, Swiss, or Parmesan cheese
croutons (see Notes)

Warm the oil in a large, heavy skillet or in a soup pot on medium-high heat. Add the onions and stir well. Cook, stirring frequently, until the onions soften. Stir in the salt and lower the heat to medium-low. Continue to cook, stirring frequently, until the onions are golden brown and caramelized, about 30 minutes. Stir in the dried thyme for the last 10 minutes of cooking.

If you caramelized the onions in a skillet, transfer them to a soup pot. Add the sherry to the skillet and stir well to deglaze the pan. Pour the dark brown, flavorful liquid into the soup pot. If the onions were cooked in a soup pot, add the sherry directly to the pot and stir well, scraping the bottom of the pot to remove all the browned bits.

Add the stock or broth, mustard, and soy sauce (and, if using, a bundle of fresh thyme). Simmer for 20 minutes. Season with black pepper, and add more mustard and soy sauce to taste.

Serve topped with grated cheese and croutons.

NOTES

Know your dried thyme—it varies in intensity and is sometimes harsh. Or, use fresh thyme: tie a small bunch of fresh thyme into a bundle with kitchen string. Add with the stock or broth, and remove before serving.

To make croutons: In a skillet on medium heat or in a microwave, briefly cook some minced garlic in olive oil and then add 1-inch bread cubes and stir until coated. Toast the bread cubes on a baking sheet in a 350°F oven for about 10 minutes. Cool before storing.

SERVING AND MENU IDEAS

Serve the soup with a crisp green salad or Summer Salad Plate (page 112). Or, begin with Seasoned Artichokes (page 263) and end with Apple Crisp (page 354) or Low-fat Lemon Pudding Cake (page 363).

Mushroom-Sesame-Tofu Soup

This is one of our early "hippie" dishes, and it still hits the spot on a damp, chilly day. It's really almost a stew. The celery, mushrooms, and tofu make it nice and chunky, the peanut butter and tahini make it rich and filling.

Back in the 1970s, many paths led to vegetarianism: ecological, humanitarian, and spiritual. Mitch Weiss's new vegetarianism brought him into our midst, and he stayed to become a skilled cook and one of the practical backbones of our business. We're indebted to Mitch for being one of the shapers and sustainers of Moosewood in its earliest years.

This soup is a pleasure to make—while each ingredient cooks, there's just enough time to prep the next ingredients to go into the pot. It's good right away, and then leftovers just keep getting better in the refrigerator for a couple of days.

We make it with both peanut butter, for heartiness, and tahini, for smoothness, but if you don't have both on hand, use whichever you have and just add more to achieve the consistency and intensity of flavor you like. If you're using only tahini, add some dark sesame oil for an interesting flavor.

Yields 9 cups
Time: 40 minutes

2 tablespoons vegetable oil
2 cups chopped onions
½ teaspoon salt
1½ cups thinly sliced celery
3 cups sliced cremini or white mushrooms (12 ounces whole)
2 tablespoons peeled grated and fresh ginger
1 teaspoon Tabasco or other hot sauce, more to taste
3 bay leaves
one 28-ounce can diced tomatoes
1 cup water
7 to 8 ounces tofu (one-half block)
¼ cup peanut butter
¼ cup tahini
¼ cup soy sauce
1 cup hot tap water

In a covered soup pot on medium heat, warm the oil. And the onions and salt and cook, stirring frequently, for about 5 minutes. Add the celery and cook for 5 minutes. Stir in the mushrooms and cook, stirring frequently, for about 5 minutes, or until the mushrooms begin to soften. Stir in the ginger and hot sauce. Add the bay leaves, tomatoes, and water and stir well. Bring to a boil, then lower the heat and simmer for about 5 minutes. Cut the tofu into 1-inch cubes and add to the soup. Return to a boil, reduce the heat, and simmer briskly for 10 minutes.

In a small bowl, stir the peanut butter and tahini together with the soy sauce and hot water until smooth. Stir into the soup. Add more hot sauce to taste.

SERVING AND MENU IDEAS
Serve with cornbread (pages 283 and 284) or whole wheat bread for a satisfying meal. Strawberry-Rhubarb Crumble (page 353) or Apple Crisp (page 354) is good for dessert.

Mulligatawny

Beautiful and aromatic Mulligatawny has been a Moosewood favorite from the beginning. Its golden, creamy, coconut broth is studded with colorful vegetables. Make it as spicy, or not, as you wish.

Back in 1973, Joan Adler, now a Moosewood cook since 1974, was working at the library down the street from the restaurant. She ate lunch at Moosewood frequently. One noon, a cup of mulligatawny transformed her life—well, at least it was the catalyst for the awakening of Joan's appreciation of food beyond the 1950s fare of her childhood. That mulligatawny had the lure of a snake charmer. She began to have lunch at Moosewood every day, and it wasn't long before she was in the Moosewood kitchen.

Yields 9 cups
Time: 55 minutes

2 tablespoons vegetable oil
1½ cups chopped onions
1 teaspoon salt
1 tablespoon peeled and grated fresh ginger
2 teaspoons ground turmeric
2 teaspoons ground coriander seeds
1 fresh hot pepper, minced, or ¼ teaspoon cayenne
    or ½ teaspoon red pepper flakes
4 cups water
1 cup diced carrots
1 cup diced potatoes
1 cup seeded and diced bell peppers
1 cup diced fresh tomatoes
½ cup cooked rice
1 cup unsweetened coconut milk
2 tablespoons fresh lemon or lime juice
3 tablespoons chopped fresh cilantro

Warm the oil in a covered soup pot on low heat. Add the onions and salt and cook until the onions have softened, about 10 minutes. Stir in the ginger, turmeric, coriander, and hot pepper and cook briefly. Add the water, carrots, and potatoes and bring to a boil. Reduce the heat to a rapid simmer, cover the pot, and cook for 10 minutes.

Add the bell peppers, tomatoes, and cooked rice. Simmer for about 5 minutes, or until all the vegetables are tender. Finally, stir in the coconut milk, lemon juice, and cilantro and heat to a simmer. Add more salt and/or lemon juice to taste.

VARIATIONS
- If you don't like cilantro, omit it, but add some chopped parsley or scallions because the green flecks look really nice in the golden broth.
- Add some chickpeas for a heartier, main dish soup.
- Add some grated coconut.

NOTE
If you don't have any cooked rice on hand, add an additional ½ cup of water and ¼ cup of raw white rice such as basmati or jasmine to the pot with the potatoes and carrots.

SERVING AND MENU IDEAS
This makes a great lunch or supper served with pappadam or bread, or a good starter for Indian, North African, or Caribbean meals.

Miso Soup

Our partner Maureen Vivino, whose influence runs through all of the Moosewood Collective cookbooks, favors simple meals in her home kitchen, and she's never caught without miso. She does all sorts of things with miso, but the good old standby is soup. We've published quite a number of recipes for miso soups, ranging from simple broths to hearty vegetable-packed soups. This one is easy, nourishing, and attractive and has just enough different textures and tastes to make it interesting.

Usually miso soup starts with a dashi, a Japanese-style soup stock, although in a pinch, you could make do with just water. However, both of our suggestions for dashi use pantry items—either dried shiitake mushrooms or dried kombu seaweed—so an easy and flavorful dashi can always be at hand. Kombu dashi has the briny, sea vegetable taste we associate with much of Japanese cuisine. Shiitake dashi is earthier and richer. Either dashi is enhanced and warmed with the addition of ginger. Either dashi will make a fine miso soup, or use both a piece of kombu and a few dried mushrooms to make a broth.

Yields 6 cups
Time: 25 minutes

DASHI
5 cups water
6 slices fresh ginger
1 cup thinly sliced onions
6 dried shiitake mushrooms or ½ ounce dried
    kombu (8- to 10-inch piece) or a combination

SOUP
4 ounces tofu (firm or soft), cut into small cubes
1 cup packed baby spinach leaves
¼ cup miso, (see page 380)

TOPPINGS
chopped scallions
a few drops of dark sesame oil

Place all of the dashi ingredients in a covered soup pot and bring to a boil. Lower the heat and simmer for 15 minutes.

Remove the pieces of ginger and the kombu, if using, and discard. If using shiitakes, remove from the hot dashi and, when cool enough to handle, trim off and discard the stems and slice the caps into thin strips, then return to the dashi. Add the tofu and bring to a simmer. In a small bowl, stir together the miso and a ladleful of the dashi and then stir into the soup. Repeat with more miso, to taste. Add the spinach and as soon as the spinach has wilted, turn off the heat to preserve the miso's healthful enzymes.

Sprinkle the toppings onto each cup or bowl of soup.

VARIATIONS
- Add 2 or 3 tablespoons of sake or dry sherry to the soup.
- Add sliced snow peas, cooked soba noodles, mung bean sprouts, or sesame seeds when you add the spinach.

SERVING AND MENU IDEAS
In Japan, miso soup is most often served toward the end of a meal composed of at least several other modestly sized dishes, and it is usually accompanied by a small bowl of plain rice. It may be served at any meal, including breakfast. We're here to testify that miso soup for breakfast is delicious and healthful; it can grow on you and become a habit.

At Moosewood, where we often mix and match cuisines, we might serve Miso Soup with a green salad with Japanese Carrot Dressing (page 305), or with Winter Salad Plate (page 110), or with Edamame-Wasabi Spread (page 42) and rice crackers. We might pair it with California Pita (page 76). Rice is always welcome, either plain or Sesame Jeweled Rice (page 290).

Corn Chowder

This creamy, golden soup is a year round favorite at Moosewood. This recipe makes a brothy chowder—if you like it thick, add either less liquid or more potatoes.

In the summer, made with corn freshly cut from the cob, this chowder is especially sweet and flavorful. It's very easy to freeze fresh corn (see page 375), so do that when you have more corn than you can eat—you'll be glad for the reminder of summer when you make this chowder in the middle of winter.

Yields about 9 cups
Serves 4 to 6
Time: 55 minutes (a little longer if using fresh corn)

2 tablespoons olive oil
1½ cups chopped onions
1½ cups diced celery
½ teaspoon salt
½ cup diced carrots
3 cups diced potatoes
3 cups water
½ teaspoon dried thyme or 1 teaspoon fresh
3½ cups fresh corn kernels or 1 pound frozen
1 cup milk
3 ounces cream cheese
ground black pepper
2 teaspoons chopped fresh dill (optional)

Warm the oil in a covered soup pot on low heat, add the onions, celery, and salt and cook until soft, about 10 minutes. Stir in the carrots when they're prepped.

Add the potatoes, water, and thyme, if using dried. Increase the heat and bring to a boil, then reduce the heat and simmer for about 5 minutes, or until the potatoes begin to soften. Add the corn and thyme, if using fresh, and simmer for another 5 or 6 minutes until the vegetables are tender.

Ladle about 2 cups of the soup into a blender, add the milk and cream cheese, and whirl until smooth. Be careful—start at the lowest speed because hot soup in the blender can be explosive! Pour the purée back into the pot and reheat gently.

Season with more salt and black pepper to taste. If you're adding dill, stir it in now.

VARIATIONS
- Add some diced bell peppers with the carrots.
- For corn and cheddar chowder, add a cup of shredded cheddar cheese to the blender with the milk and cream cheese.
- You can replace the carrots and potatoes with diced sweet potatoes.

NOTE
Fresh corn makes a deliciously sweet and "corny" soup. The average ear of corn yields about ½ cup kernels, so for this recipe, about 7 ears of corn will do it.

Texas Barbecue Bean Soup

We love the flavors of sweet and tangy barbecue sauce and chipotle peppers in adobo sauce in this hearty soup. We recommend barbecue sauce without additives, or look at Barbecued Tofu Pita (page 82) to make your own.

Make the soup with two types of beans: white, red, pinto, black beans, black-eyed peas—whatever is on hand.

Yields 8 cups
Time: 1 hour

2 tablespoons vegetable or olive oil
2 cups chopped onions
1 cup diced celery
4 garlic cloves, minced
1 teaspoon salt
1 large red or green bell pepper, seeded and diced
2 tablespoons chipotle peppers in adobo sauce
 (or 1 fresh hot pepper, minced)
2 teaspoons dried oregano
1 teaspoon dried thyme
2 teaspoons ground cumin seeds
½ teaspoon ground black pepper
2 cups water
one 15-ounce can diced tomatoes
two 15-ounce cans beans (about 3 cups beans),
 rinsed and drained (see headnote)
1 cup fresh or frozen corn kernels
⅓ cup barbecue sauce

Warm the oil in a covered soup pot on low heat. Add the onions, celery, garlic, and salt and cook for 10 to 15 minutes, stirring occasionally, until the onions are very soft. Add the bell peppers, chipotles, oregano, thyme, cumin, and black pepper and cook on medium heat for 5 minutes, stirring occasionally.

Stir in the water and tomatoes and bring to a boil. Reduce the heat and simmer, covered, for about 10 minutes, or until the vegetables are tender. Add the beans, corn, and barbecue sauce, bring back to a simmer, and cook for at least 10 minutes.

SERVING AND MENU IDEAS

Serve with shredded Monterey Jack or cheddar cheese or with some Chipotle Cream (page 310) or sour cream. We like to serve this soup with cornbread (pages 283 and 284).

West African Peanut Soup

This soup is rich and velvety smooth and a beautiful orangey-brown color. Since the early years at Moosewood, it's been a perennial customer request, and it always shows up multiple times on surveys of our fans' favorites. For many Moosewood cooks, it's a good old standard at home.

Peanut soups and sauces are found throughout West Africa. Moosewood cook Nancy Lazarus developed West African–style peanut soup for our *Sundays at Moosewood Restaurant* cookbook, and more than thirty years later, she developed this revised version to reflect how we do it today, a bit simpler and still divinely delicious.

Yields 9 cups
Time: 1 hour

1 tablespoon vegetable oil or olive oil
2 cups chopped onions
1 cup diced celery
1 teaspoon salt
2 tablespoons peeled and grated fresh ginger
1 tablespoon Tabasco, or other hot sauce, or 1 fresh hot pepper, minced
4 cups peeled chopped sweet potatoes (about 1½ pounds whole)
3 cups water
3 cups tomato juice
1 cup smooth peanut butter
¼ cup chopped fresh cilantro
chopped scallions or chives

Warm the oil in a covered soup pot on medium heat. Add the onions, celery, and salt and cook, stirring frequently, until softened, 10 to 15 minutes. Stir in the ginger and hot sauce or hot pepper. Add the sweet potatoes and water and stir well. Bring to a boil, cover, and simmer until the vegetables are very tender, about 20 minutes.

Add the tomato juice and peanut butter to the pot. In a blender in batches, or using an immersion blender, purée the soup until smooth. Add the cilantro and reheat gently. Add more salt and hot sauce to taste.

Serve topped with scallions or chives.

SERVING AND MENU IDEAS
Serve with cornbread (pages 283 and 284) and a crisp green salad with one of our signature dressings (pages 301 to 306).

Red Lentil Soup

Lately, our favorite way to make warm, golden lentil soup flecked with red and green and wonderfully fragrant with cilantro and spices is this, a blending of the two recipes we've previously published.

Red lentils don't stay red when they are cooked; they turn a nice golden color, and in this soup we add turmeric to enhance that color. Ground cumin and coriander are both fresher and more aromatic and flavorful if you keep whole cumin and coriander seeds in your pantry and, when they are called for in a recipe, toast them in an unoiled skillet or on a tray in a toaster oven until headily fragrant.

Yields 9 cups
Time: 45 minutes

1½ cups dried red lentils
5 cups water
1 teaspoon ground turmeric
2 bay leaves
4 garlic cloves, coarsely chopped
2 slices peeled fresh ginger
2½ teaspoons salt
3 tablespoons olive oil
1½ cups finely chopped onions
¼ teaspoon red pepper flakes
1½ cups diced carrots
1 cup diced potatoes
2 teaspoons ground cumin seeds
2 teaspoons ground coriander seeds
1 cup water
½ cup seeded and diced red bell peppers
2 cups chopped fresh tomatoes, or one 14-ounce can diced tomatoes
2 tablespoons fresh lemon juice
⅓ cup chopped fresh cilantro
ground black pepper

Rinse the red lentils in a sieve. Place them in a soup pot with the water, turmeric, bay leaves, garlic, ginger, and 1 teaspoon of the salt and bring to a boil, stirring occasionally as they come to a boil. Reduce the heat to a simmer and cook, covered, until soft, 15 to 20 minutes, stirring occasionally.

Meanwhile, warm the olive oil in a covered skillet or saucepan on medium-low heat. Add the onions and red pepper flakes and cook, stirring often, for about 10 minutes. Increase the heat, add the carrots, and cook for about 2 minutes. Stir in the potatoes, cumin, and coriander and cook, stirring constantly, for about 2 minutes. Stir in the water and bell peppers and bring to a boil. Reduce the heat and simmer for about 10 minutes, or until the vegetables are tender. Add the tomatoes and simmer for another 5 to 10 minutes.

Remove the bay leaves and ginger slices from the cooked lentils and discard them. Stir in the cooked vegetables. Stir in the lemon juice, cilantro, and the remaining 1½ teaspoons salt. Season with black pepper to taste.

NOTE
This soup tends to get thicker as it sits—just add more water for the consistency you like and then adjust the lemon and salt to taste.

SERVING AND MENU IDEAS
This soup is so delicious and satisfying that it can be the meal. Of course, it would be nice with a green salad or vegetable. Some bread might be welcome. Then some Creamy Vegan Rice Pudding (page 364) for dessert . . . ummm. This is also, a great starter for any North African or West African or Latin American or Indian dish.

Curried Lentil Soup

A hearty, warming soup studded with colorful veggies—as spicy or mild as you wish.

We think it's possible that although we've served this soup hundreds of times over the years, it's never been exactly the same twice. When we do a vegetable curry, we often try to make enough that leftovers can be used the next day in a lentil soup. And when we're starting from scratch, Moosewood cooks have a lot of latitude to indulge their own tastes and preferences. Linda Dickinson, the Moosewood curry queen, developed this recipe for home cooks—at the bottom of the recipe, read about all of the ways you can vary it.

Yields about 10 cups
Time: 50 minutes

1½ cups dried brown lentils
4 cups water
1 teaspoon ground turmeric
½ teaspoon salt
2 tablespoons vegetable oil
1 teaspoon black mustard seed (optional)
1½ cups chopped onions
2 garlic cloves, minced or pressed
1 tablespoon peeled and grated fresh ginger
½ teaspoon salt
1 cup diced carrots
1 cup diced potatoes
1 teaspoon ground cumin seeds
1 teaspoon ground coriander seeds
1 teaspoon ground cinnamon
½ teaspoon ground turmeric
¼ teaspoon ground cardamom
¼ to ½ teaspoon cayenne, or a fresh hot pepper, minced
3 cups water or vegetable stock
1 cup seeded and diced bell peppers (any color)
½ cup unsweetened coconut milk
2 to 3 tablespoons fresh lemon juice
¼ cup chopped fresh cilantro (optional)
plain yogurt (optional)

In a saucepan, bring the rinsed lentils, water, turmeric, and salt to a boil. Reduce the heat and simmer, covered, until the lentils are tender, 30 to 40 minutes. Stir occasionally and add more water if necessary.

Warm the oil in a soup pot on medium heat. Add the mustard seeds, if using, and cook until they start to pop. Add the onions, garlic, ginger, and salt, cover and cook on low heat until the onions are tender, about 10 minutes. Add the carrots, potatoes, cumin, coriander, cinnamon, turmeric, cardamom, and cayenne and cook briefly, stirring constantly to prevent burning.

Add the water or stock and bring to a boil, then reduce the heat and simmer until the vegetables are barely tender, 5 to 10 minutes. Stir in the bell peppers and continue to simmer until all the vegetables are tender.

When the lentils are soft, stir them and their remaining cooking liquid into the vegetables. Add the coconut milk, 2 tablespoons of the lemon juice, and the cilantro, if using. Add more lemon juice and salt to taste.

Serve the soup with a dollop of yogurt, if you like.

VARIATIONS

- Use any color of lentils; the cooking time may vary. Or, you can use green or yellow split peas instead of lentils; peas take longer to cook than lentils.

- Any vegetable combo works. Use your favorites or whatever is languishing in the veggie bin of your refrigerator: sweet potatoes, cauliflower, zucchini, green beans, spinach, tomatoes, green peas—all good choices. Just include a variety of colors. Add diced tomatoes or chopped spinach near the end of cooking.

- About spicing, if you have a favorite curry powder, use a couple of tablespoons in place of the spices, but keep the grated ginger and garlic. The mustard seeds are mostly for fun. Or, you could go in a Thai direction and use a commercial Thai curry paste. If you do that, you could add chopped basil in place of, or in addition to, cilantro.

Chilled Cantaloupe-Amaretto Soup

Pale peachy-colored, frothy, and refreshing, this soup is wonderful in midsummer when melons and peaches are fully ripe and sweet. When fresh peaches are unavailable, you can substitute frozen sliced peaches. The advantage of frozen fruit is that the soup will be instantly cold and ready to serve. This is an elegant first course for brunch or supper on the patio.

Yields 6 cups
Prep time: 25 minutes
Chilling time: 1 hour or more

1 medium cantaloupe (about 4 cups cubed)
2 cups peeled and chopped fresh ripe peaches or
    frozen sliced peaches
¾ cup peach juice
1 cup half-and-half
3 tablespoons fresh lemon juice
⅛ teaspoon ground cinnamon or ¼ teaspoon
    freshly grated nutmeg, or a pinch of each
½ teaspoon pure almond extract
¼ cup amaretto liqueur
sugar, agave syrup, or honey, if needed

Peel and seed the melon and cut into cubes. Peel, pit, and chop the peaches if using fresh.

Working in batches in a blender or food processor, purée all of the ingredients until smooth. The blender makes the smoothest soup. Stir together the batches and taste. For a slightly sweeter soup, whisk in a spoonful of sugar, agave syrup, or honey.

Chill thoroughly before serving. Well covered and refrigerated, this soup will keep for a couple of days.

VARIATION

- Replace the half-and-half with almond milk. The soup will be a little thinner, and you should taste it before adding the almond extract because you might want only a drop or two.

NOTES

You can freeze very ripe peaches whole. When ready to use, run the peach under warm water and the skin will easily rub off. Then the peach is easy to cut into pieces and blend.

When melons are at their very best in your area, seed and cube a very ripe one and freeze it. Then you can enjoy the flavor of a summer melon even in the wintertime. With frozen melon cubes (and frozen peaches), the soup will not only be instantly cold, but slightly frothy enough to serve like an elegant smoothie in a fancy cocktail glass.

SERVING AND MENU IDEAS

Having a big Italian meal? This soup makes a good palate refresher between the pasta and fish courses. It's a good summer wedding soup. Served with biscotti, it's a dessert soup.

Gazpacho

Easy, quick, light, and satisfying. Cool, savory, and tomato-sweet. Perfect for a hot summer day when tomatoes are in season. At the restaurant, gazpacho is one of our most popular soups during July and August when our terrace is open.

Yields 8 cups
Prep time: 30 minutes
Chilling time: at least 1 hour

1 quart chilled tomato juice
1 cucumber, peeled, seeded, and diced
   (about 1 cup)
2 cups diced fresh tomatoes
¼ cup finely chopped scallions
1 garlic clove, minced or pressed
¼ cup fresh lemon juice
2 tablespoons extra-virgin olive oil
2 tablespoons chopped fresh basil
2 teaspoons ground toasted cumin seeds
   (page 380)
1 teaspoon salt
Tabasco sauce or other hot sauce
2 ripe avocados, pitted and cubed (optional, but so
   yummy)

Combine all of the ingredients in a tureen, large bowl, or nonreactive pot. Chill for at least an hour.

VARIATIONS
- Instead of basil, use fresh tarragon, cilantro, or parsley.
- Try lime juice instead of lemon juice.
- Add cooked corn kernels.

SERVING AND MENU IDEAS
Gazpacho plus salad and a hunk of bread: it's great lunch! Gazpacho is the perfect starter for all sorts of dishes, for example, a quesadilla (page 196), Habas Verdes con Queso (page 142), Pecan-crusted Fish (page 233), to name but a few.

Two Tofu Salad Pitas
BLTease Sandwich Spread
Saigon Sandwich
California Pita
Antipasto Pita
Deviled Egg Salad
Spring Egg Salad
Muffuletta
Tempeh Reuben
Barbecued Tofu Pita
Roasted, Toasted Ciabatta

Two Tofu Salad Pitas

Although they are very different in the end, we realized that two of our best pita fillings start out the same way. So, we're giving them to you as one recipe. It's the dressings that make the difference.

Ira's Lunch has been a favorite at the restaurant, and at home with our families, for at least twenty-five years. We call it "Ira's Lunch" because Moosewood cook Linda Dickinson created it as a sandwich filling, a substitute for chicken salad, for Ira Rabois, her husband, to pack in his lunch box. The inspiration for "Thai Tofu" came one day when we had leftover Thai salad dressing in the Moosewood kitchen.

This recipe calls for Tofu Kan–style Baked Tofu (page 201). In and around Ithaca, we are very fortunate to have Tofu Kan made by Ithaca Soy. It's somewhat similar to other flavored baked tofu products available nationally, yet its flavor and consistency are unique . . . perfect for these fillings. So we developed a recipe for tofu kan so that anyone can make our favorite tofu kan recipes and it will be like it's from the Moosewood kitchen.

Yields about 4 cups filling, enough for 4 whole pita sandwiches
Prep time: Ira's Lunch: 15 minutes; Thai Tofu: 20 minutes

PITA FILLING
one recipe Tofu Kan–style Tofu (page 201)
     (two 7-ounce slabs)
1 cup seeded and diced red bell peppers
½ cup diced celery
⅓ cup sliced scallions

IRA'S LUNCH DRESSING
½ cup mayonnaise
1 to 2 tablespoons fresh lemon juice
1 tablespoon chopped fresh dill (optional)
salt
ground black pepper

THAI TOFU DRESSING
½ cup unsweetened coconut milk or
     pineapple juice
¼ cup peanut butter
1 tablespoon soy sauce
2 tablespoons fresh lime juice
2 tablespoons chopped fresh cilantro
     and/or basil
1 fresh hot pepper, seeded and minced
1 teaspoon peeled and grated fresh ginger
     (optional)
salt
ground black pepper

4 pita breads
salad greens (lettuce, spinach, spring mix)

On the coarse side of a handheld grater, grate the Tofu Kan. In a bowl, toss the grated tofu kan with the bell peppers, celery, and scallions.

If you're making Ira's Lunch, add the mayonnaise and lemon juice to the grated tofu kan filling and stir well. Stir in dill, if using, and season with salt and black pepper to taste.

If you're making Thai Tofu, whirl all of the dressing ingredients in a blender until smooth. Add the dressing to the grated tofu kan filling and stir well. Season with salt and black pepper to taste.

To serve, cut the pitas in half, open the pockets, and toast. While the pita is warm, stuff each half with greens and about ½ cup of filling.

SERVING AND MENU IDEAS
Both are delicious as snacks or appetizers with crackers and vegetable sticks or tomatoes. Thai Tofu is great with Thai Butternut Soup (page 58) or West African Peanut Soup (page 65). Add tomato slices to a pita filled with Ira's Lunch or Thai Tofu. Delicious with Corn Chowder (page 63) or Creamy Herbed Potato Soup (page 49).

BLTease Sandwich Spread

We're not sure who came up with this idea back in the early days at Moosewood when vegetarians were looking for substitutes for their favorite old standbys, but we do remember who named it. Put this filling in a sandwich with lettuce and tomato, and it not only approximates the flavor of a BLT, but is even better. Jeremy Werbin, a great punster and a member of the Zobo Funn Band so loved by Ithacans in the '70s, was working at Moosewood as a waiter and busser; he took a first, tentative bite, moaned with pleasure, and sighed, "BLTease." We've held onto that original name, but now it's a thing of its own—we don't even think of bacon when we eat it.

For a few years, we collaborated with Cornell University Dining Services to revive a cafe in Anabel Taylor Hall, and this was one of the hits—people came from the other side of campus for a BLTease pita.

Sometimes we like BLTease plain, for the smooth mouthfeel, but usually we add bell peppers and celery for some crunch and extra flavor.

Yields about 2½ cups
Time: 15 minutes

1 heaping cup grated tofu kan-style Baked Tofu (page 201)
4 ounces smoked cheddar cheese, shredded (about 1 cup heaping)
⅓ cup mayonnaise
½ red bell pepper, seeded and diced
½ cup diced celery
1 tablespoons finely chopped scallions

Coarsely grate the tofu kan and smoked cheddar using a handheld grater. Add the mayonnaise and stir well. Stir in the bell peppers, celery, and scallions. Add more mayonnaise to taste if needed.

SERVING AND MENU IDEAS

For lunch, a snack, or a light supper, stuff a pita with BLTease and lettuce and tomato. Or, serve it on a slice of bread or toast, open-faced. It is excellent on crackers, as a stuffing for celery sticks, or served as a dip with crudités.

Saigon Sandwich

Here's a delicious, addictive spread inspired by Vietnamese *banh mi* sandwiches and created at Moosewood by menu planner and cook, Jenny Wang. It may seem to be an odd combination, but just try it—before your meal is done, you'll be thinking about when you can have it again.

At first glance, the recipe looks "involved," but actually, it's pretty simple. Banh mi are traditionally made with baguettes, but the filling is good in pitas, sliced whole wheat bread, Kaiser rolls, or various other types and shapes of bread.

Yields 3½ cups filling, enough for 6 sandwiches
Time: 35 minutes

PICKLED CARROTS
1 cup grated carrots
¼ cup rice vinegar
1 tablespoon sugar
½ teaspoon red pepper flakes or 1 teaspoon
    minced fresh hot peppers
a sprinkling of salt

TOFU FILLING
1 heaping cup grated Tofu Kan-style Baked Tofu
    (page 201)
1 heaping cup shredded smoked cheddar cheese
½ cup seeded and diced red bell peppers
½ cup diced celery
1 tablespoon finely chopped scallions
⅓ cup mayonnaise
2 tablespoons fresh lime juice
½ teaspoon finely grated lime zest
¼ cup minced fresh cilantro and/or basil

baguette or other French bread, sliced bread,
    pitas, or rolls

EXTRAS
shredded lettuce
shredded cabbage
thinly sliced cucumber
sliced avocado
sliced tomatoes
chopped mint leaves
more cilantro or basil

In a small bowl, stir together the grated carrots, vinegar, sugar, red pepper flakes or hot peppers, and salt. Set aside for at least 20 minutes. (You can make "pickled" carrots a day or two ahead, and they will be nicely pickled.)

In a separate bowl, stir together the tofu kan, smoked cheddar, bell peppers, celery, and scallions. Add the mayonnaise, lime juice, lime zest, and cilantro or basil and mix well.

Slice the bread and prepare at least a couple of the extras listed.

Stir the carrots, with the pickling liquid, into the tofu kan mixture. Spread the spread on the bread, add the extras, close it up, and enjoy.

SERVING AND MENU IDEAS
Saigon Spread is also very good on crackers for an appetizer or snack. Or serve it as a salad on a bed of lettuce, with a cup of soup and some bread. Soups that pair well: West African Peanut Soup (page 65), Red Lentil Soup (page 67), and Thai Butternut Squash Soup (page 58).

California Pita

Moosewood is located in the Finger Lakes region of New York State, where our cloudy skies and long winters are legendary. So we intentionally include items on the restaurant's late-fall, winter, and early-spring menus that will temporarily transport our customers to sunnier climes. Happily, this delicious sandwich with its bright color and flavor does the trick, and it has always been one of the best-selling items on the lunch menu.

Yields 2½ cups filling, enough for 2 whole
  pita sandwiches
Time: 10 to 15 minutes

2 tablespoons fresh lime or lemon juice
1 tablespoon olive oil
1 garlic clove, minced or pressed
dash of cayenne (optional)
2 large Hass avocados
1 cup peeled, seeded, and diced cucumbers
1 to 2 cups diced tomatoes
2 tablespoons minced scallions or red onions
¼ cup chopped black or green olives (optional)
¼ cup chopped fresh cilantro (optional)
salt

2 whole pitas
lettuce leaves
shredded Monterey Jack or cheddar cheese
  (optional)

In a bowl, whisk together the lime juice, oil, garlic, and cayenne, if using. Slice around each avocado lengthwise down to the pit. Twist the halves apart and with the tip of the knife pop out the pit. Hold the avocado half in the palm of your hand and score the flesh into cubes. Using a spoon, scoop the cubes out of the skin into the bowl. Repeat with the other halves. Toss with the dressing. Gently stir in the cucumbers, tomatoes, scallions, and olives and cilantro, if using. Toss well. Season with salt and add more lime juice to taste.

Halve the pita bread and toast it. Line each half with a lettuce leaf and fill with a generous ½ cup of filling. Top with cheese, if you like.

Antipasto Pita

Tasty and colorful, like a salad in a sandwich. Anything you would put on an antipasto platter can be cut, chopped, shredded, or torn and dressed for a delicious pita sandwich. Here's how we usually make antipasto pita filling at the restaurant.

Yields about 6 cups filling, enough for 4 or
    5 whole pita sandwiches
Time: 25 minutes

DRESSING
¼ cup olive oil
3 tablespoons vinegar (red wine or apple cider)
1 garlic clove, pressed (optional)
½ teaspoon Dijon mustard
1 teaspoon dried oregano
1 tablespoon finely chopped fresh parsley or basil
¼ teaspoon salt
a sprinkling of ground black pepper

FILLING
1 cucumber peeled, seeded, and diced
½ red bell pepper, seeded and diced
1 large tomato, diced
12 pitted black or green olives, finely chopped
2 celery stalks, diced
½ cup cooked or canned chickpeas, drained
1 tablespoon chopped fresh parsley
1 tablespoon chopped fresh basil
½ cup chopped peperoncini
one 14-ounce can artichoke hearts in brine,
    drained and chopped

4 or 5 pita breads
lettuce leaves

In a large bowl, whisk together the dressing ingredients. As you prepare the veggies, add them to the bowl. Toss well and let sit for at least 10 minutes.

Cut the pitas in half and toast lightly. To serve, while the pitas are still warm and soft, stuff each half with a lettuce leaf and filling.

VARIATIONS
- Add chopped seasoned seitan, or cubes of mozzarella or provolone cheese.
- Make it Greek: add some chopped fresh dill and top with feta cheese.

Deviled Egg Salad

Still around 'cause it's still so good. Stuff it in a pita with lettuce and tomato or between slices of toasted whole-grain bread. Make it an appetizer with crackers and crudités. Serve it as a main dish salad on a bed of greens, or fill tomato or bell pepper shells with it. What more is there to say? After forty years, it's still what our customers want for lunch. And, eggs aren't on the "bad" list anymore. And, it's very pretty; in fact, much prettier than your average egg salad.

Yields 2 cups
Time: 25 minutes

6 large eggs
¼ cup mayonnaise
2 to 3 teaspoons Dijon mustard
¼ cup diced celery
¼ cup seeded and diced red bell peppers
2 tablespoons thinly sliced scallions
¼ teaspoon salt
ground black pepper

Place the eggs in a saucepan with cold water to cover and bring to a boil. Reduce the heat to a simmer and cook for 10 to 12 minutes. Pour off the boiling water, cover with cold water, and crack the shells to facilitate peeling. Set aside.

While the eggs cook, combine the mayonnaise, mustard, celery, bell peppers, scallions, and salt in a bowl. When the eggs are cool enough to handle, peel and coarsely chop them. Add them to the dressing mixture and stir gently to combine. Season with black pepper to taste. Serve immediately or chill.

VARIATIONS

- Greek Egg Salad: Add 1 to 2 tablespoons chopped kalamata olives and some chopped fresh dill.
- Creole Egg Salad: Add fresh thyme and a few splashes of Tabasco sauce. Replace the salt with Old Bay Seasoning.
- Mexican Egg Salad: Use Chipotle Aioli (see page 259) instead of plain mayonnaise, omit the Dijon, and add chopped fresh cilantro.
- Italian Egg Salad: Add 1 to 2 tablespoons of minced sun-dried tomatoes and chopped fresh basil.

NOTE

Toasted nuts (see page 380) would be fine in any version: chopped almonds or walnuts or whole pine nuts. Basically, any ingredient that appeals to you is worth a try. Add a couple tablespoons and see if you like it. How about capered egg salad?

Spring Egg Salad

We love to make this dish in the spring when we can use locally grown asparagus and chives. The tarragon and Dijon make it ambrosial.

If you walk into our cafe, you will likely find Moosewood partner Neil Minnis making exotic infusions for mixed drinks and genial conversation with our customers. Many of us also know Neil to be an exquisite cook; he developed this sandwich filling for our *Moosewood Restaurant New Classics* cookbook and we've been grateful for it since. Sometimes we stuff tomatoes or baby bell peppers with it.

Yields 2½ cups
Time: 30 minutes

6 large eggs
8 ounces asparagus (about 1 cup of ½-inch pieces)
⅓ cup mayonnaise
1 tablespoon Dijon mustard
2 teaspoons minced fresh tarragon
¼ teaspoon salt
sprinkling of ground black pepper
¼ cup seeded and diced red bell peppers
2 tablespoons snipped fresh chives or thinly sliced scallions

Place the eggs in a saucepan, add cold water to cover, and bring to a boil. Reduce the heat to a simmer and cook for 10 to 12 minutes. Pour off the boiling water, cover with cold water, and crack the shells to facilitate peeling. Set aside.

While the eggs cook, rinse the asparagus, break off the tough ends, and slice the tender spears into ½-inch pieces. Steam or blanch the asparagus until just tender, 3 to 5 minutes. Set aside to cool.

In a bowl, stir together the mayonnaise, mustard, tarragon, salt, and black pepper. Add the bell peppers and chives. When the eggs are cool enough to handle, peel and chop them. Add the eggs and cooled asparagus to the bowl and stir well. Taste and adjust the seasonings as needed, and enjoy!

VARIATIONS
- Replace the tarragon with 1 tablespoon of chopped fresh dill.
- Replace some or all of the mustard with fresh lemon juice.

SERVING AND MENU IDEAS
Serve between slices of whole wheat bread, in a pita, or wrapped in a flour tortilla with lettuce and tomato slices.

Muffuletta

To Louisianans and food tourists, the muffuletta sandwich is as synonymous with New Orleans as its musical and sultry streets. The traditional muffuletta is a sandwich of Sicilian origins and of heroic proportions. An Italian round sesame bread is layered with olive salad, cured meats, and cheeses, then cut into wedges for eating. At Moosewood, we make it with a variety of different breads and cheeses, and often make it vegan with Tofu Kan (see page 201) or seitan in place of cheese.

Yields 2 cups olive salad
Time: 40 minutes

OLIVE SALAD
1 cup green olives
½ cup toasted walnuts
1 garlic clove, minced or pressed
⅓ cup minced celery
¼ cup finely sliced scallions
¼ cup chopped fresh parsley
¼ teaspoon red pepper flakes
¼ teaspoon dried oregano
2 to 3 tablespoons extra-virgin olive oil
2 tablespoons red wine vinegar

ciabatta, focaccia, French or Italian bread (or your favorite)
lettuce leaves or arugula
tomato slices
sliced cheese such as fresh mozzarella, mild provolone, Swiss, or Jarlsburg

In a food processor, pulse the olives and walnuts until coarsely ground, but not yet a paste. In a bowl, combine the ground olives and walnuts with the garlic, celery, scallions, parsley, red pepper flakes, oregano, olive oil, and vinegar.

Cut the bread for sandwiches. Spread both the top and bottom pieces of the bread with the olive salad. Layer on tomato and cheese slices and greens. Close it up and dig in.

VARIATIONS
- In place of cheese, use slices of Tofu Kan–style Baked Tofu (page 201) or seitan.
- At Moosewood we often add roasted onions and zucchini to our Muffulettas: toss sliced onions and sliced zucchini with olive oil and a sprinkling of salt. Spread on an oiled baking sheet in a single layer and roast at 400°F for about 20 minutes.

SERVING AND MENU IDEAS
For a nice appetizer, serve Muffuletta olive salad on crostini, topped with fresh mozzarella and tomatoes. We especially like roasted plum tomatoes (see Roasted, Toasted Ciabatta page 84).

Tempeh Reuben

We've been making this sandwich for decades! Seasoned tempeh is piled high on whole wheat toast, and topped with good sauerkraut and plenty of melted Swiss cheese, and then slathered with our Russian dressing. It's irresistible: the cooks have to make lots of "samples" for the staff.

All sorts of tempeh are now available, but we prefer plain soy tempeh that we can flavor our own way by marinating it a bit. We give you two ways to prepare the seasoned tempeh, pan-fried on the stovetop and baked in the oven.

Use the seasoned tempeh on its own to top your favorite stir-fry, to add protein to a green salad, or simply as a healthful snack.

> Yields 3 open-faced sandwiches; about 2 cups of seasoned tempeh; 1 generous cup of Russian Dressing
> Time: 40 minutes (if pan-frying) or 50 minutes (if baking)

SEASONED TEMPEH
8 ounces plain soy tempeh
2 tablespoons soy sauce
2 tablespoons red wine or apple cider vinegar
½ teaspoon ground fennel seeds
¼ teaspoon ground black pepper
1 or 2 tablespoons vegetable or olive oil

RUSSIAN DRESSING
½ cup mayonnaise
½ cup chopped tomatoes
1 teaspoon Dijon mustard
2 tablespoons ketchup or tomato paste
¼ teaspoon salt
2 tablespoons chopped scallions
ground black pepper
1 tablespoon apple cider vinegar (optional)

1 cup shredded Swiss cheese
3 slices whole wheat, whole-grain, or rye bread
1 cup drained sauerkraut

Cut the tempeh into ¾-inch cubes and place in a shallow bowl. Whisk together the soy sauce, vinegar, fennel, and black pepper. If you're going to bake the tempeh, add 1 tablespoon of oil. Pour the marinade over the tempeh cubes, stir gently to coat, and set aside for 15 to 30 minutes.

Meanwhile, make the Russian dressing: Whirl the mayonnaise, tomatoes, mustard, ketchup, salt, and scallions in a food processor or stir together by hand in a bowl. Season with black pepper and more salt to taste, and stir in the vinegar if you want the dressing a little tangy. Refrigerate until ready to use. Shred the Swiss cheese.

If you're pan-frying the tempeh, heat 2 tablespoons of oil in a large skillet until a tiny pinch of tempeh dropped in sizzles. Gently stir the tempeh in the bowl and with a slotted spoon lift it out of any remaining marinade and carefully place it in the hot oil (it may splatter). Fry for 8 to 10 minutes, stirring and turning often, until brown. Transfer to paper towels to drain.

If you're baking the tempeh, gently stir it and place on an oiled rimmed baking sheet or dish with any remaining marinade and bake in a preheated 375°F oven until browned, about 25 minutes. Stir every 10 minutes or so.

To assemble the sandwiches, toast the bread. Pile a generous ½ cup of tempeh, generous ¼ cup of sauerkraut, and generous ¼ cup of shredded Swiss cheese on each bread slice. Put the sandwiches in a hot oven or under the broiler until the cheese has melted. Serve topped with Russian Dressing.

SERVING AND MENU IDEAS
This sandwich would be good with Creamy Herbed Potato Soup (page 49).

Barbecued Tofu Pita

Barbecued Tofu Pita is a popular lunch item at Moosewood. We drench tofu and peppers and onions in barbecue sauce and serve it in a warm whole wheat pita pocket, lined with a leaf lettuce to hold in the sauce. Sometimes we serve Barbecued Tofu on a plate, on rice, or with cornbread, and with greens or slaw on the side.

We make our own barbecue sauces, and this is one place where cooks can be creative, adding their own touches. Use our recipe or your favorite barbecue sauce.

At the restaurant, we often oven-roast the bell peppers, onions, and spices and bake the tofu. The oven method takes longer. But at home, pan-frying in oil is a quick and easy way to brown veggies and gives the tofu or tempeh a meaty surface and crusty edge.

The last step is tossing everything with a sweet, zesty sauce.

Yields 4 cups filling, enough for 4 whole pita
    sandwiches
Time: 45 minutes

one 14- to 16-ounce block firm tofu (see page 387)

2 tablespoons vegetable oil
1 large onion, sliced
1 large garlic clove, minced or pressed
½ teaspoon salt
2 medium bell peppers, seeded and chopped

BARBECUE SAUCE
⅓ cup tomato paste (3.5 ounces)
3 tablespoons brown sugar
2 teaspoons ground coriander seeds
1 teaspoon ground fennel seeds
1 to 2 tablespoons mustard (Dijon or spicy brown)
2 tablespoons apple cider vinegar
2 tablespoons soy sauce
½ cup water
2 teaspoons Tabasco or other hot sauce

2 tablespoons vegetable oil
1 to 2 tablespoons soy sauce

4 whole pita breads
lettuce leaves

First, press the tofu if you have time. It isn't essential to press the tofu for this recipe, but it will more readily absorb flavors if pressed (see page 388).

In a large skillet or soup pot, warm the vegetable oil on medium heat. Add the onions, garlic, and salt and cook for 5 minutes, stirring often. Add the bell peppers and cook, stirring often, until the onions are lightly browned and soft and the peppers are tender and getting brown around the edges, about 10 minutes. Remove from the heat and set aside.

Meanwhile, make the sauce: In a bowl, combine the tomato paste, brown sugar, coriander, fennel, mustard, vinegar, soy sauce, water, and Tabasco. Set aside.

Cut the pressed tofu into 1-inch cubes. In a large skillet on medium heat, warm the oil and pan-fry the tofu cubes in a single layer for 3 to 5 minutes, then turn them over carefully with a spatula, sprinkle them with soy sauce, and pan-fry for another 3 to 5 minutes until they turn brown and get a little crisp.

Add the vegetables and barbecue sauce to the tofu and heat the mixture until everything is piping hot.

Serve in warmed pitas lined with lettuce leaves.

VARIATION

- Instead of tofu, use 8 ounces of tempeh cut into ½-inch cubes (see page 387). Tempeh will take a little longer than tofu to pan-fry and may need a little more oil to make it brown and crisp. Mix the soy sauce with an equal amount of water, because tempeh really soaks it up.

SERVING AND MENU IDEAS

These pita sandwiches are pretty substantial and can stand on their own, but Lime-Cilantro Slaw (page 252) makes a nice counterpoint. Or make a southern-style combo plate: serve Barbecued Tofu on brown rice with Vegan Mashed Sweet Potatoes (page 278) and Quick Sautéed Greens (page 268), or with Vegan Cornbread (page 284), corn on the cob, and Cucumbers Vinaigrette (page 256). Use the barbecue sauce for Dixie Tofu-Pecan Loaf (page 209) or put some on Moosewood's Classic Tofu Burgers (page 89).

Roasted, Toasted Ciabatta

This sandwich is one of the restaurant's most popular, especially in cool weather. We vary the vegetables and the cheeses, as there are many excellent combinations. And if we have some pesto (see page 322), aioli (see page 309), or Olivada (page 39) on hand, all the better. Any of them makes a flavorful addition to this sandwich.

We use ciabatta from our local bakery, but whole wheat or rye bread or baguettes are also good choices.

Yields 4 sandwiches
Prep time: 10 minutes
Roasting time: 20 to 25 minutes
Assembly time: 5 to 10 minutes

DRESSING
3 tablespoons olive oil
2 tablespoons balsamic or red wine vinegar
½ teaspoon salt
½ teaspoon dried oregano or thyme
¼ teaspoon ground black pepper

ROASTED VEGETABLES
1 onion, sliced
1 medium bell pepper, (any color), seeded and sliced
two 5-ounce portobello mushroom caps, rinsed and sliced

4 plum tomatoes, stems removed, halved lengthwise
1 tablespoon olive oil

1⅓ cups shredded cheese, such as cheddar, mozzarella, Havarti, provolone, Fontina
one 14- to 16-inch ciabatta
mayonnaise and/or Dijon mustard (optional)

Preheat the oven to 400°F. Lightly oil a baking sheet.

In a bowl, whisk together the dressing ingredients, and then toss with the prepped onion, bell pepper, and portobellos. Spread the vegetables out on the prepared baking sheet and roast until tender, 20 to 25 minutes.

On a separate baking sheet, arrange the tomatoes, cut side up. Brush the tops with olive oil and sprinkle with salt and pepper. Roast until soft and juicy, 15 to 20 minutes. When cool enough to handle, slip the skins from the tomatoes.

While the vegetables are roasting, cut the ciabatta in half lengthwise. If you want, spread the cut side with mayonnaise and/or mustard. Put the halves back together and cut the ciabatta into 4 equal pieces. Place the bread pieces, cut side up, on another baking sheet and sprinkle each top piece with ⅓ cup cheese.

When the roasted vegetables are done, heat the bread in the oven until the cheese has melted and the bread is warm, just a couple of minutes. Layer the bottom of each sandwich with about a quarter of the vegetables and a roasted tomato half. Close up the sandwiches and enjoy.

VARIATIONS
- Roast eggplant, zucchini, or fennel for the sandwiches.
- Replace the cheese with Classic Hummus (page 37) or White Bean and Basil Spread (page 40).
- We often add some arugula or spinach leaves or some chopped fresh basil.

SERVING AND MENU IDEAS
Often, just a sandwich is enough. But then there's soup—we like all kinds of soup with our sandwiches. A smooth, simple soup like Cream of Asparagus (page 51) or Cream of Spinach (page 54) is good. Then there's Gazpacho (page 70) on a hot summer day and French Onion Soup (page 59) on a crisp fall day. It's so hard to choose . . .

Curried Red Lentil Burgers
Moosewood's Classic Tofu Burgers
Falafel Burgers
Mushroom-Tofu-Pecan Burgers
Southwestern Bean Burgers

Curried Red Lentil Burgers

These golden burgers have a nutty flavor and handsome speckles of red. They are always a hit with our lunch crowd.

We actively support companies that offer fair trade products, so we especially like Alter Eco's Red Quinoa. Of course, any variety or brand of quinoa is fine. Or, see the rice variation.

Yields 6 large burgers
Prep time: 1 hour
Baking time: 20 minutes

⅔ cup quinoa
1 cup dried red lentils
2 tablespoons olive oil
2 cups water
1 teaspoon ground turmeric
1½ teaspoons salt
1½ cups finely chopped onions
3 garlic cloves, minced or pressed
1 cup seeded and diced red bell peppers
1 tablespoon peeled and grated fresh ginger
1 tablespoon curry powder
1 teaspoon ground cinnamon
1 tablespoon fresh lemon juice
¼ cup finely chopped fresh cilantro
1 cup toasted cashews

Rinse and drain the quinoa. Rinse and drain the lentils and set aside.

In a saucepan on medium-high heat, warm 1 tablespoon of the oil. Add the quinoa and sauté for 1 minute. Add the lentils and water and bring to a boil, stirring often. (Red lentils sink to the bottom of the pan and then burn easily, so watch carefully.)

Add the turmeric and ½ teaspoon of the salt, and simmer, covered, on low heat until the quinoa is cooked, the lentils are soft, and the water has been absorbed, about 20 minutes. (If there is any liquid left, drain before adding to the burger mix.)

While the lentils and quinoa cook, warm the remaining 1 tablespoon of oil in a skillet or saucepan on medium heat, add the onions and garlic and cook until softened, about 5 minutes. Add the bell peppers, ginger, curry powder, cinnamon, and the remaining 1 teaspoon of salt and continue to cook for about 5 minutes, stirring frequently and adding a little water if needed to prevent sticking.

In a large bowl, combine the cooked quinoa and lentils, the cooked onions and peppers, and the lemon juice and cilantro. In a food processor, whirl the cashews until coarsely ground. Add them to the bowl and mix well.

Preheat the oven to 400° F. Lightly oil a baking sheet.

Shape the mix into 6 burgers and place on the prepared baking sheet. Bake for about 20 minutes, or until firm.

VARIATION

• You can substitute brown or basmati rice for the quinoa. Skip the quinoa step. Begin by cooking red lentils in the water and proceed with the recipe, adding 2 cups of cooked rice to the food processor when you grind the cashews.

SERVING AND MENU IDEAS

We usually serve Red Lentil Burgers topped with Mango Salsa (page 315) or a fruit chutney and yogurt. Sometimes we serve them with Spinach Raita (page 312) or Tzatziki (page 311). Our Favorite Tomato-Cilantro Salsa (page 314) is also good on these burgers.

Moosewood's Classic Tofu Burgers

Our all-time favorite, luscious burgers the way we make them now: Vegan and wheat-free.

Tofu burgers have been a favorite at the restaurant since we can remember. Our customers often call to ask, "Are tofu burgers on the menu today?" They love 'em! In the early years, we almost always served them on a thick slice of whole wheat toast with lettuce, tomato slices, and Russian dressing. Now we serve them various ways; some suggestions follow the recipe.

Because of the increase in the number of our customers who are either gluten intolerant or trying to reduce their consumption of wheat, we've developed ways to make our various kinds of tofu burgers without the bread crumbs we used to use in our published recipes and in the restaurant. Dicing the vegetables small, finely grating the tofu in a food processor, and grinding the walnuts all help to make a mix that will hold its shape.

This recipe makes eight large burgers, or you can shape the mix into smaller patties or "meatballs." We're happy when we have extra burgers and can freeze them for later (see Notes).

Yields 8 burgers
Prep time: 45 minutes
Baking time: 30 to 40 minutes

two 14- to 16-ounce blocks firm tofu (see page 387)
2 tablespoons vegetable oil
2 cups diced onions
½ teaspoon salt
1 teaspoon dried oregano
1 cup grated carrots
½ cup seeded and diced bell peppers (any color)
1 cup coarsely ground toasted walnuts
3 tablespoons soy sauce
2 tablespoons Dijon mustard
2 tablespoons dark sesame oil
¼ cup tahini
¼ teaspoon ground black pepper
¼ cup chopped fresh basil

First press the tofu for at least 30 minutes (see page 388).

While the tofu presses, prepare the rest of the burger mix, and when you're ready to grate the tofu, discard the expressed liquid.

In a covered skillet on low heat, warm the oil. Add the onions, sprinkle with the salt and oregano, and cook on low heat for 7 or 8 minutes, stirring occasionally. Add the carrots and bell peppers and cook, covered, until the vegetables are tender, stirring occasionally, about 8 minutes. Transfer the vegetables to a large bowl.

Finely grate the pressed tofu in a food processor and add it to the bowl of cooked vegetables along with the walnuts, soy sauce, mustard, sesame oil, tahini, pepper, and basil. Mix well and add more soy sauce to taste.

Preheat the oven to 375°F. Lightly oil a baking sheet.

Using about a cup per burger, shape the mix into 8 burgers. Set the burgers on the prepared baking sheet and bake until firm and browned, 30 to 40 minutes.

NOTES

The burgers will be a little sturdier if you use bread crumbs, about ⅔ cup for this recipe, especially if the tofu you use is soft. Gluten-free bread and bread crumbs are available, so if you're avoiding wheat and gluten you have that option.

To freeze these burgers, simply wrap cooled, baked burgers in plastic wrap and put them in the freezer. To reheat, bake on an oiled baking sheet, right from the freezer, at 350°F for 20 to 30 minutes until heated through—the time will depend on how fat your burgers are.

VARIATIONS

- **"Meatballs"**—Add ground fennel seeds to the cooking onions, shape the mix into small balls and bake for about 20 minutes for 1½-inch balls. These are great with spaghetti and Tomato-Basil Sauce (page 324).

- **Tofu "Meat" Loaf**—See the recipe on page 208.

- **Reuben Burger**—Top with melted Swiss cheese, sauerkraut, and Russian Dressing (page 81), and serve pickles on the side.

- **Mediterranean Burger**—Top with Caramelized Onions (page 313) and melted Gruyère or Fontina cheese.

- **Monterey Burger**—Top with Avocado Salsa (page 314) Simple Smooth Guacamole (page 35), or Our Favorite Tomato-Cilantro Salsa (page 314), and melted Monterey Jack, Pepper Jack, or cheddar cheese.

SERVING AND MENU IDEAS

Serve these luscious vegan burgers in a bun or on rice or toast.

Falafel Burgers

Falafel Burgers are extremely popular at the restaurant. By combining tofu and chickpeas with lemon juice, tahini, some spices, and red bell peppers we've created a great burger, a new take on traditional falafels. We like to coat Falafel Burgers with sesame seeds because they add a nice crunchiness. Usually, we serve them on rice or bulghur pilaf with Lemon-Tahini Dressing.

We've found that grating the tofu with a food processor helps the burger mix hold together without the bread crumbs or eggs we used to use in our recipes. Another thing we've learned after making hundreds of burgers and after years and years of cooking in the restaurant is how handy scoops are. We use various size scoops for all sorts of things, an 8-ounce scoop is perfect for these burgers, but a half cup measuring cup will work as well. (An 8-ounce scoop holds about 4 ounces leveled off.)

Yields 8 burgers
Prep time: 45 minutes
Baking time: 35 to 40 minutes

one 14- to 16-ounce block firm tofu (see page 387)
2 tablespoons olive oil
1½ cups finely chopped onions
3 garlic cloves, minced or pressed
1 teaspoon salt
¼ teaspoon red pepper flakes, or a pinch of cayenne
1 cup seeded and diced red bell peppers
2 tablespoons dark sesame oil
2 teaspoons ground turmeric
1 tablespoon ground coriander seeds
one 15-ounce can chickpeas, rinsed and drained (1½ cups)
¼ cup fresh lemon juice

1 to 2 tablespoons soy sauce
¼ cup tahini
¼ cup chopped fresh parsley (optional)
¼ to ⅓ cup sesame seeds

First, press the tofu for at least 15 minutes (see page 388).

Meanwhile, in a skillet on medium-low heat, warm the olive oil. Add the onions and garlic, sprinkle with the salt and the red pepper flakes, and cook for about 7 minutes, stirring often. Add the bell peppers and cook for about 5 minutes, stirring occasionally, until the onions and peppers are soft; add a splash of water, if necessary, to prevent the vegetables from sticking. Stir in the sesame oil, turmeric, and coriander, and cook for 1 minute, stirring constantly.

In a food processor, pulse the chickpeas until crumbly and put them into a large mixing bowl. Using the shredding disk, grate the tofu and add it to the bowl. Add the lemon juice, 1 tablespoon of the soy sauce, the tahini, and parsley, if using. Add the cooked onions and peppers to the bowl and stir well. Taste and add more soy sauce if needed.

Preheat the oven to 375°F. Lightly oil a baking sheet.

Using a scant 8-ounce scoop or a scant ½ cup measuring cup, shape the mixture into 8 burgers. Put the sesame seeds on a plate, coat each burger with the seeds, and place it the prepared baking sheet. Using the palm of your hand, gently flatten each burger a bit. Bake in until golden and firm, 35 to 40 minutes.

SERVING AND MENU IDEAS

Our favorite way to serve Falafel Burgers is on a bed of rice or Bulghur Pilaf (page 294) drizzled with Lemon-Tahini Dressing (page 304) and topped with Cucumber-Tomato Salsa (page 315).

Mushroom-Tofu-Pecan Burgers

We like the succulence of the mushrooms and the flavor of the pecans and herbs—the signatures of this tofu burger. We've changed the recipe to make a delicious burger for people who need to avoid wheat (no bread crumbs) and we've boosted the flavor a bit.

At Moosewood, we serve these patties on brown rice topped with shredded Fontina or cheddar cheese and a heap of Caramelized Onions (page 313). So delicious! The burgers are crumbly, rather than firm, which is a good thing served like we do. But sometimes you want a firm patty that will hold up in a sandwich. We've experimented with it a lot, and our best suggestion is to add an egg to the mixture.

Yields 8 burgers
Prep time: 50 minutes
Baking time: 35 minutes'

one 14- to 16-ounce block firm tofu (see page 387)
1 tablespoon vegetable oil
1½ cups finely chopped onions
½ teaspoon salt
1 teaspoon dried thyme
1 teaspoon dried marjoram (optional)
4 cups chopped mushrooms, white or cremini
   (about 16 ounces whole)
1 cup rolled oats
¾ cup pecans
3 tablespoons soy sauce
¼ cup chopped fresh dill
¼ teaspoon ground black pepper

First, press the tofu for at least 15 minutes (see page 388).

Warm the oil in a skillet on low heat. Add the onions, salt, thyme, and marjoram, if using, cover, and cook until the onions are soft, about 10 minutes, stirring occasionally. Stir in the mushrooms and increase the heat to medium. Stir until the mushrooms begin to release juice, about 2 minutes. Reduce the heat, cover, and cook until tender, about 10 minutes. You don't want to cook away the liquid, so keep the heat low and the skillet covered.

Put the oats into a large mixing bowl, and when the mushrooms are done, pour them over the oats and let them sit. This helps soften the oats.

Meanwhile, toast the pecans (see page 380) and set them aside to cool. With a food processor, grate the tofu and add it to the mushroom-oat mixture. Pulse the toasted pecans to a coarse meal; stop before they become a paste. Add the pecans, soy sauce, dill, and black pepper to the mix and stir well. Add more salt to taste.

Lightly oil or spray a baking sheet. Shape the mixture into burgers by filling a scoop or ½ cup measuring cup and dropping the mixture onto the baking sheet. Use the palm of your hand to flatten each patty, and pat around the circumference to compact the edges. Bake in a preheated 350°F oven until firm and browned, about 35 minutes.

SERVING AND MENU IDEAS

Serve like we do in the restaurant (see the headnote), or on whole wheat toast with barbecue sauce, or ketchup, or mustard and mayonnaise, and maybe tomato or avocado slices.

Southwestern Bean Burgers

When we serve these burgers at the restaurant with melted cheese and fresh tomato or avocado salsa, they are always a favorite with our customers. Beauty is not an attribute of these burgers undressed, but when they're covered with toppings, they look quite lovely—it's what's on the inside that counts.

Yields 8 burgers
Prep time: 40 minutes
Baking time: 30 minutes

2 tablespoons vegetable oil
1½ cups finely chopped onions
½ teaspoon red pepper flakes
1 teaspoon salt
2 garlic cloves, minced or pressed
2 cups seeded and diced bell peppers (any color)
2 teaspoons ground toasted cumin seeds
   (see page 385)
1 teaspoon dried oregano
1½ cups crumbled corn tortilla chips
   (about 6 ounces)
two 15-ounce cans small red or black beans,
   rinsed and drained (about 3 cups)
1 teaspoon finely grated orange zest
½ cup fresh orange juice

Warm the oil in a large skillet on medium-low heat. Add the onions, red pepper flakes, salt, and garlic and cook, stirring occasionally, for about 10 minutes, or until the onions are soft. Adjust the heat so that the onions cook but do not stick or scorch. Add the bell peppers, increase the heat for a minute or two to get the peppers hot, then reduce the heat and cook for about 6 minutes, stirring occasionally. Add the cumin and oregano and cook, stirring often, for about 4 minutes, until the bell peppers are tender.

While the onions and bell peppers cook, whirl the tortilla chips in a food processor until they are coarse crumbs. Put them into a large bowl. Pulse the beans in the food processor until mashed but not puréed. Add them to the mixing bowl.

When the bell peppers and onions are done, add them to the mixing bowl. Stir in the orange zest and orange juice and mix well. Add more salt to taste.

Preheat the oven to 375°F. Lightly oil a baking sheet.

Using a scoop or a generous half cup measuring cup, shape the burgers and place them on the prepared sheet. Using the palm of your hand, slightly flatten the burgers. Bake for about 30 minutes, or until the burgers are firm.

SERVING AND MENU IDEAS
Melt cheddar or Monterey Jack cheese on the burgers and serve on a bed of Spanish Rice (page 287). Top with your favorite tomato salsa or Our Favorite Tomato-Cilantro Salsa (page 314), or Avocado Salsa (page 314) and sour cream. Lime-Cilantro Slaw (page 252) is a nice crunchy accompaniment.

MAIN DISH SALADS

Sichuan Noodles

Way back in the very early days of the restaurant, two Moosewood cooks, Ashley Miller and Bob Love, took Chinese cooking classes where they learned to make these spicy peanut butter–coated noodles. They were instantly popular with our customers then and still are today, although today the rest of the world has caught up and you can find similar dishes at grocery store deli counters. Our Sichuan Noodles are easy to make at home and we think they are much tastier than what you can buy.

Serves 4
Time: 25 minutes

½ pound linguine, or soba or udon noodles
1 cucumber, peeled, seeded, and sliced into thin
   crescents
½ cup finely chopped scallions
mung bean sprouts (optional)

PEANUT DRESSING
⅓ cup peanut butter
⅓ cup warm water
2 tablespoons soy sauce
3 tablespoons vinegar (rice, cider, or white)
1 tablespoon dark sesame oil
1 teaspoon Chinese Chili Paste with Garlic
   (see page 374)

To cook the linguine, bring a large covered pot of salted water to a boil. Prepare the cucumber and scallions. In a small bowl, stir together the dressing ingredients.

When the water boils, cook the noodles until al dente. Some of us break the linguine in half before cooking it because we think it makes it easier to eat when you do. Drain the pasta and toss it with the dressing, cucumbers, and scallions. Garnish with mung sprouts, if you wish. Serve warm or chilled.

The noodles absorb the dressing over time, so if you made Sichuan Noodles ahead, or are serving leftovers, taste them and stir in a little water, and maybe more vinegar, soy sauce, and chili paste as needed.

SERVING AND MENU IDEAS
Most often, we serve Sichuan Noodles with Gingered Broccoli and Carrots (page 273) and Moosewood's Best Baked and Pan-fried Tofu (page 202). Quickly blanched snow peas or sugar snap peas are a great addition to the noodles because of their contrasting crisp texture.

Peruvian Quinoa and Vegetable Salad

Quinoa is a nutritious, quick-cooking grain that wasn't even on our radar when Moosewood opened forty years ago. Today, though, we're cooking with it as much as we can, finding more ways to use it all the time. This is a substantial salad, a complete and nutritious one-dish meal. Shiny black beans, golden corn, red tomatoes, and green flecks of cilantro make it colorful. It's always a Moosewood customer favorite when we serve it as part of a "salad du jour," and it makes a great light dinner for a warm summer night.

Yields 6 cups
Serves 4 to 6
Time: 50 minutes

QUINOA
1 cup quinoa
1 teaspoon oil
¼ teaspoon salt
1½ cups boiling water

DRESSING
¼ cup vegetable oil
3 tablespoons fresh lime or lemon juice
½ teaspoon salt

VEGETABLES
1 tablespoon vegetable oil
½ cup finely chopped onions
2 garlic cloves, minced or pressed
1 cup seeded and diced red, yellow, or orange
   bell peppers
1 cup diced zucchini
¼ teaspoon salt
1 cup frozen or fresh corn kernels
2 teaspoons ground coriander seeds
2 teaspoons ground cumin seeds
½ teaspoon red pepper flakes (optional)
1 cup finely chopped fresh tomatoes
one 15-ounce can black beans, rinsed and drained
   (about 1½ cups)
⅓ cup chopped fresh cilantro

If your quinoa isn't prerinsed, rinse and drain it well in a sieve—this removes any bitter residue from the grains. Warm the oil in a saucepan on high heat, add the drained quinoa, sprinkle with the salt, and stir for a minute. Add the boiling water and bring back to a boil. Reduce the heat to low and cook, covered, for about 15 minutes, or until the water has been absorbed. Remove from the heat and let sit, covered, until the grains are tender, about 5 minutes.

While the quinoa is cooking, make the dressing and prep the vegetables. When the quinoa is done, toss it with about half of the dressing and put it in the refrigerator to cool. It will cool more quickly if you spread it out. Reserve the rest of the dressing.

To cook the vegetables: Warm the oil in a large skillet. Add the onions and cook on high heat for about 2 minutes, stirring constantly. Add the garlic, bell peppers, zucchini, and salt and sauté for about 4 minutes. Add the corn, coriander, cumin, and red pepper flakes, if using, and stir well, and cook until the vegetables are tender, about 3 minutes.

Stir the cooked vegetables into the quinoa. Toss with the remaining dressing and the tomatoes, beans, and cilantro. Add more salt and lime juice to taste. Serve at room temperature or chilled.

VARIATIONS
- In place of the onions, use ¼ cup finely chopped scallions (stir into the vegetables with the fresh tomatoes) or ¼ cup finely diced red onions (toss with the hot quinoa if you want to eliminate the raw "bite" they can have).
- Substitute finely chopped parsley for the cilantro.
- During cooler days when you welcome warmth from your oven, use this "salad" as stuffing for roasted bell pepper halves. Serve topped with melted cheese and Smooth Hot Sauce (page 320). If you make the salad intending to stuff peppers, it's nice to substitute diced carrots for the diced bell peppers.

SERVING AND MENU IDEAS
This salad is delicious served with Simple Smooth Guacamole (page 35) and cheddar or Monterey Jack cheese.

Thai Noodle Salad

Short or long rice noodles are the most authentic for this dish, but at the restaurant we use fusilli pasta, which we think works best for catching the dressing and vegetables. We have found fusilli-shaped rice noodles and white or tricolor wheat pasta.

Serves 6 to 8
Prep time: 45 minutes
Sitting time: 20 minutes

1 pound fusilli, or other shape pasta

VEGETABLES
2 tablespoons vegetable oil
2 carrots, cut into 2-inch-long matchsticks
    (about 1½ cups)
1 red bell pepper, cut into 1½-inch-long
    matchsticks (about 2 cups)
1½ cups asparagus, cut into 1-inch pieces, tips and
    tender stalks (about 12 ounces whole)
1½ cups sliced fresh shiitake mushrooms
    (4 ounces whole)

THAI DRESSING
2 teaspoons finely grated lime zest
¼ cup fresh lime juice
1½ tablespoons rice vinegar
1 tablespoon vegetable oil
1 cup unsweetened coconut milk
1 fresh hot pepper, coarsely chopped
2 tablespoons chopped fresh cilantro,
    Thai basil, or regular basil
1 scallion, coarsely chopped
2 garlic cloves, pressed or chopped
1 teaspoon ground coriander seeds
1½ teaspoons salt
2 tablespoons brown sugar

Cook the pasta in a large pot of salted boiling water until al dente. Drain and transfer to a large serving bowl.

While the pasta cooks, warm the oil in a large skillet on medium-high heat. Add the carrots and sauté for about 2 minutes. Add the bell peppers, asparagus, and mushrooms and continue to sauté for 3 minutes. Add 2 tablespoons of the pasta cooking water, cover, and cook until the vegetables are tender but still brightly colored, about 2 minutes.

Purée all of the dressing ingredients in a blender until smooth.

Add the vegetables and dressing to the pasta and mix well. Set aside at room temperature for 20 minutes to allow the flavors to develop.

This salad is best served at room temperature.

VARIATIONS
- If you'd rather cook the vegetables in water, just blanch each for 30 seconds in a small pot of boiling water, then submerge in very cold water to set the color, and drain.
- You can make your life a little bit easier by substituting 1 tablespoon store-bought Thai curry paste for the hot peppers, garlic, and coriander in the dressing.

SERVING AND MENU IDEAS
Thai Noodle Salad looks and tastes great garnished with chopped peanuts, scallions, and bean sprouts. It's really good with Thai Baked Tofu (page 205).

Rice Salad with Herbs and Vegetables

Vibrant and fresh rice salads can reflect the season or can be inspired by what you find in your vegetable bin. Green or yellow beans, peas, mushrooms, celery are all good. Add some nuts or dried fruit. Add olives or capers. If you have an herb garden, play around with the herbs; try chives, basil, tarragon, marjoram, mint, or oregano. Go Italian, Greek, Tex-Mex, or Chinese. Keep it fresh and you can't go wrong.

Happily, our favorite rice salad is usually the one we're eating at the time. Here's a nice, basic rice salad to get you started.

Yields generous 7 cups
Serves 4 to 6
Time: about 1 hour

RICE
2 cups brown rice, rinsed and drained
2 tablespoons olive oil
½ teaspoon salt
3 cups water

DRESSING
½ cup extra-virgin olive oil
2 garlic cloves, pressed
2 tablespoons fresh lemon juice
3 tablespoons vinegar (red wine vinegar or apple cider vinegar)
2 teaspoons Dijon mustard
½ teaspoon salt
¼ teaspoon ground black pepper

VEGETABLES
1 cup diced carrots
1 cup seeded and diced bell peppers (any color)
1 cup diced fresh fennel bulb
1 cup chopped fresh parsley
½ cup chopped scallions
½ cup minced fresh dill

First, make the rice: Stir the rice, olive oil, and salt in a saucepan on high heat for a minute. Add the water, cover, and bring to a boil. Reduce the heat to low and simmer, covered, until the water has been absorbed and the rice is tender, about 45 minutes.

While the rice cooks, prepare the rest of the ingredients: In a large bowl, whisk together all of the dressing ingredients. Steam the carrots until tender and add them to the bowl. As you prep the bell peppers, fennel, parsley, scallions, and dill, put them into the bowl.

When the rice is done, transfer it to the bowl and toss thoroughly. (Important: warm rice absorbs the dressing flavors better than cold rice, so if you're using refrigerated cooked rice, warm it up before adding to the bowl.)

Serve warm, at room temperature, or chilled.

SERVING AND MENU IDEAS
Serve in a bowl or on a bed of greens with colorful tomato wedges, black olives, and a sprinkling of toasted pine nuts. Top with finely grated Parmesan or serve with Herbed Chèvre Spread (page 43), a wedge of Brie, or cubes of Jarlsberg, Lemon-Herb Baked Tofu (page 204, or Tofu Kan–style Baked Tofu (page 201). Rice salad and soup is always a good meal. During the hot days of summer, try it with Gazpacho (page 70) or Chilled Cantaloupe-Amaretto Soup (page 69).

Asian Rice Salad

This is an interesting and unusual rice salad not to be found in any deli bar. It's studded with brightly colored crunchy vegetables, soft and creamy avocado, and cubes of tofu, and is seasoned with wasabi, ginger, and sesame.

There's a lot going on when you cook this dish—a pan on the back of the stove, a dish of marinating tofu, and then another pan on the stove, vegetables to chop, a cup of marinade, remembering to add the edamame to the rice. The first time you make it, it may seem a bit frantic, but then you see that it all comes together just as the rice finishes. You stir the rice into the bowl, and you're done.

Yields 7 cups
Serves 4 to 6
Time: about 1 hour

RICE
1½ cups brown rice, rinsed and drained
2 teaspoons vegetable oil
2¼ cups water
½ teaspoon salt
¾ cup frozen shelled edamame

MARINATED TOFU
2 tablespoons soy sauce
1 tablespoon rice vinegar
1 tablespoon peeled and grated fresh ginger
8 ounces firm tofu (½ block)

VEGETABLES
1 cup grated carrots
1 cup seeded and diced bell peppers, preferably red
½ cup sliced scallions

DRESSING
2 tablespoons rice vinegar
1 tablespoon vegetable oil
1 teaspoon dark sesame oil
1 teaspoon wasabi powder, or more to taste, dissolved in an equal amount of water

2 teaspoons vegetable oil
1 tablespoon toasted sesame seeds (optional)
1 ripe avocado, peeled and sliced or cubed
salad greens

In a small, heavy saucepan with a tight-fitting lid on high heat, sauté the rice in the oil for a minute, stirring to coat the grains with the oil. Add the water and salt, bring to a boil. Reduce the heat to low, and cook, covered, for 30 minutes. At that point, add the frozen edamame to the pan, cover, and finish cooking the rice. Both the rice and edamame should be done in another 15 minutes.

Combine the marinade ingredients in a shallow bowl. Cut the tofu into ½-inch cubes and add to the marinade. Stir gently with a rubber spatula to coat well and set aside for 15 or 20 minutes.

While the tofu marinates, place the carrots, bell peppers, and scallions in a large bowl. Whisk together the dressing ingredients and pour over the vegetables.

When the tofu has marinated, warm 2 teaspoons of oil in a skillet on medium-high heat and add the tofu and the marinade. Cook, stirring often, until the liquid has evaporated and the tofu cubes are starting to brown. Add the hot cooked tofu to the bowl with the vegetables and toss.

When the rice and edamame are done, add them to the bowl with the other ingredients. Sprinkle in the sesame seeds, if using, and toss gently. Set aside to cool.

Serve at room temperature or chilled, on a bed of greens topped with avocado slices or cubes.

VARIATIONS

- In place of one of the vegetables listed, add some diced cucumbers or shredded daikon radish (but it won't be as pretty).
- Use green peas instead of edamame. Add them to the rice about 5 minutes before the rice is done.
- Replace the marinated cooked tofu cubes with Tofu Kan–style Baked Tofu (page 201).
- Garnish the salad with crumbled or thinly sliced nori seaweed.
- Garnish with sautéed shrimp and pickled ginger.

SERVING AND MENU IDEAS

For a hearty lunch or light dinner, start with a bowl of Miso Soup (page 62). Or, serve this salad with Teriyaki Fish (page 241). Or, serve roasted winter squash (see pages 271 and 272), or Asian Greens (page 269) with this salad.

Indonesian Rice Salad

This attractive, tropical salad is always a hit. Sweet, tangy and colorful, it can serve as a main course or side dish. It keeps well and travels well to picnics and dish-to-pass events.

During the early years at Moosewood, when we ventured very far from home, it was often difficult to find good vegetarian fare. So, while off on a long ocean voyage, Moosewood founders Judy Barringer and Kris Miller were especially grateful to one of the ship's cooks, Sri Wasano, who took pity and concocted some special dishes just for them. They lived happily for days on an Indonesian rice salad he made and, when they got back, we began serving it in the restaurant. We're all grateful for the kindness and the culinary skills of Sri Wasano.

With leftover rice, Indonesian Rice Salad is quickly made. If cooking rice from scratch for this recipe, cook 2 cups of short-grain brown rice in 3 cups water, to yield 4 cups cooked. Next time you're making rice for dinner, remember that deliberately planning leftovers is almost always a good idea.

Yields about 9 cups
Serves 6
Time: 25 minutes

RICE

4 cups cooked brown rice, cooled to room
    temperature
½ cup raisins or currants
2 celery stalks, thinly sliced on the diagonal
⅓ cup thinly sliced scallions
1 cup seeded and finely chopped red and/or green
    bell peppers
1 cup pineapple chunks (fresh or unsweetened
    canned)
one 8-ounce can water chestnuts, drained and
    sliced
1 cup toasted cashews or peanuts
2 tablespoons toasted sesame seeds (see page 386)

DRESSING

⅓ cup vegetable oil
3 tablespoons dark sesame oil
2 tablespoons soy sauce
2 tablespoons apple cider vinegar
½ cup orange juice or pineapple juice
1 garlic clove, minced or pressed
½ teaspoon red pepper flakes or a pinch of
    cayenne

2 cups fresh mung bean sprouts (optional)
2 cups lightly steamed snow peas or sugar snap
    peas (optional)

In a large serving bowl, combine the rice, raisins, celery, scallions, bell peppers, pineapple, water chestnuts, cashews, and sesame seeds. In a bowl, whisk together the oils, soy sauce, vinegar, orange juice, garlic, and red pepper flakes. If you prefer, you can purée the dressing ingredients in a blender. Pour the dressing over the salad and toss well.

Serve at room temperature or chill for about 30 minutes. Garnish with sprouts and/or snow peas, if you like. They look especially nice sprinkled in a ring just inside the rim of the serving bowl.

SERVING AND MENU IDEAS

Indonesian Rice Salad is well paired with Cream of Spinach Soup (page 54) or Chilled Cantaloupe-Amaretto Soup (page 69), and it's really good with Moosewood's Best Baked and Pan-fried Tofu (page 202) or Tofu Kan-style Baked Tofu (page 201).

Tabouli Salad

The clear, fresh flavors of parsley, lemon, and mint make this a dish of which we never tire. Traditionally, this Middle Eastern salad is mostly vitamin-rich parsley with just a little bulghur wheat for added texture and color. But many people in this country like the proportions reversed with more chewy wheat in the mix. Our recipe calls for 2 cups of parsley, which puts it in the mid-range on the spectrum. If your bunch of parsley yields more or less than we call for, use whatever you have, or more or less to taste.

Bulghur is wheat grain that has already been boiled, dried, and cracked so that it has a shorter cooking time than many other grains. Bulghur wheat, aka cracked wheat, comes in different grades of coarseness. At Moosewood, we prefer the texture of a coarse bulghur, but there may not be much choice at your market, and really, any grade will do fine in this dish. You can replace the bulghur with quinoa for a nice quinoa "tabouli."

Recipes for bulghur call for differing amounts of boiling water. Until you know the particular bulghur you're working with, we recommend that you start with 1 cup water per 1 cup bulghur and then add more if needed. That may take extra time, but it's better than draining off extra water, especially in a recipe like this that works best when the bulghur is dry enough to absorb the moisture of the other ingredients without being waterlogged.

Fresh mint is our first choice here, but dried mint works well, too. Just use a mint herbal tea bag.

Yields 4 cups
Serves 6
Time: 30 minutes

1 cup boiling water
1 cup bulghur wheat
1 garlic clove, minced or pressed
½ teaspoon salt
2 teaspoons chopped fresh mint or ½ teaspoon dried mint
⅓ cup fresh lemon juice
¼ cup extra-virgin olive oil
2 cups lightly packed finely chopped fresh parsley
1 cucumber, seeded and diced
½ cup thinly sliced scallions
2 tomatoes, diced

In a heatproof bowl, pour the boiling water over the bulghur, garlic, salt, and dried mint, if using. (If using fresh mint, add it later.) Cover the bowl and set it aside for 20 minutes. Taste the bulghur. It should be softened and dry, so that it will absorb the moisture from the vegetables and the lemon juice without making the tabouli too wet. If the water has been absorbed, but the grains are still crunchy, add some more boiling water, cover, and set aside for 10 minutes.

Meanwhile, in a large bowl, stir together the lemon juice and olive oil. Add the parsley, cucumbers, and scallions.

When the bulghur has absorbed the water and softened, stir it with a fork to fluff the grains. Add it to the bowl and mix well. Add fresh mint, if using, and more salt to taste.

Tabouli tastes best after sitting for at least 30 minutes at room temperature or in the refrigerator. Add the tomatoes just before serving, or garnish with them.

SERVING AND MENU IDEAS

Tabouli Salad is a fine accompaniment for many Mediterranean-style dishes. Serve it with Classic Hummus (page 37) and/or Peppercorn and Lemon Marinated Feta (page 23) or Herbed Chèvre Spread (page 43), black olives, and pita bread. We also like to pair it with Creamy Herbed Potato Soup (page 49) and Tofalafels (page 25) or Vegan Spinach–Artichoke Heart Dip (page 36).

Moroccan Couscous Salad

This is one of our most reflexive go-to salads for dish-to-pass occasions and photo-ops. It's simple to make, universally liked, and awfully pretty.

Yields 6 cups
Serves 4 to 8
Time: 45 minutes

COUSCOUS
1½ cups couscous
1½ cups water
1 tablespoon olive oil
1 teaspoon salt

VEGETABLES
1 cup diced carrots
1 cup seeded and diced red bell peppers
⅓ cup finely chopped red onions
½ cup finely chopped fresh parsley
2 tablespoons finely chopped fresh mint or
    1 teaspoon dried mint
½ cup currants

DRESSING
¼ cup olive oil
1 teaspoon finely grated lemon zest
2 tablespoons fresh lemon juice
2 tablespoons orange juice
½ teaspoon ground cinnamon
½ teaspoon salt

½ cup chopped toasted almonds (optional)

Pour the couscous into a heatproof bowl. Bring the water to a boil, and pour it over the couscous. Using a fork, stir in the olive oil and salt. If using dried mint, add it now. Cover and set aside for 5 to 10 minutes.

While the couscous softens, steam the carrots and peppers until tender, about 5 minutes. Fluff the couscous with a fork, breaking up any lumps. Add the steamed carrots and peppers and the red onions, parsley, and currants to the couscous. If using fresh mint, add it now.

Whisk together the dressing ingredients. Pour the dressing over the couscous and toss well.

Serve at room temperature or chilled. This salad will keep in the refrigerator for 4 or 5 days.

Just before serving, sprinkle with toasted almonds, if you like, or pass them at the table as a garnish.

SERVING AND MENU IDEAS
Serve as part of a combo plate with Spanakopita Bites (page 26) and Seasoned Artichokes (page 263). Moroccan Couscous Salad is good stuffed in a ripe juicy tomato or an avocado half.

Four Season Salad Plates

Salad plates made up of a mix of greens topped with various fresh and roasted vegetables, nuts, cheese, and a flavorful dressing are a regular feature on Moosewood's lunch menu. A lot of our regular customers look for them and like to tell us which are their favorites, and sometimes they give us their ideas for good combinations of toppings, hoping to see their salad plate on the menu. With quite a bit of discussion, we've come to the consensus that these four are the most popular, but you'll notice that we just *had* to tell you about some of the variations we do, hoping that will inspire you to have as good a time as we do thinking about ways to make a bed of greens delectable.

AUTUMN SALAD PLATE

When we make roasted squash for a composed salad at Moosewood, we make extra because customers ask for it as a side dish and the staff likes to gobble up the leftovers. The sugars in squash caramelize when roasted, yielding a crisp surface and a creamy, super-sweet under-layer. There are many good varieties of squash to choose from for roasting. Some of our favorites include acorn, delicata, kuri, butternut, buttercup, and sweet dumpling.

This autumn salad plate is balanced, unified, and accented by a delicious pear-and-thyme dressing. Red-skinned Bartlett pears are very pretty on this plate, and sweet and juicy, but use the best pears you have available.

Serves 4 as a main dish: 8 as a side dish
Time: 45 minutes

TOPPINGS
about 2 pounds winter squash (see headnote)
1 tablespoon olive oil or vegetable oil
¼ cup pepitas (pumpkin seeds)
4 ounces sharp cheddar
2 ripe pears
1 tablespoon fresh lemon juice
¼ cup dried cranberries

Pear-Thyme Dressing (page 305)

about 8 cups salad greens (arugula, spinach, lettuce, and/or baby greens)

Preheat the oven to 400°F. Lightly oil a rimmed baking sheet.

Scrub the winter squash, and peel it, or don't. Halve it through the stem end and scoop out the seeds. Cut the halves horizontally into ½-inch slices. Small squash give you nice crescents, but if the squash is large, cut the slices into halves or thirds. In a large bowl, toss the squash pieces with the oil. Lay the squash out on the prepared baking sheet about ½ inch apart, and sprinkle with salt. Bake until easily pierced with a fork, about 20 minutes. Remove from the oven and set aside to cool.

While the squash bakes, spread the pepitas out on a small baking tray and, if they are not already salted, sprinkle with salt. Toast in the oven for about 5 minutes, or until somewhat puffed and crunchy. Set aside to cool. Slice or cube the cheese. Quarter the pears lengthwise, remove the core, and slice thinly. To keep the cut surfaces of the pears from turning brown, sprinkle them with lemon juice. Make the dressing.

On a large platter or individual plates, make a bed of the greens. Arrange the roasted squash, pear slices, and cheddar on top. Drizzle on the dressing or pass it at the table and sprinkle with the pepitas and cranberries.

VARIATION
- Gorgonzola, blue cheese, and chèvre also are delicious on this salad plate.

SERVING AND MENU IDEAS
This salad can be served as a main dish or as part of a hearty harvest meal.

WINTER SALAD PLATE

In this salad, the sweetness of roasted beets and red onions is paired with the rich flavor of balsamic vinaigrette and the fresh taste of the greens. We like to include arugula in the mix of greens for its sharp contrast to the sweet beets.

We often serve this salad with locally produced chèvre or goat feta, but blue cheese is also a good choice. This dish is also an excellent appetizer, and makes enough to serve eight.

Yields 1 cup vinaigrette
Serves 4 as a main dish; 8 as a side dish
Time: 45 minutes

TOPPINGS

3 or 4 medium beets (about 1 pound)
4 teaspoons olive oil
salt
ground black pepper
1 large red onion
½ cup chopped toasted walnuts
¾ cup crumbled chèvre, blue, or feta cheese

BALSAMIC AND DIJON VINAIGRETTE

⅔ cup olive oil
3 tablespoons balsamic vinegar
1 tablespoon Dijon mustard
3 tablespoons water
¼ teaspoon salt
⅛ teaspoon ground black pepper
1 teaspoon pure maple syrup, sugar, or agave syrup (optional)

about 8 cups salad greens (arugula, spinach, lettuce, baby greens)

Preheat the oven to 400°F. Lightly oil 2 rimmed baking sheets.

Rinse and peel the beets. Cut them into halves or quarters and then into ½-inch-thick slices. Toss with 2 teaspoons of the olive oil. Spread out the beets on a baking sheet and sprinkle with salt and black pepper. Peel the onion, cut it in half, and then into thick slices. Toss the onions with the remaining 2 teaspoons of olive oil, spread out on the other baking sheet, and sprinkle with salt and pepper. Roast the vegetables until tender and browned about 30 minutes, stirring after 15 minutes. The onions will probably be done first.

While the vegetables are in the oven, toast and chop the walnuts and crumble the cheese. Make the vinaigrette: Whirl all of the ingredients in a blender until thick and creamy. Or, whisk together all of the ingredients by hand in a small bowl. The dressing should be pourable; add more water if needed. Set aside.

On a large platter or individual plates, make a bed of the greens. Top with the roasted beets and onions, then sprinkle on the walnuts and cheese. Pass the dressing at the table.

VARIATION

• Replace half of the olive oil in the dressing with roasted walnut oil—really yummy!

SERVING AND MENU IDEAS

Serve with bread for mopping up the plate. Creamy Hungarian Mushroom Soup (page 55), Creamy Herbed Potato Soup (page 49), or Egg Salad sandwiches (pages 78 to 79) make it a satisfying meal.

SPRING SALAD PLATE

This is our favorite salad plate for springtime. We like it best with these few simple ingredients. It's elegant in the sense that an equation can be elegant in its simplicity. The shallot vinaigrette ties the flavors together.

Yields 1 cup vinaigrette
Serves 4 as a main dish; 8 as a side dish
Time: 30 minutes

TOPPINGS

1½ pounds asparagus
1 tablespoon olive oil
1 cup hazelnuts
⅓ cup snipped fresh chives
7 ounces chèvre

SHALLOT VINAIGRETTE

⅔ cup olive oil (extra-virgin is nice)
½ cup diced shallots
¼ cup red wine vinegar or apple cider vinegar
3 tablespoons chopped fresh basil and/or tarragon
3 tablespoons water
½ teaspoon salt
¼ teaspoon ground black pepper

about 8 cups salad greens (arugula, spinach, lettuce, or baby greens)

Preheat the oven to 400°F. Lightly oil a rimmed baking sheet.

Snap off the tough ends of the asparagus and cut the spears in half. Toss with the olive oil and spread out in a single layer on the prepared baking sheet. Roast until tender and somewhat browned, 8 to 15 minutes, depending on the thickness of the spears.

While the asparagus roasts, toast the hazelnuts (see page 380), snip the chives, and crumble the chèvre or cut it into small cubes. Make the vinaigrette: In a small saucepan on medium heat, warm ⅓ cup of the olive oil. Add the shallots and cook until soft, 1 or 2 minutes. In a bowl, whisk the remaining ⅓ cup of olive oil with the vinegar, basil, tarragon, water, salt, and black pepper. Whisk in the cooked shallots and oil. If you prefer a smooth dressing, purée it in a blender.

On a large platter or individual plates, make a bed of the greens. Lay the roasted asparagus across the greens, scatter about little chunks of chèvre, sprinkle with the hazelnuts and chives. Pass the shallot vinaigrette at the table.

VARIATIONS

- If you just can't stop at the toppings we suggest, here are some ideas for other things to add to the plate: steamed snow peas or sugar snap peas, diced bell peppers, radish coins, sliced hard-boiled eggs. For some color, add thinly sliced radicchio to the greens.
- Instead of the chèvre, you could sprinkle the salad with finely grated Parmesan.
- Instead of plain chèvre, put a dollop or two of Herbed Chèvre Spread (page 43) on each salad plate.

SUMMER SALAD PLATE

During fresh tomato season, we never tire of this salad. Ripe, juicy tomatoes are enhanced with a thread of green, fruity extra-virgin olive oil. We like arugula as the bed of greens because its slightly bitter sharpness contrasts nicely with mild, creamy fresh mozzarella. Watercress, spinach, radicchio, or lettuce work well, too.

With different shapes, colors, and sizes of heirloom tomatoes and both green and purple fresh basil, this is a truly spectacular-looking salad. Cracked black pepper and coarse or flaked salt, such as Malden Sea Salt, really make a difference in taste and appearance.

If you refrigerate a tomato salad, cover it well and, just before serving, bring it back to room temperature.

Serves 4 as a main dish; 8 as a side salad
Time: 20 minutes

TOPPINGS
1 pound fresh mozzarella balls
1½ to 2 pounds fresh tomatoes
extra-virgin olive oil
12 fresh basil leaves, minced or cut into chiffonade
    (about 2 heaping tablespoons)
coarse or flaked salt
cracked black pepper

about 8 cups salad greens (see headnote)

Slice the mozzarella and tomatoes into thin rounds or half-rounds of a similar size. Mince the basil leaves or cut them into chiffonade (see page 374).

On a large platter or individual plates, make a bed of the greens. On top of the greens, arrange rows or rings of alternating and slightly overlapping slices of mozzarella and tomatoes. Drizzle a thin stream of olive oil over the salad. Sprinkle on the basil and salt and black pepper.

Serve at room temperature.

VARIATIONS
- When our tomatoes are particularly irregular or we have small mozzarella balls and the alternating, overlapping thing won't look so nice, we cut the tomatoes and mozzarella into a ½-inch dice, mix them together, and tumble them over the bed of greens.
- Add more to the salad, such as: artichoke hearts, toasted pine nuts, olives, roasted red pepper strips, red onion slivers, capers, chickpeas, croutons, or fresh raw kernels of corn cut from the cob.

SERVING AND MENU IDEAS
Pass a cruet of balsamic vinegar at the table. This salad is a lovely summer entrée with a good crusty bread to sop up the juices. Or, serve after a soup, such as Corn Chowder (page 63) or Creamy Herbed Potato Soup (page 49), or before a simple pasta, such as Pasta Aglio e Olio (page 226).

Mexican Salad Plate

Many of our lunchtime regulars regularly order our main dish green salads. They're really just a big tossed salad with lots of good stuff piled on top. Most of our salad plates reflect the season and feature whatever produce is being harvested locally, but this one is great any time of year, both for a Fourth of July spread and for Super Bowl Sunday. If you're feeding a crowd, put a bowl of tortilla chips in the center of the table and surround it with all the colorful components.

Yields 1 generous cup dressing
Serves 2 to 4
Time: 40 minutes or more (depending on what you choose to include)

one 15-ounce can red kidney beans or black beans, rinsed and drained (about 1½ cups)
2 tablespoons vegetable oil or olive oil
2 tablespoons apple cider vinegar
1 teaspoon ground coriander seeds

DRESSING
2 garlic cloves, minced or pressed
1 hot pepper, minced, or ¼ teaspoon cayenne (optional)
⅓ cup chopped fresh cilantro, or basil and scallions
½ teaspoon salt
1 generous teaspoon freshly grated orange zest
¼ cup fresh orange juice
2 tablespoons fresh lemon juice
1 tablespoon apple cider vinegar
¾ cup vegetable oil (up to half can be olive oil)
ground black pepper

about 8 cups salad greens (spinach, lettuce, baby greens)
1 bell pepper, (any color), seeded and cut into ¼-inch-wide strips, strips cut crosswise in half
1 ripe avocado, sliced, or Simple Smooth Guacamole (page 35)
cherry tomatoes or plum tomatoes sliced into rounds
sliced or shredded cheddar or Pepper Jack cheese

OTHER TOPPING IDEAS
Spanish or black olives
orange or grapefruit sections
diced cucumbers
chopped scallions
extra chopped cilantro
toasted pepitas
tortilla chips

Place the beans in a bowl and stir in the oil, vinegar, and coriander. Set aside to marinate.

In a blender, purée all of the dressing ingredients except for the oil, black pepper, and salt. Slowly add the oil in a thin, steady stream while the blender is running. Add black pepper and more salt to taste. Set aside

Compose the salad on dinner plates. Make a bed of greens on each plate and top with the bell peppers, avacado, tomatoes, and cheese and any other toppings you choose. Pass the salad dressing at the table.

SERVING AND MENU IDEAS
Gazpacho (page 70) is perfect with this salad. Cornbread (see pages 283 and 284) is also a good accompaniment.

Armenian Roasted Eggplant Salad

Roasted vegetables, cucumbers, rosemary, and olive oil are typical ingredients in Armenian cuisine, but then many countries of the Near East and Mediterranean may lay claim to succulent, big-flavored salads like this. It's a beautiful dish, glossy and colorful, and the soft roasted vegetables and crunchy celery make for an interesting texture. It's typical of dishes created by our partner and talented cook Laura Branca, who brings her Armenian heritage to our literal and figurative "table." Picture a small, beautiful woman mixing an enormous bowl of some pilaf or other and coming up with a lovely, perfectly seasoned dish every time.

Yields 7 cups
Serves 4 to 8
Time: 1½ hours

1 medium eggplant (about 1½ pounds)
1 fresh fennel bulb
2 cups seeded and diced red or yellow bell peppers
2 cups diced onions
3 garlic cloves, pressed or minced
1 to 2 tablespoons chopped fresh rosemary
3 tablespoons olive oil
½ teaspoon ground fennel seeds
salt
ground black pepper

DRESSING
¼ cup extra-virgin olive oil
1 tablespoon fresh lemon juice
2 tablespoons apple cider or red wine vinegar
2 tablespoons chopped fresh basil (optional)
½ teaspoon salt
ground black pepper

1 large cucumber, peeled, seeded, and diced
2 cups diced celery

finely chopped fresh parsley
crumbled feta cheese
black olives

Peel the eggplant and cut it into ½-inch cubes. You should have about 6 cups. Cut off the stalks and base of the fennel bulb. Cut it in half, end-to-end, and remove the core if it is tough. Peel away any tough or discolored outer layers of the bulb. Chop the bulb into 1-inch pieces.

Preheat the oven to 450°F.

In a large bowl, toss the eggplant, chopped fennel, bell peppers, and onions with the garlic, rosemary, olive oil, and ground fennel seeds. Sprinkle with salt and black pepper. Spread the vegetables evenly on two lightly oiled rimmed baking sheets. Bake for 15 minutes, and then turn the vegetables over with a spatula, and continue to bake until the eggplant and bell peppers are tender and lightly browned, up to 15 minutes.

While the vegetables roast, in a large bowl, whisk together all of the dressing ingredients. Add the diced cucumber and celery. When the roasted vegetables come out of the oven, add them to the bowl and toss well.

Serve at room temperature or chilled, garnished with parsley, crumbled feta, and/or olives.

NOTES
This salad can be made a day ahead and stored, well covered, in the refrigerator.

If you prefer larger, chunkier vegetables, bake at 400°F for 35 to 40 minutes.

SERVING AND MENU IDEAS
Serve as an appetizer or as a main dish salad on lettuce leaves with warm pita wedges or crunchy pita chips.

To make it part of a Fertile Crescent combo plate, serve with Moroccan Carrot Salad with Currants (page 257) and Tofalafels (page 25). And it makes a great filling for pita sandwiches.

Gado Gado

In various languages and dialects in Indonesia, the words *bumbu katchang* refer to a spicy peanut sauce, while the words *gado gado* refer to a one-dish meal that incorporates the delicious sauce. For decades at Moosewood, we've served our very popular gado gado plate, steamed and raw vegetables on a bed of spinach topped with a spicy peanut sauce, and it's pretty close to what you would find among some Indonesian variations of gado gado. There, the peanut sauce almost always includes dried shrimp paste, but we make a vegetarian version. And since we do like our vegetables, we probably use more than you would be served in Indonesia, but there would also usually be tempeh or tofu and maybe hard-boiled eggs.

Yields about 4 cups of sauce; enough for
    6 to 8 servings
Time: 50 minutes

GADO GADO PEANUT SAUCE
1 tablespoon vegetable oil
1 cup finely chopped onions
1 bay leaf
½ teaspoon salt
1 or 2 fresh hot peppers, minced,
    or ½ to 1 teaspoon cayenne
1 or 2 garlic cloves, minced or pressed
1½ tablespoons peeled and fresh grated ginger
1 teaspoon ground coriander seeds (optional)
2 tablespoons tamarind concentrate (see page 386)
2 cups water
1 cup unsweetened coconut milk
3 tablespoons apple cider vinegar
2 cups smooth peanut butter
2 tablespoons brown sugar
2 tablespoons soy sauce

VEGETABLES
broccoli spears, diagonally sliced carrots, strips of red, yellow, or orange bell peppers, chopped green cabbage, potato wedges, and sugar snap peas
fresh spinach leaves

EXTRAS
mung bean sprouts, baked tofu (page 201 and 202), hard-boiled eggs cut into wedges, tomato wedges

To make the peanut sauce: Warm the oil in a covered saucepan on low heat. Add the onions, bay leaf, and salt and cook for 5 minutes. Stir in the hot peppers or cayenne, garlic, ginger, coriander, if using, and tamarind concentrate, and continue to cook for 5 minutes, stirring occasionally. Add the water, coconut milk, and vinegar, increase the heat to a low simmer, and cook, covered, for 3 minutes. Stir in the peanut butter and sugar until the sauce is smooth, bring to a simmer and cook, covered, on low heat, stirring occasionally, for 10 minutes. Remove the bay leaf. Stir in the soy sauce, and add more to taste.

While the sauce is cooking, prepare and steam vegetables you like until they are just tender.

Serve Gado Gado on a large serving platter or on individual plates. Spread a bed of spinach leaves on the platter or plates. Arrange steamed and raw vegetables on top—they can be warm, room temperature, or cool. Add some of the extras. Serve the peanut sauce in a separate bowl or ladle some over the vegetables and pass more at the table.

VARIATIONS
- Serve the peanut sauce and steamed vegetables on rice instead of spinach.
- Stuff pita bread with fresh spinach, baked tofu or chopped hard-boiled eggs, and tomatoes, and top with peanut sauce.
- Serve the sauce as a dip for crisp-fried tempeh or chunks of ripe juicy pineapple.
- Leftover sauce, which will keep for at least a week in the refrigerator, can be the inspiration for a number of other dishes. We often use it as the base for a West African-style peanut soup or stew (see pages 65 and 127).
- Add some canned crushed pineapple to the sauce and serve it on rice with fresh spinach and baked tofu.

Mediterranean Lentil Salad

Not a flamboyantly beautiful dish, but elegant nevertheless. This earthy, nutritious salad is quite delicious hot or cold.

French green lentils (also called Puy lentils, *lentilles du Puy*, and *lentilles vertes du Puy*) are small and dark green. They remain tidy little disks when cooked. As with any lentils, the cooking time varies with different batches: when they were harvested, how long they've been on the shelf, etc. You'll find French lentils in the market with the other dried lentils. In this recipe, brown lentils will work and are tasty, but not as handsome—they don't hold their shape as well.

Yields 4 cups
Serves 4 to 6
Time: 40 minutes

LENTILS
1 cup dried French green lentils, rinsed
3 cups water
½ teaspoon salt
2 bay leaves
2 garlic cloves, minced or pressed
½ teaspoon dried thyme

VEGETABLES
⅓ cup sun-dried tomatoes (not packed in oil) (optional)
½ cup diced celery or fresh fennel bulb
½ cup seeded and diced red, yellow, or orange bell peppers
¼ cup minced red onions
½ cup chopped fresh parsley (optional)
1 cup diced fresh tomatoes

DRESSING
⅓ cup olive oil
3 tablespoons vinegar (preferably red wine vinegar)
1½ teaspoons Dijon mustard
1 teaspoon ground fennel seeds
½ teaspoon salt
⅛ teaspoon ground black pepper

In a saucepan, bring the lentils, water, salt, bay leaves, garlic, and thyme to a boil. Reduce the heat and simmer for 20 to 30 minutes, until the lentils are tender, stirring occasionally and adding a small amount of water, if needed, to prevent scorching.

Meanwhile, in a small bowl, cover the sun-dried tomatoes with boiling water and set aside for at least 15 minutes.

In a larger bowl, stir together the celery, bell peppers, red onions, and parsley. Set aside the fresh tomatoes until just before serving.

Whisk together the dressing ingredients and set aside. When the sun-dried tomatoes have softened, drain them and mince them and add to the bowl.

When the lentils are tender, drain off any remaining liquid. Remove and discard the bay leaves. Toss the lentils with the vegetables and the dressing.

Stir in the fresh tomatoes just before serving. Add more salt and/or black pepper to taste. Serve warm, at room temperature, or chilled.

VARIATION
• With a little stock and some extra seasonings, leftovers can easily become lentil soup.

SERVING AND MENU IDEAS
Serve the lentils on a bed of spinach or salad greens, surrounded with olives and cucumber slices. Top with fresh mozzarella or Peppercorn and Lemon Marinated Feta (page 23).

Serve with a side of marinated asparagus (see marinating method on page 266) or sautéed escarole (see cooking directions for sautéed greens on page 268). Or, add a wedge of Brie, some toasted walnuts, and crusty bread with olive oil for dipping.

Thai Vegetable Curry

Thai vegetable curry is a frequent weekend entrée at Moosewood where it's always popular with our customers. Pretty much any combination of vegetables will work, so experiment and use whatever vegetables you have on hand or simply love—just be sure to have 10 to 12 cups total. Sweet potatoes are especially nice to use because their sweetness nicely balances the lime. Sometimes we substitute pineapple juice for the coconut milk, but most of us prefer it with coconut milk.

Yields about 8 cups
Serves 4 to 6
Time: 45 minutes

1 tablespoon vegetable oil
1½ cups chopped onions
2 garlic cloves
1 teaspoon salt
1 tablespoon peeled and grated fresh ginger
1 cup water
4 cups peeled and cubed sweet potatoes
   (about 1½ pounds whole)
4 cups bite-size cauliflower florets
1½ cups chopped fresh tomatoes
one 14-ounce can unsweetened coconut milk
1 tablespoon Thai curry paste, plus more as needed
finely grated zest of 1 lime
2 tablespoons fresh lime juice
½ cup chopped fresh cilantro and/or basil

Warm the oil in a covered soup pot on medium heat. Stir in the onions, garlic, and salt, and cook for about 7 minutes, stirring often. Add the ginger and cook for 1 minute, stirring constantly. Add water and the sweet potatoes and cauliflower, cover, and bring to a boil. Reduce the heat to a rapid simmer and cook, covered, for about 6 minutes, stirring often. Add the tomatoes, coconut milk, Thai curry paste, and lime zest and bring back to a rapid simmer. Cook, covered, until all of the vegetables are tender, about 2 minutes. Stir in the lime juice and cilantro or basil and add more salt and curry paste to taste.

SERVING AND MENU IDEAS
Serve the vegetable curry on rice topped with Thai Baked Tofu (page 205) and/or toasted peanuts or cashews.

Lentil-Vegetable Sambar

Traditional south Indian sambars are spicy, thick with lentils or split peas, studded with vegetables, and often served with rice and yogurt to soothe the palate. Here is our favorite sambar, not so spicy as most in India, unless you choose to make it so. Other vegetables often used in sambars include shallots, eggplant, green beans, green peas, potatoes, and tomatoes. Use this recipe as a base and experiment with your favorite vegetables.

While both fenugreek seeds and tamarind are normally used in sambars, if you don't have one or the other, don't worry. It's fine to omit the fenugreek and replace the tamarind with 2 or 3 tablespoons of fresh lemon or lime juice.

Yields 8 cups
Serves 6
Time: about 1 hour

LENTILS
1 cup dried brown lentils
3½ cups water
1 teaspoon ground turmeric
1 teaspoon salt

VEGETABLES
2 tablespoons vegetable oil
1 teaspoon black mustard seeds
1 teaspoon cumin seeds
½ teaspoon fenugreek seeds (optional)
2 cups chopped onions
1 fresh hot pepper, minced, or ½ teaspoon cayenne
1 teaspoon salt
2 teaspoons ground coriander seeds
1 teaspoon ground cinnamon
½ teaspoon ground turmeric
4 cups cauliflower, cut into bite-size pieces
3 cups sweet potatoes, peeled and cut into 1-inch cubes
1½ tablespoons tamarind concentrate (page 386) dissolved in 1 cup hot water
1½ cups seeded and chopped red bell peppers
1 cup unsweetened coconut milk
¼ cup chopped fresh cilantro

Rinse the lentils and combine them with the water, turmeric, and salt in a medium saucepan. Bring to a boil, reduce the heat to low, and simmer, covered, until the lentils are tender, usually 30 to 40 minutes.

While the lentils cook, heat the oil in a large pot on medium heat and add the black mustard seeds, cumin seeds, and fenugreek seeds, if using. When the mustard seeds start to pop, stir in the onions, hot peppers, and salt, and cook on low heat, covered, until the onions are translucent, about 8 minutes. Add the coriander, cinnamon, and turmeric and cook for a minute or two, stirring constantly. Stir in the cauliflower, sweet potatoes, and tamarind water, and bring to a boil. Reduce the heat to a simmer and cook, covered, for 5 or 6 minutes. Add the bell peppers and coconut milk. Return to a simmer and cook until all the vegetables are just tender, about 5 minutes.

When the lentils are done, drain off any liquid and stir them into the vegetables. Stir in the cilantro and add salt to taste.

SERVING AND MENU IDEAS
Serve on rice, with yogurt or Spinach Raita (page 312) and Date-Coconut-Lemon Chutney (page 312) or Quick Banana Chutney (page 310).

Summer Vegetable Curry

When you take it steaming straight from the stovetop to the table, this is one delectable dish. A medley of summer vegetables, including corn, which gives the curry a pleasant sweetness. With its bright array of colors, this looks great served on golden rice (use saffron or turmeric, or a little of both to get the color).

The vegetables should be just tender, not mushy, and the spinach bright green, so the magic in making this fresh and delicious curry exceptional is in how you cut and cook the vegetables. We give you very specific prepping directions. But the exact amounts aren't that critical, so use that whole zucchini, even if the cup measure is more or less than listed. And by the way, this curry is good the next day, too—mellow rather than bright.

Yields 8 or 9 cups
Serves 4 to 6
Time: 50 minutes

2 tablespoons vegetable oil
1 large onion (2 to 3 cups sliced)
2 garlic cloves, minced
1 tablespoon peeled and grated fresh ginger
1 teaspoon salt
2 teaspoons ground cumin seeds
2 teaspoons ground coriander seeds
1 teaspoon ground cinnamon
1 teaspoon ground turmeric
½ teaspoon ground fennel seeds
½ teaspoon ground cardamom
¼ teaspoon cayenne or 1 fresh hot pepper, minced
1 cup sliced carrots
3 cups sliced zucchini or summer squash
1 red bell pepper, seeded
1½ cups water
2 cups chopped fresh tomatoes
1½ cups corn kernels
4 cups chopped fresh baby spinach (about 8 ounces)
¼ cup chopped fresh cilantro

Before you begin to cook, slice the onion, mince the garlic, grate the ginger, measure out the spices, and cut the carrots. Then you can start to cook and prep as you go, and you'll stay ahead of it—even if you have to pick through the spinach. To prep the onion, slice in half end to end and then cut into ½-inch-thick slices. Cut the carrots into ¼-inch-thick rounds, half-rounds, or quarters, depending on the diameter of the carrots. Same with the zucchini. Chop the bell pepper into roughly 1-inch pieces.

In a large covered skillet or soup pot on low heat, warm the oil. Add the onion, garlic, ginger, and salt and cook for 5 minutes. Increase the heat to medium, add the spices, and stir for a minute or two. Add the carrots and 1½ cups of water and bring to a simmer. Cover and simmer gently for 3 or 4 minutes. Add the bell peppers and zucchini, stir well, cover, and cook for about 5 minutes, stirring frequently. Stir in the tomatoes, cover, and cook until the tomatoes have begun to release liquid. Stir in the corn and cook, covered, for 5 minutes. Add the spinach and cilantro and stir until the spinach has wilted but is still bright green. Serve right away.

SERVING AND MENU IDEAS
Serve on rice topped with yogurt, currants, and cashews.

Instead of yogurt, try Spinach Raita (page 312), instead of currants try Quick Banana Chutney (page 310), or Date-Coconut-Lemon Chutney (page 312).

Winter Curry

All winter long, we serve some version of this curry at least once a week. The vegetables we choose may include cauliflower, winter squash, potatoes, sweet potatoes, eggplant, spinach, carrots, bell peppers, chickpeas, tomatoes, and green peas. Once in a while, we'll put lots of different vegetables into the curry, but usually, we like to keep it more simple, with just two or three major players.

However, we love a complex spice mixture in a winter curry. That aroma of Indian spices is warming and gives a sense of well-being. The spices in this recipe reflect what we usually do in the restaurant. But, we realize that at home you might not keep all of these spices on hand—if you don't include a couple of the spices, the curry will still be good—just a little different.

In the winter, we crave green and we almost always garnish a curry with barely cooked, still bright, green peas. The peas aren't simply a decoration; besides looking beautiful as an accent to the other colors, the peas also add sweetness and an interesting mouthfeel. The toppings we suggest for serving are more than mere garnishes, but you don't *have* to have all of them.

Yields 10 cups
Serves 6 to 8
Time: 1 hour

3 tablespoons vegetable oil
½ teaspoon black mustard seeds
2 cups chopped onions
3 garlic cloves, minced or pressed
1½ teaspoons salt
1 tablespoon peeled and grated fresh ginger
2 teaspoons ground cumin seeds
2 teaspoons ground coriander seeds
½ teaspoon ground cardamom seeds
1 teaspoon ground cinnamon
½ teaspoon ground fennel seeds
½ teaspoon red pepper flakes or ¼ teaspoon cayenne (more or less to taste)
2 teaspoons ground turmeric
5 cups peeled and cubed butternut squash or sweet potatoes (¾-inch pieces) (about 2 pounds, whole)
6 cups cauliflower florets
1 cup water
1 cup unsweetened coconut milk
3 cups chopped fresh tomatoes or one 15-ounce can diced tomatoes
1 to 3 tablespoons fresh lemon juice (optional)
2 cups green peas

In a large pot on medium heat, warm the oil. Add the mustard seeds and when they begin to pop, add the onions, garlic, salt, and ginger and stir well. Cover and cook on low heat for 5 minutes. Stir in the spices and continue to cook, covered, until the onions are very soft, about 5 minutes. Add the squash and stir well. Cover and cook for about 5 minutes, stirring occasionally. Add the cauliflower and stir well. Stir in the water and coconut milk and bring to a boil. Reduce the heat and simmer, covered, for about 10 minutes. Add the tomatoes and simmer until the vegetables are tender. Add lemon juice to taste.

Right before you serve the curry, steam the green peas until bright green and just tender.

SERVING AND MENU IDEAS
Serve the curry on a bed of rice, topped with the peas and a dollop of plain yogurt and sprinkled with currants and toasted cashews.

For a dinner party, serve the curry and rice in large bowls garnished with chopped cilantro and/or scallions, and serve Lentil Dhal (page 282), Spinach Raita (page 312), and Date-Coconut-Lemon Chutney (page 312) or banana or mango slices, in smaller serving bowls surrounding them. Crisp and flavorful pappadums are a wonderful addition. You can find them in the Indian section of supermarkets. In a large skillet, quickly fry each pappadum in a ¼-inch of hot oil, a couple of seconds each side, turn them with tongs and transfer to paper towels to drain.

Caribbean Stew

This is a bright and spicy stew with layers of flavor. Besides being a joy to dine upon, Caribbean Stew is packed with nutrients and antioxidants from all those beautiful sweet potatoes, cabbage, peppers, and kale.

Yields: 7 cups
Serves 4
Time: 1 hour

2 tablespoons vegetable oil
1½ cups chopped onions
1 teaspoon salt
¼ teaspoon freshly grated nutmeg
¼ teaspoon ground black pepper
2 tablespoons peeled and grated fresh ginger (see Variations)
1 fresh hot pepper, minced
2 cups chopped cabbage
1½ cups seeded and chopped bell peppers (any color) (¾-inch pieces)
several fresh thyme sprigs or ½ teaspoon dried thyme
2 cups peeled and cubed sweet potatoes (¾-inch cubes)
one 15-ounce can diced tomatoes
3 cups finely chopped kale
1 teaspoon finely grated lime zest
1 tablespoon fresh lime juice
2 tablespoons chopped fresh cilantro

Warm the oil in a covered soup pot on low heat. Add the onions with the salt, the nutmeg, black pepper, ginger, and hot peppers and thyme, if using dried, and cook for 10 minutes, or until the onions are translucent. Stir in the cabbage and bell peppers, cover, and cook for another 10 minutes. Add the sweet potatoes and enough water to just cover them, 1 or 2 cups. If using fresh thyme, tie the springs into a little bundle with kitchen string and add it to the pot. Bring to a boil and cook at a rapid simmer for 10 minutes, or until the sweet potatoes are tender. Add the tomatoes, kale, lime zest, lime juice, and cilantro and simmer for a final 10 minutes. Remove and discard the thyme sprigs.

VARIATIONS

- We almost always use fresh ginger in our savory dishes. Joan Adler, a Moosewood cook who has a very discriminating palate, found when she was well into prepping vegetables for this stew that she didn't have enough fresh ginger at home. So she forged ahead with the ground ginger she had in her cupboard, and it worked! So in a pinch, in some dishes like this one, we know that you can substitute dried ginger for grated fresh ginger. Use 1 teaspoon dried ginger.
- Add 1 cup sliced fresh or frozen okra when you add the kale.

SERVING AND MENU IDEAS

Serve on a bed of rice, Coconut Rice (page 289), or Annatto Rice (page 289) topped with toasted and salted peanuts or cashews, or tofu baked in a Jerk Sauce (page 319) or the cilantro version of Lemon-Herb Baked Tofu (page 204).

Eggplant Mykonos

This handsome and healthful vegetable stew can be the centerpiece of a Mediterranean meal. Make a little cucumber salad while the Mykonos simmers. Put some olives on the table and uncork a nice red wine. Have wedges of watermelon for dessert.

If you plan to serve Mykonos on rice, start it first.

Yields 8 cups
Serves 6 to 8
Time: 45 minutes

2 tablespoons olive oil
2 cups chopped onions
4 garlic cloves, minced or pressed
½ teaspoon red pepper flakes (optional)
1 teaspoon salt
2 teaspoons ground fennel seeds
6 cups cubed eggplant (¾-inch cubes)
    (1 medium eggplant, about 1½ pounds)
2 cups seeded and chopped red and/or
    green bell peppers
one 28-ounce can diced tomatoes
1 cup water
¼ teaspoon ground black pepper
3 cups coarsely chopped spinach (6 ounces)
1 tablespoon fresh lemon juice
1 tablespoon chopped fresh dill

Warm the oil in a covered soup pot on low heat. Add the onions, garlic, red pepper flakes, if using, and salt and cook until the onions are translucent, about 10 minutes. Add the ground fennel and cook for a couple of minutes. Add the eggplant cubes and cook for 8 to 9 minutes, stirring often. Add the bell peppers, tomatoes, and water, cover the pot, and simmer, stirring frequently, until the eggplant is soft and tender, 10 to 15 minutes. Stir in the black pepper, spinach, lemon juice, and dill and simmer for a couple of minutes until the spinach has wilted but is still bright green.

SERVING AND MENU IDEAS

Serve Eggplant Mykonos on rice, couscous, bulghur, or orzo and top with crumbled feta or chevre cheese.

Start with Olivada (page 39) on crostini. On the side, serve Tzatziki (page 311), Middle Eastern Carrot Salad with Mint (page 257), or Cucumbers Vinaigrette (page 256). Have some Baklava (page 348) or fruit for dessert.

Groundnut Stew

Groundnut stew is a staple of West Africa and a favorite at Moosewood Restaurant. It's a good everyday supper, a thick stew to serve on a bed of rice, couscous, polenta, grits, millet, or even quinoa. We want to thank Judy Barringer, inveterate traveler, founder of Moosewood Restaurant, and a Moosewood cook, for opening our eyes and palates to the flavors of Africa.

The amount of cayenne or red pepper flakes listed makes a moderately hot dish; add more or less to taste. And of course, you could always use fresh hot peppers. Tomatoes slow down the cooking of sweet potatoes, so check that the sweet potatoes have begun to soften before adding the tomatoes. You can make groundnut stew with fewer or more vegetables than listed, and the amounts can be a little more or less. So go ahead and use that whole zucchini—unless it's a giant.

Yields about 11 cups
Serves 6 to 8
Time: 55 minutes

2 tablespoons vegetable oil
2 cups chopped onions
2 garlic cloves, minced or pressed
1 teaspoon salt
2 teaspoons ground coriander seeds
2 tablespoons peeled and grated fresh ginger
¼ teaspoon cayenne or ½ teaspoon red pepper flakes or 2 teaspoons Tabasco
3 cups peeled and cubed sweet potatoes (1-inch pieces)
3 cups chopped cabbage
1 cup chopped zucchini or yellow summer squash
1 red or green bell pepper, seeded and chopped
2 cups water
one 28-ounce can diced tomatoes
¾ cup peanut butter
one 8-ounce can unsweetened, undrained crushed pineapple
¼ cup chopped fresh cilantro
2 to 3 tablespoons fresh lemon juice

Warm the oil in a covered soup pot on low heat. Add the onions, garlic, and salt and cook while you begin to prep the vegetables. After about 10 minutes, stir in the coriander, ginger, and cayenne. Increase the heat to medium and add the sweet potatoes, cabbage, zucchini, and bell peppers as you prep them, stirring well after each addition and adding a splash of water, if needed, to prevent sticking. Add the water, stir well, and increase the heat. Simmer, covered, for about 10 minutes, then stir in about half of the tomatoes. Simmer until the vegetables are tender, about 10 minutes.

Whirl the remaining tomatoes and the peanut butter in a blender until smooth. Stir into the stew along with the pineapple and cilantro and return to a simmer. Add lemon juice and salt to taste.

VARIATIONS

- Stir in some chopped greens. Add substantial greens such as collards and kale near the end of the first simmer, or add more tender greens such as mustard greens and spinach just before the peanut butter.
- Add 2 cups whole or chopped okra.
- Pineapple gives groundnut stew a luscious sweetness, but it's fine without.
- If you have leftovers, you can convert groundnut stew to a nice peanut soup: just purée with some water to a nice, smooth consistency and reheat. Serve with a hot sauce.

SERVING AND MENU IDEAS

Serve on rice, couscous, or other grain listed in the headnote. Top with chopped scallions and serve with baked tofu (see page 203) or hard-boiled eggs.

Moroccan Vegetable Stew

Colorful, aromatic, and sweet, this stew was introduced to the restaurant by Moosewood cook and menu planner Joan Adler after she discovered Paula Wolfert's books on North African cooking. That was back in the '70s. Paula Wolfert was Joan's bedtime reading for weeks.

Having a big pot of slowly simmering aromatic vegetables in the kitchen is a wonderful thing. Stews with eggplant and sweet potatoes are vulnerable to scorching—frequent stirring, adequate liquid, a tight-fitting lid, low heat, and patience will do the trick. A heavy-bottomed pot or a flame tamer is helpful, too.

Yields 8 cups
Serves 6 to 8
Time: about 1 hour

¼ cup olive oil
2 cups chopped onions
½ teaspoon salt
2 garlic cloves, minced or pressed
1 teaspoon ground turmeric
1 teaspoon ground cinnamon
½ teaspoon cayenne or red pepper flakes
½ teaspoon paprika (sweet, hot, or smoked)
4 cups peeled and cubed sweet potatoes (1-inch cubes) (2 large, about 1½ pounds)

1½ cups water
one 15-ounce can diced tomatoes
3 cups cubed eggplant (¾-inch cubes) (one 1-pound whole eggplant)
1 cup seeded and chopped bell peppers (any color)
2 cups chopped zucchini or yellow squash
one 15-ounce can chickpeas, undrained (about 1½ cups beans)
pinch of saffron
½ cup currants or raisins
1 to 2 tablespoons fresh lemon juice

In a stew pot, warm the olive oil on medium-low heat. Add the onions and salt, and cook, covered, for 5 minutes. Stir in the garlic, turmeric, cinnamon, cayenne, and paprika, cover, and cook for 3 or 4 minutes. Add the sweet potatoes, stir in the water, bring to a vigorous simmer, and cook for 5 minutes. Add the tomatoes and eggplant, cover, and simmer for 10 minutes, stirring often. Add the bell peppers, zucchini, chickpeas, saffron, and currants. Cover and simmer, stirring often, until the sweet potatoes and eggplant are tender, about 15 minutes. Stir in lemon juice to taste.

SERVING AND MENU IDEAS
Serve on couscous or with toasted pita bread. Top Moroccan Stew with chopped toasted almonds and wedges of hard-cooked egg. A sprinkling of finely chopped parsley or scallions also looks pretty.

Navajo Stew

Warm colors and a smoky flavor make this simple stew a completely satisfying meal. This is one of the most requested recipes on our Facebook page and we love telling people how easy it is to prepare. If you love cilantro, be sure to make Cilantro-Yogurt Sauce (page 310), it is an awesome topping!

Yields 8 cups
Serves 4 to 6
Time: 45 minutes

2 tablespoons olive oil or vegetable oil
2 cups chopped onions
3 garlic cloves, minced
1 teaspoon salt
1 red, green, or orange bell pepper, seeded and chopped
1 tablespoon ground cumin seeds
2 teaspoons ground coriander seeds
4 cups peeled and cubed sweet potatoes (1-inch cubes) (1½ pounds whole)
2 cups water
one 15-ounce can diced tomatoes
2 tablespoons canned chipotles in adobo sauce
½ cup chopped fresh cilantro
1½ cups cooked black beans or red beans (one 15-ounce can, rinsed and drained)
1 cup fresh or frozen corn kernels (optional)

Warm the oil in a covered soup pot on low heat. Add the onions, garlic, and salt, and cook, stirring occasionally, until the onions are soft, about 10 minutes. Stir in the bell peppers, cumin, and coriander and cook for a couple of minutes. Add the sweet potatoes and water, cover, and bring to a boil. Reduce the heat and simmer for about 10 minutes, or until the sweet potatoes are tender.

Meanwhile, purée the tomatoes, chipotles, and cilantro in a blender.

When the vegetables are tender, stir in the tomato purée and the beans. Add corn, if you like. Bring to a simmer, stirring occasionally.

SERVING AND MENU IDEAS

Top each serving with Cilantro-Yogurt Sauce (page 310), plain yogurt, or sour cream, or shredded Monterey Jack or cheddar cheese. Serve this stew with cornbread (see pages 283 and 284), flatbread, or tortilla chips. Also nice on rice.

Andean Vegetable Stew on Quinoa

Quinoa cooks up light and fluffy and makes a perfect companion for this saucy, spicy stew with its warm flavor and fragrant spices.

Quinoa is a high-protein, gluten-free grain from the Andes, with a nutty flavor. It's a good idea to rinse quinoa under cool running water before cooking, because it has a naturally occurring bitter coating that is mostly removed during processing—rinsing removes any remaining bitterness.

Yields 3 cups quinoa; 6 cups stew
Serves 4
Time: 50 minutes

QUINOA
1 cup quinoa
1 teaspoon vegetable oil or olive oil
1⅓ cups water
½ teaspoon salt

STEW
2 tablespoons vegetable oil or olive oil
1½ cups chopped onions
2 garlic cloves, minced or pressed
1 cup chopped carrots
½ teaspoon salt
1 teaspoon ground cumin seeds
1 teaspoon ground coriander seeds
1 teaspoon dried oregano
½ teaspoon red pepper flakes, or ¼ teaspoon cayenne, or 1 fresh hot pepper, minced
1 bell pepper, (any color), seeded and cut into 1-inch pieces
1½ cups chopped zucchini or yellow squash
1 cup fresh or frozen corn kernels
one 15-ounce can diced tomatoes, or 3 cups chopped fresh tomatoes
1 cup water or stock
shredded cheddar or Monterey Jack cheese (optional)

In a fine-mesh strainer, rinse the quinoa well under cool running water. Place the drained quinoa in a saucepan on medium-high heat. Add a teaspoon of oil and stir to coat. Continuing to stir, cook for a minute, then add the water and salt and bring to a boil. Reduce the heat to low, cover, and simmer until the water has been absorbed, 15 to 20 minutes. Stir with a fork to fluff the quinoa and set aside.

While the quinoa simmers, in a saucepan on medium-high heat, warm the oil. Add the onions and garlic and cook for about 5 minutes. Add the carrots and salt and continue to cook, stirring often, for another 5 minutes. Add the cumin, coriander, oregano, and red pepper flakes and cook for a minute, stirring constantly to prevent the spices from scorching. Add the bell peppers, zucchini, corn, tomatoes, and water or stock. Bring to a rapid simmer, reduce the heat, cover, and cook until the vegetables are tender, about 10 minutes. Season with more salt to taste.

Serve the stew on a bed of the quinoa. Top with cheddar or jack cheese, if you like. Sprigs of cilantro or chopped scallions make a pretty garnish.

VARIATIONS
- This combination of vegetables is what we like at Moosewood, but you could omit something, like the zucchini or corn, and add more of something else. Diced potatoes are fine, or some black beans or red beans.
- Stir in some chopped fresh cilantro.
- Make the stew spicy or not by adjusting the amount of hot peppers, red pepper flakes, or cayenne.

SERVING AND MENU IDEAS
Serve the cilantro version of Lemon-Herb Baked Tofu (page 204) on top of this stew in addition to or instead of cheese.

Green Bean, Potato, and Fennel Ragout

This stew is fragrant with flavors of southern France: thyme, tarragon, saffron, and orange. It is a popular weekend stew at the restaurant. It's such a pleasant and delicious stew that we think of it again and again, in all seasons.

We find a lot of variation in the amount of time needed to cook green beans to the perfect tenderness, sometimes having to do with the particular variety and sometimes with their freshness. We suggest you taste them often to determine when they are just the way you like them. In the restaurant, because we are making such large quantities, we often steam green beans separately and add them when we are ready to serve. The ragout will be even more colorful if you use unpeeled red-skinned potatoes.

Yields 8 cups
Serves 4 to 6
Time: 1 hour

2 leeks (see page 379)
1 medium to large fennel bulb
4 cups cubed potatoes
1 pound green beans
several fresh thyme sprigs
2 tablespoons olive oil
2 cups water or stock
1½ teaspoons salt
1 orange
one 15-ounce can diced tomatoes
generous pinch of saffron
2 tablespoons chopped fresh tarragon or
    3 tablespoons chopped fresh basil
¼ teaspoon ground black pepper

First, prep the vegetables. Chop the white and tender green parts of the leeks (about 1½ cups). Cut the fennel bulb into ¼-inch slices and then cut the slices to about an inch long (about 2 cups). Cut potatoes into stew-size chunks. Trim the green beans and cut into 2-inch pieces (about 3 ½ cups). Tie the sprigs of thyme into a little bundle with kitchen string.

In a stew pot, sauté the leeks in the oil for 4 minutes. Stir in the fennel and potatoes and cook for about 2 minutes, stirring often. Add the water, bundle of thyme, salt, and green beans, cover, and bring to a boil. Reduce to a simmer and cook for 10 minutes, stirring occasionally. While the stew simmers, zest and juice the orange. Add the tomatoes, orange zest, and saffron, bring back to a simmer, and cook until the vegetables are tender, about 10 minutes. Stir in the orange juice, fresh tarragon or basil, and black pepper. Before serving, remove and discard the thyme springs.

VARIATIONS
- Substitute chopped onions for the leeks.
- Substitute ½ teaspoon dried thyme for the fresh thyme. Add with the fennel.
- Use 2 cups chopped fresh tomatoes instead of canned.

SERVING AND MENU IDEAS
Serve with crusty bread and Brie. Or serve on a bed of couscous, and top with crumbled chèvre.

Ratatouille

A timeless, French classic which puts the bounty of late summer to good use. But you can make it in winter, too, since most of the vegetables are available then, and it will make you think of summer. Ratatouille satisfies as a main dish or a side.

Some fresh herbs are a must and you can vary your ratatouille by choosing a different herb or herb combination each time you make it. This dish improves with time, so don't hesitate to make it a day or two ahead.

Yields 8 cups
Serves 6
Total time: 50 minutes

1 medium eggplant (about 1½ pounds), peeled and cubed (about 6 cups)
4 tablespoons extra-virgin olive oil
1 teaspoon salt
1 large onion, coarsely chopped (about 2 cups)
3 garlic cloves, chopped
½ teaspoon dried oregano and/or ground fennel seeds
2 red and/or yellow bell peppers, seeded and chopped (about 3 cups)
2 cups chopped zucchini
¼ cup red wine
one 28-ounce can diced tomatoes
ground black pepper
3 tablespoons chopped fresh basil or 1 to 2 tablespoons minced fresh tarragon

Preheat the oven to 400°F.

In a large bowl, toss the eggplant cubes with 2 tablespoons of the olive oil and the salt. Spread the eggplant cubes out on a rimmed baking sheet and roast until the eggplant is soft, about 15 minutes. Remove from the oven and set aside.

While the eggplant roasts, warm the remaining 2 tablespoons of olive oil in a large pot on medium heat. Add the onions, garlic, oregano and/or fennel, and a sprinkling of salt, and cook, stirring often, until the onions are translucent, about 10 minutes. Stir in the bell peppers and zucchini and cook for another 10 minutes, stirring to prevent sticking. Stir in the roasted eggplant, red wine, and tomatoes and simmer, stirring occasionally, for 20 minutes. Season with black pepper and more salt to taste. Stir in the basil or tarragon just before serving.

VARIATIONS

- If the eggplant skin is nice, peel it in strips, because the black shiny skin looks nice.
- Of course, in keeping with summer's bounty, fresh tomatoes can be used, about 4 cups chopped.
- Add green beans or substitute yellow summer squash for the zucchini.
- Make the ratatouille with thyme or rosemary.

SERVING IDEAS

Serve topped with grated, shredded, or crumbled cheese such as Parmesan, cheddar, Fontina, feta, or chèvre. Serve in a bowl with crusty rustic bread, or on rice or couscous.

Jambalaya

The roux makes this a *fabulous* rich and flavorful stew.

Cajun brown roux are easy to make if you have patience and a good stirring wrist. As you stir and cook a Cajun roux, it goes through three stages: off-white, golden brown, and dark brown. Each has a distinct flavor. For this recipe, we're going for golden brown, about the color of peanut butter, which takes about 30 minutes of stirring. That seems like a lot, but it can be satisfying, and there's no other way to get that wonderful nutty flavor.

Yields 10 cups
Serves 8
Time: 1 hour

3 tablespoons olive oil
2 cups chopped onions
3 garlic cloves, minced or pressed
2 bay leaves
1 teaspoon salt
¼ teaspoon cayenne, or more to taste
1½ cups chopped celery
2 cups chopped carrots
2 cups seeded and chopped bell peppers
    (any color)
2 cups cubed zucchini
2 cups chopped fresh tomatoes
10 ounces frozen baby okra, whole or sliced
1 teaspoon minced fresh thyme
4 cups water
2 tablespoons chopped fresh basil
¼ teaspoon ground black pepper

BROWN ROUX
⅓ cup olive oil or vegetable oil
½ cup unbleached white all-purpose flour

In a covered soup pot on low heat, warm the oil. Add the onions, garlic, bay leaves, salt, and cayenne and cook for about 10 minutes, or until the onion are soft. Stir in the celery, carrots, bell peppers, and zucchini and cook for about 5 minutes. Add the tomatoes, okra, thyme, and water and simmer for 20 to 25 minutes. Stir in the basil and black pepper.

While the jambalaya simmers, make the roux: In a heavy skillet on medium-high heat, warm the oil to just below the smoking point. Test the temperature by sprinkling a pinch of the flour onto the hot oil. If it spreads out, the temperature is fine. If it smokes, the temperature is too high and you should reduce the heat. Whisk in the flour to form a paste. Reduce the heat to low and stir constantly with a wooden spoon. That's *very* low. Don't be tempted to try to speed up the process by increasing the heat. It won't work. If the roux burns even slightly, it will be bitter, and you'll have to throw it out and start over. So be patient; this is a process and you can't rush it. The roux will slowly darken, and a nutty flavor will develop. The medium-brown roux we want is about the color of peanut butter and will take between 20 and 30 minutes of cooking and stirring.

Remove it from the heat and let it cool for at least 5 minutes. Then whisk a couple of ladles of broth from the stew into the roux and continue to whisk until it is smooth.

Stir the roux back into the jambalaya and simmer for 5 more minutes.

SERVING IDEAS
Serve Jambalaya on rice or with crusty bread. Top with smoked cheese to keep those Cajun flavors going.

Cuban Black Beans

Caribbean Black-eyed Peas

Caribbean Red Beans

Our Best Chili

Habas Verdes con Queso

Basque Beans

Greek Lemon-Mint Beans and Vegetables

Creole Red Beans

Ghanaian White Beans and Vegetables with Fiery Pepper Sauce

Beans and Greens

Cuban Black Beans

We have probably made these beans thousands of times at home and at the restaurant. This is a good, basic recipe which can be altered by adding your favorite seasonings—chipotle peppers, thyme, oregano, cilantro, smoked paprika. If you have leftovers, you can easily transform them into a soup by adding tomato and orange juice.

Yields 7 cups
Serves 6 to 8
Time: 45 minutes

3 tablespoons vegetable oil or olive oil
2 garlic cloves, minced or pressed
1½ cups finely chopped onions
½ teaspoon red pepper flakes
1 teaspoon salt
2 teaspoons ground cumin seeds
1 teaspoon ground coriander seeds
1 cup diced carrots
1 cup seeded and diced bell peppers (any color)
one 15-ounce can diced tomatoes

three 15-ounce cans black beans, rinsed and drained (about 4½ cups)
1 tablespoon finely grated orange zest
½ cup fresh orange juice

Warm the oil in a large skillet or soup pot on medium heat. Add the garlic, onions, red pepper flakes, and salt and cook, covered, for 6 minutes, stirring occasionally. Add the cumin, coriander, and carrots, cover, and cook for 3 or 4 minutes, stirring occasionally. Add the bell peppers and cook, covered, for 3 minutes. Stir in the tomatoes and bring to a simmer. Cook, stirring occasionally, until all of the vegetables are tender, about 10 minutes.

Stir in the black beans and orange zest and juice. Cover and simmer until hot, about 5 minutes.

SERVING AND MENU IDEAS
We like to serve Cuban Black Beans on Annatto Rice (page 289) with Smooth Hot Sauce (page 320). It's good topped with Cilantro-Yogurt Sauce (page 310) or Chipotle Cream (page 310) or simply with a dollop of sour cream.

Caribbean Black-eyed Peas

When it's summertime, we think of this as a hot weather dish. In the winter, we want it because it will both warm us up and make us think of more tropical climates. On New Year's Day, we want to eat black-eyed peas for good luck, and this is a delicious way to do that.

Yields 4 cups
Serves 6
Time: 40 minutes

2 tablespoons vegetable oil or olive oil
2 cups chopped onions
4 garlic cloves, minced
1 heaping tablespoon peeled and grated fresh
    ginger
1 teaspoon minced fresh thyme, or a scant
    ½ teaspoon dried thyme
½ teaspoon ground allspice
4 cups cooked black-eyed peas, see Note (or three
    15-ounce cans, rinsed and drained)
1 cup orange juice
Salt
ground black pepper

Warm the oil in a large skillet or saucepan on medium heat. Add the onions and garlic and cook for about 6 minutes, stirring frequently, until the onions are golden and soft. Add the ginger, thyme, and allspice and cook for 5 minutes. Add the drained cooked black-eyed peas and the orange juice and simmer on low heat for 15 minutes, stirring occasionally to prevent sticking. Season with salt and black pepper to taste.

NOTE

For this recipe cook 2 cups of dried black-eyed peas in 4 to 5 cups of water until tender. The cooking time varies with different batches of dried peas. When soaked for a few hours, they usually cook in about 30 minutes. You can cook them without soaking, also; it usually takes 45 minutes to an hour, sometimes longer.

SERVING AND MENU IDEAS

Serve Caribbean Black-eyed Peas on a bed of Annatto Rice (page 289) and top with Mango Salsa (page 315) and maybe a dollop of sour cream.

Caribbean Red Beans

A colorful combination of red and green. Kale makes this dish handsome. It's a complete meal, although a crisp salad is always nice.

Yields 6 cups
Serves 4 to 6
Time: 55 minutes

2 tablespoons olive oil
1½ cups diced onions
4 garlic cloves, minced
½ to 1 teaspoon red pepper flakes or 1 minced
    fresh hot pepper
½ teaspoon ground allspice
½ teaspoon dried thyme
one 28-ounce can diced tomatoes
two 15-ounce cans red kidney beans or small red
    beans, rinsed and drained (about 3 cups)
3 cups stemmed, rinsed, and chopped kale

Warm the oil in a saucepan on medium heat. Add the onions and cook for a few minutes, stirring occasionally. Add the garlic, red pepper flakes, allspice, and thyme. Lower the heat, cover, and cook, stirring occasionally, until the onions are very soft, about 10 minutes. Add the tomatoes and beans and bring to a simmer. Simmer for about 10 minutes. Stir in the chopped kale and cook until the kale is just tender and still bright green, 5 to 10 minutes. Add salt to taste.

SERVING AND MENU IDEAS

Serve the red beans on a bed of rice, preferably Coconut Rice (page 289), and top with Cilantro-Yogurt Sauce (page 310), Chipotle Cream (page 310), avocado slices, or Simple Smooth Guacamole (page 35). Garnish with some cilantro sprigs.

Our Best Chili

February is frigid in the Finger Lakes region of upstate New York. To counter the cold weather blues and blahs, Ithaca holds a Chili Fest. Local restaurants, caterers, and carry-outs showcase their favorite chilis, and happy consumers taste their way through the numerous chili stalls, imbibe local microbrews, and try to stay astride the mechanical bull. Sated, the people then vote for the "best" chili in a set of categories. We don't mind mentioning that Moosewood has won first place three times in the vegetarian category.

We like this festive yellow, red, orange, and black chili topped with Chipotle Cream (page 310); it's also really delicious with Cilantro-Yogurt Sauce (page 310).

Yields 8 cups
Time: about 1 hour

2 tablespoons vegetable oil
1 cup chopped onions
3 garlic cloves, minced or pressed
1 teaspoon salt
1 cup diced carrots
2 cups seeded and chopped red bell peppers
1 fresh hot pepper, seeded and minced
1½ tablespoons ground cumin seeds
1 tablespoon ground coriander seeds
1 teaspoon dried oregano
1 cup fresh or frozen corn kernels
one 28-ounce can diced tomatoes
one 15-ounce can red kidney beans, rinsed and drained
one 15-ounce can black beans, rinsed and drained

Warm the oil in a covered soup pot on low heat. Add the onions, garlic, and salt, and cook until soft, about 10 minutes. Add the carrots and bell peppers, increase the heat to medium-high and cook for 5 minutes, stirring often. Stir in the hot peppers, cumin, coriander, and oregano and cook for 5 minutes more, stirring occasionally so the spices won't stick.

Add the corn, tomatoes, kidney beans, and black beans. Bring the chili to a boil, reduce the heat, cover, and simmer, stirring often, for at least 30 minutes.

SERVING AND MENU IDEAS

Top each bowl of chili with a dollop of Cilantro-Yogurt Sauce (page 310); it's both beautiful and delicious.

Serve with a simple green salad and Moosewood Restaurant's House Cornbread (page 283), Vegan Cornbread (page 284), or tortilla chips.

Habas Verdes con Queso

Both creamy and spicy, this lima bean and vegetable dish has been a perennial favorite at the restaurant since the very early days, and it's a great unfussy dish for home, too. It's economical and easy, and a lot of fun to eat with crisp corn tortilla chips as your utensils.

At the restaurant, we make Habas Verdes with dried limas. It's creamy beige, and although you come upon a whole lima occasionally as you eat it, most of the limas break down, soft and mushy. At home, we sometimes make it with canned butter beans or limas to save time. Not exactly the same dish but also good.

Yields about 7 cups
Serves 6 to 8
Time: 40 minutes

4 cups cooked lima beans or butter beans
    (see Note)
2 tablespoons olive or vegetable oil
2 cups chopped onions
½ teaspoon salt
3 garlic cloves, minced or pressed
1½ cups diced carrots
1½ cups seeded and diced green and/or red bell
    peppers
1 fresh hot pepper, minced or ½ teaspoon cayenne
one 15-ounce can diced tomatoes or 1½ cups
    chopped fresh tomatoes
2 teaspoons ground cumin seeds
1 teaspoon sweet paprika (optional)
6 ounces cream cheese

corn tortilla chips

Drain freshly cooked beans, or rinse and drain canned beans. Set the beans aside.

Warm the oil in a covered saucepan on medium-low heat. Add the onions, salt, and garlic and cook until the onions are translucent, about 10 minutes, stirring occasionally. Add the carrots, cover, and cook for 5 minutes. Add the bell peppers and hot peppers and cook, covered, for about 5 minutes. Add the tomatoes, cumin, and paprika, cover, and simmer, stirring occasionally, until the vegetables are tender, about 10 minutes. Add the beans and heat thoroughly. Cut the cream cheese into several chunks and add to the bean mixture. Stir until the cream cheese melts. Add salt to taste.

Surround individual serving bowls of Habas Verdes con Queso with enough tortilla chips to serve as scoops.

NOTE
2 cups of dried limas yields about 4 cups cooked. (See page 372 for cooking directions.) Three 15-ounce cans of butter beans or lima beans, drained, yield about 4 cups.

SERVING AND MENU IDEAS
Garnish with fresh cilantro and pass your favorite hot sauce at the table for those who like it spicier. Good with crisp Lime-Cilantro Slaw (page 252) or some Quick Sautéed Greens (page 268). Habas Verdes is also a good appetizer or snack.

Basque Beans

You won't find a dish like this in a compendium of classic Basque dishes, but our palates are drawn to the marriage of French and Spanish cuisines that underlie Basque gastronomy. We've combined the Basque favorites of leeks, white beans, hot peppers, and sherry with spinach and tomatoes to create a colorful repast. Sausage is another favorite ingredient—we add fennel seeds to suggest its fragrance and flavor.

Yields 5 cups
Serves 4 to 6
Time: 45 minutes

3 tablespoons extra-virgin olive oil
4 cups chopped leeks (4 medium leeks)
   (see page 379)
4 garlic cloves, minced or pressed
1 teaspoon salt
½ teaspoon red pepper flakes or ½ fresh hot
   pepper, minced
½ teaspoon ground fennel seed
¼ teaspoon crushed or crumbled saffron threads
½ cup dry sherry
one 15-ounce can diced tomatoes
one 15-ounce can cannellini or butter beans,
   undrained
4 cups fresh baby spinach (6 ounces)
ground black pepper

Warm the olive oil in a skillet or soup pot on medium-low heat. Add the leeks, garlic, and salt, and cook, stirring often, for 5 minutes. Add the red pepper flakes, fennel, and saffron, and cook, stirring constantly, until the leeks have softened, about 5 minutes. Add the sherry, tomatoes, and beans. Cover and bring to a boil, then reduce the heat and simmer for 20 minutes, stirring occasionally.

Stir in the spinach a handful at a time and cook until it has wilted. Add black pepper to taste.

VARIATION
- Use 2 cups chopped onions instead of leeks.

SERVING AND MENU IDEAS
We often top Basque Beans with feta, Parmesan, or ricotta salata cheese and serve it on Polenta, Cheesy and Vegan (page 296). You could also put it on rice, couscous, bulghur, or pasta. Or, serve it in a bowl with rustic bread.

Greek Lemon-Mint Beans and Vegetables

This dish is simple, hearty comfort food with lots of great flavor. Please improvise—add rosemary instead of dill, or green beans instead of zucchini, for example. However, we promise that if you just make the recipe as is, you will enjoy an easily prepared, completely satisfying supper.

Yields 8 cups
Serves 6 to 8
Time: 45 minutes

1½ cups chopped onions
2 garlic cloves, minced or pressed
1 teaspoon salt
2 tablespoons olive oil
2 cups diced carrots
1½ cups seeded and diced red or green bell peppers
2 cups diced zucchini
¼ teaspoon red pepper flakes
one 14-ounce can artichoke hearts in brine, drained and chopped
one 15-ounce can white beans, rinsed and drained (1½ cups)
one 15-ounce can diced tomatoes, or 2 cups diced fresh tomatoes
2 tablespoons minced fresh mint, or 2 teaspoons dried
1 tablespoon minced fresh dill
¼ cup fresh lemon juice
salt
ground black pepper

In a large covered skillet or soup pot on medium-low heat, cook the onions, garlic, and salt in the oil until the onions are translucent, about 10 minutes. Add the carrots and bell peppers and continue to cook for about 3 minutes, or until the carrots begin to soften. Add the zucchini and red pepper flakes and dried mint, if using, and cook for about 3 minutes. Stir in the artichoke hearts, beans, and tomatoes, cover, and simmer until all the vegetables are tender but still brightly colored, about 10 minutes. Stir in the fresh mint, if using, and the dill and lemon juice. Season with salt and black pepper to taste. You may want more mint and dill.

SERVING AND MENU IDEAS

Serve on a bed of orzo, couscous, or rice, topped with feta cheese or chèvre. You don't really need anything else, except maybe a salad.

Creole Red Beans

Creole Red Beans is a spectacular dish that's simple to make. It's a very linear recipe. You get started, and then if you work along at a steady but relaxed pace, each thing leads into the next until you have a pot of beans simmering on the back of the stove for a few minutes while you grate some cheese or make a nice salad.

In the restaurant, we always serve Creole Red Beans on brown rice—if you want to, too, remember to start the rice first.

Yields 5 cups
Serves 4 to 6
Time: 45 minutes

2 tablespoons vegetable oil
2 cups chopped onions
1 teaspoon dried oregano
½ teaspoon red pepper flakes
1 cup diced celery
2 teaspoons salt
1 cup diced carrots
½ teaspoon ground allspice
1½ cups seeded and diced bell peppers (any color)
one 6-ounce can tomato paste
1 tablespoon Dijon mustard
¼ cup apple cider vinegar
¼ cup brown sugar
two 15-ounce cans small red beans or red kidney beans, rinsed and drained (3 cups)
½ teaspoon ground black pepper

Warm the oil in a pot on medium-high heat. Add the onions, oregano, and red pepper flakes and cook for 5 minutes, stirring often. Add the celery and 1 teaspoon of the salt and cook for 5 minutes. Stir in the carrots and allspice, cover, and cook for 5 minutes. Stir in the bell peppers, cover, and cook for 5 minutes.

While the vegetables cook, in a small bowl, stir together the tomato paste, mustard, vinegar, sugar, and the remaining 1 teaspoon salt. Add this sauce and the beans to the pot, cover, and simmer on low heat, stirring occasionally, for 15 minutes. Stir in the black pepper.

SERVING AND MENU IDEAS

Serve on brown rice, topped with grated cheddar or smoked cheese or sour cream and/or Cucumber-Tomato Salsa (page 315). We also like to serve Creole Beans with sautéed kale or collards (see page 268).

Ghanaian White Beans and Vegetables with Fiery Pepper Sauce

Although we regularly serve this dish in the restaurant, we've never published a recipe for it. To reduce the quantity for home cooks and develop the recipe we give you here, we referred to an oil-stained, ragged, and yellowed handwritten recipe that cooks in the Moosewood kitchen have been using for about twenty years.

Annatto oil gives the dish a golden hue, and its flavor is somewhat reminiscent of the distinctively flavored red palm oil widely used in West Africa. We use it in both the beans and the fiery sauce. But, it's OK to skip the annatto and use plain vegetable oil—it just won't be our *favorite* Ghanaian White Beans.

We consider Fiery Pepper Sauce integral to the dish. It is unique, looks like a relish, and in hotness should live up to its name. But if you don't want to fool with it, the beans and vegetables would be good with your favorite hot sauce, too. And in that case, we'd add some thyme to the beans. You can make Fiery Pepper Sauce while the beans and vegetables simmer or ahead of time. It will keep refrigerated for several days.

Yields about 10 cups beans; about 2 cups
    Fiery Pepper Sauce
Serves 6
Time: 1 hour

ANNATTO OIL
4½ tablespoons vegetable oil
1 teaspoon annatto seeds

BEANS AND VEGETABLES
2 cups chopped onions
1 cup diced celery
2 garlic cloves, minced or pressed
1 teaspoon salt
2 tablespoons annatto oil or vegetable oil
1 cup diced carrots
2 cups diced zucchini
1 to 2 cups seeded and diced red bell peppers
one 28-ounce can diced tomatoes
two 15-ounce cans small white beans, rinsed and
    drained (3 cups)
½ cup chopped fresh cilantro
1 lime or lemon

FIERY PEPPER SAUCE
2 green bell peppers, seeded and roughly chopped
1 large onion, roughly chopped (about 2 cups)
2 fresh hot peppers, chopped
2 tablespoons annatto oil or vegetable oil
1 teaspoon salt
2 teaspoons red pepper flakes or ½ teaspoon cayenne

To make the annatto oil: In a small pan on medium heat, warm the oil and annatto seeds, swirling the oil frequently until hot. The oil will be a rich reddish color. Be careful not to scorch. Strain the annatto seeds out of the oil and discard them.

To make the beans and vegetables, in a covered soup pot on medium heat, cook the onions, celery, garlic, and salt in the annatto oil for 5 minutes. Stir in the carrots and cook for 5 minutes. Add the zucchini and bell peppers and cook for 5 minutes. Add the tomatoes, bring to a low boil, and simmer for 10 minutes. Stir in the white beans and cilantro and return to a simmer. Zest the lime or lemon and juice it. Add the zest and juice, and simmer for at least 10 minutes more.

To make the Fiery Pepper Sauce: In a food processor, whirl the bell peppers, onions, and hot peppers until there are no large pieces, but it is not fully puréed. In a large heavy skillet, warm the oil on medium-high heat. Carefully add the processed peppers and onions including the juice; it will splatter in the hot oil. Stir in the salt and red pepper flakes. Cook, uncovered, stirring frequently, for about 15 minutes, or until very soft. As the sauce thickens, you may need to lower the heat to prevent scorching.

SERVING AND MENU IDEAS
Serve the beans and vegetables on a bed of rice or Annatto Rice (page 289), topped with a generous dollop of Fiery Pepper Sauce.

Beans and Greens

Beans and greens together are a soulful combination in many ethnic cuisines. This simple, earthy dish from southern Italy is light, fresh, nutritious, and always satisfying. In every season. And so quick. Almost any kind of beans work here, but butter beans are our favorite because their mild creaminess goes well with lemon. For escarole, you could substitute curly endive, mizuna, kale, or broccoli rabe.

You can make the beans ahead of time (refrigerate if it will be a while before you serve), but the greens are best cooked at the last minute.

Serves 4 to 6
Time: 20 minutes

BEANS
two 15-ounce cans butter beans, rinsed and
    drained (3 cups)
2 tablespoons fresh lemon juice
1 tablespoon extra-virgin olive oil
½ teaspoon red pepper flakes (optional)
salt
ground black pepper

GREENS
1 large head escarole (about 1 pound)
1 tablespoon extra-virgin olive oil
4 to 6 garlic cloves, minced or pressed
salt
ground black pepper

To make the beans: In a food processor, pulse the beans, lemon juice, and olive oil until well blended, but not puréed. Add the red pepper flakes, if using, and season with salt and black pepper to taste. Set aside.

To make the greens: Rinse the escarole well and shake or pat almost dry. Chop the escarole coarsely, cutting through the leaves in two directions. In a large skillet on medium heat, warm the olive oil. Add the garlic and cook for just a minute, or until golden. Add some of the greens and stir, and then as the greens in the pan begin to wilt, add more until they're all in the pan. Increase the heat and cook, stirring frequently, until the greens are wilted and bright green, just a couple of minutes. Season with salt and black pepper to taste.

Serve Beans and Greens, side by side, on a platter and accompany with crusty bread. The beans can be served at room temperature, chilled, or hot. The greens should be cooked right before serving.

SERVING AND MENU IDEAS
Serve with olives and fresh mozzarella and tomatoes (see page 112). To make crostini, spread the beans on toasted slices of Italian or French bread and top with the greens. Beans and Greens can also be served as an antipasto before pasta with Tomato-Basil Sauce (page 324) or Puttanesca Sauce (page 322). Or, toss the beans and greens with pasta and top with a drizzle of olive oil and some Parmesan. Fresh fruit is the perfect dessert, maybe sliced melon or juicy pears or grapes.

Mushroom Frittata

Spanish-style Tortilla

Fritada de Espinaca

Caramelized Onion Pie

Mushroom Piroshki

Pizza Rustica

Mushroom Frittata

Frittatas are so versatile. They're good hot, at room temperature, and even cold. Serve them for dinner, lunch, brunch, breakfast. They're perfect for picnics, dish-to-pass meals, and sandwich fillings. Almost every vegetable is a candidate for a frittata, and most cheeses work well.

In this recipe, we infuse the milk for the custard with fresh thyme because it's such a nice and easy way to deal with those twiggy sprigs and we love the flavor of thyme. But if you don't have fresh thyme, check out the variations for how to use dried.

Serves 6 to 8
Prep time: 50 minutes
Baking time: 50 minutes

2 cups milk
2 or 3 sprigs fresh thyme
2 large potatoes, sliced ½ inch thick
    (about 3 cups sliced)
4 tablespoons olive oil
6 garlic cloves, minced or pressed
salt
3 cups sliced mushrooms (12 ounces whole)
2 cups sliced onions
½ cup seeded and sliced bell peppers (optional)
    (any color)
6 large eggs
3 ounces cream cheese
1 tablespoon Dijon mustard
½ teaspoon salt
¼ teaspoon ground black pepper
½ cup shredded cheddar cheese (2 ounces)
½ cup shredded smoked cheddar cheese (2 ounces)

Warm the milk and sprigs of thyme in a small sauce pan on low heat to just below a simmer; do not boil. Set aside.

Preheat the oven to 400°F. Lightly oil two rimmed baking sheets and a 13 × 9 × 2-inch baking pan.

In a bowl, toss the potato slices with 2 tablespoons of the oil and half of the garlic. Spread out in an even layer on a baking sheet, sprinkle with salt, and roast for about 20 minutes, until tender.

In the same bowl, toss the mushrooms, onions, and bell peppers, if using, with the remaining 2 tablespoons oil and garlic. Spread out in an even layer on the second baking sheet and roast until tender, about 15 minutes.

While the vegetables roast, make the custard. Remove the thyme sprigs from the milk; it's fine if some leaves are left floating in the milk, but be sure to fish out and discard the twigs. In a blender, whirl the thyme-infused milk and the eggs, cream cheese, mustard, salt, and black pepper until smooth.

When the vegetables come out of the oven, reduce the oven temperature to 350°F. Layer the potatoes in the prepared baking pan. Spread the onions, mushrooms, and bell peppers, if using, on top of the potatoes. Sprinkle with the shredded cheeses. Pour the custard over all.

Bake for about 50 minutes, or until the custard is set and the top is golden brown. Serve hot or at room temperature.

VARIATIONS
- If you want to use dried thyme instead of fresh, add 1 teaspoon of dried thyme to the onions and mushrooms before roasting.
- Use different vegetables: asparagus, zucchini, cauliflower, broccoli, eggplant, sun-dried tomatoes, kale, chard, spinach . . .
- Experiment with different cheeses: Fontina, Gruyère, Swiss, Jack, Havarti . . .

SERVING AND MENU IDEAS
Serve with Cucumbers Vinaigrette (page 256), Beet Salad (page 258), or Tomato, Cucumber, and Artichoke Heart Salad (page 256) on the side. Or, try it with Roasted Brussels Sprouts (page 275) or Roasted Cauliflower (page 274).

Spanish-style Tortilla

Over the years, Moosewood Restaurant has held numerous brunches for the benefit of various local and not-so-local organizations. Our cooks, waiters, bartenders, and dishwashers donate their time on Sunday morning, when the restaurant is normally closed, to prepare and serve the meal. The organization does the publicity and sells tickets, usually on a sliding scale, and we do the rest. We've held brunches for groups as varied as the Ithaca Free Clinic, CUSLAR (Committee on U.S.-Latin American Relations), Multicultural Resource Center, the local Planned Parenthood, and an NGO in Rwanda where one of our former waiters worked. It's a lot of work, we can serve about 150 people in two seatings before we have to clean up and get ready to prepare the dinner meal for our regular customers, but it's good fun and good food for everyone involved. Spanish-Style Tortilla is one of our recent favorite dishes to serve at these brunches. It's always a hit, especially with some Chipotle Aioli (page 259) on top.

Yields one 9-inch pie
Serves 6
Initial Prep time: 15 minutes
Roasting time: 20 to 25 minutes
Assembly prep time: 15 minutes
Baking time: 30 minutes

5 cups white potatoes, cut into ¼- to ½-inch-thick slices
2 cups onions, sliced into ½-inch-thick wedges
2 teaspoons sweet paprika (see Variations)
½ teaspoon red pepper flakes
2 garlic cloves, minced or pressed
1¼ teaspoons salt
2 tablespoons olive oil
4 large eggs
½ cup milk
¼ teaspoon ground black pepper
½ cup lightly packed shredded cheddar cheese
½ cup lightly packed shredded Parmesan cheese

Preheat the oven to 425°F. Spray or oil a large rimmed baking sheet or two smaller ones (you need enough surface to spread out the potatoes and onions for roasting) and a 9-inch pie plate.

In a large bowl, mix the potatoes and onions with the paprika, red pepper flakes, garlic, and 1 teaspoon of the salt. Drizzle with the olive oil and mix well. Spread the seasoned potatoes and onions in a single layer on the prepared baking sheet. Roast for 20 to 25 minutes until tender and browned. Remove from the oven and set aside. Reduce the oven temperature to 350°F.

Whisk together the eggs, milk, ¼ teaspoon salt, and black pepper until smooth.

Layer half of the roasted potatoes and onions in the prepared pie plate. Sprinkle with the cheeses and cover with the remaining potatoes and onions. Pour the egg custard evenly over all; it will generously fill the pie plate. Bake until golden brown and fairly firm, about 30 minutes. Let the tortilla sit for about 10 minutes; it will continue to cook and set. Cut into wedges and serve warm or at room temperature.

VARIATIONS

- Some people like to use smoked paprika as some of the paprika. We find that if you use more than about a teaspoon of smoked paprika in this recipe, it can taste a little bitter.
- We like to use both cheddar and Parmesan cheese, but either one alone would be fine, too. You could also try smoked cheddar or Manchego.

SERVING AND MENU IDEAS

Serve hot or at room temperature, in wedges topped with a generous dollop of Chipotle Aioli (page 259). Nice with a simple green salad or some fresh fruit. Spanish-style Tortilla can also be served cold for a picnic or a packed lunch.

Fritada de Espinaca

This Sephardic specialty is usually made for a Sabbath brunch called *desayuno*, but we have been serving it at Moosewood for any day's lunch or dinner for over two decades, since our friend Janice Weltman shared her family's recipe with us. Over the years, we've played around with the cheeses, and this recipe gives you our favorite mixture: each cheese contributes a distinctive flavor, or in the case of the cottage cheese, makes the texture just right.

We have also prepared huge batches of this delicious, golden, baked casserole for large gatherings and celebrations. We once made it to serve more than 1,000 guests at an Organic Trade Association's gala dinner. Very quickly, word got around to check out the delicious spinach frittata at Moosewood's station. People's responses were icing on the cake for us: we already thought we'd really pulled something off just to have prepped and baked that much espinaca. It really is a simple, easy recipe, a snap to do at home.

Serves 6 to 8
Prep time: 25 minutes
Baking time: 45 to 60 minutes

½ cup bread crumbs (see page 373) or matzo meal
20 ounces fresh baby spinach (about 14 cups)
6 large eggs, beaten
½ teaspoon ground black pepper
¼ teaspoon freshly grated nutmeg
1 cup cottage cheese
1 cup packed shredded feta cheese (5 ounces)
2 cups shredded sharp cheddar cheese (8 ounces)
½ cup shredded Parmesan or Pecorino Romano cheese

Preheat the oven to 350°F. Oil a 13 × 9 × 2-inch baking pan. Dust the bottom of the pan with ¼ cup of the bread crumbs or matzo meal.

Rinse the spinach and, while it's still wet, steam it in a covered pot until just wilted. Drain it in a colander, pressing out the excess liquid. Turn the spinach out onto a cutting board and when it's cool enough to handle, squeeze out more liquid, then chop it.

In a large bowl, mix the spinach with the eggs, black pepper, nutmeg, cottage cheese, feta cheese, cheddar cheese, remaining ¼ cup bread crumbs, and ¼ cup of the Parmesan. Spread the mixture evenly in the prepared pan. Sprinkle the top with the remaining ¼ cup Parmesan.

Bake for 45 to 60 minutes until the top is firm to the touch. Cut into squares or triangles. Serve warm or at room temperature.

NOTES

Sephardim traditionally use kashkaval cheese in this recipe. If you can find it, use it in place of the cheddar and Parmesan.

In place of fresh spinach, you can use two 10-ounce packages frozen chopped spinach, defrosted, and excess liquid squeezed out.

SERVING AND MENU IDEAS

Serve as a main dish, side dish, or appetizer. This is delicious with Tomato, Cucumber, and Artichoke Heart Salad (page 256) or Middle Eastern Carrot Salad with Mint (page 257) or Beet Salad (page 258).

Caramelized Onion Pie

This pie offers a great play of textures and nicely balanced flavors: each forkful is a fusion of flaky pastry, silky sweet onions with hints of mustard and thyme, creamy custard, and a crisp, browned cheesy top.

Yields one 9-inch pie
Serves 6
Prep time: about 1 hour
Baking time: 30 to 40 minutes

Our Favorite All-Purpose Piecrust for a 9-inch pie (page 356)

FILLING
1½ tablespoons olive oil
4 cups thinly sliced onions
¾ teaspoon salt
1½ teaspoons minced fresh thyme or ½ teaspoon dried thyme
4 large eggs
2 tablespoons unbleached white all-purpose flour
1 generous teaspoon Dijon mustard
⅛ teaspoon ground black pepper
1¼ cups milk
1 cup packed shredded sharp cheddar or Gruyère cheese (4 ounces)
¼ cup packed shredded smoked cheddar or smoked Gouda cheese

Make the piecrust dough. While the dough chills, you'll have time to prepare the filling. And you may have time to roll the dough out while the onions finish caramelizing.

Warm the olive oil in a large, heavy skillet on medium-high heat. Add the onions, ½ teaspoon of the salt, and dried thyme (if you're using fresh thyme, it will be added later) and sauté for about 5 minutes, or until the onions become translucent. Reduce the heat to low and cook the onions until they are very soft, browned, and sweet, about 30 minutes. Don't cover the skillet while cooking, and stir every few minutes. Add a splash of water if the onions start to stick or brown too fast. The trick is to let them brown (by not stirring too often), but not scorch. Stir more often toward the end, scraping the bottom of the pan.

While the onions caramelize, whisk together the eggs, flour, mustard, the remaining ¼ teaspoon salt, the black pepper, and milk. Shred the cheeses. Roll out the pie dough and fit it into the pie plate.

Preheat the oven to 400°F.

To assemble the pie: Mix together the cheeses and the onions and spread over the piecrust. If you're using fresh thyme, sprinkle it on top. Pour the custard over all. Bake until the filling is set and the top is crusty and golden, 30 to 40 minutes. Allow the pie to sit for 10 minutes before serving.

SERVING AND MENU IDEAS
So many dishes are "perfect" beside this pie: Cranberry Sauce (page 311), Cucumbers Vinaigrette (page 256), plain sliced tomatoes, any of our Not so Plain Green Vegetables (page 266), Sweet and Sour Cabbage Two Ways (page 280), a crisp salad with crunch (celery, pears, apples) dressed with Pear-Thyme Dressing (page 305). Gazpacho (page 70), Caramelized Onion Pie, and Fruit Skewers (page 368) make a really nice brunch.

Mushroom Piroshki

Traditional piroshki are yeasted buns, fried or baked, that are both celebratory and street food popular throughout Russia and Ukraine. Similar pastries are also made in the Balkans, central Eurasia, and Scandinavia. Piroshki are filled with savory, and sometimes sweet, fillings. At Moosewood we make large entrée-size pastry pockets, rather than the traditional smaller piroshki, and we've shortened the prep time by using a rich pie pastry, in the Estonian tradition, instead of a yeasted dough.

Moosewood cook Sara Robbins began as a baker at Moosewood within weeks of the restaurant opening, and her baking skills have stood her, and us, in good stead. She's a marvel at adeptly turning out trays of beautiful big piroshki.

In this recipe, we stuff piroshki with a creamy mushroom, potato, and cheese filling, but the mushrooms can be replaced by asparagus, broccoli, cabbage, or any other vegetable that piques your fancy. Naturally, the cheeses and herbs can be played with, too.

Yields 8
Prep time: 1½ hours, including making pie dough
Baking time: 20 to 30 minutes

2 batches Our Favorite All-Purpose Piecrust for a 10-inch pie (page 356)
2 cups peeled and diced potatoes
8 ounces cream cheese
2 tablespoons vegetable oil
1 cup chopped onions
½ teaspoon salt
½ teaspoon caraway seeds or a scant ½ teaspoon ground caraway
¼ teaspoon ground black pepper
4 cups coarsely chopped mushrooms (16 ounces whole) (see Note)
1 cup shredded sharp cheddar cheese (4 ounces)
1 to 2 tablespoons chopped fresh dill
1 large egg, beaten with 1 tablespoon water
sesame seeds or poppy seeds (optional)

Prepare two batches of pie dough. Divide the dough into eight equal portions and pat each into a flattened ball. Cover with plastic wrap and refrigerate.

In a saucepan, cover the potatoes with salted water and boil until soft. Drain the potatoes and return them to the pan. Put the cream cheese in the pan to soften. Cover and set aside.

While the potatoes cook, warm the oil in a large covered skillet on medium-low heat. Add the onions, salt, caraway, and black pepper and cook for about 10 minutes, stirring occasionally to prevent sticking. Add the mushrooms, increase the heat to medium-high and sauté for about 6 minutes, or until the mushrooms are tender and somewhat browned and their liquid has evaporated.

Mash the potatoes with the cream cheese in the saucepan. Stir in the mushrooms, cheddar cheese, and dill.

Preheat the oven to 400°F. Lightly oil two baking sheets.

Remove the dough from the fridge. Have the egg wash, a pastry brush, and sesame seeds or poppy seeds, if using, close at hand. On a lightly floured surface, roll out each piece of dough into an 8-inch circle; it's OK if the edges are irregular. Place ½ cup of filling on the half of the circle nearest you along the midline. With the back of a spoon, spread the filling to about 1½ inches from the curved edge. Lift the empty half of the dough over the filling to form a half-circle with the curved edges lined up. With your fingers lightly press down around the edges to define the filling, then fold over the outer edges to meet the filled part of the pastry. Lightly crimp the edges with a fork to seal the dough. Carefully transfer the piroshki to the prepared baking sheet. Don't crowd the piroshki; space them at least a couple of inches apart. Brush the tops of the piroshki with the egg wash and sprinkle with seeds, if using.

Bake for 20 to 30 minutes until puffy and golden. Cool on the baking sheet for a couple of minutes, and then transfer with a spatula to a platter. Serve warm or at room temperature.

NOTE
We usually use white or cremini (Italian brown) mushrooms or a combination. It's very tasty with some dried mushrooms added.

SERVING AND MENU IDEAS
Serve with Sweet and Sour Red Cabbage Two Ways (page 280) or Beet Salad (page 258), Cucumbers Vinaigrette (page 256), and/or applesauce. Also delicious with a green salad drizzled with one of our dressings (pages 301 to 306).

Pizza Rustica

This dish is a cross between a quiche and a pizza; tender pie crust is filled with savory Italian cheeses, tomato sauce, and fresh basil and topped like a pizza with bell peppers and olives—delicious. We started making it in the very early days of Moosewood when we frequently used *The Vegetarian Epicure* by Anna Thomas. We've made it our own, but we'd like to thank Anna Thomas for the inspiration.

Very pungent olives may be too dominating a flavor; use black or green olives that you like. Yellow bell peppers look especially pretty.

Yields one 9-inch pie
Serves 6
Prep time: 40 minutes; more if you make the sauce
Baking time: about 1 hour

Our Favorite All-Purpose Piecrust for 9-inch pie (page 356)
3 large eggs
14 to 16 ounces ricotta cheese
¼ teaspoon ground black pepper
½ teaspoon salt
½ cup packed shredded Parmesan cheese
2 cups shredded mozzarella cheese (8 ounces)
3 tablespoons chopped fresh basil
1½ cups Tomato-Basil Sauce (page 324) or your favorite tomato sauce (see Note)
1½ cups seeded and chopped bell peppers
½ cup chopped pitted olives

Make the dough for the piecrust, and while it chills, prepare the filling. In a mixing bowl, beat the eggs and stir in the ricotta, black pepper, salt, Parmesan, mozzarella, and basil.

Roll out the piecrust and fit it into a 9-inch pie plate. Fill it with the cheese mixture. Spread the tomato sauce evenly over the cheese. Sprinkle the bell peppers and olives evenly over all.

Bake in a preheated 400°F oven for 25 minutes. Then reduce the heat to 375°F and bake until the filling is set, 30 to 40 minutes. The pie will serve more easily if you allow it to sit for 10 minutes.

VARIATION
- Top with a sprinkling of capers or with chopped red onions.

NOTE
Our Tomato-Basil Sauce is delicious in this pizza. We like to make the sauce smooth and thick, so we cook at it for at least 20 minutes at a vigorous simmer. It's good with the optional fennel.

SERVING AND MENU IDEAS
Serve Pizza Rustica with any (or many) of these sides: Quick Sautéed Greens (page 268), Cucumbers Vinaigrette (page 256), Roasted Cauliflower (page 274), Confetti Kale Slaw (page 255), Seasoned Artichokes (page 263).

CASSEROLES

Chilaquiles Casserole

This casserole is a big favorite at Moosewood Restaurant and a family favorite in our homes. It is healthful, filling, colorful, and quite tasty. It's a gluten-free dish, and if you substitute soy or rice "cheese," it can be vegan as well.

Serves 6 to 8
Prep time: 35 minutes
Baking time: 30 minutes

2 cups chopped onions
1 tablespoon vegetable oil
3 cups seeded and finely chopped bell peppers (any color)
1½ cups fresh or frozen corn kernels
1 teaspoon ground cumin seeds
1 teaspoon ground coriander seeds
3 cups cooked black, small red, or pinto beans (or two 15-ounce cans, rinsed and drained)
1 teaspoon salt
½ teaspoon ground black pepper
4 cups coarsely crumbled corn tortilla chips
2 cups Smooth Hot Sauce (page 320) or your favorite Mexican-style salsa
2 cups shredded sharp cheddar cheese (8 ounces)

Preheat the oven to 375°F. Lightly oil a 13 × 9 × 2-inch baking pan.

In a large covered saucepan on medium heat, cook the onions in the oil, stirring occasionally, until translucent, about 8 minutes. Add the bell peppers, cover, and cook for 5 minutes. Stir in the corn, cumin, coriander, beans, salt, and black pepper and cook, covered, until hot, about 5 minutes.

To assemble the casserole: Spread half of the crumbled tortilla chips in the bottom of the prepared baking pan. Spoon the bean and vegetable mixture over the tortilla chips. Spread on half of the hot sauce or salsa. Sprinkle with 1 cup of the cheese. Finish with the remaining tortilla chips, the remaining hot sauce or salsa, and the remaining 1 cup cheese.

Bake until the cheese is bubbling and beginning to brown, about 30 minutes.

VARIATIONS

- Add a layer of chopped, blanched greens, such as kale or spinach, on top of the beans and vegetables layer.
- Use Refried Beans (page 281) for even more flavor.

SERVING AND MENU IDEAS

Garnish with sour cream, Chipotle Cream (page 310), Cilantro-Yogurt Sauce (page 310), chopped olives, slices of avocado with lime juice, or Simple Smooth Guacamole (page 35). Serve with Lime-Cilantro Slaw (page 252), a green salad, Confetti Kale Slaw (page 255), or Quick Sautéed Greens (page 268). Fruit Skewers (page 368) are a perfect light dessert with this substantial entrée.

Mexican Corn and Cheese Casserole

This golden casserole with a sweet corn flavor and easy-to-prepare instructions is a wonderful supper dish to make with kids.

Serves 6
Prep time: 30 minutes
Baking time: 35 minutes

2 tablespoons vegetable oil or olive oil
1½ cups diced onions
½ teaspoon salt
¾ cup diced carrots
1 cup seeded and diced bell peppers (any color)
3 generous cups fresh or frozen corn kernels
    (16-ounce package frozen)
1 teaspoon ground cumin seeds
1 teaspoon ground coriander seeds
½ teaspoon red pepper flakes (optional)
5 large eggs
1 cup milk
¼ teaspoon ground black pepper
1½ cups shredded cheddar cheese (6 ounces)

Preheat the oven to 375°F. Lightly oil an 11 × 7 × 2-inch baking pan.

In a covered saucepan warm the oil on medium heat. Add the onions, sprinkle with ¼ teaspoon of the salt, and cook for about 8 minutes, stirring occasionally. Add the carrots and cook, covered, for about 5 minutes. Add the bell peppers and corn, reserving 1 cup of the corn to blend into the custard. Stir in the cumin, coriander, and red pepper flakes, if using. Cover and cook, stirring occasionally, until the vegetables are tender, about 7 minutes.

Meanwhile, in a blender, purée the eggs, milk, remaining ¼ teaspoon of salt, the black pepper, and the remaining 1 cup of corn until smooth.

When the vegetables are done, spread them evenly in the prepared baking pan, pour the custard on top, and sprinkle with the cheese. Bake, uncovered, for about 35 minutes, or until golden. Test the custard by inserting a knife in the center: if it comes out clean, the casserole is ready.

SERVING AND MENU IDEAS
This tastes fine on its own, but is even nicer served with Our Favorite Tomato-Cilantro Salsa (page 314) or Smooth Hot Sauce (page 320) or Tomatillo Sauce (page 320). Simple Smooth Guacamole (page 35) and tortilla chips are good on the side. It's also nice with Green Beans with Lemon Zest Dressing (see page 266) .

Rumbledethumps

Rumbledethumps is the Scottish version of Irish colcannon and English bubble and squeak—all are potato and cabbage pies devised as a way to use up leftovers. It's a dish to satisfy your craving for comfort food; rich and filling, it could be your ticket to fulfilling your dream of having just mashed potatoes for dinner.

When Tom Walls, who was a Moosewood cook for many years, wrote his recipe for Rumbledethumps for *Sundays at Moosewood Restaurant,* he claimed to have tried all of over one zillion versions. Tom, try this one!

Our hearty, luscious version is a rich casserole of leeks or onions and cheddar-mashed potatoes rumpled up with healthy chunks of cabbage and broccoli and topped with bubbly melted cheese. Some cooks add a pinch of nutmeg, others a spoonful of Dijon mustard. Sometimes, we swap kale for the cabbage or broccoli.

Serves 4 to 6 as a main dish; 8 to 10 as a side
Prep time: 30 minutes
Baking time: 15 minutes

6 cups peeled and chopped potatoes
2 teaspoons salt
3 cups chopped green cabbage
3 cups chopped broccoli
2 tablespoons butter
3 cups chopped leeks (3 medium leeks) (page 379) or 2 cups chopped onions
3 ounces cream cheese
½ cup milk or reserved potato-cooking water
2 cups shredded sharp cheddar cheese
1 tablespoon Dijon mustard or ¼ teaspoon freshly grated nutmeg (optional)
⅛ teaspoon ground black pepper

Put the potatoes and 1 teaspoon of the salt in a covered soup pot with enough water to generously cover and bring to a boil on high heat. Reduce the heat and simmer until the potatoes are tender, about 15 minutes.

Meanwhile, in another pot, blanch the cabbage and broccoli in boiling water until just tender, 6 or 7 minutes. Drain, and set aside.

In a covered saucepan or skillet on medium-low heat, melt the butter, add the leeks or onions, and cook until soft. Set aside.

Preheat the oven to 350°F. Butter a 13 × 9 × 2-inch baking pan.

When the potatoes are done, drain them, reserving a cup of the cooking water. Mash the potatoes in the pot that you cooked them in with the cream cheese and milk or potato-cooking water. The mashed potatoes should be fairly stiff and not too smooth. Stir in 1 cup of the cheddar, the remaining 1 teaspoon salt, and the mustard or nutmeg. Fold the cabbage, broccoli, and leeks into the potatoes until thoroughly mixed. Add the black pepper and season with more salt to taste.

Spread the mixture into the prepared baking pan and top with the remaining cheddar cheese. Bake, uncovered, until thoroughly hot and golden brown, about 15 minutes.

VARIATION

- In place of cabbage or broccoli, use 5 cups of chopped kale.

NOTE

If you want to prepare Rumbledethumps in advance of baking, assemble it, cover the baking pan with aluminum foil, and refrigerate. Bake, covered, at 350°F for 25 minutes, then uncover and either bake for another 15 minutes or place under the broiler to brown the top.

SERVING AND MENU IDEAS

Serve with fresh fruit or a tossed green salad, or Cucumbers Vinaigrette (page 256), or Beet Salad (page 258). Stout is probably the proper beverage.

Zucchini-Feta Casserole

Therese Tischler, a Moosewood founder and a superlative cook, had a hand in creating this casserole and many other long-standing favorites. Although casseroles are usually thought of as hearty winter fare, this one is lighter and puts to good use the abundance of the zucchini, tomatoes, and fresh herbs abundant at summer's end. At the restaurant, we serve it year round and customers are always asking for the recipe.

When we put it to a vote whether people like it better made with rice or bulghur, it was pretty much a tie, so we decided to give you directions for both. See the Variation for the bulghur pilaf version.

Serves 6 to 8
Prep time: 1 hour
Baking time: 45 minutes

RICE PILAF LAYER
1 teaspoon olive oil
¾ cup brown rice, rinsed and drained
1½ cups water
¼ teaspoon salt
¾ cup chopped toasted walnuts
¼ cup dried currants
2 tablespoons chopped fresh mint
1 tablespoon fresh lemon juice

ROASTED VEGETABLE LAYER
2 cups sliced onions
6 cups sliced zucchini rounds (¼ inch thick)
2 cups sliced tomatoes (¼ inch thick)
2 garlic cloves, minced or pressed (optional)
1 teaspoon dried oregano or 1 tablespoon chopped fresh oregano
¼ teaspoon salt
¼ teaspoon ground black pepper
2 tablespoons olive oil

3 large eggs, lightly beaten
1½ cups crumbled or shredded feta cheese (7 ounces)
1½ cups cottage cheese
2 tablespoons chopped fresh dill

To make rice pilaf: Warm the oil in a medium saucepan and briefly sauté the rice until it emits a nutty aroma. Add the water and salt, cover the pot, and bring to a boil. Reduce the heat and simmer until tender, 35 to 45 minutes. Fluff the rice and remove it from the heat. Stir in the walnuts, currants, mint, and lemon juice.

While the rice cooks, roast the vegetables.

Preheat the oven to 400°F. Lightly oil a large rimmed baking sheet, or two smaller ones.

Combine the sliced onions, zucchini, and tomatoes with the garlic, if using, the oregano, salt, black pepper, and olive oil in a large bowl. Mix until the vegetables are well coated with the oil and seasonings. Pour the vegetables onto the prepared baking sheet, spread them out, and roast until the tomatoes and zucchini are juicy, about 25 minutes. When the vegetables are done, remove them from the oven and lower the oven temperature to 350°F.

While the vegetables roast, stir together the eggs, feta, cottage cheese, and dill and set aside. Lightly oil a 13 × 9 × 2-inch baking pan.

To assemble the casserole, spread the pilaf evenly on the bottom of the prepared baking pan. Top with the roasted vegetables. Spoon the feta-cottage mixture evenly over the vegetables. Bake, uncovered, for 45 minutes, or until the eggs are set and the top begins to turn golden. Let the casserole sit for at least 10 minutes before serving.

VARIATION

- To make bulghur pilaf: Put 1 cup of bulghur and ¼ teaspoon of salt into a bowl, pour 1 cup of boiling water over it, cover, and set aside for at least 15 minutes. Fluff with a fork and stir in the walnuts, currants, mint, and lemon juice.

SERVING AND MENU IDEAS

This casserole is especially nice with Cucumbers Vinaigrette (page 256). We also like it with Middle Eastern Carrot Salad with Mint (page 257) and Beet Salad (page 258).

Country Moussaka

Nostimos! Telios! This Greek-influenced casserole with its golden béchamel topping and enticing aroma is a great dish. Really delicious.

There are three parts that will be assembled in layers before baking: roasted vegetables, a tomato sauce, and a béchamel sauce. None of the parts is difficult to prepare, it just takes some time. We hope you'll find it well worth the effort—our customers have certainly found it well worth our effort for nearly forty years.

Serves 6 to 8
Prep time: 1 hour, 10 minutes
Baking time: 45 to 50 minutes
Resting time: 15 minutes

ROASTED VEGETABLES

1 large or 2 medium eggplant (about 3 pounds)
3 medium zucchini (about 1½ pounds)
2 tablespoons olive oil
a sprinkling of salt and ground black pepper

TOMATO SAUCE

1½ tablespoons olive oil
1 cup finely chopped onions
2 garlic cloves, minced or pressed
½ teaspoon salt
1 cup seeded and diced bell peppers (any color)
one 28-ounce can crushed or diced tomatoes
½ teaspoon ground cinnamon
1 teaspoon dried oregano
⅛ teaspoon ground black pepper
2 tablespoons chopped fresh dill

BÉCHAMEL SAUCE

¼ cup butter
¼ cup unbleached white all-purpose flour
2 cups milk, heated
¼ teaspoon freshly grated nutmeg
¼ teaspoon salt
2 large eggs, beaten

1¼ cups shredded or crumbled feta cheese
4 tablespoons raw couscous
⅔ cup shredded Parmesan cheese

Preheat the oven to 400°F. Lightly oil two rimmed baking sheets.

To make the roasted vegetables: Either peel the eggplant or don't, as you prefer, and slice both the eggplant and the zucchini into ¾-inch-thick rounds. Place them in a single layer on the prepared baking sheets. Brush the tops with the olive oil and sprinkle with salt and black pepper. Bake until tender, about 30 minutes. If, when you take the eggplant and zucchini from the oven, you're close to assembling the casserole, reduce the oven temperature to 350°F; if not, turn off the oven.

To make the tomato sauce: In a covered saucepan on low heat, warm the olive oil. Add the onions, garlic, and salt, and cook for 5 minutes, then stir in the bell peppers and continue to cook, covered to prevent sticking, until the onions are translucent. Add the tomatoes, cinnamon, oregano, and black pepper and simmer on low heat for about 20 minutes, or until you are ready to assemble the casserole. Stir in the dill.

To make the béchamel sauce: Melt the butter in a small, heavy saucepan. Whisk in the flour and cook on low heat for 1 or 2 minutes, stirring constantly to prevent scorching. Gradually pour in the hot milk, continuing to whisk, and cook until the sauce is thick and smooth, 3 or 4 minutes. Remove from the heat, and stir in the nutmeg, salt, and beaten eggs.

To assemble the casserole: Oil a 13 × 9 × 2-inch baking dish. Preheat the oven to 350°F if not already on. Pour half of the tomato sauce into the baking dish and cover with the eggplant slices. Sprinkle with half of the feta cheese and 2 tablespoons of the couscous. Top with the remaining tomato sauce. Layer the zucchini slices, then the rest of the feta cheese and the remaining 2 tablespoons couscous. Pour the béchamel sauce evenly over the top and sprinkle with the Parmesan cheese.

Bake at 350°F, uncovered, until golden and bubbly, 45 to 50 minutes. Let sit for about 15 minutes before serving.

NOTE
You can make this dish a day or two in advance. Bake it for 40 minutes and refrigerate it covered. Then, rewarm in a 350°F oven, loosely covered with aluminum foil, for about 30 minutes. Let it sit for at least 15 minutes before serving.

SERVING AND MENU IDEAS
Serve with a green salad, an assortment of olives, and some warm pita bread.

Polenta Casserole

This attractive casserole with a golden cheese topping has a bottom layer of polenta seasoned with Parmesan cheese, oregano, and red pepper flakes. You can vary the casserole with different vegetables and cheeses, but in our favorite version we layer kale and mushrooms that have been cooked in olive oil with onions and garlic, fresh tomatoes, and basil, and of course, plenty of cheese. By the way, simmering polenta is as hot as molten lava—keep the flame low, use a long-handled spoon and an oven mitt, and don't let the (spitting) bubbles scald your hand.

This casserole is perfect for a dish-to-pass. It can be completely assembled a day or two before you need it and stored in the refrigerator. It will then take a little longer to bake.

Serves 6 to 8
Prep time: 45 minutes
Baking time: 20 minutes

POLENTA
4 cups water
½ teaspoon salt
2 tablespoons olive oil or butter
½ teaspoon dried oregano
⅛ to ¼ teaspoon red pepper flakes (optional)
1½ cups cornmeal
½ cup shredded Parmesan cheese

VEGETABLES
2 tablespoons olive oil
2 cups chopped onions
2 garlic cloves, minced or pressed
1 teaspoon salt
½ teaspoon dried oregano
¼ teaspoon ground black pepper
2 cups stemmed and chopped kale or spinach
3 cups sliced mushrooms, white or cremini (12 ounces whole)

2 cups shredded mozzarella or mild provolone cheese, or a mixture
1 cup diced fresh tomatoes
⅓ cup chopped fresh basil
½ cup shredded Parmesan cheese

Put the water, salt, olive oil or butter, oregano, and red pepper flakes, if using, in a heavy-bottomed saucepan and bring to a boil. Whisk in the cornmeal as you pour it into the boiling water in a steady stream. Bring back to a boil, reduce the heat to a very low simmer, and cook, stirring occasionally, until the texture is smooth and creamy, 15 to 20 minutes. Remove from the heat and stir in the Parmesan cheese.

Preheat the oven to 350°F. Oil a 13 × 9 × 2-inch baking pan. Spread the polenta evenly in the pan and set it aside while you prepare the vegetables.

In a large soup pot or skillet on medium heat, warm the oil. Add the onions, garlic, salt, oregano, and black pepper, cover, and cook for 5 minutes, stirring occasionally. Stir in the kale (if you're using spinach, add it later), cover, and cook for 5 minutes, stirring occasionally. Stir in the mushrooms and cook, covered, until the vegetables are tender. If you're using spinach, stir it in when the mushrooms are juicy, and cook just until it has wilted. Remove from the heat and set aside.

To assemble the casserole: Sprinkle 1 cup of the mozzarella over the polenta. Spread the cooked vegetables evenly on top. In a small bowl, mix together the tomatoes and basil and then spread the mixture on top of the cooked vegetables. Finally, sprinkle the remaining cup of mozzarella and the Parmesan evenly over the tomato-basil layer.

Cover the casserole dish and bake for 10 minutes. Uncover and bake until the cheese is golden brown and the casserole is thoroughly hot, about 10 minutes. Let the casserole sit for 10 minutes before serving.

VARIATIONS
- Replace some or all of the kale and mushrooms with other vegetables such as diced eggplant, bell peppers, and zucchini. Choose your current favorite vegetables, or maybe what's languishing in the fridge or abundant in your garden. You need about 5 cups total.
- Use Pecorino Romano, ricotta salata, or feta cheese for some of the cheese.

SERVING AND MENU IDEAS
This casserole and a simple green salad is all you need for a great meal. For an extra treat, add Seasoned Artichokes (page 263) and some Chocolate Ricotta Moose (page 346) for dessert.

STUFFED VEGETABLES

Quinoa-stuffed Roasted Peppers

Quinoa is a high-protein, gluten-free grain indigenous to South America. It readily absorbs flavors. In keeping with its place of origin, we usually flavor it with cumin and coriander, maybe some cilantro and hot peppers, but in this recipe we give it a Mediterranean slant with saffron and tarragon.

The quinoa pilaf is tasty on its own as a side dish. Or, use it to stuff other vegetables. The roasted peppers can be stuffed ahead of time and then heated when you're ready to serve.

Yields 6 large stuffed pepper halves
Serves 4 to 6
Prep time: 45 minutes
Final baking time: 10 to 15 minutes

QUINOA PILAF

1 cup quinoa
1 garlic clove, minced or pressed
2 teaspoons olive oil
1⅓ cups water
¼ teaspoon salt
pinch of saffron

3 large bell peppers (any color)
olive oil, for brushing

1 tablespoon olive oil
1½ cups finely chopped onions
¼ teaspoon salt
⅔ cup diced carrots
2 cups chopped mushrooms (about 8 ounces whole)
¼ cup currants
1 tablespoon chopped fresh tarragon
1 tablespoon fresh lemon juice
salt and black pepper
4 ounces chèvre, crumbled

Preheat the oven to 400°F. Lightly oil a rimmed baking sheet.

Rinse and drain the quinoa in a fine-mesh strainer under cool running water. In a covered saucepan on high heat, cook the quinoa and garlic in the oil for about 1 minute, stirring constantly. Add the water, salt, and saffron and bring to a boil. Reduce the heat to low and cook, covered, until the water has been absorbed and the quinoa is tender, about 15 minutes. Stir the quinoa to fluff and set aside.

While the quinoa cooks, prepare the bell peppers. Cut them in half lengthwise, leaving the stems on to help them hold their shape, and remove the seeds and inner membranes. Brush the inner and outer surfaces with olive oil and place the pepper halves, cut side down, on the prepared baking sheet. Roast until softened but still firm and not collapsing, about 15 minutes. Set aside to cool and reduce the oven temperature to 350°F.

While the peppers roast, warm the oil in a saucepan on medium heat, add the onions and cook, covered, for 3 or 4 minutes. Sprinkle with the salt, stir in the carrots, and continue to cook, covered, for another 3 or 4 minutes. Stir in the mushrooms and cook, covered, until all of the vegetables are tender, about 5 minutes.

Combine the cooked quinoa, vegetables, currants, and tarragon. Stir in the lemon juice, and season with salt and black pepper to taste.

Fill the roasted pepper halves with the quinoa pilaf and top with some of the chèvre. Place the peppers in a lightly oiled baking pan, loosely cover with aluminum foil, and bake just until the peppers are thoroughly hot, 10 to 15 minutes.

VARIATIONS

- If you prefer not to have cheese, omit the chèvre and serve the peppers with Tomato-Basil Sauce (page 324) or your favorite tomato sauce.
- Use crumbled feta cheese or shredded Parmesan in place of the chèvre.
- Replace the tarragon with 2 or 3 tablespoons of chopped fresh basil.

SERVING AND MENU IDEAS

Cucumbers Vinaigrette (page 256), Tomato, Cucumber, and Artichoke Heart Salad (page 256), or one of our Not So Plain Green Vegetables (page 266) makes a perfect accompaniment.

Mushroom-Tofu-Pecan Stuffed Vegetables

We are often asked to recommend a holiday dish, especially for Thanksgiving, that will please vegans and vegetarians. This is a great one; it will make everyone happy. For a beautiful presentation, try stuffing the colorful combination of orange winter squash and red bell peppers.

If you have a smaller group, just halve the recipe's ingredients.

Yields 8 stuffed acorn squash or bell pepper halves
Serves 8
Prep time: 1 hour and 15 minutes
Final baking time: 20 minutes

one 14- to 16-ounce block firm tofu (see page 387)
4 medium acorn, delicata, or buttercup squash, or 4 large bell peppers (any color) (or a combination of the two)
2 tablespoons vegetable or olive oil
½ teaspoon ground fennel seeds
3 tablespoons soy sauce
3 tablespoons dry sherry or white wine (optional)
4 cups ½-inch bread cubes
2 tablespoons vegetable oil
3 cups chopped onions or leeks
2 cups chopped celery
4 cups sliced mushrooms (16 ounces whole)
1 teaspoon ground dried sage
1 teaspoon dried thyme
1 teaspoon dried marjoram
1 teaspoon salt
¼ teaspoon ground black pepper
½ cup water
1 cup toasted and chopped pecans
2 cups shredded cheddar, smoked cheddar, or Fontina cheese (optional)

If the tofu is firm and fresh, there is probably no need to press it. Otherwise, press it for at least 15 minutes (see page 388).

Preheat the oven to 400°F. Lightly oil a rimmed baking sheet sheet.

Cut the squash or peppers in half from stem end to blossom end. Leave the stems on the pepper halves to help them hold their shape. Remove the seeds. If using squash, arrange it cut side down in the prepared baking sheet, add about ½ inch of water, and cover with aluminum foil. Bake just until tender, about 40 minutes for most acorn squash, but the time will vary depending on size and type. If using bell peppers, brush the halves with oil inside and out and bake cut side down (no water, no cover) for 15 to 20 minutes until tender but still holding their shape. Remove from the oven and set aside. Reduce the oven temperature to 350°F.

While the squash or peppers bake, in a bowl, whisk together the oil, ground fennel, soy sauce, and sherry, if using. Cut the tofu into ½-inch cubes and gently toss with the marinade. Set aside for 15 minutes. Toast the bread cubes on a rimmed baking sheet in the oven for about 5 minutes. Set the bread cubes aside. Spread the tofu cubes on the baking sheet and bake for 30 minutes, stirring once or twice, until slightly browned and chewy.

In a large covered pot on medium heat, warm the oil. Add the onions and celery and cook, stirring often, until the onions are soft, about 8 minutes. Add more sherry, if you like. Add the mushrooms, sage, thyme, marjoram, salt, black pepper, and water, cover, and cook for about 10 minutes.

Add the baked tofu and toasted bread cubes to the cooked vegetables and toss. Stir in the pecans. Remove from the heat and set aside for a few minutes to allow the bread cubes to soften and the flavors to meld. Add more salt and black pepper to taste.

Turn the baked squash or peppers over on their baking sheet and mound about 1 cup of the stuffing in each half. Sprinkle with shredded cheese, if you like, cover, and bake at 350°F for about 20 minutes.

VARIATIONS

- Substitute rice or a red rice pilaf or wild rice pilaf (pages 293 and 294) for the bread cubes.
- Rather than stuffing vegetables, you can bake the stuffing in an oiled 2-quart baking dish. Cover the baking dish and place it in a larger baking pan. Pour in hot water to come halfway up the sides. Bake at 325°F for about 20 minutes.

SERVING AND MENU IDEAS

Our favorite Cranberry Sauce (page 311) is our favorite thing to serve with these stuffed vegetables. Serve with lots of colorful side dishes, such as Green Beans with Lemon Zest Dressing (page 266).

Greek Stuffed Tomatoes

We love this filling with its base of rice enhanced with salty feta nicely balanced by sweet currants and tangy lemon. Add the flavor of the tomato that contains it and yum . . . you can also use it to stuff eggplant and bell pepper halves, grape leaves, and zucchini canoes. If you have leftover rice, the filling is that much easier and quicker to make.

Yields 8 large stuffed tomatoes
Serves 8
Prep time: about 1 hour
Baking time: 30 minutes

1 cup rinsed and drained brown rice (2½ cups cooked brown rice)
2 teaspoons olive oil
½ teaspoon salt
1½ cups water

1 cup finely chopped onions
2 garlic cloves, minced or pressed
1 tablespoon olive oil
½ cup diced celery
¼ teaspoon salt
¼ cup pine nuts
¼ cup currants
2 tablespoons chopped fresh dill
2 to 3 tablespoons fresh lemon juice
½ cup crumbled feta cheese
ground black pepper

8 large tomatoes

In a saucepan on high heat, stir together the rice, oil, and salt, and cook for a minute, stirring constantly. Add the water and bring to a boil. Reduce the heat to very low, stir once, and simmer, covered, until the water has been absorbed and the rice is tender.

Meanwhile, in a skillet on low heat, cook the onions and garlic in the oil for about 5 minutes. Add the celery, sprinkle with the salt, and continue to cook until the onions are translucent, about 5 minutes. Stir in the pine nuts and currants and cook for a couple of minutes. Transfer to a bowl and stir in the dill, 2 tablespoons of lemon juice and the feta and set aside.

To prepare the tomatoes: Core them and cut off about the top inch of each one. Using a spoon, scoop out the seeds and pulp; take care not to break through the shell of the tomato. Sprinkle the inside of each tomato with salt and black pepper and place in a lightly oiled baking pan.

When the rice is done, add it to the bowl with the rest of the filling and stir well. Add more salt, black pepper, and lemon juice to taste.

Spoon the filling into the tomatoes, cover the baking pan with aluminum foil, and bake at 350°F for about 20 minutes, then uncover and continue to bake until the filling is hot, about another 10 minutes.

VARIATIONS

- For an excellent appetizer, cut small plum tomatoes in half from the stem end to the blossom end, scoop out the seeds and pulp, and fill the tomato shells with the rice mixture.
- Replace the pine nuts with ⅓ cup chopped walnuts.
- Omit the feta.

SERVING AND MENU IDEAS

Serve with a simple green salad, one of our Not So Plain Green Vegetables (see page 266), or Tzatziki (page 311). For a mezze feast, serve with an array of olives, Peppercorn and Lemon Marinated Feta (page 23), Classic Hummus (page 37), and toasted pita.

Indian Stuffed Eggplant

This dish is unusual and satisfying and it remains one of Moosewood's elegant favorites. The serving of an entire half of an eggplant mounded with an exotically spiced potato and vegetable filling will silence anyone who thinks vegetarian food is bland, boring, and not filling enough. One doesn't usually think of eggplant and Indian spices as comfort food, but this dish offers all the comfort of yummy mashed potatoes studded with diced vegetables and aromatic spices.

We admit it is a bit of a production, not something you would make on an ordinary Tuesday evening after work, but the steps are all uncomplicated and for special occasions or for more leisurely weekend cooking, your time will be rewarded with a really delightful dish.

If you're serving fewer than eight, instead of halving the recipe, think about making the full amount of filling and saving the extra for other meals. It's quite versatile. You can bake the filling in filo dough or pie dough to make not-fried samosas. You could add diced tomatoes instead of peppers and use the filling to stuff roasted pepper halves. Or, stuff small plum tomatoes to serve as an appetizer. Some of us make the filling to eat on its own. Both at home and in the Moosewood kitchen, sometimes it's an effort to resist "tasting" the filling over and over before it goes into the oven!

Serves 8
Prep time: about 1 hour and 20 minutes
Final baking time: 20 to 30 minutes

4 eggplants (about 1 pound each)
2 tablespoons vegetable oil
½ teaspoon salt
6 cups peeled and sliced white potatoes
2 teaspoons ground turmeric
2 cups finely chopped onions
3 garlic cloves, pressed or minced
1 cup diced carrots
1 cup seeded and diced red bell peppers
2 teaspoons ground cumin seeds
2 teaspoons ground coriander seeds
½ teaspoon cayenne
¼ teaspoon ground cloves or ground cardamom
1½ tablespoons peeled and grated fresh ginger
1 cup green peas
12 ounces cream cheese, at room temperature
    (vegan cream cheese works, too)
1 tablespoon fresh lemon juice, more to taste

Preheat the oven to 375°F. Oil two rimmed baking sheets.

Slice the eggplants in half lengthwise. Score the flesh in a crosshatch pattern and lightly sprinkle with salt. Brush the cut surface generously with oil and place the eggplant halves on the baking, sheets, cut side down. Brush the skins with oil. Bake, uncovered, until the flesh is tender and golden brown, 35 to 40 minutes.

While the eggplants bake, make the potato-vegetable filling. In a saucepan, cover the potatoes with water and stir in 1 teaspoon of the turmeric and ½ teaspoon salt. Cover and bring to a boil. Reduce the heat and cook until tender, about 15 minutes.

Heat the oil in a saucepan on medium-low heat. Cook the onions and garlic, sprinkled with salt, for about 10 minutes, covered, stirring occasionally. Add the carrots and a tablespoon of water, cover, and cook for 5 minutes. Add the bell peppers and cook, covered, for 3 or 4 minutes. While the vegetables cook, mix together the cumin, coriander, cayenne, cloves, ginger, and the remaining 1 teaspoon of turmeric in a small bowl. Stir the spice mixture into the vegetables and cook on low heat for a minute or two. Stir in the peas and cook, covered, until all of the vegetables are tender, 2 or 3 minutes.

When the potatoes are done, drain them. In a large mixing bowl, mash the potatoes with the cream cheese and lemon juice. Add the vegetable mixture to the mashed potatoes and stir well. Add more salt and/or lemon juice to taste.

When the eggplant halves are done, flip them over with a spatula and make a well in each by pushing the flesh to the sides a little. Mound some filling onto each eggplant half right out to ¼ inch from the edges. Transfer them to clean, oiled baking sheets or pans. Bake at 350°F until piping hot, 20 to 30 minutes.

SERVING AND MENU IDEAS

Serve the stuffed eggplant topped with yogurt or Spinach Raita (page 312) and Date-Coconut-Lemon Chutney (page 312). Sometimes at home, we make just the filling and serve it, as a side dish. See the headnote for more ways to use the filling.

Italian Polenta-stuffed Peppers

Platters of red, green, orange, and yellow bell peppers filled with golden, green-flecked polenta are beautiful and festive.

Yields 8 stuffed pepper halves
Serves 4 to 8
Time: about 1 hour and 15 minutes

4 large bell peppers (assorted colors are pretty)
olive oil, for brushing

POLENTA
3½ cups water
1 teaspoon salt
¼ teaspoon red pepper flakes
2 garlic cloves, minced or pressed
1½ teaspoons ground fennel seeds
1 teaspoon dried oregano
1 cup cornmeal
¼ cup chopped fresh basil
1½ cups shredded mild provolone cheese
½ cup shredded Parmesan cheese

Preheat the oven to 400°F. Lightly oil a couple of baking pans or a large, rimmed baking sheet: whatever you have that will hold the pepper halves.

Cut the peppers in half lengthwise. Remove the seeds, but leave the stems on so that the peppers will hold their shape during baking. Brush lightly with oil inside and out. Arrange the pepper halves, cut side down, on the prepared baking pans. Bake for 15 to 20 minutes until the peppers are tender but still hold their shape. Remove from the oven and set aside to cool.

While the peppers bake, make the polenta. In a heavy saucepan, bring the water, salt, red pepper flakes, garlic, fennel, and oregano to a boil. Add the polenta in a slow, steady stream while whisking briskly. Reduce the heat to low and simmer for 20 to 30 minutes (the time will vary depending on your cornmeal), stirring often, until thickened and creamy. As the polenta thickens you may need to reduce the heat and stir more often. Stir in the basil, and provolone and add salt to taste. Let the polenta mixture sit for about 10 minutes to allow it to thicken more; this will make it easier to fill the pepper halves.

Fill the baked pepper halves with the polenta-cheese mixture. Sprinkle the tops with Parmesan and return the peppers to the oven for 10 to 15 minutes until the cheese has melted and the peppers are thoroughly hot.

VARIATIONS
- Use Fontina in place of provolone.
- Add finely chopped sun-dried tomatoes to the polenta while it simmers.
- Stir finely chopped raw spinach into the polenta with the cheese.

SERVING AND MENU IDEAS
Top with Tomato-Basil Sauce (page 324), Puttanesca Sauce (page 322), or your favorite tomato sauce, with a side of Quick Sautéed Greens (page 268). For a Mediterranean feast, start with Olivada (page 39) or White Bean and Basil Spread (page 40) and crusty bread, and add Mediterranean Lentil Salad (page 118) or Beans and Greens (page 148), and Tomato, Cucumber, and Artichoke Heart Salad (page 256) to the table.

Asian-style Stuffed Portobellos

What an easy plant-based entrée that can be easily doubled or tripled to serve a multitude of friends and family. Or perhaps your family has some newly minted vegan kids coming home for the holidays— this recipe will be your go-to favorite recipe to please them. Gluten-free, too (with wheat-free soy sauce).

If you plan to serve the mushrooms on a bed of brown rice, remember to get it started before baking the mushrooms.

Serves 4
Prep time: 25 minutes (with already pressed tofu)
Baking time: 40 minutes

one 14- to 16-ounce block firm tofu (page 387)
4 portobello mushrooms (about 5 inches in
    diameter)
4 tablespoons soy sauce
4 teaspoons dark sesame oil
1 cup seeded and diced red bell peppers
½ cup minced scallions
¼ cup peanut butter
2 teaspoons peeled and grated fresh ginger
½ teaspoon Chinese Chili Paste with Garlic (see
    page 374) or Sriracha hot chili sauce (optional)
Simple Sweet and Sour Sauce (page 319)

First, press the tofu for at least 15 minutes (see page 388).

Preheat the oven to 350°F. Oil a large baking pan.

While the tofu is pressing, remove the mushroom stems and gently rinse the caps to remove any dirt. In a small bowl, mix together 3 tablespoons of the soy sauce and 3 teaspoons of the sesame oil. Brush the mushrooms on both sides with the mixture. Place the caps, gill side up, in the prepared baking pan.

When you are ready to grate the tofu, discard the liquid that has accumulated in the bowl. Grate the tofu and transfer it to a large bowl. Add the bell peppers, scallions, peanut butter, ginger, chili paste or chili sauce, if using, the remaining soy sauce, and the remaining 1 teaspoon of the sesame oil and mix thoroughly.

Mound one quarter of the filling on each mushroom, pressing with your fingers to compact.

Bake for 35 to 40 minutes until the mushrooms release juice and the filling is firm and slightly browned.

While the mushrooms bake, prepare the Simple Sweet and Sour Sauce.

SERVING AND MENU IDEAS
Serve the mushrooms on a bed of rice, or soba or udon noodles, topped with a generous drizzle of the sauce. Garnish with snow peas, sliced scallions, and/ or bean sprouts. Asian Greens (page 269) are great on the side.

Curried Squash Roti

Asparagus-Leek Strudel

Aegean Strudel

Tofu-Spinach Borekas

Black Bean–Sweet Potato Burritos

Two Quesadillas

Spinach-Cheese Burritos

Curried Squash Roti

Butternut squash is plentiful here in Central New York, and we've never gotten tired of creating new ways to prepare it. It has a beautiful sunset-orange color, a distinctive, mild, sweet flavor, and it cooks quickly. While packaged frozen squash is available and saves you having to peel and seed the squash, the rich sweetness of fresh squash is superior.

This dish reflects the influence of India on Caribbean cuisine. Over twenty years ago, Moosewood partner and Caribbean beach-comber, Ned Asta, turned us on to roti—pastry turnovers with a variety of highly seasoned savory fillings. We season good old New York State butternut squash with onions and peppers and an exotic spice mix and wrap it all up in flour tortillas. Sometimes, in place of squash, we make it with sweet potatoes, or even a combo of sweet and white potatoes. Each has its virtues, but butternut has the lightest texture and loads of nutritional benefits. We top roti with a tropical salsa and a cool dollop of sour cream.

Serves 8
Prep time: 40 minutes
Baking time: 15 to 20 minutes

1½ teaspoons ground cumin seeds
½ teaspoon ground turmeric
¼ teaspoon cayenne
⅛ teaspoon ground cloves
½ teaspoon ground cinnamon
1 teaspoon curry powder
6 cups peeled and cubed butternut or other winter
    squash (about 2½ pounds whole)
2 tablespoons vegetable oil
1½ cups finely chopped onions
1 teaspoon salt
1 cup seeded and diced red bell peppers
1 tablespoon peeled and grated fresh ginger
2 tablespoons fresh lemon juice
1 tablespoon minced fresh cilantro (optional)
eight 8-inch flour tortillas

In a small bowl, mix together the cumin, turmeric, cayenne, cloves, cinnamon, and curry powder. Set aside.

In a covered saucepan, bring the squash to a boil with a pinch of salt and enough water to cover. Lower the heat and simmer for about 10 minutes until soft.

While the squash cooks, heat the oil in a heavy skillet on medium-low heat. Add the onions and salt, cover, and cook for 5 minutes. Stir in the bell peppers, ginger, and spice mix, cover, and cook on low heat, for 10 minutes. Stir frequently, and if needed to prevent sticking, add some of the squash cooking water.

When the squash is done, drain it and mash with the lemon juice and cilantro. Stir in the cooked onions and peppers, and season with salt to taste.

Preheat the oven to 350°F. Lightly oil a 13 × 9 × 2-inch baking pan.

Place a scant ⅔ cup of the squash filling on the lower half of a tortilla and roll it up one of two ways: Roll into a cylinder with the ends open. Or fold like an envelope: fold the bottom up and over the filling, fold each side over the filling, and then roll it up. Place the roti, seam side down, in the prepared baking pan. Repeat with each tortilla and allow the rotis to lean against each other. Lightly brush the tops with oil. Cover the baking pan with aluminum foil and bake until hot, 20 to 30 minutes.

SERVING AND MENU IDEAS
Serve the roti with Annatto Rice (page 289) or Coconut Rice (page 289) and top with sour cream and Our Favorite Tomato-Cilantro Sauce (page 314), Avocado Salsa (page 314), or Mango Salsa (page 315).

Asparagus-Leek Strudel

A savory filo strudel is often our customers' end-of-the-week choice, when they are looking for something comforting yet elegant. A sumptuous filling topped with puffy, golden filo, the presentation always elicits a "wow!"

Strudels offer endless opportunities for creativity by varying the vegetables, cheeses, and herbs. Strudels look impressive, and with a little experience filo is really easy to work with. Just remember that the thin sheets of filo become brittle when exposed to the air, so work in a draft-free place if you can, and if you're interrupted or are not working quickly, cover the stack of filo with a barely damp towel. We give you instructions for a large, flat strudel to serve several people, but experiment with the filo: You can make individual little tortas folded in a triangle shape, or rolls, large or small.

Serves 6 to 8
Prep time: 1 hour
Baking time: 40 minutes
Sitting time: 10 minutes

FILLING

2 tablespoons olive oil
4 cups rinsed and thinly sliced leeks
   (see page 379)
4 cups 1-inch pieces asparagus (2 pounds whole)
2 tablespoons finely chopped fresh tarragon
¼ teaspoon ground black pepper
8 ounces cream cheese, at room temperature
2½ cups shredded dilled Havarti cheese
1 cup shredded sharp cheddar cheese
4 large eggs

FILO

16 sheets filo dough, about 12 × 7-inch (about ¾ pound)
3 tablespoons butter, melted
3 tablespoons olive oil
1 teaspoon sesame seeds or fennel seeds (optional)

In a large skillet or a soup pot on medium-low heat, warm the oil. Add the leeks with a sprinkling of salt and cook gently for about 5 minutes. Add the asparagus, stir, cover, and cook on medium heat until the asparagus pieces are bright green and tender, about 5 minutes. Remove from the heat and stir in the tarragon and black pepper. Using a rubber spatula, stir the cream cheese into the hot vegetables until the vegetable mixture becomes creamy. Add the Havarti and cheddar and stir until well mixed. Season with salt and pepper to taste. Beat the eggs until evenly colored and then stir them into the filling.

Preheat the oven to 350°F. Heat the butter and oil together until hot (the mixture brushes on more easily when hot). Place the butter-oil mixture and a pastry brush within easy reach of a work surface. Lightly brush a rimmed baking tray, about 9 × 13 inches, with the butter-oil mixture. Remove the filo from the box and lay the filo sheets on a dry surface near the baking sheet, the butter-oil mixture, and the filling. Work quickly because exposed filo dries out and becomes brittle; if you're interrupted, cover the stack of filo with a damp towel.

Lay 2 sheets of filo horizontally on the prepared baking sheet, allowing the filo to drape over the sides (see Note). Lightly brush the top sheet with the butter-oil mixture. Repeat three more times for a total of 8 filo sheets in four layers made up of

2 sheets each. Spread the filling evenly over the filo on the baking sheet. On all four sides, fold the overhanging filo up over the filling and brush the outer sheets with the butter-oil mixture. Lay 2 sheets of filo horizontally on top to cover the filling and to drape over the sides. Brush with the butter-oil mixture. Repeat three more times for a total of 8 filo sheets in four layers made up of 2 sheets each. On all four sides, tuck the extra filo under the bottom of the strudel. Sprinkle the top with sesame or fennel seeds, if you like.

Bake until golden and puffy, about 40 minutes. Let sit for at least 10 minutes before cutting into squares and serving.

NOTE

It's convenient when the filo you have drapes over your baking sheet a couple of inches on all sides, so that the rim of the baking sheet can support the finished strudel. But the dimensions of baking sheets and sheets of filo vary, so it doesn't always work out that way. It's OK if the strudel is smaller than the baking sheet. What's important in assembling the strudel is that the filling is encased with filo dough. The bottom layers of filo should wrap up the sides and over the filling, and the top layers should tuck under the strudel.

VARIATIONS

- Replace 1 cup of the asparagus with 1 cup of seeded and diced red bell peppers.
- Use dill instead of tarragon.
- Many different cheeses work in this filling—just do a blend of mild and sharp.
- Replace half of the cream cheese with 1½ cups of cottage cheese and add a tablespoon of flour.

SERVING AND MENU IDEAS

Serve this rich and creamy strudel with something crisp and refreshing: a lovely green salad; Cucumbers Vinaigrette (page 256); Tomato, Cucumber, and Artichoke Heart Salad (page 256); or one of our Not So Plain Green Vegetables (see page 266).

Aegean Strudel

Rich, golden, flaky strudel fresh from the oven elicits accolades and appreciation. We can't begin to estimate how many strudels we've served at Moosewood, but it must be thousands. We have dozens and dozens of variations—we're always trying different vegetable and cheese combinations.

Aegean Strudel is similar to spanakopita, but uses additional vegetables. We like the combination of spinach, zucchini, and artichoke hearts flavored with oregano and dill.

We've recently discovered the quarter-sheet pan, which is just the right size for strudel at home. Six cups of filling is perfect for this size baking tray, so use that amount and experiment with your favorite cheeses and vegetables.

Serves 8
Prep time: 1 hour
Baking time: 45 to 55 minutes

FILLING

10 cups fresh baby spinach (16 ounces)
2 tablespoons olive oil
1 cup finely chopped onions
3 garlic cloves, minced or pressed
1 teaspoon dried oregano
½ teaspoon salt
2 cups diced zucchini
4 large eggs
one 14-ounce can artichoke hearts in brine, drained and finely chopped
8 ounces cream cheese, at room temperature
2½ cups crumbled or shredded feta (12 ounces)
3 tablespoons unbleached white all-purpose flour
2 tablespoons chopped fresh dill
¼ teaspoon ground black pepper

FILO

¼ cup butter
¼ cup olive oil
20 sheets filo dough, about 12 × 7-inch (about 1 pound)
1 teaspoon fennel seeds or sesame seeds (optional)

Rinse and drain the spinach. In a large pot on medium-high heat and stirring constantly, cook the spinach with the water that clings to the leaves just until wilted. Turn out into a colander and set aside to drain.

In a skillet on medium-low heat, warm the olive oil. Add the onions, garlic, oregano, and salt and cook for 5 minutes, stirring occasionally. Add the zucchini and cook, stirring occasionally, until the zucchini is tender, 5 or 6 minutes. Remove from the heat.

In a large mixing bowl, beat the eggs. Add the chopped artichoke hearts, cream cheese, feta, cooked zucchini, flour, dill, and black pepper and mix thoroughly. With your hands, squeeze more liquid from the cooked spinach, add the spinach to the bowl, and stir well.

Preheat the oven to 350°F. Heat the butter and oil together until hot; this makes brushing it easier. Place the butter-oil mixture and a pastry brush within easy reach of a work surface. Lightly brush a rimmed baking sheet, about 9 × 13 inches, with the butter-oil mixture. Remove the filo from the box and lay the filo sheets on a dry surface, near the baking sheet, the butter-oil mixture, and the filling. Exposed filo dough dries out and becomes brittle, so work quickly. If you are interrupted while laying out the strudel, cover the filo with a dampened towel.

Brush the top sheet of filo with the butter-oil mixture. Pick up the top 2 sheets (one buttered and the second one not) and place them so that they're centered on the baking sheet with of filo dough draping over the sides (see Note). Repeat four times, brushing the top sheet with the butter-oil mixture and picking up 2 sheets at a time, for a total of 10 filo sheets. (If it's easier for you, lay 2 sheets of filo on the baking sheet first, and then brush the top one.)

Spread the filling evenly over the filo in the baking sheet. Fold all four sides of the overhanging filo up over the filling and brush with the butter-oil mixture. Top with the remaining filo, again 2 sheets at a time laid on top horizontally to cover the filling and brushing each layer as before. Fold under the overhanging filo, and use the pastry brush all around the perimeter to gently tuck in all the filo. Sprinkle the top with sesame or fennel seeds, if you like.

Bake until golden and puffy, 45 to 55 minutes. Let the strudel sit for at least 10 minutes before cutting and serving. We like to cut the strudel into 4 equal rectangles and then cut each of those pieces on the diagonal to make 8 triangular-shaped servings.

NOTE

It's convenient when the filo you have drapes over your baking sheet a couple of inches on all sides, so that the rim of the baking sheet can support the finished strudel. But the dimensions of baking sheets and sheets of filo vary, so it doesn't always work out that way. It's OK if the strudel is smaller than the baking sheet. What's important in assembling the strudel is that the filling is encased with filo dough. The bottom layers of filo should wrap up the sides and over the filling, and the top layers should tuck under the strudel.

SERVING AND MENU IDEAS

We can think of so many great side dishes to serve with this delicious strudel. Try it with Seasoned Artichokes (page 263) or Roasted Cauliflower (page 274) or Cucumbers Vinaigrette (page 256) or Beet Salad (page 258) or one of our Not So Plain Green Vegetables (see page 266). A simple green salad is also nice.

Tofu-Spinach Borekas

We're confident that you'll like these flaky baked tofu- and spinach-filled filo rolls, flavorful with the slight sweetness of the currants, carrots, and cinnamon and accented with lemon and fresh dill. This recipe gives directions for entrée-size borekas. You can make little appetizer-size filo pastries, too, (see Spanokopita Bites page 26).

There are a number of ways to spell *boreka* and an even larger number of cuisines that share an affection for this family of baked or fried filled filo pastries. Borekas are found in the cuisines of the countries that were part of the Ottoman Empire, especially in North Africa and throughout the Balkans, and in some Jewish traditions.

Serves 8 or more
Prep time: about 1 hour
Baking time: 30 to 40 minutes

two 14- to 16-ounce blocks firm tofu (see page 387)
10 cups baby spinach (16 ounces)
1 tablespoon olive oil, plus ⅓ to ½ cup for brushing
2 cups finely chopped onions
2 or 3 garlic cloves, minced or pressed
1 teaspoon salt
2 cups diced carrots
½ cup currants
1 teaspoon ground cinnamon
½ teaspoon ground black pepper
2 tablespoons soy sauce
1 tablespoon fresh lemon juice
⅓ cup chopped fresh dill
one 16-ounce package filo dough (12 × 17-inch sheets)
2 tablespoons sesame seeds

First press the tofu for at least 15 minutes (see page 388).

Rinse the spinach, drain it, and place it in a large pot with whatever water clings to the leaves. Cook, covered, on medium-high heat, stirring often, until the leaves have wilted, about 4 minutes. Turn out into a colander and set aside to drain.

Warm 1 tablespoon of the olive oil in a large skillet. Add the onions, garlic, and salt, cover, and cook on medium-low heat, stirring occasionally, for about 5 minutes. Stir in the carrots, cover, and cook, stirring occasionally, for about 8 minutes. Tip the condensation that develops on the lid into the skillet to prevent sticking. Stir in the currants and cinnamon, cover, and cook for a minute or two.

Meanwhile, grate the tofu in a food processor or by hand and place in a large bowl. Squeeze more liquid out of the spinach and put it on a cutting board. Coarsely chop the spinach and add it to the bowl of grated tofu along with the black pepper, soy sauce, lemon juice, and dill and mix well. Stir the cooked vegetables into the tofu mixture and stir well.

Lightly oil or spray a large rimmed baking sheet or two smaller ones. Preheat the oven to 375°F.

To make the borekas, place the bowl of filling and a pastry brush next to a dry work surface. Warm the oil in a microwave oven or in a small pan on the stovetop until it's hot but not smoking; this makes it easier to spread. Unfold the stack of filo sheets with a short side nearest you. Brush the top sheet with oil. About 3 inches from the bottom, evenly mound a cup of filling in a line that runs from side to side, leaving about 3 inches on each side uncovered. Lift the bottom edges of 3 sheets of filo up and over the filling. Fold the sides over the filling all along to the top of the stack, and brush with oil. Roll up the filling and filo to the top, to make a "package." Place the filo roll, seam side down, on the baking sheet and brush the outside with oil.

Assemble the rest of the borekas, working down the stack of filo 3 sheets at a time. Leave some space between the borekas on the baking sheet; they shouldn't touch each other.

Sprinkle each boreka with sesame seeds. On the top of each boreka, make a shallow diagonal slice through the top layers of filo down just to the filling; this allows some steam to escape and also makes it easier to cut the baked roll in half. Bake for 30 to 40 minutes until golden brown and crisp.

Serve borekas warm or at room temperature.

SERVING AND MENU IDEAS
We like to serve these flaky filo rolls with Roasted Cauliflower (page 274) and/or Beet Salad (page 258) and a crisp green salad.

Black Bean–Sweet Potato Burritos

These plump and savory burritos are popular with all our customers—vegan and non-vegan, alike. Try them with Simple Smooth Guacamole (page 35) or a zesty Avocado Salsa (page 314). And if you're not vegan, pass some shredded cheese or sour cream, as well.

We use 10-inch tortillas for these burritos, but if they're not available, or if you prefer smaller ones, that's fine, you'll just get more burritos. The filling can be made a day or two in advance.

Serves 6
Prep time: 45 minutes
Baking time: 30 minutes

6 cups peeled and cubed sweet potatoes
   (about 2½ pounds)
2 tablespoons vegetable or olive oil
2 cups chopped onions
3 garlic cloves, minced or pressed
1 fresh hot pepper, minced (for a milder "hot,"
   seeded first)
1 teaspoon salt
1 tablespoon ground cumin seeds
1 tablespoon ground coriander seeds
two 15-ounce cans black beans, drained and rinsed
   (3 cups)
1 tablespoon fresh lemon juice
½ cup chopped fresh cilantro
six 10-inch flour tortillas

In a covered saucepan, bring the sweet potatoes to a boil in salted water to cover. Reduce the heat and simmer until tender, about 15 minutes. Drain well. Mash. Set aside.

While the sweet potatoes are cooking, in a covered saucepan on low heat warm the oil. Add the onions, garlic, hot peppers, and salt and cook until the onions are soft, about 10 minutes. Stir in the cumin and coriander and cook for another minute or two.

Preheat the oven to 350°F. Lightly oil a large baking pan.

Combine the mashed sweet potatoes, the onion-spice mixture, and the black beans. Stir in the lemon juice and cilantro. Season with salt to taste.

Place about 1 cup of filling on the bottom half of each tortilla and roll up. The sides can be left open, or the sides can be folded over as you roll to form a tidy package. Arrange, seam side down, in the prepared baking pan. Lightly brush the tops of the burritos with oil and cover with aluminum foil. Bake for 25 to 30 minutes until hot.

VARIATIONS

- Add a seeded and diced bell pepper to the onions as they cook.
- Replace the fresh hot pepper with ¼ teaspoon of cayenne or ½ teaspoon of red pepper flakes.
- For a smoky flavor, use a minced canned chipotle pepper with a spoonful of adobo sauce.
- Stir a cup of corn kernels into the filling.
- Use corn tortillas instead of flour for a gluten-free alternative.

SERVING AND MENU IDEAS

Serve on a bed of rice and top with Smooth Hot Sauce (page 320) and chopped scallions. Maybe add some grated cheese or a dollop of sour cream.

Two Quesadillas

Everyone loves quesadillas. They can be an appetizer, snack, lunch, or dinner. Here are two ideas for delicious quesadilla fillings. Embellish the fillings or create new combinations with avocado, olives, fresh cilantro, scallions, hot peppers, and tomatoes. And, of course, you can go to Refried Beans (page 281) for a classic filling.

If you have two skillets for heating the quesadillas, that will speed things up.

CREAMY MUSHROOM QUESADILLAS

Serves 4
Time: 30 minutes

1 tablespoon vegetable oil
2 cups chopped onions
3 cups sliced mushrooms (12 ounces whole)
1 teaspoon salt
¼ teaspoon ground black pepper
3 ounces cream cheese, at room temperature
½ cup shredded sharp cheddar cheese

four 8- or 10-inch flour tortillas
1 cup salsa

To make the filling: Warm the oil in a skillet or saucepan on medium-high heat. Add the onions and sauté for about 5 minutes. Stir in the mushrooms, salt, black pepper, and cumin, cover, and cook on medium heat for a few minutes. Uncover, stir, and continue to cook until the mushroom juices have evaporated. Turn off the heat and stir in the cream cheese and cheddar.

Spread about ½ cup of the filling on one half of a tortilla, leaving a ½-inch border around the outer edge. Fold the tortilla over the filling to form a half-moon shape. Repeat with the other 3 tortillas.

Lightly oil a large skillet on medium heat. When the skillet is hot, cook the quesadillas for a minute or two on each side, or until golden brown. Serve topped with your favorite salsa.

SWEET POTATO QUESADILLAS

Serves 4
Time: 30 minutes

2 tablespoons vegetable oil
1 cup finely chopped onions
2 garlic cloves, minced or pressed
½ teaspoon salt
3 cups peeled and grated sweet potatoes
½ teaspoon dried oregano
2 teaspoons ground cumin seeds
1 fresh hot pepper, minced, or ⅛ teaspoon cayenne
1 cup fresh or frozen corn kernels
1 cup shredded sharp cheddar cheese (optional)

four 8- or 10-inch flour tortillas
1 cup salsa

To make the filling: Warm the oil in a covered skillet or saucepan on medium heat. Add the onions, garlic, and salt, and cook, stirring occasionally, until the onions are soft, about 8 minutes. Add the grated sweet potatoes, oregano, cumin, and hot peppers, cover, and cook for about 10 minutes, stirring often to prevent sticking. Add a splash of water if needed. Stir in the corn and heat through. Season with salt to taste.

Spread about ½ cup of the filling and ¼ cup of cheese, if using, on one half of a tortilla, leaving a ½-inch border around the outer edge. Fold the tortilla over the filling to form a half-moon shape. If the tortilla doesn't stick together around the edges, brush some oil along the bottom inside edge. Repeat with the other 3 tortillas.

Lightly oil a large skillet on medium heat. When the skillet is hot, cook the quesadillas for a minute or two on each side, or until golden brown. Serve topped with your favorite salsa.

VARIATION

- If you want to serve quesadillas as appetizers, spread the filling on 2 tortillas, press a second tortilla on top of each, and cook on each side in a skillet as directed, or brush lightly with oil and bake for about 10 minutes at 400°F. Cut each quesadilla into 6 wedges.

SERVING AND MENU IDEAS

Try either of these quesadillas with Our Favorite Tomato-Cilantro Salsa (page 314) or Avocado Salsa (page 314). Mango Salsa (page 315) would be especially good with mushroom quesadillas and Tomatilla Sauce (page 320) would be especially good on sweet potato quesadillas. Garnish with Chipotle Cream (page 310) or sour cream, if you like.

Spinach-Cheese Burritos

We thank Anna Thomas, whose recipe in *Vegetarian Epicure* was the inspiration for these burritos decades ago. We're still making them at Moosewood and they continue to be a popular weekend entrée. We usually make them with flour tortillas, but for those who are avoiding wheat or simply like the taste of corn, we give you a variation that uses corn tortillas. We like them both ways.

Serves 4 to 6
Prep time: 30 to 35 minutes
Baking time: 20 to 25 minutes

1 tablespoon vegetable oil or olive oil
2 cups chopped onions
3 garlic cloves, pressed or minced
1 teaspoon ground coriander seeds
10 cups baby spinach (about 1 pound), rinsed
   and drained
½ teaspoon dried oregano (optional)
3 ounces cream cheese, at room temperature
10 ounces Monterey jack, Swiss, or cheddar
   cheese, shredded (2½ cups)
eight 8-inch flour tortillas
Smooth Hot Sauce (page 320), Our Favorite
   Tomato-Cilantro Salsa (page 314), or your
   favorite salsa

In a large covered soup pot or skillet on medium heat, warm the oil. Add the onions and garlic and cook, stirring occasionally, until softened but not browned, about 7 minutes. Add the coriander and cook, stirring constantly, for 1 minute. Add the well-drained spinach and the oregano, if using, increase the heat, and cook, uncovered, stirring frequently, until the spinach is just wilted. Turn off the heat and add the cream cheese, stirring until it has melted.

Put the shredded cheese in a bowl and stir in the spinach-cream cheese mixture.

Preheat the oven to 375°F. Lightly oil a 13 × 9 × 2-inch baking pan.

Tortillas are often soft and supple, but if they're brittle and crack when you fold them over, soften them by warming in the oven for a couple of minutes or in the microwave for a few seconds. Place ½ cup of filling on the lower half of a tortilla, roll it up, and place it, seam down, in the prepared baking pan. Continue with the rest of the filling and tortillas. Brush the tops lightly with oil and cover the baking pan with aluminum foil.

Bake for 20 to 25 minutes until hot.

Serve topped with hot sauce or salsa.

VARIATIONS

- Use about sixteen 6-inch corn tortillas. Brush both sides with oil and put them in a single layer on a baking sheet. Warm them in a preheated 375°F oven until they are soft and pliable, about 1½ minutes. (Otherwise, corn tortillas are likely to crack when you roll them.) Use about ¼ cup of filling for each tortilla and roll and bake as you would the flour tortillas.
- In place of onions, use about a cup of chopped scallions and cook them in the oil with the garlic for 2 or 3 minutes, then add the spinach.
- Add a cup of seeded and finely chopped red bell peppers to the onions for the last 4 or 5 minutes of cooking.
- Add chopped cilantro to the filling with the cheese, or serve topped with chopped cilantro.
- To give the filling a little kick, add minced fresh hot peppers or red pepper flakes or cayenne to the cooking onions.

SERVING AND MENU IDEAS

Serve these burritos on Spanish Rice (page 287) with Lime-Cilantro Slaw (page 287). Bowls of Sopa de Lima (page 57) would be a great beginning.

Tofu Kan–style Baked Tofu

Moosewood's Best Baked and Pan-fried Tofu

Lemon-Herb Baked Tofu

Thai Baked Tofu

County-style Soft Tofu

Mushroom Mapo Tofu

Tofu "Meat" Loaf

Dixie Tofu-Pecan Loaf

Tofu Kan–style Baked Tofu

Ithaca Soy makes a wonderful product called Tofu Kan. It's a bronze-colored baked tofu with a chewy outer crust, a firm, creamy inside, and a simple flavor that makes it very versatile. At Moosewood, we grate it for sandwich spreads and slice it to go on salads and vegetable plates and in pitas. We've never found anything comparable among other commercial baked tofus, and it has frustrated us to think that tofu kan is essential to some of our recipes and that some of our readers won't get the same dish we love so much. Nancy Lazarus, a long-time Moosewood cook, went on a quest to develop a recipe for a baked tofu that our readers can make to use in our dishes that call for tofu kan. Here is a close cousin of our beloved Ithaca Soy Tofu Kan that you can make yourself at home.

Please use fresh tofu if you can (see page 387). Because of the long baking time, a glass or ceramic flat-bottomed baking pan is best. If you don't have one, use your most substantial pan. By the time the baking is done, the marinade will have been absorbed by the tofu and also evaporated, leaving a startling-looking residue on the pan. Never fear—as soon as you remove the tofu, fill the baking pan with water, and after it sits for 10 minutes or so, cleanup will be easy.

Yields two 7- or 8-ounce slabs
Pressing time: 1 to 2 hours
Prep time: 10 minutes
Baking time: 1½ to 2 hours

one 14- to 16-ounce block firm or extra-firm tofu
   (see page 387)
¼ cup soy sauce
2 teaspoons brown sugar
1 cup hot tap water

Press the tofu in the refrigerator for an hour or two (see page 388).

Stir together the soy sauce, brown sugar, and water, until the brown sugar has dissolved.

Drain the tofu and cut it horizontally into 2 slabs. Pour the marinade into an unoiled 8- or 9-inch square, nonreactive, heavy baking pan. Place the tofu slabs in the pan and spoon some marinade onto the tops.

Bake at 350°F until the liquid has been absorbed, 1½ to 2 hours; the baking time varies with different tofus and in different ovens. Every 30 minutes, turn the slabs of tofu over and spoon some of the marinade on top. At some point after an hour, you may think that the liquid will never be gone and the tofu won't become firm, but more time will do it.

Cool the tofu kan to room temperature; it will firm up more as it cools. Store well wrapped in the refrigerator for up to a week.

NOTES

Recipes in this book that call for tofu kan:
—Ira's Lunch Pita (page 73)
—Thai Tofu Lunch Pita (page 73)
—BLTease Sandwich Spread (page 74)
—Saigon Sandwich (page 75)

SERVING AND MENU IDEAS

Serve tofu kan sliced in a sandwich or on a salad, add it to a stir-fry it or eat it plain as a snack. It's our "deli meat" of choice.

Moosewood's Best Baked and Pan-fried Tofu

Both at the restaurant and at home, Moosewood cooks make various flavored tofus for snacks or sandwiches or to serve with salads, rice and steamed vegetables, gado gado, roasted vegetables . . . the list goes on. Serve hot, warm, or at room temperature. Seasoned tofu is a great snack to keep in the refrigerator.

For forty years, we've been cooking and loving tofu—here are our favorites recipes. We give you both oven and stovetop methods, because each is useful in its own way: if the oven is already heated up for something else, why not take advantage of an empty rack? If it's hot outside and you don't want to heat up the kitchen along with the oven, try the stovetop way.

The 3-ingredient basic marinade is what we usually use. But sometimes we want additional flavor, and we each have our own favorite. Generally, we add just one of the extra flavors, although chili paste and ginger go together very nicely. At a fourth grade taste test in one of our local elementary schools, the basic marinade plus ketchup was the hands-down favorite. What is it about kids and ketchup? Maybe the sweetness.

At Moosewood, we bake tofu in our convection oven, which makes it chewy on the outside and soft and succulent on the inside. But a conventional oven can achieve a similar effect. Baked tofu is easy: just pop it in the oven and stir a couple of times. Stovetop tofu is quicker, but you need to be right there with it, turning it often. Stovetop tofu can be soft and moist, or chewy or crisp, depending on the heat, timing, and the marinade you use.

Serves 4
Prep time: 10 minutes
Baking time: 30 to 60 minutes
Stovetop time: 10 to 15 minutes

one 14- to 16-ounce block firm tofu (see page 387)

BASIC MARINADE
1 tablespoon vegetable oil
1 tablespoon dark sesame oil
3 tablespoons soy sauce

OPTIONAL ADDITIONS
1 tablespoon peeled and grated fresh ginger
2 teaspoons Chinese Chili Paste with Garlic or Tabasco (see page 374)
2 tablespoons ketchup
2 tablespoons fresh lemon juice
1 tablespoon vinegar
1 to 2 tablespoons minced chipotles in adobo sauce (omit the sesame oil and increase the vegetable oil to 2 tablespoons)

Baked Tofu

Preheat a conventional oven to 400°F, convection to 375°F. Lightly oil a baking pan large enough to hold the tofu in a single layer; 9-inch square, 9 × 7-inch, 11 × 9-inch, and 13 × 9-inch pans work well.

In the baking pan, stir together the marinade ingredients. Cut the tofu (no need to press) into cubes, triangles, or strips. Put them in the baking pan and gently turn to thoroughly coat with the marinade. Bake uncovered until firm, browned, and chewy. To expose all sides to the hot air, turn gently every 10 or 15 minutes. It will take 30 to 60 minutes, depending on the size of the tofu pieces and how browned and chewy you like it.

Pan-fried Tofu

Cut the tofu (no need to press) into small cubes, about ¾-inch. Mix together the marinade. Use a 10-inch or larger skillet or heavy pan.

For crisp tofu nuggets, heat ¼ cup oil on medium-high heat. Add the tofu cubes and cook for 6 or 7 minutes, stirring every minute or so. Add soy sauce and sesame oil and any other marinade ingredients (except more oil) and stir well. Cook, stirring frequently, for a couple of minutes.

To make softer tofu cubes, marinate the tofu cubes for 5 minutes or longer. Warm about 2 tablespoons of oil in the skillet on medium-high heat. When the oil is warm, add the tofu and marinade and cook, stirring often, for 10 to 15 minutes until the tofu is firm and browned. Depending on your skillet, you may need to lower the heat after a couple of minutes.

NOTE

We don't recommend adding grated ginger to pan-fried tofu because it tends to scorch. If you're doing a ketchup version, stir the ketchup in for only the last minute or two: lower the heat and stir constantly—the ketchup will glisten at first and then become a bit duller; remove from the skillet at that point to prevent scorching.

SERVING AND MENU IDEAS

Serve with almost anything. At the restaurant, we always put baked tofu on plates of Sichuan Noodles (page 97), Indonesian Rice Salad (page 105), or Gado Gado (page 117). Make a salad with chopped romaine, tomatoes, avocado, and cukes with cubes of baked or pan-fried tofu and Japanese Carrot Dressing (page 305). Serve on top of Groundnut Stew (page 127).

Lemon-Herb Baked Tofu

This tofu makes a delicious snack, so when we're making some for a meal, we usually make extra. It will keep in a closed container or a plastic bag in the refrigerator for 4 or 5 days, although it takes self-control to keep it that long. It's a great sandwich filling or topping for salads, and a nice side for grain salads or simple rice and steamed vegetables.

When you take the tofu out of the oven, don't groan at the crusty deposit on the baking pan, thinking that it's going to be a hard cleanup. Put the pan in the sink, fill it with water, and let it soak for 5 minutes—the crust will dissolve and it will be easy to wash the pan.

Serves 4
Prep time: 15 minutes
Baking time: about 1 hour

one 14- to 16-ounce block firm tofu (see page 387)
¼ cup fresh lemon juice
2 tablespoons soy sauce
2 tablespoons olive oil or vegetable oil
½ cup water
1 tablespoon minced fresh rosemary or ¼ cup
    chopped fresh cilantro
¼ teaspoon ground black pepper

Preheat the oven to 400°F.

In a nonreactive baking pan large enough to hold the tofu in a single layer (a 9-inch square or 9 × 7-inch baking pan is perfect), stir together the lemon juice, soy sauce, oil, water, rosemary or cilantro, and black pepper. Cut the tofu (no need to press) into cubes, triangles, or strips. Put them in the baking pan and gently turn to thoroughly coat with the marinade.

Bake, uncovered, for 45 to 60 minutes. After about 30 minutes, gently stir the tofu. Take the tofu out of the oven when it has browned and most of the marinade has been absorbed.

Serve right away, or warm, or at room temperature, or chilled.

VARIATIONS
- Sometimes, we add about a tablespoon of minced scallions to the marinade.
- And, sometimes when we make the cilantro version, we add a minced fresh hot pepper.

SERVING AND MENU IDEAS
For a simple Italian-style meal, serve the rosemary version of this tofu with Polenta, Cheesy and Vegan (page 296) and Quick Sautéed Greens (page 268). For a simple dinner with a Mexican theme, make the cilantro version and serve it with Spanish Rice (page 287) and Lime-Cilantro Slaw (page 252).

Thai Baked Tofu

Easy-to-make and flavorful, baked tofu is a tasty, high-protein filling for sandwiches or topping for stews and sautés, and is a great addition to combination platters and composed salad plates. We like to have some around just for snacking, maybe to dip into yummy Peanut Sauce (page 25).

Serves 4
Prep time: 10 minutes
Baking time: 30 to 40 minutes

one 14- to 16-ounce block firm tofu (see page 387)

MARINADE
2 tablespoons vegetable oil
3 tablespoons soy sauce
2 garlic cloves, pressed or minced
1 teaspoon finely grated lime zest
3 tablespoons fresh lime juice
1 tablespoon sugar, honey, or pure maple syrup
1 to 2 tablespoons Thai green or red curry paste
   (see page 387)

Cut the tofu (no need to press) into cubes, triangles, or sticks. Lightly oil a baking pan that will hold the tofu in a single layer; a 9-inch square or 9 × 7-inch baking dish works well.

In a small bowl, whisk together the marinade ingredients. In the baking dish, gently toss the tofu with the marinade until all the surfaces are coated.

Bake, uncovered, in a preheated 400°F oven for 30 to 40 minutes, gently stirring after 20 minutes. When it is done the tofu will be firm with crisp edges, and the marinade will have been mostly absorbed. Serve hot or at room temperature.

SERVING AND MENU IDEAS
Bake a batch to accompany Thai Noodle Salad (page 100) or Indonesian Rice Salad (page 105). Thai Baked Tofu is also great on a Gado Gado plate (page 117) or to top Thai Vegetable Curry (page 121). It's good for jazzing up a plain dish like rice and steamed vegetables.

Country-style Soft Tofu

Country-style Soft Tofu comes together in only about 15 minutes and is exactly the kind of comforting meal for at home that many of us crave again and again. The taste is savory with a touch of Sichuan heat, and the texture is smooth and custardy. Stir-fried baby bok choy is our favorite thing to eat with Country-style Soft Tofu.

Serves 3 or 4
Time: 15 minutes

one 14- to 16-ounce block soft tofu (see page 287)
1 cup water
4 teaspoons cornstarch
2 tablespoons soy sauce
2 teaspoons dark sesame oil
½ teaspoon rice vinegar, apple cider vinegar, or white vinegar
¼ to ½ teaspoon Chinese Chili Paste with Garlic (see page 374)
⅓ cup chopped scallions

Cut the tofu into 1-inch cubes and set aside. In a saucepan, stir the water and cornstarch with a fork until the cornstarch dissolves. Add the soy sauce, sesame oil, vinegar, and chili paste. On medium-high heat, cook the sauce, stirring constantly until it simmers, darkens, and thickens, about 3 minutes. With a wooden spoon, gently stir in the tofu cubes and lower the heat. Simmer for about 4 minutes to heat the tofu. Add the scallions to the pan and stir gently. Serve immediately on rice or noodles.

VARIATIONS
- When the sauce has thickened and you're adding the tofu, stir in about ½ cup of sliced snow peas or fresh or frozen green peas.
- Although soft tofu is easier to work with, you can use silken tofu in this dish. Silken tofu is slippery and difficult to cut into neat cubes, but it's fine if it falls apart a bit. Be sure to stir the delicate tofu into the sauce with a wooden spoon.

SERVING AND MENU IDEAS
The soft consistency of this saucy tofu goes best with chewy, short-grain brown rice, but that takes about 45 minutes to cook, so either plan ahead or serve the tofu with udon noodles or a shorter-cooking rice such as jasmine. Succulent baby bok choy can be stir-fried in a few minutes (see page 269) and is the perfect side dish, as is Sesame Spinach (page 264) and Green Beans with Lemon Zest Dressing (page 266).

Mushroom Mapo Tofu

Traditional Sichuan *mapo doufu* is made with ground meat, which gives a bumpy texture that contrasts with smooth soft tofu. *Po* means old woman, and *ma* is short for *mazi*, a pockmarked person—Chinese legend says that the dish originated in Chengdu at the roadside inn belonging to a lady with a pock-marked face. In that city today, there are several *Chen mapo dofu* restaurants that specialize in the famous dish.

We make our mapo-inspired spicy vegan sauce with onions and mushrooms. It's a wonderful mix of flavors and textures. Because the mushrooms are smooth and soft, we like the contrast of firm tofu, but soft tofu is good, too. Sichuan mapo is very spicy, usually with chili oil or paste and Sichuan peppercorns, but make it as mild or as spicy as you like, and you can use whatever "hot" you like or have on hand: cayenne, Tabasco, red pepper flakes, etc.

Also not traditional, we like our mapo with a steamed green vegetable, in the restaurant almost always broccoli. Chinese greens such as choy sum (Chinese broccoli), or broccoli rabe, or whole green beans are good also.

Serves 4 to 6
Time: 50 minutes

cooked brown rice

TOFU

2 tablespoons peeled and grated fresh ginger
1 tablespoon Chinese Chili Paste with Garlic
    (see page 374)
¼ cup soy sauce
2 tablespoons white, apple cider, or rice vinegar
¼ cup sherry
3 tablespoons tomato paste
1 tablespoon dark sesame oil
1 cup water
one 14- to 16-ounce block firm tofu
    (see page 387)

VEGETABLES

¼ cup vegetable oil
2 cups chopped onions
4 cups chopped or sliced mushrooms (16 ounces)
    (see Note)
2 tablespoons cornstarch dissolved in
    2 tablespoons water

6 cups broccoli spears
toasted walnuts
diagonally sliced scallions

If you don't have cooked rice on hand, cook some first (see page 384).

In a bowl, stir together the grated ginger, chili paste, soy sauce, vinegar, sherry, tomato paste, sesame oil, and water. Cut the tofu (no need to press) into 1-inch cubes and add to the bowl. Using a rubber spatula, gently turn the tofu to cover with the sauce. Set aside.

Heat the oil in a wok or large skillet or soup pot on medium-high heat, add the onions and sauté for about 5 minutes, until softened. Add the mushrooms and sauté for about 5 minutes, until softened. Add the tofu and sauce and bring to a low boil. Reduce the heat and simmer, covered, for about 10 minutes.

Meanwhile, steam the broccoli. Prepare the walnuts and scallions.

Add the dissolved cornstarch to the mushrooms and tofu, bring back to a simmer, and stir gently until the sauce thickens and becomes clear.

Serve on individual plates: arrange the steamed broccoli on a bed of rice, top with mapo tofu, and sprinkle with walnuts and scallions.

NOTE

Use any mushrooms you like, or a mixture: moonlight, cremini, fresh shiitake, even portobello (slice the cap in half horizontally, then both vertically and horizontally into ½-inch nubs).

SERVING AND MENU IDEAS

Serve with a simple green salad and Japanese Carrot Dressing (page 305) or Ginger-Miso Dressing (page 306). Garnish with mung sprouts and/or quickly blanched sugar snap peas or snow peas.

Tofu "Meat" Loaf

Early on, when we made "American Diner Food" one of our ethnic Sunday night menus, the Moosewood Blue Plate Special was born: tofu "meat" loaf and mashed potatoes with mushroom gravy and a side of peas and carrots. It started as a joke, but it's become such a beloved standard at the restaurant that we now put it on the menu without even a hint of irony.

We bake tofu loaf in a 13 × 9 × 2-inch baking dish rather than a loaf pan because that gives each piece a larger chewy surface.

Serves 8
Prep time: 45 minutes
Baking time: 35 minutes

two 14- to 16-ounce blocks firm tofu (see page 387)
2 tablespoons vegetable oil
2 cups diced onions
½ teaspoon salt
1 teaspoon dried oregano
1 cup grated carrots
½ cup seeded and diced bell peppers (any color)
1 cup coarsely ground toasted walnuts
3 tablespoons soy sauce
2 tablespoons Dijon mustard
2 tablespoons dark sesame oil
¼ cup tahini
¼ teaspoon ground black pepper
¼ cup chopped fresh basil

First, press the tofu for at least 20 minutes (see page 388).

In a covered skillet, warm the oil on low heat. Add the onions, sprinkle with the salt and oregano, and cook for 7 or 8 minutes, stirring occasionally. Add the carrots and bell peppers and cook, covered, until the vegetables are tender, stirring occasionally, about 8 minutes. Transfer the vegetables to a mixing bowl.

Preheat the oven to 350°F. Oil a 13 × 9 × 2-inch baking pan.

Grate the pressed tofu by hand or in a food processor and add it to the cooked vegetables with the walnuts, soy sauce, mustard, sesame oil, tahini, black pepper, and basil. Mix well and add more soy sauce to taste.

Spread the mixture evenly into the prepared baking pan and smooth the top. Bake at for about 35 minutes, or until the loaf is firm and the top browned.

SERVING AND MENU IDEAS
Serve tofu loaf with Vegan Mashed Potatoes (page 278) and Mushroom Gravy (page 327) or Caramelized Onion Gravy (page 325) and a side of peas and carrots.

Dixie Tofu-Pecan Loaf

First at Moosewood there was the ever-popular "Blue Plate Special," our classic tofu walnut burger mix made into a loaf, served with mashed white potatoes, mushroom gravy, and peas and carrots. Now there's Dixie Blue Plate Special with a similar tofu loaf made with pecans, seasoned differently, topped with some barbecue sauce or onion gravy and served with mashed sweet potatoes and garlicky sautéed greens or coleslaw. It's clear that our customers think that Moosewood venturing south is a good thing.

Serves 6 to 8
Prep time: 35 minutes
Baking time: 40 minutes

two 14- to 16-ounce blocks firm tofu (see page 387)
2 tablespoons vegetable oil
2 cups diced onions
1 cup diced celery
1 teaspoon salt
1 teaspoon dried thyme
½ teaspoon dried oregano
¼ teaspoon red pepper flakes, plus more to taste
1 cup toasted pecans
1½ cups seeded and diced red bell peppers
2 tablespoons Dijon mustard
½ cup chopped fresh parsley
3 tablespoons soy sauce
¼ teaspoon ground black pepper
2 tablespoons barbecue sauce or ketchup (optional)

First, press the tofu for at least 20 minutes (see page 388).

In a large, covered skillet on low heat, warm the oil. Add the onions, celery, salt, thyme, oregano, and red pepper flakes to taste, and cook, covered, stirring occasionally, for 10 minutes.

While the onions cook, whirl the toasted pecans in a food processor until coarsely ground. Transfer to a large mixing bowl. Grate the tofu in a food processor or with a handheld grater and add to the bowl. Preheat the oven to 375°F. Lightly oil a 13 × 9 × 2-inch baking pan.

Stir the bell peppers into the onions and herbs, cover, and cook until tender, about 5 minutes. Add to the bowl with the tofu and pecans. Stir in the mustard, parsley, soy sauce, black pepper, and barbecue sauce or ketchup, if using. Season with salt and black pepper to taste.

Spread the tofu mixture evenly in the prepared pan and smooth the top. Bake until firm and browned, about 40 minutes.

SERVING AND MENU IDEAS
Serve topped with Caramelized Onion Gravy (page 325) or Barbecue Sauce (page 82) with sides of Vegan Mashed Sweet Potatoes (page 278) and Quick Sautéed Greens (page 268); collards would be especially appropriate. Or, while the oven is on, make some Roasted White and Sweet Potatoes (page 29), forego the gravy, and serve with Lime-Cilantro Slaw (page 252) or Confetti Kale Slaw (page 255).

Spinach Lasagna

There are few dishes as intoxicating as the sight and smell of a golden, bubbling lasagna.

We prepare this lasagna with our Tomato-Basil Sauce to which we add bay leaf, ground fennel seeds, and sometimes wine. We add chopped fresh, uncooked spinach to the filling because the taste of the spinach is truer, the prep time is shorter, and you have one less pot to wash. The final result resembles the tricolors of the Italian flag: red, white, and bright green. *Buon appetito!*

We make lasagna with uncooked noodles, and as long as there's enough sauce, they cook nicely as the dish bakes.

Serves 9
Prep time: 30 minutes if using premade sauce, an additional 15 to 20 minutes if making sauce (the sauce can simmer while the filling is prepared)
Baking time: 1 hour to 1 hour and 15 minutes

5 to 6 cups Tomato-Basil Sauce (page 324) or other tomato sauce
2 cups shredded mozzarella cheese (8 ounces)
2 cups shredded Parmesan cheese (5 ounces)
2 large eggs
about 16 ounces ricotta cheese
¼ teaspoon freshly grated nutmeg (optional)
7 cups chopped fresh baby spinach (about 12 ounces)
¾ pound lasagna noodles

Start making the tomato sauce if you don't already have it. In a bowl, mix together the mozzarella and Parmesan cheeses and set aside about a cup of the mixture to sprinkle on top of the lasagna later. In a larger mixing bowl, beat the eggs. Add the ricotta, mixed mozzarella and Parmesan, nutmeg, if using, and chopped raw spinach. Mix thoroughly.

Preheat the oven to 350°F. Oil a 13 × 9 × 2-inch baking pan. Spread 1½ cups of tomato sauce across the bottom of the pan. Top with a layer of lasagna noodles; we usually break some noodles and use them to fill in any empty spaces. Spread half of the spinach-cheese filling on the noodles. Spread another 1 cup of tomato sauce over the filling. Top with noodles and the remaining filling. Add the final layer of noodles and top with 2½ cups of sauce. (You can add more sauce if it will fit in your pan.)

Cover the pan with aluminum foil; dome the foil so that it doesn't touch the sauce. Bake until the noodles feel tender when a knife is inserted, probably an hour or more. Remove the foil when the noodles are tender, sprinkle the reserved cup of mozzarella and Parm on top, and bake for an additional 5 to 10 minutes until the cheese has melted. Let the lasagna sit, uncovered, at room temperature for 10 to 15 minutes before serving.

SERVING AND MENU IDEAS
What more could you want besides a green salad or simple vegetable side dish (see page 266)

Vegetable-Tofu Lasagna

At Moosewood, lasagna is very popular, and we usually feature at least two variations per week. In this vegan lasagna, seasoned whipped tofu replaces the traditional ricotta layer, and mushrooms and spinach stand in for mozzarella. This is a very flavorful dish—even the non-vegans don't miss the cheese—really!

As with all our lasagnas, the noodles are added uncooked. As long as there's adequate sauce, they cook beautifully as the dish bakes.

The lasagna can be assembled a day ahead of time and refrigerated. When chilled, bake at 325°F for about 1½ hours.

Serves 8
Prep time: 45 minutes if using premade sauce, about an hour if making sauce
Baking time: about 1 hour

Tomato-Basil Sauce (page 324) or 5 to 6 cups of your favorite tomato sauce
2½ tablespoons olive oil
1 pound mushrooms, sliced (about 5 cups)
1 teaspoon salt
2 tablespoons sherry or red wine (optional)
8 cups baby spinach (about 12 ounces)
one 14- to 16-ounce block firm tofu
1½ tablespoons soy sauce
2 garlic cloves, minced or pressed
½ teaspoon dried oregano
1 teaspoon ground fennel seeds
¼ teaspoon ground black pepper
½ cup chopped fresh basil
¾ pound lasagna noodles

If you're making Tomato-Basil Sauce, do that first, and go on with the recipe as it simmers.

In a large saucepan or skillet on medium heat, warm 1 tablespoon of the oil. Add the mushrooms and sauté for a couple of minutes. Stir in ½ teaspoon of the salt and the sherry or wine, if using, cover, and cook until the mushrooms are tender and juicy, about 5 minutes. Set aside.

Finely chop the spinach and set aside. Crumble the tofu into a food processor. Add the remaining 1½ tablespoons of olive oil, soy sauce, garlic, oregano, fennel, black pepper, and the remaining ½ teaspoon of salt. Whirl until the tofu mix is smooth and creamy, using a rubber spatula to scrape down the sides. Add the basil and process briefly to mix.

Preheat the oven to 350°F. Oil a 13 × 9 × 2-inch baking pan.

Spread 1½ cups of the tomato sauce over the bottom of the pan. Top with a layer of lasagna noodles; we usually break some noodles and use them to fill in the empty spaces in the noodle layer. Spread on half of the tofu filling, and then half of the mushrooms and chopped raw spinach. Spread another 1½ cups of tomato sauce over the vegetables. Top with noodles, the remaining tofu mix, and the rest of the mushrooms and spinach. Add a final layer of lasagna noodles and top it with 2 to 3 cups of tomato sauce.

Cover the pan with aluminum foil; dome the foil so that it doesn't touch the sauce. Bake until the noodles feel tender when a knife is inserted, about 1 hour.

VARIATIONS

- Make with different or additional vegetables. At the restaurant, we might add zucchini, fresh fennel, or bell peppers to this dish. Or, replace the spinach with sautéed kale or broccoli rabe. Asparagus is good, too.
- Use Puttanesca Sauce (page 322) instead of Tomato-Basil Sauce.
- For a gluten-free version, use rice lasagna noodles. We recommend cooking them first.

SERVING AND MENU IDEAS

Serve with one of our Simple Side Vegetables Simply Embellished (page 264) or Roasted Brussels Sprouts (page 275) and a crisp green salad.

Pasta al Cavalfiore

We confess that while preparing this dish you will dirty a lot of pots and bowls and the preparation is not quick and easy. But your efforts will be rewarded with a big, beautiful casserole that is golden and bubbly and looks like elegant mac and cheese delicious comfort cuisine—great to take to a dish-to-pass or add to a party buffet.

Serves 8 (more as a side dish)
Prep time: 1 hour and 15 minutes
Baking time: 40 minutes

CHEESE SAUCE
½ cup butter
½ cup unbleached white all-purpose flour
1 quart milk, heated
¼ teaspoon freshly grated nutmeg
1 tablespoon Dijon mustard
1 teaspoon salt
¼ teaspoon ground black pepper
2 cups shredded Parmesan cheese

2 tablespoons olive oil
2 cups chopped onions
3 garlic cloves, minced or pressed
2 tablespoons sherry, white wine, or water
1 medium head cauliflower, cut in florets
1 teaspoon salt
3 cups chopped fresh tomatoes
½ cup chopped fresh basil
3 tablespoons fresh lemon juice
1 pound chunky pasta (shells, penne, ziti, fusilli)
2 cups shredded mozzarella cheese

To prepare the cheese sauce: Melt the butter in a heavy saucepan on medium heat. Whisk in the flour and cook, stirring constantly, for a couple of minutes. Slowly add the heated milk, whisking constantly until the sauce thickens. Stir in the nutmeg, mustard, salt, pepper, and Parmesan and remove from the heat.

Bring a large pot of salted water to a boil for the pasta.

Meanwhile, in a large pot on medium heat, warm the oil. Add the onions and garlic and cook, covered, stirring frequently, until the onions are translucent, about 8 minutes. Stir in the sherry, wine, or water. Add the cauliflower and salt, cover, and cook, stirring often, until the cauliflower is tender, about 10 minutes. Stir in the tomatoes, basil, and lemon juice and remove from the heat.

When the water for pasta is at a rolling boil, cook the pasta until al dente. Drain.

Preheat the oven to 375°F. Oil a 13 × 9 × 2-inch baking pan.

In a large mixing bowl or one of the pots, combine the pasta, vegetables, cheese sauce, and half of the mozzarella cheese. Add more salt and pepper to taste. Spread the pasta mixture in the baking pan. Sprinkle the remaining mozzarella cheese on top. Bake, covered, for 20 minutes, then remove the cover and bake for 20 to 25 minutes until bubbling and golden on top.

VARIATIONS
- In place of chopped fresh tomatoes, use two 15-ounce cans or one 28-ounce can of diced tomatoes, drained.
- Instead of baking a casserole, stir the cooked vegetables into the cheese sauce and ladle the sauce over individual portions of cooked pasta. Top with the grated mozzarella.
- OK, we know this is called *cavalfiore* but in the Moosewood tradition of messing around with recipes, you could replace the cauliflower with zucchini or yellow squash and the tomatoes with red bell peppers. Or, chopped spinach or chard (keep the tomatoes). Or, mushrooms. Or broccoli. Or . . .

SERVING AND MENU IDEAS
Anything more than a crisp green salad may put you into a stupor.

Macaroni and Cheese with Broccoli

There's a TV commercial for boxed mac and cheese that shows adults sneaking bites from their kids, to the anger and dismay of the kids and the rueful guilt of the parents, who still love this dish as much as they did when they were children. The point is that everyone loves macaroni and cheese. A point we want to make is that if you make it yourself from scratch, you control the quality of the ingredients (no powdered cheese or additives), you end up with a batch big enough for the whole family, it doesn't take a lot longer to make, and, wow, does it taste better. We use whole-grain pasta and plenty of broccoli.

Sometimes we bake mac and cheese, sometimes we don't. Eat it as soon as you put the cheese sauce in the pasta and it's smooth and slippery. Bake it and it's more solid with a delicious chewy crust.

Serves 6 to 8
Prep time: 30 minutes
Baking time: 20 to 25 minutes

1 recipe Cheese Sauce (page 324)
12 ounces broccoli crowns, chopped into bite-size pieces (about 4 cups)
1 pound elbow pasta or fusilli
salt
ground black pepper to taste
1 cup fine bread crumbs (see page 373)
1 cup shredded sharp cheddar cheese

Bring a large pot of salted water to a boil for cooking the pasta. Make the cheese sauce. When the pasta water boils, add the pasta and stir. After 4 minutes, add the broccoli to the pasta pot. When the pasta is al dente, drain the pasta and broccoli. Combine the pasta, broccoli, and cheese sauce.

Preheat the oven to 350°F. Butter or oil a 13 × 9 × 2-inch baking pan or large casserole dish. Spread the pasta-broccoli-cheese mixture evenly in the baking pan. Sprinkle the bread crumbs over the top, then sprinkle with the grated cheddar. Bake for about 25 minutes, until the cheese is bubbling and the top is lightly browned.

VARIATION

- You can serve this dish right after stirring the cheese sauce into the pasta and broccoli, and forego baking it.

SERVING AND MENU IDEAS

Serve with a green salad with sliced apples or pears and/or grapes and Pear-Thyme Dressing (page 305). Or with sliced tomatoes or Cucumbers Vinaigrette (page 256).

Eggplant-Mushroom Marsala

We've been making this dish at Moosewood for forty years. It is a vegetable-laden sauce with the sweet and rich undertones of its signature ingredient, Marsala wine. We serve it over egg noodles with a generous sprinkling of Parmesan. It is also delicious on polenta or a creamy, simple risotto.

Marsala may seem like an expensive ingredient, but it is essential here. It usually comes in a screw-top bottle and it keeps well after opening. You will find it useful in many dishes; just a little adds a distinctive, rich flavor.

You can probably keep up with the chopping as you go, getting the next ingredients ready just as you need to add them to the pot. Or, for a more relaxed time, have all the ingredients ready before you begin to cook. Put water on to boil for the polenta or noodles when you begin to cook the onions and all will be ready together.

Serves 6
Time: 50 minutes

3 tablespoons olive oil
2 cups chopped onions
3 garlic cloves, minced or pressed
1 bay leaf
1 teaspoon salt
4 cups cubed eggplant (½-inch cubes) (1 eggplant, about 1¼ pounds)
1 red, yellow, or orange bell pepper, seeded and chopped
1 pound cremini or white mushrooms, sliced (about 5 cups)
1 teaspoon dried oregano
one 28-ounce can diced tomatoes
1 cup Marsala wine

2 tablespoons cornstarch dissolved in 2 tablespoons cold water
2 tablespoons chopped fresh basil
freshly ground black pepper
12 ounces egg noodles
finely grated Parmesan or Pecorino Romano cheese

In a soup pot or large skillet on medium-high heat, warm the oil. Add the onions, garlic, bay leaf, and salt and cook for about 5 minutes, stirring occasionally. Add the eggplant and bell pepper and cook for 5 minutes, stirring frequently. Add the mushrooms, oregano, and tomatoes, stir well, cover, and bring to a simmer. Simmer, covered, for 10 minutes. Add the Marsala and simmer, covered, until the vegetables are tender, about 10 minutes. Remove and discard the bay leaf.

Meanwhile, cook the egg noodles.

Just before serving, stir the dissolved cornstarch into the eggplant and mushrooms and cook, stirring constantly, just until the sauce has thickened; if the sauce is simmering steadily, this happens very quickly. Add the basil and season with black pepper and more salt to taste.

Serve on egg noodles, and top with finely grated cheese.

VARIATION

- Serve this sauce on polenta (page 296).

SERVING AND MENU IDEAS

In place of, or in addition to, cheese, top with a dollop of sour cream. A good appetizer to nibble on is Olivada (page 39) with toasted baguette rounds or with crudités. Try something light and fruity for dessert, like Low-fat Lemon Pudding Cake (page 363) served with fresh berries.

Vegetable Stroganoff

Traditionally, stroganoff is a beef and sour cream dish that originated in Russia in the nineteenth century. We're sure you'll appreciate our Moosewood vegetarian version of this creamy, chock-full-of-vegetables sauce flavored with red wine, paprika, and dill—and never miss that beef.

Serves 6
Time: 1 hour and 10 minutes

1 tablespoon vegetable oil
1½ cups chopped onions
1 tablespoon sweet paprika
½ teaspoon salt
½ teaspoon dried marjoram
1½ cups carrots cut into ½-inch-thick half-moons
½ cup dry red wine
6 cups mushrooms cut into halves or quarters
   (about 24 ounces)
4 cups bite-size cauliflower florets
one 15-ounce can diced tomatoes
1½ cups seeded and chopped red bell peppers
2 tablespoons cornstarch dissolved in
   2 tablespoons cold water
2 tablespoons soy sauce
3 tablespoons chopped fresh dill, more to taste
½ teaspoon black pepper
¾ cup sour cream
12 ounces egg noodles

The goal in this recipe is for the sauce and the noodles to be done at about the same time. But, we can't tell you exactly when to put on a large pot of salted water to boil for cooking the noodles. It depends upon how quickly your stove will boil water and how long the egg noodles you're using take to cook. Generally, we'd put the water on about the time we add the cauliflower to the cooking stroganoff vegetables. When the water boils, cook the noodles until al dente and drain.

In a soup pot on low heat, warm the oil. Add the onions, paprika, salt, and marjoram and cook, covered, for about 10 minutes, stirring occasionally. Add the carrots and cook, covered, for 5 minutes. Condensation usually forms on the inside surface of the pot lid; when you lift the lid to stir, let the water drip into the pot to keep the vegetables from sticking, and if it's not enough, just add a splash of water. Add the wine and mushrooms and increase the heat until the wine begins to simmer, then reduce the heat, cover, and cook at a low simmer for 5 minutes, stirring occasionally. Stir in the cauliflower and cook, covered, for 5 minutes. Stir in the tomatoes and bell peppers, return to a simmer, and cook, covered, until the vegetables are tender, 5 to 10 minutes. Stir in the dissolved cornstarch and cook, stirring constantly, just until the sauce has thickened. If the sauce is simmering steadily, this happens very quickly. Stir in the soy sauce, dill, black pepper, and sour cream. Add more salt or soy sauce, black pepper, and dill to taste.

Serve the stroganoff sauce over the egg noodles.

VARIATION

- You can adjust the proportions of the vegetables to your liking with the exception of the tomatoes, as long as you have about 14 cups of vegetables (including the onions). For instance, if you love mushrooms, add more, or substitute cabbage for the cauliflower, or don't use bell peppers at all and increase the amount of some other vegetable.

SERVING AND MENU IDEAS
Serve with a simple green salad with one of our homemade dressings (see pages 301 to 306).

Pasta Tutto Giardino

Tutto giardino means "the whole garden," and the beauty of this lavish, creamy vegetable sauce is that you can make it with your favorite vegetables from the garden or market as the season progresses. The sauce is easy and very pleasing. It's great on fettuccine, and we also serve it on chunky pastas like penne, shells, ziti, orecchiette, and farfalle. One customer who loves this sauce serves it with farfalle (bow ties) and calls it "Butterflies in the Garden."

Serves 6
Time: 45 minutes

2 tablespoons olive oil
1½ cups diced onions
2 garlic cloves, pressed or minced
1½ teaspoons salt
1 cup diced carrots
1½ to 2 cups seeded and diced bell peppers
    (1 red, yellow, orange, or green)
3 cups sliced mushrooms, white or cremini
    (12 ounces)
2 cups diced zucchini or yellow squash
½ teaspoon dried oregano
1 cup dry white wine
1 cup diced fresh tomatoes
¼ cup chopped fresh basil
1 cup asparagus (cut into 1-inch lengths), or fresh
    or frozen peas
½ cup butter
½ cup unbleached white all-purpose flour
2 cups hot milk
ground black pepper
1 to 2 teaspoons fresh lemon juice (optional)
1 pound pasta
finely grated Parmesan cheese

In a soup pot on medium-low heat, warm the oil. Add the onions, garlic, and salt and cook for 3 or 4 minutes. Add the carrots, cover, and cook for 4 minutes, stirring occasionally. Stir in the bell peppers, mushrooms, zucchini, oregano, and wine. Cover and cook until the vegetables are just tender, 8 to 10 minutes, stirring occasionally. Stir in the tomatoes and basil. Turn off the heat. If you're using asparagus or fresh peas, steam them separately until just tender, and stir into the vegetable mixture. If you are using frozen peas, stir them into the hot vegetable mixture.

To cook the pasta, bring a large pot of salted water to a boil. Add the pasta and cook until al dente.

While the pasta cooks, melt the butter in a saucepan on medium-high heat. Whisk in the flour and cook, stirring constantly, for a minute or two. Gradually add the milk, and cook, stirring constantly until thickened. Stir the white sauce into the vegetable mixture and reheat on low. Add more salt and pepper to taste. Stir in a little lemon juice to brighten the flavor, if you like. If the sauce is too thick, add a little more milk.

When the pasta is al dente, drain it.

Serve the pasta topped with the sauce and finely grated Parmesan.

SERVING AND MENU IDEAS
Most evenings, we'd be happy with just a plate of Pasta Tutto Giardino for supper, but a crisp salad, too, would be nice to munch on.

Pasta Fazool

Traditionally, *pasta e fagioli* is a hearty soup, but at Moosewood we make a hearty sauce with the vegetables and beans and serve it over pasta. Substitute or add any vegetable that you like—zucchini and fresh fennel would be great. Leftovers can be thinned with more water and tomatoes and served as a satisfying soup.

This is one of the recipes we chose for the Ithaca City School District's Cool School Food Program, a team effort to improve school lunch menus by introducing healthful and delicious plant-based options. Wynnie Stein from Moosewood worked with the team using local organic beans and fresh kale from the school district's garden. The program conducted tasting days when the elementary school students voted on a proposed finished recipe by filling out ballots with a smiley or frowny face. Hundreds of children voted resoundingly with a smile to have this recipe appear permanently on the monthly menu. Makes us happy and proud.

Serves 6
Time: 45 minutes

1 pound short, chunky pasta (shells, penne, or fusilli)

SAUCE
2 tablespoons olive oil
1½ cups finely chopped onions
1 cup diced celery
2 garlic cloves, minced or pressed
⅛ cup red wine (optional)
1 cup diced carrots
1 cup seeded and diced bell peppers
¼ teaspoon red pepper flakes
½ teaspoon ground black pepper
1 teaspoon salt
1½ teaspoons ground fennel seeds
2 teaspoons dried oregano or 2 tablespoons chopped fresh
1 cup water
one 28-ounce can diced tomatoes
two 15-ounce cans white, pinto, or pink beans, rinsed and drained (3 cups)
2 tablespoons chopped fresh basil
4 packed cups coarsely chopped fresh kale or spinach
finely grated Parmesan or Pecorino Romano cheese (optional)

Bring a large pot of salted water to a boil, add the pasta and cook until al dente. Try to time cooking the pasta so it is done when the sauce is.

Meanwhile, make the sauce: In large saucepan on medium heat, warm the oil. Add the onions, celery, and garlic and cook, stirring frequently, until the onions have softened, about 8 minutes. Stir in the wine, if using. Add the carrots and bell peppers and continue to cook for a few minutes. Stir in the red pepper flakes, black pepper, salt, ground fennel, oregano, and water and cook, covered, until the vegetables are tender, about 5 minutes. Add the tomatoes and beans and bring to a low boil. Reduce to a simmer and cook, covered, for about 10 minutes. Stir in the basil and kale or spinach and continue to cook, covered, for about 5 minutes, or until the greens are soft but still brightly colored.

Drain the pasta. Either ladle the sauce over individual bowls of hot pasta, or mix everything together in a large serving bowl. Top with the finely grated cheese.

SERVING AND MENU IDEAS
Serve with a simple green salad. Start with Olivada (page 39) or Vegan Spinach–Artichoke Heart Dip (page 36) and crostini, and finish with Italian Sesame Cookies (page 343) and fresh fruit.

Pasta Primavera

Although it can be enjoyed any time of year, this colorful dish is intended to celebrate the delicate fresh vegetables associated with spring. So, we don't smother them in a heavy cream sauce or add any strong seasonings. Rather, we simply lightly sauté the slender sticks of vegetables and make it a little bit saucy with tomatoes and wine.

Most of the vegetables are cut into matchstick shapes about the same length as penne or rigatoni so that they cook quickly, complement the pasta, and are easy to eat. But you could use fusilli or farfalle or just about any other shape of pasta.

Serves 6
Time: 40 minutes

1 pound asparagus
1 pound chunky pasta
   (whole wheat is nice)
1 tablespoon olive oil
6 garlic cloves, minced or pressed
1 small red onion, thinly sliced
2 small carrots, peeled and cut into 2-inch
   matchsticks
1 red bell pepper, seeded and cut into 2-inch
   matchsticks
2 small zucchini, cut into 2-inch
   matchsticks
2 cups chopped tomatoes
¼ cup dry white wine
1 teaspoon salt
1 cup fresh or frozen green peas
½ cup sliced fresh basil
ground black pepper
about 1 cup grated Pecorino Romano or
   Parmesan cheese

The goal here is for the pasta and the sautéed vegetables to be done at about the same time. You need to manage both a pot of water for the asparagus and the pasta, and a large skillet or other heavy pan for sautéing the vegetables. First, prep the vegetables and grate the cheese, and while you're doing that, put a large covered pot of salted water on to boil and cook the asparagus.

Break off and discard the tough ends of the asparagus spears and cut them into 2-inch pieces. When the water is at a boil, cook the asparagus for a minute or two until vivid green and barely tender. Remove the asparagus with a slotted spoon and set aside. Keep the water boiling to be ready for the pasta.

In a large skillet or pan on medium-high heat, warm the oil. Add the garlic, red onions, and carrot sticks. Sauté for a minute or two, stirring frequently. Stir the pasta into the pot of boiling water, and cook. Add the bell peppers and zucchini to the skillet and continue to sauté for a few minutes. Add the cooked asparagus and the tomatoes and wine, which will quickly bubble and steam. Add the salt and finish cooking the vegetables until just tender. Stir in the peas and basil. If you are using frozen peas rinse them with boiling water before adding. Season with black pepper and add more salt to taste.

When the pasta is al dente, drain it, reserving about ¼ cup of the cooking water.

In a large serving bowl, toss the pasta with about half of the grated cheese and the reserved cooking water. Drizzle the pasta with a little olive oil if you like. Top the pasta with the vegetables, sprinkle on the rest of the cheese, and serve right away.

SERVING AND MENU IDEAS
After all of those healthful vegetables why not indulge in some Chocolate Ricotta Moose (page 346) or Vanilla Cheesecake (page 338)?

Pasta with Asparagus and Lemon Sauce

If you love asparagus, love lemon, and love pasta, this is a great recipe for you to try. It's wonderful—simple, quick, healthy, delicious. The sauce is thick and velvety, a beautiful lemony-green, and its flavor is the essence of asparagus. One pot and a blender, and you're good to go.

Use extra-virgin or a fruity, flavorful olive oil. Real lemon lovers should add the lemon zest. Use any shape pasta—we usually make this dish with mezze penne or penne, campanelle, casareccio, gemelli, rigatoni, or fusilli because those shapes mirror the shape of asparagus tips. Whole wheat rigatoni is one of our favorites for this dish.

Serves 6
Time: 35 minutes

1½ to 2 pounds asparagus
1 pound pasta (see headnote)
2 teaspoons lightly packed, finely grated lemon
    zest (optional)
⅓ cup fresh lemon juice
⅓ cup extra-virgin olive oil
½ teaspoon salt
¼ teaspoon black pepper
1 cup shredded Parmesan cheese, more to pass at
    the table

Bring a large pot of salted water to a boil. Meanwhile, rinse the asparagus well to remove any sand from the tips. Snap off and discard the tough ends. Cut off and set aside the tips (about 1½ inches long).

When the water comes to a boil, cook the asparagus tips until just tender, 3 or 4 minutes. Remove them with a slotted spoon and set aside. (Or, put the tips in a colander or sieve and dunk that in the boiling water—no fishing out required.) Put the asparagus spears into the boiling water and cook until tender, usually 6 or 7 minutes. Remove them with a slotted spoon or tongs and place them in a blender. Cook the pasta in the same water until al dente.

While the pasta cooks, whirl the asparagus spears, lemon zest, if using, lemon juice, olive oil, salt, and black pepper in the blender until smooth.

When the pasta is done, drain it. In a large serving bowl, toss the pasta with the sauce, asparagus tips, and Parmesan. Serve immediately. Pass more Parmesan at the table.

SERVING AND MENU IDEAS
Start with White Bean and Basil Spread (page 40) or Vegan Spinach-Artichoke Heart Dip (page 36) on toasted bread rounds and serve with a tomato salad, a green salad, or a fruit salad, or a simple side, such as sliced tomatoes or beets.

Quick Uncooked Tomato Sauce for Pasta

First put on the pot for cooking the pasta, because this oh-so-fresh-tasting raw sauce is made in a blender in fewer minutes than it takes to boil the water and cook the pasta. The little cubes of fresh mozzarella, just beginning to melt in the hot pasta, are luscious. When tomatoes are in season and gardens are bursting with fragrant basil, we just can't get enough.

It's important in a dish this simple to use fine ingredients—a good, fruity, green extra-virgin olive oil, ripe garden tomatoes, good pasta, and freshly ground or cracked black pepper. Whole wheat butterfly pasta is our favorite with this sauce. The sauce is also good with other dishes, such as sautéed summer vegetables, baked potatoes, and omelets.

Yields about 5 cups sauce
Serves 4 to 6
Time: 20 minutes

5 cups chopped ripe tomatoes
¼ cup chopped fresh basil
2 garlic cloves, pressed
¼ cup extra-virgin olive oil
1 teaspoon salt
⅛ teaspoon ground black pepper
8 ounces fresh mozzarella cheese
1 pound pasta (farfalle or other short, chunky shape)
½ cup grated Parmesan or Pecorino Romano cheese (optional)

Bring a large covered pot of salted water to a boil.

Put 2 cups of the tomatoes into a large serving bowl. Put the rest into a blender. Put half of the chopped basil into the bowl with the tomatoes; the rest goes in the blender. Add the garlic, olive oil, salt, and black pepper to the blender and whirl until smooth. Pour the blender sauce into the serving bowl. Cut the mozzarella into small cubes and add them to the bowl.

When the water comes to a rapid boil, cook the pasta just until al dente. Drain the pasta, add it to the serving bowl, and toss well. Top with grated cheese, if you like, and serve immediately.

VARIATIONS
- Add about 2 cups of sliced mushrooms, raw or lightly sautéed.
- To make a completely raw meal, leave out the cheese and make fettuccine-like strands of zucchini in place of pasta. You need a spiral slicer, such as a Benriner Turning Vegetable Slicer, to make this mock noodle.

SERVING AND MENU IDEAS
Serve with a tossed green salad, one of our Not So Plain Green Vegetables (page 266), or Confetti Kale Slaw (page 255).

Twelve Quick Pastas

In every Italian cook's repetoire there is an easy pasta dish, called *aglio e olio* (garlic and oil), that is good any time and can be made on the spur of the moment with a few simple ingredients always on hand.

We owe a tremendous debt to Susan Harville, Moosewood cook, partner, dessert maker, and Italian food aficionado. Sometime in the mid-1970s, Susan fell in love with Italian food (she named her son Emilio), and she has been devising simple, elegant, and mouthwatering meals ever since for family and friends. The expectant diners eagerly await the big bowl of her latest delicious, hot pasta concoction that she will hurry to the table moments after she has tossed it all together. We asked her to write down some of those dishes for this book—we made her stop at only twelve.

With Pasta Aglio e Olio as the base, these dozen delicious pasta dishes can all be made in the time it takes to boil water and cook pasta. For consistency, we'll assume you use 1 pound of pasta (whole wheat pasta works well in all), good-quality extra-virgin olive oil, and minced fresh garlic. Exact measurements are not important.

Serves 4 to 6
Time: 20 to 25 minutes

PASTA AGLIO E OLIO

Use spaghetti or linguine or other long-strand pasta. Sauté plenty of minced garlic (say, 6 or 8 cloves or more) in extra-virgin olive oil (maybe 3 or 4 tablespoons) for a minute, until golden. Don't let it scorch. Toss the garlic and oil with hot drained pasta, along with finely grated Pecorino Romano or Parmesan cheese, salt, and ground black black pepper.

PASTA AL VESUVIO

Start with Aglio e Olio, but to the garlic and oil add chopped fresh parsley (about a cup), a couple of tablespoons of pine nuts, some grated lemon zest, and ½ teaspoon, or more, of red pepper flakes. Cook just until the parsley has wilted but is still bright green. Toss with hot pasta along with salt, ground black pepper, and grated cheese.

PASTA WITH OLIVES PIQUANT

Mince about 1½ cups of assorted deli olives (some kalamatas, some big green ones, some stuffed with pimientos, garlic, lemon peel, or almonds—all are good) by hand or in a food processor, pulsing just a few times so that the olives are finely chopped but not pasty. Add the olives, along with a little minced fresh parsley and maybe ¼ teaspoon of red pepper flakes, to the garlic and oil. Save a cup of pasta cooking water when you drain the pasta so you can swirl the last bits of olive out of the skillet. Toss everything with the hot pasta and sprinkle on grated cheese, if you like.

FETTUCCINE WITH FRESH HERBS

You'll need a little more extra-virgin olive oil, say ¼ cup, in which to sauté the garlic for a minute until it starts to turn golden. Add about ½ cup each of minced fresh parsley, minced fresh basil, and minced fresh chives. Cook the fresh herbs for only about 30 seconds, stirring constantly. Ladle about ½ cup of hot pasta cooking water into the pan and set aside. Toss the drained pasta with the oil and herb mixture, salt, ground black pepper, and grated Pecorino Romano or Parmesan cheese.

PASTA WITH ZUCCHINI AND LEMON

While the pasta water comes to a boil, slice 6 to 8 small, tender, young zucchini (about 4 cups) and juice a lemon. Add the zucchini to the garlic and oil and sauté until the zucchini is golden brown. Sprinkle it with salt and ground black pepper, add the lemon juice, and remove from the heat. Toss the hot drained pasta with grated Pecorino Romano (1 to 2 cups) and top with the zucchini.

PASTA WITH BROCCOLI

Use a short, chunky pasta. While the pasta water comes to a boil, finely chop a lot of broccoli. Sauté the broccoli in the oil for about 5 minutes before adding garlic. Then season with salt, ground black pepper, and add a couple of spoonfuls of hot pasta cooking water to steam the broccoli to tenderness. Top the cooked pasta with the broccoli and about a cup of grated Pecorino Romano, Parmesan, or ricotta salata cheese or with crumbled feta or Gorgonzola cheese.

VARIATIONS

- Cook seeded and chopped red bell peppers with the broccoli or add a couple chopped fresh tomatoes at the end.
- Add about ½ cup of chopped black olives and ¼ teaspoon of red pepper flakes.
- Add about a cup of shelled cooked edamame or small red beans and/or about a cup of toasted walnuts.

PASTA WITH CHARD

Use ziti or another chunky pasta and about 1½ pounds of ruby, rainbow, or green chard. While the pasta water comes to a boil, cut the chard stems into ½-inch slices and chop the leaves. Sauté the stems first for a minute or two before adding the garlic and leaves. Cook for about 5 minutes, or until the leaves are wilted but still brightly colored. Season with salt and ground black pepper, and a pinch of red pepper flakes, if you like. Top the pasta with the chard and grated Pecorino Romano, Parmesan, or Asiago cheese or crumbled ricotta salata. Another nice addition to pasta with chard is dried cherries soaked in a few tablespoons of hot pasta water while the pasta cooks, plus some toasted walnuts.

PASTA WITH BEANS AND GREENS

Use a short chunky pasta, such as orecchiette, penne, fusilli, or ditalini. Sauté about 1 pound of rinsed and chopped fresh greens, such as escarole, endive, mizuna, mustard greens, or broccoli rabe with olive oil and garlic. until the greens are wilted but still bright green. Add a little pasta cooking water if needed. Add a 15-ounce can of rinsed and drained beans, such as butter beans, pinto, Roman, or cannellini beans. Season with salt and ground black pepper, and add a couple of pinches of dried

rosemary or oregano. Toss everything with the pasta and top with grated Pecorino Romano, Parmesan, or sharp provolone, and/or top with chopped fresh tomatoes.

PASTA WITH GRAPE TOMATOES AND FETA

Use a short, chunky pasta. While the pasta-cooking water comes to a boil, slice about 2 pints of grape tomatoes in half lengthwise. Sauté garlic in olive oil until golden, about 1 minute. Add the tomatoes and cook for 3 or 4 minutes until the tomatoes are somewhat softened but not falling apart. Toss the hot pasta with about ¾ cup of crumbled feta cheese and enough reserved cooking water to coat the pasta. Top with the tomato-garlic mixture and sprinkle with ground black pepper.

VARIATIONS

- Add about 2 cups of fresh green beans, cut in half crosswise on a diagonal, to the pasta cooking water after the pasta has been added and it has returned to a boil. Drain the pasta and beans together, or add about 2 cups of chopped fresh spinach to the pasta water just a minute before the pasta is drained.
- Begin by soaking about ½ cup of sun-dried tomatoes in a little boiling water until softened, 10 to 15 minutes. Cut the sun-dried tomatoes into thin strips and add them, along with a few tablespoons of their soaking water, to the skillet of grape tomatoes and garlic.
- Top the pasta with toasted pine nuts.

QUICK TOMATO SAUCE

Cook some minced garlic in a couple of tablespoons of olive oil until golden, then add about 2 cups of finely chopped onions and cook on medium heat until golden, 5 or 6 minutes. Add salt and ground black pepper and two 28-ounce cans diced tomatoes or chopped plum tomatoes with their juice. Add a few leaves of fresh basil, if you like. Simmer until the pasta is cooked. Purée if you like.

- For a quick puttanesca sauce, add a few tablespoons of capers and sliced olives, and some oregano and red pepper flakes.
- For a quick arrabbiata sauce, add about a cup of seeded and diced bell peppers along with the onions and then add 1 teaspoon of red pepper flakes. Purée the sauce, or part of the sauce, in a blender until smooth.

ROASTED RED PEPPER SAUCE

Use penne or another chunky pasta. Cook a finely chopped onion and garlic in oil. When the onion is golden, add about 1½ cups of finely chopped fresh or canned tomatoes and some sliced, jarred roasted red peppers and minced fresh basil. Cook for a couple of minutes and then purée half of the sauce in a blender and return it to the pan. Add ¼ cup of chopped fresh parsley. Season with salt and ground black pepper to taste. Top the pasta and sauce with Gorgonzola or another blue cheese or grated Pecorino Romano or Parmesan cheese.

PASTA WITH PEAS AND ONIONS

Here's a naturally sweet pasta dish without any garlic. Use a pasta shape that can catch and hold peas, such as orecchiette or shells. While the pasta water comes to a boil, cut 4 medium onions lengthwise into thin slices and cook them in a little olive oil until they begin to brown. Season with salt and ground black pepper. Add about 4 cups of peas with a couple of spoonfuls of the hot pasta water. Toss the drained pasta with grated Pecorino Romano cheese and top with the peas and onions.

Coconut-Lime Cashew-crusted Fish

Dukkah-crusted Fish

Pecan-crusted Fish

Spicy Chipotle Cornmeal-crusted Fish

Not Fried Fish

Fish Cakes

Flounder Rollatini

Flounder Florentine

Spicy Caribbean Fish

Teriyaki Fish

Malaysian Fish

Oven-poached Fish with Leeks and Wine

Fish Basilico

Asian-style Fish in Parchment

Fish "Tostadas"

Creamy Seafood Stew

Coconut-Lime Cashew-crusted Fish

We only occasionally fry fish in the restaurant. We think overall that baking with a minimum of oil is a healthier way to go. But that doesn't mean that we're immune to the pleasures of a sizzling, crisp, crusty coating and a tender, flaky interior—the hallmarks of well-fried food. To that end, we've developed a number of marinated fish dishes with crunchy toppings. We bake the fish at a high temperature, and a trick for achieving a crisper bottom and sides is to preheat the oiled baking pan for about 5 minutes before putting in the fish.

Serves 4 to 6
Prep time: 20 minutes
Marinating time: 1 hour
Baking time: about 25 minutes

2 pounds firm fish fillets
3 tablespoons fresh lime juice
one 14-ounce can unsweetened coconut milk
1½ cups cashews, toasted
1 cup unsweetened grated coconut
1 teaspoon salt
⅛ teaspoon cayenne or ground black pepper
3 tablespoons chopped scallions

Rinse and drain the fish. In a shallow dish, whisk together the lime juice and coconut milk. Add the fish, turn to coat both sides, and allow to marinate for at least 1 hour.

Meanwhile, in a food processor, whirl the cashews until finely ground. Add the coconut, salt, and cayenne or black pepper and pulse a few times until the mixture is well combined. Set aside.

About 30 minutes before you are ready to serve, preheat the oven to 400°F and preheat an oiled baking pan large enough to hold the fish fillets in a single layer. Dredge each marinated fillet in the coconut-cashew mixture, making sure to coat all sides, and place in the preheated baking pan (see headnote). Sprinkle with the chopped scallions. Bake for about 25 minutes, more or less depending on the thickness of the fillets, or until the coating is light golden brown and the fish is flaky and tender.

SERVING AND MENU IDEAS
Top with Mango Aioli (page 309) or Lime-Dijon Aioli (page 309). If you'd like it a little spicy, try it with Mango Salsa (page 309). Serve with Vegan Mashed Potatoes and Sweet Potatoes (page 278) and Quick Sautéed Greens (page 268).

Dukkah-crusted Fish

Dukkah is an Egyptian nut and seed mixture that is usually used as a dip with bread and vegetables. Many versions of the mixture can be found for sale in small markets in Cairo and elsewhere. Our first taste of it was brought back from a little store in Adelaide, South Australia, of all places. When we created our own recipe for the spice mix, we realized how good it would be on fish.

Serves 4 to 6
Prep time: 20 minutes
Baking time: 20 to 30 minutes

2 pounds firm fish fillets
2 tablespoons olive oil
2 tablespoons fresh lemon juice
⅓ cup almonds
⅓ cup hazelnuts
⅓ cup sesame seeds
1 tablespoon ground toasted cumin seeds
1 teaspoon ground black pepper
½ teaspoon salt
1 tablespoon minced fresh thyme

Rinse the fish fillets and place them in a large bowl. Whisk together the oil and lemon juice and pour it over the fish. Turn the fillets a couple of times to coat. Set aside to marinate while you prepare the nut and seed mixture.

In the bowl of a food processor, whirl the almonds and hazelnuts until coarsely ground. Add the sesame seeds, cumin, black pepper, salt, and thyme and whirl until well mixed.

Preheat the oven to 400°F. Oil a baking pan large enough to hold the fillets in a single layer.

After the fish has marinated for about 15 minutes, place the fillets in the prepared baking pan. Discard any leftover marinade. Top each fillet with 3 to 4 tablespoons of the nut and seed mixture. Bake until the fish flakes easily with a fork, 20 to 30 minutes depending on the thickness of the fillets.

SERVING AND MENU IDEAS

Serve with Bulghur Pilaf (page 294) and Roasted Cauliflower (page 274), or with Greek Lemony Roasted Potatoes (page 276) and Beet Salad (page 258) or Moroccan Carrot Salad with Currants (page 257), or with Quick Sautéed Greens (page 268) and Dilled Potatoes Vinaigrette (page 277), or with Moroccan Couscous Salad (page 107) . . . the choices are endless.

Pecan-crusted Fish

This easy and elegant way to prepare fish owes its inspiration to the South, where fresh fish, buttermilk, pecans, and fresh thyme are familiar ingredients. Buttermilk provides a moist, creamy coating that the pecan crust will adhere to. If you don't have buttermilk on hand, plain yogurt works just as well.

We serve this extremely popular dish often; the fish has a mouthwatering crust without frying it in oil, and the flavors are versatile enough that we can serve it with mashed sweet potatoes and garlicky greens for a Southern treat, or with mashed white potatoes and green beans for an East Coast dinner, or with seasoned rice and a fruit salsa for a Caribbean twist.

Serves 6
Prep time: 20 minutes
Baking time: 30 minutes

2 pounds firm fish fillets
1 cup buttermilk
¼ cup olive oil or vegetable oil
3 garlic cloves, minced or pressed
1 cup unseasoned bread crumbs (see page 373)
1 cup pecans
¼ cup finely chopped fresh parsley
2 teaspoons minced fresh thyme or 1 teaspoon dried thyme
1 teaspoon sweet paprika
½ teaspoon salt
⅛ teaspoon cayenne

Rinse the fish fillets and place them in a large, shallow dish. Pour the buttermilk over them and set aside.

Warm the oil in a skillet, add the garlic, and sauté just until it sizzles and turns golden. Stir in the bread crumbs and sauté for 3 or 4 minutes until golden and crisp. Put the bread crumbs into a large, shallow dish. In a food processor, pulse the pecans until ground but still bumpy (like cracked wheat). Add the pecans, parsley, thyme, paprika, salt, and cayenne to the bread crumbs and mix well.

Preheat the oven to 400°F. Oil a baking sheet or baking Pan large enough to hold the fillets in a single layer.

Using a fork or tongs or your fingers, lift each fillet out of the buttermilk marinade, letting the excess drain off, and dredge each fillet in the pecan–bread-crumb mixture to coat completely. Place the coated fillets skin side down in the prepared baking pan or sheet, leaving a little space between each fillet so that the coating can brown.

Bake covered for 10 minutes, and then uncovered for 10 to 20 minutes, until the coating is light brown and crisp and the fish is tender and flaky.

SERVING AND MENU IDEAS
Serve each fillet garnished with a little finely chopped parsley or a pretty sprig of fresh thyme and a wedge of lemon. Pass Tabasco or other hot sauce at the table. Really nice served with Mango Salsa (page 315) or Mango Aioli (page 309).

Spicy Chipotle Cornmeal–crusted Fish

Although at Moosewood we almost exclusively bake the fish we serve, in this recipe, we pan-fry it for a nice, crispy crust and because it's quick and easy. Our favorite way to serve this fish is with Mango Aioli (page 309). It's also good plain or with good old ketchup or tartar sauce.

In Ithaca, we can get locally grown and ground cornmeal and the flavor and texture of freshly ground cornmeal is wonderful. We hope you can find good-quality cornmeal where you live.

Serves 4 to 6
Time: 30 minutes

2 pounds firm fish fillets
2 tablespoons vegetable oil, plus oil
    for pan-frying
2 tablespoons fresh lemon or lime juice
3 tablespoons chipotles in adobo sauce
2 garlic cloves, minced or pressed (optional)
1½ teaspoons salt
1 cup cornmeal (see pages 382 and 383)
½ teaspoon ground black pepper

Rinse the fish and cut it into 4 or 6 portions. In a blender or food processor, whirl the oil, lemon or lime juice, chipotles in adobo to taste, garlic, if using, and 1 teaspoon of the salt. The more chipotle peppers, the less adobo sauce you need and the spicier your fish will be. Place the mixture in a shallow bowl. Add the fish and generously coat the fillets with the chipotle sauce. Put the cornmeal, remaining ½ teaspoon salt, and pepper into another shallow bowl or large plate. Dredge each piece of fish on all sides in the seasoned cornmeal.

Unless you have a very large skillet, you'll probably have to pan-fry in two skillets or in batches. Fill a nonstick or well-seasoned skillet ¼ inch deep with oil. Warm on medium-high heat until the oil is hot but not smoking. Cook the fish for 3 to 4 minutes on each side, depending on the thickness, until the fish flakes with a fork. Transfer to paper towels to drain. If you have another batch to fry, keep the cooked fish in a warm oven.

SERVING AND MENU IDEAS
Serve this delectable fish with mashed or roasted white or sweet potatoes or Dilled Potatoes Vinaigrette (page 277) and Quick Sautéed Greens (page 268). Green Beans with Lemon Zest Dressing (page 266) also taste good as a side vegetable.

Not Fried Fish

A surprising number of our partners, six out of nineteen, grew up in or have close family ties to the state of Maryland, and with that comes sentimental ties to the seasonings of the Chesapeake region. Dave Dietrich, our most recent transplant from Maryland—albeit twenty-two years ago—feels right at home with Old Bay Seasoning. Now, there's always a can of Old Bay on our spice shelf and fish dishes, stews, and chowders seasoned with it are popular menu items. Here's one of our favorites, an easy, down-home fish dish.

Serves 6 to 8
Prep time: 10 to 15 minutes
Marinating time: at least 20 minutes
Baking time: 10 to 12 minutes

2 pounds firm fish fillets
2 tablespoons Old Bay Seasoning (see page 380)
¼ cup fresh lemon juice
4 garlic cloves, minced or pressed
¼ cup olive oil
2 cups finely ground whole wheat or white bread crumbs, or cornbread crumbs
1 heaping tablespoon chopped fresh thyme or 2 teaspoons dried thyme

Rinse and drain the fish. In a small bowl, whisk together the Old Bay, lemon juice, garlic, and olive oil. Place the fish in a large bowl, pour in the marinade, turn the fish to coat all sides, and marinate for 20 minutes or longer.

While the fish marinates, toast the bread crumbs on a baking sheet at 350°F for 5 to 10 minutes, until crisp. Check after 5 minutes, and shake the pan or stir if they need more time; watch that they don't burn. Remove the crumbs from the oven and set them aside to cool and dry. Increase the oven temperature to 425°F.

When the bread crumbs have cooled, transfer them to a bowl or large plate and stir in the thyme. Generously oil a large, rimmed baking tray or a couple of baking pans large enough to lay out the fillets with space all around each. Heat the baking sheet or pans in the oven for 5 minutes, and then set the hot pan near the bowl with the herbed crumbs.

Working quickly, gently shake excess marinade from each fillet, dredge it in the bread crumbs, and lay it on the pan, placing the fillets side by side without touching. Bake for 10 to 12 minutes until the fish is flaky and the topping is crisp.

SERVING AND MENU IDEAS
Serve with corn on the cob (page 265) and Chopped Broccoli Salad (page 251) or Lime-Cilantro Slaw (page 252). You can also do a variation on fish and chips by serving Not Fried Fish with oven-roasted potatoes (see page 29).

Fish Cakes

When fish cakes are on the menu at Moosewood, they sell out in a nanosecond. The inspiration for our first recipe for fish cakes made with potatoes came from Davina Stein, a great cook who even back in the 1950s, when everyone else was using canned salmon, made delicious fish cakes with fresh fish. It doesn't matter whether we make them with salmon or cod or whether we include shrimp or catfish, there is something tremendously satisfying about these baked patties that are crunchy on the outside and creamy within. Fish cakes are an excellent way to use leftover fish and potatoes.

At the restaurant, we top fish cakes with an herbed or spiced aioli, following our inspiration of the day, or to go with whatever side dish we're serving beside the fish cakes.

Yields 10 fish cakes
Serves 5 to 10
Prep time: 1 hour
Baking time: 25 minutes

1½ pounds firm fish fillets
2 tablespoons olive oil or vegetable oil
1 cup finely chopped onions
2½ cups diced or thinly sliced peeled potatoes
1 cup diced carrots
1 cup water
1 teaspoon salt
1 large egg, lightly beaten
1 tablespoon mayonnaise
1 tablespoon Dijon mustard
1 tablespoon fresh lemon juice
1 tablespoon chopped fresh dill
½ teaspoon ground black pepper
1½ cups bread crumbs (see page 373)

Preheat the oven to 375°F. Oil a baking pan large enough to hold the fish fillets.

Arrange the fish, skin side down, in the pan. Sprinkle with a little salt and black pepper, and bake, uncovered, until the fish flakes easily with a fork, 10 to 20 minutes, depending on the thickness. Remove from the oven and set aside.

While the fish bakes, warm the oil in a covered skillet or saucepan on medium-low heat. Add the onions and cook for 10 minutes, stirring frequently to prevent sticking. Stir in the potatoes, carrots, water, and salt. Cover and cook at a low boil until the potatoes and carrots are soft, about 15 minutes, stirring occasionally. When the vegetables are soft, drain them if there is still liquid in the pan.

If necessary, skin the baked fish. In a large mixing bowl, using a handheld potato masher, mash the drained vegetables and the fish—don't overdo it: bits and pieces of carrots and onions are good. Add the beaten egg, mayonnaise, mustard, lemon juice, dill, black pepper, and ¼ cup of the bread crumbs and mix thoroughly.

Oil a large rimmed baking sheet or 2 or 3 baking pans. Pour the remaining bread crumbs into a shallow bowl. Form ½-cup patties. Cover each patty with bread crumbs. The mixture tends to be a little on the wet side, so for easy handling, rest each patty in the bowl of crumbs and sprinkle crumbs on the top. Gently transfer each patty to the baking pan, placing the fish cakes 2 to 3 inches apart. Bake for about 25 minutes, or until the cakes are firm to the touch and the outside is crisp.

SERVING AND MENU IDEAS

In the restaurant we usually top fish cakes with Herbed Aioli (page 309), Chipotle Aioli (page 259), or Lime-Dijon Aioli (page 309). We serve them with roasted white or sweet potatoes and some seasonal vegetable or crisp cabbage salad. They are also great served on a whole-grain bun or Kaiser roll, topped with aioli or coleslaw. And in the summer, how about fish cakes with an ear of sweet corn and a sweating glass of cold lemonade or limeade?

Flounder Rollatini

Flounder is perfect for rolling because the fillets are thin and boneless. These chunky fish rolls filled with a savory filling are a crowd-pleaser for fish lovers.

Serves 4 to 6
Prep time: 25 minutes
Baking time: 30 minutes

FILLING
⅓ cup finely chopped toasted almonds
½ cup shredded Parmesan cheese
⅓ cup chopped fresh parsley
⅓ cup chopped fresh basil

2 pounds flounder fillets (2- to 4-ounce fillets)
3 tablespoons butter
2 tablespoons fresh lemon juice

Preheat the oven to 375°F. Oil a 9-inch square or an 11 × 7-inch baking pan.

In a bowl, mix together the almonds, Parmesan, parsley, and basil.

If any of the fillets are large, cut them in half; when rolled, they should be about 2 inches thick. Rinse the flounder and place each fillet, skinned side up, on a flat work surface. Sprinkle filling on the wide end of each fillet and roll it up. Arrange the flounder rolls, seam side down and close together, in the prepared baking pan. Melt the butter and stir in the lemon juice. Pour the lemon butter over the rolled fillets and cover the pan.

Bake for 25 to 30 minutes until the fish is white, feels firm to the touch, and flakes easily with a fork.

SERVING AND MENU IDEAS
Serve the flounder rolls on rice, couscous, or orzo, or with Risotto Milanese (page 299), with a simple vegetable on the side—whatever is in season. For inspiration, look at Not Plain Green Vegetables (page 266) and Simple Side Vegetables Simply Embellished (page 264).

Flounder Florentine

Flounder Florentine has been one of our most loved fish dishes for a long, long time. It's simple, elegant, and quick and easy to make at home. It can be assembled beforehand and kept in the refrigerator, making it a great dish for dinner guests.

Sometimes we add chopped toasted almonds to the filling; sometimes we use dill instead of tarragon. Often, we top Flounder Florentine with chopped tomatoes stirred together with a splash of olive oil and some chopped fresh basil.

Serves 4 to 6
Prep time: 25 minutes
Baking time: 20 minutes

FILLING
2 tablespoons olive oil
1 cup minced onions
5 cups baby spinach (8 ounces)
1 tablespoon chopped fresh tarragon
2 tablespoons fresh lemon juice

2 pounds flounder fillets (2 to 4 ounces each)
2 tablespoons fresh lemon juice
salt
ground black pepper
2 tablespoons melted butter or olive oil

Warm the oil in a saucepan on medium-low heat. Add the onions and cook, stirring frequently, for about 5 minutes, or until translucent.

Meanwhile, chop the spinach. Stir the spinach and tarragon into the onions and cook just until the spinach has wilted, about 2 minutes. Remove from the heat and add the lemon juice. Set aside to cool.

Preheat the oven to 375°F. Oil a baking pan (11 × 7 inch or 9-inch square).

Rinse the flounder and lay out the fillets, skinned side up, on a flat work surface. Spoon about a tablespoon of the filling onto the wide part of each fillet and roll it up. Place the rolls, seam side down and close together, in the prepared baking pan. Drizzle the lemon juice over the rolls, sprinkle with salt and black pepper, and drizzle with the melted butter or the olive oil. Bake covered for 20 to 25 minutes until the fish is tender but firm to the touch.

SERVING AND MENU IDEAS
Serve on brown rice, orzo, or couscous or with Greek Lemony Potatoes (page 276) or Dilled Potatoes Vinaigrette (page 277). Good with Seasoned Artichokes (page 263) or Roasted Cauliflower (page 274) or Roasted Brussels Sprouts (page 275).

Spicy Caribbean Fish

We added coconut milk to this spicy sauce that we've been making for fish since the early days of the restaurant and decided that we loved it that way. And even though it's good without it, those of us who like cilantro love it in this sauce. Make the sauce as spicy or as mild as you like; some of us like to use spicy habanero chiles without seeding them, some prefer a milder hot pepper, and some always scoop out all the seeds and any membranes in any and all hot peppers to make them milder. At the restaurant, we tend to go for not too spicy to please the majority of our customers.

Yields about 2 cups sauce
Serves 4
Prep time: 30 minutes
Baking time: 20 to 30 minutes

SAUCE
1 tablespoon vegetable oil
1 cup finely chopped onions
1 teaspoon salt
1 fresh hot pepper, minced
1 garlic clove, minced or pressed
½ teaspoon dried thyme
2 cups diced fresh tomatoes
½ cup unsweetened coconut milk
1 teaspoon finely grated lime zest
2 tablespoons fresh lime juice
3 tablespoons chopped fresh cilantro
    (optional)

1½ pounds firm fish fillets
ground black pepper

In a saucepan on medium heat, warm the oil. Add the onions and salt. Cook for 5 minutes, stirring often. Add the minced hot pepper, garlic, and thyme and cook for about 3 minutes, stirring often. Stir in the tomatoes, increase the heat, and cook until the tomatoes begin to get juicy, about 2 minutes, stirring often. Add the coconut milk, bring back to a simmer, and cook for 2 minutes. Stir in the lime zest, lime juice, and cilantro, if using. Set the sauce aside to cool.

While the sauce is cooling, preheat the oven to 400°F. Rinse the fish fillets and place in an oiled baking pan large enough to hold the fillets in a single layer. Sprinkle with salt and black pepper.

Pour the sauce over the fish fillets and bake for 15 to 30 minutes until the fish flakes easily with a fork. The baking time will vary depending on the thickness of the fish fillets and whether or not the sauce is hot when you pour it on the fish (see Note).

NOTE

It's fine to make this sauce ahead of time, but don't pour it over the fish while it's still hot if you're not ready to bake the fish. Either wait until the sauce is cool to add it to the pan of fish you've refrigerated, or store the sauce separately and cover the fish with it when you are ready to bake it.

SERVING AND MENU IDEAS

This fish is good served on a bed of rice that will absorb all of the flavorful sauce, or with Roasted White or Sweet Potatoes (see page 29). Often, we garnish with chopped scallions and lime wedges and serve it with Coconut Rice (page 289) and Lime-Cilantro Slaw (page 252) or sautéed kale (see page 268).

Teriyaki Fish

Savory, sweet, and tangy, teriyaki sauce is perfect for fish, vegetables, and tofu. It's so easy to make that you'll wonder why you ever bought it in jars. (And, no mystery ingredients when you make it yourself.) You might want to make a double batch because refrigerated teriyaki sauce lasts almost indefinitely.

Yields about 1¼ cups sauce
Serves 4 to 6
Prep time: 10 to 15 minutes
Marinating time: 30 minutes
Baking time: 15 to 20 minutes

TERIYAKI SAUCE

½ cup soy sauce
½ cup dry sherry or sake
¼ cup rice vinegar
1 tablespoon peeled and grated fresh ginger
2 garlic cloves, pressed or minced
2 tablespoons brown sugar

2 pounds firm fish fillets

Combine the teriyaki sauce ingredients in a small, nonreactive saucepan and bring to a boil. Reduce the heat, and simmer for a minute, then set aside to cool.

While the sauce is cooling, rinse the fish and lay out the fillets in an oiled nonreactive baking pan large enough to hold the fillets in a single layer. Pour the cooled sauce over the fish through a strainer to remove the ginger and garlic. Refrigerate for 20 to 30 minutes to allow the fish to absorb flavor.

Preheat the oven to 375°F.

Bake the fish fillets in the sauce until the fish flakes easily with a fork, 15 to 20 minutes, depending on the thickness of the fillets.

VARIATIONS

- Grill the fish after marinating. This works best with thicker fillets. Baste occasionally with the marinade as the fish cooks.
- Replace the sherry in the teriyaki sauce with mirin and reduce the sugar to 1 to 2 teaspoons, to taste.
- Add some chili paste or chili oil to give the sauce a kick.
- Some dark sesame oil is also good.
- Cook shrimp quickly in the sauce.
- Replace the fish with tofu cubes or strips.

SERVING AND MENU IDEAS

Serve on a bed of rice or soba noodles, garnished with chopped scallions and a sprinkling of toasted sesame seeds. Add some Gingered Broccoli and Carrots (page 273) or Asian Slaw (page 253) and life is good . . .

Malaysian Fish

In Malaysia, this very tasty sauce is served on grilled whole fish and called *Ikan Percik*. At Moosewood, we bake the fish in the brownish gold sauce. The finished dish is pretty and tasty sprinkled with a chiffonade of fresh basil, cilantro, or mint.

Serves 5 or 6
Prep time: 20 minutes
Marinating time: 30 minutes
Baking time: 30 minutes

2 pounds firm fish fillets
½ cup minced onions
2 garlic cloves, minced or pressed
2 teaspoons peeled and grated fresh ginger
1 fresh hot pepper, minced
½ cup unsweetened coconut milk
¼ cup tamarind concentrate (see page 386)
1 teaspoon ground turmeric
1 teaspoon salt
a sprinkling of ground black pepper

Rinse the fish and lay it out in a lightly oiled baking pan large enough to hold the fillets in a single layer. Combine the onions, garlic, ginger, hot peppers, coconut milk, tamarind, turmeric, salt, and black pepper in a bowl. Spread the sauce evenly over the fish. Cover and refrigerate for 30 minutes.

Preheat the oven to 400°F.

Bake the fish fillets, uncovered, until the fish flakes easily with a fork. The baking time, generally 20 to 30 minutes, depends on the variety and thickness of the fish.

VARIATION

- To make the sauce to spread on grilled fish (or tofu), stir all of the ingredients in a wok or small skillet on medium-low heat until hot, thick, and fragrant.

SERVING AND MENU IDEAS

Serve on jasmine rice, brown rice, or Coconut Rice (page 289). Delicious with sides of Middle Eastern Carrot Salad with Mint (page 257) and Spinach Raita (page 312). Attractive and delicious topped with whole or chopped fresh cilantro, basil, and/or mint leaves. And because they taste so good with the sauce, top with bite-size slices or matchsticks of various crunchy and not crunchy vegetables and fruits, such as mango, carrots, cucumbers, snow peas, or mung sprouts.

Oven-poached Fish with Leeks and Wine

This dish has a rich and flavorful broth, so we like to serve it on rice or couscous to soak up the mellow leek, thyme, and wine flavors.

Farmers mound soil around the base of leeks to extend the length of the white part, and some of it gets between the layers as the leeks grow. We've tried different techniques for removing the grit, and we think the one described in the Guide (see page 379) is easiest and most foolproof.

Serves 4 to 6
Prep time: 25 minutes
Baking time: 15 to 30 minutes

3 medium leeks
2 tablespoons olive oil
1 teaspoon salt
¾ cup dry white wine
several sprigs of fresh thyme
2 pounds firm fish fillets
ground black pepper
2 tablespoons capers

Clean and chop the leeks (see page 379). You should have about 3 cups chopped. In a heavy skillet on high heat, sauté the leeks in the oil with the salt, stirring constantly for 3 or 4 minutes. Add the wine, stir well, cover, and bring to a simmer. Add the thyme sprigs, reduce the heat, cover, and simmer gently for 5 minutes. Uncover and remove from the heat.

Preheat the oven to 376°F. Oil a nonreactive baking pan large enough to hold the fish fillets in a single layer.

Rinse the fish fillets, place them in the prepared baking pan, and sprinkle them with salt and black pepper. Spoon the leeks (and wine with the sprigs of thyme) around and between the pieces of fish. Sprinkle the capers over the tops of the fillets. If you love the taste of thyme, lay a fresh sprig on each fillet. Cover and bake for 15 to 30 minutes, depending on the thickness of the fillets, until the fish flakes easily with a fork.

VARIATIONS
- If you'd rather use dried thyme, add ½ teaspoon to the sautéing leeks.
- After sprinkling the fillets with salt and pepper, spread some chopped fresh tomatoes over them and then sprinkle with the capers.

SERVING AND MENU IDEAS
Serve on rice topped with a dollop of Herbed Aioli (page 309) and with a side of Quick Sauteed Greens (page 268). Or, for a nice summery meal serve this fish with Dilled Potatoes Vinaigrette (page 277) and Chopped Broccoli Salad (page 251). Another time try it on Couscous (page 300) with Roasted Cauliflower (page 274) or Roasted Brussels Sprouts (page 275).

Fish Basilico

The secret to Moosewood's popular, flavorful bread-crumb toppings is that we make our own bread crumbs using hearty whole wheat bread. The coarser crumb adds great texture, stands up to assertive seasonings, and well, we think whole wheat just tastes better.

Serves 4 to 6
Prep time: 15 minutes
Baking time: 20 to 25 minutes

¼ cup olive oil
3 large garlic cloves, minced or pressed
1 teaspoon finely grated lemon zest
2 cups whole wheat bread crumbs (see page 373)
¼ cup chopped fresh basil
⅔ cup shredded Parmesan cheese
1 teaspoon salt
¼ teaspoon ground black pepper
2 pounds firm fish fillets
¼ cup fresh lemon juice

Preheat the oven to 350°F. Lightly oil a baking pan large enough to hold the fish fillets in a single layer.

Warm the oil in a large skillet on medium-high heat. Add the garlic and cook for just a minute until it sizzles. Immediately stir in the lemon zest and bread crumbs and stir to break up any lumps. Keep stirring until the crumbs are golden and crisp. Stir in the basil and continue to cook for 1 minute. Transfer the mixture to a bowl. Stir in the Parmesan, salt, and black pepper.

Place the fish, skin side down, in the prepared baking pan. Pour the lemon juice over the fillets and spread the bread-crumb topping evenly over the top of the fish. Bake, covered, for 10 minutes; uncover and continue to bake until the fish flakes easily with a fork, 10 to 15 minutes.

VARIATIONS

- Fish Nicosia—When you sauté the bread crumbs, add a pinch of cayenne, 2 teaspoons of ground cumin seeds, and 1 teaspoon of ground coriander seeds. When juicy, fresh tomatoes are in season, chop 2 tomatoes and spread over the fish before topping with the bread-crumb mixture. Omit the Parmesan. Bake as directed.

SERVING AND MENU IDEAS

Serve with Greek Lemony Potatoes (page 276) or mashed potatoes (see page 278). Take a look at Simple Side Vegetables Simply Embellished (page 264) to get inspiration for interesting side dishes.

Asian-style Fish in Parchment

Don't be intimidated by these parchment packages, they're really quite easy to make. A burst of aromatic steam is released as each packet is opened. And inside, the fish and vegetables have been perfectly cooked, bathed in the savory sauce. And there's no nasty baking pan to clean!

This recipe can easily be increased to serve as many as you wish. And, of course, use your favorite fish.

Serves 2
Prep time: 20 minutes
Baking time: 20 to 25 minutes

2 firm fish fillets or steaks (about 6-ounces each)
2 tablespoons soy sauce
2 teaspoons peeled and grated fresh ginger
2 teaspoons dark sesame oil
2 tablespoons rice vinegar or fresh lemon juice
1 cup thinly sliced carrots
1 cup seeded and thinly sliced bell peppers
    (preferably red or yellow)
2 tablespoons sliced scallions

Preheat the oven to 425°F. Rinse the fish and set aside to drain. In a small bowl, whisk together the soy sauce, ginger, sesame oil, and vinegar or lemon juice. Prepare the carrots, bell peppers, and scallions.

Make two packets, one for each fillet. To make each packet: Fold a 12 × 15-inch sheet of parchment paper in half to form a 12 × 7½-inch rectangle. Trim off the corners on the side opposite the fold and then open the parchment. Near the center of the parchment next to the fold, layer half of the carrots and bell peppers and 1 fillet, drizzle it with half of the sauce, and sprinkle on 1 tablespoon of the scallions. Fold the empty half of the sheet of parchment over the fish. Starting at one side of the fold and working your way around the open edges, curl up and crimp the parchment to form a sealed half-moon–shaped packet.

Place the packets on a baking sheet and bake for about 20 minutes, or a few minutes longer for thick fillets. The parchment paper will become puffed and golden brown. Since it is difficult (if not impossible) to open and then reseal the parchment, it's best to err on the side of longer baking to ensure that the fish is cooked through. Because the parchment locks in the cooking juices, the fish and vegetables will remain moist and flavorful.

Once the fish is baked, it is best to serve it immediately. The packets contain a lot of juices, so put them right on large dinner plates and let each person open their own at the table.

VARIATIONS
Vary the vegetables in the packet: thinly sliced bok choy or kale is good, as are a few sliced fresh shiitakes. Some sliced water chestnuts could be added for crunch and a little chili paste or oil added for heat. But keep the amount of vegetables to about 1 cup, so the packet isn't overfilled, making it difficult to fold.

SERVING AND MENU IDEAS
Serve with soba or udon noodles or rice, with sides of sautéed fresh shiitakes and Asian Greens (page 269) or Asian Slaw (page 253). Other possibilities include Sugar Snap Peas and Radishes with Orange and Mustard (page 264), Green Beans with Ginger (page 265), Sesame Spinach (page 264).

Fish "Tostadas"

This dish is a wonderful jumble of crispy tortilla chips, savory bites of fish, spicy and juicy salsa, and mellow avocado. Eating it is a messy, crumbly business. We think of it as a casual dining experience filled with taste and texture sensations—just have plenty of napkins on hand.

For years at the restaurant, we served fish tostadas the usual way, with the toppings piled on a whole fried tortilla. But we noticed that sometimes the plates were coming to the dishwasher with the tortilla still on them, uneaten. We realized that some of our customers weren't comfortable picking up the tortilla and eating it out of hand, but also had trouble cutting through all those toppings to the tortilla. So, we tried it this way, with large tortilla chips for scooping up the filling or munching separately. Problem solved; clean plates.

Serves 4 to 6
Time: about 1 hour

1½ pounds firm fish fillets
¼ cup fresh lemon juice
¼ cup olive oil or vegetable oil
2 garlic cloves, minced or pressed
½ teaspoon salt
¼ teaspoon ground black pepper

eight 6-inch corn tortillas
½ cup olive oil or vegetable oil

¼ cup cornmeal
1 tablespoon ground coriander seeds
1 tablespoon ground cumin seeds
2 teaspoons dried thyme or 1 tablespoon chopped fresh thyme
1 teaspoon salt
⅛ teaspoon cayenne
⅛ teaspoon ground black pepper

shredded lettuce
salsa
avocados, peeled, pitted, and cubed

Cut each fish fillet into bite-size pieces. Place the fish pieces in a large, shallow bowl. Whisk together the lemon juice, olive oil, garlic, salt, and black pepper. Pour the marinade over the fish and refrigerate for at least 20 minutes or up to several hours.

While the fish marinates, prepare the tortilla chips. Cut each tortilla into quarters. Heat the oil in a large, heavy skillet on medium-high heat. Fry several quarters at a time, using metal tongs to carefully flip them over, until golden brown and crisp on both sides. Transfer to paper towels to drain, then sprinkle with salt. Reserve the oil in the pan for frying the fish.

On a platter or baking sheet, combine the cornmeal, coriander, cumin, thyme, salt, cayenne, and black pepper. Dredge each piece of fish on all sides in the seasoned cornmeal. Reheat the oil in the frying pan. Add the fish in batches and fry for about 3 minutes on each side, or until the fish is done and the coating is crisp. Add more oil if needed.

Construct each "tostada" by laying the tortilla chips around the perimeter of a dinner plate and then in the middle, make a bed of shredded lettuce and top it with several pieces of fish, some salsa, and avocado cubes.

SERVING AND MENU IDEAS
We like to serve these tostadas on a bed of Spanish Rice (page 287). Use Lime-Cilantro Slaw (page 252) instead of the shredded lettuce—the tastes and textures are harmonious and completely delicious. A good prepared salsa is fine to use, but if you have the time, try our easy, fresh Mango Salsa (page 315) or Our Favorite Tomato-Cilantro Salsa (page 314) or Smooth Hot Sauce (page 320). And then, a dollop of Chipotle Aioli (see page 259) or Mango Aioli (page 309) on top is perfect! Fresh corn on the cob is also perfect.

Creamy Seafood Stew

If you're yearning for that "old Cape Cod" feeling, this is the dish for you. We like this stew with both fish and shellfish. See what fish you find at the market that's fresh and reasonably priced and not on the "don't buy" list. We call for scallops or shrimp, but could you add some clams or mussels in the shell? Sure, if you like them—clean them and add to simmering stew just before serving.

Lovely looking with colorful vegetables.

Yields 10 cups
Time: 50 minutes

2 tablespoons olive oil or butter
2 cups chopped onions
1 teaspoon salt
1 cup diced carrots
1 cup diced celery
1 medium zucchini or yellow squash, diced
    (about 2 cups)
1 bell pepper, seeded and diced (about 1½ cups)
    (any color)
4 cups diced white potatoes
one 16-ounce bottle or can clam juice
    (sometimes called broth)
1 cup water
½ cup dry white wine or sherry (optional)
½ teaspoon ground black pepper
1 tablespoon chopped fresh dill
1½ pounds firm fish fillets, cut into bite-size pieces
4 ounces cream cheese
1 cup milk
12 ounces scallops, or peeled and deveined shrimp

Warm the oil or butter in a covered soup pot on low heat. Add the onions and salt and cook for 5 minutes. Add the carrots and celery, increase the heat to medium, and cook, covered, for 5 minutes. Add the zucchini and bell pepper and cook, covered, for 5 minutes. Add the potatoes, clam juice, water, and wine, if using, stir well, and bring to a simmer. Simmer, covered for 10 minutes. Add the black pepper, dill, and fish and simmer, covered, for 5 minutes.

While the fish cooks, in a blender, whirl the cream cheese, milk, and about a cup of hot broth until smooth. Stir this mixture into the stew and bring it back to a simmer. Add the scallops or shrimp just before serving and simmer for 2 or 3 minutes.

SERVING AND MENU IDEAS
Bread and salad are all you need.

Chopped Broccoli Salad

Lime-Cilantro Slaw

Asian Slaw

Confetti Kale Slaw

Cucumbers Vinaigrette

Tomato, Cucumber, and Artichoke Heart Salad

Middle Eastern Carrot Salad with Mint

Moroccan Carrot Salad with Currants

Beet Salad

Sweet Potato Salad with Chipotle Aioli

Chopped Broccoli Salad

A novel addition to the coleslaw tradition—bad poetry, good salad.

Yields 4½ cups
Serves 6 to 8
Prep time: 25 minutes
Sitting time: 30 minutes

1 pound broccoli (about 4 cups chopped)
½ cup mayonnaise
2 teaspoons pure maple syrup or other sweetener
4 teaspoons apple cider vinegar
¼ teaspoon salt
⅛ teaspoon ground black pepper
¼ cup currants
1 cup seeded and finely chopped bell peppers (any color)
2 tablespoons sliced scallions or snipped fresh chives (optional)

Slice off the thick bottoms of the broccoli and peel away any tough skins from the stems. Finely chop the florets and small stem shoots. Cut larger stems lengthwise into halves or quarters and then thinly slice.

In a medium serving bowl, whisk together the mayonnaise, sweetener, vinegar, salt, and black pepper. Fold in the broccoli, currants, bell peppers, and scallions, if using. Set aside to allow the flavors to meld for at least 30 minutes.

Our Favorite Slaws

We are amazed looking through all of our cookbooks at just how many slaw recipes we have. We make slaw often because we love its fresh, tart crunch with so many different dishes. Here are two that we turn to time and time again. Both of these are cabbage slaws with a clean, crisp flavor. They'll help you fall in love with cabbage, if you aren't already.

The truth is this: often, a very simple slaw is the basic best. Keep it simple and it won't compete, but will be a refreshing break from the more complex flavors of a main dish. That said, notice all our variations. Sometimes you want a complex slaw for a simple main dish or sandwich or snack.

To slice the cabbage, use a good sharp knife to cut the head of cabbage in half. Remove the core and place a half-head flat side down on the cutting board. Cut across the grain into ⅛- to ¼-inch slices. Then cut across the pile of sliced cabbage into pieces about 2 inches long. Or, you can make quick work of it with a mandoline.

We make simple slaws with other vegetables, and fruits, too: broccoli, kale, celery, fennel, celeriac, jicama, daikon, turnips, parsnips, beets, firm pears, apples, to name the most usual.

LIME-CILANTRO SLAW

This cabbage slaw is tart and refreshing with lime and delicious in its simplicity. We love the way this slaw looks made with both green and red cabbage and the bright green scallions and cilantro. One large, juicy lime yields about 3 tablespoons of juice; if your limes are small or not so succulent, you'll need two.

Cabbage varies in its sweetness so be sure to taste your slaw and add more sugar as needed.

Yields 4 cups (shrinks down as it sits and wilts)
Serves 4 to 6
Time: 15 minutes

4 cups thinly sliced cabbage (green, red, or both)
  (see headnote)
½ cup chopped scallions
¼ cup chopped fresh cilantro

DRESSING
1 tablespoon olive oil or vegetable oil
finely grated zest of 1 lime
3 tablespoons fresh lime juice
1 teaspoon sugar
½ teaspoon salt

In a bowl, combine the cabbage, scallions, and cilantro. In a separate small bowl, whisk the dressing ingredients. Add the dressing to the cabbage and stir well. Add more sugar and/or salt to taste.

Serve right away or refrigerate. Serve chilled or at room temperature.

VARIATIONS
- Make it hot: Add minced fresh hot peppers, or cayenne or red pepper flakes.
- If you don't like cilantro, leave it out; if you love it, pile it in there.
- Use white or apple cider vinegar instead of lime juice.
- Add finely chopped bell peppers and/or grated carrots.
- Use finely chopped red onions in place of scallions.
- Add garlic, ground cumin seeds.
- Add shredded jicama.
- If you like creamy coleslaw, add some mayonnaise or sour cream.

ASIAN SLAW

If your carrots are quite sweet, you may want to reduce the brown sugar, and if your cabbage is not-so-sweet you might want to add more.

Yields 3 cups
Serves 4
Time: 20 minutes

3 cups thinly sliced cabbage (see headnote)
1 cup shredded carrots
⅓ cup chopped scallions

DRESSING

2 tablespoons vegetable oil
1 teaspoon dark sesame oil
2 tablespoons vinegar (rice, white, or apple cider)
1 teaspoon peeled and grated fresh ginger
1 tablespoon soy sauce
2 teaspoons brown sugar
dash of chili oil or Chinese Chili Paste with Garlic (see page 374) (optional)

Combine the cabbage, carrots, and scallions in a bowl. In a separate bowl, whisk together all of the dressing ingredients. Pour the dressing over the vegetables and toss well.

Serve right away or refrigerate. Serve chilled or at room temperature.

VARIATIONS

- Add about ½ cup of julienned bell peppers.
- In place of or in addition to carrots, add shredded firm pears, Asian pears, or apples.
- Add shredded daikon.
- Wilt the slaw (just a bit): Heat the oil to just below smoking and pour it over the vegetables, then stir in the rest of the dressing ingredients.

SERVING AND MENU IDEAS

Lime-Cilantro Slaw is a perfect foil for bean-y, cheese-y Mexican dishes, such as Spinach-Cheese Burritos (page 198) and Bean Tostadas (see page 281) or Fish "Tostadas" (page 246). It's also good with Spicy Caribbean Fish (page 240) and Chilaquiles Casserole (page 161), or for that matter, with sandwiches, potato salad, fries, roasted or grilled vegetables—the list goes on and on.

Asian slaw is the perfect accompaniment to Asian-style Stuffed Portobellos (page 183), Teriyaki Fish (page 241), Sichuan Noodles (page 97) and Country-style Soft Tofu (page 206).

Confetti Kale Slaw

A colorful, fresh-flavored slaw. Sweet and tangy. We call it confetti because that's what it looks like: kind of fluffy.

Slice the kale into thin pieces for the most tender slaw. Several of the vegetables are described as shredded, but by that sometimes we mean shredded with a hand grater and sometimes shredded with a sharp knife. It could get confusing, so we give you specific instructions for prepping the vegetables.

Yields 8 cups
Serves 6 to 8
Time: 30 minutes

DRESSING
½ cup orange juice
¼ cup fresh lemon juice
1 tablespoon apple cider vinegar
¼ cup olive oil
¼ teaspoon salt
¼ teaspoon ground black pepper

1 large firm apple, shredded (1 to 2 cups)
1 cup shredded green or red cabbage
1 cup shredded carrots
1 cup minced celery
¼ cup minced scallions
3 cups shredded kale, packed

To make the dressing: Whisk together the orange juice, lemon juice, vinegar, olive oil, salt, and black pepper in a large bowl.

Prepare the apple and vegetables and place them in the bowl as you go: Peel the apple or don't, and shred it on the large-holed side of a hand grater. To prevent the apples from discoloring, toss well with the dressing. Thinly slice the cabbage and then cut across the slices about every inch. Peel the carrots and shred on the large-holed side of a hand grater. Mince the celery. Mince the scallions.

To shred the kale: Rinse the kale leaves and shake off excess water. Strip the leaves from the large stems and pile on a chopping board. Gather the kale into a compact mass and thinly slice it. Then cut down across the slices, chopping the kale into 1- to 2-inch pieces. Go after those larger pieces of kale that got away from you when you were slicing it. Add the shredded kale to the bowl and toss well.

Delicious served right away, but the sweetness intensifies as it sits. This slaw will keep in the refrigerator for 2 or 3 days.

SERVING AND MENU IDEAS
This slaw is excellent beside a main dish that's rich and cheesy or bland and smooth, such as Macaroni and Cheese with Broccoli (page 217), a cheese omelet, baked potatoes with sour cream, or strudel. It's also good with something spicy, and makes a cheese sandwich something special—put the slaw in the sandwich or serve as a side dish.

Cucumbers Vinaigrette

Especially in summer, when cucumbers are at their best, this is our go-to side dish for many of our richer entrées. By varying the herbs, you vary the ethnicity. It can accompany a host of main dishes, and it's a snap to make. We serve it alongside creamy, cheesy strudels, casseroles, tarts, and turnovers.

Yields 2 cups
Serves 4
Time: 15 minutes

2 medium cucumbers, peeled and seeded if the
    seeds are large
¼ cup apple cider vinegar
1 tablespoon sugar
½ teaspoon salt
2 teaspoons chopped fresh dill, basil, or oregano
    or 1 teaspoon chopped fresh tarragon, mint, or
    thyme
a sprinkling of ground black pepper
2 tablespoons finely sliced scallions or snipped
    fresh chives

Peel the cucumbers, cut in half lengthwise, scoop out the seeds if they are large, and slice into ⅛- to ¼-inch-thick rounds or half-moons, or dice. In a serving bowl, whisk together the vinegar, sugar, salt, herbs, and black pepper. Fold in the cucumbers and scallions. Serve chilled or at room temperature.

Tomato, Cucumber, and Artichoke Heart Salad

This delicious salad complements almost anything. Dill and mint are our favorite flavors for it, but it's good with one or the other, or a different herb, or no herbs at all.

Yields about 6 cups
Serves 6
Time: 20 minutes

¼ cup olive oil
2 tablespoons vinegar (apple cider or red wine)
1 garlic clove, pressed or minced
1 tablespoon chopped fresh dill
2 tablespoons chopped fresh mint
one 14-ounce can artichoke hearts in brine
1 or 2 cucumbers
2 cups fresh tomato wedges or chunks
1 or 2 scallions, thinly sliced
salt
ground black pepper

In a serving bowl, whisk together the olive oil, vinegar, garlic, dill, and mint. Drain the artichoke hearts and cut each into quarters. Toss with the dressing in the bowl.

As you prepare the vegetables, add them to the bowl. Peel the cucumber, cut in half lengthwise, scoop out the seeds if they are large, and slice. Cut the tomatoes into wedges, or if the tomatoes are large, chunks. Slice the scallions. Toss well and season with salt and black pepper.

Serve chilled or at room temperature.

SERVING AND MENU IDEAS

This salad is very versatile, at Moosewood we would serve it next to Zucchini-Feta Casserole (page 164), Tofu-Spinach Borekas (page 192), Mushroom Frittata (page 151), Caramelized Onion Pie (page 155), Tabouli Salad (page 106), and Fritada de Espinaca (page 153) to name but a few.

Middle Eastern Carrot Salad with Mint

This is one of Moosewood's absolute favorite side salads. It is light, healthful, and delightfully refreshing. And it's pretty: bright glistening orange carrots flecked with mint and parsley. We'd be hard-pressed to think of many dishes that this salad does not complement.

Yields 2½ cups
Serves 4 to 6
Time: 15 minutes

3 cups shredded carrots (1 pound)
3 tablespoons fresh lemon juice
1 tablespoon agave syrup, sugar, pure maple syrup, or honey
2 tablespoons olive oil
½ teaspoon ground coriander seeds
2 tablespoons minced fresh mint leaves
¼ teaspoon salt
chopped fresh parsley and/or dill (optional)

In a bowl, stir together the carrots, lemon juice, sweetener, oil, coriander, mint, and salt. You can serve the salad right away, but the flavors develop if it sits for at least 15 minutes, and the next day it's even more delicious.

Serve sprinkled with parsley and/or dill, if you like. Serve at room temperature or chilled. Refrigerated, the salad keeps very well for 2 to 3 days.

SERVING AND MENU IDEAS
Perfect with North African, Greek, Middle Eastern, Tex-Mex, Indian, Central American, North American, and Southeast Asian foods. This carrot salad is a lovely contrast to a smooth soup, a savory casserole, quiche or strudel, or any spicy food.

Moroccan Carrot Salad with Currants

Flecked with currants and aromatic with cinnamon and orange, this pretty salad is light and refreshing and extremely easy to make. The carrots can be coarsely grated, as we've done at Moosewood, but you can also cut them into very thin matchsticks for a crunchy, pretty alternative.

Yields 2½ cups
Serves 4 to 6
Time: 20 minutes

3 cups shredded carrots (1 pound)
⅓ cup dried currants
1 tablespoon olive oil
¼ teaspoon salt
1 orange
1 tablespoon fresh lemon juice
½ teaspoon ground cinnamon
1 tablespoon agave syrup, sugar, pure maple syrup, or honey
ground black pepper
chopped fresh parsley or scallions (optional)

Stir together the carrots, currants, oil, and salt. Zest and juice the orange, and stir 1½ teaspoons of the zest and all of the juice (⅓ to ½ cup) into the carrots. Add the lemon juice, cinnamon, and sweetener. Season with black pepper and stir well. Set aside for at least 15 minutes for the flavors to develop.

The salad can be served at room temperature or chilled, topped with parsley and/or scallions, if you like. This carrot salad keeps in the refrigerator for 2 or 3 days.

SERVING AND MENU IDEAS
This sweet, fruity, crunchy salad is nice with something very savory, rich, or spicy. It's good with Country Moussaka (page 166), Zucchini-Feta Casserole (page 164), Mushroom Piroshki (page 156), and Spanish-style Tortilla (page 152), to name just a few.

Beet Salad

Try a combination of colorful beets in this simple, gorgeous salad—perhaps an heirloom variety like Chioggia or golden and red beets.

If your beets still have their green leaves, sauté them in olive oil with a little garlic and serve them as a side dish, or use young, tender beet leaves raw in a salad.

Yields 2 cups
Time: about 1 hour

1 pound beets (about 4 medium)
2 tablespoons minced scallions
2 teaspoons chopped fresh dill
2 to 3 tablespoons apple cider vinegar or fresh
    lemon juice
1 teaspoon honey or sugar (more or less to taste)
olive oil (optional)
salt
ground black pepper

Cut off the stems of the beets to about an inch, scrub them, and place them in a pot with water to cover. Bring to a boil, cover, reduce the heat, and simmer until easily pierced with a sharp knife. The cooking time will vary depending on the variety, size, and how long the beets have been stored. We suggest you start checking to see if they are done after 30 minutes.

Drain the beets and rinse with cold water until cool enough to handle. Slip off and discard the skins and stems, and slice the beets. In a bowl, toss the sliced beets with the rest of the ingredients. Some beets are very sweet and no honey or sugar is needed, so taste before you add any sweetener. When the beets are starchy, we add a drizzle of olive oil.

Serve chilled or at room temperature.

VARIATION
- Sometimes we add peeled, seeded, and sliced cucumbers to this salad.

SERVING AND MENU IDEAS
For a main dish, serve the beets on a bed of arugula, spinach, or field greens, topped with feta or goat cheese and sprinkled with toasted walnuts or Spiced Nuts (page 21). Beet Salad is also good next to many dishes, serve it with Mushroom Piroshki (page 156), Kasha and Mushroom Pilaf (page 295), and Rumbledethumps (page 163).

Sweet Potato Salad with Chipotle Aioli

We've always made potato salads, both classic and ones that push the potato salad envelope. As potato salads go, this is certainly not the same old, same old. Different and delicious, the spicy, tangy dressing nicely balances the sweetness of the potatoes. It's a welcome addition to picnics and parties.

Yields 6 cups
Serves 4 to 6
Time: 40 minutes

5 cups peeled and diced sweet potatoes
  (about 2 pounds)
1 cup diced celery
1 cup seeded and diced red bell peppers
¼ cup minced scallions or red onions (optional)

Chipotle Aioli
1 or 2 garlic cloves, minced or pressed
1 tablespoon olive oil
½ cup mayonnaise
1 tablespoon chipotles in adobo sauce
1 tablespoon fresh lime or lemon juice

In a soup pot, cover the potatoes with cool salted water. Bring to a boil on high heat, reduce to a vigorous simmer, and cook, covered, until tender, about 5 minutes. (The size of the cubes will determine the time they take to cook.) Drain the sweet potatoes, and spread them out to cool.

Put the celery, bell peppers, and scallions in a serving bowl. When the potatoes have cooled a bit, add them to the bowl.

To make the Chipotle Aioli: Cook the garlic in the olive oil in a microwave oven or on the stovetop, just until it sizzles. Place it in a food processor with the mayonnaise, chipotles in adobo sauce, and lime juice and whirl until well combined. Add more chipotles to taste.

Toss the vegetables with the chipotle aioli. Add salt to taste.

Serve at room temperature or chilled.

SERVING AND MENU IDEAS
This multipurpose salad is really good with Southwestern Bean Burgers (page 93), Moosewood's Classic Tofu Burgers (page 89), Fish Cakes (page 237), and Pecan-crusted Fish (page 233), to name a few. For a delectable light summer dinner or lunch, serve with Lime-Cilantro Slaw (page 252) and pan-fried or baked tofu (see page 202)

SIDES

Seasoned Artichokes

Moosewood cook Eliana Parra, who loves artichokes and grew up in Chile where they grow abundantly, has fond memories of whiling away the time sitting around the table with family and friends, chatting and pulling off the leaves of giant globe artichokes, dipping them in olive oil and lemon juice, and nibbling the tender ends. There is something relaxing and social about eating artichokes—you just can't rush it.

At Moosewood, we most often serve artichokes with a little cup of lemon butter, but artichokes also taste great with garlicky herbed aioli, olive oil and vinegar or lemon juice, or almost any favorite salad dressing.

To eat an artichoke: Remove the leaves one by one, dip the fleshy pad at the bottom of the leaf in sauce and scrape the tender flesh off with your teeth. Discard the rest of the leaf. When you get down to the heart of the artichoke, you'll encounter the choke where the tips of interior leaves are small and spiny and where there are tough fibers that no one eats. Scoop out this choke with a spoon and discard it to reveal the true heart of the artichoke, the thick little saucer-shaped base of the leaves that gives you a few bites of concentrated artichoke flavor after all that nibbling at the leaves.

Artichokes come in different sizes and some cook quickly and others take a long time to get tender. We suggest a range of cooking times, because there is no way to tell until they start cooking..

Yields 4 artichokes
Prep time: 10 to 15 minutes
Cooking time: 30 to 60 minutes

2 or 3 garlic cloves, coarsely chopped or smashed
2 or 3 bay leaves
1 teaspoon whole black peppercorns
1 teaspoon salt
juice of half a lemon or 2 tablespoons red wine
    vinegar or apple cider vinegar
1 teaspoon fennel seeds (optional)
4 artichokes

Put a large pot of water with the garlic, bay leaves, peppercorns, salt, lemon juice or vinegar, and fennel seeds, if using, on the stove top to boil.

Trim the artichokes: With a sharp knife, cut off the top inch or so where the leaves are tightly bunched. Cut off the artichoke stems evenly so that they will sit upright in a pot. For a "groomed" look, use kitchen scissors to snip off the sharp tips of each leaf, although once cooked they won't be so sharp. Some artichokes have leaves with rounded tips; they may be called "thornless." Rinse the prepped artichokes.

Place the artichokes into the pot of water as you trim them. Artichokes float and bob around if they don't fit snugly in the pot. If your pot is large, put a colander on top to hold them down in the water. When the water boils, reduce the heat and simmer until the outer leaves are easy to pull off and the bottom of the stem can be easily pierced with a knife. This takes between 30 and 60 minutes depending on the size and quality of the artichokes.

Drain the artichokes and serve them hot.

VARIATIONS

- You can also cut cooked artichokes in half, from the stem to the top, scoop out the choke and marinate them with olive oil, red wine vinegar, or lemon juice and some minced fresh herbs such as dill, tarragon, or parsley.

SERVING AND MENU IDEAS

Serve with lemon butter or with extra-virgin olive oil and lemon. Or make Herbed Aioli (page 309) to dip the leaves in.

Seasoned Artichokes complement lots of dishes. Try them with Quinoa-stuffed Roasted Peppers (page 173), Moroccan Couscous Salad (page 107), or Beans and Greens (page 148).

Simple Side Vegetables Simply Embellished

When the harvest is in and you're looking for something a little different to do with all the fresh vegetables, even though you thought you would never tire of them simply steamed, look here for inspiration. With the addition of one or two extra flavors you have a new and interesting dish. Here are a few examples of what you can do.

PEAS AND ESCAROLE

Sauté shredded escarole in oil or butter until wilted but still bright green. Toss with cooked sweet peas seasoned with salt and pepper.

SESAME SPINACH

Toss steamed spinach with dark sesame oil, soy sauce, and toasted sesame seeds.

ASPARAGUS WITH PINE NUTS AND BALSAMIC VINEGAR

Top steamed asparagus spears with melted butter and balsamic vinegar and sprinkle with toasted pine nuts.

SUGAR SNAP PEAS AND RADISHES WITH ORANGE AND MUSTARD

Stir together orange juice, orange zest, Dijon mustard, and salt. Sauté sugar snap peas or snow peas and sliced radishes in oil for a minute, add some water, cover, and cook until just tender. Drain and add the orange and mustard, and maybe some minced red onions or scallions. Season with salt and pepper.

KALE OR COLLARDS WITH CRANBERRIES

Sauté chopped kale or collards in olive oil with garlic until it wilts. Add some water and chopped dried cranberries, cover, and cook until tender. Season with salt.

LEMONY SUMMER SQUASH

Sauté shredded zucchini, yellow squash, or other summer squash with garlic in olive oil for just a few minutes, until tender. Stir in fresh lemon juice, lemon zest, and season with salt and pepper. Stir in some sour cream or grated Parmesan.

PEPERONATA

Slice at least two colors of bell peppers lengthwise. Slice onions lengthwise, about half the amount of the peppers. Sauté the onions in olive oil for 5 minutes, Add the peppers and some garlic and sauté for about 10 minutes, or until the peppers are soft. Season with salt and pepper. You can add some chopped tomatoes during the last 5 minutes of cooking.

CURRIED CORN

Sauté some onions and add curry powder and fresh corn kernels cut off the cob. Heat up with unsweetened coconut milk and fresh lime juice, and season with salt and pepper.

CORN ON THE COB TOPPINGS

- Tex-Mex: On the hot corn, spread mayonnaise and drizzle with fresh lime juice and hot pepper sauce, top with grated Parmesan.
- Chipotle Mayonnaise: Stir 2 tablespoons of fresh lime juice and 2 tablespoons of minced chipotles in adobo sauce into about a cup of mayonnaise.
- Red Pepper Butter Sauce (page 321)
- Ginger-Mint Butter: Add peeled and grated fresh ginger, minced fresh chives, and minced fresh mint leaves to melted butter.

CARROT COINS AND ORANGE

Steam or boil carrot rounds until tender. Drain and stir in some butter or olive oil and orange marmalade or pomegranate jelly. Maybe add some chopped chives or scallions. Season with salt.

GREEN BEANS WITH GINGER

Stir soy sauce, peeled and grated ginger, and dark sesame oil into cooked green beans.

SPINACH AND MUSHROOMS

Sauté garlic, minced red onions, and chopped mushrooms in olive oil until the mushrooms are tender. Pour directly from the pan onto a bowl of baby spinach. Toss until the spinach has wilted. Season with salt.

ROASTED BRUSSELS SPROUTS WITH PECANS

Stir together Dijon mustard, lemon juice, olive oil, minced red onions, and salt. Toss Roasted Brussels Sprouts (page 275) with toasted pecans or walnuts and the dressing.

WINTER SQUASH AND CRANBERRIES

Toss roasted cubes of winter squash (page 110) with diced raw celery and apples and a little Cranberry Sauce (page 311). Season with salt and pepper.

POTATOES WITH LEMON AND CAPERS

Toss boiled potato cubes with olive oil, fresh lemon juice, lemon zest, and whole or chopped capers. Season with salt and pepper.

BEETS WITH HORSERADISH SOUR CREAM

Toss boiled or roasted beets with a dressing made of sour cream, a little olive oil, horseradish, vinegar, minced scallions, and salt and pepper.

Not So Plain Green Vegetables

It takes almost no time to make a simply dressed green vegetable that will really enhance a meal. Serve hot or at room temperature as a side vegetable, or chilled as a salad.

All three dressings work on all three of the green vegetables, and each can be used on vegetables of other colors as well, such as cauliflower and carrots. The dressings can all be made in about 5 minutes while the vegetable cooks.

Because lemon juice and vinegar dull the color of green vegetables, we use only finely grated lemon peel, which doesn't have that effect, in the dressing. Sometimes, we serve lemon wedges on the side or sprinkle on some vinegar at the last minute. In dishes this simple, use the finest-quality oil: fruity extra-virgin olive oil or delicious walnut oil.

GREEN BEANS WITH LEMON ZEST DRESSING

An intensely flavored dressing with zing that works on all sorts of cooked vegetables—really delicious on sautéed mushrooms (use less oil) and on steamed cauliflower.

Serves 4
Time: 15 minutes

1 pound green beans, stem ends trimmed

LEMON ZEST DRESSING
3 tablespoons extra-virgin olive oil
1 garlic clove, minced
½ teaspoon Dijon mustard
¼ teaspoon ground black pepper
¼ teaspoon salt
1 tablespoon finely grated lemon zest
rounded ¼ teaspoon ground fennel seeds

Steam or boil the green beans until tender. Meanwhile, in a small bowl, stir together the oil, garlic, mustard, black pepper, salt, lemon zest, and fennel.

Toss the hot beans with the dressing, coating all evenly. Add more salt and black pepper to taste. Serve hot, at room temperature, or cold.

VARIATION
• Replace the ground fennel with 2 teaspoons of minced fresh tarragon or dill.

BROCCOLI WITH WALNUT DRESSING

Walnut oil has a distinctive flavor; this dressing can transform plain steamed vegetables from mundane to magnificent.

Serves 4
Time: 15 minutes

1 pound broccoli

WALNUT DRESSING

3 tablespoons walnut oil or extra-virgin olive oil
½ teaspoon Dijon mustard
¼ teaspoon salt
¼ teaspoon ground black pepper
¼ cup finely chopped toasted walnuts

2 teaspoons balsamic vinegar

Cut the broccoli into bite-size spears. Steam or boil the broccoli until tender.

Meanwhile, in a small bowl, stir together the oil, Dijon mustard, salt, and black pepper. Add the walnuts.

When the broccoli is tender place it in a serving bowl. Pour the walnut dressing over the broccoli and toss. Add more salt and black pepper to taste. Serve hot, at room temperature, or cold. Just before serving, sprinkle with balsamic vinegar.

ASPARAGUS DRESSED WITH GARLIC AND OIL

When we say garlic, we mean it! If you don't love lots of garlic, use less.

Serves 4
Time: 15 minutes

1 pound asparagus, tough ends snapped off
3 tablespoons extra-virgin olive oil
6 garlic cloves, minced
salt
ground black pepper
lemon wedges

Steam or boil the asparagus spears until tender. Warm the oil in a skillet on medium heat, add the garlic, and cook for a minute or two, just until golden. Remove the garlic from the oil and set aside.

Place the asparagus on a serving platter. Drizzle the garlic-infused olive oil over the asparagus. Sprinkle the cooked garlic in a strip across the middle of the asparagus spears. Sprinkle with salt and pepper. Place lemon wedges around the edges. Serve hot, at room temperature, or cold.

SERVING AND MENU IDEAS

The green beans are great beside Quick Uncooked Tomato Sauce on Pasta (page 225). For an elegant brunch serve the asparagus next to an omelet or with Spanish-style Tortilla (page 152). The broccoli is an excellent side for a grain salad, such as Rice Salad with Herbs and Vegetables (page 101). Pair any of them with Moosewood's Classic Tofu Burgers (page 89) and Vegan Mashed Potatoes and Sweet Potatoes (page 278) with Mushroom Gravy (page 327).

Quick Sautéed Greens

We think we crave the taste of greens because our bodies crave the nutrients. Dark leafy greens have health-giving concentrations of vitamins and minerals. In general, the darker the green, the more nutritious, but it's a good idea to eat a variety of greens because they each have a different nutritional profile.

Each type of greens is flavorful and appealing in its own way. Chard is mild, sweet, and earthy, and rainbow and ruby chard are quite colorful and beautiful. Kale very often appears on those top ten superfoods lists because it is a powerhouse of nutrition. We cut out and discard tough kale stems; kale leaves range from smooth to crinkly, from delicate to substantial. Collards are also extremely nutritious with a grassy flavor. Broccoli rabe has a bitter sharpness that may be an acquired taste, but once acquired, may be craved. We use the stems, leaves, and florets of broccoli rabe. Sometimes when the flavor is especially sharp we blanch broccoli rabe before sautéing.

The cooking time varies depending on the type of greens and how young, fresh, and tender they are. Do a taste test to decide how long to cook. Most are done in 5 or 6 minutes.

Serves 4 to 6
Time: 15 minutes

about 8 cups chopped chard, kale, collards, or
    broccoli rabe
2 tablespoons olive oil (regular or extra-virgin)
4 garlic cloves, minced
a pinch or two red pepper flakes (optional)
½ teaspoon salt
ground black pepper

Cut the stems of chard crosswise into ½-inch pieces and coarsely chop the leaves. Remove the tough stems of kale or collards and discard; then coarsely chop the leaves. Cut bunches of broccoli rabe crosswise, separating out the lower stems to cook first.

In a large skillet on medium-high heat, warm the oil. Add the garlic and red pepper flakes and sauté briefly, for a minute or two. Add the stems of chard or broccoli rabe and sauté for a minute or two. Add as many chopped leaves as you can comfortably stir in the skillet. As the leaves wilt, add more. Sauté until the greens are limp and tender but still bright green. Season with the salt and a sprinkling of black pepper. Serve immediately.

VARIATION
*   For a little extra spark and some Southern style, add a splash of vinegar just before serving. Vinegar will dull the bright green color a bit in time.

SERVING AND MENU SUGGESTIONS
Quick Sautéed Greens is a good, quick side dish for a cheesy rich entrée, such as Macaroni and Cheese with Broccoli (page 217) or Pasta al Cavalfiore (page 216) or for Fish Cakes (page 237) or Caribbean Red Beans (page 139). Make a Southern garden vegetable dinner: serve Quick Sautéed Greens with Sweet Potato Salad with Chipotle Aioli (page 259) or Roasted White and Sweet Potatoes with Chipotle Aioli (page 29), Lemony Summer Squash (page 264), sliced tomatoes, and Cornbread (see page 283 and 284).

Asian Greens

Here is a quick and tasty treatment for green leafy vegetables such as bok choy, Chinese cabbage, and spinach. While you're chopping them, the fresh raw greens look like a massive amount, but when cooked, they wilt and reduce to just a small mass. The wealth of powerful nutrients in greens is maintained or even improved when cooked.

Serves 4 to 6
Time: 10 to 15 minutes

1 pound baby bok choy (about 12 small heads)
    OR
1½ pounds Chinese cabbage (½ large head)
    (8 cups chopped)
    OR
2 pounds spinach (about 20 cups)

2 tablespoons soy sauce
1 tablespoon dark sesame oil
2 tablespoons dry sherry, Chinese rice wine, or
    water
2 to 3 tablespoons vegetable oil
6 garlic cloves, minced
2 teaspoons peeled and grated fresh ginger
    (optional)
1 tablespoon toasted sesame seeds (optional)

Prepare all of the ingredients and have them near at hand before you turn on the heat and begin to stir-fry.

Rinse the greens well to remove any grit. Cut each head of baby bok choy lengthwise into quarters, leaving the leaf stems attached at the root end. Cut Chinese cabbage once or twice lengthwise and then crosswise into ½-inch strips. For large spinach leaves: remove tough stems and coarsely chop. For baby spinach: do nothing.

In a small bowl, stir together the soy sauce, sesame oil, and sherry wine or water and set aside.

In a large skillet or wok on medium-high heat, warm the vegetable oil. Add the garlic and ginger, if using, and sizzle, stirring constantly for about 10 seconds, then add the greens. Toss to coat with oil and stir-fry until the greens are wilted and bright green. If the greens don't all fit in at first, as the greens in the pan wilt, add more until they're all in. (The root ends of baby bok choy remain crisp-tender.) Pour in the soy sauce mixture and stir well to coat. Sprinkle with toasted sesame seeds, if you wish. Serve immediately.

SERVING AND MENU IDEAS
Serve Asian Greens alongside Country-style Soft Tofu (page 206) and brown rice. Or try it as a quick, last-minute side dish for Asian-style Stuffed Portobellos (page 183) or Teriyaki Fish (page 241) or Asian Rice Salad (page 102).

Roasted Vegetables

Roasted vegetables of all sorts are very popular with Moosewood customers. They are also very versatile. The combination of vegetables chosen, the sauces used to dress them, and what they are served with all can be varied. Try vegetables roasted with Mediterranean Dressing on a bed of polenta (page 296) or orzo, and top with grated Parmesan or Pecorino Romano cheese. Serve vegetables roasted with Moroccan Spice Dressing (see page 272) on lemony couscous (see page 300), topped with crumbled feta or chopped almonds. Vegetables roasted with Savory Hoisin Dressing are perfect on a bed of rice or stir-fried greens, topped with baked tofu (see page 202).

Perfectly roasted vegetables are speckled brown and beginning to crisp on the outside, succulent and juicy on the inside, and sweeter than if they had been cooked some other way.

Whatever vegetables you choose, cut 10 to 12 cups worth. That may sound like a lot, but some of the volume will be reduced as they roast. We sometimes separate the harder vegetables, such as potatoes and carrots, and start them roasting first, or even blanch them briefly first. But most of the time we just toss everything together. So have fun!

Serves 6
Prep time: 25 minutes
Roasting time: 35 to 45 minutes

1 large onion
2 medium potatoes
1 large sweet potato
2 bell peppers (different colors are nice)
2 to 3 cups mushrooms (10 ounces)
1 medium zucchini

MEDITERRANEAN DRESSING

⅓ cup olive oil
¼ cup red wine vinegar or balsamic vinegar
4 garlic cloves, minced or pressed
1 teaspoon salt
1 teaspoon ground fennel seeds
¼ teaspoon ground black pepper
1 tablespoon minced fresh rosemary

SAVORY HOISIN DRESSING

¼ cup vegetable oil
¼ cup soy sauce
¼ cup rice vinegar or 3 tablespoons apple cider vinegar
3 tablespoons hoisin sauce
1 tablespoon peeled and grated fresh ginger

MOROCCAN SPICE DRESSING
⅓ cup olive oil

¼ cup fresh lemon juice

2 teaspoons sweet paprika

1 teaspoon ground turmeric

1 teaspoon cumin seeds (whole or ground)

1 teaspoon salt

¼ teaspoon cayenne

3 garlic cloves, minced or pressed

½ teaspoon ground cinnamon

Preheat the oven to 425°F. Lightly oil two rimmed baking sheets.

Peel the onion and cut it in half lengthwise and then into thick crescent-shaped slices. Cut the potatoes in half lengthwise and then into ½-inch-thick slices. Peel the sweet potato and slice the same way. Cut the bell peppers in half lengthwise, stem and seed them, and cut into either chunks or thick slices. Small mushrooms may be left whole, cut larger ones in half. Slice the zucchini in half lengthwise and then cut into chunks.

Prepare one of the dressings by whisking together the ingredients.

In a large bowl, toss the prepared vegetables with the dressing of your choice. Spread out the vegetables in a single layer on the prepared baking sheets. Roast for about 15 minutes. Stir and return to the oven to finish roasting. Check again in about 15 minutes; the vegetables may be done then or may require more time. When all of the vegetables are tender, remove them from the oven and pile them on a serving platter.

VARIATIONS
*   Other vegetables good for roasting include carrots, cauliflower, winter squash, asparagus, green beans, Brussels sprouts, summer squash, hot peppers, corn—almost anything except leafy vegetables.

SERVING AND MENU IDEAS
Serve roasted vegetables as an entrée as suggested in the headnote. Serve on a bed of greens for a salad plate. Or, serve as a side with, say, mac and cheese, fish, or a burger.

Gingered Broccoli and Carrots

At Moosewood, we pair this colorful and healthful side with Sichuan Noodles (page 97) and Moosewood's Best Baked and Pan-fried Tofu (page 202) for one of our most popular salad plates.

To retain the bright green of the broccoli, don't dress the vegetables with the marinade until about half an hour before serving. You can vary the amount of broccoli and carrots you use, or use other vegetables, such as snow peas, red bell peppers, and asparagus. Just be sure to have a total of about 6 cups of prepped vegetables.

Serves 4
Prep time: 20 minutes

2 or 3 broccoli crowns (about 4 cups of spears)
2 medium carrots (about 2 cups sliced)

GINGER MARINADE
1 teaspoon peeled and grated fresh ginger
2 tablespoons vegetable oil
1 teaspoon dark sesame oil (optional)
1 garlic clove, minced or pressed
2 tablespoons rice vinegar
2 teaspoons soy sauce

Cut the broccoli into spears. We recommend using broccoli crowns, but you can also use a head of broccoli, just peel the large stems. Peel the carrots and cut them on the diagonal into slices about ¼ inch thick. Steam the vegetables until crisp-tender and spread them out on large plate or a platter to cool.

In a small bowl, whisk together the marinade ingredients and pour over the vegetables. Mix well. If you have time, it's nice to let the vegetables marinate for about 20 minutes before serving. Serve at room temperature or chilled.

SERVING AND MENU IDEAS
This is a bright vegetable side dish for Tofukabobs with Peanut Sauce (page 32), Moosewood's Classic Tofu Burgers (page 89), Asian-style Stuffed Portobellos (page 183), or Teriyaki Fish (page 241). To round out a meal, serve it with a sandwich such as Deviled Egg Salad (page 78) or Ira's Lunch Pita (page 73).

Roasted Cauliflower

Blasting cauliflower in a hot oven intensifies its natural sweetness and brings out an irresistible flavor. It's kind of remarkable—even people who say they don't like cauliflower can't get enough of it. It's like French fries: you think maybe you'll have a couple, and then you keep going back.

We just love roasted cauliflower: plain; herbed or spiced; curried; with onions and red bell peppers; with lots of garlic, a little garlic, or no garlic; dressed with lemon juice or balsamic vinegar; topped with Parmesan. While the oven is hot, roast some sweet potatoes—yum, a wonderful flavor combination.

Serves 6
Prep time: 15 minutes
Roasting time: 30 minutes

1 large head of cauliflower, cut into 2-inch-wide
    florets (6 to 10 cups)
2 to 3 tablespoons olive oil
salt
ground black pepper

Preheat the oven to 425°F. Lightly oil a rimmed baking sheet.

In a large bowl, toss the cauliflower with 2 to 3 tablespoons of oil, depending upon how large your head of cauliflower is. Spread the florets out in a single layer on the prepared baking sheet. Sprinkle with salt and pepper.

Roast, stirring occasionally, for 25 to 35 minutes until tender and golden-brown. Stir after 15 minutes. (When you stir the cauliflower, take it out of the oven and close the door so that the oven temperature will stay high.) The cauliflower is done when it's lightly browned and tender, but not falling apart.

Serve warm or at room temperature.

VARIATIONS
- Before roasting, toss with:
  —pressed, minced, crushed, or whole garlic cloves
  —sliced onions
  —sliced red bell peppers
  —minced fresh rosemary or thyme
  —dried oregano
  —ground coriander, cinnamon, and turmeric
  —turmeric and peeled and grated fresh ginger
  —curry powder or garam masala or berbere spice mix
  —ground caraway
- Sprinkle roasted cauliflower with:
  —shredded Parmesan or crumbled feta cheese
  —chopped fresh chives
  —capers
  —hot sauce

SERVING AND MENU IDEAS
Cauliflower roasted with coriander, cinnamon, and turmeric is delicious with Tofu-Spinach Borekas (page 192), Indian Stuffed Eggplant (page 179), or Fritada de Espinaca (page 153). Roast cauliflower with rosemary and serve with Fish Basilico (page 244), Aegean Strudel (page 190), or Italian Polenta-stuffed Peppers (page 181).

Roasted Brussels Sprouts

"Brussels sprouts—yuk!" That's how some of us, and many of the people around us, used to respond before we started roasting them. Now, "yuk" has become "yum." So try them with your favorite picky eater—no promises, but it's worth a try! "Brussels sprouts—yum!"

Our hands-down favorite "dressing" for Roasted Brussels Sprouts is horseradish butter.

Serves 4 to 6
Prep time: 10 minutes
Roasting time: 15 to 20 minutes

1 pound Brussels sprouts
2 tablespoons olive oil
¼ teaspoon salt
⅛ teaspoon ground black pepper

2 tablespoons butter or olive oil
Plus one of the following:
1 generous tablespoon prepared horseradish, more to taste
1 garlic clove, pressed
1 tablespoon minced fresh chives,
1 tablespoon minced fresh dill,
2 tablespoons chopped toasted pecans or almonds

Preheat the oven to 400°F. Lightly oil a rimmed baking sheet.

Rinse the Brussels sprouts and cut off the bottoms. Discard any dry or discolored outer leaves and cut each sprout in half lengthwise. Toss with the oil, salt, and black pepper. Arrange, cut side down, on the prepared baking sheet. Roast until just tender, 15 to 20 minutes.

While the sprouts are roasting, heat the butter or olive oil and stir in the horseradish (or other ingredient).

Pour the horseradish (or other) butter or oil over the roasted Brussels sprouts and serve.

VARIATIONS
If you use only oil (no butter), roasted Brussels sprouts are a good both hot and at room temperature.
- Sometimes at Moosewood we roast chunks of carrots along with the Brussels sprouts and toss it all with horseradish butter or oil—very pretty.
- Sometimes at home when we don't want to turn on the oven, we cook the Brussels sprouts on the stovetop in a large skillet, adding a splash of water as needed to cook them to perfection, and then we dress them with flavored butter or oil.

Greek Lemony Potatoes

Aromatic and infused with the flavor of lemons, these are scrumptious. They travel well and are good at room temperature, making them a nice choice for a dish-to-pass.

Any white or yellow-fleshed potato works. Peel or don't peel. Red-skinned potatoes taste great and hold their shape cooked this way, but take longer to cook.

Sometimes at home, when we take Greek potatoes out of the oven, we stir a chiffonade of spinach into them and top them with crumbled feta and call it supper. Yummm.

Serves 6
Prep time: 15 minutes
Baking time: 1 hour to 1½ hours

6 cups cubed potatoes (peeled or not, 1 to 1½-inch chunks)
1 teaspoon finely grated lemon zest
½ cup fresh lemon juice
2 tablespoons olive oil
2 garlic cloves, minced or pressed
1 teaspoon dried oregano
1½ cups hot water
1 teaspoon salt
¼ teaspoon ground black pepper

Preheat the oven to 425°F. In a 13 × 9 × 2-inch nonreactive baking pan (ceramic, glass, stainless steel, or enameled), stir the potatoes with the lemon zest, lemon juice, oil, garlic, oregano, hot water, salt, and black pepper. Bake until the water has evaporated and the potatoes are tender. The length of time in the oven depends on the variety of potato, the pan you're using, and how closely packed the potatoes are: usually a little more than an hour. After about 30 minutes in the oven, stir every 10 minutes or so. Add more water if the potatoes begin to stick before they're done. Season with more salt and black pepper to taste.

SERVING AND MENU IDEAS
Serve next to Falafel Burgers (page 91), Flounder Florentine (page 239), or Fish Basilico (page 244). Or make a sunny Mediterranean-combo plate by serving these great lemony potatoes with Spanakopita Bites (page 26) and Seasoned Artichokes (page 263).

Dilled Potatoes Vinaigrette

These simply dressed potatoes are an all-time favorite, especially during hot, sultry summer days, crisp autumn evenings, and cozy winter nights . . . So, there you have it. Eat them anytime.

Red-skinned potatoes are especially attractive, but any kind of potato will work just fine. Dress the potatoes while they're hot; that way they are infused with the flavor of the dressing. These are delicious served hot, at room temperature, or chilled.

Serves 6
Time: 25 minutes

5 cups cubed white potatoes
½ cup olive oil
¼ cup red wine vinegar
1½ teaspoons salt
¼ teaspoon ground black pepper
1 cup diced celery
½ cup finely chopped scallions or red onions, or snipped fresh chives
¼ cup minced fresh dill

In a soup pot, cover the potatoes with cool salted water and add the salt. Bring to a boil on high heat, reduce to a vigorous simmer, and cook, covered, until the potatoes are tender, about 7 minutes.

While the potatoes cook, in a serving bowl, whisk together the oil, vinegar, salt, and black pepper. Place the celery and scallions or red onions in the bowl.

When the potatoes are done, drain well. Add them to the serving bowl and toss with the oil and vinegar while still hot. Stir in the dill and season with more salt and black pepper to taste.

VARIATION
- Mix it up with various fresh herbs: some combination of minced fresh tarragon, dill, basil, cilantro.

SERVING AND MENU IDEAS
A good side for fish or Barbecued Tofu Pita (see page 82). Nice on a bed of greens with hard-boiled eggs and tomato wedges. Serve beside Moosewood's Classic Tofu Burgers (page 89). Serve as one of several salads, such as Chopped Broccoli Salad (page 251), Moroccan Carrot Salad with Currants (page 257) and Beet Salad (page 258) for a sumptuous picnic.

Vegan Mashed Potatoes and Sweet Potatoes

We associate mashed potatoes, whether made from white or sweet potatoes, with family holiday meals, and there are many people, both adults and kids, who consider them their most favorite comfort food. At Moosewood, mashed potatoes are an extremely popular side dish. We make them creamy, with plenty of butter and milk or cream, and vegan, healthful and flavorful enough on their own that you don't need to slather them with butter. Since vegan mashed potatoes are a little less common that's what we give you here.

VEGAN MASHED WHITE POTATOES

Any variety of potato will work, but we recommend a yellow, buttery-flavored variety, such as Yukon Gold, or ask a farmer at your local farmers' market for a recommendation. We predict that you won't need any embellishment for these mashed potatoes, but there are vegan substitutes for butter, cream cheese, and sour cream in case you want them to be richer.

Keep in mind that leftover mashed potatoes will give you a head start on many creamy, puréed soups. The potato cooking water can also be used to provide flavor in many soups.

Serves 6
Time: 20 minutes

8 cups water
1 teaspoon salt
6 garlic cloves
2 bay leaves
6 cups peeled and chopped potatoes
1 to 2 tablespoons extra-virgin olive oil
salt
ground black pepper

Put the water, salt, garlic cloves, and bay leaves into a covered pot. Bring to a boil on high heat. While the water heats, prep the potatoes, adding them to the water as you chop them. When the water boils, lower the heat and simmer for 10 to 12 minutes until the potatoes are tender.

Place a colander over a large bowl and drain the potatoes, collecting the cooking water in the bowl. Remove and discard the bay leaves. Using a hand held potato masher or an electric mixer, mash the potatoes and garlic with the olive oil and enough of the reserved potato water (probably about a cup) to achieve the consistency you like. Season with salt and black pepper. Serve immediately or reheat just before serving.

VARIATION

- Use soy milk instead of reserved potato cooking water to mash with the potatoes. Soy milk has a slightly nutty flavor, the potato cooking water adds more pure potato flavor.

VEGAN MASHED SWEET POTATOES

In 1992, the Center for Science in the Public Interest ranked sweet potatoes higher in nutritional value than any other vegetable, but that's only one more reason to love them.

Sometimes we want plain mashed sweet potatoes, but they're also really delicious with a little coconut milk and lime, and with maple syrup and adobo sauce. We couldn't decide which is our favorite, so we leave it up to you to decide.

Serves 6
Time: 25 minutes

6 cups peeled and chopped sweet potatoes
    (about 2½ pounds whole)
8 cups water
2 bay leaves
1 teaspoon salt
3 tablespoons unsweetened coconut milk
1 tablespoon fresh lime juice
    or 3 tablespoons pure maple syrup and
    ½ teaspoon adobo sauce from chipotle peppers
    in adobo, more to taste
ground black pepper

While you peel and chop the sweet potatoes, put the water, bay leaves, and salt on to boil in a covered pot. As you cut the potatoes, add them to the water. When the water boils, reduce the heat and simmer for 10 to 12 minutes until the potatoes are tender.

Drain the potatoes in a colander. Remove and discard the bay leaves. Using a handheld potato masher or an electric mixer, mash the potatoes with either the coconut milk and lime juice or with the maple syrup and adobo sauce. Season with salt and black pepper. Serve immediately or reheat just before serving.

NOTE

Many of us didn't believe our fellow cook, Lisa Wichman, when she suggested using an electric mixer to beat the potatoes, rather than the tried-and-true potato masher, but it works and the potatoes are creamier. Less elbow grease is required, but then, mashing old style is good for the pecs.

SERVING AND MENU IDEAS

Mushroom Gravy (page 327) and Caramelized Onion Gravy (page 325) are perfect pooled on mashed potatoes. Add Moosewood's Classic Tofu Burgers (page 89) made into a loaf and you have Blue Plate Special. For a Dixie Blue Plate Special, serve mashed sweet potatoes with Dixie Tofu-Pecan Loaf (page 209). For a satisfying fish dinner, pair Pecan-crusted Fish (page 233) with mashed potatoes and Sweet and Sour Red Cabbage Two Ways (page 280) or try Spicy Chipotle Cornmeal-crusted Fish (page 235) with mashed sweet potatoes and Quick Sautéed Greens (page 268).

Sweet and Sour Red Cabbage Two Ways

Many of us who have worked at Moosewood over the years have family roots in Eastern Europe. This colorful side dish really evokes the old world for us, and is a wonderful companion to Mushroom Piroshki (page 156), strudels, and even just mashed potatoes.

In the restaurant, we make sweet and sour cabbage the slow way, bringing out the full sweetness of onions and cabbage and adding other flavors to make it go best with whatever it will be served beside. At home, we often want sweet and sour cabbage fast and easy, and not only because we're in a hurry to eat. If we're having something that has complex flavors, we may want the clean, simple flavor of plain cabbage, sweet and sour. Also, we like the cabbage with a little "resistance," al dente, if you will. So, to give you our favorite, we have to give you two recipes.

SWEET AND SOUR RED CABBAGE

Serves 4 to 8
Prep time: 25 minutes
Simmering time: 30 minutes to 1 hour

2 tablespoons vegetable oil
1 large onion, peeled, halved, and thinly sliced into
    half-moons (about 2 cups)
1 teaspoon salt
8 cups thinly sliced red cabbage (a 2-pound head)
¾ cup apple juice or cider
¼ teaspoon ground black pepper
1 teaspoon whole caraway seeds
⅓ cup currants or raisins
¼ cup apple cider vinegar
1 tablespoon brown sugar or other sweetener of
    choice
1 tablespoon chopped fresh dill

Warm the oil in a covered pot larger than 2-quart. Add the onions and salt and cook on low heat until the onions are soft, about 10 minutes, stirring occasionally. Stir in the cabbage, cover, and cook, stirring occasionally, for 10 minutes.

Add the apple juice, black pepper, caraway, currants, vinegar, and sugar and cook, covered, on low heat for about 30 minutes, stirring occasionally. At this point the cabbage and onions should be greatly reduced in volume and very flavorful. They become sweeter the longer they cook, so if you have the time let them cook for 15 to 30 minutes more. Stir in the fresh dill, and add more vinegar and sugar to taste.

FAST AND EASY SIMPLE SWEET AND SOUR RED CABBAGE

Serves 4 to 8
Prep time: 10 minutes
Simmering time: 15 minutes

8 cups thinly sliced red cabbage (a 2-pound head)
2 tablespoons vegetable or olive oil
1 teaspoon salt
¾ cup water
⅓ cup apple cider vinegar or white vinegar
3 tablespoons brown sugar

Slice the cabbage halves across the leaves, then cut the slices into 1- to 2-inch pieces.

Warm the oil in a larger than 2-quart pot on medium-high heat. Add the cabbage and salt and sauté for about 5 minutes, or until the cabbage begins to soften and cook down in volume; stir very frequently, if not constantly. Add the water, reduce the heat to low, cover, and simmer for 15 minutes, stirring occasionally, mainly to check that there's enough liquid to steam the cabbage and prevent sticking.

Stir in the vinegar and brown sugar. At this point, the cabbage will be tender, with some "tooth." Eat right away, or keep warm, covered, on low heat until you're ready to eat.

SERVING AND MENU IDEAS
First and foremost, serve some next to our wonderful Mushroom Piroshki (page 156). It's also delicious with Caramelized Onion Pie (page 155), Mushroom-Tofu-Pecan Stuffed Vegetables (page 175), and Kasha and Mushroom Pilaf (page 295).

Refried Beans

Refried beans can be used in oh so many ways: in quesadillas or burritos, in Chilaquiles Casserole (page 161), in a pita with some tomato salsa and cheese, or in our favorite way at the restaurant—as a component of bean tostadas, a frequent and always popular dinner entrée at Moosewood. For our tostada, we pile refried beans on crisp corn tortillas, with Lime-Cilantro Slaw (page 252) or with shredded lettuce, then we add some Smooth Hot Sauce (page 320) and/or Avocado Salsa (page 314) or Simple Smooth Guacamole (page 35), some grated cheese, and maybe sour cream or chopped olives. Sometimes we serve the tostadas with a side of Spanish Rice (page 287), or more often, we put the tostada on a bed of rice to keep the whole yummy pile of stuff from sliding off the plate as the waiters hurry them to the customers.

Yields about 4 cups
Time: 30 minutes (with already cooked beans)

2 tablespoons vegetable oil
2 cups diced onions
2 garlic cloves, minced or pressed
½ teaspoon salt
1½ teaspoons ground toasted cumin seeds
4 cups drained cooked pinto beans, liquid reserved (three 15-ounce cans) (to cook dried beans, see page 372)
1 tablespoon soy sauce
¼ teaspoon ground black pepper

In a large, covered skillet on low heat, warm the oil. Add the onions, garlic, and salt and cook, stirring occasionally, until the onions are very soft, about 15 minutes. Stir in the cumin and cook for 2 minutes. Add the beans and mash with a hand-held potato masher. Add the reserved liquid, a tablespoonful at a time, to achieve the consistency you like. Stir in the soy sauce and black pepper and cook, covered, on low heat until the beans are hot. Add more salt or soy sauce and more black pepper to taste.

VARIATIONS

- We like refried black beans, too. Sometimes we add a little finely grated orange zest and/or orange juice to them.

Lentil Dhal

Dhal (also *dal* or *dahl*) can be made with red or brown lentils, green or yellow split peas, chickpeas, or beans. At Moosewood we usually make dhal with brown or green lentils.

Flavorful, aromatic dhal makes a wonderful accompaniment to vegetable curries. Serve with brown basmati or jasmine rice and a little chutney and raita or yogurt for a greater dinner.

Yields about 5 cups
Serves 6 to 8
Time: 45 to 55 minutes (depending on the lentils)

1½ cups dried green or brown lentils
4½ cups water
1 teaspoon ground turmeric
½ teaspoon salt

2 tablespoons vegetable oil
2 cups diced onions
2 garlic cloves, minced or pressed
½ teaspoon salt
1 tablespoon peeled and grated fresh ginger
1 teaspoon ground turmeric
1 teaspoon ground cumin seeds
¼ teaspoon cayenne or red pepper flakes
2 tablespoons fresh lemon juice
¾ to 1 cup unsweetened coconut milk

Place the lentils, water, turmeric, and salt in a large saucepan. Bring to a boil, reduce the heat, and simmer, covered, until tender, 40 to 50 minutes. Drain and return to the pan.

While the lentils are cooking, warm the oil in a skillet on medium-low heat. Add the onions, garlic, and salt, and cook for a couple of minutes, stirring frequently. Add the ginger, turmeric, cumin, and cayenne, and cook, covered, until the onions are translucent and start to brown, about 10 minutes.

Stir the onions and spices, lemon juice, and ¾ cup of the coconut milk into the drained lentils and heat thoroughly. If the dhal is too stiff, add a little more coconut milk.

SERVING AND MENU IDEAS

Serve with Summer Vegetable Curry (page 123), Winter Curry (page 124), or Indian Stuffed Eggplant (page 179). Leftover Lentil Dhal is good stirred into Mulligatawny (page 61).

Moosewood Restaurant's House Cornbread

Here is a big batch of dense, moist, slightly sweet cornbread. We don't make it every day at the restaurant, but often. When customers see it on the menu, usually with some stew or bean dish or under Mexican vegetables, many ask for a piece or two à la carte, so we always make extra. And, if there are any leftovers, we freeze them to use later to make stuffing or cornmeal crumbs for coating fish.

We use whole-grain organic cornmeal and whole wheat pastry flour, but if regular whole wheat flour is what you have on hand, that works well, too. Some of us prefer not using any white flour and eliminate it in this recipe by substituting 2 cups of whole wheat pastry flour. Others of us like to substitute coarsely ground polenta for half of the cornmeal. We can't help messing with a good thing.

Yields one 13 × 9 × 2-inch pan cornbread
Prep time: 15 minutes
Baking time: 25 minutes

1½ cups cornmeal
1 cup whole wheat pastry flour or whole wheat flour
1 cup unbleached white all-purpose flour
1½ tablespoons baking powder
1 teaspoon baking soda
1 teaspoon salt
3 large eggs
⅓ cup pure maple syrup or packed brown sugar
2 cups buttermilk
⅔ cup milk
⅓ cup melted butter or vegetable oil

Preheat the oven to 425°F. Butter a 13 × 9 × 2-inch baking dish.

In a large bowl, sift together the cornmeal, whole wheat and white flours, baking powder, baking soda, and salt. In a separate bowl, beat the eggs, add the maple syrup, buttermilk, milk, and melted butter and whisk together.

Make a well in the dry ingredients and stir in the wet ingredients just until blended. Do not overmix. Spread the batter evenly in the prepared pan and bake for 25 minutes, or until firm and lightly brown on top.

Vegan Cornbread

When we're cooking at Moosewood, we're lucky that we often have the flexibility to be creative and try a new technique or experiment with new ingredients and ideas. We've experimented a lot while making cornbread that's vegan, and so far, this simple recipe is our favorite and most delicious you-won't-believe-it's-vegan cornbread recipe. It's sweet, but not too sweet, with a moist and tender texture.

Some of us like to whip together a batch of cornbread and bake it while we're getting ready for work. It's easy to do and the results—well, warm, fragrant cornbread for breakfast: what could be better than that?

Yields one 9-inch round or 8-inch square
   cornbread
Prep time: 15 minutes
Baking time: 20 minutes

1 cup unbleached white all-purpose flour
1 cup cornmeal
2 teaspoons baking powder
½ teaspoon baking soda
½ teaspoon salt
¼ cup vegetable oil
¼ cup packed brown sugar
1¼ cups plain soy milk
1 tablespoon apple cider vinegar

Preheat the oven to 400°F. Lightly oil a 9-inch pie plate or round baking pan or an 8-inch square baking dish.

Sift the flour, cornmeal, baking powder, baking soda, and salt into a mixing bowl. In a separate bowl, whisk together the oil, brown sugar, and soy milk.

As soon as you mix the wet and dry ingredients, the leavening starts working, so don't delay getting the batter into the oven. Stir the wet ingredients into the dry ingredients just until mixed. Add the vinegar and stir until well mixed. Pour the batter into the prepared pan and bake until golden and a knife inserted in the middle of the cornbread comes out clean, about 20 minutes.

VARIATIONS

- You can substitute whole wheat pastry flour for the all-purpose white flour.
- Just before adding the vinegar to the batter, stir in some finely diced scallions, seeded and diced red bell peppers, and/or corn kernels; up to a half cup each. This cornbread might take a little longer to bake.

Spanish Rice

Annatto Rice

Coconut Rice

Sesame Jeweled Rice

Black Rice Pilaf

Red Rice Pilaf

Wild Rice Pilaf

Bulghur Pilaf

Kasha and Mushroom Pilaf

Polenta, Cheesy and Vegan

Risotto Milanese

Couscous

Spanish Rice

Using just a few ingredients, humble brown rice can be transformed into a highly seasoned companion for Mexican, Latin American, Caribbean, Creole, and Cajun dishes. Or it can be served as a main dish by embellishing the cooked rice with toppings such as avocado cubes, shredded Monterey jack cheese, salsa, and lime wedges.

Yields 4 cups
Time: about 1 hour

2 tablespoons olive oil
½ cup finely chopped onions
2 garlic cloves, minced or pressed
½ teaspoon minced fresh hot peppers or a
    generous pinch of cayenne
½ teaspoon whole cumin seeds
1½ cups brown rice, rinsed and drained
½ teaspoon salt
3 cups water

EXTRAS
½ cup chopped Spanish olives
3 tablespoons chopped fresh cilantro
1 cup diced fresh tomatoes
½ cup finely chopped scallions

In a saucepan with a tight-fitting lid on medium heat, warm the oil. Add the onions, garlic, hot peppers, and cumin and sauté for 5 minutes. Add the rice, salt, and water, stir well, and bring to a boil. Reduce the heat to very low and simmer, covered, for about 45 minutes, or until the water has been absorbed and the rice is tender. Stir in any or all of the extras.

VARIATION
• Substitute ½ cup of tomato purée for ½ cup of the water.

SERVING AND MENU IDEAS
Serve with Black Bean–Sweet Potato Burritos (page 195), Two Quesadillas (page 196), Spinach-Cheese Burritos (page 198), Southwestern Bean Burgers (page 93), or Spicy Caribbean Fish (page 240).

Annatto Rice

We still think it's magical the way annatto (achiote) seeds change the color of oil to a lovely sunset orange. Some of us make annatto oil at every opportunity, just to see it happen. You can make extra oil and keep it in your refrigerator; it will keep for several weeks.

Yields 6 cups
Serves 6
Time: about 1 hour

2 tablespoon vegetable oil or olive oil
1 teaspoon annatto seeds (see page 371)
2 cups chopped onions
1 teaspoon salt
2 cups brown rice, rinsed and drained
3 cups water

In a 2-quart saucepan on low heat, warm the oil and annatto seeds, swirling occasionally, until the oil becomes a golden orange color. Strain the oil through a sieve to remove the seeds. Discard the seeds and return the strained oil to the pan.

Add the onions and salt and cook, covered, on medium-low heat, stirring frequently, until the onions are soft but not browned, about 10 minutes. Add the rice and water to the pan and stir well. Cover and bring to a boil, then reduce the heat to low and simmer until the rice is tender, about 45 minutes. Add salt and pepper to taste.

SERVING AND MENU IDEAS
Serve with Cuban Black Beans (page 137) or Caribbean Black-eyed Peas (page 138). Serve as a bed under Spinach-Cheese Burritos (page 198), Black Bean-Sweet Potato Burritos (page 195), or Caribbean Stew (page 125).

Coconut Rice

Rice is so versatile. When you add a few extra ingredients while it cooks, its depth and flavor can enhance the simplest of dishes. We think you'll love the fragrance of this rice—there is nothing is quite like the aroma of coconut.

Yields 6 cups
Serves 6
Time: about 1 hour

2 cups brown rice, rinsed and drained
2 teaspoons vegetable oil or olive oil
1 teaspoon ground turmeric
½ teaspoon salt
2½ cups water
1 cup unsweetened coconut milk

In a saucepan on medium-high heat, stir together the rice, oil, turmeric, and salt for a minute. Add the water and coconut milk and bring to a boil. Reduce the heat to low and simmer, covered, until the liquid has been absorbed and the rice is tender, about 45 minutes.

VARIATION
• If you're in a hurry or prefer it, you can make coconut rice with white rice: reduce the coconut milk to ¾ cup and simmer until the liquid has been absorbed, about 15 minutes.

SERVING AND MENU IDEAS
Serve this rice with Caribbean Red Beans (page 139), Summer Vegetable Curry (page 123), or Curried Squash Roti (page 187). Or have some with Thai Baked Tofu (page 205).

Sesame Jeweled Rice

This pretty side dish is a standby accompaniment to many of the Asian-inspired dishes we serve. Brown rice is studded with colorful diced vegetables and toasted sesame seeds, and dark sesame oil adds flavor and fragrance. If you love fried rice, try this healthful, not-fried alternative.

Most of the prep happens while the rice cooks. Leftovers can be brightened up by adding a few more peas and scallions.

Yields 6 cups
Serves 6 to 8
Time: about 1 hour

3 teaspoons dark sesame oil
1½ cups brown rice, rinsed and drained
3 cups water
¾ cup finely diced carrots
½ cup seeded and finely diced red bell peppers
⅔ cup minced scallions
2 tablespoons sesame seeds
1 cup frozen green peas
1 tablespoon soy sauce

In a 2-quart saucepan with a tight-fitting lid on low heat, warm 1 teaspoon of the oil, add the rice, and stir so that the grains are coated with the oil. Add the water, cover, and bring to a boil. Reduce the heat to low.

While the rice simmers, prepare the carrots, bell peppers, and scallions. Toast the sesame seeds in a single layer on a dry pan in a toaster oven for 2 or 3 minutes, or toast them in a dry skillet on the stovetop until fragrant and beginning to brown.

When the rice has been simmering for 25 minutes, spread the carrots on top of the cooking rice and continue to simmer, covered. When the carrots are al dente, after about 10 minutes, spread the bell peppers and frozen peas on top of the carrots, cover, and continue to cook until the rice is tender and the water has been absorbed, about 10 minutes. Remove from the heat, add the scallions, sesame seeds, 2 teaspoons of sesame oil, and the soy sauce, and stir well. Cover and let the flavors meld for a few minutes before serving. Add more soy sauce to taste.

SERVING AND MENU IDEAS
Serve this lovely rice with Asian-style Stuffed Portobellos (page 183), Teriyaki Fish (page 241), Asian-style Fish in Parchment (page 245), or some of Moosewood's Best Baked and Pan-fried Tofu (page 202) with a side of Asian Greens (page 269) or Asian Slaw (page 253). It makes a simple meal beside scrambled eggs or an omelet.

Black Rice Pilaf

"Thai black rice," "purple sticky rice," and "Chinese Forbidden Rice" are all names for the rice we first discovered in rice pudding in a Thai restaurant. The brown and black, multicolored grains of raw rice cook into a purple-black pilaf with a sweet aroma and slightly sticky texture.

While cooking, the slices of ginger will float to the top of the rice, making it easy to remove them before stirring in the veggies.

Yields 4 cups
Serves 4 to 6
Time: 1 hour

1 cup brown rice, preferably short grain
½ cup Thai black rice
1 tablespoon vegetable oil
4 slices fresh ginger
½ teaspoon salt
2¼ cups water

½ cup seeded and diced red bell peppers
½ cup sliced scallions
1 tablespoon soy sauce
1 to 2 tablespoons toasted sesame seeds (optional)

Rinse the two varieties of rice in a fine-mesh strainer under cool running water and set aside to drain. Warm the oil in a saucepan with a tight-fitting lid on medium-high heat. Add the rice and ginger and sauté for a minute, stirring to coat the grains of rice with the oil. Add the salt and water, stir well, cover the pan, and bring to a boil. Reduce the heat to low and simmer, covered, until the water has been absorbed and the rice is tender, about 45 minutes.

When the rice is done, remove the ginger and stir in the bell peppers, scallions, and soy sauce, and the sesame seeds, if using. Let the rice sit, covered, for at least 5 minutes, then serve.

SERVING AND MENU IDEAS

Serve with Moosewood's Best Baked and Pan-fried Tofu (page 202) and Asian Greens (page 269) or Gingered Broccoli and Carrots (page 273). It's also good with Teriyaki Fish (page 241) or Asian-style Fish in Parchment (page 245).

Red Rice Pilaf

Wehani rice is a reddish-brown variety of basmati rice with a chewy texture and nutty flavor. We often pair this pilaf with Southern dishes and sometimes we stuff tomatoes or roasted bell peppers with it.

Yields 4 generous cups
Serves 4 to 6
Time: about 1 hour

1 cup brown rice
½ cup wehani rice
1 tablespoon olive oil
½ teaspoon dried thyme
½ teaspoon salt
2¼ cups water

½ cup seeded and diced red bell peppers
½ cup sliced scallions
½ cup chopped toasted pecans
salt
ground black pepper

Rinse the two types of rice in a fine-mesh strainer under cool running water and drain. Warm the oil in a saucepan on high heat. Add the rice and sauté for a minute or two, stirring to coat the grains with the oil. Add the thyme, salt, and water and bring to a boil. Reduce the heat to low and simmer, covered, until the water has been absorbed and the rice is tender, about 45 minutes.

Stir in the bell peppers and scallions. Let the rice sit, covered, for about 5 minutes. Stir in the pecans and season with salt and black pepper to taste just before serving.

VARIATIONS
- Replace the scallions with chopped parsley.
- Add a little Tabasco or other hot sauce or cayenne to kick up the heat.
- Add some currants or chopped dried apricots to give a little sweetness to the pilaf.

SERVING AND MENU IDEAS
Serve with Not Fried Fish (page 236) or tofu baked in Jerk Sauce (page 319) with Simple Smooth Guacamole (page 35) and tender fresh collard greens (see page 268).

Wild Rice Pilaf

Wild rice comes from a tall, aquatic North American perennial grass, not related to rice. It has been an important food, sometimes considered sacred, for some American Indians for a very long time. It is now commercially grown and is considered a delicacy by many. We like its unique flavor and texture and often combine it with brown rice in dishes like this pilaf. We use wild rice in salads, soups, and pilafs.

Yields 4 cups
Serves 4 to 6
Time: about 1 hour

1 cup brown rice, preferably long grain
½ cup wild rice
1 tablespoon olive oil
1 bay leaf
1 or 2 garlic cloves, minced or pressed
2¼ cups water
½ teaspoon salt

1 tablespoon olive oil
1 cup diced onions
½ cup diced celery
½ cup diced carrots
¼ cup chopped fresh parsley
salt
ground black pepper

Rinse both kinds of rice in a fine-mesh strainer under cool running water and set aside to drain. Warm the oil in a saucepan on high heat. Add the rice, bay leaf, and garlic and sauté for a minute, stirring constantly. Add the water and salt, stir well, cover the pan, and bring to a boil. Reduce the heat to low and simmer, covered, until the water has been absorbed and the rice is tender, about 45 minutes.

While the rice is cooking, in a skillet or saucepan on medium-high heat, warm the oil. Add the onions, and sauté for 3 or 4 minutes. Add the celery and carrots, sprinkle lightly with salt, cover the pan, and cook on low heat until all of the vegetables are just tender, about 5 minutes. Set aside.

When the rice is done, stir in the sautéed vegetables and the parsley. Season with salt and black pepper.

VARIATIONS
- Replace the parsley with 2 tablespoons of chopped fresh dill.
- At the end, instead of additional salt, add soy sauce to taste.
- Add about ½ cup of chopped toasted nuts, such as almonds or walnuts.
- Add some dried cranberries.

SERVING AND MENU IDEAS
Serve wild rice pilaf at Thanksgiving stuffed in a baked delicata or acorn squash, or next to Mushroom-Tofu-Pecan Stuffed Vegetables (page 175) or Oven-poached Fish with Leeks and Wine (page 243) and Roasted Brussels Sprouts (page 275).

Bulghur Pilaf

We love the chewy texture of bulghur and we love that it's a quick-cooking whole grain. This flavorful pilaf has many uses; see some of our ideas at the end of the recipe below. For those who are avoiding wheat, the seasonings work just as well with rice. Look for whole-grain bulghur, not refined, for the best taste and nutrition.

Yields about 7 cups
Serves 6 to 8
Time: 30 minutes

1 tablespoon olive oil
1 cup diced onions
1 garlic clove, minced or pressed
½ teaspoon salt
2 teaspoons minced fresh rosemary
2 cups coarse bulghur wheat
2½ cups boiling water
ground black pepper

Warm the olive oil in a saucepan on low heat. Add the onions and garlic and sprinkle with the salt. Cook, covered, stirring occasionally, until the onions are soft, about 10 minutes. Add the rosemary and bulghur, increase the heat, and cook, stirring constantly, for about a minute to toast the bulghur and coat the grains. Pour in the boiling water, using caution because it will bubble and sputter. Stir well, bring back to a boil, reduce the heat to low, cover, and cook for 10 minutes.

Stir the bulghur and taste to see if it is done. It may need a few more minutes of cooking time and/or a little more water. Season with salt and black pepper. Serve hot or at room temperature.

VARIATIONS

- Stir in some chopped fresh parsley for colorful green flecks.
- Instead of rosemary, use 2 teaspoons minced fresh thyme or ½ teaspoon dried.
- To make a more elaborate dish, add ½ teaspoon finely grated orange zest, ½ cup dried cranberries or finely chopped dried apricots, and 2 teaspoons of fresh lemon juice. Serve topped with toasted almonds.

SERVING AND MENU IDEAS

Serve under Falafel Burgers (page 91). Use Bulghur Pilaf at room temperature as part of a salad plate with Peppercorn and Lemon Marinated Feta (page 23) and Tomato, Cucumber, and Artichoke Heart Salad (page 256). For dinner some night, make some Quick Sautéed Greens (page 268) and some tofu (see Moosewood's Best Baked and Pan-fried Tofu, page 202) to go with Bulghur Pilaf. For Thanksgiving, make the cranberry variation with parsley as a lovely side dish. In the summer take it on a picnic.

Kasha and Mushroom Pilaf

People seem to hold strong opinions about kasha; they either like it or they don't. It has a unique flavor that's hard to describe. If you're in the love-it camp, you'll love this pilaf. The mushrooms and soy sauce give it depth, the parsley some color, the onions cooked in butter a special flavor and richness. We think it tastes better to coat the grains with an egg and roast them in the skillet before cooking.

Yields 4 generous cups
Serves 4 to 6
Time: 30 minutes

2 tablespoons butter
1 cup diced onions
½ teaspoon salt
1 large egg
1 cup kasha (see page 379)
4 cups chopped mushrooms (16 ounces whole)
1½ to 2 cups boiling water
1 tablespoon soy sauce
¼ cup minced fresh parsley
¼ teaspoon ground black pepper

In a large covered skillet on low heat, melt the butter. Add the onions, sprinkle with the salt, and cook, covered, for 10 minutes, stirring occasionally.

While the onions cook, beat the egg in a small bowl. Add the kasha and stir well to coat the grains. Set aside.

Add the mushrooms to the onions, increase the heat to medium, and cook, stirring frequently, until the mushrooms begin to release some liquid. Cook, uncovered, stirring occasionally, until the mushrooms are tender, about 8 minutes. Add the kasha to the skillet and stir constantly until the grains are dry and separate. Pour in 1½ cups of boiling water—use caution, it splatters a bit. Bring to a simmer and cook, covered, until the water has been absorbed, about 10 minutes. Taste to see if the kasha is tender; if not, add ¼ to ½ cup boiling water and continue cooking.

When the kasha is done, stir in the soy sauce, parsley, and black pepper. Season with more salt and black pepper to taste.

VARIATIONS

- You can make this with vegetable oil instead of butter, but we do like that buttery flavor.
- To make Kasha Varnishkas: Cook farfalle pasta and stir it into the kasha pilaf. Season with butter and salt.

SERVING AND MENU IDEAS

On a wintery evening this would be good served with Sweet and Sour Red Cabbage Two Ways (page 280) and some of Moosewood's Best Baked and Pan-fried Tofu (page 202). Maybe some Creamy Herbed Potato Soup (page 49) to start.

Polenta, Cheesy and Vegan

In some areas of northern Italy, polenta is a staple food, surpassing pasta. We love its creamy, comforting taste and texture, and its versatility. Polenta's smooth texture and mild flavor is a good medium for the addition of sharper flavors and textural accents. Sometimes we add spinach, spicy greens, fresh corn kernels, or sun-dried tomatoes to our polenta, and also an assortment of cheeses and fresh and dried herbs. At Moosewood, polenta often serves as a bed for Mediterranean or Mexican stews, and we also use it as a stuffing for bell peppers, as a layer in casseroles, and for polenta cutlets and croutons.

We make polenta with unrefined, unenriched whole-grain cornmeal. In this coarsely ground meal, the germ of the kernel, where most of the vitamins, protein, and other nutrients reside is still intact. We are tremendously lucky to have a farmer in our area who grows and dries organic corn, and a miller who grinds it. If you can find locally grown and milled corn, try it, you'll taste the difference.

Yields 4 cups
Serves 4 to 6
Time: depends on the cornmeal

CHEESY POLENTA

3 cups water
1 teaspoon salt
2 tablespoons butter or olive oil
1 cup cornmeal (page 382)
½ cup grated Parmesan or sharp cheddar cheese
ground black pepper

Put the water, salt, and butter or oil in a heavy-bottomed saucepan and bring to a boil. Start with 3 cups of water, but keep an eye on the polenta as it simmers, because you might need to add more water, depending on the grind and kind of cornmeal. Whisk in the cornmeal as you pour it into the boiling water in a steady stream. Bring back to a boil, reduce the heat to a very low simmer, and cook, stirring occasionally, until the texture is smooth and creamy, 15 to 30 minutes. We can't tell you just how long it will take because cornmeal is so varied.

Remove from the heat and stir in the cheese. Season with black pepper and add more salt to taste. Pictured right with Peperonata (page 264).

VEGAN POLENTA

2 tablespoons olive oil or vegetable oil
2 garlic cloves, finely chopped or minced
¾ teaspoon ground fennel seeds
1½ teaspoons salt
⅛ teaspoon ground black pepper
3 cups water
1 cup cornmeal (page 382)

In a heavy-bottomed saucepan on high heat, warm the oil. Add the garlic, fennel, salt, and black pepper and sizzle for just a minute, taking care not to scorch the garlic. Carefully add the water and bring

to a boil. Start with 3 cups of water, but keep an eye on the polenta as it simmers, because you might need to add more water, depending on the grind and kind of cornmeal. Whisk in the cornmeal as you pour it into the boiling water in a steady stream. Bring back to a boil, reduce the heat to a very low simmer, and cook, stirring occasionally, until smooth and creamy, 15 to 30 minutes. We can't tell you just how long it will take because cornmeal is so varied.

VARIATIONS

- **Polenta Cutlets**—Pour the hot polenta into a lightly oiled, rimmed baking sheet (13 × 9 × 1-inch) to about ¾-inch depth and refrigerate for 30 minutes. Preheat the oven to 375°F. Cut the firm, chilled polenta into triangles or rectangles. Transfer the cutlets to a lightly oiled, larger baking sheet that will allow at least ½ inch between each cutlet. Bake for 15 minutes. Remove the baking sheet from the oven, turn over the cutlets, lightly brush with oil and sprinkle with cheese, if desired. Return the baking sheet to the oven for 5 minutes. Depending on the size of the cutlets, they can be served as tasty appetizers, or served as a side grain. Polenta cutlets are yummy drizzled with Tomato-Basil Sauce (page 324) or Puttanesca Sauce (page 322).

- **Polenta Croutons**—Chill Cheesy Polenta for 30 minutes as directed for Polenta Cutlets and then cut the polenta into 1-inch cubes. Preheat the oven to 350°F degrees. Toss the cubes with oil and bake them for 30 minutes. Turn the cubes over and bake for another 10 minutes. Cool on the sheet to room temperature. Garnish soups, stews, and salads with polenta croutons, or serve as snacks.

- **Vegan Polenta Plus**—Mix in a vegan cheese at the end. And/or add ⅓ cup of diced sun-dried tomatoes and ½ cup of fresh or frozen corn kernels for the last 10 minutes of cooking.

- **Herbed Polenta**—Thyme, basil, and oregano all taste good in polenta. Add dried herbs to the cooking water; stir in finely minced fresh herbs when the polenta is done.

Risotto Milanese

Risotto Milanese is the classic cheesy saffron risotto. Much has been written about preparing the perfect risotto, but we've found that letting go of the worrisome striving to create perfection has helped us to make a most delicious risotto with just a few simple ingredients and techniques—in fact we are sure that simplicity is what was intended when this exquisite dish was first crafted. Basically, the rice's starch is released and transformed by slowly adding the liquid, producing the finished risotto's creamy consistency.

For a great vegetarian risotto, use homemade vegetable stock (see page 389) or Imagine Food's No-Chicken Broth. Use a good arborio or carnaroli rice.

Yields 6 cups
Serves 4 to 6
Time: 45 minutes

1 quart vegetable stock or broth (see page 389)
1 cup water
generous pinch of saffron
2 tablespoons olive oil
1 cup finely diced onions
2 cups arborio or carnaroli rice
½ cup dry white wine
3 tablespoons butter
¾ cup shredded Parmesan cheese
ground black pepper
salt

In a saucepan, bring the stock and water to a steady simmer. Add the saffron.

Warm the olive oil on medium-high heat oil in a large, heavy saucepan, Add the onions and sauté for about 4 minutes, or until softened. Add the rice and stir thoroughly. Add the wine and stir for a minute or two.

Ladle in simmering stock, ½ cup at a time, stirring the rice often with a long wooden spoon and making sure the liquid has been absorbed before each new addition. Continue cooking and adding stock until the rice is tender but firm to the bite, moist and clinging together, 20 to 25 minutes total. The amount of liquid you need may vary, depending on the rice.

Gently beat in the Parmesan, black pepper, salt. the remaining 2 tablespoons butter, which helps wrap those flavors around the grains. If you don't want to use butter, add more olive oil.

VARIATIONS

- **Spinach-Feta Risotto**—When most of the broth has been absorbed, stir in 10 ounces (7 cups) of washed baby spinach, in batches if necessary, and cover until the spinach has wilted but is still bright green. Substitute 1 cup crumbled feta cheese for the Parmesan.

SERVING AND MENU IDEAS

Serve with a simple juicy tomato salad, garlicky greens (page 268), tossed green salad, or one of our Simply Dressed Green Vegetables (page 264). Serve with Flounder Florentine (page 239) or Roasted Vegetables (page 271).

Couscous

Couscous is a staple ingredient of North African cuisine and its history can be traced back to the eleventh century. Couscous is traditionally crafted by hand using crushed semolina in a lengthy process of shaking the semolina mixture through a series of sieves to produce pasta beads of a similar size. Traditional couscous is steamed in a couscoussière or over a long-simmering soup or stew in a pot with a vented lid that prevents steam condensation from dropping into the couscous and making it gummy.

The couscous we find in our stores is made of wheat and is "instant" (precooked), and it truly is quick-cooking and easy to prepare. At Moosewood, we like best the nutty, wholesome flavor of whole wheat couscous. We also like couscous that's marketed as Israeli and sometimes Middle Eastern couscous, with its larger toasted pasta balls that cook on the stovetop like bulghur or rice. Store dry couscous well sealed in the refrigerator or freezer.

Couscous should be light and fluffy, not gummy and not gritty. We can't explain why so many recipes and package directions call for so much liquid: we always start with equal measures of dry couscous and boiling water or stock, and rarely need to add more.

A bowl of couscous is like a blank canvas: take inspiration from what's in your pantry and refrigerator or garden to make a couscous salad or pilaf. See our suggestions following the recipe.

Yields 4 cups
Time: 10 to 20 minutes

1½ cups couscous
1 teaspoon salt
1½ teaspoons olive oil
1½ cups boiling water or vegetable stock
    (see page 389)

Place the couscous, salt, and oil in a heatproof bowl. Add the boiling water or stock and stir briefly. Cover (we usually use a plate) and set aside for 5 minutes. Uncover and fluff with a fork to break up any lumps. If the couscous isn't tender, add a bit more boiling water, cover, and allow the couscous to steam for a few minutes more. Fluff again and serve.

VARIATIONS

- To infuse the couscous with flavor:
  —Add to the water while it comes to a boil: fresh thyme sprigs, a pinch of saffron, dried mint, or a cinnamon stick.
  —Add to the dry couscous before adding the boiling water: finely grated lemon zest or orange zest, chopped fresh mint.

- Here are some things you can add to make couscous salad or pilaf:
  —currants or dried apricots, pistachios (steam the couscous with orange zest and cinnamon)
  —rehydrated sun-dried tomatoes, black olives, red onions, fresh basil, feta cheese
  —mint, cucumbers, red onions, tomatoes
  —red bell peppers, scallions, tomatoes, fresh basil
  —sliced snow peas, peeled and grated fresh ginger, chopped cilantro, fresh lime juice
  —toasted pine nuts, fresh spinach, fresh lemon juice
  —chickpeas, spinach or chard, raisins
  —roasted vegetables, feta cheese
  —parsley, mint, scallions, chickpeas, fresh lemon, lime, and/or orange juice, olive oil
  —almonds, dates, cilantro, lemon, saffron in the water

SERVING AND MENU IDEAS

This recipe makes enough couscous to serve as a bed for Moroccan Vegetable Stew (page 129), Greek Lemon-Mint Beans and Vegetables (page 145), Flounder Rollatini (page 238), Flounder Florentine (page 239), or Oven-poached Fish with Leeks and Wine (page 243).

Moosewood's Creamy Green Dressing

Lemon-Tahini Dressing

Feta-Garlic Dressing

Japanese Carrot Dressing

Pear-Thyme Dressing

Ginger-Miso Dressing

Moosewood's Creamy Green Dressing

This creamy, green, slightly sweet dressing has been our signature house dressing for many years. Customers sometimes ask if they could please just buy a quart or so of it to take home.

The recipe has undergone some changes over the years—we now use quite a bit more spinach and basil than we did originally, we use milk instead of buttermilk, and we don't add any garlic—but the basic concept remains the same. And, it remains our most popular dressing.

Yields 2 generous cups
Time: 10 minutes

¾ cup vegetable oil
3 tablespoons apple cider vinegar
1 tablespoon honey or maple syrup
2 teaspoons Dijon mustard
½ teaspoon salt
½ cup packed fresh spinach leaves
¼ cup packed fresh basil leaves, more to taste
¾ cup milk

Combine all of the ingredients except for the milk in a blender and whirl until smooth. With the blender running, pour in the milk in a steady stream. The dressing will thicken and be a lovely shade of green. Add salt and more fresh basil to taste.

Although you can serve the dressing immediately, we usually let it sit for a while so the flavors can meld. It will keep for about a week refrigerated.

VARIATIONS

- At the Moose, we use only canola oil in the dressing, but if you prefer, use ¼ cup of olive oil and ½ cup vegetable oil. Don't use extra-virgin olive oil; it's too strong for this dressing.
- Replace the milk with buttermilk.
- If you don't like sweet dressing, reduce the amount of sweetener.

Lemon-Tahini Dressing

This creamy dressing has been a Moosewood standard for many years and is popular with vegans and omnivores alike. At the restaurant, we always add cumin, but it's also delicious without.

Yields 1¼ cups
Time: 10 minutes

½ cup water
3 tablespoons fresh lemon juice
2 teaspoons red wine vinegar or apple cider vinegar
1 tablespoon olive oil
½ cup tahini
1 garlic clove, minced or pressed
½ teaspoon salt
a generous pinch of ground black pepper or cayenne
½ teaspoon ground cumin seeds (optional)

Combine all of the ingredients in a blender and process until smooth and creamy. Or whisk the ingredients in a bowl until smooth.

The dressing will keep in the refrigerator for up to 2 weeks.

VARIATIONS

- Reduce the salt and add 1 or 2 teaspoons of soy sauce.
- Stir in a tablespoon of minced parsley or fresh dill.
- Omit the vinegar and add another tablespoon of lemon juice.

SERVING AND MENU IDEAS

This dressing is great on tossed salad, of course, but also on Moosewood's Classic Tofu Burgers (page 89), Tofalafels (page 25), Falafel Burgers (page 91) and stuffed grape leaves. It's good for dipping with toasted pita and crudités. Or blend with chickpeas for a delicious hummus, or with roasted eggplant for baba ganouj.

Feta-Garlic Dressing

This is the dressing for those of us who can't get enough feta or garlic. It's ranch dressing for the rugged. Quarter a ripe juicy tomato, or roast up some potato wedges, asparagus spears, or cauliflower florets, and let the dipping begin!

Yields 2 cups
Time: 15 minutes

¾ cup grated feta cheese, packed
¾ cup milk
¼ cup apple cider vinegar
2 garlic cloves, minced or pressed
⅛ teaspoon ground black pepper
¾ cup olive oil
2 tablespoons minced fresh dill

In a blender on low speed, purée the feta, milk, vinegar, garlic, and black pepper for a minute. With the blender running, slowly add the olive oil in a thin, steady stream. The dressing will thicken as it sits. Stir in the dill.

Japanese Carrot Dressing

This brightly colored dressing makes a beautiful topping for dark leafy greens and is easy to make. Put Japanese Carrot Dressing on shredded iceberg lettuce and you have that Japanese restaurant bento box salad. It's thicker than most dressings and makes a nice dip for steamed snow peas, sugar snap peas, or green beans.

Yields 1¼ cups
Time: 15 minutes

½ cup packed grated carrots
¼ cup chopped onions or scallion bulbs
½ cup vegetable oil
3 tablespoons rice vinegar
1½ tablespoons peeled and grated fresh ginger
1 tablespoon soy sauce
1 teaspoon dark sesame oil
2 tablespoons water
¼ teaspoon salt
1 teaspoon brown sugar (optional)
ground black pepper

Combine all of the ingredients, except for the brown sugar and black pepper, in a blender and whirl on low for a few seconds, then increase the speed to medium or high and purée until smooth. Taste the dressing—if the carrots are very sweet, you may not want any additional sweetener. Otherwise, add the brown sugar, if using, and whirl again briefly. Season with black pepper and add more salt to taste.

This dressing will keep for several days in the refrigerator.

SERVING IDEAS
Serve this dressing not only on green salads, but also as a topping for plain fish or roasted beets or Brussels sprouts.

Pear-Thyme Dressing

Once upon a time, one of our most innovative cooks, Jenny Wang, decided to experiment with using a pear that was a little too ripe to serve sliced onto a lunchtime salad du jour to make a dressing. We loved the results, both the flavor and the fact that the pear adds creaminess without extra fat.

The taste and color of the dressing varies depending on the flavor and color of the pear you use. A red-skinned pear will make a dressing with flecks of red. A green pear, especially if you use the lime juice variation, will give a lovely green hue. And don't think you have to wait for a pear to get overripe before you make this dressing, a perfectly ripe pear, or even a slightly underripe pear will do, too.

Yields 1 generous cup
Time: 10 minutes

1 pear
2 teaspoons minced fresh thyme
2 tablespoons water
2 tablespoons apple cider vinegar
½ teaspoon salt
⅛ teaspoon ground black pepper
⅓ cup olive oil
1 teaspoon Dijon mustard (optional)
1 to 3 teaspoons honey or maple syrup (optional)

Core the pear and cut it into chunks, no need to peel it. Put the pear, thyme, water, vinegar, salt, and black pepper into a blender and purée. With the blender running, slowly pour in the oil. Taste, and add mustard and honey or maple syrup, if you like.

VARIATIONS
- Use fresh lime juice instead of apple cider vinegar.
- Substitute an equal amount of tarragon for the thyme.

SERVING AND MENU IDEAS
A great dressing for sharper tasting greens like arugula. Use this dressing for Autumn Salad Plate (page 109).

Ginger-Miso Dressing

Yields 2 cups
Time: 15 minutes

Creamy, salty, tangy, and piquant, this salad dressing is a Moosewood favorite on both sides of the serving window. We have staff who blissfully end their shift with a bowls of grated carrots and slices of Tofu Kan–style Tofu (page 201) smothered with generous ladles of Ginger-Miso.

For many years, we called this dressing "floating cloud," because we loved that name of a similar dressing in *The Book of Miso,* by William Shurtleff and Akiko Aoyagi. We've revised it many times, and we published our changing versions in three previous cookbooks. This is the recipe we use in the Moosewood kitchen today, cut down to size for home cooking, of course.

The quality and type of the miso is important. Look for a sweet white or light miso. South River makes a good, organic white miso.

5 level tablespoons light miso
3 tablespoons peeled and grated fresh ginger
¼ cup dark sesame oil
¼ cup apple cider vinegar
¼ cup water
¾ cup vegetable oil (not olive oil)

In a blender on low speed, whirl all of the ingredients, except for the vegetable oil, for a minute. With the blender running, slowly pour in the oil in a thin, steady stream. The dressing becomes thicker and creamy.

SERVING AND MENU IDEAS

Besides being one of our favorite dressings for green salads, Ginger-Miso Dressing is a natural with steamed vegetables and tofu. It is also tasty when used to baste grilled vegetables and fish. We use it as dressing in pita sandwiches, for example: baby spinach, grated carrots and cucumbers, hard-boiled eggs, and tofu or tempeh.

CONDIMENTS AND SALSAS

Mango Aioli

Herbed Aioli

Lime-Dijon Aioli

Cilantro-Yogurt Sauce

Quick Banana Chutney

Chipotle Cream

Tzatziki

Cranberry Sauce

Spinach Raita

Date-Coconut-Lemon Chutney

Caramelized Onions

Our Favorite Tomato-Cilantro Salsa

Avocado Salsa

Cucumber-Tomato Salsa

Mango Salsa

Mango Aioli

We've said it before—we love mangoes! Their flavor, their nutrition, their color. When we first whirled them with mayonnaise and lime, it was love at first taste.

Yields about 1 cup
Time: 5 minutes

½ cup fresh or frozen mango chunks, thawed
½ cup mayonnaise
½ teaspoon finely grated lime or lemon zest
2 teaspoons fresh lime or lemon juice

Whirl all of the ingredients in a food processor until smooth.

SERVING AND MENU IDEAS

Serve this aioli with Spicy Chipotle Cornmeal-crusted Fish (page 235) and Coconut-Cashew-crusted Fish (page 231). It is good on roasted sweet potatoes. Or for a Caribbean-inspired meal, make some Coconut Rice (page 289), bake tofu with Jerk Sauce (page 319), and arrange a platter of colorful steamed vegetables with Mango Aioli on the side.

Herbed Aioli

We often have at least one kind of aioli in our reach-in refrigerator at the restaurant. We use aioli like this one for roasted or steamed vegetables, in egg salad, on sandwiches, to top fish cakes, for cooked artichokes, in slaws. We're sure you can find many uses for it at home as well.

Yields about 1 cup
Time: 10 minutes

1 cup mayonnaise
1 garlic clove, minced or pressed
2 tablespoons snipped fresh chives or finely
    chopped scallions
1 tablespoon chopped fresh dill, basil, tarragon, or
    other fresh herb
½ teaspoon finely grated lemon zest
1 tablespoon fresh lemon juice

Whisk together all of the ingredients. For a mellower garlic flavor, sizzle the garlic in 1 tablespoon of olive oil just until golden on the stovetop or in a microwave oven before adding it.

Lime-Dijon Aioli

The French word *aïoli,* comes from the old French words "ai," which means garlic and "oli," which means oil. We're happy to combine them in our most French version of aioli, full of garlic with a touch of Dijon mustard and fresh thyme and tinged green with lime juice. We like it on Fish Cakes (page 237), and Coconut-Cashew-crusted Fish (page 231). Sometimes for lunch at the restaurant, you'll find a salad plate with a medley of steamed vegetables, such as potatoes, carrots, broccoli, asparagus, and bell peppers, on a bed of fresh spinach, with hard-boiled egg and an aioli like this one.

Yields about 1 cup
Time: 5 minutes

1 cup mayonnaise
1 teaspoon Dijon mustard, more to taste
2 tablespoons olive oil
3 garlic cloves, minced or pressed
2 tablespoons fresh lime juice
1 teaspoon minced fresh thyme (optional)

In the bowl of a food processor or in a small bowl using a whisk, combine the mayonnaise, mustard, olive oil, garlic, lime juice, and thyme, if using. If you prefer the mellower flavor of cooked garlic, sizzle it in the oil in a microwave or on the stovetop before adding it.

Cilantro-Yogurt Sauce

This pretty green sauce, so tangy and refreshing, makes stews, chili, stuffed vegetables, and curries special. So simple, so quick.

Yields 2 cups
Time: 5 minutes

2 cups plain yogurt
½ cup chopped fresh cilantro
¼ teaspoon salt
pinch of sugar (optional)

Purée everything in a blender until smooth and bright green.

SERVING AND MENU IDEAS

Use as a topping however you would sour cream or yogurt. Serve with Navajo Stew (page 130), Our Best Chili (page 141), and Summer Vegetable Curry (page 123).

Quick Banana Chutney

Delicious and so quick and easy to make. Nice with curries or other spicy dishes.

Yields about 1 cup
Time: 15 minutes

3 ripe or very ripe bananas
1 teaspoon finely grated lemon zest
1 to 2 tablespoons fresh lemon juice
¼ teaspoon ground cinnamon
pinch of ground cardamom
pinch of salt

In a nonreactive saucepan, mash the bananas with a fork or handheld potato masher. Stir in the lemon zest, lemon juice, cinnamon, cardamom, and salt. Bring to a boil, stirring occasionally. As they heat, the bananas will release moisture. Lower the heat and simmer, stirring occasionally, for 10 minutes. The chutney will gradually thicken as steam escapes—it looks like oatmeal cooking. Cool to room temperature.

Store, covered, in the refrigerator. It will keep for at least a week.

Chipotle Cream

This creamy, spicy topping may be just the thing you need to add some extra spark to many dishes. We have offered it as a topping for the chili we serve at our local Chili Fest contest, and we think it just might have helped us win. See Our Best Chili (page 141).

Try a dollop on a simple quesadilla made with beans and salsa, or an an omelet, on Black Bean–Sweet Potato Burrito (page 195), or on Southwestern Sweet Potato–Corn Soup (page 56).

Yields about ¾ cup
Time: 5 minutes

1 chipotle pepper in adobo sauce or to taste
¾ cup plain yogurt
2 ounces cream cheese
1 teaspoon salt

Whirl all of the ingredients in a food processor until smooth.

Tzatziki

Recipes for the combination of cucumbers, yogurt, and herbs and spices are so popular in so many cuisines that we've made versions from India, Armenia, North Africa, and Scandinavia, but we come back again and again to this classic from Greece. This is a lovely accompaniment to Mediterranean and Middle Eastern dishes. It has a cooling effect when served with a spicy meal.

Traditionally, the cucumbers for tzatziki are salted and drained to prevent watery tzatziki, but Greek yogurt is so thick that you can skip that step. We do squeeze the grated cucumbers by hand. The flavor and fragrance of the fresh mint leaves is refreshing.

Yields about 3½ cups
Serves 6 to 8
Time: 15 minutes

2 or 3 large cucumbers, grated (about 3 cups)
14 to 16 ounces plain Greek yogurt
2 garlic cloves, minced or pressed (optional)
2 tablespoons minced fresh mint leaves
½ teaspoon salt
ground black pepper

Peel the cucumbers, cut them in half lengthwise, and scrape the seeds out with a spoon. Using a hand grater or a food processor, grate the cucumbers and set aside. In a bowl, stir together the yogurt, garlic, mint, salt, and black pepper to taste. Squeeze the grated cucumbers by the handful and add to the bowl. Stir well. Serve chilled.

SERVING AND MENU IDEAS
Serve next to Greek Stuffed Tomatoes (page 177), Aegean Strudel (page 190), and Falafel Burgers (page 91). We've served it with Winter Curry (page 124) and Indian Stuffed Eggplant (page 179) as well.

Cranberry Sauce

Fresh cranberry sauce is beautiful, has a bright sweet and tangy taste, and it's so easy to make. The gelatinous cylinder that comes out a can is only a very distant cousin. We love cranberries with orange. This, our favorite recipe for cranberry sauce, has apples and maple syrup. We use fresh orange zest and juice, but orange juice straight out of the carton is good, too.

Fresh cranberries are in our markets October through December. At other times of the year, when we crave cranberry sauce, we can usually find frozen ones in the supermarket.

Yields 4 cups
Time: 20 minutes

12 ounces fresh or frozen cranberries (about 2 cups)
2 cups peeled and cubed crisp, sweet-tart apples, such as Crispin
2 teaspoons finely grated orange zest
⅓ cup water
¾ cup fresh orange juice
⅔ cup maple syrup

Rinse and drain fresh cranberries and remove any leaves, stems, and soft or wrinkled cranberries. Frozen cranberries can go straight into the pan.

In a covered saucepan on medium-high heat, bring the cranberries, apples, orange zest, and water to a boil. Remove the cover, reduce the heat, and simmer until the cranberries burst and the sauce thickens, about 10 minutes. Stir in the orange juice and maple syrup and remove from the heat. The sauce will continue to thicken as it cools.

SERVING AND MENU IDEAS
Serve the sauce with baked or roasted winter squash. Use as a condiment in sandwiches. It's delicious with sautéed mushrooms and spinach. Serve some on the side of Mushroom-Tofu-Pecan Stuffed Vegetables (page 175), Kasha and Mushroom Pilaf (page 295) and Mushroom Piroshki (page 156).

Spinach Raita

Raita cools and refreshes the palate when eating curry and other spicy Indian dishes, and adds interest to the meal as a whole. Raita is prime fusion fare—an equally good accompaniment to Caribbean, African, and Middle-Eastern cuisines. On the home front, raita enhances roasted vegetables, especially potatoes (sweet and white), and grilled fish.

We've made this raita three ways and like them all: using thick Greek-style yogurt, using regular yogurt we drained for 1 hour, and using regular yogurt straight from the carton. The Greek-style yogurt produces a thick spread, good for dipping with crackers, chips, and vegetable sticks. It can also be slathered on sandwich bread in place of mayonnaise. The drained yogurt is creamy and thick, good as a side or as a dip for flat bread. And raita made with regular yogurt, not drained, is light and refreshing.

Yields a generous 2 cups
Serves 4 as a side dish
Time: 10 minutes (more if draining the yogurt)

6 cups baby spinach (about 9 ounces)
1 tablespoon butter or vegetable oil
½ teaspoon whole cumin seeds
½ teaspoon black mustard seeds
¼ teaspoon ground cardamom
¼ teaspoon ground black pepper
2 cups plain yogurt, drained yogurt, or Greek yogurt (see headnote)
salt

Rinse the spinach. In a pot on medium heat, steam the spinach, stirring a couple of times, until wilted, about 5 minutes. Drain the spinach in a colander, pressing out the excess water. Place the drained spinach on a cutting board and when it is cool enough to handle, squeeze out more liquid and chop coarsely. Set aside in a bowl.

While the spinach cools, melt the butter in the smallest skillet you have. Add the cumin seeds, black mustard seeds, cardamom, and black pepper and sizzle the spices on medium heat until the mustard seeds begin to pop. Remove from the heat.

Add the yogurt to the bowl of spinach and stir in the spices. Mix well and season with salt to taste.

NOTE
To drain yogurt, place a sieve or colander lined with cheesecloth or coffee filters over a pot or bowl. For 2 cups of thickened yogurt use 3 cups of yogurt. Refrigerate for about an hour. For thicker yogurt, drain longer. Draining overnight will yield a yogurt of Greek-style thickness.

SERVING AND MENU IDEAS
Serve with any curry. We especially like this raita with Lentil-Vegetable Sambar (page 122), Indian Stuffed Eggplant (page 179), and Curried Squash Roti (page 187).

Date-Coconut-Lemon Chutney

This is an easy, uncooked chutney, one that we've been serving at Moosewood since the early years. It has delightful flavor, is very simple to make, and is the perfect accompaniment to almost any curry.

Yields 1 generous cup
Time: 20 minutes

1½ cups finely chopped pitted dates (8 ounces)
¼ cup unsweetened shredded dried coconut
3 tablespoons fresh lemon juice, more to taste
1 tablespoon peeled and grated fresh ginger, more to taste
1 teaspoon ground coriander seeds
¼ teaspoon salt
2 tablespoons finely chopped parsley (optional)

Place the chopped dates in a bowl and pour ⅓ cup boiling water over them. Cover and set aside for about 5 minutes to soften. The dates should be quite soft. If they're too firm, add a little more boiling water and let them sit longer.

Stir in the remaining ingredients. Add more ginger and lemon to taste. The chutney should be both sweet and tangy.

NOTE

If the dates you have are especially dry or if you don't want to finely chop them by hand, soften them in the boiling water, stir in the other ingredients, and put the mixture in a food processor and pulse until the chutney is the consistency you like.

VARIATION

Use 1 teaspoon of ground fennel seeds instead of the coriander.

SERVING AND MENU IDEAS

Serve with Lentil-Vegetable Sambar (page 122), Indian Stuffed Eggplant (page 179), Winter Curry (page 124), Summer Vegetable Curry (page 123), or Curried Red Lentil Burgers (page 87).

Caramelized Onions

Caramelized onions with their deep, rich, sweet flavor and deep, rich, golden brown color are a wonderful thing. A wonderful thing for onion soup, of course, and also for pizzas, sandwiches, casseroles, savory pies, frittatas, and omelets, and for stirring into polenta, serving next to mashed potatoes, or topping a veggie burger. The list goes on and on. Long, slow cooking brings out and browns the natural sugars in the onions.

Some people say that you have to cook onions for an hour or more to get good, sweet, brown caramelized onions, and others claim to do it in 10 minutes, but in our experience, with a heavy skillet and a little attention, you can do it in about half an hour. Caramelized onions freeze well for up to several months, so why not buy a big bag of onions and spend an evening cooking up a big mess of them, letting them cool, and packaging them in freezer bags.

Yields 1½ cups
Time: 35 minutes

1 large onion (about 4 cups sliced)
1 tablespoon vegetable or olive oil
½ teaspoon salt

Cut off the root and top end of the onion. Peel it. Cut it in half from top to root and cut each half from top end to root end into slices about ¼ inch wide.

In a large, heavy skillet on medium-high heat, warm the oil. Add the onions, sprinkle with the salt, and cook, stirring constantly, until the onions begin to soften and the color darkens a bit, about 4 minutes. Reduce the heat to low and cook, uncovered and stirring every few minutes, until the onions are very soft and golden brown, about 25 minutes. Add a splash of water if the onions start to stick or brown too fast. The trick is to let them brown (by not stirring too often), but not scorch. Stir more often toward the end, scraping the bottom of the pan. A minute or two before the cooking is done, add a couple of tablespoons of water to help deglaze the pan (the water will evaporate).

SERVING AND MENU IDEAS

Caramelized Onions are perfect on Mushroom-Tofu-Pecan Burgers (page 175) and Moosewood's Classic Tofu Burgers (page 89). Check out our suggestions in the headnote for various other uses.

Our Favorite Tomato-Cilantro Salsa

This is a quickly made fresh salsa inspired by *pebre*, a Chilean salsa that came to us by way of Eliana (Nana) Parra, who arrived in Ithaca from her native land, Chile, in the 1970s. Nana came to Moosewood without English, but with energy and efficiency and—*pebre!* It was, and is, a marvel to see her turn out a multitude of empanadas and pebre in short order. At the end of the recipe, you'll find some recipes that are enhanced with this fresh salsa, but there are a hundreds more excuses to eat some.

Yields about 2 cups
Time: 20 minutes

¼ cup minced red onions
½ teaspoon salt
1 small hot pepper, minced
1 garlic clove, minced or pressed
1 tablespoon vegetable oil
2 cups diced fresh tomatoes
1 tablespoon red wine vinegar
1 tablespoon minced fresh cilantro, more to taste

Put the red onions in a bowl and sprinkle with the salt. In a microwave oven or on the stovetop in a very small saucepan, cook the hot peppers and garlic in the oil until sizzling; keep an eye on it, it doesn't take long. Pour this hot mixture over the red onions and stir well. (This helps to take away the bite of raw onions.) Add the tomatoes, vinegar, and cilantro and stir well. For the best flavor, let the salsa sit for at least 10 minutes before serving. Stir in more cilantro, if you like.

VARIATION
• If you'd like a saucier salsa, whirl the tomatoes briefly in a food processor.

SERVING AND MENU IDEAS
Try this salsa with a quesadilla (see page 196), or on Refried Beans (page 281), Spinach-Cheese Burritos (page 198), Cuban Black Beans (page 137), Southwestern Bean Burgers (page 93), or Fish "Tostadas" (page 246), or simply as a dip for tortilla chips.

Avocado Salsa

At the restaurant, we always have a case of avocados ripening, and as soon as they're perfectly soft and flavorful, they go on the menu—often as this salsa. When we serve it with tortilla chips it's one of our customers' favorite appetizers. And it's a refreshing and colorful way to garnish roti, burritos, frittatas, and other Caribbean or Latin American dishes.

Yields 2½ to 3 cups
Time: 15 minutes

2 ripe avocados, cubed
1 cup diced fresh tomatoes
½ cup seeded and diced bell peppers (any color) or peeled, seeded, and diced cucumbers
¼ cup minced red onions or scallions
¼ cup fresh lime or lemon juice
¼ teaspoon salt
1 tablespoon olive oil (optional)
2 tablespoons chopped fresh cilantro (optional)
¼ teaspoon cayenne (optional)

In a bowl, stir together the avocados, tomatoes, bell peppers or cucumbers, scallions, lemon juice, and salt. Let sit for about 10 minutes for the flavors to blend. Taste, and add any of the optional ingredients and more lime or lemon juice and salt if you like.

Cucumber-Tomato Salsa

This is a simply made, bright-tasting, mild salsa. We especially like it with Creole Red Beans (page 146) and Falafel Burgers (page 91). You could also cut the vegetables a little bigger and serve it as a side salad for any rich, cheesy main dish, such as Rumbledethumps (page 163) or Macaroni and Cheese with Broccoli (page 217).

Yields 3 cups
Time: 20 minutes

2 cups diced fresh tomatoes
1 cup peeled, seeded, and diced cucumbers
¼ cup snipped fresh chives, or finely chopped scallions or red onions
½ teaspoon salt
1 teaspoon minced fresh thyme or 1 teaspoon dried oregano
1 tablespoon olive oil
2 teaspoons fresh lemon juice or red wine vinegar, or a combination
¼ teaspoon ground black pepper
1 tablespoon minced fresh parsley (optional)

Put all of the ingredients in a bowl and mix well. Add more salt and black pepper to taste. If you use dried oregano, let the salsa sit for at least 10 to 15 minutes before serving.

Mango Salsa

We love mangoes! We use them every opportunity we get. In this recipe their sweetness is nicely balanced with the sharp heat of hot peppers and the tang of lime. Make the salsa as hot or as mild as you like.

Yields 5 cups
Time: 25 minutes (less with frozen mangoes)

3 cups diced mango chunks (2 ripe mangoes, peeled and diced, or a 16-ounce package of frozen mango chunks, thawed and diced)
1 small cucumber, peeled, seeded, and diced
1 cup diced fresh tomatoes
½ cup seeded and diced bell peppers (any color)
1 teaspoon olive oil
2 garlic cloves, minced or pressed
1 fresh hot pepper, minced
2 tablespoons fresh lime juice
1 tablespoon chopped fresh cilantro (optional)
1 tablespoon chopped scallions (optional)
salt
ground black pepper

In a bowl, combine the mangoes, cucumber, tomatoes, and bell peppers. To mellow and marry the flavors, heat the oil, garlic, and hot peppers in a microwave or on the stovetop just until the garlic sizzles. Stir the garlic–hot pepper oil and the lime juice, and cilantro and scallions, if using, into the mango-vegetable mixture.

VARIATION
- Sometimes we add some cubes of fresh pineapple in addition to the mango.

SERVING AND MENU IDEAS
Perfect with Caribbean Black-eyed Peas (page 138) or Cuban Black Beans (pages 137). Try some on Curried Red Lentil Burgers (page 87) or Indian Stuffed Eggplant (page 179). And make sure to try it as a dip with corn tortilla chips.

Jerk Sauce

Simple Sweet and Sour Sauce

Tomatillo Sauce

Smooth Hot Sauce

Red Pepper Butter

Puttanesca Sauce

Three Pestos

Tomato-Basil Sauce

Cheese Sauce

Caramelized Onion Gravy

Spinach Béchamel

Mushroom Gravy

Jerk Sauce

Jerk sauce is a Jamaican-style barbecue sauce with complex flavors. The sauce is spicy, sweet, salty, and tangy all at the same time. After you've made it once, make it your own favorite jerk sauce by adjusting the seasonings to suit your taste.

Traditionally, jerk sauce is used as a marinade for grilled meat, but we've found many other uses for it. We use it as a marinade for grilled or baked tofu, roasted vegetables, and fish or shrimp.

Yields 1 cup
Time: 10 minutes

1 cup chopped onions or scallions
1 fresh hot pepper, chopped
3 tablespoons apple cider vinegar or red wine
    vinegar
3 tablespoons vegetable oil
3 tablespoons soy sauce
2 garlic cloves, sliced
1 tablespoon peeled and grated fresh ginger
1 teaspoon dried thyme
1 teaspoon ground allspice
1 teaspoon ground cinnamon
1 tablespoon brown sugar

Combine all of the ingredients in a blender and whirl until smooth.

VARIATIONS

- Add a couple tablespoons of chopped fresh cilantro.
- Replace some of the vinegar with fresh lemon or lime juice.
- Add some rum.
- Ground cloves can stand in for the allspice.
- If 1 hot pepper isn't enough, add more. If your hot pepper is very hot, too hot for you, add less or remove the seeds.

Simple Sweet and Sour Sauce

Lovely color and great flavor for a minimum of effort! This sauce will enliven any Asian-style stuffed vegetable or stir-fry.

Yields about 1½ cups
Time: 5 minutes

1 cup orange or pineapple juice
1 tablespoon soy sauce
1 tablespoon apple cider vinegar or rice vinegar
1 teaspoon peeled and grated fresh ginger
1 tablespoon brown sugar
1 tablespoon cornstarch dissolved in 1 tablespoon
    cold water

In a small nonreactive saucepan, combine the orange or pineapple juice, soy sauce, vinegar, ginger, and brown sugar and bring to a boil. Whisk in the dissolved cornstarch. Reduce the heat and stir for a couple of minutes until the sauce thickens and becomes clear. Serve hot.

SERVING AND MENU IDEAS

This sauce transforms plain steamed vegetables into something special. Make a meal of rice, vegetables, and some of Moosewood's Best Baked and Pan-fried Tofu (page 202) drizzled with some of the sauce. Serve the sauce on Asian-style Stuffed Portobellos (page 183).

Tomatillo Sauce

Tomatillos look like small, hard, green tomatoes encased in thin, papery husks. They're easy to grow and have become plentiful in our Ithaca Farmers' Market. They can be used cooked or raw and their distinctive flavor is a little sour. We offer you two methods for cooking them in this recipe, one stovetop and one roasted in the oven. If your oven is on anyway, it's a little simpler to use the roasting method, but either way works just fine.

This simple green sauce is a tasty, interesting condiment and a nice change from tomato salsa. Make it as spicy as you like.

Yields 1½ generous cups
Time: 35 minutes

1 pound fresh tomatillos (about 3 cups coarsely chopped)
2 tablespoons vegetable oil
1 cup finely chopped onions
1 garlic clove, minced or pressed
¾ teaspoon salt
1 minced fresh hot pepper
2 teaspoons ground coriander seeds
½ teaspoon ground cumin seeds
1 teaspoon sugar
2 tablespoons chopped fresh cilantro

Peel off and discard the husks from the tomatillos. Rinse, core, and coarsely chop.

Stovetop Method
Warm the oil in a covered saucepan, add the onions, garlic, salt, and hot peppers (let your taste be the guide for how much to use and whether to seed or not). Cook, covered, on low heat for about 8 minutes, stirring occasionally. Stir in the coriander and cumin and cook, covered, for 2 minutes. Stir in the chopped tomatillos and ¼ cup of water. Increase the heat until the mixture begins to simmer vigorously, then cover and simmer on low heat, stirring occasionally, until the tomatillos have broken down and are saucy, about 15 minutes.

Purée in a food processor or in a blender. Stir in the sugar and cilantro.

Oven-Roasting Method
Preheat the oven to 425°F. Lightly oil a baking sheet.

In a mixing bowl, toss together the chopped tomatillos, oil, onions, garlic, salt, hot peppers, coriander, and cumin. Spread the mixture out on the prepared baking sheet and roast until the tomatillos are soft, about 20 minutes. Purée in a food processor or in a blender. Stir in the sugar and cilantro.

SERVING AND MENU IDEAS
Use Tomatillo Sauce as a dip for corn tortilla chips, or instead of a tomato-based hot sauce for Refried Beans (page 281) or Spinach-Cheese Burritos (page 198). Or use it as a condiment for Mexican Corn and Cheese Casserole (page 162) or anytime you want a flavor boost for a Mexican-style dish.

Smooth Hot Sauce

We love and depend on this spicy, full-bodied sauce. If you use red bell peppers, it's bright red; with green bell peppers, it's a rusty brown. Either way, it's delicious and one of our staples. This recipe makes 4 cups of sauce, and it keeps well in the refrigerator for at least 2 weeks, and longer in the freezer.

There are those among us who are connected to people who think it's not a meal without hot sauce. Sure, in the store there are lots of choices of little bottles and big bottles of hot sauce, and we do keep some in our homes. But, when you make your own hot sauce, you can control the ingredients, flavor, and spiciness—and you can make a lot for less.

Our earlier books have hot sauce recipes that tell you to blend all the ingredients together raw and then simmer. That works, but the flavor can be harsh if not cooked long enough. In the restaurant kitchen, where the ovens are on most of the time, some cooks roast all the vegetables and spices and then blend them with the tomatoes. Others sauté the onions and peppers in our big cast-iron skillet, and that's how most of us make hot sauce at home.

Yields about 4 cups
Time: 30 minutes

1½ tablespoons vegetable oil or olive oil
1 cup chopped onions
½ teaspoon salt
3 garlic cloves, chopped
1 cup seeded and chopped bell peppers
1 chopped fresh hot pepper, ¼ teaspoon cayenne, or ½ teaspoon red pepper flakes
one 28-ounce can tomatoes
2 teaspoons ground toasted cumin seeds (page 386)
2 teaspoons ground toasted coriander seeds (page 386)
¼ cup chopped fresh cilantro (optional)

Warm the oil in a large skillet on medium-high heat. Add the onions and salt and sauté for about 5 minutes. Add the garlic, bell peppers, and hot peppers and continue to sauté for about 4 minutes, or until the peppers have softened and the onions begin to brown. Remove from the heat.

Put the tomatoes, cumin and coriander, cilantro, if using, and cooked onions and peppers into a blender and whirl until smooth. Return to the pan, cover, and bring to a low boil. Simmer for about 10 minutes, stirring occasionally. Add salt to taste.

SERVING AND MENU IDEAS

Serve on Cuban Black Beans (page 137) or Mexican Corn and Cheese Casserole (page 162). Use in Chilaquiles Casserole (page 161), to add flavor to chili and soups, or to top stuffed peppers, omelets, and frittatas. We use this hot sauce on Latin American and Tex-Mex dishes like burritos, enchiladas, tacos, bean and vegetable casseroles, bean and rice dishes. It is also a good ingredient or accompaniment to spice up Middle-Eastern and North or West African dishes.

Red Pepper Butter

This nasturtium-orange sauce makes simple dishes elegant. Try it on plain pasta and broccoli, pasta and cauliflower, pasta and olives, pasta and asparagus, pasta and peas—pasta and almost anything! Delicious on steamed vegetables or fish, and stirred into potatoes or polenta. It's handy to have on hand; it will keep in the refrigerator for a week or more, and you can also freeze it.

The name notwithstanding, you can make this with olive oil only—no butter—for a very tasty vegan sauce. If you make it with red peppers that you've roasted yourself, a touch of extra lemon juice will balance the flavors.

Yields 2 cups
Time: 10 minutes

½ cup olive oil
5 garlic cloves
one 12-ounce can roasted red peppers, drained (1¼ cups)
½ cup butter, at room temperature (1 stick)
2 tablespoons fresh lemon juice
½ teaspoon salt
a generous sprinkling of ground black pepper
2 tablespoons chopped fresh basil or dill (optional)

Warm the olive oil in a small heavy pan on medium heat. Cook the garlic cloves until golden, about 3 minutes. Remove from the heat. (You can do this in a microwave, too.)

In a blender, whirl the roasted red peppers, butter, lemon juice, salt, and black pepper. Add the warm oil and garlic cloves and whirl until smooth. Stir the basil or dill in by hand.

Use right away or refrigerate or freeze. Thaw frozen Red Pepper Butter at room temperature and stir well before using.

Puttanesca Sauce

Puttanesca Sauce is zesty tomato sauce with body, accented with capers, kalamata olives, and red pepper flakes.

Yields 7 cups
Time: 45 minutes

3 tablespoons olive oil
1½ cups diced onions
4 garlic cloves, minced or pressed
¼ teaspoon salt
two 28-ounce cans diced tomatoes
1 tablespoon minced fresh oregano (1 teaspoon dried)
¾ teaspoon red pepper flakes
2 tablespoons capers, drained
⅓ cup chopped pitted kalamata olives
2 tablespoons chopped fresh basil (optional)

Warm the oil in a covered pot on medium-low heat. Add the onions, garlic, and salt and cook for 10 minutes, until soft. Stir in the tomatoes, oregano, red pepper flakes, capers, and olives, cover, and simmer for 20 to 25 minutes, stirring frequently. Stir in the fresh basil and add salt to taste.

SERVING AND MENU IDEAS
Serve Puttanesca Sauce over pasta with finely grated Parmesan or your favorite sharp Italian cheese. Or ladle some over Italian Polenta-stuffed Peppers (page 181), or plain fish, polenta, eggplants, or portobellos that would be enhanced by this highly flavored sauce.

Three Pestos

It's perhaps audacious to give the name "pesto" to any sauce other than the sublime Pesto Genovese. Well, chefs *are* audacious. That simple purée has inspired cooks to experiment with myriad combinations of herbs, oils, nuts, seeds, vegetables, cheeses, and even fruit. You might say this classic has launched a thousand pestos, and many have strayed far from Italy. Think Thai basil and mint with roasted peanuts. Moosewood cook David Hirsch put five pestos in *The Moosewood Restaurant Kitchen Garden* cookbook. Pesto is a good motivation for tending a garden.

Of course, we love a dollop of pesto on pasta, and we also add it to minestrones, tomato soups, and Mediterranean stews. It is a nice spread for sandwiches and crostini. We also put it in bean dips and aioli.

We're aware that pine nuts can be expensive, and because some people can have an almost allergic reaction to them, we often prepare our pestos using almonds or walnuts. This food processor method is easy and foolproof. If you use a blender to make pesto, chop the ingredients by hand first, and be prepared to stop and scrape—a lot.

PESTO GENOVESE
Yields 1½ cups
Time: 15 minutes

⅓ cup pine nuts or ½ cup almonds or walnuts, toasted (page 380)
4 cups packed basil leaves
3 chopped garlic cloves
½ cup plus 3 tablespoons shredded Parmesan cheese (the 3 tablespoons can be Pecorino Romano cheese)
½ cup olive oil (regular or extra-virgin)
salt

Pulse the pine nuts or almonds or walnuts in a food processor until chopped. Add the basil, garlic, and cheese and pulse until the ingredients are well chopped. Turn the processor on and pour in the oil in a slow, steady stream. Process to a smooth paste. Season with salt to taste.

VARIATIONS

- Sometimes fresh basil is hard to come by in large quantities. For a milder but still tasty pesto, we have substituted up to half the basil with baby spinach.
- For pesto with a slight edge, replace half the basil with arugula. When we include arugula, we blanch it in boiling water for a minute or two first to remove some of its sharpness.
- In Genoa, pesto is traditionally made with very young and tender basil leaves. At times, larger leaves can also be sharp. If that's what you've got, blanch them, as well.
- If you prefer a milder garlic flavor, sizzle it for a minute in a tablespoon of the olive oil.

ASPARAGUS PESTO

When asparagus is in season we just can't get enough of it. And when paired with some fresh tarragon, well what could be better?

Yields 1½ cups
Time: 15 minutes

1 pound asparagus
½ cup almonds, toasted (page 380)
2 chopped garlic cloves
¼ cup packed shredded Parmesan cheese
1 tablespoon chopped fresh tarragon
½ teaspoon salt
¼ teaspoon ground black pepper
¼ cup olive oil (regular or extra-virgin)

Snap off the tough ends of the asparagus spears at their natural breaking point, then slice the spears crosswise into ½-inch pieces. You'll need at least 2 cups for this recipe. Steam the asparagus pieces until bright green, about 5 minutes. Set aside.

Pulse the almonds in a food processor until chopped. Add the garlic, Parmesan, tarragon, salt, and black pepper and pulse until well chopped. Turn the processor on and pour in the oil in a slow, thin, steady stream. Process until uniform. This pesto has some texture because the asparagus does not purée to a smooth paste.

PUMPKIN SEED PESTO

We think you'll like this alternative to pesto made with tree nuts.

Yields about 1 cup
Time: 15 minutes

½ cup hulled, toasted pepitas (pumpkin seeds) (see Note)
2 chopped garlic cloves
⅛ teaspoon ground black pepper
2 packed cups fresh basil
⅓ cup shredded Parmesan cheese
⅓ cup olive oil
salt

Put the pepitas, garlic, black pepper, basil, and Parmesan in the bowl of a food processor and pulse to chop. Then, with the processor running, pour in the oil in a slow, thin, steady stream and process until smooth. Season with salt to taste.

NOTE

Pepitas are sometimes salted when you buy them, sometimes not. Add salt at the end to suit your taste.

Tomato-Basil Sauce

This is the restaurant's house tomato-basil sauce. We use it on polenta and stuffed vegetables, in our lasagnas, and as an option for "kid's" pasta. This recipe makes a generous amount, enough for a large lasagna, with maybe a cup or two left over. Although making your own sauce takes a little longer than opening a jar, you can season the sauce just the way you like it. And—it just tastes better. You can freeze any leftovers for later.

Yields about 7 cups
Time: 35 minutes

2 tablespoons olive oil
1½ cups finely chopped onions
4 garlic cloves, minced or pressed
½ teaspoon salt
1 teaspoon dried oregano (1 tablespoon fresh)
1 or 2 bay leaves (optional)
¼ cup dry red wine (optional)
two 28-ounce cans diced tomatoes
¼ to ½ cup chopped fresh basil
ground black pepper

Warm the oil in a heavy, nonreactive saucepan on medium-high heat. Add the onions and garlic and cook for a minute or two, stirring often. Sprinkle in the salt and add the oregano and bay leaves, if using, cover the pan, and reduce the heat to low. Cook until the onions are soft and translucent, 7 or 8 minutes. Stir in the wine, if using.

For a sauce like we usually make at Moosewood, whirl half of the tomatoes in a blender and leave the rest chunky. For a smoother sauce, whirl all of the tomatoes. Add the tomatoes to the pan, bring to a simmer, and cook on low heat for 10 to 15 minutes. Cook longer for a thicker sauce. Remove and discard bay leaves, if used. Stir in the basil. Season with black pepper and more salt to taste.

VARIATIONS

- Add 2 or 3 teaspoons ground fennel to the cooking onions.
- For a Greek-style sauce, replace the basil with 3 or 4 tablespoons of chopped fresh dill and add ⅓ cup chopped Kalamata olives.
- Make it spicier with 1 teaspoon of red pepper flakes.
- For a creamy sauce, purée a cup or two of the sauce with ½ cup cream cheese, and stir back into the pan.

Cheese Sauce

This sauce is a great example of one of the time-honored, delicious basics. Many of the women at Moosewood remember being taught how to make a simple roux in home economics class in the early '60s, and then to magically transform the roux into sauces. We think some of those simple lessons sparked a lifelong love of cooking, and we recommend this recipe as one of the basics to teach to your kids, boys and girls.

A roux is a classic French thickener made by cooking flour and butter into a smooth paste until the raw flavor of the flour is cooked out. It gives sauces and soups a velvety-smooth richness.

We think a great sharp cheddar is all you need for this sauce, but you might like to substitute up to a cup of shredded Parmesan, Fontina, or Gruyère to give the sauce a more complex flavor. Cheeses vary in saltiness, so we suggest you salt the sauce to taste at the end.

Yields generous 5 cups
Time: 25 minutes

10 ounces sharp cheddar cheese (2½ cups shredded)
4 cups milk
½ cup butter or olive oil
½ cup unbleached white all-purpose flour
2 teaspoons Dijon mustard

2 tablespoons dry sherry (optional)
⅛ teaspoon ground black or white pepper
generous pinch of freshly grated nutmeg
   (optional)

Shred the cheese and set aside.

Heat the milk in a saucepan to just below boiling. Meanwhile, in a heavy saucepan on medium-low heat, melt the butter until bubbling, but don't let it brown. While whisking, add the flour gradually to form a smooth roux. Cook, whisking constantly, for 3 or 4 minutes. (This cooking removes the raw flour taste; constant whisking prevents scorching).

Increase the heat to medium and whisk the hot milk into the roux, adding it about a cup at a time, and making sure the roux and milk are smooth before adding more. When all of the hot milk is in, the sauce will be smooth and thickened.

Add the shredded cheese, mustard, sherry, if using, pepper, and nutmeg. Reduce the heat and whisk until the cheese has melted. Season with salt to taste.

SERVING AND MENU IDEAS

This sauce is good on pasta, rice, stuffed vegetables, and crepes, and, of course, for Macaroni and Cheese with Broccoli (page 217). You can also add some to a creamy soup or chowder to thicken it and add more flavor.

Caramelized Onion Gravy

You are going to love this savory, rich-tasting brown gravy that is low in fat, vegan, and keeps well. When you caramelize onions, the natural sugars emerge and brown. Caramelized onions are sweet and mellow tasting.

Yields 5 cups
Time: 35 minutes

8 cups thinly sliced onions
¼ cup vegetable oil
½ teaspoon salt
1 teaspoon minced fresh thyme
1 teaspoon minced fresh rosemary
¼ cup soy sauce
½ cup dry sherry
2 cups hot water
¼ cup cornstarch
¼ cup cold water
¼ teaspoon ground black pepper

Slice the onions in half top to bottom, and then thinly slice stem end to root end. Heat the oil in a soup pot. Add the onions and cook for 3 minutes on medium heat, stirring constantly. Stir in the salt, thyme, and rosemary, and cook, uncovered, for about 25 minutes, stirring frequently. As the onions begin to stick a little to the pan, they are beginning to caramelize. Scrape them free and stir well. The onions will soften and brown—if they begin to scorch, the heat is too high. When the onions have browned and are absolutely soft, add the soy sauce and sherry and stir well. Continue to cook for 3 or 4 minutes. Stir in the hot water and bring to a simmer.

Stir the cornstarch and cold water together in a small cup or bowl until smooth. Pour into the simmering gravy while stirring and continue to stir until thickened. If the gravy isn't thick enough, mix an additional tablespoon of cornstarch with a tablespoon of cold water and stir it into the gravy while it simmers. Stir in the black pepper.

SERVING AND MENU IDEAS

Serve this flavorful gravy with mashed potatoes (see page 278). Ladle some over the Dixie Tofu-Pecan Loaf (page 209) or have some on Mushroom-Tofu-Pecan Burgers (page 92) served on rice or mashed potatoes.

Spinach Béchamel

Béchamel, or white sauce, is the thick, creamy base for many sauces and gravies. It's made by combining a simple flour and butter roux with hot milk. For this bright, beautifully green spinach béchamel, the fresh spinach should be just barely wilted, and still vivid green. The sauce can be made with dried herbs and spices, but we think that fresh thyme and basil and freshly grated nutmeg make a big difference.

Yields 4 cups
Time: 40 minutes

BÉCHAMEL SAUCE

2 cups hot milk
2 or 3 sprigs of fresh thyme or ½ teaspoon dried thyme
⅓ cup butter
⅓ cup unbleached white all-purpose flour
½ teaspoon salt
¼ teaspoon ground black pepper
½ teaspoon freshly grated nutmeg

2 tablespoons olive oil
1½ cups finely chopped onions
½ teaspoon dried thyme (optional)
½ teaspoon salt
¼ teaspoon ground black pepper
2 tablespoons chopped fresh basil
6 cups fresh baby spinach (about 9 ounces), rinsed and drained
2 to 4 tablespoons fresh lemon juice

To make the béchamel: Heat the milk in a saucepan to just below boiling. If you're using fresh thyme, add it to the milk as it heats to infuse the milk with the flavor. Remove the sprigs before adding the hot milk to the roux.

In a heavy 2-quart saucepan on low heat, melt the butter until bubbling, but don't let it brown. Whisk in the flour and cook, stirring constantly, until the roux is smooth and starting to bubble around the edges, about 2 minutes; do not let it brown. Whisk in the hot milk and keep whisking until the sauce thickens, about 2 minutes. Stir in the salt, black pepper, and nutmeg, cover, and set aside.

Warm the olive oil in a large skillet or sauce pan on medium heat. Cook the onions, dried thyme, if using, salt, and black pepper, covered, until the onions are soft but not browned, about 6 minutes. Stir frequently and when you take the cover off, let the condensation drip back into the onions. Stir in the basil and spread the spinach on top. Cover and gently steam the spinach until it has wilted but is still vivid green, 2 or 3 minutes.

In a food processor or blender, purée the spinach and onions and their liquid with about half of the béchamel until smooth and evenly green. Stir the purée back into the pan of béchamel and mix well. Add lemon juice and more salt and black pepper to taste.

SERVING AND MENU IDEAS

Serve over your favorite pasta, topped with finely grated Parmesan or feta cheese. At the restaurant, we frequently serve Fettuccine San Polo: Spinach Béchamel on fettuccine, topped with steamed cauliflower florets, chopped fresh tomatoes, and finely grated Parmesan. We also often use this sauce to make spinach lasagna béchamel by layering it with noodles and Italian cheeses. For lasagna tricolore, we layer the noodles with Italian cheeses and Tomato-Basil Sauce (page 324) and top it with Spinach Béchamel.

Mushroom Gravy

This savory, quick, vegan, gluten-free gravy is our favorite topping for a variety of dishes. We smother some of our burgers in it, as well as our much-loved tofu "meatloaf" (pages 89, 208, and 209). It's a natural on mashed potatoes, both white and sweet, and on stuffed vegetables.

We like cremini (Italian brown) mushrooms, but also often use white button mushrooms. Or mix up your mushrooms; use a combination of fresh ones and dried, and try some varieties you haven't tasted before. If using dried mushrooms, soak them first in hot water for about 20 minutes, and use the soaking liquid in the gravy.

Yields 4 cups
Time: 25 minutes

2 tablespoons vegetable oil
1½ cups diced onions
pinch of salt
4 cups sliced mushrooms (16 ounces whole)
1 teaspoon chopped fresh thyme or ¼ teaspoon
    dried thyme
¼ cup dry sherry
3 tablespoons soy sauce
1¾ cups water
¼ teaspoon ground black pepper
2 tablespoons cornstarch dissolved in ¼ cup cold
    water

Warm the oil in a cast-iron skillet or heavy-bottomed saucepan on medium-high heat. Add the onions with a pinch of salt and sauté for 5 minutes. Add the mushrooms and thyme and cook until the mushrooms are tender, about 10 minutes, stirring frequently to prevent sticking. Add the sherry, soy sauce, water, and black pepper. Cover and bring to a simmer. Add the dissolved cornstarch and stir until the gravy becomes clear and thickened.

Serve right away or remove from the heat and reheat before serving. Keep at a simmer, not a boil—liquids thickened with cornstarch lose viscosity if allowed to boil.

VARIATIONS

- In place of water, you can use stock. If it's salted, we recommend starting with 2 tablespoons of soy sauce, then tasting for salt at the end.
- Pan Asian Mushroom Gravy—Replace some of the mushrooms with Asian varieties, such as shiitake, straw, enokitake, or oyster mushrooms. Replace the thyme with 1 tablespoon grated and peeled fresh ginger, and add 1 teaspoon of dark sesame oil at the end.

Frosted Carrot Cake

Sara's Fresh Apple Spice Cake

Vegan Chocolate Cake

Our Favorite Pound Cakes

Vanilla Cheesecake

Banana Cake with Cream Cheese Frosting

Gingerbread

Moosewood Fudge Brownies

Italian Sesame Cookies

Cowboy Cookies

Chocolate–Chocolate Chip Cookies

Chocolate Ricotta Moose

Almond Shortbread

Baklava

Apricot-Almond Baklava

Strawberry-Rhubarb Crumble

Apple Crisp

Southern Nut Pie Eudora

Our Favorite All-Purpose Piecrust

Pumpkin Pie

Fresh Berry Ricotta Moose

Fresh Strawberry Sauce

Blueberry-Cherry Pie with Sour Cream Lattice Crust

Low-fat Lemon Pudding Cake

Creamy Vegan Rice Pudding

Vanilla Custard Sauce

Fresh Fruit Trifle

Savannah Banana

Truffles

Chocolate Cups

Fruit Skewers

Frosted Carrot Cake

This cake is one of our customers' favorite desserts. And what better way to eat your fruits and vegetables? It has a pound of carrots as well as pineapple and raisins.

Yields one 13 × 9 × 2 inch cake; 2 cups frosting
Prep time: about 1 hour
Baking time: about 1 hour

CARROT CAKE

1 pound carrots
one 8-ounce can unsweetened crushed pineapple
1¼ cups vegetable oil
2 cups sugar
4 large eggs
1 teaspoon pure vanilla extract
2 cups unbleached white all-purpose flour
1½ teaspoons baking powder
½ teaspoon baking soda
2 teaspoons ground cinnamon
¼ teaspoon freshly grated nutmeg
¼ teaspoon ground allspice
½ teaspoon salt
1 cup chopped walnuts
1 cup raisins

CREAM CHEESE FROSTING

½ cup butter, at room temperature
6 ounces cream cheese, at room temperature
½ teaspoon finely grated lemon zest
1 tablespoon fresh lemon juice
about 2 cups confectioners' sugar

Preheat the oven to 350°F. Butter or oil a 13 × 9 × 2-inch baking pan and dust it with flour.

To make the cake: Peel the carrots, cut them in ½- to ¾-inch chunks and pulse them in the bowl of a food processor until flaked. We've found that this method of preparing the carrots consistently works better for a cake than the more traditional way of grating or shredding them. Set the carrots aside. Put the pineapple in a colander and set aside to drain while you prepare the cake.

In a large mixing bowl, using an electric mixer, beat the oil and sugar until well combined. Add the eggs and beat well. Beat in the vanilla. In a separate bowl, sift together the flour, baking powder, baking soda, cinnamon, nutmeg, allspice, and salt. Stir the dry ingredients into the egg mixture just until all the flour is incorporated. Fold in the flaked carrots, drained pineapple, chopped walnuts, and raisins.

Pour the batter into the prepared baking pan and bake until a knife inserted in the center comes out clean, 55 to 60 minutes. Remove from the oven and cool on a rack.

To make the frosting: Using an electric mixer, beat the butter and cream cheese until creamy. Beat in the lemon zest and lemon juice. Gradually beat in the confectioners' sugar until the frosting is a good consistency for spreading and is to your taste. (If your confectioners' sugar is lumpy it's a good idea to sift it.)

When the cake is cool, spread the frosting over the top.

VARIATIONS

You can also make this a layer cake by baking the batter in two 9-inch round cake pans. They will take less time to bake, about 30 minutes. The recipe makes enough frosting for a layer cake.

The walnuts can be omitted, but we prefer the cake with them.

Sara's Fresh Apple Spice Cake

Sara Robbins started at Moosewood in 1973 as a baker and dessert maker. She brought this cake to her hiring interview. It is a beloved family recipe from her talented Aunt Minnie of Atlanta, Georgia. This coffee cake is a classic of the American South where many households swear by their own versions. It is also perfect for upstate New York, a leading grower of apples of every variety.

The cake is moist, homey, and wholesome, and the recipe is fail-safe.

Yields one 10-inch Bundt cake or a 13 × 9 × 2-inch
　　sheet cake
Prep time: 30 minutes
Baking time: about 1 hour

1¼ cups vegetable oil
2 cups lightly packed brown sugar
3 large eggs
2 teaspoons pure vanilla extract
3 cups unbleached white all-purpose flour or 2
　　cups white and 1 cup whole wheat flour
1 teaspoon baking powder
1 teaspoon baking soda
½ teaspoon salt
2 teaspoons ground cinnamon
½ teaspoon ground cardamom
3 tablespoons apple juice or cider, milk,
　　buttermilk, or water
3 cups chopped apples (peeled or not)
1 cup chopped walnuts or pecans (optional)

Preheat the oven to 350°F. Butter or oil a 10-inch Bundt pan or a 13 × 9 × 2-inch baking pan. Either dust with flour or sprinkle with sesame seeds.

In a large bowl, beat the oil and brown sugar for a couple of minutes. Add the eggs, one at a time, beating after each addition, and then beat until creamy. Add the vanilla and beat to incorporate.

In a separate bowl, sift together the flour, baking powder, baking soda, salt, cinnamon, and cardamom. Add to the sugar-egg mixture along with the liquid, and beat until smooth. Fold the apples into the batter. Fold in the nuts, if using.

Pour the batter into the prepared pan and bake for an hour or more until the cake is golden brown, fragrant, pulling away from the sides of the pan, and firm to the touch.

If you made a Bundt cake, cool it in the pan for 10 or 15 minutes and then invert onto a serving plate. Serve the sheet cake from the pan. Serve warm or at room temperature.

SERVING IDEAS

Plain, this cake is good for brunch or a snack. We usually dust it with confectioners' sugar after it has cooled. For dessert, it sure is good with whipped cream or ice cream.

Vegan Chocolate Cake

Dark and dense, moist and delicious. Over the years, we've made only minor changes to our Vegan Chocolate Cake recipe. We usually make a large, single layer cake topped with a simple chocolate glaze and we serve it right out of the pan. But sometimes we add peanut butter, or coconut or coconut milk, or raspberry purée, or orange zest and orange liqueur to the cake or to the glaze.

This recipe also makes the right amount of batter for a two-layer cake, two 9-inch round or 8-inch square pans (2 inches deep). To ensure that the cake layers come out of the pan cleanly, we recommend that you line the pans with parchment paper: oil the bottom and sides of the pans, cut the parchment paper to fit the bottom of the pan, oil it and then dust the bottom and sides with flour.

Yields one 13 × 9 × 2-inch cake or two 9-inch
   round or 8-inch square layers
Prep time: 15 minutes
Baking time: about 55 minutes

CAKE
3 cups unbleached white all-purpose flour
⅔ cup unsweetened cocoa powder (lightly packed
   with the back of a spoon)
2 cups sugar
1 teaspoon salt
1 teaspoon baking soda
1¾ cups water
2 teaspoons pure vanilla extract
1 cup vegetable oil
¼ cup apple cider vinegar

VEGAN CHOCOLATE GLAZE
8 ounces semisweet chocolate
½ cup boiling water

Preheat the oven to 350°F. Oil a 13 × 9 × 2-inch baking pan and dust it with flour.

To make the cake: In a large mixing bowl, sift together the flour, cocoa powder, sugar, salt, and baking soda. Use a whisk or spoon to thoroughly mix the ingredients together. In a separate bowl, combine the water, vanilla, and oil. Add the wet ingredients to the dry ingredients and whisk until smooth. Add the vinegar and whisk just until it is incorporated; the batter will be thinner than most cake batter. Pour the batter into the prepared pan(s). Bake for 50 to 55 minutes until a knife inserted in the middle comes out clean. With this cake it is best to err on the side of overbaking, if the middle is even slightly undercooked, the cake will sink in the middle as it cools.

When the cake has thoroughly cooled, make the glaze: Put the chocolate and boiling water in blender and let it sit for a couple of minutes to soften the chocolate. Then whirl until smooth. You can glaze the cooled cake right away, but it is best to pour the glaze into a bowl and chill for 15 to 20 minutes until it is a spreadable consistency.

Our Favorite Pound Cakes

With their fine texture and rich, buttery flavor, pound cakes have been a consistent favorite at Moosewood for most of our history.

We start with a plain, vanilla cake which is great as is with a cup of tea or perfect with fresh berries spooned on top or glazed with chocolate. It's what we use to make Savannah Banana Pudding (page 365) and Fresh Fruit Trifle (page 365).

But also, we're constantly changing a few things in the recipe to invent new cakes. Any flavor or extract is OK. You can use brown sugar instead of white. Lots of different liquids work well. In place of buttermilk, we've used milk, coffee, yogurt, sour cream, fruit juice, coconut milk, wine, whiskey, and green tea. You can add things like nuts, chocolate chips, dried fruit, coconut, citrus peel, or juicy fresh fruits (in which case, you eliminate the liquid). You can even reduce the flour by 1 cup and add 2 cups of cornmeal, for a nice polenta pound cake.

The cake can be dusted with confectioners' sugar or cocoa powder, soaked with a liqueur, glazed, or frosted. It can be served with fruit and/or whipped cream, or sliced and layered with lemon curd and decorated with candied violets or edible fresh flowers.

Yields one 10-inch Bundt cake
Prep time: 15 minutes
Baking time: 1 hour and 15 to 30 minutes

1 pound butter, softened to room temperature
2½ cups sugar
6 large eggs
2 teaspoons pure vanilla extract
4 cups unbleached white pastry flour
½ cup buttermilk or milk
1 teaspoon salt
2 teaspoons baking powder

Preheat the oven to 350°F. Thoroughly coat a 10-inch (12-cup) Bundt pan (see Note) with butter or cooking spray and dust liberally with flour.

Using an electric mixer, cream the softened butter and sugar until light. Beat in the eggs and vanilla until smooth. On a lower speed, mix in 2 cups of the flour until blended, then add the buttermilk and mix well. Sift together the remaining 2 cups of flour and the salt and baking powder. Add to the batter and beat well.

Spoon the batter into the prepared Bundt pan. Bake for 1 hour and 15 to 30 minutes until the cake is golden brown, pulls away from the sides of the pan, and is firm to the touch. A knife inserted into the center should come out clean. Check for doneness starting at an hour because the baking time varies with different pans and ovens.

Cool the cake in the pan on a rack for 15 to 20 minutes. Invert onto a serving plate to cool. Make sure the cake has dropped out of the pan, but leave the pan over the cake for about 20 minutes while it cools.

Not every 10-inch Bundt pan holds the same amount because of differences in the fluting and slope. For this recipe, we recommend a Bundt pan that holds at least 12 cups, because if the pan is too small, there is a risk that the batter will overflow during baking, making a mess in your oven.

VARIATIONS

Moosewood dessert makers have created an enormous number of pound cake variations over the years. Here are a half-dozen of our favorites. When you've invented a wild new version that you're proud of, please tell us about it.

- **Pistachio-Lemon Pound Cake**—Use pure lemon extract and add the zest of 1 lemon plus a cup of chopped pistachios. Coat the cooled cake with a simple lemon glaze that you can make by stirring together 1 cup of confectioners' sugar and 2 to 3 tablespoons of fresh lemon juice until smooth.

- **Date-Walnut-Orange Pound Cake**—Use pure orange extract and add the zest of 1 orange. Use fresh orange juice as the liquid and add I cup of chopped toasted walnuts and 1 cup of chopped dates.

- **Blueberry-Lemon Pound Cake**—Use pure lemon extract and add the zest of 1 lemon. For the liquid, use the juice of the lemon (about ¼ cup). Add 2 cups fresh or frozen blueberries. Some blueberries release a lot of moisture, so this cake may take an additional 15 minutes to bake.

- **Pecan-Cardamom Pound Cake**—Use brown sugar instead of white and use ½ cup of coffee as the liquid. Add 2 teaspoons ground cardamom, 1 teaspoon ground cinnamon, ½ teaspoon ground allspice, and ½ teaspoon ground black pepper. Add 1 cup of chopped toasted pecans. You can make a coffee glaze by mixing together 1½ cups of confectioners' sugar and ¼ cup of coffee.

- **Chocolate-Hazelnut Orange Pound Cake**—Add the zest of 1 orange and use the orange juice as the liquid. Add 1 cup of chopped toasted hazelnuts and 1 cup of coarsely chopped semisweet chocolate or chocolate chips.

- **Amaretto Pound Cake**—Use pure almond extract and either milk, cream, or almond milk as the liquid. Add 1 cup of chopped toasted almonds. When the cake has cooled, pour ½ cup of amaretto or other almond liqueur over it, and when it has soaked in, dust the cake with confectioners' sugar.

Vanilla Cheesecake

For this recipe we went to the chocolate- and butter-smudged old notebook that the restaurant dessert makers have written, used, and revised over the years. This cheesecake is that pure, creamy, rich, plain vanilla cheesecake that so many people love. And the crust is very tasty.

We usually serve it with a fruit topping, but customers often ask for the topping on the side or not at all, because they love to have that rich flavor and velvety mouthfeel uncomplicated by any extra tastes or textures.

We give you directions for using a food processor because we think that's the best and easiest method. If your processor is smaller than 9-cup capacity, you'll need to do the filling in two batches and combine the batches in a large bowl. You can also make mix the filling with a blender (lots of scraping down), or a mixer (at the start, a strain on the motor). It's helpful if the ingredients are at room temperature.

We've made lots of cheesecakes, and when they've cracked or had bubbles on top, we've worked hard to figure out why. Please read our cheesecake tips (see page 339) before you start so you'll understand why we give you the directions we do.

With this recipe, you can make a 9-inch or a 10-inch cheesecake. As counterintuitive as it may seem, the directions are the same, and the baking times differ by only fifteen minutes. A 9-inch cheesecake will be higher, and unless you like a thick crust, reduce the crust ingredients to ¾ cup oats, ¾ cup walnuts, ⅓ cup brown sugar, 3 tablespoons melted butter.

Yields one 9- or 10-inch cheesecake
Prep time: 25 minutes
Baking time: about 45 minutes
In oven cooling time: 1 hour
Room temperature cooling time: 4 hours or
    overnight
Chilling time: at least 6 hours

NUTS AND OATS CRUST
1 cup rolled oats
1 cup walnuts
½ cup packed brown sugar
¼ cup melted butter

FILLING
1½ pounds cream cheese
1 cup sour cream
1 tablespoon pure vanilla extract
¼ teaspoon salt
1 cup sugar
4 large eggs

Preheat the oven to 325°F. Generously butter the bottom and sides of a 9- or 10-inch springform pan. (See headnote about pan size.)

To make the crust: Whirl the crust ingredients in a food processor until crumbly. Spread the mixture evenly over the bottom of the pan, pressing it out to the sides and against the outside edges to about ½ inch up. Bake for 10 minutes while you prepare the filling. Then reduce the oven temperature to 300°F.

To make the filling: Cut the cream cheese into 2-inch chunks. Whirl the cream cheese, sour cream, vanilla, salt, and sugar in a food processor just until smooth. Check with a spoon for cream cheese lumps—if you find any, break them up and whirl again briefly. Add the eggs, whirl briefly, and then scrape the sides and process until smooth and evenly colored, but don't process more than necessary. Pour the filling into the springform pan and bake the cheesecake until the sides are firm and the center still moves a bit when gently shaken. A 10-inch cheesecake will take about 45 minutes, and a 9-inch about an hour. Do not overbake; the cooking process will continue during the cool-down period. Turn off the oven and open the oven door a crack. Leave the cheesecake in the oven for an hour.

Place the cheesecake, in its pan, on a countertop and cover it with a plate or a baking sheet. Let it sit at room temperature for 4 hours or overnight. Then refrigerate in the pan for at least 6 hours.

Remove the cheesecake from the pan before serving. For a clean release, run a knife dipped in water around the outside edges as you slowly release the clasp. If the bottom sticks, warm the bottom of the pan by holding it on hot water for about 15 seconds to melt the butter on the bottom of the crust just enough to release it from the pan.

SERVING IDEAS

Serve absolutely plain on a pretty plate. Or, decorate with edible flowers or slices of fresh fruit. Or, serve each slice topped with a fruit sauce, such as Fresh Strawberry Sauce (page 359). And, just so you know, cheesecake *will* hold birthday candles upright.

HOW TO AVOID CHEESECAKE CRACKS AND TWO OTHER TIPS

Cheesecakes have a tendency to crack, but they don't have to.

One cause of cracking is too much air in the batter. As the cheesecakes heats up in the oven, air bubbles expand and combine with each other and rise. When they break out of the top of the cake cracks or craters appear in the cake's surface. So, avoid overbeating the batter because overbeating incorporates additional air. Mix the batter well and eliminate cream cheese lumps before you add the eggs. To help achieve this, bring the cream cheese to room temperature or soften it by unwrapping it and placing it in a glass or ceramic bowl and microwaving for 30 to 45 seconds until slightly softened. Eggs hold air in the batter, so add them last and mix the batter as little as possible once they are in.

Another cause of a cracked surface is a too-rapid temperature change. If you heat a cheesecake too fast or cool it down too fast, it's likely to crack. So, bake the cheesecake at a low oven temperature. A water bath isn't essential, but it does assure that the cheesecake cooks slowly and evenly: Wrap the bottom of the springform pan in aluminum foil and place it in a larger pan with hot water in it, just halfway up the outside of the springform pan and bake as directed.

Don't overbake the cheesecake. When perfectly done, there will still be a 2- to 3-inch diameter wobbly spot in the middle of the cheesecake. The texture will smooth out as it cools.

Cheesecake shrinks as it cools. Hence the directions for a slow, gentle cooling down. And, generously butter the sides of the springform pan before pouring in batter to allow the cake to pull away from the pan as it cools and shrinks instead of pulling apart from the middle.

If after all this, you still have a crack, and you care what your cheesecake looks like, spread on a topping or a sauce to camouflage the crevasse.

Tip: A well-constructed, heavy springform pan is a joy to use. A leaking, tinny springform pan that imparts a metallic taste ruins, or at least taints, a cheesecake. We recommend Fat Daddio brand springform pans.

Tip: Baked plain cheesecakes freeze well. When completely chilled, wrap securely in plastic wrap and then heavy-duty aluminum foil. Do not freeze cheesecakes with garnishes or toppings. Defrost in the refrigerator.

Banana Cake with Cream Cheese Frosting

This is a simple, moist, always pleasing cake that we turn to over and over. It's a regular on Moosewood's dessert menu and one of the most requested recipes on our website. It's easy enough for any day, and judging by the requests from our customers and families, it is many people's favorite birthday cake.

The frosting recipe makes about 3 cups, a good amount for a layer cake. Halve the frosting recipe for a larger single layer cake.

Yields one 13 × 9 × 2-inch cake or two 9-inch
    round layers; 3 cups frosting
Prep time: 25 minutes
Baking time: 25 minutes

BANANA CAKE
½ cup butter, at room temperature (1 stick)
1 cup sugar
3 large eggs
2 teaspoons pure vanilla extract
2 cups unbleached white all-purpose flour
1 teaspoon baking soda
1 teaspoon baking powder
1 teaspoon salt
1½ cups mashed ripe bananas (about 4)

CREAM CHEESE FROSTING
½ cup butter, at room temperature
8 ounces cream cheese, at room temperature
4 cups confectioners' sugar (1 pound)
1 teaspoon pure vanilla extract

Preheat the oven to 350°F. Lightly butter, oil, or spray a 13 × 9 × 2-inch baking pan or two 9-inch round cake pans.

To make the cake: Using an electric mixer, cream the butter and sugar. Add the eggs and vanilla and beat until smooth and creamy. Sift together the flour, baking soda, baking powder, and salt. Add half the dry mixture and beat until smooth. Add the mashed bananas and mix. Add the remaining flour mixture and beat until smooth.

Pour the batter into the prepared pan(s). Bake until golden brown and a knife inserted in the center comes out clean, about 25 minutes for round cake pans and about 35 minutes for a 13 × 9 × 2-inch pan. Cool in the pan(s) for 15 minutes. Gently turn layer cakes out of the pans onto plates or waxed paper on a cooling rack. It's most practical to serve a single-layer cake from the baking pan. Allow the cake to cool completely before frosting.

To make the frosting: Using an electric mixer, beat the butter and cream cheese in a large mixing bowl until smooth. Add the confectioners' sugar, a cup at a time, and beat until smooth. Add the vanilla and beat to incorporate.

Spread the frosting on the cooled cake. If you're making a layer cake, first spread frosting between the two layers and then on the sides and top of the cake.

Gingerbread

Our favorite gingerbread is based on a recipe from an old Fannie Farmer cookbook, and it's been a Moosewood favorite since the very early days. We like that it's not too sweet, and we love that so many ingredients are in half-cup measurements or multiples of. Over the years, we've added more ginger and some cinnamon to the original recipe.

Sometimes at the restaurant we serve gingerbread drizzled with lemon sauce, sometimes topped with a little whipped cream, sometimes shiny with a lemon glaze. Plain or slightly embellished, it's delicious, especially when warm.

Yields an 8 × 8-inch gingerbread
Prep time: 20 minutes
Baking time: about 30 minutes

2 large eggs
½ cup sour cream
½ cup unsulphured molasses
½ cup packed brown sugar
1½ cups unbleached white all-purpose flour
½ teaspoon baking soda
1 tablespoon ground ginger
1 teaspoon ground cinnamon
¼ teaspoon salt
½ cup melted butter

Preheat the oven to 350°F. Butter or spray with oil an 8 × 8-inch baking pan.

Using an electric mixer, beat the eggs in a large bowl. Add the sour cream, molasses, and brown sugar and beat until smooth and creamy. In a separate mixing bowl, sift together the flour, baking soda, ginger, cinnamon, and salt. Beat the dry ingredients into the egg and molasses mixture until smooth. Pour in the melted butter and beat until smooth. Pour the batter into the prepared baking pan and bake until a knife inserted in the center comes out clean, about 30 minutes.

VARIATION

- If you prefer to make gingerbread cupcakes, butter a standard 12-cup muffin pan or lightly coat with cooking spray. Evenly distribute the batter among the cups (they will be full). Cupcakes will take 20 to 25 minutes to bake. Cool for about 5 minutes and then transfer the cupcakes to a cooling rack.

Moosewood Fudge Brownies

There's no question that Moosewood Fudge Brownies are not health food. We've experimented over the years with alternative brownie recipes that include whole wheat flour, rice, prunes, carob, and even chickpeas, while never taking the real thing off the menu because there really is no equivalent for butter, eggs, and fine-quality chocolate. So, they're immoderately rich and good, but as with all good things in moderation, they have a special place in Moosewood cuisine.

Moosewood's menu changes—new soups, new entrées, new desserts. You never know what will be offered—except for brownies. Brownies are the one thing we never rotate off the menu and mustn't ever run out of lest we cause some customer abject disappointment, outright disbelief, and bitter regret at their horrible, undeserved turn of fate.

In Moosewood's early years, there were customers who needed to reward themselves with a brownie after eating all those vegetables, or maybe for trying tofu for the first time. First thing, they reserved their brownie, and then ordered their meal. Today, some customers who just can't manage dessert right after their meal take a brownie to go.

Yields twenty-four 2-inch brownies
Prep time: 10 minutes
Baking time: 20 to 30 minutes

1 cup butter, melted (2 sticks)
6 ounces unsweetened chocolate (1 cup chips or
    chunks)
1 pound brown sugar (2 cups packed)
1 teaspoon pure vanilla extract
5 large eggs
1 cup unbleached white pastry flour (see Notes)

Preheat the oven to 350°F. Butter or coat with cooking spray a 13 × 9 × 2-inch baking pan.

In a small heavy saucepan, melt the butter. Add the chocolate, stir for a minute and remove from the heat. When the chocolate has fully softened, stir until smooth.

Put the brown sugar and vanilla into a mixing bowl. Add the melted butter and chocolate and beat with an electric mixer until combined. Add the eggs and beat well. Add the flour and mix until the batter is smooth.

Pour the batter into the prepared pan and bake for 20 to 30 minutes until the brownies are pulling away from the sides of the pan and the middle is still moist.

NOTES
Pastry flour makes moist, fudgy brownies. If you use all-purpose flour, the brownies will be more cakelike.

We use unsalted butter when we make brownies at the restaurant, but at home we use either salted or unsalted butter, whichever we have on hand, and we think the results are equally good.

SERVING AND MENU IDEAS
Brownies are great topped with ice cream. Crumble leftover brownies and serve on ice cream. Brownie crumbs freeze well and can go straight from the freezer to a sundae with no defrosting, for an instant dessert.

Italian Sesame Cookies

In many Italian-American homes, no holiday is complete without these golden, not-too-sweet, delicate butter cookies—biscuits, almost—to dunk in espresso, coffee, tea, wine, anisette, or milk. They're available in most Italian bakeries, but the ones you make at home are so much better.

Back in Queens, these were Moosewood cook Ned Asta's mother's favorite cookie, and Ned describes in this recipe how to make the traditional S shape that fits perfectly into the narrow top of a demitasse or liqueur glass.

These cookies can be kind of messy to make, but if you get an assembly line going and don't slop the water onto your dry, floured work surface, although your hands will be coated with sesame seeds, production will hum right along.

Yields about 40 cookies
Prep time: 45 minutes
Baking time: 25 minutes

3 cups unbleached white all-purpose flour
1 cup sugar
1½ teaspoons baking powder
½ teaspoon salt
1 cup cold butter (2 sticks)
3 large eggs
2 teaspoons pure vanilla extract
1¼ cups sesame seeds

You can make this dough in a food processor or by hand.

To make with a food processor: Put the flour, sugar, baking powder, and salt into the food processor and pulse 3 or 4 times. Cut the butter into small pieces and pulse 7 or 8 times until just crumbly. Lightly beat the eggs and vanilla together and add to the bowl. Pulse until just moistened and uniform.

To make by hand: In a mixing bowl, sift together the flour, sugar, baking powder, and salt. Cut the butter into small pieces and work it into the dry ingredients with your fingers or a pastry cutter until just crumbly. Beat the eggs and the vanilla together and add to the bowl. Mix just until the dough is moistened and uniform.

Divide the dough into 4 equal parts. Keep the dough covered with plastic wrap in the refrigerator until you're ready to shape the cookies.

Preheat the oven to 350°F. Butter or oil two baking sheets.

Lightly flour a work surface, and next to it place a cup of cold water with a pastry brush and a flat dinner plate. Put the sesame seeds in a shallow bowl, next to a baking sheet.

Roll one-fourth of the dough into a thin rope about 24 inches long. Cut into 10 pieces. Gently pinch and pull each piece to about 4 inches long and place on the dinner plate. When you have 4 or 5 on the plate, brush them with water and then roll each one in the sesame seeds to coat and place it on the baking sheet in a loose S shape. Repeat with the rest of the rope, placing the cookies about 2 inches apart. Repeat with the rest of the refrigerated dough.

Bake the cookies until firm and golden, about 25 minutes. Cool on a wire rack.

Cowboy Cookies

Our dessert makers try out a lot of different cookies at Moosewood, but most frequently they make easy Cowboy Cookies, which are sturdy, wholesome, homespun treats that might even sustain you on a hard day out on the trail.

We keep a big glass jar full of cookies near the side door that leads down the hall to the other stores in our building. Every day people from the antique shop or the toy store or the guitar workshop pop their heads in to check out the cookies of the day. When they find a beautifully frosted or filled cookie or some ethnic classic that took all morning to fill and roll and layer or some delicate airy miracle of bakers' art, they are polite about it, but what they really want most of all are Cowboy Cookies again and again.

Yields about 24 big cookies or 40 smaller cookies
Prep time: 25 minutes
Baking time: about 12 minutes per batch

2 cups unbleached white all-purpose flour (see Note)
1 teaspoon baking soda
½ teaspoon baking powder
½ teaspoon salt
1 cup butter, at room temperature (2 sticks)
½ cup sugar
½ cup packed brown sugar
2 large eggs
1 teaspoon pure vanilla extract
2 cups rolled oats
2 cups semisweet chocolate chips or chunks (12 ounces)
1½ cups raisins, dried cranberries, or chopped dried cherries (optional)
1 cup coarsely chopped toasted walnuts (optional)

NOTE

Some of us like to use pastry flour, which makes the cookies crisper.

Preheat the oven to 350°F.

In a mixing bowl, sift together the flour, baking soda, baking powder, and salt. Set aside. In a large mixing bowl, using an electric mixer, cream together the butter and sugars. Add the eggs and vanilla and beat well. Add the dry ingredients and blend well. Stir in the oats. Fold in the chocolate chips and the dried fruit and the nuts, if using. The dough will be fairly stiff.

Drop spoonfuls of dough onto unoiled baking sheets. For large cookies, place rounded blobs of dough about the size of a ping-pong ball on the baking sheets, placing then about 4 inches apart. For smaller cookies, drop rounded tablespoons of dough onto the baking sheets, placing them about 2 inches apart. Bake for 12 to 15 minutes until golden brown. Transfer the cookies to wire cooling racks. Cool completely before storing in a sealed container.

Chocolate–Chocolate Chip Cookies

With easy-to-make, big, chewy, dark chocolate cookies filled with chunks of chocolate, things are looking up in the world. For the restaurant, we make these with good-size chocolate chunks, but the more readily available chocolate chips are fine.

Yields about 24 big cookies
Prep time: 25 minutes
Baking time: 15 to 20 minutes

1 cup butter (2 sticks), at room temperature
¼ cup cream cheese
2 cups sugar
2 large eggs
1 teaspoon pure vanilla extract
2 cups unbleached white all-purpose flour
⅔ cup unsweetened cocoa powder
½ teaspoon baking soda
½ teaspoon salt
1½ cups chocolate chips or chunks (9 ounces)

Preheat the oven to 325°F. Lightly oil two baking sheets (or four if your oven will hold them).

Using an electric mixer, thoroughly cream the butter, cream cheese, and sugar. Add the eggs and vanilla and beat well.

In a separate bowl, sift together the flour, cocoa powder, baking soda, and salt. Add to the butter and sugar mixture and blend well. The dough will be fairly stiff. Using a spoon, fold in the chocolate chips.

Drop large balls of dough (about the size of small tangerines) onto the prepared baking sheets, spacing them 3 to 4 inches apart. Six cookies will fit comfortably on a standard baking sheet.

Bake for 15 to 20 minutes until the cookies feel soft in the middle, but don't collapse under a gentle touch. Cool the cookies on the baking sheet for a few minutes, then transfer them, while still warm, to a wire cooling rack. Cool completely before storing in a sealed container.

Chocolate Ricotta Moose

A velvety, rich, deep chocolate mousse-like pudding that has been frequently on the restaurant dessert menu since we can remember. Not cooked and with ricotta as the base, it's just about the quickest and easiest dessert to make, other than a bowl of fresh fruit and nuts. You can eat it right away or refrigerate it to serve later.

The presentation can be as humble or as elegant as you like. At the restaurant, we spoon the pudding into clear dessert glasses and top with whipped cream, red raspberries or sliced strawberries, and a sprig of mint. At home, we often spoon it from the mixing bowl into small bowls at the table.

The quality and flavor of the ricotta and chocolate are significant—with excellent ricotta and chocolate, it is sublime.

Yields about 4 cups
Serves 6 to 8
Time: 15 minutes

6 ounces semisweet chocolate (1 cup chips or pieces)
1 teaspoon pure vanilla extract
14 to 16 ounces ricotta cheese

1 cup heavy cream
¼ teaspoon pure vanilla extract
1 tablespoon pure maple syrup or honey or 2 tablespoons confectioners' sugar

Melt the chocolate on the stove top on very low heat or in a microwave oven. In a food processor, whirl the melted chocolate with the vanilla and ricotta until evenly colored and very smooth. You'll probably need to scrape down the sides a couple of times. Refrigerate until ready to serve.

Before serving, whip the heavy cream with the vanilla and sweetener in a bowl. Fold the chocolate-ricotta mixture into the whipped cream until evenly colored. Serve right away or chill.

Almond Shortbread

Our Moosewood dessert makers are held in high esteem—after all, dessert is some people's favorite meal of the day, and eating a luscious sweet is a sensual and emotional experience. Is it any wonder that Proust began *Remembrance of Things Past* with a madeleine pastry? Kip Wilcox is in our pantheon of most respected dessert makers. Her shortbread recipes are the basis for these delicately flavored and not-too-sweet little cookies that are our favorite shortbread, both to make and to eat.

This recipe is very versatile. You can use almost any nuts: pistachios, walnuts, pecans, hazelnuts, peanuts . . . . Vanilla is always a good extract to add, but others are good, too, say, orange extract with hazelnuts, lemon extract with pistachios, almond extract if you love that flavor . . . . And, you can roll out the dough and cut it into various shapes, or pat the dough into a pie plate and cut it into wedges (see Variations).

Yields 24 cookies
Prep time: 30 minutes
Chilling time: 30 minutes
Baking time: 20 to 25 minutes

½ cup almonds, plus 24 whole almonds for
     decoration
2 cups unbleached white all-purpose flour
¾ cup confectioners' sugar
¼ teaspoon salt if using salted butter, ½ teaspoon
     salt if using unsalted butter
1 cup butter, softened (2 sticks)
1 teaspoon pure almond extract

Toast the almonds until fragrant and lightly browned, about 10 minutes in a 350°F oven. Set them aside for a few minutes to cool. Count out 24 almonds and set aside. Put the remaining almonds and 1 cup of the flour into a food processor and process until the almonds are finely ground. Add the sugar and salt, and pulse briefly to combine.

Add the softened butter and the almond extract to the flour, and process until well blended. In ⅓-cup increments, add the remaining 1 cup flour, pulsing only briefly after each addition. Don't overwork the dough; as soon as it can be shaped and is not sticky, you're done.

Turn the dough out and divide it in two. Place each half on a piece of plastic wrap and shape it into a 6-inch log, patting the sides and the ends so the size of the log is uniform. Wrap the logs in the plastic wrap and chill for 30 minutes or more.

When the logs are chilled, preheat the oven to 350°F. Line a baking sheet with parchment paper (see page 381), or, if your baking sheet is heavy, it will be fine bare and unoiled.

Remove the plastic wrap and slice each log into 12 slices, ½ inch thick. Arrange the slices on the baking sheet, spacing them about 1 inch apart. Press a toasted almond into the center of each cookie.

Bake for 20 to 25 minutes, just until lightly colored—if you wait until they're golden in the oven, they'll be overbaked. Rotate the baking sheet after about 10 minutes so the cookies bake evenly. When the shortbread is done, place the hot baking sheet on a rack and cool for 10 minutes before removing them.

Put on a pot of coffee!

VARIATIONS
- Rather than chilling the dough in a log, you can pat it out, right on the baking sheet, into 4 rounds about 6 inches in diameter and a little less than ½ inch thick. Score each round into 6 wedges and press a toasted whole almond into each wedge. Bake for 20 to 25 minutes until just becoming golden. While still hot, cut each round into wedges and transfer the wedges to a wire cooling rack.
- Or, roll or pat the dough to a little less than ½ inch thick on a lightly floured surface. Cut into shapes with a cookie cutter and press an almond into each cookie. Bake about 1 inch apart on the baking sheet, then transfer to a wire cooling rack.

Baklava

We've developed baklava recipes that have less sugar, less honey, or less spice, and that substitute olive oil and whole wheat filo. But if you want the full effect and are willing to let your diet go to hell in a handbasket, then this one's for you. This recipe will produce a tray of golden brown pieces of baklava, about 1¼ inches deep, filled with spiced, sweet nuts and topped with flaky, crisp, buttered filo pastry, generously drizzled with a sweet spiced syrup—about 1500 calories per square inch! (Well, maybe not, but close.)

Just in case you don't have a big family or lots of neighbors or a large party to help you eat this up, we want you to know that the recipe halves easily. Use a 9 × 12-inch baking sheet and cut the filo with scissors to fit.

Covered, baklava keeps a really long time at room temperature. Somehow the syrup just preserves everything.

Yields 48 pieces
Prep time: 45 minutes
Baking time: 30 to 40 minutes
Cooling time: 20 minutes

BAKLAVA
2 cups almonds
4 cups walnuts
1 cup packed brown sugar
2 teaspoons ground cinnamon
1 teaspoon ground allspice
½ teaspoon salt

½ to ¾ cup butter, melted
1 pound filo pastry (approximately 28 sheets of filo, 12 × 17 inches)

SYRUP
1 cup honey
1 cup sugar
1½ cups water
2 teaspoons ground cinnamon
1 teaspoon ground allspice
1 tablespoon finely grated orange zest
juice of 1 orange
1 tablespoon finely grated lemon zest
2 to 4 tablespoons fresh lemon juice

Grind the almonds coarsely in a food processor, and set aside in a mixing bowl. Add the walnuts to the food processor, pulse until finely chopped, and add to the mixing bowl. Stir in the brown sugar, cinnamon, allspice, and salt and mix well.

Set up your work area with the bowl of nut filling, the melted butter, a pastry brush, and an 17 × 11-inch rimmed baking sheet. Unfold the package of filo and place it next to the baking sheet. Turn off any fans in the room. Brush the baking sheet with the melted butter.

Lay 2 sheets of filo in the baking sheet; they should fit almost perfectly, but if any filo drapes over the sides of the pan, place them so it is evenly distributed on all four sides. Brush the top sheet with melted butter. Do this three more times, 2 sheets of filo at a time, buttering the top sheet, for a total of 8 sheets of filo. Sprinkle about 1½ cups of the nut mixture evenly on the pastry. Cover the nuts with 2 sheets of filo, buttering the top sheet. Repeat, for a total of 4 sheets. Sprinkle with about 1½ cups of the nut mixture. Repeat with 4 more sheets of filo, two at a time, buttering the top sheets as before, and top with about 1½ cups of the nut mixture. Repeat with 4 sheets of filo, two at a time, buttering the top sheet. Sprinkle with the remaining nut mixture. Top with the rest of the filo, two sheets at a time, buttering the top sheet each time. The baklava will have 4 layers of nuts and 5 layers of filo. The final layer of filo will be about 8 sheets. Butter the top sheet of filo generously.

With a sharp knife, score the baklava into diamonds, or 1½-inch squares, cutting down to, but not through, the bottom layer. To make diamonds, make two diagonal cuts from corner to opposing corner. Then make cuts parallel on both sides of each diagonal about 1½ inches apart. There will be some triangles around the edges. You know how to cut squares.

Bake in a preheated 350°F oven (don't use a convection oven) until the filo is golden and crisp, 30 to 35 minutes. Check after 15 minutes to make sure the top isn't browning too quickly, and if it is, reduce the oven temperature to 325°F.

While the baklava bakes, make the syrup: Put the honey, sugar, water, cinnamon, allspice, orange zest and juice, and lemon zest and juice in a saucepan. If you like things lemony use the larger amount of lemon juice. Bring to a boil, reduce the heat, and simmer for 15 to 25 minutes until the syrup has thickened. Be careful not to let the syrup boil over.

When you take the baklava from the oven, set it aside to cool for about 20 minutes. Then pour the hot syrup over the whole baklava, and cut along the scored lines through the bottom layer so the syrup will run down to all the layers.

SERVING IDEAS
Serve Baklava at room temperature with spearmint tea, espresso, or demitasse.

Apricot-Almond Baklava

This delicious baklava has spiced ground almonds and an apricot purée layered in flaky, crisp, buttered filo pastry and drizzled with fruity honey syrup. It's not as sweet as a traditional baklava. Almonds, apricots, honey, and juice are all good foods, but honestly, Apricot-Almond Baklava might be a stretch if you're seeking nutrition rather than calories and bliss.

Assembly of filo pastry can be intimidating, but after working with it a couple of times, you gain confidence. A few wrinkles or torn sheets won't show once it's baked. Filo can last a long time unopened in the fridge, but if you're not sure when you'll use it, keep it in the freezer.

Yields 48 pieces
Prep time: 50 to 60 minutes
Baking time: 30 to 35 minutes
Cooling time: 15 minutes

BAKLAVA
2 cups dried unsulphured apricots, chopped
1½ cups apple or apricot juice
4 cups almonds
⅔ cup packed brown sugar
1 teaspoon ground cinnamon
½ to ¾ cup melted butter
1 pound filo pastry (approximately 28 sheets of filo, 12 × 17 inches)

SYRUP
1 cup honey
1 cup apple or apricot juice
1 tablespoon fresh lemon juice

Simmer the apricots and juice in a small covered saucepan for about 15 minutes, until the apricots are soft and have absorbed the juice. Stir a few times and watch closely at the end to prevent the apricots from sticking. When the apricots are soft, purée them in a food processor and set aside in a bowl.

While the apricots cook, whirl the almonds in a food processor until ground, but not a paste. Add the brown sugar and cinnamon and whirl to mix thoroughly. Set aside in a bowl.

Set up a work area with the nut mixture, the apricot purée, the melted butter, a pastry brush, and an 17 × 11-inch rimmed baking tray. Preheat the oven (don't use a convection oven) to 350°F. Unfold the package of filo and place it next to the baking sheet. Turn off any fans in the room. Brush the baking sheet with melted butter.

Lay two sheets of filo in the baking sheet, they should fit almost perfectly, but if any filo drapes over the sides of the pan, place them so that it is evenly distributed on all four sides. Brush the top sheet with melted butter. Do this three more times, 2 sheets of filo at a time, buttering the top sheet, for a total of 8 sheets of filo. Sprinkle about one-third of the almond mixture evenly on the pastry. Lay a sheet of filo on the nuts and butter the top. Repeat with 2 more sheets of filo. Evenly spread about half of the apricot purée on the top filo sheet. Lay a sheet of filo on the apricot purée and butter the top. Repeat with 2 more sheets of filo. Sprinkle on another third of the almond mixture. Top with 3 sheets of filo, buttering each sheet. Evenly spread the rest of the apricot purée on the filo. Layer on 3 sheets of filo, buttering each sheet. Sprinkle on the rest of the almond mixture and top with the remaining filo, buttering every second sheet of filo. There should be about 8 sheets of filo remaining for this final layer. Brush the top sheet generously with the butter. The baklava will have 3 layers of nuts, 2 layers of apricot purée, and 6 layers of filo.

With a sharp knife, score the baklava into diamonds or 1½-inch squares, cutting down to, but not through the bottom layer. To make diamonds, cut two diagonal slices from corner to opposing corner. Then make cuts parallel on both sides of each diagonal, about 1½ inches apart. There will be some triangles around the edges. You know how to cut squares.

Bake until the filo is golden and crisp, 30 to 35 minutes. Check after 15 minutes to make sure the top isn't browning too quickly, and if it is, reduce the oven temperature to 325°F.

While the baklava bakes, make the syrup: Combine the honey, apple juice, and lemon juice in a small saucepan. Bring to a simmer on low heat and cook for 10 minutes, until thickened. When you take the baklava from the oven, set it aside to cool for 10 to 15 minutes. Then pour the hot syrup over the whole baklava, and cut along the scored lines through the bottom layer so the syrup will run down to all the layers.

SERVING IDEAS

Serve Apricot-Almond Baklava at room temperature with spearmint tea, espresso, Turkish coffee, or apricot brandy.

Strawberry-Rhubarb Crumble

We look forward in the spring to the appearance of local strawberries and rhubarb in our markets. This crumble uses just the right amount of sweetening—enough to satisfy as dessert, but not so sweet that the flavor of the fruit is lost.

Try the crumble topping with other fruit as the season progresses, or as your taste buds dictate. Experiment with different fruit combinations. No matter what fruit you use, just be sure to have about 6 cups of slices, berries, whatever. Some of our favorites include peaches and blueberries with some lemon, peaches and mangoes with a little ginger and lime, strawberries and mangoes with cinnamon and cardamom (as in the photo opposite), apples and dried apricots with lemon—almost any combination has its fans. Of course you can make the topping with another kind of nut, but we love the rich, buttery taste of pecans the best.

We like to make extra topping and keep it in the freezer. With frozen fruit and frozen crumble topping on hand, you can quickly and easily put together a delicious dessert any time.

Serves 6
Prep time: 25 minutes
Baking time: 45 minutes

3 cups strawberries, hulled and halved or
    quartered, depending on the size
3 cups sliced rhubarb (¾ inch-thick-slices)
    (cut very wide stalks in half lengthwise
    before slicing)
¾ cup packed brown sugar
1 teaspoon ground cinnamon
1 tablespoon cornstarch

PECAN CRUMBLE TOPPING
1 cup unbleached white all-purpose flour
1 cup chopped pecans
½ cup sugar
¼ teaspoon salt
⅓ cup vegetable oil

Preheat the oven to 400°F.

In a mixing bowl, toss the strawberries and rhubarb with the brown sugar, cinnamon, and cornstarch. Set aside while you make the crumble topping.

In the bowl of a food processor, whirl the flour, pecans, sugar, and salt until crumbly. Place the mixture in a bowl and drizzle the oil over it. Thoroughly mix the oil into the flour and pecan mixture.

Give the fruit mixture a stir and distribute it evenly among six 7- or 8-ounce baking cups or ramekins. Tap the bottom of the cups gently on a hard surface to settle the fruit. Spread the topping evenly over the fruit and place the cups on a baking sheet or large baking dish (easier to handle and also will catch any juices that bubble over).

Bake until the fruit is bubbling and the topping browned, about 45 minutes. Serve hot, warm, or at room temperature.

VARIATIONS

- If you use frozen fruit, it is best to measure it before thawing, because the fruit compacts as it thaws. Add an additional tablespoon of cornstarch to help thicken the fruit. Most fruit is sweeter than rhubarb, so we suggest you use a little less brown sugar in other fruit mixtures: we usually use ½ cup for 6 cups of fruit. To blueberries, peaches, pears, or apples, we like to add a tablespoon of fresh lemon or lime juice and/or a little finely grated zest.

Apple Crisp

When we think of crisp, our first thought is of a mound of flavorful, sweet apples topped with a crunchy oat topping. For this recipe, we've made a vegan and wheat-free crisp topping that is sure to please everyone. Many supermarkets now carry gluten-free oats for those who need them.

We're in the heart of New York State apple country, and we've kept it simple and straightforward, apples with some good local maple syrup. Different types of apples take different amounts of time to bake, and the time of year (how fresh or how long in storage) makes a difference, too.

This recipe works just as well with pears, or peaches, or how about pears with cranberries, or peaches and blueberries, or strawberries and mangoes, or cherries and apples. If you can think of it, we've probably made it, and we hope you will experiment and enjoy this crisp topping with all sorts of fruit combinations. When you use softer, juicier fruit, like peaches and berries, toss the fruit mixture with a tablespoon of cornstarch.

Serves 6
Prep time: 25 minutes
Baking time: 45 to 50 minutes

6 cups peeled and sliced apples (5 or 6 apples)
¼ cup pure maple syrup or packed brown sugar
½ teaspoon ground cinnamon
½ teaspoon ground cardamom
1 tablespoon fresh lemon juice

CRISP TOPPING

1½ cups rolled oats
¼ cup packed brown sugar, pure maple syrup, or agave syrup
½ teaspoon salt
¼ cup vegetable oil

In a bowl, toss the apples with the maple syrup, cinnamon, cardamom, and lemon juice. Pile the apples into an unoiled baking pan (see Note for sizes that work). Bake in a preheated 375°F oven until the apples are bubbling, about 25 minutes for apples like Crispin, less for softer apples like McIntosh and Empire.

While the apples bake, toast the rolled oats on a tray in the oven for 10 minutes, stir them, and toast for another 5 to 10 minutes until fragrant and beginning to brown. Remove from the oven and set aside to cool. When the oats are cool, whirl ½ cup in a blender or food processor until like flour. In a bowl, mix the oat flour with the rest of the toasted oats and the brown sugar and salt. Add the oil and stir until well mixed.

When the apples are bubbling, remove the pan from the oven and stir to settle the apples into the dish a little. Spread the oat mixture evenly over the apples and bake until the apples are crisp-tender and the topping is golden brown, 20 to 25 minutes.

Serve hot, warm, or at room temperature. If the apples are especially juicy, let the crisp sit for 5 to 10 minutes so the oat topping can absorb some of the juice.

NOTE

Any of these pans will work with this recipe: 9-inch deep dish pie plate, 9.5-inch pie plate, 10-inch pie plate, 9-inch round cake pan, 8 × 8 × 2- or 9-inch square baking pan, 11 × 7 × 2-inch baking pan, 1½- or 2-quart casserole dish.

VARIATIONS

- If you don't have cardamom, substitute ¼ teaspoon freshly grated nutmeg or increase the cinnamon to 1 teaspoon.
- We like the nutty flavor and crispness of oats toasted first in the oven, but it isn't essential. And we think that whirling some of the oats to make oat flour makes a better topping, but that also isn't essential.
- You can use melted butter in place of the oil.

SERVING IDEAS

This is good as is, but is also delicious with some whipped cream or vanilla ice cream.

Southern Nut Pie Eudora

Sometime in the 1980s, Susan Harville, then and now a Moosewood dessert maker, heard that Eudora Welty, one of her favorite writers, was coming to Ithaca to read from her books. Susan made this pie to give to Ms. Welty as a token of her appreciation. Ms. Welty very graciously accepted the pie and said, ". . . the pleasure you've had from reading my work? Why, surely, it couldn't add up to a whole pecan pie!"

Southern Nut Pie Eudora went into the Moosewood Collective's first cookbook *New Recipes from Moosewood Restaurant* in 1987. We just *had* to reprint it unchanged in *The Moosewood Restaurant Book of Desserts* in 1997. And here it is again, still our favorite nut pie, just the same as the pie that Susan gave Eudora.

We also have a longstanding love affair with maple syrup. Some of us have tapped maple trees in late winter and experienced the Zen of patiently watching a bubbling sugaring pan turn thin and watery sap into golden syrup. Maple syrup is our favorite sweetener for many desserts and it works beautifully in this, our Yankee version of a Southern classic.

Serves 8
Prep time: 30 minutes including crust
Baking time: 1 hour

1 unbaked 9-inch pie crust (see page 356)
1½ cups pecan halves (sometimes we use walnuts)
¼ cup melted butter
1 teaspoon pure vanilla extract
2 tablespoons unbleached white all-purpose flour
½ teaspoon salt
3 large eggs, well beaten
1 cup pure maple syrup
1 cup half-and-half or heavy cream

Preheat the oven to 375°F.

Spread the nuts evenly across the bottom of the unbaked pie shell. In a bowl, whisk together the melted butter, vanilla, and flour. Add the salt, eggs, maple syrup, and half-and-half and mix until smooth. (Or, whirl everything in a blender.) Pour the filling over the nuts in the pie shell. When the nuts float to the top, gently push them back down to wet them so they won't burn during baking.

Bake for 50 to 60 minutes, or until a knife inserted in the center comes out clean. Let the pie cool for at least 15 minutes before slicing.

SERVING IDEAS

Serve plain or garnished with a dollop of whipped cream or a scoop of vanilla ice cream.

Our Favorite All-Purpose Piecrust

There are many different sizes of "standard" pie pans: diameters from 8 to 10 inches and depths from 1¼ to 2 inches, with volumes from 3 to 7 cups. This recipe gives you ingredient amounts for a single crust for a 9-inch standard pie plate or a 9.5-inch deep dish pie plate or a 10-inch standard pie plate.

Although at Moosewood we usually use pastry flour for piecrust, this recipe calls for all-purpose flour because we've learned that pastry flour is hard to find in some parts of the country and it's not consistent from place to place and among different brands. We developed this recipe using unbleached white all-purpose flour. But some of us still swear by pastry flour, so if you can find it in your area, give it a try and see which you prefer.

The most important thing to keep in mind when making the dough is to not to overwork it, and don't add more water than is needed because both cause a tough crust. Cold butter and ice water are important, too. Some people freeze butter for making piecrust dough.

Yields 1 single piecrust
Prep time: 15 minutes
Chilling time: 30 minutes
Rolling time: 5 minutes

FOR A 9-INCH STANDARD PIE PLATE:
1 cup unbleached white all-purpose flour
¼ teaspoon salt
6 tablespoons cold unsalted butter
2 to 3 tablespoons ice water

FOR A 9.5-INCH DEEP DISH PIE PLATE
OR A 10-INCH STANDARD PIE PLATE:
1½ cups unbleached white all-purpose flour
¼ teaspoon salt
½ cup cold unsalted butter
3 to 5 tablespoons of ice water

To make piecrust with a food processor: Put the flour and salt in the bowl of the food processor and whirl to mix. Cut the butter into ½-inch pieces and sprinkle them over the flour. Pulse until the dough is crumbly; you should still be able to feel very small but distinct pieces of butter with your fingers. Sprinkle 2 tablespoons of ice water over the flour and butter and pulse 6 to 8 times. Pinch a little of the dough with your fingertips and if it holds together there is enough water, if not add another tablespoon of water and pulse a few times. Turn the dough out and use your fingers to gather it together into a ball. Flatten the ball into a disk. You can roll the dough out right away, but it really rolls out more easily if you cover it with plastic wrap and refrigerate it for about 30 minutes.

To make piecrust by hand: Combine the flour and salt in a large bowl. Cut the cold butter into small pieces and sprinkle onto the flour. Using a pastry cutter, two table knives, or your fingers, work the butter into the flour just until it resembles coarse meal, with small pieces of butter throughout. Sprinkle the ice water over the dough, a little at a time, stirring and adding more ice water until the dough holds together when you pinch it. Use your fingertips to gather it together into a ball. Flatten into a disk and proceed as above.

To roll it out: On a lightly floured surface, roll the dough into a round by lightly pressing with a floured rolling pin from the center out to the edges. Make a round 3 or 4 inches larger in diameter than the size of your pie plate. As you work, it's a good idea to periodically check that the dough is not sticking to the surface you're rolling it on, because it's frustrating to have made a nice big round of dough only to find that you can't lift it in one piece. So, as you go, lift up an edge, and if it's beginning to stick, pick it up and sprinkle a little more flour on the rolling surface.

Fit the dough into the pie plate, cut away or fold under any excess dough, and crimp the edges with your fingers or a fork.

To freeze an unbaked piecrust: Roll out the dough and fit it into a pie plate. Wrap it well and store in the freezer for up to a month.

VARIATIONS

- You can substitute whole wheat pastry flour for all-purpose flour. You might need an additional tablespoon of ice water. And, the crust will be most tender if you refrigerate the dough overnight so that the bran hydrates fully.
- You can use salted butter instead of unsalted, but then omit the ¼ teaspoon of salt.
- To make a slightly sweet crust for a dessert pie, add 2 tablespoons of sugar.
- Some of the cooks at Moosewood use a different technique with the dough: Sprinkle on the ice water a bit at a time and with your hands, push the dough to the middle of the bowl to form a ball. Cut the dough in half, place one half on top of the other, and press down. Repeat the cutting and pressing steps three times until all of the water is incorporated and the dough clings together. Flatten into a disk and proceed as above.

Pumpkin Pie

We've made a lot of pumpkin pies a lot of different ways—various liquids, like milk, cream, half-and-half, almond milk, soy milk, coconut milk; various vegan versions; different spices; and with apples, with pears, with a pecan layer (our second favorite, the recipe is in *Moosewood Restaurant's Book of Desserts*). But when it comes down to our favorite, it's this basic pumpkin pie—maybe because it's like the ones we had as children, made with evaporated milk (you can get it organic now). After we settled on this particular recipe as our favorite, we discovered that it is almost the same as the recipe that's been on the label of Libby's canned pumpkin since the 1950s, so we suppose maybe there *is* something to that harkening back to childhood thing.

We've made delicious holiday pies with baked fresh pumpkin or squash, and some of us love sweet potatoes best. But overall, at home most of us prefer canned pumpkin because it's expedient and stressfree. We recommend real maple syrup in our pie, but brown or white sugar works, too.

Yields one 9.5-inch pie
Serves 8
Prep time: 15 minutes for the pastry; 10 minutes
    for the filling
Baking time: about 1 hour

1 unbaked 9.5-inch pie shell (see page 356)
    (see Note)

FILLING
one 15- or 16-ounce can cooked pumpkin purée
    (about 2 cups)
3 large eggs, beaten
½ cup pure maple syrup, or ¾ cup brown or white
    sugar
one 12-ounce can evaporated milk (or 1½ cups of
    other "milk")
1½ teaspoons ground cinnamon
½ teaspoon ground ginger
¼ teaspoon ground cloves
½ teaspoon salt

Make the piecrust and fit it into the pie plate.
    Preheat the oven to 425°F.

In a large bowl, whisk the filling ingredients until smooth. Pour the filling into the unbaked piecrust and bake for 15 minutes at 425°F. Reduce the oven temperature to 350°F and bake for 40 to 50 minutes more until the crust is golden and a knife inserted about 2 inches from the side comes out clean.

Cool to room temperature and then refrigerate until serving time.

NOTE
If your pie plate is 9 inches across, get out a custard cup because you'll have a little extra filling; if it's 10-inch, the filling won't be as deep.

VARIATIONS
- For an easy vegan filling, omit the eggs and substitute 12 ounces of silken tofu for the milk, and add a teaspoon of pure vanilla extract. For the crust, use margarine or vegetable shortening.
- Instead of evaporated milk, use the same amount of cream, half-and-half, or soy, rice, almond or other milk.
- Decorate with walnut or pecan halves. After the pie has baked for 30 or 40 minutes, press them around the edge of the pie press them around the edge of the pie, into the filling about a ¼ inch.
- Decorate the top with poached pear slices after about 35 minutes of baking.

SERVING IDEAS
Serve with a dollop of whipped cream or some vanilla ice cream—yum!

Fresh Berry Ricotta Moose

The bright and wonderful flavor of fresh fruit at its peak makes this fluffy, simple, quick, not-cooked "mousse" divine. It's good for brunch served in a melon wedge, welcome as dessert, and satisfying as a snack.

You can follow this recipe using any combination of strawberries, blueberries, raspberries, blackberries, cherries, and chopped peaches, or with only one fruit. We prefer a no-sugar-added fruit spread, just enough sweetening to heighten the natural fruit flavor.

Yields about 5 cups
Serves 6 to 8
Time: 10 to 15 minutes

14 to 16 ounces ricotta cheese
1 pint fresh strawberries, blueberries, or raspberries, rinsed
½ cup fruit spread or preserves made of the same berries (about 5 ounces)
1 cup heavy cream

In a food processor or using an electric mixer on high speed, whip the ricotta for about 2 minutes, until very smooth.

Set aside a few nice berries for garnishes. If you're using strawberries, hull them and cut into halves or quarters. Fold the berries and the fruit spread into the whipped ricotta. Refrigerate if not serving right away.

Just before serving, whip the cream until stiff. Fold the whipped cream into the ricotta mixture. Spoon the "mousse" into dessert cups and top each with a berry garnish. Serve chilled.

VARIATIONS
- You can substitute about a pound of frozen blueberries, cherries, or raspberries (defrosted, and if there's a lot of juice, drained). We don't recommend frozen strawberries because they don't retain a firm texture. Use a fruit spread made of the same fruit.
- You could add a little pure vanilla or almond extract to the whipped cream.

Fresh Strawberry Sauce

Really fresh tasting and not too gooey or sweet, so perfect for topping cheesecake, pound cake, or ice cream.

Yields 3 cups
Time: 15 minutes

1 quart fresh strawberries (1½ pounds)
2 tablespoons fresh lemon juice
2 to 4 tablespoons sugar

Hull the strawberries. In a blender, purée about one-fourth of the strawberries with the lemon juice and sugar. Slice the rest of the strawberries and put them in a bowl. Pour the purée over the sliced strawberries and stir well.

Serve right away or refrigerate. If you like your strawberries softened, let them macerate in the refrigerator for at least a couple of hours.

Blueberry-Cherry Pie with Sour Cream Lattice Crust

This pie makes a dramatic presentation with its rich, golden brown, puffy lattice top. We've been making a variation of this crust for about a quarter of a century.

In Ithaca, blueberries and cherries ripen at the same time of year, and they are even tastier and more beautiful when combined. Tart cherries are the best to use in pies; they are often available frozen if you can't find fresh ones. At times, we've made the pie with sweet cherries, but it's just not the same. We like about equal amounts of cherries and blueberries, but feel free to change the proportions.

Most of us love the sweet-tartness of this pie, but if you know that you like sweet fruit pies, you might want to add another ¼ cup of sugar.

The quantities in this recipe are just right for a 9.5-inch deep dish pie plate. If your pie plate is smaller, you may have extra filling and dough. If it's larger, you may be hard-pressed to roll out a large enough crust and there may not be enough filling to make a perfect pie. So, if your pie plate is bigger, increase the crust and filling ingredients by about 25 percent to have enough. If it's smaller, you may have enough for a little tart, too.

Yields one 9.5-inch deep dish pie
Pie dough prep time: 15 minutes
Dough chilling time: 30 minutes
Filling prep time: 15 minutes, longer if pitting fresh cherries
Rolling out the dough and putting the pie together time: 15 minutes
Baking time: about 1 hour

CRUST FOR 9.5-INCH DEEP DISH PIECRUST (1¾ INCHES DEEP)

2 cups unbleached white all-purpose flour
½ teaspoon salt
1½ teaspoons baking powder
1 cup cold unsalted butter, (2 sticks), if you use salted, reduce the added salt to ¼ teaspoon
½ cup sour cream

FILLING

3 cups blueberries
3 cups fresh or frozen tart cherries
¾ cup sugar
1 teaspoon finely grated lemon zest
1 tablespoons fresh lemon juice
¼ cup cornstarch

To make the piecrust: Sift the flour, salt, and baking powder into a large mixing bowl. Cut the butter into small pieces and use a pastry cutter, two table knives, or your fingers to work them into the flour until they are incorporated as small, crumbly pieces.

Stir in the sour cream and use your hands to shape the dough into a ball. Divide the dough into 2 balls, one for the bottom crust a little larger than the second one for the lattice top. Flatten them slightly into disks. Wrap individually with plastic wrap and chill for about 30 minutes.

While the dough chills, sort through the blueberries and cherries, discarding any stems and unripe or discolored fruit. Pit the cherries, if using fresh. No need to thaw frozen fruit before using. Place the fruit in a mixing bowl and add the sugar, lemon zest and juice, and cornstarch. Use a spatula to mix well and set aside.

When the dough has chilled, remove the larger disk from the refrigerator and roll it out on a heavily floured surface until it is about 13 inches in diameter. The dough is soft and needs a lot of flour on the rolling surface. Fit the dough into a 9.5-inch deep dish pie plate. Fill with the fruit. Roll out the smaller disk of dough to about a 12-inch diameter and cut it into 10 strips, each about an inch wide.

Arrange the strips on top of the fruit in a lattice pattern. Trim off any extra dough and crimp the edges.

Bake in a preheated 400°F oven for 20 minutes, then reduce the heat to 375°F and bake until the filling is bubbling and the crust is golden brown, about 40 minutes more. Allow the pie to cool for at least 10 minutes before serving.

VARIATIONS

- We love this over-the-top crust, but Our Favorite All-Purpose Piecrust for a 9.5 to 10-inch piecrust works too (page 356).

SERVING IDEAS

Not that it needs it of course, but what could be bad about having some vanilla ice cream or whipped cream on this pie?

Low-fat Lemon Pudding Cake

Luscious and yet surprisingly low in fat, this American dessert classic separates into layers during baking—a tart-sweet custard on the bottom and a spongy cake layer on top. It's pleasing any time of year. At Moosewood Restaurant, it seems to be especially popular after the winter holidays, when maybe it helps people stick to their resolutions.

We're cooks, not nutritionists, and we're not of one mind when it comes to eggs. Some of us make pudding cake with only two of the egg yolks, and others with all four yolks. The recipe works fine either way, and the difference in flavor and consistency is minor.

Serves 8
Prep time: 25 minutes
Baking time: 30 to 45 minutes

4 large eggs
¼ teaspoon salt
1½ cups buttermilk
½ cup fresh lemon juice
1¼ cups sugar
1 teaspoon pure vanilla extract
½ cup unbleached white flour, preferably pastry flour
½ teaspoon baking powder

Lightly oil eight 7- or 8-ounce ovenproof ramekins or other glass or ceramic baking cups. Place the cups in a 2 inch-deep baking pan. Bring a kettle of water to a boil. Preheat the oven to 350°F.

Separate the eggs, putting the whites into a medium mixing bowl and 2 to 4 of the yolks (see headnote) into a large mixing bowl. Using an electric mixer, beat the egg whites and salt until stiff. Set aside.

In the large bowl, beat the egg yolks, buttermilk, lemon juice, sugar, and vanilla until smooth. Sift the flour and baking powder into the bowl and beat until smooth. Gently fold the egg whites into the batter until it is fairly smooth.

Distribute the batter evenly among the baking ramekins. Pour boiling water into the baking pan, taking care to avoid getting any water in the ramekins, until the water reaches halfway up the sides of the ramekins.

Bake for 30 to 45 minutes until puffed and lightly browned on top. The baking time will depend upon your oven and your baking cups. Remove the cups from the hot water to stop cooking.

Serve warm, at room temperature, or chilled.

SERVING IDEAS
Serve plain or sprinkled with fresh berries.

Creamy Vegan Rice Pudding

A creamy beige pudding studded with bits of dried fruit, lovely topped with sliced strawberries or peaches. Rice pudding is a homey, easy-to-prepare dessert that requires little effort other than occasional stirring. It's a satisfying snack and great for breakfast. This recipe can easily be doubled.

Yields 4 cups
Serves 4 to 6
Time: 50 minutes

2 cups cooked rice, brown or white (see Notes)
1 quart unsweetened soy milk or other vegan "milk" (see Notes)
⅓ cup currants or raisins
⅓ to ½ cup sweetener: sugar, pure maple syrup, or blue agave syrup
½ teaspoon ground cinnamon
¼ teaspoon salt
1 teaspoon finely grated lemon zest (optional)
1 teaspoon pure vanilla extract

If you're using white rice, combine all of the ingredients at once, except for the vanilla, and simmer, stirring frequently, until thickened, 25 to 30 minutes.

If you're using brown rice, in a heavy saucepan combine it with the "milk" you've chosen and the currants or raisins and bring to a boil. Reduce the heat and simmer gently, stirring often to prevent sticking. When the rice has softened, 30 to 40 minutes, add the sweetener, cinnamon, salt, and lemon zest, if using, and continue to simmer for another 10 minutes. The pudding should thicken quickly now.

Remove from the heat, stir in the vanilla, and serve warm or chilled.

NOTES
The cooking instructions are different for brown and white rice, because we've found that brown rice resists becoming soft and creamy and is much better at absorbing the cooking liquid when there is no sweetener present.

Lots of options for plant-based "milk" beverages: soy, rice, oat, cashew, almond, coconut. If you use sweetened, adjust for that when you add sweetener. Don't confuse thick canned coconut milk with coconut milk beverage; look on the market shelves near the soy milks.

VARIATIONS
- Add a different dried fruit, such as dried cranberries, dried cherries, or chopped dried apricots, or no fruit at all.
- Dairy milk works fine in this recipe.

Vanilla Custard Sauce

This homey and versatile custard sauce elevates fresh fruit to a wonderful dessert. Custard sauce is an essential element of Fresh Fruit Trifle and Savannah Banana Pudding (see below), both of which are beloved at Moosewood.

Yields 2½ cups
Time: 15 minutes

2 cups milk
⅓ cup sugar
4 large eggs
1 teaspoon pure vanilla extract

In a heavy saucepan on medium heat, stir together the milk and sugar. Whisk the eggs well or whirl them in a blender for a moment until uniformly yellow. Stir the eggs into the milk and continue stirring until the custard is just under the boiling point. Remove from the heat and stir in the vanilla.

If you see that the custard has lumps, small or large, it means that the heat was too high, or you were distracted from your stirring task, or the custard got too hot at the end. You can fix it. Just whirl it in a blender for a few seconds to smooth it out. Some of us think a pinch of salt brightens the flavor; others of us would never do such a thing.

Vanilla Custard Sauce can be served warm or cold. It will keep in the refrigerator for several days.

SERVING IDEAS
Pour Vanilla Custard Sauce over fresh strawberries or blueberries, or sliced peaches. Drizzle it on poached pears or sautéed apples. It's great on Gingerbread (page 341), Our Favorite Pound Cakes (page 336), or Sara's Fresh Apple Spice Cake (page 333).

FRESH FRUIT TRIFLE
Trifle is a very traditional English dessert, customarily made with fruit jam and stale cake combined with spirits of some sort, custard sauce, and whipped cream, all layered in a clear glass bowl, often reserved for holidays and special occasions. Italian cuisine has made a place for this dessert also, calling it *Zuppa Inglese* (English Soup).

At Moosewood, we use fresh fruit rather than jam, we don't always add liquor, and the cake needn't be stale, although we're always glad for leftover pound cake, which freezes very well. We like trifle at any time of year, on ordinary days as well as ceremonial occasions. A special trifle bowl is nice, but we're happy to see trifle on the table, even if in any old mixing bowl.

To assemble a trifle, cut or break Our Favorite Pound Cakes (page 336) into bite-size pieces. If you want, drizzle a little brandy, sherry, rum, or fruit- or nut-flavored liqueur over the cake and let it soak in. Place some cake pieces in either a large bowl or individual parfait glasses or dessert cups. Pour on some Vanilla Custard Sauce. Next, layer on some fresh fruit cut into bite-sized pieces: cherries, peaches, strawberries, plums, orange sections, blueberries, raspberries, mango, or kiwi. Do each layer once or twice more. Whip heavy cream with a little pure vanilla extract and maple syrup or confectioners' sugar, and mound it on top. Decorate with a few pieces of fresh fruit. Chill until serving.

SAVANNAH BANANA PUDDING
Moosewood's Penny Goldin loves to travel and she seizes the opportunity to do "research," a euphemism for going to lots of local restaurants. She first tasted vanilla wafer and banana pudding during a trip to Savannah, Georgia. She thought, "A trifle really—and we'll call it Savannah Banana!" And we do.

To make Savannah Banana Pudding, fold bite-size pieces of Our Favorite Pound Cakes (page 336), sliced bananas, and freshly whipped cream into chilled Vanilla Custard Sauce. Make more than you think you'll need for dessert tonight, because you're sure to want more for breakfast tomorrow.

Chocolate Confections

Here are two easy ways to make impressive and personalized chocolate confections by combining your favorite nuts or dried fruits or flavored liqueurs with fine-quality chocolate. These make a delicious gift for a valentine or a nice little dessert to serve with a cup of coffee or a glass of wine. Use a food processor to chop the nuts and fruits for a speedier preparation.

TRUFFLES

Truffles are soft, melt-in-the-mouth, swoon-inducing chocolates. We give you a basic formula here, but you can invent as many variations as you can think of. You can add any kind of nut or dried fruit, emphasizing one or combining a few. Flavor the chocolate with liqueur, rum, brandy, espresso, or nothing and just go for a pure chocolate taste. Do use a fine-quality chocolate. The unsweetened cocoa provides a bitter chocolate coating on the outside that is a delectable contrast to the sweet chocolate inside.

Our favorite truffle may be a semisweet chocolate with toasted walnuts, dried cherries, apricots, and brandy (apricot brandy, if you have some). But then, we also really like the combination of milk chocolate, a hazelnut liqueur such as Frangelico, and hazelnuts. Or try dark chocolate with an orange liqueur, such as Grand Marnier, and pistachios. Or add about 1 tablespoon of instant espresso powder and a chocolate or mocha liqueur along with Brazil nuts and dried mangoes.

Yields about 30 walnut-size truffles
Prep time: 30 minutes
Chilling time: at least 1 hour

16 ounces bittersweet, semisweet, or milk chocolate (about 3 cups chips or chunks)
1 cup heavy cream
1 tablespoon flavored liqueur, rum, brandy, cognac, or espresso (optional)
1 cup toasted walnuts or other nuts, finely chopped
1 cup finely chopped dried fruit (such as apricots, figs, prunes, cherries, cranberries, or raisins)
½ cup unsweetened cocoa powder

Melt the chocolate with the cream in a microwave or a double boiler or a bowl set over a pot of barely simmering water. Stir until smooth. Add the liqueur or espresso, if using, and stir well. Add the chopped nuts and dried fruits and mix well. Spread the mixture evenly in a nonreactive 13 × 9-inch pan or two pie plates or 8-inch square pans. Cover and refrigerate for at least an hour, or until well chilled and firm. Refrigerating longer or overnight is fine.

When the chocolate is firm, spread the cocoa on a plate. Scoop out the chilled mixture by spoonfuls and roll briefly between the palms of your hands to form a ball. The balls don't need to be perfectly smooth or even perfectly spherical. We usually make them about walnut-size. If you have little candy cups, make truffles that fit nicely in them. Roll each ball in the cocoa to coat evenly.

Place each truffle in a candy cup or arrange the truffles in a cookie tin lined with wax paper. Separate the layers with wax paper. Truffles will keep in the refrigerator for at least 2 weeks. They're best served at room temperature.

VARIATION

For truffles that are perfectly smooth inside, don't add any nuts or fruits to the chocolate mixture. If you want some texture on the outside, roll them in chopped nuts or shredded coconut.

CHOCOLATE CUPS

These are even easier to make than truffles. They are really nothing more than chocolate binding together other good things, like nuts, fruits, cookie crumbs, or small candies. The chocolate mixture is poured into small fluted paper or foil candy cups and it takes that shape when cool.

If you are thinking of kids' treats, use milk chocolate and add stuff like raisins, peanuts or peanut butter chips, crisp rice cereal or cookie crumbs. For more sophisticated candies, use dark chocolate with salted pistachios and dried cranberries, or try almonds, minced dried figs, and white chocolate chips. Or maybe use white chocolate filled with slivered rose petals, candied violets, and minced dried pineapple. How about crushed peanut brittle and pieces of little pretzel sticks? Jelly beans? Candied orange peel? Crushed roasted coffee beans? Dried hot peppers?

Yields about 36 candies
Prep time: 30 minutes
Chilling time: 1 hour or more

16 ounces chocolate (bittersweet, semisweet, milk, or white)
2 cups chopped toasted nuts, minced dried fruit, crisp rice cereal or cookie crumbs, candied violets, or other good things

Melt the chocolate in a microwave or a double boiler or a bowl set over a pot of barely simmering water. Stir until smooth. Remove from the heat and stir in the nuts, fruits, cereal, and other good things you've chosen. (If you have beautiful candied violets, save them to put on top.) Drop the mixture by the spoonful into candy cups.

Chill until firm, at least an hour, longer or overnight is fine. The candies will pop out of the paper when firm. Serve at room temperature. Tightly covered and refrigerated, Chocolate Cups will keep for at least 2 weeks.

VARIATION

Pour just the melted chocolate into small fluted candy cups and lightly press in pieces of fresh fruit, such as quartered strawberries, halved cherries or grapes, or whole raspberries or blueberries. Try to coat any cut sides of the fresh fruit pieces with chocolate, but let some of the fruit show on top. Fresh fruit chocolate cups will only keep for a day.

Fruit Skewers

If you ever thought fresh fruit was sort of a boring dessert, try this. The guava and lime glaze has a delectable and mysterious taste, new to most people. Colorful, glistening fruit threaded on a bamboo skewer becomes festive finger food, great for parties and buffets. Fruit Skewers also work well as an appetizer or side dish. Or, forego the skewers and serve the guava-coated fruit in a bowl as a salad.

Bamboo skewers can usually be found in the supermarket near small kitchen utensils. A 10-inch skewer is perfect for this recipe. Find guava paste in a wide flat tin in Latin or Asian groceries and in well-stocked supermarkets.

Yields 20 fruit skewers
Time: 25 minutes

½ ripe pineapple, peeled and cored
½ ripe cantaloupe, peeled and seeded
1 small bunch seedless green grapes (at least 20)
1 small bunch seedless red or black grapes
    (at least 20)
1 pint fresh strawberries, hulled

⅓ cup guava paste (page 377)
3 tablespoons fresh lime juice

Cut the cored pineapple half into bite-size chunks—you should get at least 40 pieces—and place them in a large bowl. Cut the cantaloupe into bite-size cubes and add to the bowl. Put the grapes and strawberries into the bowl.

Purée the guava paste and lime juice in a blender to make a smooth, very thick dressing. Add the dressing to the bowl of fruit and gently toss to cover the fruit with the guava dressing.

On each skewer, spear 7 or 8 pieces of fruit. This is a somewhat messy procedure, but the finished skewers will be surprisingly dripfree. Begin and end with grapes, because they make good anchors. You'll probably only have enough strawberries to put one on each skewer, but you should be able to put two pieces each of pineapple and cantaloupe. So it will go something like: grape, melon, pineapple, strawberry, melon, pineapple, grape. Arrange the finished fruit skewers, side by side, on a large platter.

Serve soon or cover and refrigerate. Serve at room temperature or chilled.

Baking Pan Sizes and Equivalents

In our home kitchens, most of us don't have a giant cabinet full of baking pans of all sizes and shapes, so when we don't have the size pan called for in a recipe, some of us go through calculations to try to determine which of the pans that we have will substitute, and some of us just use whatever pan looks right and then deal with it when there's too much stuff to fit or the cake turns out kind of thin.

This chart of pan volumes may save you from doing some challenging arithmetic. But, substituting one size pan for another isn't simply a matter of the volumes of the pans, so read on.

If you're making a casserole or a cake and you don't have the size baking dish called for, check the volume chart, but also look at the depth and shape of the pan. Think about the relative depth of the ingredients in the dish: if the depth is greater than it would be in the pan called for, lengthen the baking time; if the depth is less, shorten the baking time. Also, the material a pan is made of, its weight, and the qualities of its surface area can make a difference in the ideal baking time and temperature.

Pie plates are all over the place in terms of their diameter and volume. The angle of the slanted sides and the depth makes a difference in volume.

Sometimes they're labeled by the diameter of the outer edges, rather than the inside measurement. Particularly with hand-thrown or thick ceramic pie plates, the actual volume may be significantly different than that of a metal or glass pie plate of the supposed same diameter. The type of crust is another thing to consider when you're trying to decide which pie plate to use: a pie plate lined with a thick oat-and nut crust will hold considerably less filling than with a thin flour crust. Also, a pie plate holds more of mounded fillings than fillings that are level, such as custards. And, to complicate things further, the actual volume of the pan and the best filling level aren't necessarily the same: some fillings need room to expand, and others settle during baking.

Springform pans come in different sizes, materials, and designs. If you already have one, you probably know its quirks and how best to use it. But if you're going to buy one, we recommend Fat Daddio's, available online and in cooking stores.

Whatever pan you're using, fill it with batter only to the level indicated in the recipe because the batter will rise. If a cake recipe calls for two 9-inch round cake pans and you want to make a square cake, use two 8-inch square pans because the volume is equivalent. Two 8 × 1½-inch square pans = two 9 × 1½-inch round pans = one 13 × 9 × 2-inch rectangular pan.

The easiest way to determine the volume of a particular pan is to see how many cups of water it holds. This is helpful when you have unusually shaped or handcrafted pans. Of course, pans rarely hold even cups of water, and since you'd rather have some space unfilled than the mess in your oven that an overflowing filling makes, round off to the next cup down: if your pan holds 9½ cups, consider it a 9-cup pan.

When it comes right down to it, some of us have a favorite pan that we just like to use. It always turns out a perfect casserole evenly cooked throughout and not too crisp around the edges, and it washes up easily or has some sentimental value. So sometimes, we adjust the recipe to the pan.

BAKING PAN VOLUMES

Here's a general guide to volumes that you can use to find substitutes for the pans called for in our recipes.

Volume of the pan, filled to level:

4 cups
8 × 1½-inch round cake pan
8 × 1½-inch round pie plate

5 cups
9 × 1½-inch pie plate
8 × 4 × 2½-inch loaf pan

6 cups
8 × 2-inch round cake pan
9 × 1½-inch round cake pan
8 × 8 × 1½-inch square pan
9 × 2-inch round pie plate (deep dish)

10 × 1½-inch round pie plate
8½ × 4½ × 2½-inch loaf pan
7½ × 3-inch Bundt pan
8 × 2-inch springform pan

7 cups
9 × 9 × 1½-inch square pan
11 × 7½-inch rectangular pan
9½ × 2-inch round pie plate (deep dish)
8½ × 3-inch Bundt pan

8 cups
9 × 2-inch round cake pan
8 × 8 × 2-inch square pan
9 × 5 × 3-inch loaf pan

9 cups
11 × 7 × 2-inch rectangular pan
9 × 3-inch Bundt pan
8 × 3-inch springform pan

10 cups
9 × 9 × 2-inch square pan
10 × 2-inch round cake pan

12 cups
10 × 10 × 2-inch square pan
12 × 8 × 2-inch rectangular pan
10 × 3½-inch Bundt pan
9 × 3-inch springform pan
10 × 2½-inch springform pan

14 cups
13 × 9 × 2-inch rectangular pan
13 × 9 × 2-inch baking dish
13 × 9 × 2-inch casserole dish
10 × 3-inch springform pan

Guide to Ingredients and Basic Cooking

ANNATTO (ACHIOTE)

A brick-red, triangular-shaped seed of a bush grown in the Caribbean and Central and South America, annatto has a mild, musky, peppery taste, though without pepper's heat. It is most often used to give foods a rich, gold coloring. At Moosewood, we use it to color rice and other grains, and it is used on a grand scale in the food industry to give color to many foods, particularly butter, cheese, and margarine. To extract annatto's color, briefly heat the seeds in oil until the oil turns red, strain the seeds, and use the oil in the preparation of your dish. Look for seeds that are red all over. Any seed that is brown or turning brown is old and tasteless and won't give your dish a lovely golden color. Store the seeds in an airtight jar away from heat.

ARTICHOKE HEARTS

Our recipes call for artichoke hearts packed in brine, not those in an oil-based marinade. Cans of artichoke hearts are not standardized by weight or count. We've used cans weighing between 13.75 ounces and 16 ounces, with 5 to 12 hearts per can. The size of canned artichoke hearts varies and they may be whole, halved, or quartered. So what does one do when trying to follow a recipe? Use what is available! For our recipes, size and number are not critical; you can use any can weighing between 14 and 16 ounces. Artichoke hearts in brine are stocked in the canned vegetables aisle of the supermarket, and sometimes in specialty or gourmet foods sections.

BAKING PANS, SIZES AND SUBSTITUTIONS

see Baking Pan Sizes and Equivalents, pages 369 and 370

BEANS

Canned Beans

Canned beans are a handy pantry item. The amount of drained beans in the same size cans of various brands (and even within a brand) can vary surprisingly. Our "standard" for a 15-ounce can is 1½ cups of drained beans. We've been dismayed to find less than a cup of beans in some cans. Our recipes' ingredient lists give both can size and cup amount, in case you cook your own beans or the can you have is a skimpy one, but it shouldn't matter too much in the finished dish unless you're doubling or tripling the recipe. The saltiness also varies, so we recommend that when cooking a bean dish with canned beans you add less salt early and then add more salt at the end if needed. We usually rinse and drain canned beans.

Dried Beans

Dried beans are also handy to have in the pantry. They can be stored indefinitely in an airtight container in a cool place (not the refrigerator or freezer), although they're best when cooked within a year. It's easy to cook dried beans; it just takes some time. Three steps: sort, soak, and simmer.

How to Cook Dried Beans and Lentils

Sort through dried beans to remove any shriveled beans and pebbles or other debris. Put the beans in a colander and rinse with cold water.

Lentils and black-eyed peas don't need to be soaked before cooking. Soak most beans in three times their volume of cold water for about 6 hours before cooking. Or, put them in a pot of cold water, bring them to a boil, and then remove from the heat and soak for 1 to 2 hours. It's a mistake to soak dried beans too long. Most recipes say overnight, but if soaked too long, beans may sour or ferment, which affects flavor and makes them difficult to digest.

Pour off the water in which the beans were soaked, and add fresh water. Bring to a boil and then simmer until tender (see chart below for a guideline to cooking time and water-to-bean ratio). When we say simmer, we mean simmer: boiling can cause the cooking liquid to overflow and the beans to break apart and the skins to separate. When dried beans boil, sometimes foam forms on the top of the cooking liquid. This foam is water-soluble protein released from the beans and it will be absorbed back into the bean cooking liquid. It is not necessary to remove the foam, but it makes a mess if it boils over, so keep an eye on it to be sure that it simmers gently.

	1 cup dried beans when cooked yields:	water-bean ratio	simmering time
Cook after soaking:			
Black beans	3 cups	4:1	1 hour
Chickpeas (garbanzo beans)	3 cups	4:1	1½ hours
Kidney beans	2¾ cups	3:1	1½ hours
Lima beans	3 cups	3:1	1 hour
Pinto beans	3 cups	3:1	45 minutes
White beans (navy, pea)	3 cups	3:1	1 hour
No soaking:			
Black-eyed peas	2½ cups	3:1	30 minutes
Lentils, brown	3 cups	2:1	30 minutes
Lentils, French green	3 cups	2:1	20 minutes
Lentils, red	3 cups	2:1	15 minutes

Don't add acidic ingredients, like vinegar, tomatoes, or tomato juice, to cooking beans until after the beans are tender and cooked completely.

Cooking times vary not only with the type of beans, but also may vary with their age (amount of time since picked and dried).

BREAD CRUMBS

Use dry, stale, or fresh whole wheat, Italian, French, rye, or sourdough bread—you name it. In a 350°F oven, toast bread slices on a dry baking sheet until dried out, about 10 minutes, turning the slices over after 5 minutes. Remove from the oven and cool to room temperature. Whirl in a food processor. Or sometimes, we first pulverize the bread in a food processor, and then spread the crumbs out on a baking sheet and bake until dry. Freeze extra crumbs, and then, before using, rebake to dry them out.

BULGHUR

Made from wheat berries that have been steamed or boiled and then dried and cracked, bulghur comes in various grinds from fine to coarse. Bulghur is probably best known in this country as the basis for tabouli salad. We also use it for other salads, for stuffings, and as a bed for stews. Bulghur cooks into a fluffy, whole grain by simply placing it in a bowl or pot, adding boiling water, and covering it and letting it sit. Store raw bulghur in a well-sealed container in a cool, dark place or in the refrigerator or freezer. This will forestall its natural oils from oxidizing and turning rancid. Bulghur is sometimes called cracked wheat. You can find it in the natural foods and international sections of supermarkets and in ethnic groceries.

How to Cook Bulghur

In our experience, different batches of bulghur need more or less water to get soft yet chewy with-out being too wet. Until you know the particular bulghur you're working with, we recommend that you start with 1 cup of water per 1 cup of bulghur and then add more if it needs it.

In a heatproof bowl, pour an equal amount of boiling water over the bulghur and sprinkle with salt. Cover the bowl and let sit for 20 minutes. Taste the bulghur; it should be softened and dry (not soggy). If the water has been absorbed but the grains are still crunchy, add some more boiling water, cover, and set aside for 10 minutes. Fluff with a fork.

BUTTER

Butter is available salted and unsalted. Unsalted is sometimes called "sweet butter." Both have their virtues. Salted butter is less expensive because it is more popular and less perishable. With sweet butter, however, you can control the amount of salt in a recipe since various salted butters have different amounts of salt (this can be critical in baking) and with sweet butter, you can eliminate salt entirely for ingredient or health reasons. It's also a matter of taste. If you grew up as some of us did on sweet butter, there's really no substitute for its clean, sweet, delicate flavor. (Sometimes as kids, the bread was a mere vehicle for the butter.) But often when we hand our friends and family a slice of sweet-buttered bread, they take a bite and ask for the salt shaker. So there you are, it's a matter of taste.

But whichever your preference, pay attention to how you store butter. It not only oxidizes quickly in warm temperatures, which leads to rancidity, but, when not well wrapped, it is a magnet for odors that affect its flavor. For the freshest, best-tasting butter, refrigerate ¼ pound in a closed glass dish and freeze the rest. If you want softened butter, 30 minutes before serving cut off the amount of refrigerated butter you'll need and bring it to room temperature. Refrigerated butter will keep for 2 to 3 weeks; frozen butter will store for up to 3 months in a ziplock plastic bag.

Our recipes call for salted butter, unless unsalted is specified.

BUYING LOCAL
see page 13

CHEESE, SHREDDED AND GRATED
see page 17

CHIFFONADE
Chiffonade refers to a knife technique for cutting basil, mint, spinach, and other herbs and green leaves into long, thin strips—delicate little ribbons. Chiffonade also refers to the little ribbons of green themselves, as in "Sprinkle with a chiffonade of basil." The word rhymes with "pod" and translated from French as "rags" or maybe "made from rags."

To cut a chiffonade, first make a neat stack of about 10 leaves all in the same direction. Roll the stack lengthwise into a tight bundle. Cut across the bundle, working methodically from one end to the other, into very thin ribbons. Fluff the chiffonade and use to garnish freely.

CHINESE CHILI PASTE WITH GARLIC
This condiment adds spark to Asian marinades, glazes, sauces, and stir-fries. It's usually a mixture of hot peppers, salt, and garlic, though some pastes contain oil and/or soy beans. Check the ingredient list, because some chili pastes contain things you may want to avoid. We like Lan Chi Chili Paste with Garlic, which is simply chilies, salt, soybean oil, and garlic. Chili paste will keep indefinitely in the refrigerator, and can be found where Asian foodstuffs are sold.

For 1 tablespoon of Chinese chili paste, substitute 2 garlic cloves, pressed, and a minced fresh hot pepper or ¼ teaspoon cayenne or ½ teaspoon ground red pepper flakes. If you're making a dish that isn't cooked, cook the garlic in a little oil until just golden and cook fresh hot peppers until soft.

CHINESE RICE WINE (SHAO HSING)
Chinese rice wine is an amber-colored mild-tasting wine made from rice. It can be found at Asian food stores and Asian liquor stores. Check ingredient lists to avoid things best not ingested. Dry sherry is an acceptable substitute.

CHIPOTLE PEPPERS IN ADOBO SAUCE
Chipotle is the Aztec word for smoke. Chipotles are dried and smoked red jalapeño peppers. Chipotles are available as whole dried peppers and also ground, but we like them best in their plumped, juicy form packed in adobo sauce in small cans. Adobo is typically a mélange of tomatoes, onions, oil, vinegar, sugar, herbs, and spices. Some sauces include ancho chiles as well as jalapeños.

There's nothing else quite like these spicy, smoky peppers in their sauce. A discreet addition of chipotles in adobo sauce gives depth and mystery to marinades, sauces, salsas, soups, and stews. It is also great in aioli, polenta, cheese spreads, bean dips—the list goes on. Chipotles are hot, so start small by slicing off part of a pepper, and then mincing or puréeing it, or for the fainter of heart, begin with a small spoonful of sauce only.

We prefer the simplest ingredient lists: look for cans free of preservatives and high-fructose corn syrup. A good brand is La Preferida, though there are many more. We've found that the sauce recipes differ, too, so sample some until you find the one you like best. Chipotles in adobo stored in a closed glass jar in the refrigerator will keep for 1 to 3 months. Chipotles in adobo sauce also freeze well. You can put a pepper and some sauce in ice cube tray units, pop them out when frozen, store in a freezer bag, and use from the freezer as needed. Look for chipotle peppers in adobo sauce in the Latin food aisle of supermarkets, in bodegas, and online at www.google.com/shopping.

CLEAN FIFTEEN LIST
see page 14

COCONUT MILK
Coconut milk is a thick, white liquid made by pressing grated, fresh, ripe coconut meat. Coconut milk is a common ingredient in many tropical cuisines, most notably Caribbean, Southeast Asian, West African, and Polynesian.

You can make coconut milk yourself, but it is readily available in cans. The coconut milk we use in our recipes is unsweetened and is available in full-fat and lower-fat (sometimes called "lite") forms. We use both. Often, a thick "cream" separates and floats to the top of full-fat coconut milk. If you're not using the whole can, shake the can before opening and that may even it out to a smooth, creamy thickness; if not, pour the whole can into a bowl and stir well.

Don't confuse coconut milk with cream of coconut, a sweetened product used in mixed drinks, or with coconut water, an up-and-coming beverage on the health food scene.

Store opened coconut milk in a tightly lidded container in the refrigerator for 1 to 2 weeks. Coconut milk freezes well. A frozen chunk can be chopped off and used directly in a recipe.

Our favorite brand of coconut milk is Thai Kitchen. It includes guar gum as a stabilizer, but not the emulsifiers and sulfite preservatives found in many other brands. It is available both organic and not at www.thaikitchen.com/products/coconut-milk/coconut-milk.aspx and www.vitacost.com, and in the Asian section of supermarkets, and at gourmet food stores and Asian groceries.

CORN
When the summer's crop of sweet corn is coming on strong, it's both economical and easy to freeze corn kernels for later in the year. But the best reason to do it is that corn you've frozen yourself, assuming it's good corn when you freeze it, is so much better than corn from the supermarket freezer case. Freeze it as soon as you can after it's picked, and when you add it to that soup in January, it will be sweet and tender, like a little taste of summer.

How to Freeze Fresh Corn
Shuck the corn and pull off most of the silk. (No blanching or cooking necessary.) With a sharp knife, cut the kernels off the cobs. To contain all the kernels, including the ones that fly off to the side as you slice, rest one end of the cob on the bottom of a large bowl and slice down the cob in strips, as close as you can without cutting into the cob. Put the kernels into a freezer bag, suck out the air to minimize frost, and pop it in the freezer. That's it.

CORNMEAL
see pages 382–383

COUSCOUS
Milled wheat that when raw looks like tiny yellow or light brown (whole wheat) pearls. We use pre-cooked "quick" whole wheat couscous that is light and fluffy and ready to eat with just a few minutes of soaking with boiling water. Couscous makes a good bed for stews, roasted vegetables, and beans. We also use it in grain salads.

How to Cook Couscous
This is for quick-cooking couscous, either whole wheat or more refined. In a heatproof bowl, pour

an equal amount of boiling water over the couscous, sprinkle with salt, and stir briefly. Cover and let sit for about 5 minutes. Fluff with a fork. Occasionally, we get a batch of couscous that needs a little more time or more water to soften. If after 5 minutes, the couscous is still crunchy, but dry, sprinkle a couple of tablespoons of boiling water over it, cover, and let sit for a few minutes more.

CREAM CHEESE

We blend soft, creamy cream cheese into soups, strudels, frittatas, and desserts. At Moosewood, we use both cream cheese and a lower-fat cream cheese, labeled "⅓ lower fat" or "Neufchâtel." For our recipes, you can use either. French Neufchâtel is a cheese made in Normandy since the 1600s, and it is similar to our cream cheese, but made with whole milk, no cream added. So, calling lower-fat cream cheese "Neufchâtel" does make some sense in terms of fat content, and it probably makes good marketing sense, but French Neufchâtel is different.

DAIKON

A long, white, smooth radish popular in China and Japan, daikon has a mild, crisp taste with a bit of a bite. It is traditionally grated and used as a condiment alongside richer fare, and is often pickled and eaten at the start of a meal as an appetite stimulant. Daikon is also grown in this country and is available in Asian food stores, the Asian section of the supermarket, produce departments, and, increasingly, at farmers' markets. It can be used like any other radish in salads and can also be cut into large enough pieces for use in stir-fries and stews. When buying, look for crisp, white daikon with uncracked skins. Peel it like a carrot before using, and store unused daikon in the crisper section of the refrigerator, in a ziplock bag to retain humidity.

DARK SESAME OIL

see page 384

DIRTY DOZEN LIST

see page 14

EDAMAME

Edamame is the Japanese name for immature green soybeans. Edamame also denotes soybeans boiled in their pods, salted, and served as a snack or appetizer. Fresh edamame are sometimes available at farmers' markets, select supermarkets, and ethnic grocery stores, but in most areas, you can more readily find frozen edamame, both shelled and in the pod.

FENNEL

We adore fresh fennel. Raw, roasted, grilled, or braised. We slice it or shave it into salads and sauté it for our Mediterranean stews. We love its sweet, mild anise flavor and its clean, crisp texture. Fresh fennel has a bright white bulbous bottom of wide, overlapping layers and tall, pale green, celery-like stalks that end in feathery fronds. Every part of the vegetable is usable. The bulb is crisp and juicy. The stalks are crunchy and, if sometimes a bit tough, can be used to flavor stocks. The feathery tops make a lovely snipped garnish, and contribute a pleasant mild herb flavor when blended into dressings or vinaigrettes. Choose unmarred bulbs with crisp stalks. Refrigerated in a well-sealed bag, it will keep for several days.

FENUGREEK SEEDS

We use fenugreek most frequently in curries, sambars, and chutneys. The light brown, oblong seeds have an earthy, musky flavor and aroma, and we usually toast and grind them before adding to a dish or spice mix. Fenugreek seeds are available where Indian and Pakistani foods are sold, and in the spice section of well-stocked supermarkets.

FILO

The ultrathin sheets of filo pastry dough are used in savory and sweet strudels, pies, turnovers, and appetizers across the Mediterranean, Middle East, and North Africa. Filo is probably best known as the pastry of baklava and spanakopita. It is a low-fat dough made simply of flour, water, and salt, sometimes with a small amount of olive oil and/or vinegar. While it is possible, if challenging, to make your own filo dough, good filo is available in the frozen food sections of many supermarkets and online (go to www.fillofactory.com), where organic and whole wheat filo sheets can also be found. Store unopened filo for up to a month in the refrigerator. Tightly rewrap in plastic after opening, and filo will keep for a few days in the refrigerator and up to a year in the freezer. Do not refreeze after thawing, or it will become brittle.

FISH
see page 17

GMOs
see page 14

GRITS

Grits are ground, dried corn with the germ removed. We use white or yellow grits in the same ways we use polenta, mostly as a bed for beans or stews. We use stone-ground, regular, or quick-cooking grits, but never instant, which not only taste insipid but also contain various additives we're leery of. Depending on the grind, grits take from 5 to 10 minutes to 2 hours to cook.

GUAVA PASTE

Guava paste is a conserve made from a very thick purée of guava pulp and sugar. Some guava pastes are very dense with a fruit leather-like consistency, while others are moister and slightly less gelatinous, more jamlike, but they are all intensely sweet with a distinctive flavor and a slightly gritty texture firm enough to slice. Guava paste is used in both savory and sweet dishes, and has found its way into U.S. culinary lexicon through our Mexican, Caribbean, and Central and South American citizenry.

We prefer brands such as Guayaquil that stick to the basics: guava, sugar, citric acid, and sometimes pectin. We've seen other brands that include high-fructose corn syrup and as many as three different artificial food colorings. It is not uncommon to have guava paste left over since recipes usually call for discreet amounts, but it keeps almost indefinitely when well-covered in the refrigerator. Check out the many recipes online that use guava paste. It is often packaged in wide, flat tins, also in packets and jars, and is available in the Latin foods section of supermarkets, in Mexican and Latin American markets, and online.

HALF-AND-HALF

Half-and-half is a homogenized commercial dairy product consisting of half light cream and half milk. Its butterfat content ranges between 10 and 12 percent. We use half-and-half in recipes when we want richness, but not as much as with full-fat cream. Half-and-half won't whip into peaks like heavy cream or whipping cream.

You can make half-and-half by combining 3 parts whole milk with 1 part heavy cream, or 2 parts low-fat milk with 1 part heavy cream.

HERBS
see page 385

HOISIN SAUCE

This Asian condiment is spoon-thick, dark, salty, and sweet. It is used in Chinese and Southeast Asian dishes, and may be best known as the sauce spread on mu shu pancakes before they are filled and rolled.

Hoisin sauce is composed of sugar, sweet potatoes, fermented soybean paste, sesame seed paste, and a range of spices. We use it as a condiment, to glaze roasted vegetables, and as an ingredient in marinades and toppings for shrimp and fish. Our favorite hoisin is made by Lee Kum Kee, packed in glass jars so the flavor stays pure. Look for it in Asian food stores and in the Asian food section of your supermarket. Tightly lidded and uncontaminated, hoisin will keep for many months in the refrigerator.

HOT PEPPERS

We enjoy the flavors of local fresh hot peppers before winter descends and we're limited to dried chiles or what's available from hundreds of miles away. Both dried and fresh chiles are pungent, but fresh chiles taste like what they are—a fresh vegetable. They lend a clean-tasting different kind of heat, fragrance, and flavor to the dishes they're in. Many varieties of hot peppers are grown and eaten all over the world. The fresh hot peppers commonly found in this country, or at least in the Southern Tier of upstate New York, are poblano, jalapeño, serrano, Scotch bonnet, and habanero. This list ranges from the mildest, poblano, to the most fiery. Scotch Bonnet and habanero are tied for hottest, on this list anyway—then there are those little Thai peppers and the king of hot, the Trinidad Moruga Scorpion.

To control the spicy heat of a dish, the first step is to taste a bit of the pepper to see how hot it is. Within the same pepper crop, even from the same pepper plant, heat will vary. Secondly, the most intense heat resides in the seeds and ribs of the pepper, so if the flesh of the chile is hot enough for you, remove the seeds, ribs, and central membranes.

Remember to protect your body parts. The spicy hot oils that cling to your hands when working with hot peppers can be extremely painful in cuts on hands and fingers and when inadvertently rubbed into eyes or lips. We often use latex or nitrile gloves when working with chiles. Immediately wash your hands in warm, soapy water after handling hot peppers.

If you bite into a chile that sets your mouth afire, avoid drinking liquid because it only disperses the heat; instead eat a piece of bread, potato, tortilla, or avocado.

LENTILS

Lentils are small disk-shaped dried legumes. One of the virtues of lentils compared with other dried beans is that they cook quickly and don't need to be presoaked. The best known and most often used are brown lentils. They absorb seasonings handily and cook in about 30 minutes. French green lentils are smaller and greener in color; their cooking time may range from 20 to 40 minutes. One virtue of French lentils is that they maintain their form beautifully during cooking and therefore look lovely in main dish salads and side dishes. Red lentils are the only hulled lentil. They start off a pretty coral color and turn yellow during cooking. Red lentils are the starchiest of the lentil family and make wonderful soups and purées. They usually cook in about 15 minutes.

For cooking directions, go to page 372.

Store lentils in airtight glass containers in a cool, dark place for up to a year. Lentils are available in packages and in bulk at natural food stores, in most supermarkets, in Middle Eastern and Indian food stores, and online.

LOCAL FOOD

see page 13

KALE

Kale is a leafy green often on "superfoods" lists. Its leaves are dark green, sometimes with a purple, red, or blue patina, and may be curly or flat, smooth or bumpy. To prep for cooking, strip the leaves off the stems: hold the stem in one hand, wrap your other thumb and forefinger firmly around the stem at the base of the leaf, and in one fast motion, pull away from the end of the stem; the leaf will come off the stem easily. Bunches of kale found in produce markets vary in weight and in the amount of large stems and wilted or yellowing leaves, so it's hard sometimes to know how much you need to buy for a particular amount, but usually, with nice, fresh kale, 1 pound will yield about 5 cups of sorted, stemmed, and chopped greens.

KASHA

Kasha has an earthy flavor and sturdy yet fluffy texture. The word *kasha* is a Slavic term for porridge that can be made from any number of grains. In this country, kasha has become synonymous with toasted buckwheat groats, which, ironically, is neither a variety of wheat nor a grain. Kasha is a cocoa-colored triangular seed from a plant in the rhubarb family. It is gluten-free.

You can store kasha in a cool, dry place for a short amount of time, but it is best to keep it in the refrigerator, where it will last up to 3 months, or in the freezer for up to 6 months. Kasha, conventional and organic, can be purchased in packages and in bulk at natural food stores and well-stocked supermarkets. It is also found in stores that market Eastern European and Jewish food products.

How to Cook Kasha

For each cup of kasha, use 2 cups of water. Bring the water to a boil, then stir in the kasha, cover, and reduce the heat. Simmer for 10 to 15 minutes, and then remove from the heat and let it sit covered for about 10 minutes. Fluff with a fork and add salt to taste.

Traditionally, kasha is stirred with a beaten egg in a skillet on medium heat for a couple of minutes, until dry and the grains are separated. Then add boiling water or broth and proceed as above: simmer for about 15 minutes, let sit for about 10 minutes, then fluff with a fork.

Untoasted buckwheat should simmer for about 10 minutes longer than kasha.

You can toast buckwheat groats in a dry skillet on medium heat: stir for about 5 minutes, until browned.

LEEKS

It's important to rinse leeks well to remove the sand and grit between the layers. Use the white and tender green parts of a leek bulb. The upper, darker green parts of leeks make good stock. A medium-size leek usually yields about 1 cup, chopped.

To most easily rinse out the grains of sand that are trapped between the layers of the leeks, remove 1 or 2 outer layers and cut off the root end. Cut off and discard the top half only of the tough upper green leaves—you'll use the rest as a "handle" while rinsing. Cut the white and light green part of the leeks in half lengthwise and then in half again into quarters. Holding the leek by the upper leaves, rinse well under cool running water, fanning the layers apart with your other hand. Cut the white and light green parts into $\frac{1}{8}$-inch slices. In a colander, rinse the sliced leeks well. Drain.

MARSALA

Marsala is a fortified wine, thick and rich, almost like brandy. It originated in Sicily in the city of Marsala. Its taste and alcohol content are altered by the addition of distilled wine or fruit juice, and it is produced at three levels of refinement depending on how long it is aged and whether or not it is aged in wood. Marsala is made from red or green grapes. We use a red Marsala in our Eggplant-Mushroom

Marsala (page 218) and white wine Marsala is often used in desserts such as zabaglione and tiramisu.

MISO

Used throughout Japanese cuisine to flavor and add healthful benefits to soups, stews, sauces, dressings, and spreads, miso is a thick paste made of fermented soy beans and/or grain. The mixture of soy with the particular grain, and the length of fermentation, makes for very different misos. Rice or white miso is golden in color and has a sweet mild taste. Barley miso is brown and is richer and more savory. Wheat or soy miso is dark brown and tastes stronger and saltier. For everyday cooking, and especially for the cook who's new to miso, we recommend rice miso. South River is one of our favorite brands, but there are many excellent choices available. If we had to have only one, we'd choose a milder light- or medium-colored miso. There's no reason you can't mix a couple of misos in one dish. Miso's healthful enzymes are destroyed by high temperatures, so once the miso is added, don't let the soup boil. Miso can be purchased at most natural food stores and where Japanese foods are sold.

NUTS

Toasted nuts have a greater depth of both texture and flavor. You can toast nuts in the oven or toaster oven, in a heavy skillet on the stovetop, or in the microwave oven. Nuts become crisper and darker as they cool, so stop the toasting process when they're a shade lighter than you want. When overbrowned, nuts develop an acrid flavor. Warm nuts are easier to chop by hand, but if using a food processor, cool toasted nuts before chopping or grinding.

How to Toast Nuts

To toast nuts in the oven or toaster oven, preheat the oven to 350°F. Spread the nuts in a single layer on a dry baking sheet and bake, stirring once or twice for even toasting, until golden and fragrant. The cooking time varies depending on the nut, so check on them periodically:

- Almonds: 10 minutes
- Hazelnuts: 12 to 15 minutes
- Macadamia nuts: 12 to 15 minutes
- Pecans: 10 to 15 minutes
- Pine nuts: 5 minutes
- Walnuts: 10 to 15 minutes
- Peanuts (shelled): 20 to 25 minutes

To toast nuts in a skillet, spread the nuts in a single layer in a dry heavy skillet on medium heat, stirring frequently. When aromatic and lightly browned, remove the nuts from the hot pan because they'll continue to cook.

To toast nuts in a microwave, spread a single layer of nuts out on a microwave-safe plate. Cook them in 1-minute intervals on full power, stirring after each minute, until the nuts begin to crisp and become fragrant. Microwaved nuts have a toasted flavor, but don't brown.

To skin hazelnuts or peanuts after toasting, let them cool a bit, and then pour the nuts onto a clean kitchen towel spread out on a work surface. Gather the towel around the nuts and rub together until most of the skins have come off. Don't worry about getting off every little bit of skin. Pick out the nuts. If you have a yard, go out there to shake the skins out of the towel.

OLD BAY SEASONING

Although we've tried, we haven't yet perfected a spice blend that matches Old Bay Seasoning. Old Bay is a seasoning mixture that originated around the Chesapeake Bay that's become synonymous with the shellfish cuisine of the Maryland, Delaware, and Virginia peninsula. At the restaurant, we not only sprinkle it on fish and seafood but use it in chowders, rubs, aioli, egg salad, and stews. Try it on fresh ears of corn or roasted potatoes.

Old Bay Seasoning is found in rectangular cans in the spice aisle of supermarkets and often where you buy fresh seafood. Online it can be purchased at www.google.com/shopping.

ORGANIC FOOD
see page 14

PAPRIKA
Paprika is a favored spice in Eastern European cuisines. Sweet or hot red peppers are dried and sometimes smoked, then ground to produce the three paprika varieties: sweet, hot, and smoked. Sweet paprika is the most ubiquitous and mild paprika, and the one we most often use. Hot paprika is not as pungent as cayenne. Look for paprika in the spice section of your food market.

PARCHMENT PAPER
Parchment paper is heavy, nonstick paper, usually brown, that's very useful and can help you avoid lots of messes. You can roll out pie or biscuit or cookie dough on it. Its most frequent use is probably as a liner for baking sheets. It's awfully nice not to have to oil (and then scrub) the baking sheet, and, especially if the baking sheet is lightweight, the parchment paper helps to keep the bottoms of cookies from browning too much. It's also good for roasted vegetables (unless you want crusty bottoms): no scraping the pieces off of the pan. Use it when roasting or baking something that's very acidic, like tomatoes, to prevent a metallic flavor.

Parchment paper makes it a snap to turn layer cakes out in one piece; use scissors to cut the parchment paper to the size of the bottom of the baking pan. You can also use parchment paper to make little packages filled with vegetables and bake-steam them in the oven (page 245). Parchment works wonderfully for separating layers of cookies or candies in a tin. With a pretty ribbon, it's beautiful emergency gift-wrapping paper.

And, it's just so nice to handle. Parchment paper is not expensive, and a roll goes a long way. It also comes in sheets. Plus, we use the same piece several times, until it gets so brittle that it starts to fall apart (unless we cooked something like onions on it). Don't butter or oil the parchment paper or the baking sheet, unless the recipe says to.

PASTA
Dried pasta is an economical pantry item that keeps almost indefinitely, so you can keep a wide selection on hand. There are a few simple and effortless things you can do to make every pasta dish better. Start with good pasta, pair it with a sauce that complements its shape, and cook it right.

We recommend that you use imported Italian pastas. The Italian federal government imposes exacting standards for ingredients and manufacturing processes: dried commercial pasta must be made with pure durum semolina flour without artificial additives, colored pastas must be made with natural vegetables, and egg pastas must contain whole eggs. In Italian factories, the temperature of the dough is kept low, with a long kneading time, and then when the dough moves slowly through extrusion machines and is pushed through holes in bronze dies, that creates pasta with a slightly rough, porous surface that sauce will cling to. Drying is controlled at a low temperature for a long time.

In the United States, there are no restrictions on the type of flour used and often the flour is over-refined, artificially enriched, and soft. Frozen vegetables or just vegetable dyes are the norm. Larger American companies' extrusion machines usually use Teflon dies and that creates a slick, glossy surface on the pasta. High-speed kneading and drying may be at a temperature high enough to risk denaturing the protein in the semolina, resulting in a softer cooked pasta.

Some American artisan pastas are extruded through bronze dies, and if you find one in your area, try it—you may find a pasta that delights you. The imported Italian-made pasta brands we like and that are widely available in this country are Bionaturae, DeCecco, and Gia Russa.

If it's been a while since you tried whole-grain pasta, try it again now. Some of the whole wheat pastas that have come on the market lately have a firm texture and nutty flavor. Every pasta dish in this book can be made with whole wheat pasta. If you're avoiding wheat, try pastas made from rice, corn, kamut, spelt, quinoa, and buckwheat.

How to Cook Pasta

Use a large covered pot filled with plenty of salted water, 5 or 6 quarts per pound of pasta, so that the water will quickly return to a boil after the pasta is added and so the pasta has room to float freely and cook evenly.

Ease the pasta into rapidly boiling water, stir to separate, and cover the pot until it returns to a full, rolling boil. Don't break long strands of pasta—just push them into the boiling water and in seconds they'll be soft enough to stir. Stir occasionally to prevent clumping. To know when pasta is done, taste it. Catch it when it is just al dente—tender but with a firm bite. This is especially important for whole-grain pastas, which become too soft when overcooked.

Drain pasta immediately in a colander, and quickly, before it starts to dry out, transfer the hot pasta to a warm serving bowl or back into the warm pot you cooked it in. Never rinse with cold water.

The many different shapes and sizes of pasta often have affectionate, humorous, and vivid names in Italian, such as angels' hair and priest chokers. Some pasta shapes are named for how they look. Orecchiette look like little ears and penne are fountain pen–shaped. Each pasta shape has a different texture, a different mouth feel. Pair a pasta and sauce based on the consistency of the sauce. Thin flat noodles, such as fettucine and farfalle, go well with delicate cream and cheese sauces. A chunky vegetable or bean sauce is best with a heartier short pasta shape, such as penne or fusilli. Bowl-shaped cuts, such as orecchiette and shells, are good for sauces with finely chopped vegetables, because the pasta catches and holds the vegetable pieces. Match long strands like spaghetti with smooth tomato and pesto sauces so that the entire strands will be coated with sauce for that slippery sensation in the mouth. That said, the lack of a perfect pasta shape never stops us from going ahead with the sauce we want to make.

PEPERONCINI

These small, sweet peppers with a mild heat are native to the Mediterranean and are sometimes marketed as Tuscan peppers. Peperoncini are most often pickled and used whole on antipasto platters or sliced for sandwiches and salads. The color ranges from chartreuse to bright red. Peperoncini are available in the condiment aisle of the supermarket.

POLENTA

Polenta is Italian cornmeal porridge, essentially cornmeal mush. Polenta is a good bed for beans and stews and delicious as a layer in casseroles.

You can make polenta with any cornmeal: yellow, white, or blue; finely ground, coarse, or stone-ground. Finer grinds of cornmeal make smooth and creamy polenta; coarsely ground cornmeal makes a nubbier, more sturdy polenta.

The type of cornmeal you use affects the water-to-cornmeal ratio, the cooking time, and the flavor and texture of the polenta. A medium grind of cornmeal usually takes about 20 minutes to cook. Coarse stone-ground cornmeal may take an hour or more. And then, there's a very finely ground or processed cornmeal that cooks in as little as 5 minutes. The very quick-cooking cornmeal is sometimes labeled polenta cornmeal, but any cornmeal, from "instant" to cornmeal flour and right up to a very coarse grind, may also be labeled "polenta cornmeal."

For polenta at Moosewood, we use whole grain, coarsely ground cornmeal, locally milled from locally grown organic, non-GMO corn; the same cornmeal we use to make cornbread. Whole-grain cornmeal retains the germ of the corn kernel, so essential oils, fiber, vitamins, and minerals are not lost. It has an honest corn taste. Bob's Red Mill Polenta, available in stores and online, is a good commercial option.

How to Cook Polenta

Notwithstanding the preceding discussion, it's easy to make polenta. Basically, all you do is stir cornmeal into boiling water and then simmer, stirring frequently, and adding more boiling water if it gets too thick too fast, until the polenta is smooth and creamy and tastes done. We recommend that you start with a 1:3 ratio of cornmeal to water, and add more water if you need to. We salt the water. To prevent lumps, add the cornmeal in a steady stream while whisking briskly. To reduce the risk of scorching, use a heat diffuser after the polenta has thickened.

QUINOA

Quinoa hails from the South American Andes and is truly an ancient grain, between 5,000 and 9,000 years old. When we first started writing about quinoa in 1994 it was the new grain on the block in this country. Quinoa is a tasty, easily digested, gluten-free grain rich in vitamins, minerals, and protein. It is a complete protein containing all essential amino acids.

Find quinoa in packages or in bulk at well-stocked supermarkets and natural food stores. Organic and conventional quinoa is available online at www.bobsredmill.com and www.myspicesage.com.

How to Cook Quinoa

Quinoa cooks in 15 to 20 minutes, and as it cooks, the external germs, which form little bands around the little flattened spheres, spiral out in crescent-shaped tails. Quinoa grows with a protective, bitter coating of saponin that keeps birds and bugs from devouring it. In processing, most of the saponin is removed, but quinoa must still be thoroughly rinsed before cooking. Saponon lathers under running water, so rinse until there are no suds. Quinoa expands about four times during cooking.

For each cup of dry quinoa, use $1\frac{1}{2}$ cups water. Rinse the dry quinoa until the water runs clear. In a saucepan on medium-high heat, warm enough oil to cover the bottom. Add the rinsed quinoa and a little salt, and stir for a couple of minutes. Stir in boiling water, cover, and simmer for about 15 minutes, or until the water has been absorbed. Turn off the heat and let sit for about 5 minutes, until tender.

RICE

Every day, we make a big pot of brown rice at the restaurant. Actually, at least two big pots. Plain brown rice serves as a good bed for all sorts of dishes, including beans, stews, burritos, and roasted vegetables. For something a little different, replace up to half of brown rice with wild rice or wehani or other red rice. We rarely make white rice, occasionally white basmati or jasmine for a dessert. We use black rice in some pilafs and puddings.

Brown rice is our bread and butter at Moosewood, our favorite rice with its chewy texture and full flavor. We like the short, plump, moist kernels of short-grain brown rice. When we want a fluffier rice, we make long-grain brown rice.

Black rice, also called sweet black rice and Chinese forbidden rice, has multicolored black and brown grains that turn almost purple when cooked. It is short-grained and high in gluten, with a sweet flavor and sticky texture.

Basmati rice, also called Texmati and "calmati," is aromatic with a nutty flavor and smooth texture.

Wehani rice is a brown rice that turns an earthy honey-red color when cooked. It is slightly chewy and its aroma is similar to that of hot peanuts.

Wild rice is not rice, but seeds of a marsh grass that have been gathered historically in North America and China. The flavor of its long black and brown grains is distinctive, but we don't know how to describe it. We mix wild rice with brown rice for pilafs and stuffings.

How to Cook Rice

Use a pan with a heavy bottom and a tight-fitting lid. If you have a heat diffuser, it's a good idea to use it under simmering rice. Because most rice expands about triple during cooking, the amount of raw rice should fill no more than one-fourth of the pan. Generally, figure ½ cup of raw rice for one serving.

For larger quantities of rice, use less water proportionately. For example, for 3 cups of raw brown rice, use 4½ cups of water.

Brown and Brown Basmati Rice
1 cup rinsed and drained brown rice
2 teaspoons olive oil
½ teaspoon salt
2 cups water

In a saucepan on high heat, combine the rice, oil, and salt. Stir for a minute or two, add the water, cover, and bring to a boil. Reduce the heat to very low and simmer for about 45 minutes, or until the water has been absorbed and the rice is firm but tender. When the rice is done, turn off the heat and take off the lid. Fluff the rice with a fork and let it sit for a couple of minutes.

Depending on the rice, the weight of the pan and how tightly it's covered, and the heat, you may need to add a little more water after 30 to 35 minutes of simmering, and if there's still water at the bottom when the rice is tender, tilt the pan to drain off the water and stir the rice and let it sit, uncovered, on very low heat for a few minutes.

White Rice, White Basmati, and Jasmine Rice
1¾ cups water
½ teaspoon salt
1 teaspoon oil
1 cup rice

Bring the water to a boil in a covered saucepan. Add the salt and oil, and stir in the rice. Cover, reduce the heat to very low, and simmer for about 15 minutes.

SESAME OIL

An amber-colored oil with a richly aromatic nutty flavor and fragrance, Asian sesame oil is usually used as a finishing oil in Asian dishes, serving as a seasoning rather than as a cooking or salad oil. Generally only a small amount is needed to complement other flavors; more will not only compete, but dominate. Sometimes called dark sesame oil, roasted or toasted sesame oil, or simply sesame oil, it is made from crushed roasted sesame seeds, the source of its dark color. It should not be confused with the cold-pressed, pale sesame oil made from untoasted seeds that is used for cooking and frying.

Like all products, Asian sesame oils vary in quality and we encourage you to experiment. One of our favorites is Jayone, from Korea. If unavailable in your food store, it can be purchased online at www.jayone.com. Asian sesame oil can be found in the international and Asian sections of well-stocked markets. It will keep for 2 to 3 months, unrefrigerated, when stored in a cool dark place, and for a long time in the refrigerator.

SPICES AND HERBS

Herbs are the aromatic leaves of various plants. Spices are flavorful and fragrant seasonings made from seeds, roots, stems, bark, buds, and fruit. Fresh herbs and freshly ground or grated spices can transform a simple dish into something delectable. But, herbs and spices are expensive and perishable, so we'd like to give you some simple tips for making the most of them.

Fresh Herbs

Fresh herbs are one of life's joys, but unless you grow herbs and can pick just what you need when you need it, you've likely had to compost a slimy half-bunch of dill or cilantro that you found in the vegetable crisper. When you have fresh herbs that you're not going to use soon, you can easily freeze them for next week or month. Purée the fresh leaves in the blender with a little water. Pour the purée into an ice cube tray, and when frozen solid, pop out the cubes and store them in a freezer bag. Be sure to label, because once puréed and frozen, the green of basil looks pretty much like the green of parsley or cilantro. Then, you can drop a frozen cube or two into your soup or sauce.

Dried Herbs and Spices

Dried herbs and most spices lose flavor and fragrance quickly because oxidization occurs and their aromatics dissipate. When you can, buy in bulk—we suggest this not so you can stock up on large quantities of herbs and spices, but so you can buy small quantities. This will save you not only a significant amount of money, but also the waste of discarding the spice if it's not used again for months. When buying in bulk, go to a store that has a lot of consumer traffic and so a high turnover of inventory. Buy whole, unground spices such as cardamom and cumin, coriander, and fennel seeds. Whole spices last longer than ground spices. Grind only what you need or will use within a couple of weeks. Store herbs and spices in airtight glass jars in a cool dark place. Discard after 6 months.

Toasting Spices

Toasting releases a spice's aromatic and flavorful oils, bringing out an earthier, richer, and fuller flavor and fragrance. In some cases, as with cinnamon and fennel, the spice becomes sweeter and mellower. Toasting spices is a way to enhance your dish and your cooking experience—and it takes only minutes.

Spices that benefit most from toasting include cumin, coriander, fennel, and mustard seeds, cinnamon, cardamom, and star anise. In general, whole spices are preferred over ground spices for toasting, because whole spices better retain their natural oils and so have more flavor to release when they're heated or ground. You can certainly toast ground spices; just keep in mind that it will take only seconds.

Don't toast different spices in the same pan at the same time because spices brown at different speeds, and so you'd be left with either some that aren't toasted or some that are scorched. Heat the spices slowly, so that they warm clear through to the center without burning the outside. Spices are ready when they smell rich and full-bodied and become slightly darker in color. Be careful not to scorch spices or they'll be bitter; they shouldn't smoke at any time during the process.

How to Toast Spices

Put spices in a cold, dry (no oil), heavy skillet or pan. Warm the pan on medium heat, and as the pan heats and the spices become fragrant, stir or shake often. Whole spices may jump a bit, and you may hear little popping sounds as they toast. When you can really smell the fragrance and as soon as the spices just start to brown, they're ready. Transfer them immediately to a bowl or plate to cool—their residual heat will keep the cooking process going a little longer. If you wait until they are very toasted in the pan, they'll become burnt and bitter once off the heat.

You can also toast spices in the oven or toaster oven. Spread the spices out on a dry tray and toast at 325°F until they're fully aromatic and slightly darker.

Grind cool, whole spices to a fine texture in a coffee grinder, spice grinder, or mortar and pestle. Toasted spices are easier to grind than untoasted spices. Once toasted, spices are best used immediately, but any extra can be stored in a well-sealed jar or plastic bag.

SWEET POTATOES

Sweet potatoes are very nutritious and high in fiber and complex carbohydrates. The color of their skin may be red, brown, purple, or tan, and their flesh ranges from white through tan, yellow, orange, reddish orange, and purple. They're on the Clean Fifteen list (page 14). They're delicious.

But here's the real reason we've included sweet potatoes in this guide: Over the years, we've been mystified at times because the sweet potatoes in a soup or stew have taken either a lot longer to cook than we expected, or never fully cooked at all. Eventually, we realized that it was happening when we cooked sweet potatoes with tomatoes. So, in dishes that include tomatoes, we cook the sweet potatoes until almost tender before adding tomatoes, or cook the sweet potatoes separately until just tender and then add them to the pot.

TAHINI

This thick, creamy sesame butter is made from hulled and lightly toasted sesame seeds. It is a familiar ingredient in the cuisines of Greece and Turkey and across the Middle East and North Africa. Here, it is probably best known as a principle ingredient in hummus. Tahini is available in tins and jars in the ethnic section of well-stocked supermarkets and in natural food stores, where it is often offered in bulk. Bulk tahini is rarely refrigerated, so buy it at a store with a rapid inventory turnover. Tahini has a high oil content and the oil will rise to the top. When opening a new jar of tahini, mix down the oil and refrigerate to keep it emulsified and to prevent rancidity.

TAMARIND CONCENTRATE (TAMARIND PASTE)

The fruity, sour extract of the tamarind tree pod is much used in the cuisines of Southeast Asia, India, and Latin America. It gives a sweet-tart kick to curries and is a standard ingredient in pad Thai and Vietnamese pho. It is the basis of beverages and soft drinks in Central and South America.

Though tamarind pulp is available in specialty

stores and can be made into the useful concentrate, it is far easier to purchase the concentrate ready-made. It is available in small containers where Asian and Hispanic foods are sold. We like Laxmi brand. It will keep for months in the refrigerator in a tightly lidded container. In most recipes, you can substitute fresh lime juice for tamarind; the flavor is different but the sour is about the same.

TEMPEH

Tempeh is naturally fermented whole cooked soybeans and very little else—maybe a bit of vinegar to start the culturing process—pressed into a meaty-tasting cake. Basic tempeh is gluten-free, though there are varieties that include wheat and other grains. Tempeh is native to Indonesian cuisine, most popular in Java, and has been eaten in Asia for hundreds of years. Tempeh is porous and readily absorbs marinades and flavorings. It has a stronger nutritional profile than tofu and other soy products because it is made of the whole bean. It is also said by some to be more digestible than other beans and bean products because the enzymatic fermentation process "pre-digests" the beans.

Tempeh can be sliced or cubed and fried or baked, or crumbled in vegetarian "burgers." Tightly wrap opened tempeh in freezer-proof plastic and it will freeze well. Tempeh is available in health food stores, some Asian food stores, and online at www.lightlife.com.

THAI CURRY PASTE

Thai curry paste is the source of many Thai dishes' rich and complex flavors and heat. Curry pastes are flavorful additions to stir-fries, soups, curries, marinades, and rice and noodle dishes.

The three most common curry pastes are green, red, and yellow, which correspond to the color of the hot pepper used, and each paste uses a different array of spices. Green curry paste, often considered the hottest paste (though this is debatable and dependent on the type of green chilies used), typically includes lemongrass, Thai ginger (galangal), keiffir lime leaves, sweet basil, and coriander root. Red curry paste is made of long red hot peppers, lemongrass and galangal, and additional chili powder and other spices. Yellow curry paste is the mildest blend, made of yellow peppers and traditional Indian spices like cumin, coriander, turmeric, and ginger. Most curry pastes also include shallots, oil, sugar, and salt.

Vegetarian cooks should look closely at ingredient lists, because classic Thai pastes include fish sauce and shrimp paste, though there are a variety of options that do not. The flavor of curry pastes varies with the paste maker, so sample a few to find the one(s) you like. They can be found where Asian foods are sold.

TOFU

All tofus are not equal. The difference between good, fresh tofu and some of the nationally available brands is significant. It's like the difference between sweet green peas just picked in your garden and canned ones, between just-pressed apple cider and bottled apple juice. When we're away from home and buy some of the national brands we find in the supermarket, we begin to understand why tofu is something they joke about on sitcoms. It is simply not that which we've come to take for granted from our hometown tofu maker, Ithaca Soy. We don't think we can overstate it: if the tofu is not so good, with the same recipe, the same other good ingredients, and the same techniques, the result is just not the same.

Good firm tofu is not chalky, not mushy, and doesn't have the texture of liverwurst. When you bake it, the outer edges are chewy and the inside is succulent. You can easily shred it on a hand grater. When you sauté it, it has a nice resistance, a "bite" like al dente pasta. It readily absorbs flavors.

If a good fresh tofu isn't available in your stores and there's a Chinese or Japanese restaurant where the tofu is delectable, ask where they get their tofu. Maybe you can get some, too. Or, ask if you can buy a block from them.

Usually, tofu comes in 14-, 15-, or 16-ounce cakes. Fresh tofu, in particular, is not cut as precisely as national and regional brands packaged in little plastic tubs, and a block of it may weigh even 18 ounces. We developed and tested our recipes with 16-ounce blocks of tofu, but the recipes should work even if you have a little more or less tofu.

How to Press Tofu

Whether or not you need to press tofu depends on both how it's used in the recipe and the quality of the tofu. Soft and silken tofus are never pressed. Firm, and even extra-firm, tofu may contain a lot of moisture, and that can affect the outcome. It may not matter too much in some recipes, for instance baked tofu—you may just have to bake it longer. But the extra liquid that some tofu holds may make something like a filling or burger mix too wet. Pressing tofu expresses some of that water, making the tofu denser and more firm. It's surprising how much liquid pools around some tofu during pressing.

At the restaurant, we almost exclusively use firm fresh tofu, and we usually press it for an hour or so before using it to make it even firmer. We put the blocks of tofu in a flat-bottomed baking pan and put another flat pan on top of it. Then we put weight in the top pan, usually a stack of plates. In our home kitchens, depending on the recipe and if we have firm fresh tofu, we often don't press it at all. Some-

times we simply press it gently between our hands, held over the sink, and that's fine for many uses.

If the tofu you have isn't a firm fresh tofu, we suggest that you always press it. Whatever tofu you have, if you're going to grate it, we recommend that you press it.

Place the block of tofu in a broad, flat bowl or casserole dish, put a plate on top of the tofu, and balance a heavy can or book on the plate. After the tofu has pressed for about 30 minutes, drain the liquid that has accumulated in the bowl. If you're not yet ready to use the tofu or if you want to press it more, refrigerate it.

How long the tofu should be pressed depends on the tofu you have. To be safe, if a recipe needs dense, firm tofu, press it until no more liquid has accumulated ten minutes after you poured the water off. In our recipes that call for firm tofu, we tell you when pressing is probably not necessary, and when you need quite firm tofu, in which case, you should press it well.

We can't think of an instance in which tofu would be pressed too long, even if it were all day or overnight. On the other hand, if you're pressed for time, just press it until you're ready for it and it will probably be ok. If you use the same kind of tofu regularly, you'll come to know how firm or wet it is.

How to Grate Tofu

First, press the tofu until it's dense, until no more liquid is being expressed. At home, we usually use a hand grater, the large-holed side. In a food processor, use the large-holed blade. Like with cheese, how much pressure you apply while grating will determine how large or fine the shred is.

VEGETABLE STOCK

Every day at the restaurant, we make vegetable stock for soups and stews. At home, most of us make soups with water or with one of our favorite convenience products: quart boxes of organic vegetable, mushroom, or mock chicken broth, like Imagine and Pacific brands. Still, there's nothing as good as a fresh homemade vegetable stock. When we make it at home, we make a big pot and freeze the extra in quart freezer bags.

How to Make Vegetable Stock

Simmer chunks of vegetables in water for about an hour. Strain through a sieve or a colander and use right away or refrigerate in a closed container for up to 4 days or freeze for up to several months.

10 cups water
2 onions, peeled and quartered
2 potatoes, washed and thickly sliced
2 carrots, coarsely chopped
2 celery stalks, thickly sliced
2 garlic cloves, smashed
2 bay leaves
½ teaspoon salt
several whole black peppercorns

Other possibilities: sweet potatoes, zucchini or summer squash, mushrooms or mushroom stems, parsnips, apples, pears, parsley, fresh herbs.

Don't include bell peppers or eggplant (they make the stock bitter), tomatoes or other acidic fruits or vegetables (they may curdle the soup), broccoli, cauliflower, turnips, or other strongly flavored vegetables or ones whose color bleeds, like beets and greens.

WASABI

Also known as "Japanese horseradish," wasabi is a pungent root used as a condiment, most familiarly alongside sushi and sashimi. It is prepared and used in three forms: grated fresh, dried and ground into a powder, and made into a paste. True wasabi is difficult to grow outside of Japan, so what most Westerners know of wasabi is actually a mixture of horseradish, mustard, green food coloring or spinach powder, and a binding starch. Wasabi in powder and paste forms are usually located in the Asian section of supermarkets and in Asian food stores. Imported true wasabi powder is available online and at select gourmet food stores.

ZEST

In the world of food, zest is both noun and verb. As a noun, zest is the outer, colored part of citrus rind, not including its white pith. It gives a dish an intensified essence of fruit flavor. All citrus, as well as some lesser-known tropical family members, can be zested, which brings us to the verb. To zest is to cut, scrap, or grate the zest. It is not difficult to zest a piece of citrus, but it takes some care.

A handy tool is a Microplane grater, an ultrafine-toothed grater that is readily available in cooking stores and was originally only a carpenter's rasp. You can also zest on the fine-holed side of a box grater. Gently and shallowly run the outside of a whole fruit across the grater, to remove the colored part of the peel, but not the bitter white pith. You can also thinly slice the peel with a vegetable peeler and then mince it.

The Moosewood Collective

From the upper left corner going clockwise: Joan Adler, Eliana Parra, David Hirsch, Susan Harville, Wynnie Stein, Neil Minnis, Laura Branca, Penny Goldin, Linda Dickinson, Ned Asta, Jenny Wang, Lisa Wichman, Nancy Lazarus, Sara Wade Robbins, Dave Dietrich. The four members who were unavailable when the photo was taken are Kip Wilcox, Maureen Vivino, Tony Del Plato, and Michael Blodgett.

Index

Simon raised an eyebrow. 'And what tales would be rife at the moment?'

De Tosny shrugged. 'I will leave the tellers to spin their stories themselves. Suffice to say that Bishop Odo is stalking the court and casting his web as he goes.'

'Ah,' Simon nodded as if that explained everything. 'The old spider is still at his tricks then?'

'More than ever. The old king was his brother, but that did not stop him from intriguing. Now he has nephews to manipulate, and he thinks them considerably more malleable than his iron fist of a brother.' De Tosny looked around. There was no one to hear, but still he drew in his horns. 'I will talk to you later once you have settled in.' He slapped Simon on the shoulder. 'I would not like your sheep to freeze. Lamb always tastes sweetest when it is warm.' He bowed again to the women, smiled incorrigibly for Jude's benefit, and, blowing on his hands, vanished into the deepening blue twilight.

'You keep some interesting friends,' Matilda said with a gleam of amused curiosity. 'Does he really have such a bad reputation with women?'

'Only with women who have a bad reputation themselves,' Simon answered – 'but he is known to play outrageously close to the knuckle with the chaste wives and daughters of barons who attend the court. Fingers may not have been burned, but there have been some narrow escapes.'

'Is he betrothed or married?'

'Not as yet,' Simon said blandly.

Matilda nodded and said nothing, but she missed neither her sister's furious blush, nor the tone of her husband's reply. Everyone cast webs she thought, only some did it with more subtlety than others.

Matilda was accustomed to comfort and luxury. Even if her mother had leanings towards a religious life, she had also believed in maintaining the dignity of her status and the hall at

Northampton had been as well appointed as any in the land. However, nothing had prepared her for Westminster's great hall. Charcoal burned in decorative wrought-iron braziers, giving off waves of glowing red heat. The walls bore the smell of new limewash, and it gleamed, as yet unblackened by successive layers of smoke. Embroidered woollen hangings ran in horizontal bands along the walls, and colourful shields and banners decorated the higher reaches. Lower down, obscuring some of the hangings, great swags of evergreen had been hung to enhance the festive season and resinous forest scents added to the melange assaulting Matilda's nose. The floor was thickly strewn with dried reeds and scattered with herbs that gave off a pleasant aroma as they were trampled underfoot. The gardener in Matilda identified lavender, bergamot and rue.

There were one or two women in the hall, but they were vastly outnumbered and, to Matilda's astonishment, outdressed by the men. She had to prevent herself from staring as a plump baron traipsed past. His tunic of salmon-pink wool with yellow silk sleeve linings was wearing him rather than the other way around. His ankle boots were of goatskin dyed green with silk lacing and he was wearing green and yellow striped hose. Luxurious dark-brown hair tumbled to his shoulders and caught glints of red in the candlelight.

'Close your mouth, sweeting, it is not seemly to gape,' Simon murmured in her ear.

'You must have thought us very dull when you came to Northampton,' she said as another man passed, every finger adorned with gem-set rings and his tunic sparkling with hundreds of seed pearls and little gold beads.

'The old king's court was somewhat more staid, I agree, but this is the Christmas feast and an opportunity for all to dress in their most exaggerated finery.'

Matilda's own finery consisted of a gown of dark green wool embellished with a necklace of irregular polished amber beads that had once belonged to her paternal great grandmother. Jude wore wine-red with a cross of gold. Dowdy by no means, but

they resembled two nuns in comparison with the garish butterflies surrounding them. Even the bishops and archdeacons
were part of the display, their silk copes stiff and glittering with
thread of gold.

'Your father would have enjoyed this,' Simon remarked. 'He
would have outshone them all . . . and I mean that in a praise-
worthy sense.' He squeezed Matilda's hand. 'Although, truth
to say, his daughter is a more than worthy representative.'

She laughed. 'You do not need to play the courtier with me.
Male birds always have the brighter plumage, do they not?'

Simon grinned at her retort and tweaked one of her wrist-
thick braids.

'But I think you are right about my father,' she added softly.
'I remember he wore gold bracelets at his wrists. I can see them
now . . .' For a moment she was a tiny child, watching her
father push aside the well housing. She had a clear image of
his hands, the long fingers, the red hair growing strongly on
their backs, the cunningly worked bracelets and the way they
slid together and clinked musically on the bones of his wrist.
'My mother hated them, but I thought they were beautiful.'

'He wore them at his marriage,' Simon said. 'He had cropped
his hair and shaved his beard for your mother. He was going
to remove his bracelets too, but I said he should keep them.'
He smiled wryly. 'I was thirteen-years-old, what did I know?'

'Him,' she said with lucent eyes. 'You knew him.'

'Perhaps.' Simon shrugged and bit his tongue on the
comment that Waltheof had probably had more in common
with a thirteen-year-old boy than the woman he had been about
to wed.

An usher arrived to lead them to a long dais at the end of
the hall where the new king was seated with a gathering of
courtiers. The sight of William Rufus at close quarters almost
caused Matilda to stop walking but a quick prod from Simon
restored her pace. She lowered her eyes, swallowed the urge to
giggle, and, once they reached the foot of the dais, sank in a
deep curtsey.

Above her, she heard the creak of the high-backed seat as Rufus rose. She was engulfed in a powerful embrace, set on her feet, and brought eye to eye with the King, who was built like a barrel and not overly endowed with height.

'Cousin Matilda, welcome to Westminster.' Rufus' voice was as loud and harsh as the call of a crow and hurt her ears. His hair was pale sandy-blond, with a centre parting exposing a broad forehead and framing the ruddy, wind-burned complexion that had given him his nickname. He wore a tunic of clashing bright red splashed with green embroidery that reminded Matilda of a whoremonger whom her mother had once had whipped from the parish.

'I am pleased to be here, your grace,' she replied.

'God's Holy Face, but you resemble your sire – does she not, Simon?'

'Indeed, your grace,' Simon answered gravely. 'She has his courage and his joy in life.'

'But let us hope not his judgement, eh?' Rufus laughed, and his barrel belly shook.

Matilda went crimson.

'She resembles her mother too,' Rufus continued tactlessly. 'She too could give you a look that would shrivel your cods in your braies. Although I warrant she does not shrivel yours, eh Simon?'

'Not in the least, sire,' Simon's tone was level, revealing neither amusement nor anger. The courtier's mask, Matilda thought. Was this how he survived at gatherings like this?

'Aye, well she's got the hips on her to breed you some fine sons.' So dismissing Matilda, Rufus turned his attention to Jude. 'Now this one looks more like her mother, although I hope she doesn't have the temper to match.' He chucked Jude beneath the chin. 'A pretty little doe, aren't you?'

Jude blushed and looked down. Rufus let her go and turned to Simon. 'What did you do with my sweet cousin, their mother?' His tone suggested that he considered Judith anything but sweet.

Simon cleared his throat. 'The lady expressed a preference to retire to her devotions with the nuns at Elstow, sire.'

'Hah, I should think you were overjoyed. I doubt she has mellowed with the years.'

'Her leaving was to our mutual agreement,' Simon said with quiet dignity.

Rufus snorted. 'I used to wonder what my father saw in you – until that time you came to my aid when everyone else stood back. Not all that glitters is gold, is it?'

Smiling ruefully, Simon plucked at his plain reddish brown tunic. 'I most certainly do not glitter, sire.'

Rufus gave Simon a punishing blow on the shoulder. 'When you do, I will have cause to worry.' An imperative gesture furnished Simon and the two women with a place at the side of the main trestle. Goblets were set before them and expensive golden wine poured to the brim.

Matilda strove to keep her revulsion from showing on her face but the effort made her tremble. She felt as if she had been pawed over and besmirched.

Simon lightly laid his hand over hers. 'Let it slide from you like water off a duck's back,' he cautioned, murmuring in her ear so that it looked to a casual observer as if he were speaking love words. 'It is the only way.'

Matilda had an opinion on that, but a sense of self-preservation held her from voicing it. She took a long drink and prepared to endure. It was something she was good at, even if her training had been at the hands of the cloister rather than at the groin of the court.

Rufus demanded to know how the building work was progressing at Northampton and Simon gave him the relevant details. Observing the King from beneath her lashes, Matilda saw that he could not be still for a moment, that he had to twitch and gesture and interject comment. He belched and farted as if he lived on a diet of onions and cabbages, and he laughed aloud at some of the riper sounds and stenches.

How, she wondered, could her mother and this man have

sprung from the loins of the same grandparents? And how could Simon bring himself to serve such a sovereign? And yet, as she watched and listened, her hands folded in her lap, she began to see glimmers of a different personality beneath the crude and garish façade. William Rufus was acting the fool, but acting was not the same as being one.

Later, when the King had retired to an inner chamber with two handsome young attendants, Simon led Matilda and Jude among the other barons to make introductions. Matilda quickly learned that the swirl and current of court politics was as deadly as a river in spate. There were men whom Simon called friend with open smiles and relaxed manner, others he treated with wary courtesy, and some where, beneath her hand, the muscles of his arm grew as hard as iron and she could almost see the hair rise on his nape.

Roger de Montgomery, Lord of Shrewsbury, and his sons were one such group. Matilda curtseyed to them as Simon bowed. As she straightened, her gaze was trapped by the most handsome of the four men. He had hair as black as midnight water, eyes of pale, crystal grey and features that were so chiselled and clean that a stone mason would have wept. His dark colouring and strange eyes were set off by a magnificent court tunic of dark blue silk lined with the deep purple-red hue that only the richest in the land could afford. His name, she learned, was Robert de Bêlleme, and from the way Simon was standing she understood that her husband disliked him intensely.

'We heard that you had wed at the behest of England's new king,' declared Montgomery. His tone indicated that congratulations were not in order. 'And that you are to be invested with the title of Earl of Northampton.'

'You know better than I how the mill wheels of court gossip grind the corn of destiny,' Simon replied and made to move on.

Montgomery caught his sleeve. 'If I listen closely to what is said, it is because I am a prudent man. It may be that your title is not worth the air of its speaking. William Rufus has been

anointed king, but some say that it is not his right to inherit
the crown.'

Simon raised one eyebrow. 'Someone once said that it was
not his father's right to take England's crown, but I see few of
them at court today. Still,' he shrugged and smiled, 'it is a fact
of life that gossip-peddlers – like whoremongers – will always
be amongst us.' He drew his arm from beneath Montgomery's
clasp and moved, ushering Matilda and Jude before him.

'So will halfwits and cripples,' said Robert de Bêlleme in a
voice that was as precise and balanced as his features. 'But I
know which have the more value to me.'

For a moment Matilda thought that Simon was going to turn
round and lash out at his tormentors, but with formidable
control he continued to walk away. His complexion, however,
was ashen, and his eyes red-gold with fury. Matilda's own
anger, slow to kindle, burned hot at the core for the insult that
had been cast at Simon like a spear.

'How dare they,' she said through clenched teeth.

Simon strode blindly. Near the door he paused in a draught
of icy air and drew several slow, deep breaths.

'Trouble?' enquired Ranulf de Tosny, detaching himself
from another group of courtiers and joining them.

Simon shook his head. 'Only my own,' he said. 'Take care
of Matilda and Jude will you?' Without waiting for a reply he
went outside, his stride swift and uneven with the anger that
still gripped him.

'It seems that he does trust a wolf with his sheep after all,'
De Tosny said, but in a preoccupied way, his eyes on Simon.
He turned to the women. 'What happened?'

Matilda told him and De Tosny glanced towards the
Montgomerys, distaste apparent in every line of his face.

'Their blood is tainted,' he said. 'Not a good one among
them.'

'They seem to be in like company,' Matilda said angrily. 'I
used to wonder why my mother shunned the court, but now I
see that she had good reason.'

De Tosny grimaced. 'It was not always as dangerous as this. You have come at a time of change and turmoil. There is a new king on the throne, but some here believe that his older brother has the better right to sit there.'

'Meaning the Montgomerys?'

De Tosny's gaze slipped from hers. 'Among others,' he said warily. 'Robert of Normandy would not hold the reins of governance as tightly as Rufus, and certain lords would be able to take their chances.'

From his behaviour, Matilda judged that he did not want to name the 'certain lords' and was anxious not to be pressed. It was of no consequence. She would ask Simon. The thought of her husband drew her eyes to the night sky framed in the doorway.

'He needs a moment's stillness to regain himself,' De Tosny murmured as he saw her look. 'He will return soon enough.' A wry smile lit in the depths of his eyes. 'Even if he has left you and your sister with me, he is still a diligent shepherd.'

His words were intended to soothe and reassure, but Matilda's nurturing instincts remained perturbed. Murmuring her excuses, she went in search of her husband.

Outside the air was freezing and the frost had grown a coat of silver-white fur. Matilda shivered and folded her hands together inside her mantle. It was double-lined wool, but still it did not entirely protect her from the bite of the winter evening.

She found Simon not alone, as she had expected, but deep in conversation with the hugest man she had ever seen. He must have stood around two yards tall and his girth was such that it almost blotted out the horizon. His face was so fat that it resembled an inflated bladder of lard. Beside him Simon looked like a scrawny waif from the gutters.

Seeing her, the enormous baron ceased talking. The look he sent her was shrewd and for a moment lustfully appreciative. Simon turned. A frown flickered briefly and was gone. Holding out his hand, he drew her to his side.

'May I introduce my wife, Matilda, daughter of Waltheof of Huntingdon,' Simon said. 'Matilda, this is Hugh Lupus, Earl of Chester. Hugh's mother and your grandmother Adelaide are half-sisters, so you are cousins of a degree.'

Leaning forward, Hugh Lupus kissed Matilda loudly on both cheeks. 'And delighted I am to greet you . . . cousin,' he declared salaciously.

The smell emanating from the man was almost overpowering – sweat and scented oil in equal proportions that almost made her heave. His lips were wet and red and somehow slightly obscene.

'A rare beauty you have there, Simon, look at those Viking bones.' Stepping back, Hugh Lupus eyed her up and down as if she were a brood mare at Smithfield horsefair. 'You must be glad her mother rejected you, eh?'

Simon said nothing, but Matilda did not sense any anger as there had been when confronting the Montgomery clan. Indeed, there appeared to be a glint of wry amusement in his eyes. 'Overjoyed,' he said dryly.

'And you should count your blessings too, lass,' Hugh Lupus added, wagging a sausage-thick forefinger at Matilda. 'Simon is one of the best.'

'I only have to look around me to know that, my lord . . . with all respect,' she said a trifle tartly.

Hugh Lupus threw back his head and gave a great, wheezy laugh. 'Beauty and spirit,' he said. 'Almost makes me wish I had been sent to Northampton in your stead, Simon.'

'Since you're her cousin, and a man already wed into the bargain, I doubt you would have had much success,' Simon retorted.

'I seldom let such trifling matters stand in my way.' Slapping Simon on the shoulder with sufficient force to make him stagger, and winking broadly at Matilda, he went on his way.

Matilda gave a small shudder of relief. Her cousin or not, she thought she would prefer him to keep his distance. 'I was worried about you,' she said.

He turned to her, his breath a coil of white vapour in the freezing air. 'Without cause. All I needed was a moment to recover.'

'You didn't get it though.'

He pulled her against him and slipped his hands beneath her mantle to find hers and grasp them. 'Mayhap not, but Hugh Lupus is an old acquaintance. We understand each other, and he too has no love for the Montgomery clan.'

'Why do they bait you?'

He twitched his shoulders. 'I have never been at odds with the father Roger de Montgomery – until recently, but I have always had small tolerance for his son Robert and he for me. He takes men's weaknesses and mocks them. From boyhood, it has ever been his pleasure to inflict pain.' His eyelids tightened. 'I have been on campaigns with him and seen what he does to prisoners. Where there is war, there is death, I accept that; I am not a soft-hearted fool. But sparing men on the battlefield in order to torture them at leisure and for sport is a different matter.'

'Robert de Bêlleme does that?' Matilda remembered the arresting pale-grey eyes and shivered.

'And more. Your father stood up to him once on my behalf, and after that De Bêlleme did everything in his power to harm your father's standing with King William.'

Matilda bit her lip. 'And now will he harm your standing with the new king?' she asked

Simon shook his head and began to walk along the pathway between the buildings, the way through the shadows illuminated by star and torchlight. 'Not in the least,' he said. 'Rufus views the Montgomery family with suspicion, and rightly so. The Conqueror might have bequeathed this kingdom to his namesake son on his deathbed, but his eldest, Robert, claims that it should have been his.'

Matilda nodded. 'And the Montgomery's support Robert's claim. Ranulf de Tosny told me.'

Simon sighed. 'They have been reticent on the matter thus

far, but their leanings are common knowledge. It is also common knowledge that Odo of Bayeux supports his eldest nephew's claim. I do not believe he is at court now to make peace with Rufus, but rather to stir up support for Robert. I have no doubt that before the twelve nights are out I will be approached and asked to change my loyalty. That was what Hugh and I were talking about when you came upon us.' He rubbed his palms over his face and pressed his fingertips against his lips.'

'What is Robert of Normandy like?' Matilda gave him a look filled with curiosity.

'Pleasant, good-humoured, indolent. He is skilled with a sword and lance – a fine soldier, if not a fine general.' He returned her look. 'What are you thinking?'

'I was wondering if he would make a more fitting king than Rufus,' she said. 'After all, Robert is the eldest son, and Rufus is . . .' she paused, searching for a diplomatic word.

'A buffoon,' Simon finished for her. 'A coarse, loud clown with a weakness for handsome young men and the clothes of a quean.' They paused at the river's edge to watch the lapping sparkle of black water, reflected torchlight quivering on its surface. 'You are not alone in your wondering,' he said, 'but anyone who has glimpsed beyond the first impression will know that Rufus is by far the better choice for England. Robert talks, but Rufus acts. Robert can fight, but Rufus is the better general and he has a superior grasp of the day to day task of ruling. Robert would promise all to everyone, do nothing and this land would dissolve into chaos.'

'So why do such as Bishop Odo and the Montgomerys support him?'

'To their own ends. Chaos and the wherewithal to go their own way would suit them very well. They would be able to create their own little kingdoms.'

Matilda absorbed this and eyed her husband thoughtfully. 'But do you not desire a small kingdom for yourself too?'

'I have as much as I need and at the King's gift,' he said. 'To take more would only be biting off more than I could chew. Believe me, my love, Rufus is by far the better king. Hugh thinks so too, and since his lands border those of Montgomery he will be a check to their ambition.' He stooped to pick up a stone from the path and throw it into the water. There was a splash and torchlit ripples shimmered towards their feet.

'You become accustomed to negotiating the difficult waters of the court,' Simon murmured. 'The rules for survival are to say little and observe everyone – listen to what they say, both with their voices and their bodies, watch with whom they associate, and talk with the servants who are in a position to know what goes on behind locked doors.'

'You do all this?'

'When I am at court – yes.'

Matilda made a face.

'It is a skill to be learned like any other.' He faced her. 'Those who master it prosper, those who do not struggle. When you dwell at court for a long time it becomes a part of your nature. My father was King William's chamberlain and I learned the skills early. Your father did not have them, nor did he wish to learn. He took every man and woman as he found them, and in the end his trust was his downfall. He had no shield and they cut him down.'

Matilda shivered. The words found a hollow place within her stomach and lodged there like a leaden weight.

'And what if Robert's faction prevails?' she asked. 'What if they cut you down too?'

He raised his hand to stroke her cheek. 'Robert's faction will not prevail,' he said. 'And much as I loved and respected your father, I am not him.'

Matilda laid her fingers over his, but she could take no comfort from his warmth, for the winter evening had set a bone-deep chill over everything and her flesh was numb. She remembered her father telling her that all would be well, and that it had been a lie, because nothing had been well from the moment he rode out. Now Simon, in his own way, was asking her to trust him. But if she did, would she be paid in false coin and one day find herself abandoned to face the world alone?

Simon looked at her shrewdly. 'Come,' he said, 'let us go within. At least, whatever the company, the braziers are warm. Besides,' he added, trying for lightness, 'I would leif as not leave your sister in Ranulf de Tosny's care for too long a time.'

Matilda smiled, but it was only a token stretching of the lips. The sooner they were away from court, the better, she thought. and for the first time in her life she found herself sympathising with her mother.

CHAPTER 27

Nunnery of Elstow,
July 1088

The nuns were harvesting blackcurrants in the gardens beyond the west wall of the chapel. Matilda itched to join them and indulge in the satisfaction of plucking the ripe shiny fruits from the bushes, but that was servant's work, and since she was on her mother's territory she was doing her best to abide by her mother's rules. Relations between her and Judith were tepid, but Matilda had made the effort to bridge the chasm opened up by her marriage to Simon, and to her surprise her mother had built the foundations of a bridge on her own side of the divide. They would never be close, but at least they were on speaking terms.

She was not the only visitor to Elstow on this bright summer afternoon. Her grandmother, the formidable Countess Adelaide of Aumale, had been dwelling in the guesthouse for the past month, attended on by a host of servants and nuns. She was suffering from severe joint ache in her hipbones and could only get about with the aid of a walking stick and the support of a sturdy maid. The pain and the inconvenience had sharpened her naturally irascible temper until it was like a new blade.

'So then,' she said, looking Matilda up and down, 'all praise be to God that you carry a child in your belly. I was beginning to wonder if De Senlis had empty seed sacks.'

Matilda flushed and pressed the flat of her hand against her stomach. 'I am glad for your concern, belle mère,' she murmured, 'but there is no cause.' She was entering her fourth month of pregnancy. The sickness had recently abated and the exhaustion of the early months had been replaced by a feeling of wellbeing and energy. Hence she had felt suitably fortified to pay a visit to Elstow whilst Simon was absent on the King's business.

'Hah, being forced into marriage with a cripple is more than enough cause,' Adelaide snapped.

'Simon is not a cripple, and I was not forced,' Matilda said with angry indignation. 'Indeed, I was very willing, and I have not a single cause for regret.'

'Doubtless they will come later,' Adelaide retorted sourly. 'Look at your mother. Hot with lust for your father she was, burning up with it. Nothing would please her but that she had him, and look what happened. Ended up they could not bear the sight of each other.'

'Mother!' Judith said sharply. She had been listening to the exchange though taking no part, but now she launched a protest. 'You are raking over old coals. It is in the past and a matter I would rather you did not discuss.'

'Because it shows your weakness,' Adelaide said. She wagged an admonitory forefinger at her daughter. 'You could have had the cream of the young men of Normandy, but you chose that wastrel Waltheof Siwardsson instead. I always knew it would end in grief.'

'Grief or not, belle mère, his name is revered,' Matilda said fiercely. 'Pilgrims swarm to his tomb, and even Normans say that he was falsely executed. King William himself repented of the deed after it was done.'

Judith rose to her feet and walked away from the conversation, distancing herself. Matilda remained and faced her grandmother, determined to hold her ground.

'He was executed for treason,' Adelaide snapped. 'For plotting against the King and attempting to set a Danish pirate on the throne.'

'The men who instigated the plot were not executed,' Matilda pointed out. 'One still rides free, and the other languishes in prison, but they both have their lives. What about the barons who are in rebellion against William Rufus? Will they face beheading if they are defeated? I think not.' She spoke in the deliberate knowledge that her grandmother's half-brother Robert of Mortain was one of the rebels, and that it was only by the slimmest of decisions that Adelaide's husband and son had opted to support William Rufus.

Two spots of colour like badly applied rouge blossomed on Adelaide's cheeks. 'You were a small child when your father turned traitor, you could not know.' Raising her walking stick, Adelaide pointed it at Matilda. 'He ruined your mother's life with his drinking and his irresponsible ways. He could no more rule his lands than could an infant in tail clouts.'

'That was still no reason for him to die.'

'Reason enough,' Adelaide said harshly. 'He did not deserve to live, and I made sure he did not.'

There was something so chilling in her tone that it raised the wisps of hair at Matilda's nape. A creeping silence grew, and with it a terrible sense of foreboding.

Judith turned from the embrasure and paced back across the room, the hem of her charcoal-coloured gown swishing the rushes. 'Mother, what did you do?' Her voice was quiet but its cadence could have sliced stone.

'Nothing of which I am ashamed.' Adelaide glared and clutched her stick like an unsheathed sword. 'When that wastrel husband of yours was arrested, you came to court and said that you disowned him because he was a traitor. Your uncle was disposed to be lenient for your sake and merely banish him, but I knew that could not be allowed to happen. Banishment would not have meant banishment for such as him. Come a year, or two, he would have returned – likely in the company of Danish pirates to judge from his previous behaviour.' She paused to draw a breath, her bosom heaving, the gold cross she wore around her neck flashing erratically. 'I persuaded my brother that where there was leniency, there would be regret.'

'You signed his death warrant,' Judith whispered. Her complexion had turned the unhealthy hue of parchment.

Matilda stared between her mother and her grandmother and felt icy prickles run up and down her spine. The atmosphere in the room was leaden with tension.

'Don't be so foolish!' Adelaide snapped, her light brown eyes glittering. 'Your uncle would never have changed his mind on my word alone. Those of whom he sought counsel were all agreed. Your uncles Odo and Robert for certain, and Roger de Montgomery.'

'All who had their axes to grind,' Judith said harshly.

'You had your own axe to grind as well, daughter. Or perhaps sealed up in your nunnery you forget how desperate you were to be rid of your husband. You begged me to help you, and you were content when I said I would see what could be done.'

'I wanted him banished, not dead. Jesu God, Mother!' The oath burst from her and she clapped her hand to her mouth too late.

'Hah! For ten years you dwelled as mistress of his earldom. Not until your uncle died did you relinquish your grip – and only then out of your own folly.' Adelaide's face was pinched with malice. 'Does not the Bible say that a man should not remove the mote of sawdust from his neighbour's eye until he has removed the plank of wood from his own? You are as guilty as I am, daughter – more so because you could not bind Waltheof to your side and prevent him from folly. He was weak, you should have moulded him. When you could not it was left to me to do the only thing possible and make sure we were rid of him for good!'

'No, Mother, you did it for yourself,' Judith cried. 'For your precious son, because you wanted to see him Earl of Huntingdon!'

'And you complied, daughter . . . do not missay me, for you are only looking at your own reflection.'

The cold prickles down Matilda's spine worked inwards to her belly. Suddenly she felt so sick that there was scarcely time to leap to her feet and reach the corner where she retched violently into the rushes. Her vision turned speckled black at the edges and her knees buckled.

'Now see what you have done!' she heard her mother snap. 'If she miscarries, you can add another murder to your tally.'

Dimly Matilda felt her mother's arms fold around her, and she tried to thrust her away. 'Do not touch me!' she gasped. 'I want none of you.'

Judith avoided Matilda's half-fainting efforts at rejection and gripped the harder. 'Whether you do or not, you have no choice,' she said grimly. 'Now calm yourself. You do not want to harm the child.'

The last words sank into Matilda's mind and anchored her by a thin thread to reason. For the sake of the baby she managed to draw a steadying breath. Through her struggle for composure, Matilda realised that Judith too was fighting for a degree of balance as if she was teetering on the edge of a high drop. Her mother's breathing was as shaky and uncertain as her own, and she could feel the tremors pass through her flesh as if they were one body, as once they had been when Judith had carried her in her womb.

Behind them there was a rustle of straw as Adelaide pushed herself to her feet and, leaning heavily on her stick, limped from the room without another word. Judith started to pull away but Matilda would not let her go and clung to her fiercely. Digging her fingers into the dark wool of her mother's sleeve, she forced her to meet her gaze. 'Swear to me that you had no part in my father's death,' she whispered. 'Swear to me.'

Her mother's throat worked. 'That I cannot do,' she whispered, 'although I wish to God that I could.' She closed her eyes. 'You were so young, and you adored him as much as he adored you. You never knew the other side of him – the feckless fool who would drink himself into a stupor at the slightest excuse and had less than a child's grasp of the business of governance.'

'So you ended his life for that?'

Judith's eyes flashed opened. 'I did not know that my uncle would execute him. I thought that he would be banished. The guilt torments me. No matter how long I pray on my knees to God, the burden does not ease. Yes, I wanted him gone from my life, but not at the cost of his life . . . If I had known what was to happen, I would have begged my uncle to spare him.'

Matilda released her grip on Judith and sat back, tears streaming down her face. Cold, proud, unyielding as granite her mother might be, but an accounting of the truth had always been essential to her, no matter how bitter the fruit.

Judith rose to her feet and stepped away from Matilda, gathering her own composure around her like a cloak. A swift brush of her hand across her lids, a slight sniff was as much as she yielded. 'I tried,' she said, 'but it was not enough. You might as well have mated fire and ice and expected one to survive.'

'And what of me, Mother?' Matilda demanded in a choked voice. 'If I am a mingling of your blood and my father's, how am I to survive?'

Judith's face assumed its customary expression of frozen composure. 'Perhaps, out of all the women in this family, you will emerge the most unscathed because you have the ability to bend rather than break. That at least your father has given you to your advantage. Besides, whatever differences I have with your husband, he is a man of ambition, familiar with the ways of the court. And he is Norman. The challenges of your marriage will not be the same as mine.'

'Then what will they be?' Matilda whispered.

Judith shrugged. 'Simon de Senlis is like a tomcat,' she said. 'He seeks a warm hearth at which to curl up in the winter and all the comforts that home provides. But come the spring, when there is prey to pursue and territory to explore, you will not keep him. That is why I am glad that you have the ability to bend.'

Matilda knuckled her eyes again and rose clumsily to her feet. Clucking her tongue, her mother advanced to beat stalks of straw from her daughter's gown and smooth the fine tawny wool.

'I could have had him for my husband,' Judith said. 'The babe growing in your belly could now be growing in mine. Remember that. He wed you out of no more than ambition and necessity. You accepted his offer because it was convenient, because you were attracted to him as you are to all waifs and underdogs, and most of all because he was wearing your father's cloak.' She looked at Matilda, her brown eyes hard but not hostile. 'I say these things for your own good. Bear them in mind and do not let yourself become carried away on a surfeit of minstrel's tales of love. That is the way to survive.'

Hooves clattered in the guesthouse courtyard alongside the sound of male voices. Smearing away her tears, Matilda went to look out of the double-arched window slit and saw her husband dismounting with an escort of knights and serjeants. They were all wearing either mail or quilted tunics and the horses were sweating as if they had been ridden hard. She saw her grandmother hobble over to Simon and speak to him, using her stick for emphasis as usual. Simon smiled, bowed and answered her, but Matilda knew him well enough to see that the courtesy he gave to Adelaide was of polished duty not genuine pleasure.

Her mother's words had made Matilda feel wretchedly queasy because they struck at the core of her fear. They had been cruel too, even if they did have an element of truth. Despite, or perhaps because of them, her heart turned over. She needed Simon. Needed the strength of his arms, his reassuring words, and most of all she needed him to take her away from here. Spinning from the window, she hurried to the door, flung it open and ran down to the courtyard.

Simon turned, a broad grin spread across his face, and he

opened his arms. Matilda flung herself into them like a desperate fugitive grasping a sanctuary knocker. Adelaide sniffed scornfully and stumped away in the direction of the church.

'Tears?' Simon brushed his thumb across her cheek. 'What's all this?'

'Naught.' Matilda gulped, although it was a great deal more than naught. 'I will tell you later.' She squeezed him fiercely. 'It is so good to see you. When can we go home?' Her voice shook.

He held her gently at arm's length and looked her up and down. 'It is too late in the day to ride for Northampton,' he said, 'but there is naught to stop us from spending the night at Oakley . . . if that is your wish.'

Matilda rested her forehead against the cool, metal rivets of his hauberk. 'I would like that,' she said. 'If you are not too tired from the road.'

'Nothing that a cup of wine and some food will not refresh,' he said as a couple of squires led the horses away to the trough in the yard. 'We have ridden hard, but not so much that a few more miles will make any difference.'

Matilda nodded, and sensed that he had no more desire than she did to rest tonight beneath her mother's roof.

Moonlight spilled through the open shutters and cast its bluish silver light on the bed and the naked flesh of the entwined man and woman. In the aftermath of lovemaking, Simon had been telling Matilda about the fighting in the south. Bishop Odo and the Montgomery family had raised rebellion against King William Rufus, declaring that the Conqueror's first son, Robert, should be king. Rufus had mustered his supporters and hastened to deal with the insurgents. Montgomery had surrendered, but Odo had had to be prised out of Rochester like a winkle hooked out of its shell with a silver pin, only instead of a silver pin Rufus had used thirst and starvation, his endeavours aided by a plague of maggot flies.

'The garrison had to take it in turns to eat while their

comrades brushed the insects from around them,' Simon had said with a grimace. 'We could smell the city rotting from our positions outside the walls. Men, horses, dogs . . . Once you have experienced such a stench, you never forget it. That and the stink of burning are the "perfumes" of war.'

Matilda, whose own knowledge of bad smells was confined to memories of the days when the gong farmers emptied out the cess pits, shuddered at his words. Yet, she did not try to stem them. She understood his need to speak to her rather than have the memories fester within him.

'Montgomery went to negotiate with them. At first they wanted their liberty and their lands in exchange for their surrender and oath of homage, but Rufus could see that he had them in a cleft stick and he refused. He said that they might have their lives and their weapons. Those who still had horses could keep them and ride out.' Simon was silent for a moment, remembering, threading his fingers through her hair.

'They came in double file, holding on to their dignity despite the fact that they stank of the midden and their lips were cracked and their skins erupting in sores. Rufus had the victory trumpets sounded from our ranks, as loudly as the heralds could blow. The common Englishmen who had been drawn from their fields to serve in Rufus' ranks jeered and poured scorn on them, crying out that they should be hanged.'

'What did Rufus do?' Matilda asked.

'He stood back and let them give tongue with a smile on his face,' Simon said. 'What more proof did he need that he was King of the English than to let the English scream his name in approbation and bay for his enemy's blood? I think that he is a cunning general and a very shrewd politician.' He stated the assessment without admiration.

'So the danger is over now that Bishop Odo and the Montgomerys have been brought to heel.' She moved closer to him.

'For the moment. Odo may continue to scheme, but he is growing too old to involve himself in the strain of battle. When he rode out of Rochester on the surrender he was carrying his years as if they were a heavy sack on his shoulders. I do not believe that he will return to England – unless in the aftermath of an invasion if Robert prevails – which I doubt will happen. As to the Montgomery faction, they surrendered and survived by a whisker this time, but their powers in England will be checked by the likes of Hugh Lupus and Fitzhaimo of Gloucester . . . and me.' He gave a humourless smile. 'Now there's a task to relish.'

Matilda pressed her nose against his flesh and felt the tickle of his chest hair. She did not want to think of him being involved with the Montgomerys in any way. 'But you will be staying at home a while?' Hearing the anxious note in her own voice, she bit her lip. She knew that he hated to be fettered, and yet she needed a modicum of security – and following the revelations at Elstow she felt terribly vulnerable.

He spread his fingers, webbing her glittering hair across it. 'A while, yes,' he said in a soothing voice, as if he sensed her need. 'I have a castle to build, and a son to see born. Enough for any man.'

Matilda hugged him in gratitude for a moment, but then her head came up. 'What if I should bear a daughter?' she demanded. 'My mother bore two girls, and her mother before her. My uncle Stephen did not arrive until my grandmother was past her fortieth year.'

Simon shifted position to look at her. Raising his thumb, he brushed the furrow from her brow. 'If you should bear a daughter, then no matter I will still cherish her, and she will be but the first. You do not have to follow the pattern laid down by your mother and her mother before her, do you?'

'I will never follow their pattern,' Matilda vowed fiercely. 'Never.' She clenched her fists and tried to stave off the memory of the afternoon's revelations. 'If our child is a daughter, she will grow up loved and valued and the only duty I will impose on her is that she love and value others the same.'

Simon gently stroked her back. 'That seems a fine notion to

me,' he murmured soothingly. 'Pride is no bad trait to possess, but too strong a measure can taste of bitter grief. I do not believe that your grandmother was ever happy in her triumph, or even satisfied. And you have seen how it is with your mother. She has grown a shell to shut out the hurts of the world, and now it has so many layers that she is trapped within it.'

Matilda lay against him and gazed out of the shutters at the swollen white disc of the moon. She had not had to tell him much about her grandmother's part in her father's downfall. He had been a squire at court, and knew already. When she had asked him why he had not told her, he had shrugged.

'The art of keeping silent is one I have learned to value,' he had said, and would not be further drawn.

As always she was left with the worrying feeling that she did not know him at all, and the knowledge that in contrast he knew her very well indeed. Perhaps he understood about her mother's shell, she thought, because he dwelt inside one of his own, and the art of silence was part of that carapace. If only she could breach the defences and truly know him as he seemed to know her. If only she could prove her mother's words wrong.

The moon sailed across the unshuttered aperture and disappeared, leaving a dark blue sky ablaze with stars. Matilda watched the night, and for the first time felt the flutter of new life within her womb.

CHAPTER 28

Northampton, Spring 1090

Simon had put all of Northampton's wealth on show to honour the marriage of his sister-in-law Jude to Ranulf de Tosny of Conches. The trestles in the newly completed great hall were draped with bleached linen cloths. On the high table the napery was embroidered with English goldwork, and the flagons and cups set out for the guests were fashioned of silver gilt and rock crystal.

Seated beside her husband on the high dais, Matilda watched the bridal couple sip from the loving cup and eat off the same trencher. Jude's silky dark hair was uncovered in token of her virginity and fell in two thick plaits to her waist. A bridal chaplet of daisies, mayblossom and fresh greenery was bound at her brow and she wore a gown of red wool with sleeve linings of blue silk. The bridegroom seemed much taken with his wife, as well he might, Matilda thought. Jude not only looked lovely but had a sweet nature, and the lands that she brought to her marriage were enough to make any man rush to make his vows.

'I would have liked our own wedding day to be as great an occasion as this one,' Simon said and briefly covered her hand with his own.

Matilda gave him a slightly startled look. Had she seemed wistful? She thought not. 'Mayhap,' she said, 'but I do not miss gilding the lily. When we were little, Jude would plunder our mother's coffer, try on her finest veils, and most elaborate girdles. It was always my task to keep watch and make sure that she was not caught!'

Simon laughed. 'But surely you enjoy gilding the lily just a little? That shade of blue suits you well.' His gaze wandered appreciatively over her figure, as slender as if she had never borne a child.

Matilda blushed. 'A little,' she admitted, 'but I do not yearn.'

He looked amused. 'Most women of my acquaintance would sell their eye teeth to be the centre of attention tonight.'

'Indeed. And with how many women are you acquainted?'

'Enough to count my blessings.' He kissed her hand.

'Spoken like a true courtier,' Matilda said, smiling, but with an edge to her voice.

Their banter was curtailed by the arrival of Helisende, who had managed to make her way down the side of the hall, threading through servants bearing flagons and steaming platters.

'My lady, your son is awake and crying fit to bring down the rafters.'

'I have never known a child so greedy,' Simon said, looking pained.

Matilda smiled and as she rose, tugged a lock of his hair. In the more relaxed atmosphere of Rufus' rule, the short crops of the Conqueror's reign were giving way to longer styles, and Simon's tawny brown hair now rested level with the neckband of his tunic. She liked it that way, for the depths of her mind harboured a dim memory of her father's hair at that length, sweeping against his cheek as he played with her in the garden.

'He takes after you,' she said.

Simon gestured at his trencher. 'I do not how you can say that, my lady,' he declared with a glimmer of amusement. 'I am no glutton at the board.'

'I was not talking of food,' Matilda retorted pertly. She left with the sound of his chuckle chasing the shadows from her heart, and went to feed their son. At seventeen months old he was well on the way to being weaned, but still woke on occasion and nothing would content him but the comfort of suckling at her breast.

His birth had been easy, for Matilda had the large bones and wide hips of her Viking ancestors and the baby, although healthy and vigorous, was of Simon's build. He was placid and good-natured, with abundant copper-red hair and eyes of deep sea-blue. It had been only fitting to christen him for the grand-sire he so clearly resembled.

She watched him as he nursed and felt a surge of deep and tender love that was almost a physical pain. He was walking; his vocabulary was developing rapidly and soon he would not need the security of her breast. The time of dependency was fleeting and, cling tightly as she might, nothing could prevent these moments from slipping through her hands like silver into the darkness of a well.

'It is a great pity that your grandmother is not here to see what a fine child he is,' Judith remarked from the doorway.

Matilda looked up with a start. She had been so absorbed in tending to her son that she had not seen her mother arrive. 'It is an even greater pity that my father is not here to see his first grandchild,' she replied, and the generous curve of her lips was suddenly tight.

The birth of a son had for ever changed the relationship between them, for in producing a boy Matilda had accom-plished what Judith had not, and the balance of power, already in Matilda's favour, had shifted further. Indeed, following that terrible day at Elstow Judith's manner towards her daughter had changed. She had become more conciliatory, more willing to listen, and much less critical. Mention of Adelaide was still enough to strain the atmosphere, though. Adelaide had died of a flux shortly after little Waltheof was born. Matilda had not attended the funeral, for she had still been recovering from the birth, but she had been more than glad of the excuse and it bothered her conscience. She should be able to forgive, and it disturbed her that she could not.

'Indeed it is,' Judith said with a sigh. 'He loved small infants
– far more than I ever did. But then perhaps that was what
attracted me to him in the first instance – his joy and innocence.'

Matilda looked down at the suckling infant and kept very
still. It was the first time that her mother had ever spoken of
her marriage to Waltheof in less than disparaging terms.

'He was not afraid to laugh or weep,' Judith said, 'and I had
been raised in a household where to do either was unseemly.'
Her lips curved sorrowfully. 'I thought that your father could
teach me how to do both, but it proved beyond both our capa-
bilities.' Her voice stumbled, and looking up Matilda was
disconcerted to find her mother's eyes filled with tears. Perhaps
it was because the season was so close to the anniversary of his
death. The morrow's eve.

Judith blinked fiercely, clearly irritated with herself. 'I came
to remind you that we should begin the bedding ceremony –
before the men grow too gilded to stand.' She made an abrupt
gesture. 'I did not mean to speak of your father. Perhaps I have
drunk a goblet too much myself.'

The baby gave a milky belch, and a white dribble appeared
at the corner of his mouth. 'Full to the brim,' Matilda said,
aching to see her mother retreat behind the familiar wall of
frozen dignity. 'I am glad that you did,' she said softly. 'I have
so little of him to keep.'

'You have the best parts,' Judith murmured. 'I do not know
whether to envy or pity you.'

Matilda gestured the nurse to take the baby, and repinned
the deep neck opening of her gown. 'I want neither your envy
nor your pity. They won't make any difference, will they?'
Rising to her feet, she shook out the folds of the dress in a
gesture designed to end the conversation and smooth her
ruffled emotions. 'Come, or else they will begin the bedding
ceremony without us.'

The air of constraint between mother and daughter was
swiftly banished as they exchanged the peace of the women's

chamber for the hall where the wedding celebrations had developed a raucous edge. Women and men had separated off, the former surrounding the bride, the latter the laughing groom.

Matilda paused briefly at Simon's side and gave a worried glance towards Ranulf de Tosny. 'I hope he is not too far in his cups that he hurts Jude,' she murmured.

Simon squeezed her waist. 'You need not fret on that score.' He said against her ear. 'It is mostly high spirits. After the first two cups I made sure that the wine was watered. Cheaper for me that way too,' he added flippantly. 'Besides, I didn't want to be in my cups either.' His hand moved briefly over her buttocks, revealing that he was not quite as stony sober as he claimed.

Matilda laughed and pushed him away. 'We shall see,' she said with a look through her lashes, and went to join the women.

Jude was brought to the main bedchamber. Usually it was reserved for Simon, Matilda and their immediate attendants, but tonight they had vacated it in honour of the bride and groom. A new, crisp, lavender-scented sheet had been spread tightly over the feather mattress. In the morning, stained with the bride's virgin blood, it would be hammered to the wall behind the dais table as proof that her husband was the first man to touch her and that any child born nine months from this time would be of his loins. There was a covering sheet of bleached linen, a woollen blanket, and a counterpane of embroidered silk that was part of the wealth that the bride brought to her marriage, silk being literally worth its weight in gold.

With great ceremony the women stripped Jude of her garments and combed her hair until it lay in a shining skein down her back. Seeing how much she was shivering, Matilda folded her in a wrap of beaver fur while they awaited the men.

'It will be all right,' she murmured and kissed her sister's temple.

'I know it will,' said Jude, giving her a tight, nervous smile. 'Sybille told me everything . . . the way she told you. If it were left to Mama, I would be as innocent as a spring lamb. And if I had believed everything that Ranulf told me before the wedding, I'd not be a virgin now!'

That broke the tension and Matilda started to giggle. So did Jude. The raised eyebrow of disapproval they received from their mother only increased their mirth.

Footsteps sounded outside the chamber door, and the wood resounded to the thump of a fist and loud voices craving entrance, with many jests about 'forcing portals' and 'turning keys in greased locks'. Judith's frown deepened and her lips started to purse. Pushing aside the maid who had been about to admit the men, she raised the latch herself and, throwing the door wide, blocked the threshold with her body.

'I thought dragons were supposed to be hot, not cold,' slurred Ranulf's brother Roger, wavering where he stood.

Ranulf flourished a bow in Judith's direction and managed to stand upright again without falling over, revealing that he was reasonably sober. 'Madame belle mère,' he saluted her. 'I have come to claim my bride, if you will but yield her to me.'

Matilda saw that he was wearing Simon's bearskin cloak – useful because it draped him from collar to ankle, the surplus length folded like a cape around his shoulders. Beneath it, he was naked save for his shoes.

Judith inclined her head in return. 'Treat her well,' she said in a voice that cut across all their jesting and merriment like a whip, 'or you will answer to me.' She gestured stiffly for the men to enter the room then stepped back, her sleeve across her nose as if to diffuse the potent wine fumes.

'I will cherish her all my days,' Ranulf replied, although his eyes were now on his bride, not his mother-by-marriage. 'Why should I not when she has beauty and lands and she sets my heart alight?' He took Jude's hands within his own, his expression soulful, laughter dancing in his eyes.

'You would be surprised how many men find reason once they have grown bored of the taste of the fruit,' Judith retorted. Her spine as rigid as a broom handle, she returned to the middle of the room, determined that a degree of propriety should be maintained.

'Not me,' Ranulf said confidently.

Judith gave him a hard stare. 'I hold you to it,' she said, and ushered forward the priest to bless the couple and the waiting bed.

That ritual performed, Ranulf swept his bride up in his arms and placed her amid the sheets to a chorus of halloos and yells of encouragement.

'I need no help this night,' Ranulf retorted cheerfully and tossed the bearskin cloak back to Simon.

'Well, just call out if you do,' Simon grinned.

Ranulf's teeth flashed in response. 'If you hear me shouting, it will be for a different reason entirely!' he quipped, causing Jude to blush fire-red.

More whistles and bawdy comments followed, but the wedding party took the hint and trooped from the room on a final volley of advice and good wishes.

The wine continued to flow and the kitchens continued to supply bread and small pastries, stuffed figs, honey sweetmeats, and tender slivers of lamb marinated in wine, cooked on a griddle and served on skewers of beechwood.

Simon and Matilda mingled among their guests who showed no sign of flagging. Matilda danced with Earl Hugh of Chester and fended off his determined attempts to flirt, finally escaping on the arm of her uncle Stephen. The latter was only two years older than she, with a mane of thick flaxen hair, ice-blue eyes and his father's cleft chin. Folk said that he was one of the few members of the house of William of Normandy who actually looked suitable to wear a crown.

'Do not you dare call me uncle,' he said as they moved and turned in the pattern of the dance. 'It makes me feel like an ancient greybeard, and I'm scarce old enough to grow a whisker. Cousin will suffice.'

'I would not dream of giving you grey hairs,' Matilda said sweetly, and playfully tapped his arm. 'It was good of you to come.' She liked Stephen. Her mother had been avoiding him rather grimly all evening.

He bowed. 'It was good of you to invite me,' he said gallantly. 'There was a time when my parents cultivated notions of acquiring your lands for my inheritance. I would have understood if you had chose to keep me at arm's length or even barred your gates.'

Matilda warmed further to his charm and candour. 'You are welcome whenever you choose to visit,' she said. 'My husband is sure enough of his own abilities not to feel threatened. Besides,' she added with a swift glance around to make sure that her mother was not within earshot, 'we are neither of us our parents.'

'Thank sweet Christ for that!' Stephen declared, adding hastily, 'I will say nothing against my mother, God rest her soul, nor against my father, because he is not here to defend his reputation . . . but I have never been as eager as they to saddle up and ride a horse made of ambition.'

'Oh, I think everyone has ambitions,' Matilda said. 'But of differing kinds. Perhaps if you had not had everything given to you on a golden platter, you would be hungrier.'

He frowned for a moment as if to protest, but the expression was replaced by a thoughtful look. 'I suppose that is true,' he said. 'My mother was always fleeing from the fact that her mother was a laundress and my father was deposed of his own lands in Champagne. For me it has been different. I have what I want. If I strive, it is only to please them.' His eye corners crinkled attractively. 'What of your own ambition, cousin?'

Matilda smiled. 'That is easy,' she said lightly. 'To stay awake long enough to see these nuptials to their close.' She was learning from Simon, she thought. How to fend off probing questions. How to hide what she did not wish to reveal.

The dance ended and they parted. Hugh of Chester was ensconced in a corner, a girl on each ample thigh and his legs spread to allow breathing space for his crotch. Matilda avoided that part of the room. Simon was deep in conversation with

Abbot Ingulf of Crowland, and her mother was talking with members of the Tosny family. Unobtrusively, Matilda slipped among the crowds, a word here, a murmur there. Her eyes felt gritty; she was tired, but she bolstered herself with a cup of wine. What *was* her ambition? Her brow furrowed at the thought. To live without looking over her shoulder to the past. To be surrounded in the warmth of a love as deep and thick as a winter pelt. Whether or not such ambition was attainable was another matter.

Had she known it, ambition was also the subject of Simon's conversation with Abbot Ingulf.

'Indeed, I have seen strange and changing times,' the Abbot said, shifting his leg to try to ease the gout that was plaguing him. 'I was a clerk in the household of the Holy King Edward and it was there I first learned my trade. Got to know Normans too.' He bestowed Simon a wintry smile. 'It stood me in good stead because I learned that we are all the same in the eyes of God.'

'Indeed,' Simon said politely. Abbot Ingulf was garrulous and the evening was growing late. Although Simon had never needed a great deal of sleep, the length of the day was beginning to tell. He clenched his jaw to suppress a yawn.

'When King Edward died, I left the royal service,' Ingulf continued and refreshed his goblet, obviously prepared to settle into a long, enjoyable monologue. 'Harold Godwinsson had his own preferred clerks and I was still a young man with a young man's restlessness. It is true that I had travelled many roads with King Edward's court and seen more of England in my youth than most men see in a lifetime . . . but that only increased my wanderlust.' He took a swallow of wine and washed it round his mouth. 'Serving the King, there had been little time for God, so I packed my satchel, took up my staff, and went on a pilgrimage.'

Simon forgot to be bored and turned to the Abbot with a refreshed gleam in his eyes. 'Where did you go?'

'To the Holy City of Jerusalem,' Ingulf said with a ring of pride in his voice. 'And there are not many men who have done that in a lifetime either. Some say they will go, but by the time they are ready it is too late and their bodies are not strong enough to withstand the journey. Certainly I could not do it now. I doubt that my gouty leg would permit me as far as the Narrow Sea.' Ingulf leaned down to rub the affected limb.

Simon gazed at him. The spark of interest had rapidly become a flame and it licked at his core. 'What was Jerusalem like?' he demanded and poured wine into his own cup, all notion of sleep thrust aside.

Ingulf smiled. 'Not paved with gold, as some will tell you, but golden in its own way, with the sun shining on the stones and gleaming upon the roof of the Holy Sepulchre. To walk in the dust where Christ walked is the most humbling and exalted experience a man can have. I have seen Gethsemane, and the place where Our Lord was entombed.'

Ingulf spoke on and Simon listened, rapt, as the Abbot told him of the great Byzantine cities with their cisterns and fountains, of lands perfumed with exotic spices and heat and dust beyond anything that Simon had experienced.

'Of course you would have to go yourself, to truly know what it is like,' Ingulf said in a voice that was growing creaky and hoarse. Two further cups of wine had disappeared down his gullet and he was starting to slur his words. 'And while you are still young enough to do so. The way is arduous and there are many dangers.'

'I intend to,' Simon replied fervently. 'Even as a child I relished setting my feet on different ground.'

The Abbot smiled sceptically. 'Mayhap you will, and mayhap not,' he said. 'I have known many men – and some women – swear to see Jerusalem when the fire is in their eyes, but it goes no further because it is easier to dream than to do. It was simple for me. I had no master, and I could not return to royal service. But others have harder shackles to break.' He lifted his gaze and swept it meaningfully around the hall. 'You would have much to leave behind, my lord.'

Simon nodded, and some of the brightness went from his eyes, but a glimmer remained. 'Indeed I would, and I know that the time is not ripe, but the seed is a fruit and it is still growing. I will get there.'

The Abbot nodded. He tilted his cup to his mouth, found it almost empty, and set it ponderously aside without refilling it. 'The drink does as much talking as the man,' he said. 'It is not always wise to pay heed to an old fool whose tongue has run away with him.'

'Not always,' Simon agreed, 'but is it not also said *In vino veritas?*'

'Ah, you know your Roman proverbs?' Ingulf smiled. 'Truth in wine. Perhaps after all you will succeed.' He levered himself to his feet, wincing as the gout gnawed at his toes. 'I'm afraid I have a pilgrimage to make of this moment – to the privy pit.'

When he had gone, Simon sat for a brief time alone. The Abbot's tales had stirred the old restlessness, which had been lying like sediment at the bottom of a deep pool. Now it swirled through his blood with the wine, infusing him with desire.

It was late in the night, much closer to dawn than dusk, when everyone finally settled down for the night. Since Matilda and Simon had given up their chamber to the bride and groom, they had bedded down in the women's solar with several other guests.

'What were you and Ingulf talking about so deeply?' Matilda wanted to know as she curved her arm around Simon's body in the dark.

'Mmmm?' He turned slightly. 'His life before he was a monk. He used to be a royal clerk, and then he went on a pilgrimage.' Simon's voice was sleepy and deliberately indifferent. He knew that Matilda would not respond with enthusiasm to the notion of his becoming a pilgrim. She would likely see it as abandonment. Besides, he was aware that for the moment it was no more than a stirred-up dream. He folded her hand in his and pretended to settle into sleep. Within moments, the pretence had become reality.

Simon and Matilda presided over a somewhat subdued table the next morning. The bride and groom had yet to rise and only the hardiest souls had stumbled to the trestle to partake of bread, cheese and watered wine. Matilda was sleepy, but since she had not overindulged at the flagon was in a reasonable condition. Simon was rather green around the gills and she had given him an infusion of willow bark tisane to dull the worst of his headache.

'I should know better at my age,' groaned Ingulf, and gave Simon a pained look. 'Your wine is too strong and smooth, my lord. I am accustomed only to ale and water.'

Matilda did not believe that for one moment. An abbot of Ingulf's status was bound to keep a fine cellar – his guests would expect it of him.

'You were the one who sent it past your lips,' Simon retorted with a wry smile. 'I think you are annoyed at your own inability to resist temptation.'

The Abbot raised his hands, admitting culpability.

Matilda rose. 'I will go and brew a cauldron of headache remedy,' she said. 'Likely there will be many in need.' Especially Hugh of Chester she thought. By her reckoning he had sunk almost two gallons of their best wine.

She set off down the hall but was apprehended by a mud-splattered messenger. Her steward hastened to intercept the man, but she gestured him aside, signalling that she was content to deal with the matter herself.

'I am Matilda, Countess of Huntingdon and Northampton,' she said. 'Whom do you seek?'

The messenger bowed and Matilda's nostrils twitched, for he stank of smoke.

'Abbot Ingulf, my lady,' he said and showed his teeth in a grimace of distress. 'He is needed immediately at Crowland; there has been a terrible fire.'

'A fire?' Matilda pressed her hand to her throat and felt her pulse leap against her fingers. 'Dear sweet Christ . . . How much has been lost?'

'Many of the buildings my lady. The guesthouse, the dorter, the library . . .'

Matilda swallowed. 'What of the chapter house? What of my father's tomb?'

His gaze slipped from hers. 'There was some damage to the chapter house, but the tomb of Earl Waltheof is intact.'

Relief flooded through Matilda, adding to the shock and almost buckling her knees. Somehow she remained on her feet. It was the discipline of duty, so forcefully instilled in her by her mother, that carried her through the next moments. She brought the messenger to the dais; she sent servants to prepare Ingulf's mule and baggage. She murmured the right words, but it was all a façade. Behind the mask she was a little girl screaming hysterically as her father rode away.

'A rush dip was left unattended in the dorter when the brothers went to prayer at matins the day before yesterday,' the messenger said as a distressed Ingulf demanded information. 'It tipped among the floor rushes and caught alight, then set fire to the straw sleeping pallets. By the time the alarm was raised the place was ablaze and the flames had spread. We saved what books we could from the library, and we managed to stop the fire before it had done much damage to the chapter house.' Here the messenger darted a nervous look at Matilda, whose complexion was ashen. 'I say again, my lady, your father's tomb was in no way damaged.'

Matilda nodded and clenched her hands in her gown to stop them from trembling. *But it might have been*, she wanted to cry.

'It is indeed a shock and a great pity,' Simon said, and set his arm around his wife in support. 'We grieve with you.' He gave a practical shrug of his shoulders. 'But there has been no loss of life, and dwellings can be rebuilt. Indeed, it is an opportunity to do so on a finer scale. I agree that the loss of the books in the library is a tragedy, but many of them can be replaced, and you have monks among your brethren who are skilled illuminators. You could have lost so much more.'

Ingulf left soon after, armed with a promise of funds from the earldom to help rebuild the abbey. In a state of shock, Matilda saw that the wedding guests were attended to, suckled her son, conversed sensibly with all, and later was not to remember a single thing she said or did. Had there been no nuptials to supervise, she would have ridden back to Crowland with Ingulf in order to see for herself that her father's tomb was undamaged.

'He did not burn, and therefore you should not torture yourself,' Simon said, looking so sincere that she knew he was wearing his courtier's mask and humouring her.

Matilda bit her lip. 'It is with me all the time,' she said. 'I cannot help but wonder. You would do so too, were it your own flesh and blood.'

'Your father was as close to me as my own kin,' Simon said sombrely. 'My blood is mingled with his in our son. It is no use dwelling on what might have happened. You are building a castle of woe for yourself out of a single grain of sand. Ingulf says that he will have your father's bones translated to the church and buried with reverence beneath the altar. They will be safe from all harm there.' He took her arm. 'God has him in his care. You should lay your own burden down.'

She shook her head, for, although she understood what he was saying, the very authority of his reason made her want to rebel. She did not want to lay her burden down, because while she had it the connection to her father remained strong. She carried it out of love, she guarded it jealously, and the notion of relinquishing it was too frightening to contemplate.

CHAPTER 29

Crowland Abbey, Spring 1093

'You are sure you are strong enough for this ordeal?' Judith asked.

Matilda nodded and valiantly swallowed a retch. She had eaten a dish of mussels the previous day and it had severely disagreed with her. They had all wanted her to remain at her manor of Ryhall rather than making this journey to Crowland, but she had insisted. Her father's coffin was to be opened so that his bones might be washed in holy water and reinterred before the altar of the repaired monastery church of Crowland Abbey. 'I am all right,' she said. It wasn't true, but she was determined to do what she must.

Judith raised a sceptical eyebrow.

Matilda turned her head from her mother's shrewd gaze and stared at the landscape through which they rode. It was late spring, and the wetlands were beginning to dry out. Sheep grazed the higher ground of the reedy marshland and goats nibbled at the scrub and brambles. There was money to be made from wool. The weavers of Flanders paid good silver for the numerous fleeces that came out of these marshlands and was shipped on galleys from Boston to Ghent.

In front of her Simon was talking with animated pleasure to his brother-in-law. She thought that they were discussing hunting, for she had heard hawking terminology mentioned several times, then Ranulf said something about a girl called Sabina and Simon laughed and lowered his voice over the reply.

Feeling hot and sick, Matilda glowered resentfully at his spine.

'It is to be expected of men,' Judith said. 'Their ways are like children. Few of them ever grow up.' She spoke with a slight curl to her lip.

'Perhaps it is better to be a child than an adult,' Matilda murmured with an almost wistful glance at her son, who had fallen asleep on Sybille's shoulder. She would have carried him herself had she not felt so unwell.

Judith made an irritated sound to show what she thought of such reasoning.

Matilda eyed her mother. Judith had said nothing about her own feelings towards the opening of Waltheof's coffin. Perhaps she did not have any. Or perhaps the walls she had built around herself were too strong to be broached.

'Did you never miss him?' Matilda asked. 'Don't you ever feel guilty about the manner of his death?'

For a moment she thought that her mother was not going to answer, that she was going to retreat further behind her defences, but Judith sighed and drew the reins through her fingers. 'Of course I felt guilty about his death,' she said. 'And I mourned him too – because he was a child, and the death of a child always comes harder than that of an adult.' She turned slightly in the saddle to face Matilda. 'But he was the one who made his bed, no matter that others laid the covers. I come here out of duty, not to fall weeping over what has happened in the past.'

She dug her heels into her palfrey's flanks and rode on ahead, her back as straight as a rod, her hands competent on the reins.

'Has she been upsetting you again?' Jude joined her. Since there was only room to ride two abreast on the path, she had been hanging back.

Matilda gave her sister a wan smile. 'No,' she said. 'We were in need of a respite. We curdle in each other's company like milk and vinegar.'

Jude nervously stroked her mare's neck. 'How do you think it will be to look on our father's bones?'

The words sent a flash of queasy heat through Matilda's belly. She swallowed a retch. 'I do not know,' she whispered. Every time they came to Crowland, they would see Abbot Theodore's skull displayed with the deep bite of the sword cut in its cranium. The sight had seldom bothered her. She was accustomed to saints' bones and relics as an everyday part of her life, but Theodore's skull was two centuries old, was not of her flesh, and Theodore had not tossed her in the air, or sat her in his lap, or walked with her in a garden, his warm strong hand enclosing hers. To see those hands bereft of flesh, and the dark eye sockets . . . 'It has to be done,' she said. 'And I have to see it done . . . but I will be glad when this day is over.'

'I too,' Jude said sombrely.

Matilda shivered. With no break of trees or hills between Crowland and the North Sea, the wind was frozen and punishing. There were kindly days in the fens, but this was not one of them.

The fire-damaged parts of Crowland Abbey had been demolished and rebuilt in timber as a temporary measure. Stone had been cut from the quarries at Barnack and brought to the site in preparation for some serious rebuilding, and a French mason had been employed to oversee the work. The church itself was intact, and it was here that Waltheof was to be laid to rest, but first his remains had to be washed and wrapped in a fresh shroud of purple silk, provided for the purpose by Simon, who had bought it from an Italian trader in London.

Matilda had been sick twice since entering the abbey precincts. Her stomach was still rolling and the ginger in wine that the infirmarian had given her to abate the nausea had had little effect. It was as much the tension that was affecting her now as the bad mussels. Gripping Simon's arm, she clenched her teeth and held herself rigid as the inner coffin was carried to a linen-covered table and set down with great care.

Simon surveyed her white knuckles and fixed expression with troubled eyes. 'Do you want to go outside?' he murmured.

Matilda shook her head. It was beyond her to open her mouth and speak. Cold sweat dewed her brow, and her vision swam in and out of focus. The voices of the monks, softly intoning in Latin, echoed off the walls. The infirmary had been rebuilt after the fire, and the resinous scent of new wood hung in the air. Matilda hardly dared to breathe, for even the tiniest movement upset her precarious stomach.

The wooden lid was carefully removed with the gentle levering of crowbars to reveal the inner wooden coffin. Fluid filled Matilda's mouth. She forced herself to look, although her eyes were dry and stinging. Her father was never going to ride through Northampton's gates because his soul was in heaven and what remained of his body was here . . .

Between them the monks carefully eased the lid from the coffin, and to Matilda it was like the occasions when she slid the wooden cover from the well in her garden. She still threw silver to the elf because it was a tradition ingrained, but if an elf really had popped out of the well she would have run screaming. Now she was hemmed around. Could not run, could not open her mouth to scream.

They had reburied him in the robes of a Benedictine monk, dark within the darkness of the coffin, strong cloth unrotted by the years, and knotted about the body by a girdle of rope. Within the confines of the deep cowl shrouding the skull there was a glimmer of rich copper-red. Fierce, vital, still gleaming with the life that its owner had left behind. Flesh upon brow ridges, bony dark sockets sealed with sunken lids. Not entirely a skull, but not full-fleshed either.

Matilda gulped and strove to inhale, but her chest was empty of breath. A sound of swarming bees filled her ears, and although she stretched her eyes as wide as she could there was still no light. She felt Simon's arm tightening around her like a vice, thought she heard a voice calling her through the buzzing, but it was too far away, too distant for her to respond, and the darkness was stronger.

*   *   *

She woke up in the guesthouse, the scent of lavender strong in her nostrils. Jude was pressing a cloth to her brow and Simon was chaffing her hands. Matilda stared at them, her focus blurring and clearing by turns.

'It's all right,' Jude murmured. 'You fainted away when they opened our father's tomb.'

Matilda heaved and Simon quickly thrust a bowl beneath her, but her retching was dry. Shudders tore through her body. Simon cast the bowl aside and drew her against him, holding her hard until the spasms eased.

Although she was exhausted, Matilda willed herself to sit up and look at him. 'I . . . have they washed the bones?' she gulped. Her mind filled with the image of the coffin's dusky interior, the gleam of hair, the hint of features sunken within the recess of the cowl.

Simon drew his forefinger gently across her eyebrows. 'No, my love,' he said with a look at Jude. 'They have left them as they are.'

Matilda stared at Simon and her sister in bewilderment.

'It was thought for the best.' Simon took her gently by the shoulders. 'There is still some flesh on the bones,' he said, 'and as you saw his hair remains bright. He has been buried before the altar in the same state that they found him.' He did not need to add that the word would spread among the pilgrims and become exaggerated in the telling. Waltheof would be spoken of as an incorrupt, and a candidate for sainthood. Crowland's fame and wealth would increase with the size of the story. The abbey would be rebuilt on a grand scale with the coin from the pilgrimages and Waltheof would indeed rise from the dead with a vengeance.

'It is proof that he should not have died, isn't it?' Matilda searched Simon's face. 'Like when the slain bleed in the presence of their murderers?'

'Mayhap,' he said. 'But I rather think that the embalmer who dealt with him before they brought him from Winchester knew his art.'

Matilda rose from the bed. Her legs were shaking, but at least they supported her as she tottered towards the door.

'Where are you going?'

'To pray,' she said. 'To welcome my father to his new resting place.' She gave Simon a shadowed look. 'I can at least hope that he will sleep better than I do.'

He let her go. Turning to Jude, he dug one hand wearily through his hair. 'I wonder if she will ever be free,' he said wearily.

Jude shook her head to show that she did not have an answer.

'No,' Simon sighed, 'I do not know either.'

CHAPTER 30

February 1096

It was the third morning in a row that Matilda had been sick. Staggering back to bed she dabbled with the notion that she might finally be with child again. Her fluxes had always been irregular, but she thought that her last one must have been before she attended the Christmas court at Windsor. Her son was seven years old and she had begun to believe he would be an only child. There had been other symptoms too, when she thought about them. Recently she had been lethargic, sleeping longer in the morning, retiring to bed early. Ordinary tasks that she usually took in her stride had seemed inordinately difficult. She had put it down to the feeling of malaise that would begin to creep up on her as the anniversary of her father's death approached. Since the opening of his tomb it had intensified; that it had begun sooner than usual had slightly perturbed her, but she had thought it due to the distance that had recently sprung up between her and Simon.

She had tried to identify a cause but nothing came immediately to mind. It was true that she had not wanted to attend the winter feast at Windsor, but that was because of the state of William Rufus' bachelor court. Desiring to be with Simon, she had swallowed her prejudices. He had been away from home all summer on campaign against the rebellious Earl Robert of Mowbray. Rufus had insisted that all his tenants-in-chief be present for the Christmas court, so there had been no option but to endure if she wanted to be with her husband.

The visit, she conceded, had not been entirely dreadful. Ranulf de Tosny had been at the gathering and had brought Jude with him, so the sisters had been able to spend time in the pleasure of gossip and plundering the market stalls that had sprung up with rapid efficiency around the encampment of the court. The latter had been more to Jude's taste than hers, but still, she had still emerged with several bolts of Flemish wool to make tunics and gowns, a fine oak coffer decorated with wrought-iron work for the main bedchamber at Northampton, and a quite beautiful ivory figure of the Virgin for her private chapel. Not to be left out, Simon had acquired a fine dappled riding horse and a new belt for his sword. And between them, it seemed, they had finally conceived a second child.

Gingerly Matilda sat up. Her stomach rolled but she was able to leave the bed without retching. No, she thought. It had been good between them at the Christmas gathering, but something had happened there to change things. It was not that they had argued, more that since their return Simon was preoccupied and distant. Her first thought was that he had taken a mistress, but discreet enquiries and her own observation had shown it not to be the case. She had begun to worry that a grave situation was brewing. Was this how it had begun when her father had contemplated allying himself with the Danes? The long silences, the sense of being shut out? Simon had talked much with the other barons at the Christmas gathering, sometimes long into the night. At the time it had not bothered her, for she had Jude to keep her company and they had their own matters to discuss. Now, in hindsight, she wondered and worried.

Helisende helped her to dress and brought her honey-sweetened wine and dry bread. Matilda sipped the former, nibbled the latter and gradually began to feel better.

'Good for all sorts of stomach upsets,' the maid said knowingly. 'Even those that take nine months to resolve.'

'Is it as obvious as that?'

'Well, some of the women have been whispering since you

were ill yester morn, and now they're certain. And the laundress says she hasn't seen your flux linens since before the feast of Saint Lucy.'

'I should have asked them before I asked myself,' Matilda said irritably. 'Well, tell them to say nothing until I have broached the news to Earl Simon. I would rather he heard the news from me than the laundress!'

'Of course not, my lady!' Helisende looked affronted. 'They're good souls, they wouldn't say anything – and if one did, I'd use a bridle to bind her tongue.'

Matilda found a weak smile. She had no doubt, knowing Helisende, that the words were more than just picturesque. 'Is Earl Simon still in the hall?' she asked. 'Or is he about his business?'

'He was in the hall when I fetched your bread and wine, my lady.'

Matilda nodded. Now was as good a time as any to tell him about the child, she thought. Smoothing her gown, checking that her wimple was straight, she went to the curtain separating the bedchamber from the solar and wondered why she felt like a soldier girding up to do battle.

The March morning was already advanced enough for full daylight to be streaming through the open shutters and her women were busy at their spinning and needlework. Of her son there was no sign, by which she knew that he was at his lessons with the chaplain. Simon's former squire Turstan was using the attraction of his new knighthood to flirt with one of the younger maids, but when he saw Matilda he came smartly to attention, and, approaching her, bowed.

'My lady, Lord Simon said to inform you that the Lord of Aumale has ridden in with his troop and is hoping to speak with you.'

Matilda stared at the squire with the fixed gaze of a hare trapped in its form. 'Are you sure?' she asked out of her astonishment and concern.

'Yes, my lady.' He gave her a puzzled look.

Thoughts panicked through Matilda's mind and her heart thumped against her ribs. Last year there had been a plot to overthrow the King – and Simon had spent half the year in the field helping to put it down. Her stepgrandfather, Eudo of Champagne, had been implicated. There had been a strong rumour that the intention of the rebels was to put his son Stephen on the throne. The rebellion had been quashed and Stephen had indignantly professed his innocence. Some of the rebels had been imprisoned; others, including Eudo, had been dispossessed of their English lands – in Eudo's case the spit of land on the eastern seaboard known as Holderness. Stephen himself had escaped punishment, but he had been lying very low ever since.

As she followed Turstan to the hall, her unsettled stomach surged and churned. What if he wanted succour? Giving it would surely be dangerous? She wondered if Simon had become embroiled in some scheme. Certainly, it would explain his recent preoccupation. And yet his loyalty to Rufus had never been in doubt and he had nothing to gain from changing sides. Reason told her that she had nothing to fear, but her instinct said differently.

Stephen was warming himself at the central fire in the hall and talking with Simon. To say that he was living under the threat of arrest he looked inordinately relaxed. The wheat-blond hair he had inherited from his father was neatly trimmed and sleeked behind his ears; his eyes were bright, there was a smile on his lips. Simon seemed to have taken his mood, for he was smiling too. Then he caught sight of Matilda, and wariness entered his gaze.

Matilda's misgiving increased, and she found it very difficult to put on a welcoming expression as she advanced to greet their guest.

Stephen turned to her and, with a glimmer of shock, she saw the large red silk cross stitched to the left front of his tunic.

'Cousin!' Grasping her hands in his, he leaned left and right to kiss her cheeks. 'It is good to see you!'

'And you,' Matilda murmured, less enthusiastically. 'A surprise too.' She gestured a servant to bring wine. 'To what do we owe the pleasure?'

Stephen gave an incorrigible grin. 'You sound the way my mother used to when she was gathering herself for a tirade,' he said. 'Do not worry. I am not here to inveigle Simon into turning against the King. Indeed, quite the opposite. You are to be rid of me for some time, and I have come to make my farewells.' He touched the red cross on his breast.

Matilda eyed him while her suspicions grew. At the Christmas court there had been vague rumours about a crusade being called to rescue Jerusalem from the infidels. She had paid little heed at the time, but now she wished she had.

'So the cry has gone up in earnest?' Simon said, and there was a note of anticipation in his voice that set up a fresh wave of anxiety in Matilda's breast.

'Aye, ten days ago at Clermont Ferrand. Duke Robert has sworn himself to the cause, and my uncle Odo. It is to be a great undertaking.'

The servant returned with the wine and poured it, red as blood, into three silver goblets.

'And a diplomatic way of keeping out of Rufus' way until the dust has settled.' Simon gave their visitor a knowing look.

'Oh, indeed.' Stephen tilted his head in acknowledgement. 'Not only that, but a crusader's lands are sacrosanct. Any man who dares lay a finger on them while their owner is absent fighting for Christ lays himself open to excommunication.'

'Then you have nothing to lose.'

'Except your life,' Matilda said more curtly than she had intended.

Stephen shrugged. 'But if I lose it in the service of God my place in heaven will be assured. For the moment, there is nothing for me here save exile and suspicion. I may as well spend that exile profitably. Besides,' he said, 'I have a desire to tread the ground that Our Saviour trod and to cleanse my sins at the church of the Holy Sepulchre.'

Matilda could see Simon absorbing the words as if they were liquid gold. As the wanderlust gleamed in his eyes, her fear grew. 'It seems like vanity to me,' she snapped. 'It won't be like a week's hunting in a forest lodge . . . you might be gone for years . . . You might never return.'

'I know the risks,' Stephen said nonchalantly. 'That is why I have come to say goodbye.' He tilted his head and gave her a puppyish look. 'I was hoping that you would see me on my way with a Godspeed and a smile.'

Simon folded his arms. 'You should know by now that the women of the Conqueror's line seldom do anything with a smile.'

Matilda drew herself up. Simon's comment was unfair, even if she had been teary and out of sorts of late. 'Because the men we marry give us more cause for weeping than joy,' she retorted. 'Of course I will wish you Godspeed. It just seems a rather drastic measure to take to keep out of the King's way.'

'Not as drastic as the consequences of remaining,' Stephen said. 'I'd prefer to keep my freedom and my head.'

The words, spoken with a broad, unthinking grin, fell into silence. And in that silence a look of horror and contrition spread across Stephen's face. 'I . . . didn't . . . I'm sorry.'

'If you are to stay the night, you will need a chamber prepared,' Matilda said through stiff lips. She hardly dared open them because she felt so sick. 'You will excuse me.'

Somehow she managed to leave the hall before the spasms seized her and she doubled over, retching violently.

'Matilda?' Simon had followed her out. She felt his arms go around her shoulders. 'It was an unthinking mistake on Stephen's part. You should not take it so badly . . .' There was a note in his voice that was almost impatience.

'You fool,' Matilda gasped as she struggled to control the heaving. 'It is naught of my father.' It wasn't quite true, but her reaction was still much less about Waltheof than Simon believed.

'Then what? Are you ill?'

She shook her head. 'No,' she said, and managed to stand up, although her stomach was trembling like a plucked harpstring. 'I am with child.'

His eyes widened and he silently repeated her last two words. He looked her up and down. 'You are certain?'

She nodded. 'But I cannot tell you when it will be born . . . late summer or early autumn, I think. Are you not pleased?'

For answer he folded her in his arms and held her against him, but in a grip that was light, as if she were made of glass. 'Of course I am pleased! How could I be anything else when it has been so long?'

Matilda wondered if she was imagining the note of reserve in his voice and decided that she was. Why should he not be overjoyed at the news? Unless, like a swallow, he was preparing to fly. She thrust the thought aside, as if ignoring it would be enough to make the possibility go away.

'Perhaps you should lie down a while until the sickness passes,' Simon suggested tenderly. 'Helisende can see to organising a chamber for Stephen, and I can keep him entertained.'

Matilda had no strength to argue. The retching session had left her feeling as limp as wrung-out linen, and her stomach was still threatening rebellion. Besides, she knew that she would be unable to listen to Stephen's tactless enthusiasm with any degree of courtesy. She was glad to retire to her chamber and lie on the bed.

'I am sorry,' Stephen said, looking chagrined. 'I am always being told that I open my mouth without thinking. I regret that she took my words so badly.'

Simon grimaced. 'She is with child,' he said, 'and thus more susceptible to women's moods.' It was not the entire tale but it was easier to explain it to Stephen thus. To describe Matilda's insecurities since the fire at Crowland Abbey would have been pointless and painful.

'Ah,' Stephen said. 'Congratulations.'

Simon smiled wryly. 'Perhaps more than congratulations are

in order. I was beginning to think that little Waltheof would be the only arrow to my bow. Unfortunately Matilda finds the carrying a trial. Last time she was beset by sickness and bouts of weeping, and this occasion looks set to be no different.'

'Mmmm,' said Stephen, acknowledging Simon's words whilst obviously at a loss how to respond to them.

Recognising the younger man's discomfiture, aware that he was not the right person to burden with his domestic troubles, Simon slapped Stephen's shoulder. 'Enough of such business. Tell me more about your plans for your journey.' Drawing Stephen to a bench, he sat down with him, and was soon deeply engrossed in the subject of the crusade.

A bitter wind whistled around the keep walls. Late in the day, it had begun to snow and the print of flakes could be heard sifting against the latched shutters. In the candlelit bedchamber, its corners warmed by braziers, Simon swirled the heated wine in his goblet and paced the room. Sitting in bed, Matilda looked at him with fear and misgiving. He had scarcely spoken since they had retired, and because of it, because of his pacing, she knew what he would say when he opened his mouth. She could not bear the tension, and taking the battle into her own hands she pre-empted him.

'Tell me that you are not considering following Stephen and the others on this wild foray,' she said.

His brows twitched. 'It is no wild foray, but a call from the Pope on behalf of the Holy Land,' he argued. 'All men from the Christian world are being called upon to go and do their duty.'

'There is duty, and duty,' Matilda said, and vigorously rearranged the bedclothes around her.

'Sweeting, I know there is.' He took a long drink from the cup. He was wearing a linen shirt against the February cold, just as she was wearing her chemise. 'Indeed,' he said pensively. 'It is my duty that has been warring on my conscience.' Going to the flagon he poured her a measure of wine too and brought it over.

Matilda did not want the wine; her stomach was curdled enough as it was. Yet she took the cup because he had given it.

'My duty as Earl of Northampton, or my duty as a man in the service of the Lord Jesus Christ.' He gave her a wry look. 'If I have had a thorn in my hose, it is because I have been pondering the matter since Christmastide.'

Sparkles of cold panic ran down Matilda's spine. 'The King gave you this earldom in good faith,' she said as steadily as she could. 'If you take the cross with all the other rebels who are doing it to keep out of his way, you will be betraying him.'

'And if I stay, I will be betraying God.'

Matilda laughed, but the sound was not pleasant. 'Let us have this out in the open. What you want to do is go adventuring,' she scoffed. 'I know you, Simon. You want to pick flowers on the other side of the hill. You are never content. When you came to this earldom, it was all to you in the world, because it was a challenge and it was new. And so was I. Now that your position is secure, you crave new experiences. God is your excuse, not your reason!' She set her cup down on the stool at her bedside with a bang that sloshed the wine over the brim and glared at him.

Simon glared back, his brows drawn tightly down and his tawny eyes ablaze. 'I used to think that you had your father's nature, but now I begin to wonder if you are not every bit the bitch that your mother is,' he snapped. 'A less patient husband would not tolerate such words from his wife.'

'A more considerate husband would not cause such words to be spoken in the first place,' Matilda retorted. 'You must have a high opinion of yourself if you believe that you have the patience of a saint. I have bedded with you and borne you a child. I carry another in my belly. I have loved you well, and if you repay me in false coin, then I swear that I will never forgive you.' Her voice trembled and it was not just the cold that made her shake as she faced him. 'Simon, think well before you make your choice . . . think very well.'

Their eyes met and held. Neither looked away. 'I have been

thinking ever since the Christmas feast,' he said evenly.
'Stephen's visit only confirmed my decision. The call has gone
out and I have to follow it.'

She shook her head. 'You have to follow your own selfish
desire,' she said. 'That is all I see.'

'Then you are blind.' Breaking eye contact, he drank his
wine and returned the cup to the trestle. 'At the Holy Sepulchre,
I will say prayers for your father's soul and bring back a stone
from Jerusalem to lay at the foot of his tomb.'

'Do not tell me that it is for my father's sake you are considering this venture!' Matilda gasped in furious astonishment.

Simon raised his hand, palm outwards. 'Listen to me. If your
father were alive today he would have been one of the first to
sew a red cross onto his tunic. Since he cannot, I am taking his
banner to Jerusalem.'

'How can you say what my father would have done?' she
snapped.

'Because I knew him.'

The words struck Matilda like a slap across the face and
abruptly terminated the conversation. Cruel but true. Simon
had known him, and she had not. And if she thought about it
in a rational way she knew that Simon was right. Her father
would have been one of the first to sew a red cross on his cloak.

'You will follow your intention whatever I say.' She made a
weary gesture of capitulation. 'Do as you will.' She lay down,
her back to him, and drew her knees up to her chin. She was
so cold. It was as if a lump of ice was lodged in her stomach.
If Simon went on crusade, then it would fall to her to take up
his position at the centre of the wheel and she did not know if
she was strong enough. *You have no choice*, said a bossy inter-
nal voice that sounded suspiciously like her mother's. *It is your
duty.*

She heard his heavy sigh and, for a moment, was afraid that
he was going to bang out of the room. However he muttered
an oath beneath his breath and, raising the bedclothes on a waft
of cold air, joined her. His arm came around her waist, turned

her over and drew to him. He pressed his lips against her temple, her cheek, her mouth.

'I am afraid,' she whispered, and clung to him, her fingers gripping the fine textured linen of his shirt. 'I am afraid that I will bid you farewell and never see you again.' At the back of her mind was the hazy but terrifying memory of watching her father ride away to see King William. His promise to return; the emptiness of that vow.

'We cannot let fear stifle us,' he said, 'otherwise we might as well dwell in a cage.' He rubbed his hand up and down her back in a soothing motion. 'I fear the cage more than I fear the unknown.'

'So it is your fear that spurs you,' she said. 'It pushes you onward without thought for what you leave behind. Because you are lame, you must prove that there is no horizon you cannot conquer.'

His hand stopped. She heard the sharp hiss of his breath and realised with a jolt of triumph and pain that she had succeeded in thrusting past his guard.

'It is true, is it not?'

She half thought he would remove his hand, but he did not. Rather his grip tightened. 'We are all ridden by demons,' he said. 'We live with them as best we can and hope one day to throw them off.' He cupped her cheek on the side of his hand and kissed her. 'We live with each other's demons too,' he added softly. 'And perhaps that is the most difficult endurance of all.'

CHAPTER 31

Crowland Abbey, October 1096

The chanting of monks soared heavenwards on the wafts of incense. Crowland Abbey's chapel was awash with liquid autumn light, burnishing the fair-brown hair upon Simon's bent head to polished gold and gilding the embroidered purple pall that lay over Waltheof's resting place.

Outside the abbey gates a crowd of pilgrims waited to file past the tomb, but on the point of setting out on his journey to Jerusalem Simon was granted a moment alone with his father-by-marriage.

'I ask you to watch over Matilda and our children while I am gone,' Simon murmured, his hands clasped and his gaze fixed upon the pall with its surroundings of pilgrim offerings, both the grand and the tawdry. His jaw tightened as he spoke of his wife. Matters had been strained between them for several months, each of them avoiding confrontation. He had spent much of his time away from Northampton, raising funds for the journey, discussing the venture with others who were committed and dealing with outstanding business. Matilda had taken to her garden with a vengeance until she was as brown as a peasant woman and her hands were rough and work-worn. Advancing pregnancy had curtailed her frenetic activity, and in the two weeks before the birth she had merely sat beneath her precious apple tree with her sewing and her maids. Simon was not sure how either of them could bridge the distance without warping their natures out of true.

A cloud drifted across the sun and for a moment the light ceased to stream across the tomb. Simon decided that it was an act of nature, not an omen, but his mood was pensive as he crossed his breast and rose to his feet. 'I will see through your eyes as I promised,' he said. 'I will live each day as you asked.' He hesitated by the tomb, but the words that came so easily to him at court remained locked and tangled in his brain. 'Rest in peace,' he said with a swallow, and walked swiftly up the nave towards the daylight.

At the door Abbot Ingulf was waiting for him. 'God speed you on your journey, my lord,' he said with a deep bow. 'We will pray for your wellbeing daily.'

Simon returned the gesture. 'Your support is welcome,' he said graciously. 'If it is God's will that I return from this enterprise, I will not forget Crowland in my benefactions.'

Formal speeches over, the men clasped and embraced. In his way Simon had grown as fond of Ingulf as Waltheof had once been fond of Ulfcytel. He saw in the Abbot something of what he wanted for himself. Ingulf had been a courtier, a man of the world. He had wandered far and wide, seen all that he desired and had found his inner peace.

'Have a care my son,' Ingulf said, a tear in the corner of his eye. 'Come back to us whole.'

'I will do my best.' Simon gave the coarse woollen shoulder a final squeeze and left Ingulf for the abbey guesthouse, where Matilda was waiting to make her own farewells.

The birth of their daughter a month ago had been hard, and although she had travelled to Crowland with him she was still not fully recovered. The weight she had gained during the pregnancy had melted from her bones following the birth, but she did not look well.

Holding the baby in the crook of her left arm, she came to him. Named for her mother, the infant had a fuzz of dark gold hair and eyes of kitten-blue. She was a fractious scrap, with the loudest squawl Simon had ever heard. Another one in the mould of Judith and Adelaide, he had decided. The blood of the Conqueror was at its strongest in the women bred from its line.

Simon took the baby into his own arms and, praying that she did not begin bawling, leaned over to press a kiss on her smooth, small forehead.

'This will be the last time that you see her as a babe in arms,' Matilda said, her voice cracking slightly. 'When you return she will be walking and talking . . . and she will not know you.'

'There will be time enough,' Simon said, his voice impassive to hide the discomfort he felt at her words. 'While she is so little, she will not miss me.'

'There is never enough time,' Matilda said, and then stopped herself by drawing a swift, shaken breath. 'I will not send you away with recriminations . . . I made a promise to myself. But go now, swiftly, before I break that promise.'

Simon gave his daughter to Helisende and swept Matilda into his embrace, kissing her hard. Then he stooped to his son, who was watching the proceedings with solemn deep blue eyes.

'Be a good boy for your mother,' he said, 'and a fine soldier for me.'

The little boy sucked his lower lip and nodded. 'I am good,' he said indignantly.

Simon's lips twitched. He ruffled the lad's fluffy red-gold curls and stood up. 'Then be angelic,' he said, and turned to mount the horse that Turstan was holding. Drawing the reins through his fingers, he nudged the grey with his heels, clicked his tongue and, with a final salute, rode out of the abbey gates.

Some of the children who had come as pilgrims with their parents ran alongside the cavalcade, keeping pace, cheering and waving. Matilda stood where she had bade farewell, rooted to the ground. In her mind's eye she saw herself running after him, stumbling on her gown, screaming at him not to leave her. She had a vivid recollection of fighting to prevent her father from going away with his friend. Of being torn from his arms and thrown down in a pile of straw to shriek and thresh until she was exhausted.

'My lady, are you all right?'

The gentle touch on her shoulder; Helisende's concerned voice brought her around with a shudder. 'Yes,' she said, 'I am all right.' It wasn't the truth, but she could put on a brave face. After all, she was her mother's daughter.

The last horse rode out of the abbey gates, and the procession dwindled to the occasional glint of armour on the horizon. Her eyes grew dry from staring and then began to water.

'Will Papa be home soon?' Her son looked up at her, his eyes anxious with the need for reassurance.

Matilda steeled herself. 'When he has done what he must,' she said in a soothing voice that did not reflect the savage emotions roiling within her. 'Come, we will go and pray for him at your grandfather's tomb.' She placed a gentle hand on the child's shoulder and turned away from the road towards the abbey. For the benefit of the gathered pilgrims, she inclined her head to them and smiled. She bade an attendant take a purse of silver pennies and halfpennies and distribute them among the crowd with the exhortation that they pray for her husband's success. She gave Ingulf a smaller pouch of gold for the benefit of the abbey. Serene, courteous, doing her duty. Outwardly the great and gracious lady. Inwardly screaming with grief. Was this how her mother had felt?

'I thought I was different,' she murmured to Helisende as she entered the chapel, its air spiced with incense and the scent of beeswax candles. Streamers of gilded autumn light fell across the purple pall, focusing the eye on the blaze of opulence and light. 'But I am not. Simon was right. I am my mother's daughter – how could I not be? And he has in him a streak every bit as feckless as my father . . . and perhaps that is why I love him and I hate him too.'

'My lady, you do not hate him!' Helisende looked shocked. In her arms the baby stirred and made a fretful little sound.

Matilda swallowed. 'I am trying not to,' she said, and knelt at the foot of the tomb, the clay floor tiles striking cold to her knees even through the heavy woollen fabric of her gown.

CHAPTER 32

Port of Brindisi, Easter 1097

Under a spring sun much hotter and yellower than that of England, Simon watched the bustle on the dockside. Brindisi's harbour jostled with all manner of craft, tethered like a herd of horses anxious to gallop across the sunspangled plains of sea beyond the harbour mouth. Gangplanks had been run out to the vessels closest inshore, and sailors, soldiers and labourers toiled to fill the deck spaces with supplies – water barrels, firkins of wine, salt meat, weapons, dismantled tents, horses, harness, soldiers.

The Norman crusader contingent, under the banners of Robert of Normandy and Stephen of Blois, had travelled down through Italy and spent the winter months in Brindisi, assembling a fleet and making the local tavern keepers rich. While awaiting the spring and the right conditions for crossing the Adriatic Sea, many crusaders decided that they had ventured far enough from home and, ripping the crosses from their cloaks, turned back. Others, finding themselves in financial difficulties, sold their weapons and took employment wherever they could find it to earn a crust and a bed for the night.

Beset by neither a waning of enthusiasm nor lack of funds, but filled with a certain degree of impatience, Simon had spent the winter exploring his surroundings, familiarising himself with the region – the handsome dark-eyed people, the food with its warm flavours of olive and citrus. He enjoyed the strange, boiled pastries they made, bland in themselves but superb when blended with meat and spices and washed down with the robust red wine of the area.

Whilst eating and drinking in the various hostelries around the harbour he had picked up a liberal smattering of the language and daily practice had improved his accent and his understanding. Weather permitting, he had ridden out with a guide to explore the countryside and the coastline surrounding the port.

On the days when rain lashed the walls of his lodging house and a bitter wind swirled smoke around the room, guilty thoughts of England and Matilda drove him to send for a scribe and write her letters detailing his progress – or lack of it. On these days too, he would think wistfully of her warmth in his bed and the soothing gentleness of her oiled fingers on his damaged leg. It was with great righteousness and a hint of self-mockery that he wrote to her of his chastity. He had slept alone since leaving England. Not that such endurance was entirely the result of an effort to remain pure while engaged in Christ's business. Simon's oath to God was aided by the fact that the available women were less than appealing and free with their favours. He had no desire to sport where a hundred others had sported before him.

A crowd had gathered on the wharfside to watch the first soldiers and supplies embark, their destination the port of Durazzo on the Byzantine coast. A warm breeze was blowing off the sea, and the sailors were using their oars to row the galleys out of the harbour mouth. Each pull and scoop raised small puffs of white water upon the glittering blue. Simon joined the group of onlookers, among them Duke Robert of Normandy and Stephen of Aumale. The latter made room for Simon at his side and Simon found himself standing against a slender man of middle years, with gaunt features and black hair silvering at the temples. Immediately Simon stiffened. He knew that Ralf de Gael was a crusader, had even seen him from a distance, but this was the first time that their paths had directly crossed. While he recognised De Gael, the Breton lord obviously did not remember him, but then Simon had been a green youth at the time of Waltheof's death and beneath De Gael's notice. Twenty years later the boy was long into manhood and the former Earl of Norfolk was growing old.

De Gael smiled at Simon. 'I am not a good sailor,' he said. 'I will be glad when this leg of our journey is completed.'

'So will we all.' Simon forced himself to be civil. 'It has been a long wait through the winter.'

They watched the ships sculling out of the harbour. Gulls wheeled and screamed overhead. Someone made a comment to Robert of Normandy and he laughed aloud. De Gael looked at Simon through lids narrowed with the twin efforts of focusing and remembering.

'Forgive me,' he said. 'I feel that I should know you?'

Simon turned his gaze from the sea to fix it on the man who had trapped his friends in treason and escaped to Brittany to live a full and prosperous life. 'Likely you remember me from the Conqueror's court,' he replied impassively. 'I was a squire of the chamber and my father was one of King William's chamberlains.'

A glint of recognition lit in the eyes and De Gael snapped his fingers. They were elegantly manicured and adorned with fine gold rings. 'Ah, the lad who broke his leg – I remember now!'

'The lad whom Waltheof of Northumberland saved from having his ribs smashed into his lungs by a bolting horse,' Simon said, hunting De Gael's face for a response. The smile that had been about to break vanished. De Gael's right hand closed around his sword belt in a defensive gesture.

'I remember that too,' the Breton murmured. 'It was the most brave and foolhardy act I have ever witnessed.' He fiddled with the tongue of leather folded over the belt buckle. 'I was glad that I had not attempted it myself, but I felt diminished that I had not done so.'

Simon eyed him warily. Part of De Gael's ability to charm

lay in his self-deprecating manner. He was ever the first to trample on his own pride and men . . . and women were disarmed by the trait.

'And how did you feel when Waltheof died?' Simon asked softly, unwilling to be taken in. 'Did you feel diminished then, my lord?'

The dark eyes blazed and dull colour suffused the fine, knife-blade cheekbones. 'By what right do you question me?' he demanded.

'By the right of blood,' Simon answered. 'I am wedded to Waltheof's eldest daughter, and my son is his grandson and namesake. Waltheof did not live to see his daughter grow up and wed nor his grandchildren born because he was foolish enough to trust a man who was supposed to be his friend.'

De Gael stared. His jaw was rigid. 'You have no right to judge me,' he said hoarsely. 'Only God can do that.'

'And I am sure that God will,' Simon said coldly. He made to walk away, but De Gael grasped his sleeve.

'You do not understand. Waltheof was indeed my friend and not a day goes by that I have not regretted what happened. If I could return to my youth and undo that moment, I would.'

'Likely so,' Simon retorted, and steeled himself against the pleading in the other man's tone. 'Since you would still hold the title of Earl of Norfolk too.' He shook himself free. 'My wife carries the memory of her father like a shackle, and there is nothing I can do to free her. Do you know what destruction you wrought with your scheming?'

'Far less destruction than the tyrant who sat on the throne and persecuted from on high,' De Gael snapped. 'It was an ill-conceived and ill-timed idea, but it was born of genuine grievance.'

Simon made a disparaging sound. 'And it died in disaster.'

'I know that. I count myself at fault and, although you will not believe this because I can see that you think the worst of me, I took a crusader's vow to atone for my past. In Jerusalem I will pray for Waltheof's soul and make my peace. If I die on the road, my bones will testify my sincerity.'

Simon strove to maintain his contempt for De Gael, but against his efforts found himself warming to the man's candour. It might be false – De Gael had a slick way with words – but there seemed to be a genuine chord of sadness in the older man's voice.

'I am sorry for Waltheof's daughter. She was a pretty little thing,' De Gael continued. 'I know that he doted on her and she adored him.' He gave a wry grimace. 'I am afraid that she disliked me. Even then she knew that I was responsible for taking her father away from her.'

Simon thought of Matilda's strength and the counterbalance of her terrible vulnerability, most of it brought about by this man. De Gael was not entirely to blame, though. Others had played their part. 'I do not think that time has wrought any change of opinion, my lord,' he said. 'Ask your forgiveness of God, and be content with that. I do not think that we have anything more to say to each other that will be of profit . . .'

De Gael sighed heavily. 'I . . .'

Whatever else he was going to say was cut off by a loud expletive from Stephen of Aumale, who had been doing his best not to listen to the exchange between Simon and the former Earl of Norfolk.

'God's Holy Bones, the poor bastards!'

Following Stephen's pointing finger, Simon saw that one of the transport ships heavily laden with soldiers had capsized midway between the shelter of the harbour and the open sea. Small figures bobbed briefly in the water before vanishing in the swell. A few fortunate ones had managed to gain a grip on the mast, but, unable to swim and dragged down by the weight of their garments, the majority were drowning. Other vessels coming hard about were rowing frantically towards the stricken ship to pick up those who were clinging on.

'God have mercy on their souls,' muttered De Gael, signing his breast and shaking his head. Among the horrified watch-

ers on shore there were mutters of foreboding, and declarations
that it was an ill omen.

'It is a test of our fortitude!' Robert of Normandy bellowed,
striking a pose. 'Those of you who are faint-hearted can crawl
home with your tails between your legs. Our compatriots are
even now in heaven with the Saviour! A ship may be lost, but
what is a single one among many?' He strode along the dockside, exhorting and rallying. Watching him at work, Simon
could well understand how men had been seduced into
rebelling against William Rufus to try to make this man King
of England. Robert of Normandy might be small and stout,
with receding hair, but there was a certain glamour about him.
His character was known to be lazy and indolent, but the
crusade had fired his blood and he was proving a more adequate
leader now than he had ever done at home.

The few survivors of the sudden, brutal shipwreck were
brought ashore together with those bodies that the crews of the
other vessels had been able to hook from the water. Robert's
chaplain and Archbishop Adehmar came forward to attend the
dead, stepping carefully around the drenching pools of seawater that streamed from the corpses.

A woman, her clothes sodden, her black hair dripping
around her face, knelt over one of the dead men and howled
for him. The sound raised the hair on Simon's nape, and as he
stared he was assailed by a chill of recognition. It was almost
twenty years since last he had seen her, but still he knew the
oval face and wide, grey-violet eyes: Sabina, the falconer's
daughter with whom he had conducted that first affair of innocence and aching, unrequited lust.

Pushing through the crowd to her side he looked down at
the dead man whose head she was cradling in her lap. Time
had put a badger-stripe of grey in his beard and given him a
paunch to droop over his belt, but Simon still recognised the
serjeant who had taken his place in the soft darkness of the
mews. Stitched to his tunic was the ubiquitous cross of red
linen, its edges frayed and faded from wear and exposure to

light. Seawater had made spiky clumps of his lashes, and beneath half-closed lids his eyes were glazed with death.

Someone leaned down to Sabina with a sympathetic word and was batted vigorously away. 'He is my husband!' she snarled like a she-wolf. Leaning over the dead man, she kissed his face and dug her hands into his streaming hair. 'Why didn't God take me as well?' She prostrated herself over his body, kissing and touching in a frenzy as if her desperation would restore him to life.

Clucking his tongue in pity, Ralf de Gael turned away.

Simon stooped to her. 'Sabina?'

The gaze she turned on him was unfocused and wild. Her lips curled back in a snarl. 'Let me be!' she spat.

'Sabina, look at me. It's Simon.' He touched her shoulder and, like the man before him, was flung off. 'Please, I can help you.'

The faintest glimmer of lucidity shone through her shock and grief. 'No one can help me,' she choked. 'Saer's dead. I should have died too. Go away.' She laid her hand upon her husband's cold throat as if she could conjure a heartbeat beneath her fingertips and rocked herself back and forth, tears mingling with the salt water streaming down her face. 'We were supposed to see Jerusalem together and pray for our children!'

Simon watched her for a moment. Like Ralf he could have turned away and pretended it was none of his business, but it would indeed be a pretence, and one his conscience would make him pay for later. Rising from his crouch, he beckoned to two serjeants from his troop. 'Bring a stretcher,' he commanded, 'and bear this man to the nearest church.' Removing his cloak, he draped it around Sabina's shoulders. The blue fabric, the white bearskin, gave her complexion the same grey cast as the corpses laid on the wharfside.

The other survivors of the capsizing were being found dry garments and given hot wine to drink. The crusader fleet continued to load up supplies and put out to sea. Ship's horns bellowed out as the vessels communicated with each other.

Robert of Normandy embarked on a large drakkar with round shields overlapped along the side to increase the height of the freeboard. His chaplains and stewards organised prayers for the dead and the hasty digging of graves.

The first terrible wave of grief over, Sabina sat silently by her husband while she waited for him to be taken and buried. She had washed the salt from his hair and beard, had used her bone comb to ease out the tangles, and now she sat with her hands folded and her expression blank.

Simon gave her a cup of wine and she looked at it as if she did not know what it was. 'I did not want to come on this journey, but he thought it would make a difference,' she said, her voice husky from the strain of screaming. 'He thought if only we could petition God at his most holy altar and show how much we loved him that he would forgive us our sins and reward us . . .' She took a hesitant drink from the cup, her hand shaking so badly that she could scarcely hold the rim to her lips. 'Our sins must be greater than we had ever imagined, for look what God has wrought . . .'

'Hush,' Simon murmured. 'It was the work of man not God that tumbled your ship. It was laden with too many people and too low in the water.'

'Then why was I saved and my husband drowned? Why didn't I die with him?' Her voice rose and cracked. 'Do not tell me that God is merciful, for I will not believe you!' She swiped her sleeve across her eyes and sniffed.

'I will tell you nothing,' Simon said and touched her hand. 'There is a place for you in my household until you are recovered enough to decide what you want to do.'

'I do not need your pity.' She raised her head and looked at him proudly through a glitter of tears.

His heart turned over. For an instant she reminded him so much of Matilda that he found it difficult to speak. 'It is not out of pity that I am offering,' he replied, 'but out of old friendship. I have lodgings in the town. You are welcome to spend the night while you decide whether you want to go on or return home.'

She continued to look at him and colour burned up in Simon's face.

'It is an honourable offer,' he said. 'To take advantage is not my intention.'

'I know that.' She gave a cracked laugh. 'We always drew back from the edge, didn't we?' Even with his cloak around her shoulders, she was shivering violently.

The chaplain arrived to escort her husband's body to his grave. A low moan rose in Sabina's throat.

'Come,' Simon said gently, and drew her to her feet. 'Let us bury him with dignity.' He gave her hand a squeeze. 'And when it is done, I know an apothecary who will give you something to help you sleep.'

She leaned on him heavily. 'It will take more than an apothecary to help me,' she said grimly.

Sabina's fragile condition led Simon to decide to bring her with him. Despite the dangers waiting on the road to Jerusalem, the way home for a woman alone was probably more hazardous. Even taking a couple of stout serjeants for escort was no guarantee of safety, and Sabina was so engulfed by her grief that she was not capable of looking out for herself.

On the crossing from Brindisi to Durazzo she curled up against the gunwale and hid her face from the sea. When Simon stooped to hand her a cup of wine and ask how she was faring, she shook her head.

'Not well,' she said, but took the cup with trembling hands and drank it to the lees. Simon sat down beside her, leaning his back against the ship's side and shifting his shoulder blades until he was comfortable. He said nothing, making it clear that he was content to sit and not make demands on her. Finally Sabina broke the silence.

'It was Saer's notion that we take the cross,' she said tremulously. 'He thought that if we showed our devotion to God he would bless us with more children.' She tightened her hand around the cup until her knuckles showed white. 'We had three you know – two boys and a girl.'

The 'had' was telling. Simon touched her shoulder in a gesture of sympathy and felt it quiver.

'One son and our infant daughter died of fever two summers ago. I did everything to try to save them, but it wasn't enough.' Her eyes were desolate. 'I consulted a herbwife. Saer brought an apothecary and a doctor, but they could do nothing. Other children in the village died too . . .' She swallowed hard. 'Our eldest son survived, only to cut himself on a scythe blade at harvest time and die of the stiffening sickness . . .'

'I am sorry,' Simon said, knowing that the words were inadequate. It was a fact of life that many children did not survive the journey into adulthood. His mother had lost two sons between bearing Garnier and him, one stillborn, the other succumbing to a childhood illness. But common occurrence was no comfort to parental grief.

'You do not understand,' Sabina said, baring her teeth. 'We tried to salve our wounds and comfort our loss by conceiving another child, but Saer . . .' She bent her head so that all he saw was the top of her wimple and a few wind-whipped strands of black hair. 'The loss of his son unmanned him. That was one of the reasons he took a crusader's vow – in the hope of finding a cure. Instead all he found was his death.' She let the empty cup roll onto the deck and, bowing her face into her cupped hands, rocked back and forth with muffled cries of distress.

Simon gathered her in his arms. He said nothing, for words would have been trite and inadequate.

She clung to him and wept harshly against his breast until she was exhausted. Simon gently eased out from beneath her and, tucking his cloak around her body, left her to sleep out her grief.

'A regular champion of waifs and strays,' said Stephen of Aumale, who was one of the other passengers on their vessel. His gaze was speculative.

Simon tried to look nonchalant. 'I knew her and her parents

many years ago at court. My conscience would not let me abandon her.'

Stephen raised his fair brows and his lips twitched with amusement. 'A very tender conscience,' he said. 'Matilda would be proud of your devotion.'

Simon gave him an irritated scowl. 'She was an old friend in need,' he said curtly. 'Read no more into the situation than that.'

'Oh, I don't,' Stephen said, but not as if he meant it. 'I am sure it is your Christian duty to succour her in every way you can.'

Before Simon could retort Stephen had moved off down the ship, his tread blithe and carefree. Simon cursed softly beneath his breath. He deliberately avoided looking at the vulnerable huddle that was Sabina and went instead to stand at the steer-board with the helmsman.

CHAPTER 33

September 1097

'I s there really an elf in the well?' Young Waltheof peered into the wattle-lined tunnel with its twinkle of water deep below.

Matilda smiled, reliving her own fascination, remembering how she had scrutinised the mysterious, uncovered darkness with her father watchfully at her side. 'Who can say?' she said. 'Your grandfather told me that the elf was shy and never came out when there were people about, but that he should be paid to keep the water sweet.' Grasping the linen rope, she drew the bucket to the surface and poured the water into a waiting earthenware jug. 'Here.' She gave the child a small silver ring. 'Throw this in to him and make a wish.'

Waltheof screwed up his face to think. 'I want a dog like Hector,' he said. 'With a tail like a curly feather.'

Matilda rolled her eyes. Hector was a menace to all. That the menace was due to sheer friendliness and exuberance rather than malice was no consolation. The 'curly feather' of a tail had a propensity for swishing cups and bowls off tables, while the other end would indiscriminately devour whatever came its way in between slobbering over any human in sight. Hector was the result of an unfortunate meeting between one of the keep's boarhound bitches and a huntsman's spaniel dog that was so randy it would tup anything that stood still to be mounted. Matilda was in no haste to see the mistake repeated, even for the sake of her son. Fortunately Hector had been the single pup from the mating and Matilda's chaplain had taken him for companionship. The prospect of another such in her bower did not bear thinking about.

The silver ring vanished in a single glint of metal and a minute plink as it struck the surface of the water. Ripples shivered and were still. The boy leaned hopefully over the well opening. 'If I'm very quiet, perhaps he will come out,' he said hopefully.

'Never,' Matilda said. 'The light blinds his eyes.' Her lips twitched slightly. The notion of her son sitting quietly for longer than it took to blink was impossible. Besides, she did not want him lingering beside the open well cover. She knew what a fascination it had held for her in her own childhood. 'Drop the bucket back,' she said.

'Won't it hit him on the head?'

'No, he lives too far down in the water.'

The boy nodded acceptance and threw the bucket down with gusto so that it landed with a vigorous splash. Matilda made her own wish as the ripples surged and settled. Gesturing a nearby gardener to slide the heavy well covering back over the hole, she hefted the jug and bore it towards the endive and lettuce bed. The leaves were wilting in the September sun, which in the mid-afternoon still bore the strength of summer. Helisende sat in the shade of the apple tree, her attention on the baby. In the last week little Maude had found her feet and was beginning to totter unsteadily around, her fat pink toes plumping purposefully through the cool green grass.

Matilda watched her daughter pull herself up and use Helisende's knee as a balance before launching herself. Three steps, four, and she sat down with a bump, but only to struggle up again and totter towards her mother, arms outstretched, a beaming smile on her face.

Matilda set the water jar down and, making cooing sounds of encouragement, held out her arms. 'Your papa should be here to see you,' she said, and as her throat tightened she felt resentment and longing stir within her. Her son thought it was a great adventure that his father had gone off to war. He would play 'crusades' with the other boys, galloping around on his hobbyhorse, waving his toy sword in the air and slaughtering imaginary Saracens. Sometimes Matilda thought that the only difference between a boy's game and a man's game was that the latter involved real danger and grief and the former could be stopped the moment that injury occurred or the participants grew tired. But one was the training for the other, and that worried her.

The baby staggered the last important step and Matilda swung her up in her arms, welcoming the warm, solid weight. Girls had a different set of worries and burdens to bear, she thought. Her daughter struggled and clamoured to be set down so that she could totter her way back to Helisende. Matilda smiled at her sturdy determination, waited to see her triumphant arrival, then stooped to her water jar.

She was watching the last drops soak into the soil when a Benedictine monk was brought to her by one of the hall stewards. The man was somewhat dusty from travel and the crown of his head shone pink from exposure to the burn of the sun. Matilda greeted him courteously and drew him to the shade of the bench beneath her apple tree. A swift command sent a servant hurrying to fetch water for washing and wine for refreshment.

'You are welcome brother . . .'

'Matthias,' he completed for her with a grave inclination of his head. 'I will not trouble your presence long, my lady. My journey is to Crowland, but I am glad of a respite for myself and my mule.'

'Have you come far?' Matilda enquired politely. She was accustomed to visitors but they were usually secular. Monks and priests preferred to rest in the abbeys and convents of their orders.

'From Winchester,' he said. 'I have letters for Abbot Ingulf.' Unfastening his leather travelling satchel, he produced a folded, salt-stained parchment, tied with narrow thongs of rolled leather and closed with a red wax seal. 'This was given into my keeping by a fellow monk who had carried it from Normandy. It has been in many hands along the way, so I am told, but it comes originally from Earl Simon on his blessed mission.'

Matilda had taken the package from him as he spoke. Now she began to tremble. A letter from Simon. His hands had touched this as they delivered it to the first messenger in the chain. He had pressed his seal ring deep into the liquid wax to make an impression. He was still alive – or had been when this was written, and he had been thinking of her. Letters had arrived regularly until Eastertide, many from a place named Brindisi, but she had heard nothing since then.

Brother Matthias regarded her with concern. 'My lady . . . are you all right?'

She gave the monk so dazzling a look that it seemed to him he had been smiled upon by the Madonna herself.

'Yes,' Matilda whispered through a sudden burgeoning of tears and thought that perhaps there really was an elf in the well.

Matilda did not open the letter at once. To do so under the scrutiny of the monk and beset by the surrounding distractions of everyday life would have destroyed the pleasure and unsettled her concentration. She preferred to wait and anticipate.

It was the cool of the evening when she returned to the garden, a lantern lighting her way to the bench beneath the apple tree. Brother Matthias had eaten a large portion of squab pie, washed it down with a pint of cider, and then departed for the monastery at St Ives to seek a night's lodging. The children were abed with Helisende to watch over them. A night breeze rustled the leaves and from the direction of the orchard a little owl let out several piercing shrieks. But they were familiar sounds that comforted rather than disturbed her. She had never been afraid of the dark, only of being left alone.

With damp, unsteady fingers she took the small knife from

the sheath at her belt and cut the leather thongs binding the parchment. Breaking the seal, she opened the casing and found that it enclosed two more folded sheets of parchment, closely but neatly written in deep brown ink. Simon could read and write, but only when forced. This was the hand of a scribe, elegant and in formal Latin. Judith's interest in the Church meant that Matilda had been taught to read the language. At the time it had seemed a chore, but now she was grateful for her mother's foresight and insistence. She would have hated to summon her own scribe to read aloud the words that needed to be either savoured or suffered in private.

The lantern cast a wavering dark gold shadow over the words. Picking it up by its chain, she hooked it over the lowest branch of the tree and angled herself so that the light shone full on the writing.

Earl Simon to Countess Matilda, whatever warm greetings her mind can imagine.

Let your heart be comforted that I have travelled on this blessed journey without harm so far as I have reached. We came to the great city of Constantinople that is ruled by the Emperor Alexius. Although he received our leaders with smiles and gifts, truth to say, he is prudent and jealous of his great and beautiful city. We were not permitted to enter freely and wander at our will, but always under escort in small groups of no more than five or six at a time. My love, Constantinople is a place of great wonder that surpasses anything I have ever seen or that you could imagine. Some say that the streets are paved with gold. That is an untruth, but indeed, there is gold everywhere, and ivory and silk in every bright colour of the rainbow and beyond. The churches drip with wealth and the merchants go clothed in purple like kings. Truly it is a remarkable sight and my eyes have grown sore so much have I stared.

I confess my love, that I have bought you neither silk nor gold from the great capital of Byzantium, for I know such tokens of wealth impress you not. But I have secured something else that I

*hope will bring you great joy and that, God willing, I will live
to place in your hands.*

Matilda grimaced as she read this. The only think that could
bring her great joy was Simon's return. She had no difficulty
imagining his pleasure at discovering the wonders of
Constantinople. What was written here was only the echo of
his wonder. A moth blundered in front of the lantern and cast
a fluttering shadow as it strove to burn its wings on the dazzle
of candlelight. Matilda grabbed swiftly and felt the frantic
beating of soft wings within the cage of her fist. Opening her
hand, she cast the pale insect far into the dark, and again
lowered her gaze to the letter.

*We left the city after a sojourn of ten days and sailed across
the arm of the sea that surrounds the city and is called the Bosporus.
It is said that the sea around Constantinople is cruel to voyagers,
but on the day that we sailed it was as calm as a duck pond. After
landing, we took horse for the Turkish-held city of Nicaea, and
it is from there that I write to you. I have seen hard battle, but
through God's great mercy I yet live and with no wounds to trouble
my body. The Turkish leader, Quilij Arslan, came upon us in an
attempt to relieve the siege, but we scattered his army to the four
winds and hope that negotiations will yet win the city for us. We
are told that from Nicaea to Jerusalem is but a march of five
weeks, and only the city of Antioch between to stop us.*

*You should know that I have made my peace with Ralf de
Gael. He is here amongst us with a company of Breton lords and
has spoken to me of his grief and regret over your father's death.
I will speak more of this when I return, but I thought that you
should know of this detail and think upon it. Lord Ralf has ever
been a man of charm and easy words, but I truly believe that the
matter of your father's death has lingered on his conscience.*

Matilda raised her head from her reading and leaned her
head against the rough bark of the tree. She felt a small stab of

resentment. Well and good if Simon had made his own peace with De Gael, but she hoped that he had not made it on her behalf too. Her nature might be generous and loving, but in the matter of forgiving Ralf de Gael she was not prepared to be charitable. Indeed, she was irritated that Simon should mention him at all when this letter was all she had of him for months yet to come. He had spoken of hard fighting too, his manner offhand, but she knew that such indifference on the page was not necessarily the truth.

I trust that you are in good health, my love, and that our children are thriving. I hold you all dearly in my thoughts and wish that I could hold you in my arms too. Christ willing, that joyous time will not be too far away. Until then, may God keep you safe.

He had signed his name at the bottom of the missive, his hand neat and compact, showing none of the boldness and generosity of love that she craved. The last paragraph expressed tender sentiments but in an obligatory fashion, or perhaps she was expecting too much? A letter had to go through many hands on a journey of this length, and it was not unlikely that intimate details might be read by others.

With a soft sigh she folded the parchment and sat with it in her lap. The sky darkened from dusk to true dark, but she remained where she was, wondering what Simon was doing, how he was faring and if he truly was thinking of her the way that she was thinking of him.

CHAPTER 34

Dorylaeum, Anatolian Plateau, June 1097

The night sky was a heavy blue, thickly populated with stars. Beside the small settlement of Dorylaeum on the trade route through Antioch to Jerusalem, the crusader army had encamped for the night – or half of it had. To ease the foraging conditions, the leaders had split the army. The Norman contingent were the vanguard, the southern French and Lorrainers were marching a day behind.

Simon had pitched his tents beside a spring of sweet water and the soft sound it made as it bubbled up from beneath the ground was cool and soothing. The day had been as hot as a bread oven, but with the sunset had come a chill wind and he was glad of the warmth of the white fur cloak. Hundreds of campfires surrounded his position, islands of orange heat and light in the stony darkness. The voices of men, the notes of flute and bagpipe, the high-pitched laughter of women rose and mingled on the night air with smoke and cooking smells.

Four days ago they had marched from Nicaea. The wounded had remained behind, and under the supervision of the Byzantine army were restoring and repairing the defences damaged during the siege. Absently rubbing his left leg, he wondered if he should have stayed with them. The area surrounding the old healed break was red and inflamed. It had been troubling him for more than a week and was gradually worsening. A physician had told him to wash the area in strong, hot vinegar twice a day, but thus far the treatment was having no effect.

'Your leg is bothering you?'

He turned from his musing to regard Sabina, who had emerged from her small canvas shelter and was studying him anxiously.

'A little,' he said in an offhand manner designed to make little of the difficulty. 'There are times when it has flared up before, but it has always subsided.'

'But usually you have been able to tend and rest it,' she said. She shook out the goatskin rug she held in her hands and knelt down on it before the fire.

'That I can do when we come to Antioch.'

'If you reach it alive,' she said grimly. 'This campaign eats men whole.' She tossed two lumps of charcoal from the supply sack into the small circle of glowing heat and watched the sudden dance of flame.

'Indeed, but no one who set out expected the road to Jerusalem to be easy,' Simon replied and studied her from his eye corner. For the first weeks after her husband's drowning she had moved through the world with as much animation as a child's straw doll, uncaring, interested in nothing. Gradually, however, she had begun to emerge from her trance. It was a slow, painful process. Seldom a day went past when she did not weep for her loss, usually when she was at prayer, but in the between times she had found a kind of balance. Occasionally she even smiled.

In return for Simon's care and protection, she had undertaken the task of laundress and cauldron tender to him and his men. She had her own small shelter, which she pitched beside theirs, and although she mostly preferred to keep aloof she would occasionally join their fire with a piece of mending, or come, like now, to warm herself and contemplate.

'Mayhap, but it is a hard road for a man to travel just to feel righteous about himself,' she said softly. 'You should turn back, before it is too late.'

Simon laughed without humour. 'My leg is not as bad as all that,' he said. 'Besides, I am not just travelling this road in order to feel righteous about myself.'

'Then for what?' Her eyes were dark in the firelight, her skin cast in pale gold. Between her slightly parted lips he could see the moist gleam of her teeth.

He hesitated. 'I am not sure that you would understand,' he said. 'Certainly my wife did not.'

A faint smile curved her lips. 'I am not your wife.'

There was something of her old spirit in the remark, and Simon felt a spark kindle beyond the compassion and pity that had been his response towards her thus far. 'But you are a woman.'

'I see. And more likely to understand your wife than you.' Her smile deepened.

'I suppose so, yes.'

'Then tell me, and let us know for sure.'

The challenge hung between them in the soft night air and Simon realised that if he took it up the level of intimacy between them would change. He needed the diversion. He did not want her to retreat to her shelter and her shell. Taking a stick of kindling, he drew a spiral pattern in the soil. 'I broke my leg when I was a young squire in King William's household,' he said. 'For weeks on end, I had to lie abed while the bones knitted. It was a bad break and, although it did mend, the damage was irreparable. I was left with a limp and frequent pain. Some of this you must already know from the past.'

Sabina nodded. 'But you concealed it well,' she said. 'When we were younger I never gave it any consideration. To me you were just the King's squire Simon, with a new hawk to train and a certain way about you . . .' She looked down quickly, and the firelight made shadowy fans of her dark lashes.

'As I remember, you had a certain way about you too,' Simon said softly.

'It was a long time ago.' She plucked at the goatskin on which she was sitting as if performing a task of monumental importance.

'Not so long,' he said. 'I still have Guinevere in the mews at Huntingdon, and she still flies truer than many a younger hawk.'

'She was a good bird, and you trained her well,' Sabina said. 'Even if you were distracted on occasion.' She glanced at him, then down again.

Across the night a woman's throaty laugh floated from one of the other campfires. Simon rubbed his leg and tried to ignore the heaviness in his groin. If not arousal, it ran the sensation very close.

'You were telling me why you are here,' Sabina prompted.

'It is because of those weeks that I spent cooped in a small room with only the walls for company. I had visitors, I had my lessons and other such joys to pass the time, but everyone and everything had to come to me. I was a prisoner, and even at that tender age I realised how much I had always taken for granted until then.'

She nodded thoughtfully. 'So now you seize every opportunity for new experience that comes your way lest it pass you by?'

'It is more than that, and less,' he said. 'I cannot bear to feel enclosed by four walls, and that is what happens when I stop. Matilda, my wife . . . I love her dearly, but she is content to dwell within the four walls that I fear. For her they represent security, not imprisonment.'

'That is true, I think, of many women and men,' Sabina said. 'The women build nests to raise their children, and the men go out into the world.'

He laughed at first, but as he reflected on her words realised how true they were. 'But you did not remain behind when your husband took the Cross?' He phrased the words as a question.

'No,' she said. 'I followed him because I did not want him out of my sight. Besides, I had no nest to protect and no nestlings to nurture any more.' Abruptly she rose and retired to her small shelter. He heard the swish of the flap dropping, and knew that she had retreated because she was hurt and wanted to cry. For one wild moment he contemplated going after her to comfort her pain, but common sense pinned him down and the moment passed.

Sighing, Simon tossed more charcoal onto the flames. Recently, a small inner voice had been suggesting that he was a long way from home, and that Matilda had been right to suggest that the grass on the other side of the hill was not necessarily better just because it looked different. His mouth curved as he imagined her in her precious garden, surrounded by the damp, scented blooms of a northern summer. The letter he had written during their rest in Nicaea would not reach her until the leaves were turning to brown and the apples on her tree ripening a speckled red and gold. By the time she cut the seal, he might be in Jerusalem . . . or he might be dead. And all because he had to know what lay over the horizon.

To one side, four members of his troop were playing dice. He considered lecturing them about the profanity of their game but decided not to bother. They would only go behind his back. Even men filled with religious devotion needed their distractions.

He finished the wine and eased to his feet. A throbbing pain shot through his leg, making him gasp and swear.

'My lord?' One of the dice players raised his head, and eyed him anxiously.

'It is naught,' Simon said brusquely. 'Go back to your sport.' He limped to his own tent and ducked through the flap, waving away Turstan when the young man would have attended him. 'I need nothing else this night,' he said. 'Do whatever you wish.'

'Sir.' Turstan saluted and went to join the dice players.

Simon reached for his wineskin and took several long swallows of the dark Byzantine brew. Careful to avoid jolting his leg, he eased down onto his pallet and closed his eyes. The stuffing was made from several fleeces culled from the flocks that grazed on the fenland at his manor of Ryhall and suddenly it seemed to him that he was standing among the flocks, inhaling their ammoniac smell, and listening to their bleating as they grazed the rich summer meadow. His legs were sound and he went striding among them, seeking the path that ran towards the woods on the far side. The sheep scattered, bleating reproachfully, and he became aware of a figure standing on the edge of the woods, waiting for him. A tall man, copper-haired, blue-eyed, wearing a cloak with a white fur lining. His fist grasped a huge battleaxe, held in a way that said he was on guard but not about to strike. A red line, thin as scarlet thread, encircled his neck.

Simon stared. He was not afraid. He knew that he must be dreaming and that he could wake himself if he so chose. But he wanted to see where the dream led.

As if reading his thoughts, Waltheof smiled. 'Just one step further,' he said. 'Is that not what you have always wanted, Simon? One more step to prove that you are as able as any man with two sound legs?'

Simon looked down. 'I do have two sound legs,' he said.

'And I have a head on my shoulders.' Waltheof answered, and turning on his heel walked into the dark forest. Simon hesitated, then followed him. It was what he was meant to do, he was sure of it. Otherwise, why would Waltheof have been waiting for him?

The trees closed around them and Simon's eyes widened to full stretch, trying to pick out the path under the darkness of the branches.

'Where are we going?' he demanded.

'Patience,' his companion said. 'I have something to show you.' He took him deeper still so that light and air seemed little more than memories. The musty, overpowering smell of fungus and woodrot was all pervading. Somewhere a pack of wolves was howling and the hair prickled erect on his nape as he realised that the sound was coming closer.

Waltheof strode on grimly and Simon fixed his gaze to the flash of white that was the lining of the bearskin cloak because

that was all he could see. Behind him he swore he detected the
soft pad of paws on the leaf litter of the forest floor. Waltheof
stopped and Simon bumped into him. He was solid and alive,
not a being without substance as Simon had half expected.

The wolves were very near; the sound of their howling filled
the wood, bouncing off the trees, filling his head. Rancid breath
heated the back of his neck. Simon groped at his belt but he
carried not so much as a knife to defend himself. He looked at
Waltheof, at the huge Dane axe in his hand.

'I cannot help you,' Waltheof said. 'You chose to follow me
into the unknown. Now you face it.' Before Simon's gaze, his
companion's solidity melted away. Something thudded at his
feet, and looking down Simon saw the gleam of a skull as it
came to rest against the toe of his boot. It grinned at him full
stretch, no lips to conceal the hugeness of its mockery. And
beyond it he perceived other skulls gleaming, row upon row,
filling a clearing in the trees.

'God help me,' he croaked through a parched throat. The
wolves attacked. Their howls claimed the hollow of his own
skull and although he could not see them he could feel their
vicious teeth and claws ripping the life out of him.

'My lord, wake up, wake up!'

Gasping, choking Simon burst out of his nightmare into the
cold, pure air of reality. The mauling of the wolves became
Turstan's hands shaking him, but the howls remained. Sharp,
loud, ululating.

'My lord, wake up. The Turks are upon us!'

'What?' Simon struggled off his pallet. Pain roared down his
leg like a lion, and for a moment he could not move. By the flick-
ering light of a cresset lamp set dangerously on a campstool he
saw that Turstan was wearing a quilted gambeson and mail shirt.

'Quilij Arslan is here with his entire army!' The young man's
voice was pitched high and almost breaking with excitement
and fear. 'He's surrounded the camp!'

Simon's heart had already been pounding from the vividness
of his nightmare. Now it drummed in his ears and his leg throbbed

in time with each hard, swift stroke. Turning awkwardly, he reached for his own padded tunic and hauberk.

Turstan helped him with swift efficiency, his fingers nimble despite his high state of agitation.

'They have not attacked yet?' Foolish question. Once witnessed, a Turkish assault could never be forgotten. They sped in on their swift, manoeuvrable little horses, fired arrows from their short but deadly bows, and whisked out of range again, maddening as gnats, constantly biting and darting away. Their swords were curved like shallow half-moons and so sharp that they could slice off a man's wrist and he would not notice until he saw the blood and his severed flesh twitching on the ground at his feet.

'No, my lord – but it cannot be long. As soon as first light strikes the horizon . . .'

First light, so that the archers could see to mark their targets and the horses would not stumble on the ground. Latching his swordbelt, collecting his helm, his eyes still crusted with sleep, Simon ducked out of his tent, gazed eastwards and saw a thin oystershell rim of dawn on the horizon.

Sabina was already out of her shelter. Sleeves rolled up, she was briskly assembling costrels and pails.

'There is always need of water if there is to be a battle,' she said by way of greeting.

Simon nodded brusquely. 'See if you can find linen for bandages too – raid my coffers if you must.'

She acknowledged him with a wave of her hand, her back already turned as she headed for the spring to fill her vessels.

Simon heeled about and limped towards the tents of the Norman leaders. They needed to organise with unprecedented speed. As soon as the light hit grey, the Turks would attack.

He arrived at the muster point at the same time as Ralf de Gael and Stephen of Aumale, both of them mail-clad and looking pensive and alert. Count Bohemond of Taranto, one of the senior Norman leaders, sat on his horse before his tent, flanked on either side by Robert of Normandy and Stephen of

Blois. Bohemond was a tall, muscular warrior with brutal features and a voice that could pierce a shield wall at fifty paces, a man whom others followed confidently into battle, for, although this was a holy crusade, Bohemond of Taranto was graced with the Devil's own luck.

Now he raised that magnificent voice and bellowed their battle plan across the paling sky. 'There are too many of them to face on horseback,' he cried. 'If we ride out to meet them, they will sow our ranks with death from their bows. I have sent a messenger with all speed to Raymond of Toulouse that he may bring the rest of our army to our succour.'

'So if we do not attack, what do we do? Sit here like trussed chickens and let them take us?' demanded a vociferous knight standing next to Simon.

Bohemond looked irritated. 'We form a defensive ring until the others arrive to reinforce us,' he said. 'Let the women and the footsoldiers draw in all our tents and pitch them close by the spring. The women and those who are unable to fight will receive the wounded and supply water to the fighting men. Let the knights with the best armour dismount and form a ring of steel around the camp.'

'That is preposterous!' shouted the knight. 'I would rather die charging the enemy than play the coward.'

'No one is asking you to play the coward,' Bohemond retorted, baring his square white teeth. 'By your own words, you play the fool. If you seek to be the most courageous, then take up your shield and join the front line.'

The knight glowered, spat on the ground and shouldered his way back through the gathering.

'Those who want to die for Christ now can go with him,' Bohemond cried. 'Those of you who want to live to see Jerusalem, follow my command.'

A few knights, mostly the companions of the first one, turned and left, but most men stood their ground and remained to receive more detailed orders.

Ralf de Gael laid a slender hand on Simon's shoulder. 'I saw the way you were limping when you came to the meet,' he murmured. 'I hope that you are not going into the fight.'

Simon stiffened beneath De Gael's concerned touch. By his suggestion, the Breton lord had just made the outcome inevitable. 'I can stand,' he said coldly, 'and likely make a better task of hefting a shield than walking hither and yon bearing pails of water.'

De Gael looked wry. 'It was not my intention to hurt your pride, rather to save your body,' he said.

'My lord, the intentions you have never had have always been the ones that are most damning,' Simon snapped and, turning his back on the Breton, went to organise his troops. Although pain tore through his leg, he forced himself to stride out, full aware that De Gael was watching him.

Just before the sun broke over the horizon the Turks attacked, swooping upon the crusader camp on their light, swift horses. Even while his gut somersaulted with a rush of fear at their assault, Simon still found a space to admire their athletic, almost languid grace as they fired arrows from the backs of their galloping mounts. Some rode in closer and hurled javelins over the tops of the Norman shield wall, seeking to penetrate the closed ranks.

Men screamed and fell as they were hit; others ran into the gap to take their place. Simon's kite shield, blazoned with a simple cross of gold on a red background, protected him from chin to ankle. Even if an arrow did pierce the seasoned lime-wood, it still had to punch through his mail and quilted linen undertunic before it found flesh. However, there was a price to pay for being so well protected. As the sun climbed in the sky, it heated the iron rivets on hauberks until they burned to the touch, and turned burnished steel helms into cooking pots. Sweat poured out of Simon like water from a leaky bucket, and the weight of his shield grew so heavy that it was almost like bearing a full-grown man on his left arm. He gulped hot air through his mouth and gained no respite. Sweat streamed into his eyes, stinging with salt, blurring his vision until he saw everything through a veil of salty moisture he could ill afford to lose. His leg pulsed and throbbed until bearing weight upon it was agony, but bear it he did, for to have withdrawn would have endangered the defensive line.

Every hour the front ranks retired to the back of the line for a respite from the assault of arrows and javelins while the women and non-combatants came amongst them with cooling horns and ladles of water from the spring. Staggering, feeling sick and disoriented, Simon gave up his place to the knight who touched his shoulder, and went to take a brief rest.

Sabina was waiting for him, a bucket at her feet. 'You must drink slowly else you will spew it all back up,' she told him as she dipped a wooden cup and held it out brimming. His hand was shaking so badly that he could scarce unfasten his mail aventail and lift the cup to his lips. More than half of the precious liquid spilled down his chin.

'You are not well.' Her grey eyes filled with concern. 'You should not be among the fighting men.'

'Christ, not you as well,' he snarled. 'I am as fit to fight as any soldier out there. Even if my body weakens, my spirit will hold me to the task.'

'Your stubborn spirit,' she amended grimly, but did not try to dissuade him further. 'Sit,' she said, indicating a campstool. 'And do not say that you have no desire to do so. All I need do is push you and you will fall down.'

Simon tried to glare at her, but his eyes crossed. He tottered the two steps to the stool and slumped down upon it. Not just his hands were trembling, but his entire body. He handed the empty cup back to Sabina and she refilled it. But instead of giving him the cup to drink, she gently removed his helm and poured the water over his head. Simon gasped, as much with pleasure as shock. The cold deluge trickled down the back of his neck and seeped into the sweat-soaked fleece of his gambeson. Twice more she doused him before she let him drink again. Simon was so parched that he thought that however much liquid he absorbed, it would never be enough to satisfy.

Taking his helm, Sabina began binding it with torn strips of wet linen. 'To stop the heat of the sun,' she said. 'And you should wear a tunic over your mail, like some of the Byzantines do.' She handed him a length of silk cloth in which she had slit a head opening. It was a tabard, improvised from some of the cloth Simon had brought from Constantinople. He had intended it as a gift for Matilda, a dress length to make a court robe. The cut had ruined it for such use, but he did not complain. Anything that mitigated the appalling heat of the battlefield was a blessing.

'Do you want food?'

Simon shook his head as he donned the silk over his mail and tucked it down through his swordbelt. The very mention of the word made him feel violently sick.

'Will we succeed?' she asked, 'or are we going to be massacred here?' Her voice was calm and flat. She had faced death when the galley had capsized, and seen it claim her children and her husband. It had marched as her constant companion, and for the moment she was numb.

Simon shrugged. 'If the second army can reach us in time then all will be well,' he replied, 'but I do not know for how long our men can hold the ground in this heat. Still,' he added quickly, 'the Saracens do not have an infinite supply of arrows and javelins. They must run out if we can only hold them off for long enough.' With an effort he lurched to his feet and swayed. The pain in his leg was agonising. Sabina filled his carrying costrel with water and he drank another cupful before he slipped his left arm through the leather grips on his shield.

There was a yell from the Norman ranks and Simon jerked round. Beside him Sabina craned on tiptoe to see what was happening. A conroi of horsemen forty strong had broken out from the Norman lines and was charging down on a retreating cluster of Saracen archers. Bohemond, who had arrived that moment at the springs to check on the wounded and take a drink, hurled his cup to the ground.

'God's Holy Face, the fools!' he roared. 'I gave no order. Who dares defy me?' He thrust his way through the battle lines like a plough through soil. A horn sounded to call the men back, but went ignored.

The Norman horses were slower than the light desert mounts of the Turks and were unable to catch the fleeing bowmen. A fresh wave of Saracens rode out to support their comrades and intercepted the Normans with a fierce rain of arrows. The knight's charge broke up in confusion as a hail of deadly barbs hit horses and men. Scimitars flashing, the Turks took advantage and moved in for the kill.

Simon watched one man fall, an arrow in his shoulder. His foot was tangled in the stirrup leather and his panicking horse dragged him across the stony ground at a hard gallop. His screams for help pierced the sky, and then the screams stopped as a rock shattered his spine. Sabina looked away.

'God have mercy,' Simon whispered as he watched scimitars flash in the harsh white light, and men fall. A handful of knights managed to break out of the ring of death and galloped back to their own lines, their shields quilled with arrows. The wounded were brought through to the water stations by the spring, and Simon recognised the impetuous knight who had been defying Bohemond at the dawn muster. Now his teeth were bared in agony and a black-feathered Saracen shaft protruded from his collarbone, the point forced in so deeply that extracting it would likely be impossible.

It was a high price to pay for folly, Simon thought, and he knew that he was in no case to pass judgement, for he had committed enormous follies of his own and was about to compound them. Hefting his shield, gripping his spear, he limped back into the dusty hell of the battle.

Towards noon Simon's shield took an arrow that punched through the limewood and his mail and sliced a flesh wound beneath his ribs. The impact of the barb made him reel, and because he was unbalanced due to his inflamed leg he went down. He heard the thunder of hooves, and from the corner of his eye saw a Turkish soldier swooping in, spear raised to throw. With a final, tremendous effort, Simon twisted his damaged shield back into position across his body. The spear thrummed home, opening up a jagged hole in the wood and pinning him to the ground through mail and gambeson. The move wrenched his leg and he heard himself scream. Red and black spots danced before his eyes and he briefly lost consciousness.

His awareness returned as he heard Sabina's voice urging him to drink and felt the rim of a cup against his lips. She was supporting his shoulders against her kneeling form and her violet-grey eyes were swimming with tears. He took a choking swallow of water and a tremor shook him. 'My shield . . .' he croaked. 'Have Turstan find my spare one.'

'Of course,' she murmured. 'He has just gone to look for it. You might as well let me tend you while you wait.'

He knew from the soothing tone of her voice that Turstan had done no such thing, but he was half insensible and in too much extremity to do more than mouth a feeble protest. An almighty roar went up from their ranks and he struggled to rise, certain that Quilij Arslan's men had broken through. The sound grew louder, crashing upon him, filling his ears.

'Be still.' Sabina laid a calming hand on his shoulder and pressed him back down. 'And be glad. The second army has come. We are saved.'

Her words joined the noise of cheering in Simon's head and seemed to swell inside his skull until he thought it would split. His awareness drifted and, although his eyes were open, they saw not the pitched tents and the busy women but a tall man with copper hair and a red ring at his throat, watching him, a poised battleaxe in his hand.

No matter how hard Simon had worked to hold his position during the battle of Dorylaeum, it was after the Turks had been defeated that his own real battle began. As well as the flesh wounds he had suffered, his left leg was now badly infected and he was drifting in and out of delirium.

'We cannot bring him with us to Antioch, the road is too difficult,' said Ralf de Gael when he paid a visit to Simon's camp. The army was due to march on the following morning and head towards Antioch, but the way led across harsh terrain where there was no water and the heat was intense. There was no room for stragglers on the march.

Sabina glanced at Simon, who was dozing feverishly in the shade of an open tent. 'Others have already told me, my lord,' she said softly. 'I know that if he takes such a route it will be his last journey. He must go home, whether he wills it or not.' She turned back to De Gael. 'I am willing to stay with him and tend to his wounds along the way. It was my husband's vow to see Jerusalem, not mine. I have no oath to keep.'

De Gael was silent and she wondered if she had said something wrong, for high colour flooded along his narrow cheekbones. With thin, graceful fingers he unfastened the leather pouch from his waist and tossed it to her. 'Here,' he said. 'This will help you on your journey.'

She caught it, and through the soft brown leather felt the solid reassurance of gold bezants. The crusaders who had been capable at the end of the battle two days ago had pursued the fleeing Turks and caught up with their baggage lines. Men who had been beggars at dawn had become as rich as kings by dusk.

'I do not need your charity, De Gael,' Simon croaked from his pallet. He had woken and turned a little to face the Breton, but it was obvious that the move had cost him dear. His complexion was pallid and droplets of sweat dewed his brow.

'I was not giving it to you but to the woman,' De Gael retorted, and walked over to Simon, his gait somewhat stiff from the muscles he had strained in the battle. 'If she is to care for you, then she deserves some reward to keep her loyal.'

Sabina's eyes blazed indignantly at the Breton lord's insinuation.

Simon gave a mirthless laugh. 'You set her worth too cheaply, my lord,' he said hoarsely.

De Gael looked puzzled. 'You mean I should offer her more?'

'I mean that her value lies in more than just gold.' Simon gave Sabina a look that in spite of its fever glaze struck her like an arrow.

'I see,' said the Breton with an arch of his brows.

'No, you do not. You have never seen.' Simon's lips curled in a grimace, but of pain rather than contempt. His eyes squeezed shut.

'My lord, he should be left to rest,' Sabina murmured, and was swiftly at Simon's side. Wringing out a cloth in a bowl of water, she laid it across Simon's brow. Her underlip was caught unconsciously between her teeth and two deep frown lines incised the space between her fine, dark brows.

De Gael nodded. 'I will take your prayers for yourself and Waltheof with mine to Jerusalem,' he said, 'and ask God to be with you on your journey home.' When Simon did not respond, except to gasp, De Gael hesitated then walked away, an air of resignation to his step.

Sabina let out her breath in relief, for his presence had set her on edge. Glancing round to make sure that she did not have an audience, she hitched up her skirt at the hip and tied the purse of gold to the waist belt of her braies.

'I have often heard men say that women keep their greatest treasure under their skirts, but now I have seen it with my own eyes,' Simon murmured weakly. His lids had opened again, but he was barely lucid. She saw the effort it was costing him as pride warred with debilitating pain.

She took the cloth from his brow, refreshed it in the bowl and replaced it. 'You stand need to waste your breath on folly when the journey will take all your strength and endurance,' she scolded. 'You do not have to pretend with me.'

He swallowed, feverish sweat shining on the movement of his throat. 'It is not for your sake that I am pretending,' he said through gritted teeth. 'But for my own.'

CHAPTER 35

Biting her lip, Sabina admitted Father Gilbert to the room in Nicaea where Simon lay. Fever had stripped his flesh to the bone, and she was terrified that he was going to die. In the mews she had dealt with the ailments of hawks, had saved the weakly ones from starvation by hand feeding them, had bathed infected eyes, had dealt with parasites and moult, all without difficulty. But she had been unable to save her children from fever and stiffening sickness and her husband from drowning. Now the man who had been her first sweet love was fading before her eyes, despite all that she could do.

The priest was here to confess Simon and shrive him of his sins lest his time was nigh. Sabina closed the door on the chamber and went into the courtyard behind the house. There was a marble fountain – nothing as grand as the marvels they had seen in Constantinople, but pleasing still. She sat down on a bench beneath a fig tree that offered cool green shade from the heat of the day, but she could not settle, and seconds later rose to pace the circumference of the courtyard, which, for all its pleasantness, felt like a prison. The Norman chirugeon who had attended Simon this morn had declared morosely that there was nothing to do but fetch an axe and chop off the infected leg. Simon had been lucid enough to declare that he would rather die than face such an ordeal. Indeed, he would rather be dead than lose his leg and the chirugeon had been dismissed, muttering darkly that only a priest could serve Simon now.

Sabina had heard that there was a Byzantine physician in the town, but the crusader troops were wary of his remedies and distrusted him as they distrusted all Greeks. It was rumoured that he fraternised with infidels. Aubrey, Simon's master-at-arms, had refused to fetch him, saying that he would not let a foreigner butcher his master. But with nothing left to lose Sabina was growing more inclined by the minute to seek him out.

The sun had shifted a degree on the dial when the priest emerged from Simon's chamber, his expression grave. Sabina saw Aubrey step forward to speak with him, then cross himself at the grave shake of the priest's head.

Sabina recognised the signals for they had been part of the preliminaries when her children were dying. 'I will not let it happen,' she said, clenching her fists in her gown and not caring that her words verged on blasphemy. Some priests said that it was God's will whether a man lived or died, and that caring for the sick should be more by way of comfort than hoping to save. But she was unable to embrace that notion with equanimity.

Father Gilbert left the house and she hurried after him, calling out in the hot, dusty street.

He turned, his silver brows raised in question. 'Daughter?'

Sabina wiped her wet palms on her gown. 'Please,' she said. 'Do you know where I can find the Byzantine physician?'

He considered her thoughtfully. 'If your purpose is to help your lord, I doubt that anyone but God can save him now,' he said. 'He will not agree to the removal of the limb and that is the only thing that might secure his life.'

'Even so.' She made a small gesture serve for the rest.

'Your zeal commends you, daughter, but mayhap it is misplaced.'

Sabina drew herself up. 'Mayhap it is, but I will not know unless I try. I have heard that the Byzantines know much of the ancient lore of healing. If this man cannot help then I have lost nothing. And if he can cure my lord, then it will not have been a lost opportunity.'

'You speak boldly for a woman.' Father Gilbert's tone was

more speculative than hostile. He folded his arms within his habit sleeves and considered her out of incisive blue eyes.

'I speak as I must. Lord Simon de Senlis was charitable to me beyond measure in Brindisi. Now loyalty binds me to do what I can for him in return.'

The priest nodded. 'You are not then his mistress,' he said drily.

'Indeed not!' Indignation burned Sabina's face. 'I am a widow of respectable reputation!' The words rang facetiously in her own ears. How respectable her reputation would be by the time she arrived home was open to debate.

'Then your loyalty towards this man does you great credit,' the priest said, inclining his tonsured head. 'I am acquainted with the house of the Byzantine physician and I will take you there.' He raised a forefinger, cutting off her words of gratitude. 'I will warn you that his services do not come cheaply and that he has a contempt for us at least as great as the contempt that we harbour for his kind.'

'I have enough to pay for his services,' Sabina responded, 'and I care not for his nature providing only that he is a competent doctor.'

The priest shrugged. 'That is open to debate, daughter, and a risk you take.' He began to walk, his sandalled feet sending out puffs of dust. Bowing her head, as was modest in the presence of a priest, Sabina accompanied him through the winding streets of Nicaea until they came to an arched alleyway with dwellings either side, their doors brightly painted and their stone walls fortress-thick. Dark-eyed black-haired children played a ball game in the narrow street. A woman was beating a woven mat out of an upstairs window and a small shower of dust and reed fragments shimmied to the ground. Disturbed from its basking by the debris, a brown lizard shot up the wall and disappeared into a dark crevice.

Pausing at a door that was coloured deep red, Father Gilbert knocked loudly. 'I am looking for Alexius the physician!' he cried, 'I have a sick man who needs his skills!'

The woman who had been beating the mat gave Sabina and her companion an unfriendly look and, retreating into the dark arch of the room, fastened the shutters with a smart rap. The children disappeared down an even narrower side alley, like the lizard into its crevice.

'Greeks!' snorted the priest. 'Now you understand why it is a waste of time.'

Sabina set her lips. 'I will not give up so easily,' she said and raised her own hand to knock at the red door.

Even before her knuckles had connected, a man appeared from around the side of the house, his expression decidedly grumpy. He was moving his tongue around the inside of his mouth as if clearing food from his palate, and indeed, a few crumbs of bread were trapped within his luxuriant black beard. A loose robe of blue linen with silk borders billowed around his tall, narrow frame.

He looked his two visitors up and down with irascible dark brown eyes. Sabina guiltily lowered her hand and put it behind her back.

'Can a man not eat his food in peace?' he demanded sourly. 'You Franks, you are barbarians!' He spoke Norman French with a heavy accent, but since Sabina could not even begin to comprehend Greek she was not going to carp at such a minor flaw.

'I am sorry to disturb you,' Father Gilbert said somewhat stiffly, 'but there is a sick man in need of your services and our errand is one of Christian mercy.'

'Hah, why come to me? You have your own physicians who are quite capable of "Christian mercy".' His tone was decidedly scornful. 'I have no desire to interfere with their learned treatments.' Flicking crumbs from his beard, he started to turn away.

'Wait . . . please – they have said that the only way is to remove his leg . . . and I know it will surely kill him,' Sabina cried.

Alexius the physician snorted down his nose. 'That is what

your healers always say. They hack pieces off people more readily than common street butchers.' However his manner thawed slightly. 'I will come,' he said. 'But I will promise nothing. You Franks only send for me in the last resort, when it is usually too late. Wait while I finish my meal and fetch my satchel. A few moments will make no difference.' He disappeared again.

'I warned you, daughter,' Father Gilbert said wryly.

Sabina managed a wan smile. 'In truth I can bear with his manner if he is able to do something for my lord.'

'Only last week, I stood by and watched your Frankish chirugeons kill a man,' said Alexius as he followed Sabina through the large wooden gates and into the courtyard of the house where Simon was lodged. 'He had taken a spear wound to the thigh and I had been treating him with poultices, but your people insisted that he would only recover if the limb was removed.' He gave a snort of derision. 'Needless to say, he parted company with this life almost as swiftly as they parted him from his leg with a war axe.'

'My lord has refused to submit to the knife,' Sabina said. 'He says that if he is going to die, it will be with his body intact.'

'Wise man,' said Alexius facetiously.

They entered the sick room, which was darkened because the shutters had been closed against the hot beat of the sun. Simon was thrashing in the midst of a fevered dream. Turstan, who was keeping watch at his bedside, leaped to his feet and looked anxiously at Sabina and the newcomer.

'It's all right,' Sabina said quickly. 'Master Alexius is here to help Lord Simon.'

'If he is not beyond help,' the Greek confirmed pessimistically and striding to the shutters unfastened the latch and threw them wide to admit a surge of hot, yellow sunshine. 'And that I cannot tell if I cannot see what needs to be done.'

Simon had cried out and thrown his forearm across his eyes at the sudden burn of light. Sweat glistened on his body, making it seem as if he had just emerged from a pool, and his eyes were an opaque fever-glazed gold.

The physician approached the bed and, drawing aside the light cover, gazed the length of his patient's body. He made a soft clicking noise between the slight gap in his front teeth and shook his head.

Sabina's stomach plummeted. 'Can you do anything for him?' she asked.

'I can do much for him, but whether he will live is another matter.' Removing his satchel, Alexius pushed back his sleeves. 'I will need hot water and fresh linen bandages.'

Sabina nodded and went to the door.

'And if you have some good, clear wine, then that too.' He stooped over Simon's bandaged, massively swollen leg and once more clucked his tongue.

'You are not taking it off!' Simon gasped and struggled upright against the soaked sheets and bolsters.

'Of course I am not,' Alexius said, his nostrils flaring with indignation. 'I am not one of your barbarous Frankish chirugeons.' He pressed one long, firm hand against Simon's brow. 'Your fever is high, I see, but not so great that you do not know what is happening to you. I am going to give you a drink that will dull your pain, and then I am going to clean and drain your leg and poultice the wound.'

Simon lay back, panting, and bared his teeth in the terrible semblance of a smile. 'Do you then challenge the priest who came here to shrive me in preparation to greet death?'

Alexius mirrored the smile with his own lack of mirth. 'It was the priest and the woman who came to fetch me,' he said. 'Father Gilbert's task is the comfort and saving of souls. My concern is with the flesh.'

Sabina returned with the requested items. She had thought that the wine was a vehicle for mixing the physician's nostrums – indeed, it was, but most of it disappeared down Alexius' throat in very short order and only a scant cupful was left for the patient.

'Drink this,' said Alexius, handing Simon a chalcedony cup filled with hot wine and herbs. 'It will make you sleep.'

'What's in it?' Turstan demanded suspiciously, his hand hovering close to his sword hilt.

Alexius gave him an irritated look. 'I believe it is what you Franks call a potion of dwale. It contains the juice of hemlock, white poppy and henbane, together with vinegar and briony.'

'Jesu, you will kill him!' Turstan started forward, an inch of steel showing at the rim of his scabbard.

'Put up!' Simon gasped at the young man. 'Think you if he kills me that he expects to leave this room alive!'

'It is the quantities that are crucial, not the contents,' Alexius said, unperturbed. 'A man can kill himself on wine alone if he drinks enough. This will do no more than dull your master's wits whilst I do what must be done.'

Turstan slotted the sword back into the scabbard but his frown remained. Filled with misgivings of her own, Sabina watched the physician hold the cup to Simon's lips. The taste must have been foul, for Simon grimaced, but he drank steadily until it was all gone.

Very soon his eyelids drooped and when Alexius raised Simon's arm and let it drop there was not the slightest response. Save for the rise and fall of his chest, the man on the bed might as well have been dead.

Alexius turned his attention to the infected leg and with a dexterity and speed too swift to follow set about draining and poulticing the wound. The stench was appalling and Sabina had to draw her wimple across her face. Turstan visibly paled, but steadfastly held his ground. Alexius seemed not in the least disturbed, all his concentration bent upon his task.

'I can see that this leg has been broken long ago,' the Greek said. 'The ill humour stems from this old injury.' He washed out the crater left by the abscess with warm salt water. 'Now it needs to be poulticed and bandaged,' he said, and snapped his fingers and pointed, indicating that she should pass him the hot water and the bandages.

Sabina forced herself through the barrier of her revulsion and came to the bedside with the items. Even lanced and cleaned, the wound looked so terrible that she did not think it could ever heal.

Alexius tested the heat of the water with his wrist and, with a satisfied grunt, poured about a quarter of it into a wooden bowl. Taking what looked suspiciously like a large hunk of mouldy bread from his satchel he broke it into pieces in the water and mashed it around until it formed a gluey, bluish-grey mass. This he packed into the wound and bound it firmly in place with the fresh bandages.

'So,' he said. 'We replace the dressing twice a day for a week and see how matters progress.' With a grunt of satisfaction he washed his hands in the remaining water and then applied himself to tending Simon's minor injuries from the battle at Dorylaeum. These he smeared with a thick application of honey before lightly bandaging.

'Leave him to sleep now,' he said. 'I am afraid that when he awakens he will have sore need of the pot, for his bowels will void the potion in a vigorous manner.' He gathered up his instruments and returned them to his satchel. 'I will come again this evening before the curfew.'

Sabina saw him to the door and presented him with one of the gold bezants given to her by Ralf de Gael.

Alexius smiled dourly as he took it. 'At least you pay in good Byzantine gold and not the common silver of the Franks,' he said.

'You do not think much of us, even though your emperor summoned us to help him against the Turks,' Sabina was stung to retort.

'I think you are a barbaric hoard,' Alexius said. 'And our emperor asked for a few trained mercenaries, not the rabble of zealots that has washed up against his walls. But I cannot fault your courage, or the endurance of your fighting men and the women who follow in their dust.' Inclining his head to her, he departed, a tall thin figure striding out like an ungainly wading bird.

Sighing, Sabina closed the door and returned to her vigil in the sickroom. She had done her best. Now it truly was in the hands of God and a Byzantine physician who obviously cared deeply about his craft, if not his patients.

CHAPTER 36

Nunnery of Elstow, Christmas 1097

'Is there news?'

Matilda had known that her mother was going to ask, but even so the question made her tense. 'Only the letter that arrived in September when they were preparing to leave Nicaea.' She shivered. The day was bitterly cold with snow threatening in the raw wind, but her mother had lit only the most meagre of fires in her chamber. Judith could have had grand apartments and as much charcoal on her fire as she desired, but she chose to live a Spartan life, bereft of colour. The embroideries of which she had once been so fond had been banished into one of two plain coffers standing against the side of the room, leaving the walls bare of all adornment save a large crucifix. Even the shutters were plain, with no hangings to exclude the draughts that blew through the wooden joints.

Moving with the stiffness of rheumatic joints, Judith went to one of the coffers, threw back the lid and drew out a green woollen mantle.

'Here, put this on. You are too soft.' She handed her daughter the garment and scooped more charcoal into the brazier with a small shovel. 'Your uncle Stephen wrote that they had a great victory against the Turks at a place called Dorylaeum, but that was in the summer. News takes so long to travel.' She crossed herself. 'I pray daily for their success and their safe return.'

'So do I.' Matilda thrust her head through the embroidered opening of the mantle and shook the folds down over her body. Little Matilda, who had been standing pressed against her skirts, now made a game of hiding under the bottom edge of the voluminous woollen garment.

Sour humour twisted Judith's lips. 'So now, as I once was, you are a Countess with a great burden of responsibility. There are dark shadows beneath your eyes, daughter. Are you sure that the task is not too great for you?'

Matilda shook her head. 'If there are dark shadows beneath my eyes it is because I do not sleep well alone,' she said. 'I do not have your love of solitude.'

Her mother gave a contemptuous sniff. 'Sooner or later, we all must sleep alone,' she said.

'I know that, and I would rather it was later. As to the matter of ruling my lands . . . I watched you do it when I was a child and I have absorbed much. I know which men Simon trusted and I trust them in his stead to see that matters run smoothly.'

Judith's eyes brightened with warning. 'So smoothly that you do not see that they may be stealing from you. It is never wise to trust anyone.'

For an instant her words conjured the spectre of Waltheof into the room. Moving stiffly, Judith came to stand behind her grandson and laid her vein-mottled hands upon his shoulders, thus suggesting without words that Matilda should have a care for the sake of future generations.

'I am not cheated,' Matilda said with quiet dignity. 'I do not close myself in my chamber and shut my ears. I keep myself busier than a bee in a hive, because only then, when I am utterly worn out with writs, courts, deeds and accounts, can I snatch a few hours' sleep. I know every servant's duty to me. I do not drive my people the way that I drive myself, but they know what I expect of them.' She gave a humourless smile. 'God help me, mother, but sometimes I feel as if your shadow stands at my shoulder.'

Judith's lips compressed. 'I can see how much you resent me,' she said. 'Even now, when we have made our peace. But I am not the shadow standing at your shoulder. You need to seek elsewhere for that.'

Matilda's complexion reddened as she absorbed the implication. It made her feel defensive because it was partly true. Perhaps she would never be free of either parent. 'I do not resent you,' she said. 'We are of the same flesh, that is all. In years to come, I see myself standing where you stand now . . . and it frightens me.'

Judith shook her head. 'Then you fear without cause, daughter,' she said, with what was almost grim humour. 'In my place you would build up the fire and embrace the comfort of a mantle. You do not have the taste for austerity . . . The passions you have are your father's, and they lie elsewhere. Go and live your life . . . not mine, or his.'

The somewhat awkward silence that followed her words was broken by the sound of the matins bell calling the nuns to worship. It was with a mutual sense of relief that mother and daughter went to join them, each having been given food for thought.

In church, Matilda knelt beside her mother and prayed for Simon's safe homecoming. Little Matilda wriggled like an eel and was only prevented from shouting at the top of her voice by the bribe of a piece of honeycomb to suck. Waltheof behaved beautifully, and seemed totally absorbed in the chants and the ritual. With shining eyes and parted lips, he hung on every part of the service. The sight was so odd in a small boy that it sent a frisson down Matilda's spine. Judith noticed it too, for, as they left the church she said, 'It is not usual for firstborn sons to enter the Church, but have you given thought to the notion?'

'I have.' Matilda watched her son skipping along the path, his shoes making scuff lines in the dirt. 'But it is too early to tell, and if I do not bear Simon another son Waltheof will have to live a secular life, whatever his vocation.'

Judith narrowed her eyes, the better to focus on her small grandson. 'You had best pray that your husband returns,' she said softly, 'and that you are both still fecund, for the child has a true devotion, and that is rare indeed.' There was such a desolate look in her eyes that all Matilda's irritation vanished, and in its stead she felt a surge that was almost compassion.

Simon opened his eyes and while his mind roused to the notion of a new day looked at the ceiling. It was painted with gold stars on a blue background so that it seemed to his waking gaze that he was looking at a night sky. The illusion was marred by a hanging lamp of opaque glass suspended on a chain and giving off a soft, translucent glow from the scented oil burning within. He let his stare travel around the room, taking in the richly coloured frescoes adorning the walls, the bed hangings of iridescent silk, the embroidered covers that had been stitched to mirror the strange ceiling. There had been so many night-mares and strange dreams of late that it took him some time to remember where he was and why.

'Good morrow, my lord,' said Sabina. 'I see you are awake at last.' She came to him across the room, her black hair tightly braided but uncovered in the privacy of the chamber. She was carrying a basket containing fresh bread, its surface painted with honey and slivers of nut, and a cup brimming with wine.

Simon sat up against the bolsters and felt the silk slide sensu-ously against his skin. 'I think so.' He managed a grin. 'It is difficult to sort dream from reality in a chamber like this.' He took the knife that lay in the basket and carved a chunk from the loaf. The warm, yeasty smell made his mouth water. After almost dying in Nicaea he had a fresh appreciation of the wonders of being alive. It seemed as if all his senses had been stripped of a dusty layer of familiarity and were now as sharp and new as the colours of spring. Hunger was perhaps the most intense. He had been too ill to eat for weeks and now his body was putting on the flesh it had lost to the burn of fever. Alexius the Byzantine physician had known his craft, and it was his knowledge, coupled with Sabina's vigilant tending, that had saved his life. After the draining of the abscess and within a couple of applications of the mouldy bread poultices, the fever had diminished and Simon's leg had begun to heal. Two weeks after Alexius' first visit, they had left Nicaea for Durazzo. Simon acknowledged that, despite his recovery, he was not strong enough to return to the crusade trail. The army was laying siege to Antioch, and conditions were such that anyone who took sick died. If he rode to Antioch, he would become one more mouth to feed, followed by one more corpse to bury. Even if the hills were greener on the other side – which now he doubted – for the nonce he no longer wanted to see them.

Sabina sat down on the enamelled coffer at the bedside and leaning over helped herself to a chunk of the bread. Sunlight poked through the slats in the shutters and shone on her braids, putting a rainbow sheen on the raven-black. Her eyes were the soft, violet-grey of a dove's breast and her face the pure oval of a Madonna's, but she ate with the gusto of a soldier. The contrast touched and amused him. When a delicate flush tinged her cheek, he realised that his scrutiny was too intense and he sent his gaze beyond her into the splendour of the room. Astonishing what a gold coin could buy. This dwelling belonged to a silk merchant who was absent on business and it was as magnificent as any palace in England. The walls were painted with figures so lifelike that Simon sometimes thought that he could see them breathing. The colours were deep and rich, and the artist had not stinted to use gold in the paint that delineated embroidery on the fine garments. The effect was opulent and heavy. Exquisite taste, but in the end too much for the eye to take in and the mind to absorb.

'Turstan has gone to the wharves,' Sabina said. Her voice was hesitant. 'Apparently there is a ship due to sail for Brindisi on the late tide.'

'Ah,' Simon nodded. It was the next step of their journey, back across the Bosphorus. He had told Turstan that they would begin searching for a ship today, and the young man was plainly eager to be about the task. Sabina, however, did not share that eagerness.

'The thought of a sea voyage troubles you?'

She forced a smile. 'Of course it does,' she said. 'I cannot help but remember . . . but I have no choice unless it be to stay here.' Abruptly she rose and paced to the window. 'I can endure. I have the strength.'

Simon studied her slender frame. 'I know you do,' he said quietly. 'I owe my life to it. If you had not fetched that physician . . . if you had not stayed at my side and tended me through the fever . . .'

She gave a harsh little laugh. 'That was not strength,' she said. 'That was fear. If I had lost you the way that I lost everyone else who was dear to me . . .' She folded her arms and hugged herself tightly, her back still turned.

'But you didn't lose me,' he said. 'And I am in your debt.'

'You owe me nothing.' Her knuckles tightened against the side seams of her gown. 'I was merely repaying what was owed, and if you offer me your kindness and gratitude I will kick you.'

A lazy heat wound through Simon's groin. It was a sensation that was becoming increasingly frequent as he drew away from sickness into full health. 'Neither of those,' he said hoarsely.

She turned then to look at him. The sunlight shone through her pupils, turning her eyes to the colour of opals. There was a long silence in which the tension built like steam under the lid of a cauldron. One step further. Simon swallowed. His mouth was dry, his groin hot and heavy. She licked her lips and moved closer, drawn as if there was an invisible thread looped around her belt.

Once out of the slanting sunlight, her eyes were quenched to dark violet. His lust became a physical pain, all the sharper for having been quenched for so long. Instead of running

slowly, the sap was leaping through his veins, congesting them
until he thought they would burst.

She paused at the foot of the bed and looked at him. Naked
from his sleep, his body was still thin from his illness, each rib
delineated, but there was wiry strength in the long muscles of
his arms and his flat, firm belly. Face, throat and hands were
tanned oak-brown by the burn of the Eastern sun; the rest was
as pale as new milk. His gaze was like molten wine. She wanted
to push her hands through his sleep-tangled hair and lie with
him. Touch him, confirm the life force flowing through both
of them. It had been so long since she had been held and wanted
and loved. Her cheeks burned. There was moisture between
her thighs.

He extended his hand. With trembling fingers she took it,
felt sweat leap between them and then the wild, hot burn of
longing, and longing assuaged.

CHAPTER 37

Sabina and Simon rode into the convent of Evreux at the same time as the rain. The November skies were grey and heavy with moisture and a bitter wind was blowing from the north. The nunnery boasted a fine timber guesthouse, with feather stuffing in the pallets rather than straw, and wax candles that burned with a clear, yellow light. There was water provided for washing and a deep fire pit in the centre of the room sent out wafts of brazen heat.

Sabina sat on one of the pallets in the guest dormitory. There were twenty in all, arrayed down either side of the room. Someone's travelling satchel and a clean pair of shoes had claimed one of the mattresses, but for the nonce she was the only occupant. The stables were situated beneath and a glance out of the arched window showed her two lay workers busy in the cobbled yard, their hoods raised against the drizzle. She watched Simon cross the yard and speak to one of them. His limp was more pronounced since the old leg injury had flared up and he could no longer make even the slightest pretence of hiding it. However it had worked to his advantage. The mention he had been on crusade and at the battle of Dorylaeum, coupled with evidence of injury, meant that the doors of abbey guesthouses and castles alike had been flung open to them with effusive welcome.

She watched the familiar gesture he made of pushing his hair back off his face, his other hand clasped around his belt. Her stomach twisted. She was going to miss him terribly . . . but it was for the best.

That morning in Durazzo was branded in her memory. Their lust had been incandescent, so fierce that the first time it had lasted no more than a dozen racing heartbeats. The second time the blaze had been slower to kindle, a lazy burn of pleasure that had grown hotter by steady, calculated degrees until the time had arrived to free the fire and let it immolate them.

It had to happen, she thought. In a way, it had been the closing of a circle that had begun in her father's mews when they were little more than children. There was no regret on either side, but they had not lain together again and they had avoided situations during the journey up through Italy and France where they might have succumbed.

She heard him climb the wooden staircase to the dormitory and listened to his steps, alternately firm and hesitant. By the time he opened the door, she was on her feet and facing it. A nunnery guesthouse was not a setting to put temptation in their way, but it was the first time they had been alone in each other's company since Durazzo.

'You are sure you want to stay here?' he said, casting a glance around the chamber.

She folded her hands together and faced him squarely. 'Quite sure.'

He cleared his throat. 'You know there is a place for you in my household, should you wish it.'

She shook her head. 'You mean well, but you are wrong. Where would I go – home in your entourage to your wife? What would I do? I have no skill with an embroidery needle, nor any desire to become a lady of the bower.'

He winced at her assessment. 'Mayhap you are right,' he sighed, 'but I would not have you think that I intend abandoning you. The least I can do is offer you a roof and protection.'

'It is noble of you, but I need neither. You took me in when

Saer died and I was grief-wild. I like to think that I repaid your support in full measure when you were sick. There are no debts. We settled the last of them that day in Durazzo.'

Their eyes met. She saw understanding in his, and a renewed blaze of gold like fire. 'You truly desire to become a nun?' he asked. 'After everything that you . . . that we . . .' He made a gesture that served for the rest, a gesture that encompassed the bed.

'After everything,' she said firmly, although her cheeks reddened. 'And not because I have suddenly grown penitent or ashamed. I have thought about taking the veil ever since the road to Dorylaeum.' She looked down at her clasped hands. 'Between then and Durazzo, between Durazzo and now I have done much praying and thinking and my mind is set. If the nuns of Evreux will have me then I will join them – for the peace of my soul, and for the love of God who has taken so much and given it back. For Saer and my children who did not live.' Her voice almost wobbled but with a supreme effort she steadied it and found a smile.

He turned to the window, and biting his thumbnail gazed out. The sound of the rain rustled around them and the voices of the grooms floated through the open shutters. 'I have no doubt that the Abbess will welcome you with open arms,' he said. 'A purse of Byzantine gold and the company in which you have arrived are sure to guarantee you a position.'

'Who knows. One day I may become an abbess myself.'

He made a shrugging gesture. 'If you set your mind to the matter, I do not doubt you will succeed. But to renounce the world . . .' He looked at her sombrely over his shoulder. 'It is a great stride to take.'

She came to the window and, wrapping her arms around him, laid her head on his breast. If the grooms looked up, they would see the embrace, but she did not care. 'No,' she said, with a tremulous smile. 'Like that day in Durazzo – it is but a single step.'

Waltheof genuflected, rose to his feet, and carefully laid the garland of evergreen and red-berried holly at the foot of his grandfather's tomb. He loved coming to Crowland, and it was always with great solemnity and sense of occasion that he would enter the chapel and make his offering. His mother visited the abbey several times a year. The last occasion had been late summer and the place had been crammed with pilgrims and dusty travellers, all present to venerate the bones of his grandfather, who, by the ordinary people at least, was viewed as a saint. The blind had been made to see, so it was said, and the lame to walk. Propped against the wall near the tomb were several crutches left by grateful folk who claimed to have been cured by their visit to the tomb. To have such power, even in death, fascinated the boy.

Today, he and his family had his grandsire to themselves. A light snow was sifting down outside, the wind was bitter and most folk were hugging their hearths and waiting out the winter like hibernating animals. Waltheof, however, was warm within several layers of wool and a hooded mantle lined with marten fur. His little sister was grizzling, but then she was a baby and always did. His mother crossed herself and rose from her own knees. Briefly she laid her hand on the silk pall covering the tomb housing, her gesture tender and sad.

Waltheof thought that she looked very pretty. She was wearing her best winter gown of reddish-gold wool with little lozenges of gold thread embroidered at the hanging cuff and deep neck opening. Her veil was fluted and bound at her brow with a braid band stitched with small garnets, and her thick, bronze-coloured braids were twined with red ribbons. In a way that he couldn't understand she reminded him of the statue of the blue-cloaked Madonna in the church at Northampton. The clothes and colours were different, but in his young mind some element still drew the two together.

They left the church house and trooped out into the frozen air. Waltheof gazed up through fluttering lashes at the light fall of snowflakes and stuck out his tongue in the hopes of catching one and feeling it melt.

There were riders waiting in the courtyard. Smoky steam rose from the nostrils of their horses and harnesses jingled as the beasts stamped their hooves on the frozen ground. One of the men had dismounted and was gazing intently towards him and his mother and sister. He looked familiar to Waltheof, but the boy could not quite place him. His mother had stopped, although her gown and mantle still swished gently with the impetus of her last step. She was as rigid as the Virgin statue, and twice as pale.

'Dear, sweet Jesu,' she whispered. Her hands opened and closed at her sides. He watched the movement of her fingers, fascinated by the gleam of light on her gold rings. And then she cried, 'Simon!' in a breaking voice, and ran to fling her arms around the man whom now Waltheof suddenly recognised.

At his back, Helisende lightly placed her hand on his shoulder. 'Your papa is home from the crusades,' she told him, a shiver of emotion in her own voice. 'Praise God. Now perhaps all will be well.'

The snowfall grew heavier and more persistent. Although they could have stayed at the guesthouse in Crowland, and Ingulf would have been more than pleased to house a newly returned crusader and exchange stories, Simon was uneasy with the surroundings, and preferred to ride on to the hunting lodge at Fotheringhay.

During the journey he spoke little. He took Waltheof up before him, wrapping the child tenderly in his cloak. Little Matilda clamoured to ride on his saddle too and he obliged, but the novelty quickly wore off and she soon demanded to be returned to the familiar arms of her mother.

By the time they reached the hunting lodge the snow was fetlock deep on the horses and the snowflakes were almost as large as communion wafers.

'Won't last,' said the cheerful gatekeeper who came out to welcome them, a lantern wavering on the ash pole in his hand.

'Be gone in a couple of days. Will you be wanting the huntsmen to mark some game for you, my lord?'

Simon nodded. 'Some of the men might wish to hunt, and
it would be good to have fresh meat for the table.' He gently
lowered his son to the ground and then swung carefully from
the saddle. His leg was aching with the cold and he was tired,
hungry and, if the truth were known, unsettled. Matilda had
changed during his absence. Some of the yielding softness had
gone from her character, leaving it closer to the bone. Her edge
was a little steelier now, more of her mother's weight in the
scales when it had been her father's nature that tipped the
balance before. Her manner was brisk and accustomed as she
spoke to the gatekeeper and then to the attendants who had
made haste to prepare the hunting lodge with only a short
advance warning by the herald she had sent ahead. But then,
Simon thought, he had left her to her own devices, and she had
been forced to stand alone.

A blazing fire had been kindled in the lodge's central hearth
and a cook was hastily assembling a cauldron of leek pottage
while an assistant mixed dough for savoury griddlecakes.
Simon rubbed his hands and held them out to the fire. Aping
him, Waltheof did the same before dancing off to investigate
the other rooms in the lodge.

Matilda brought Simon a brimming cup of wine. They had
said little to each other since the first, breathless greeting. It
was all held behind a dam, waiting for the first breach to be
made, and the words to come pouring through in an unstop-
pable tumult.

He took the cup and their fingers touched in the exchange.
A pink flush rose from her throat to her face and Simon felt a
responding warmth in the area of his crotch. He also felt a flicker
of guilt, but even for the sake of unburdening his conscience
he was not going to tell her about Sabina. Some things were
better left unsaid.

'What made you turn back?' she asked. 'I thought to be a
crusader's widow for a long time yet.'

The wine was a strong Gascon red and made Simon's throat sting. 'You were nearly a widow in truth,' he said. 'My leg became infected and I was only saved by the skills of a Byzantine physician and some dedicated nursing. By the time I was well enough to leave my bed, our army had moved on. I did not have the health to follow. Had I done so, my bones would be bleaching on a plain in Anatolia.'

A look of alarm widened her eyes but he saw her fight it down. Nor did she insist on finding him a chair or begin to fuss around him. Familiar ground had indeed shifted during his absence.

'Those of my men who wanted to stay have joined the troops of Stephen of Aumale.'

'Not Ralf de Gael?' Suddenly her voice was sharp with challenge.

He shook his head. 'No, I have no Bretons in my troop, and my English knights would leif as not follow De Gael.'

'Yet you made your peace with him?'

'Yes, I made my peace with him. What else was I to do? Challenge him to a trial by combat?' He breathed out hard. 'Every man makes mistakes in his life. God knows I have committed my own share of folly. De Gael took the cross to atone for the part he played in your father's death. I know that he has always been able to charm the birds out of the trees with that smooth tongue of his, but I can tell when a man is lying and when he is telling the truth, and I believe De Gael is genuinely remorseful.' He looked at her. 'Are you so unforgiving and vindictive that you will cling to your past grievances for the rest of your life?'

She gave him a narrow look. 'My English family are fond of their blood feuds,' she said. 'It is a tradition we have clung to time out of mind.'

'You would rather I had put my blade through De Gael's breast?'

'No.' She shook her head. 'He is not worth the sullying of good steel and the damning of your soul. Nor is he worth the bother of my hatred. He is *nithing* to me. Beneath my contempt.' She looked at him. 'Whatever you think, that is one demon that no longer rides me so hard.' She had spoken proudly, but her eyes had grown suspiciously liquid.

Simon's heart moved within him, stirred by compassion and love. Setting his cup down on the hearthstone, he pulled her round and drew her into his embrace. Her own arms swept around his neck and she clung tightly. He buried his face against the soft skin of her throat beneath the veil and felt the beating of her pulse. There was a faint perfume of lavender, and lemon balm, clean, enticing, unbearably erotic. She moved her head sideways and his lips slid across hers. He tasted the salt of her tears and through it felt the leaping response of her need. Her mouth was open, her thighs straining against his.

Their embrace was wild and primitive, no room for anyone or anything else, but eventually they had to surface to gasp for breath and with separation came a modicum of awareness. The servants, heads lowered and eyes discreetly averted, were going about the business of preparing the lodge for the guests. His men were arranging their baggage between the aisles of the hall and unrolling straw mattresses. Only the woman tending the cooking pot was close enough to hear what was being said and she was very busy with her griddle cake dough.

Waltheof came bounding back from his exploration and rushed up to his parents, a large deer antler clutched in his fist.

'See what I found!' he cried.

The need to focus on the child further restored sanity. Simon took the antler and admired it. Matilda smoothed her gown and wiped her eyes. While she composed herself, Simon explained to the boy in a less than steady voice that the number of tines on the antler meant that the stag had been six years old when he shed these particular horns.

'I daresay if we search the woods we might come across more sheddings if the huntsmen have not picked them up,' he said.

'Now?'

Simon grinned at his son's enthusiasm and shook his head. 'No, lad. My old bones need to rest first, and while the snowfall might not be as thick among the trees I have no desire to venture out again in this growing blizzard. Still,' he ran his fingers along the grooved yellowish-brown stem of the antler, 'this section here will make a fine hilt for a knife, and that can be made beside the hearth.'

The child nodded excitedly and dashed off to show his find to Helisende and his little sister.

Stooping to the hearth, Simon picked up his wine and found that it had grown warm from its proximity to the flames. 'When I was taken sick, I dreamed of your father,' he said, and gently shook the cup to swirl the dark contents. 'He came to me and showed me that the other side of the hill could hold terror as well as freedom. I do not know if it was a true vision or just a fevered dream, but it was one of the reasons I turned back.'

'And what of your crusader's vow?' she asked. 'Will you have a priest absolve you?'

'Mayhap.' He gave an uncomfortable shrug. To be quit of the vow entirely would be to close a door. He had been relieved to turn back – the wanderlust no longer rode him hard – but he still needed to see through the open portal. He watched his small son skip across the room and return to his side, the antler clutched in his hand. 'For the nonce I have a notion to build another church in Northampton and give thanks for my safe homecoming.'

Matilda relaxed and the expression in her eyes grew soft and warm.

'Can I help to build it too?' Waltheof demanded.

Simon smiled and ruffled the boy's red-gold curls. 'Of course you can,' he said. 'Looking after it will be one of your duties when you are a grown man.'

The boy beamed as if he had been given a present of great worth.

'You like buildings, do you?' Simon asked, diverted by Waltheof's enthusiasm.

'I like churches,' he said, and hared off again to show his

prize piece to one of the knights who was entering the hall after stabling his horse.

'My mother says that he has a natural vocation, and I believe she is right,' Matilda murmured. She looked through her lashes at her husband. They were spiky from her tears, but the effect, along with the slight reddening, only served to make the dark lapis colour of her pupils more luminous. 'One he cannot fulfil while he is an only son.'

Simon met the sidelong appraisal, and heat flared at his crotch, hot and deep. 'Then it behoves us to do something about it,' he said.

She looked over her shoulder. The last of the soldiers to enter from outside was just closing the door on a world of whirling whiteness. Candles glowed in all the sconces and the central hearth threw out a cheery red light. 'We have the time,' she said softly, and took his hand in hers. 'For a while, at least, whatever the state of the other side of the hill, you are not going to reach it.'

Matilda looked at the collection of small, innocuous brown bulbs that Simon had tipped out on the bed from their cloth pouch. 'What are they?'

He pillowed his hands behind his head and gave her a smile lazy with the repletion of lovemaking. 'For that you will have to take the word of the man who sold them to me. He says that if you bury them in the garden during the autumn they will produce the first flowers of spring. Milk flowers he called them, and he said that the blooms are white and delicate, but robust nonetheless.'

'I will plant them the moment we are home,' she vowed, and scooped them carefully back into their pouch.

'You see,' he said, 'even when I was chasing my demons I thought of you and your garden.'

Matilda was less than impressed. 'And I thought of you every day,' she said. 'I rubbed my knees raw at first with prayer and lamentation.' Setting the pouch carefully to one side, she faced him. 'But I learned to live with it. It was like grieving. The ache did not go away but it became less in time. My children needed me, so did the people. Much as I wanted to crawl into the darkness and lick my wounds, I couldn't.' Aware that her tone was growing accusatory and shrewish, she drew back from further recrimination. She had him now; that was all that mattered. And she could so easily have lost him. The scar on his leg and the hollow where the poison had eaten the flesh away was evidence of that.

'I did not mean to sound clever that I thought of you,' he said softly and unpillowed his hand to stroke a tendril of her hair. 'Perhaps it was more in the way of atonement for the way we had parted . . . and perhaps I was wondering what I was doing so far from home. When I bought them I wanted to imagine you planting those bulbs in your garden.'

Matilda was swept by a wave of tenderness and remorse. Leaning forward, she kissed him. 'You are home now,' she said. 'Let us not brood.' Deliberately lightening her tone, she drew away. 'I have gifts for you, too.'

'Other than the one you have already given me?' he grinned suggestively.

Matilda laughed and blushed. 'I do not think that I could dwell in a convent like my mother,' she admitted.

'Perish the thought.'

She went to her small travelling chest and raising the lid drew out a shirt of fine linen chansil and a tunic of blue Flemish wool, embroidered with a pattern of English interlaced work at cuff and hem and throat. 'I took the measurements from a tunic you left behind,' she said. 'It kept my fingers busy when I had naught to do.' She did not add that for a time she had slept with his old tunic clutched in her arms for comfort, or that the act of making him a new one had been a way of adjusting to his absence.

'More than busy,' he said gruffly as he took the garments and examined the delicate stitchwork with wonder. 'I have never set eyes upon such fine needlecraft!'

Matilda warmed beneath the admiration in his tone and rejoined him on the bed. 'I don't know,' she teased, picking up the leg of one his hastily discarded hose. 'You seem to have sewn a very neat patch on this.'

The hesitation that followed was infinitesimal but it changed the atmosphere. What had been warm and intimate was suddenly strained. 'I cannot take the credit,' he said. 'One of the laundresses did our mending.' Suddenly he was very busy, donning the shirt, trying on the tunic.

'One of the laundresses,' Matilda repeated, with slightly narrowed eyes.

'She sewed and washed clothes for everyone,' he said in a cloth muffled voice. When his head emerged through the neck opening of the tunic, his gaze did not quite meet hers.

Matilda said nothing. She decided not to ask if Simon had been faithful to her during his absence. Crusaders might take a vow to be chaste while they were soldiers of Christ, but she knew that many did not succeed in keeping their oath. Simon might not be a sexual predator, but she knew his predilection for pastures new. Still, a laundress was no threat to her position, and there had been no sign of such a woman among his entourage. Thus she spoke no more on the matter, and if she did not dismiss it from her mind, neither did she dwell on it with anguish.

CHAPTER 38

Northampton, Christmas 1097

'Shall I put it here?' Waltheof asked. He wafted a brightly coloured knot of braid at his mother then stood on tiptoe to place it in the bare branches of the apple tree.

'Yes, sweetheart, just there,' Matilda paused in her own decoration of the tree to watch her son stretch out, the tip of his tongue protruding between his lips as he concentrated. She smiled wistfully. Her mother had never held with the ceremony of honouring a tree so that it would be fruitful during the next season. It was as pagan as the elf in the well, she said; nonsense, not to be tolerated. But her father had always permitted his people to 'wassail' the trees and Matilda had encouraged the custom.

Simon lifted his small daughter and helped her hang a row of silver bridle bells along a sturdy twig. 'This time last year I was kicking my heels in Brindisi and waiting for the spring,' he said. 'It seems a lifetime ago.'

'It is a lifetime ago.' Stooping to the basket at her feet, Matilda picked up some false apples carved of wood by one of the knights who had a skill in such things. She handed them to their son and glanced at her husband. 'You regret turning back, don't you?' she said shrewdly.

Simon wriggled his shoulders. 'In some small part, yes,' he admitted. 'I swore a vow, and I have always prided myself on holding to my word.'

'If you had held to it, you would likely be dead.' Matilda gave a small shiver.

'Yes, but honourably so,' he said with a wry smile. Taking one of the wooden apples he helped little Matilda to loop it on a high branch of the apple tree.

She bit her lip. 'Is that why you have not asked the priest to absolve you of your oath – because your business is unfinished?'

Simon pondered for a moment. 'While my vow remains open,' he said at last, 'it means that I have not given up. Mayhap it is more of a sop to my conscience than anything else, but if I go and ask for absolution it will mean that I have yielded.'

Matilda said nothing more. She did not really believe that he would set off again on another crusade to fulfil his oath, but she found it hard not to keep demanding constant reassurance. Hard, but not impossible. She had learned much during his absence, not least that she was strong if she had to be. It was only a matter of time before he would have to leave on the King's business anyway. There was war in Normandy, and Matilda daily expected a summons that Simon would have no choice but to answer.

That afternoon the second part of the ceremony was carried out and all the occupants of the hall gathered in the frosty garden grounds. Cups of steaming mulled cider were ladled out from a large cauldron and everyone joined hands and danced around the tree, exhorting it, as a representative of all the apple trees in the orchard, to grow strong and be fruitful in the coming year.

Dusk encroached, turning the world to silver blue as the first star shone in the sky. Laughing, filled with the pleasure of the moment, Matilda moved among the crowd. The hot cider had filled her with a delicious glow, and it almost seemed to her that her tree was glowing too, for the lanterns set around its base had gilded it with light.

Waltheof and some of the castle's children were playing a

game of chase, winding in and out amongst the adults, their squeals high-pitched and carrying in the twilit air. Little Maude toddled after them, bundled up in various layers of clothing topped by a sheepskin mantle.

Simon curved his arm around Matilda's waist from behind and nuzzled aside her wimple to kiss her throat. Smiling, she turned in his embrace and offered him her lips.

From the direction of the courtyard the sound of a shout and the whinny of a horse carried on the clear, cold air. Simon lifted his head from Matilda's like a hound catching a scent. She resisted the urge to hold him more tightly and turned with him to face the sound of intrusion.

'Surely the King will not summon you to Normandy so close to the winter feast?' She was unable to prevent the note of desolation in her voice.

But the summons was not for Simon, it was for her. From Elstow. Her mother was sick with a fever of the lungs and beyond any help but God's. If Matilda wanted to bid farewell, then she must come at once.

Dazed, she made sure that the messenger was given a cup of mulled cider and bade him to take food from the trestle laid out to one side of the tree.

'I must go to her,' she said.

Simon glanced at the sky, which had deepened beyond turquoise and into sapphire. 'At night?' he asked dubiously. His words emerged on a puff of white vapour.

'The morning may be too late.' She looked at him. 'I have to do this – for my sake and hers.'

He studied her thoughtfully, then gave a nod of acceptance. 'You will need torches for the road and a stout escort. Go and make yourself ready for the journey and I will order the horses saddled.' Squeezing her arm, he left.

The people danced around her tree, singing the Wassail, making merry. She felt as if she were looking through a window on a bright and gilded scene from which she had been forcibly expelled. Grimly, she pulled her gaze from the celebration and left the enchantment of the garden for the bleak and practical world beyond.

'You do not have to come,' she said to Simon when she found him in their bedchamber, donning a pair of thick chausses over the pair he was already wearing. He was also apparelled in the thick, quilted gambeson he usually wore under his armour.

'I want to,' he said. 'I have never truly made peace with your mother. Besides, you cannot go alone.'

Matilda felt a flash of resentment, keen as a recent wound. She went to her coffer and drew out woollen hose, and a thick pair of naal-binding socks. 'I have grown accustomed to my own company,' she said a trifle tartly.

He reached for the braid leg bindings to wind between ankle and knee. 'Don't you want me to accompany you?'

She bent her head to remove her boot and draw the sock over the one she was already wearing.

'Matilda?'

She lifted her head. 'Of course I want you to come,' she snapped. 'But at your own behest, not from duty or pity, or because you think I'm a lost sheep who will bleat her way over the edge of a cliff if not supervised.' She turned to the other foot, her movements abrupt and her face hidden by the folds of her wimple. 'And because I want you with me, I feel guilty. I have seen how you have been limping on that leg today because the cold is gnawing your bones.'

Simon's smile was humourless. 'Ah then, my love, you have sealed the bargain. You should know better than to cite my leg as a reason why I should stay at home.' In the absence of his squire, he flipped a leg binding around his own calf with expert speed and tucked in the end. 'Nothing you can say or do will keep me now.'

'Nothing I could say or do could keep you before,' she retorted and with a grimace tried to stamp her way into her boot, the fit now made much tighter by the additional sock. 'God's wounds,' she muttered through her teeth.

Simon came to her, and, bending on his good knee, took her

foot in his hands and applied leverage. She felt his grip at her
ankle, warm, hard and sure. It was not the touch of a man in
a state of weakness. 'Yes, my leg pains me,' he said, 'but it
would do so whether I came with you or remained here. I have
your father's cloak; I will be warm enough.'

Her foot shot into the boot and he fastened the horn toggle
at the side. She touched his hair, and watched the gold strands
shimmer among the brown. 'It is your cloak now,' she
murmured as he performed the same service to her other foot.

'Is it?' He gave a vexed smile. 'Even now I am not certain.'
He eased to his feet. He was adept at controlling the response
to his pain, but she saw the betraying tightening of his eyelids
and winced for him. There were meanings beneath the words,
like rocks under the deception of calm water, or bodies in a
shallow grave.

'You have always had your own way of wearing it,' she
offered.

He started towards the door. 'You need not sweeten the
potion,' he said. 'I knew the burdens when I fastened it at my
shoulders.'

'All of them?' she too rose, and followed him. There was a
tension in the air, like the quiver after the last note on the harp
when a song was ended.

'No, not all,' he admitted, 'but still, I knew what I was
doing.'

She believed him. She had seldom seen Simon nonplussed or
ill at ease, whatever the situation. It came from being a squire at
old King William's court, she thought. That, and a feline degree
of self-containment that she had never been able to win past.

He set his arm lightly across her shoulders. 'And I have never
regretted it.'

It was Matilda's turn to smile and tighten her lids. 'You do
not need to sweeten the potion either.' She drew out of his arms,
proving that she could do so, and went down to the waiting
horses.

*   *   *

Judith's room at Elstow was almost as cold as the outside air, where frost was growing on the trees like silver moleskin and the air was as sharp as crystal in the lungs.

Entering on the heels of the anxious infirmarian, Matilda's teeth continued to chatter. 'Why is there no brazier?' she demanded.

The nun shook her head and looked apologetic. 'The Lady Judith said that there was no point in having one. We tried to bring one in and light it, but she grew so angry and distressed that Mother Abbess said that we should respect her wishes.'

Her dying wishes. The words hung unspoken but as tangible as the white vapour that puffed from Matilda's nose and mouth. The room was as bare as a crypt. The walls were barren of all save a crucifix – Christ in hollow-ribbed suffering keeping watch over stark, limewashed plaster. Two plain coffers stood near the bed, one holding a thick wax candle that burned with a steady golden flame in the midnight deep. Seated next to it, her eyes red and puffy with weeping and the rest of her face pinched with cold, was her mother's maid, Sybille. There was a silver goblet in her hand, half full of some dark-coloured liquid. On the bed itself Judith was propped up high against the bolsters to aid her breathing. Spots of feverish colour stained her cheekbones, but otherwise her complexion was ashen. Her grey-streaked hair lay in a single braid, coiled to the left and lying like a rope over her faltering heart. Within their gaunt sockets her eyes were closed, but she was conscious and aware, for her hands were occupied with a set of prayer beads and her lips were moving as she recited the psalms.

Matilda moved to the bedside, Simon following in her wake. The crackle of their feet on the rushes did not disturb Judith's concentration and she continued to murmur.

'Oh, my lady, thank Christ you have come. I did not know if you would!' Sybille rose stiffly to her feet and embraced Matilda, tears running down her face. 'She has been waiting for you! A messenger has gone to your sister too, but she will not arrive for several days yet and my lady does not have that time to wait.'

'Sybille, hush. You always did have a tongue like a bell clapper.' Judith's voice was weak and reedy, and by the end of the sentence she was fighting for breath.

'Mama.' Matilda pushed out of the maid's arms and knelt at the bedside. She took her mother's frozen, skeletal hands and chaffed them in hers. 'You should have sent for me sooner.'

'So that you could watch me die for longer?' A spark kindled in Judith's eye caverns. 'Where would be the point in that?'

Matilda rubbed her thumb over Judith's icy knuckles. 'To be with you,' she said. 'To offer succour and comfort.' There was a tightness in her throat, but it was more a familiar response to being near her mother than anything of grief. Even at the end, Judith could not be conciliatory.

The sound of the dying woman's struggle to breathe filled the room. 'I need neither succour nor comfort,' Judith gasped. 'I have grown so accustomed to being without that their lack disturbs me not.' Her lips curved in the travesty of a smile. 'Instead I have my pride . . . or I had it.' She swallowed jerkily. Matilda took the half-cup of wine and held it to her mother's lips. Judith took a moistening sip, no more, and leaned her head against the piled bolsters while she gathered strength. 'Still, I am glad you have come.' Her voice was a faded whisper that trailed off as her eyes fixed on a point beyond Matilda's shoulder and widened with a blending of fear and astonishment.

'Come out of the shadows,' she croaked hoarsely, 'I do not see well . . .'

Simon stepped forward, and the candlelight around the bed illuminated the blue of his cloak, glittered on the braid border, and cast a yellow glow on the white fur lining. His shadow wavered on the limewashed wall, fuzzy and distorted so that it looked more ursine than human.

'Madame, belle mère,' he said and, advancing to the bed, stooped to kiss her cold brow.

Matilda felt her mother shudder, and knew without being

told that Judith had for a moment believed that the presence of her former husband stalked the room.

'I am guilty,' Judith wheezed. 'I have been shriven, but still I am guilty . . . God might forgive me, but I will never forgive myself.'

'Hush, do not distress yourself,' Matilda murmured. 'You cannot make an end like this . . .' She squeezed the cold hands beneath hers and tried to imbue them with some vestige of her own warmth and life. Softly in the background, she could hear Sybille's choked sobs. 'My . . . my father would not want to see you like this.'

'Of course not . . . your father is a saint!' There was a bitter note in the thin voice. 'He is revered for what I took to be his weakness.'

Matilda steeled herself not to leap to her feet and turn her back on her mother. Not to pour out all of her own bitterness and resentment. Her struggle must have shown in her eyes, however, for she caught Simon's gaze on her in troubled compassion. He gave a slight shake of his head, offering both wordless support and the advice that she should say nothing.

Biting her lip, she held her place, and was suddenly glad that they had not arrived sooner.

'I loved him,' Judith whispered, and two tears suddenly spilled from her eyes and rolled down her gaunt cheeks. 'Despite all, I loved him.' There was no breath in her to cry, and her thin body shook with the rigours of her struggle.

In terror Matilda watched her, thinking that she was going to die of this moment. Shriven perhaps, but far from at peace. However the spasms ceased, and although Judith gasped like a fish too long out of water, her eyes were yet lucid. She extended one palsied hand to touch the white fur of Simon's cloak. Her fingers closed in the harsh guard hairs and dug through to the snow-softness beneath.

'Then that is all that matters,' Simon said and, unfastening the catch, laid the cloak across her body. 'You have to let all else go.'

She looked at him and seemed slowly to absorb his words, for her breathing calmed a little and her clutch became less desperate on the fur.

'Was Waltheof able to do that?' she wheezed.

'Yes,' said Simon without hint of a stumble or pause and meeting her gaze squarely.

'You tell me what I want to hear . . .'

'I tell you the truth.'

She made a disparaging sound, but her crisis was fought and won and she had regained her control. 'I am glad that you are my daughter's husband and not mine,' she said, and stroked the lining of the cloak.

'So am I,' Simon said.

Judith almost smiled at the remark. 'I hear you have not revoked your crusader's vow,' she said after a pause to gather strength.

'No, belle mère,' Simon said gravely, 'I have not revoked it.'

'Then pray for me.'

'Gladly.' Simon dipped his head in acknowledgement and moved from the bed, leaving the cloak draped across her body. If he was cold without its enveloping warmth, he gave no sign. Matilda was moved by his compassion and filled with pride and awe. She supposed it was the result of his life as a courtier. Being a squire to the Conqueror had been excellent training for everything that life . . . and the leaving of life could hurl at him.

Judith closed her eyes and slept, but even in slumber did not relinquish her grip on the cloak.

From the abbey the matins bell sounded, calling the nuns to stumble from their pallets in the dorter and walk in procession to the chapel. Simon went quietly from the room and returned with his second cloak – an affair of dark green wool trimmed with the contrasting red of squirrel and lined for warmth with sheepskins. He also brought a flagon of hot wine, a small loaf and a half wheel of yellow cheese.

'Food?' he murmured.

Matilda shook her head. Her stomach was tied in a knot and she could not think of eating, but she took the wine with gratitude and drank a warming mouthful. There was ginger in it, and she welcomed the trickle of heat it sent through her frozen body. Sybille drank too, cupping her hands around her goblet and sniffing with cold. She too refused the food that Simon offered. Shrugging, he settled himself on the second coffer and ate a portion of bread and cheese.

'On campaign you eat to keep your strength, no matter if the sight of food revolts your belly,' he said, but made no more effort to force the women.

Twice more as the night drew on Matilda heard the abbey bell summoning the nuns to prayer. The candle burned down on its spike and Sybille brought out a new one from the aumbry in the corner. Matilda saw that there were more candles in the recessed cupboard – at least half a dozen of golden beeswax, and as thick as a strong man's wrist.

'Kindle them all,' she commanded the maid. 'We may not have heat, but at least we can have a blaze of light.'

Sybille did as she bade, emptying the aumbry of its contents and seeking out extra wrought-iron spikes. 'My lady would say that it is a terrible waste,' she said with an apprehensive glance at the bed.

'For this once I think that the cost is justified,' Matilda answered. 'Let her path be lit fittingly.' Rising from the bedside, she lit a candle from the guttering one on the coffer and from it kindled the rest until the room was huge with light.

From the abbey the prime bell rang out, once more beckoning the nuns to their devotions. Outside the chamber a grey winter dawn was breaking. Simon rose to his feet and, murmuring that he was going outside for a piss, limped stiffly from the room.

As the door closed softly behind him, Judith raised her lids as if they weighed as greatly as pennies made of lead. Her gaze fixed upon the brightness of the candles, and then with effort, slid to her daughter.

'A profligate waste,' she murmured rustily.

'A fitting salute,' Matilda retorted, and lifted the cup of wine from the coffer to offer her mother a drink.

Judith made a feeble gesture of denial. 'Leave be,' she whispered. 'I am beyond that . . .' Her hand groped and sought upon the coverlet, found the edge of the fur cloak and clutched it. A look of relief softened the lines on her face. 'I dreamed of your father,' she said, and a faint smile wavered on her lips like a reflection blurred in water. 'He was wearing this . . . and unlike me, he had not grown old . . .'

Matilda wondered uneasily if her mother was going to have another seizure of grief, but the smile remained, and when the dying woman breathed, 'I loved him,' there was a kind of sad understanding in her face. 'But not enough.' There was another soft breath that stirred the fur on the white pelt, and one that did not, followed by a sound like a key grating in a lock. Then there was silence. The candles flickered, their light glinting in the shine of Judith's fixed stare.

'Mother?' Matilda leaned over the still form on the bed. She took one of the cold wrists in hers and searched along the delicate blue vein for the pulse of life, but found nothing. Very gently, she pressed the open lids shut.

Sybille rose stiffly from her kneeling position at the other side of the bed and, easing a cramp in her spine, went to unfasten the latch and throw wide the shutters on a grey dawn sky. 'To aid her soul's passage,' she declared. Her face was wet, but then Sybille had always been swift to show emotion, the opposite of the mistress she had served for forty years.

The daylight streamed weakly into the room, taking away some of the glory from the candle's blaze and casting a pallid light on Judith's body. A cold draught guttered the flames and Matilda could almost fancy that it was indeed her mother's soul leaving its earthly shell and drifting heavenwards. She felt numb. There was no sting of tears, no rush of grief. Nothing, save perhaps a regret as cold and sad as the air blowing through the room.

Leaving the bedside, she joined Sybille at the open shutters and put her arms around the woman's shoulders. The light was steadily paling in the east, and she could see the lay workers going about their business. The smell of new bread from the bakehouse wafted suggestively past her nostrils. She saw Simon talking to one of the knights of their escort as the two men trudged back up the path from the latrines. Simon's hands were tucked in his belt in a stance that was so familiar it sent a small leap of emotion through her.

'Only time I ever knew her happy were in the first days of marriage to your father,' Sybille sniffed. 'But they were as different as a cat and a dog. I knew it would end in grief, more's the pity for both their sakes. I pray she finds her peace with God now.' She made the sign of the cross on her breast.

Matilda echoed the maid's gesture. 'I hope so too,' she murmured, but the words came by rote. Sense and meaning would come later – or perhaps not at all.

'I should fetch the priest and the Mother Abbess.' Sybille wiped her eyes on her sleeve. 'My lady will want to lie in the chapel . . .'

'No, let me do that,' Matilda said quickly. 'You knew her the best of us . . . You were her closest companion. It is fitting that you should prepare her for her final resting place.'

Sybille nodded. 'Yes, Lady Matilda. I would be honoured to see to laying her out.'

'Good then. Do you make a start and I will join you presently.' She kissed the maid's damp cheek and was briefly engulfed in the choking hold of a fresh wave of Sybille's emotion. In truth she was glad that at least there was someone to weep for her mother.

Descending to the bailey, she went to intercept Simon and bring him the news that Judith had died.

He had finished speaking with the other knight, and now he came towards her, his hands still gripping his belt, his stride stiff and uneven in the frosty morning cold. Even though her feelings were frozen, something must have shown on her face, for his step quickened and his thin brows drew together in concern.

'She has gone,' Matilda said as he reached her. 'And I am glad for her. Perhaps now she will have the peace she never found in life.' The muscles of her face felt stiff, as if the cold had invaded and frozen them.

He folded his arms around her. 'God rest her soul,' he murmured. 'I know it was troubled.'

Matilda pressed her face into the russet wool of his tunic. 'Sybille is composing her body ready for chapel,' she said. 'I must make arrangements for masses to be said for her soul and see that alms are distributed in her name.' She rubbed her cheek against his breast. 'Everything stops while we wait for death to come, and then everything becomes as busy as a beehive.' She gave a little shiver. 'And then everything stops again,' she said softly. 'And that perhaps is a worse silence than the first.'

He rubbed his fingertips gently at the small of her back. 'But only as winter comes before spring,' he said. 'If you can weather the cold, then the season will turn.'

'I am in the winter now,' she said. 'I feel nothing. I am frozen.'

'Well, half of that is because you have been sitting all night in a room so cold that it would turn fire to ice in the snap of a finger,' he remonstrated. 'And you wouldn't eat any food to fuel your belly when I offered. At least ask some hot gruel of the nuns before you set about your tasks.'

'I thought it was women who were supposed to be scolds,' she found the spark to murmur.

'I was caring, not scolding,' Simon retorted.

The words lit the tiniest flicker of warmth at Matilda's core. 'You might have married her,' she said.

'But I didn't.' He sought downwards and found her cold lips with his own. She felt their pressure, the warmth of his mouth, breathing life into hers. Her fingers caught and gripped as a stab of heat shattered the ice encasing her vitals. She made a sound in her throat, half pleasure, half anguish, and he absorbed it into the strength of their kiss. She swayed where she stood, locked in longing and a need so great that it almost felled her.

The sound of the draw bar sliding back from the main gate and the entry of a horseman on a blowing bay courser made Simon break the kiss and lift his head. Leaning against him, her body a mass of tingling sensation, Matilda watched the rider approach. He wore a thick, fur-lined cloak against the winter cold, and a hood of charcoal-coloured wool. The pommel of a sword shone with a dull steel light at his belt.

She felt Simon tense against her, and looking into his face saw that he was gazing at the newcomer with recognition in his eyes.

'Beric?' he said. 'What brings you here to Elstow? Is there news?' His right arm departed the embrace to extend towards the man; his left remained on her waist and turned her to face the intrusion. 'A king's messenger,' Simon muttered out of the side of his mouth for her benefit.

The man dismounted with a little jump, for his horse was tall and he was not. He was powerfully built, though, and looked as if he knew how to use the weapon at his belt.

'Not so much news, my lord, as a summons.' He reached into the satchel slung from left shoulder to right hip and produced a vellum packet from which dangled the royal seal of King William Rufus. 'He wants you in Normandy. They told me at Northampton's gates that you had come here.'

Simon took the packet from the outstretched hand. Matilda watched the gesture and was transported back to small childhood with such a vivid jolt that she almost gasped. She saw Ralf de Gael riding into the courtyard and felt her father's arms slacken around her as his attention diverted to his friend. She remembered the fury and pain she had felt – and the anguish of being punished for her tantrum while her papa rode off to hunt with his friend. And after that everything had changed.

The power of the feeling, coupled with lack of food and sleep and the long, draining vigil at her mother's deathbed, buckled her knees and she sagged against Simon in a half-swoon. He bore her up with an exclamation of concern and she heard him call out across the courtyard. Moments later she found herself being borne away by the porteress and her novice assistant, who murmured over her in concern. To her protests that she was all right and her feeble struggles to be free of them they paid no heed, but brought her to the infirmary and sat her in a cushioned curule chair near the fire; and it seemed to her that the wheel had turned full circle.

A bowl of hot oat gruel and two cups of sweet mead later, she began to feel slightly better and insisted to the nuns tending her that she did not want to lie down and rest. 'I need to be busy,' she said.

'Aye, it must be a shock, losing your poor lady mother,' clucked the infirmaress, a plump hen of a woman with comfortable, pleated features and shrewd blue eyes. 'Best if your hands and mind are occupied until you're ready to think about matters.'

'Indeed,' Matilda said, but it was not the shock of her mother's death that had felled her.

Leaving the infirmary, she went to the chapel and found that preparations were already afoot to transport her mother's body from her chamber to lie in state before the altar. She spoke to the Mother Abbess about prayers, accepted condolences with appropriate murmurs and downcast lids, and then sped in search of Simon, filled with an irrational fear that he might already have left.

He was in the stables, arranging to have a loose shoe on his horse's off-hind hoof reshod. When he saw her he left his conversation with the groom and she saw the apprehension fill his eyes.

'You are feeling better?' He took her hands in his.

'Enough to do what I must,' she said with a half-smile that was brave rather than possessed of any humour. She gestured to the horse, which the groom was preparing to lead out into the yard. 'You do not need to tell me. I know that you will ride out of here before the bells ring the hour of nones.'

He sighed and released one of her hands so that he could push his hair off his forehead. 'The King desires me to act as one of his commanders in the field and the summons is urgent. I've already sent a rider out to Huntingdon with an order of muster. Now I have to return to Northampton and do the same. Matilda, I . . .'

Quickly she raised her palm and laid it against his lips. 'Do not seek to sweeten the potion,' she said. 'You too are bound to do as you must.'

A look of relief flickered in his eyes. Obviously he had expected her to weep and cling. The part of her that was the child had every intention of doing so, but the woman held that part in check with grim determination. 'Promise only that you will send word to me of where you are and what you are doing.' She managed to keep her voice on an even keel. 'It is the silences that are the hardest to bear.'

The groom clopped the horse into the yard, swung astride, and turned it towards the gates.

'Smith'll have him shod in a cat's whisker, m'lord,' he said.

Simon nodded and flipped the man a silver coin from his pouch. 'I'll be at prayer in the chapel.'

Saluting, the groom rode out.

Simon turned to Matilda and drew her into the knee-deep hay of the stable just vacated by his horse. 'I promise.' He pulled her into his arms, and ignoring the toing and froing of servants and grooms kissed her until she was hot and melting and breathless. 'Wherever we are in the field, I promise.' Through her gown and his chausses and tunic she could feel how hard he was, and she rubbed against him with a small gasp. To be doing this while her mother was being prepared to lie in state in the chapel might indicate a lack of decorum, but the need to confirm the life force coursing through her own veins was just as strong . . . and abetted by the knowledge of Simon's imminent departure. If they did not make their private farewells now, there would be no other time.

Although it was he who had instigated their lovemaking, it

was Matilda who took control. She broke the embrace, but only to draw him into the stables, to the farthest stall, which was full of clean, fresh hay.

'My mother would be shocked,' she whispered as she pulled him down to her, 'but I will do my penance later.'

'No,' Simon said as he cupped her face in his hands and paused on the threshold of wild lust for a moment of tenderness. 'Deep in her heart, your mother would have been envious. Do no penance, but rejoice.'

CHAPTER 39

Castle of Gisors, Norman Border, March 1098

R emoving his helm, shrugging his shield from his shoulders, Simon limped into the Great Hall at Gisors. His temper was almost at boiling point, and it was taking all of his will to hold it down.

The object of his rage was sitting with his boots propped upon the dais trestle, drinking from a handsome silver-gilt cup. Cloak, helm and swordbelt were laid at one side in readiness to ride. Robert de Bêlleme, Simon's *bête noire*, was also a battle commander at Gisors, and indeed the man responsible for the redesigning of what had been a poxy border keep into what was swiftly becoming an imposing fortress. His skills as an engineer and architect were outstanding. That did not, however, prevent Simon from loathing him. De Bêlleme had changed sides more often than the tables were turned in a busy great hall. Whilst Robert of Normandy was still occupied on the crusade, De Bêlleme was content to serve William Rufus, but Simon doubted the loyalty would last. The baron's nature was too fickle for that. The only light in the darkness was that De Bêlleme was about to leave Gisors for the war that William Rufus was conducting against Helias of La Fleche in Maine.

'Your man Gerard de Serigny has burned yet another

village!' Simon snarled as he dumped his helm on the table and slung a leather armguard after it. 'What is the point of building this castle to hold the border if we then lay waste to the area that supplies it and make enemies of the people? Have you no control over the foraging parties you send out?'

De Bêlleme narrowed his silvery eyes. 'If De Serigny has burned a village, then it must have been harbouring French sympathies,' he said. 'It's possible to find lice even in the cleanest hair. And you know how fast they breed.' He made a cracking gesture with index finger and thumb.

Simon gave a growl of disgust and reached across De Bêlleme for the flagon, forcing the Baron to lean back and inhale a whiff of stale armpit. 'It was no more harbouring French sympathies than you would know honour if it walked up to you and smacked you in the face.' Simon snapped. Sloshing wine into a cup, he threw himself down on the bench that ran the length of the dais. 'I trust Gerard de Serigny is leaving with you.'

De Bêlleme finished his own wine, tossed the cup to his squire for cleaning, and rose to his feet. Unlike Simon, who was newly returned from patrol and spattered with mud, De Bêlleme glittered like a statue in a church, not a speck of rust on his hauberk, not a spatter of mud on cloak or tunic hem. 'No,' he said with a taunting smile. 'Serigny is remaining here, seconded to Hugh Lupus. I can spare a conroi, and whatever you think, you need men like him. At least they do not get caught by the French.'

Simon's anger bubbled closer to the top of the cauldron. A fortnight since he and Hugh Lupus had been caught on the border by a large troop of French soldiers. Their ransoms had been a formality, swiftly paid by William Rufus, but De Bêlleme had been rubbing it in ever since. 'There is no chance of that while they are raiding villages close to home, is there?' he retorted.

De Bêlleme gave an exaggerated sigh. 'You were an irritating brat, De Senlis, and you've not changed except to grow older and even less competent than you were as a squire.'

'That dish of frumenty I threw down your neck was delib-

erate,' Simon answered. 'And I count my competence somewhat less rancid than your honour . . . . my lord.' He inclined
his head to emphasise the sarcasm but there was no deference.
These days, being an earl, he outranked De Bêlleme.

'I have neither the time nor the inclination to bandy words
with you,' De Bêlleme sneered, and, taking his feet off the
trestle, he pinned his cloak and swept together helm and sword.

'Mayhap not, but you will have them with De Serigny before
you go, or I will do it myself – and with more than words if
necessary.'

De Bêlleme glared at Simon. 'Do you know what happened
to the last man who tried to tell me my business?'

Simon gave an exaggerated shrug. 'Doubtless you impaled
him on a stake in the dungeon or strung him from the battle-
ments by his own guts.' He met the pale gaze calmly, although
his heart was hammering and he could feel his palm itching
with the need to hold a sword between himself and De
Bêlleme.

De Bêlleme made an impatient sound. 'I loathe you,' he said,
'but this once I will speak with De Serigny. We will not always
be allies, Simon de Senlis. Remember it well.'

His spurs scraped the bench as he stepped over it and strode
from the dais. Simon watched him out of the hall with a stare
that was fixed and cold, but when the baron was gone his spine
melted and he slumped on the bench. There was icy sweat in
his armpits and even if his hand was itching to hold a sword
his palm was so damp that it would have fouled his grip. He
knew men who had a similar response to snakes. With him it
was Robert de Bêlleme.

He drained his cup and poured himself a fresh measure,
waving away the squire who would have attended him. 'Go and
prepare a tub,' he said. 'I stink like a midden.'

The lad trotted off, but moments later and far too soon to
have accomplished his errand, he returned to the dais with a
sealed parchment in his hand. 'Earl Simon, a messenger asked
me to give you this. Says it is a personal matter.'

Simon took the package and squinted at the seal, but it was not one that he recognised. He thought about leaving it until after he had bathed. There were always messengers, always supplicants, always someone wanting something. But he knew that now it was in his hand it would niggle at him. *A personal matter.* He thought at first of Matilda – but it wasn't her seal. 'Did the messenger say where he came from?' he questioned.

'From the convent of the Holy Redeemer in Evreux, my lord.'

Simon's expression did not change. He thanked the lad and dismissed him to his original errand, then slit the seal and unfolded the package.

When he had finished reading the single page of scribe-written brown lines, he threw back his head, closed his eyes, and softly groaned.

Simon drew rein outside the convent and dismounted. Behind him his conroi did the same, but since they did not expect to be admitted they settled down to wait in the lee of the outer wall.

Simon handed his bridle to Turstan and went to rap the lion's head knocker on the nunnery's heavy oak door. The brass ring in the lion's mouth was solid and smooth in his fingers, anchoring him to the reality of why he was here. Above the knocker, a small door opened in the thickness of the wood and a nun peered out at him, her face framed in a white wimple overlaid by a dark veil.

'Simon de Senlis, Earl of Northampton and Huntingdon,' he said to her. 'I am expected.'

A key grated in a lock and a bolt slid back. The nun opened the main door sufficiently to admit him and no wider. Simon suppressed a grimace. The job of porteress was always given to a nun with the mentality of a goodwife guarding her chicken run from foxes. She honoured him with a dip of her head and the suggestion of a curtsey, but only after she had frowned round the door at his men and locked up behind him.

'I will take you to Mother Abbess,' she said. Her mouth was prim and tight as if pulled with a drawstring. Clearly the reason for him being here was known and not approved – whatever his rank. She led him through the warren of buildings to the Abbess' private solar. Other nuns were about their duties in the space between prayers, indoor pursuits today of spinning, weaving and sewing, since it was not fit weather for gardening. He received swift glances and lowered lids. They would not talk about him behind his back, because they were sworn to speak only as necessary, but he could feel the weight of their speculation.

The Abbess' solar was a pleasant room, warmed by braziers and hung with colourful religious embroideries. The coffers along the side of the room released a scent of beeswax from their gleaming surfaces. It was such a contrast to Judith's chamber at Elstow that it enforced Simon's realisation of how much his mother-by-marriage had mortified herself in her last years.

The Abbess was seated in a high-backed chair, her hands folded in her lap and wrapped around a set of beautiful agate prayer beads. A large gold cross shone on her breast against the dark wool of her habit. Rising to her feet, she greeted Simon cordially, and bade the porteress fetch Sabina.

'I must thank you for coming so swiftly, my lord, and in person,' she said, resuming her seat and gesturing him to a second chair padded with an embroidered cushion. Turning to an exquisite silver flagon, she poured a generous measure of wine into one of two matching goblets and handed it to him.

'You thought I might send a proxy?' he said with raised brows.

'Not to missay your honour, but I thought it likely, my lord. I did not know if you would have the time – or the interest.'

'For this I would,' he said grimly and took a drink of the wine. As he had expected, it was superb. 'After all, the responsibility is mine.'

'Not all men would see the matter in that particular light,

my lord. We see plenty of distressed young women at our gates who have been abandoned by their lovers and left to deal with the consequences themselves. And on many occasions the father owns more than a ploughshare.'

'I did not abandon Sabina,' Simon said, his colour rising. 'Indeed, I offered her a place under my roof, but she was set on joining your community . . . I did not know until your letter arrived that she had borne a child.' He met her gaze steadily. 'She is not my habitual mistress, cast off to a nunnery when the arrangement no longer suited. This infant was born of a single occasion of weakness.'

She was not going to let him off the hook so easily. 'And yet Sister Sabina says that you know each other well.'

'We do . . . but not as lovers.'

The nun looked sceptical. He could not blame her. 'He is a fine, healthy baby. We could raise him here and send him for fostering in a monastery when he is old enough, but it is not wise to keep an infant among nuns when one of them is his mother. Even if he is bastard born, he is the son of an earl, and Sister Sabina desires that you foster him in your own household . . . I assume that your very presence here attests that you are willing?'

Simon set his empty cup back on the table and shook his head at her offer of more. 'Of course I am willing,' he said.

There was a tap on the door and Sabina entered, a swaddled bundle lying along her left arm, cradled against her heart. Simon stared at her. She had always been attractive in her ordinary gown and wimple, but the nun's garb made her look like a Madonna. The oval face, the pure features, the grey-violet eyes with their thick black lashes. He could almost see dumbfounded peasants kneeling at her feet in worship. And he would have been tempted to join them. Her hands were slender and beautifully shaped, ringless too. She had removed Saer's wedding band.

Simon rose to his feet. His heart was hammering against his ribs and his throat was tight. The words that had always come

so easily before now deserted him. He swallowed. 'Why did
you not send to me sooner?' he demanded.

She met his gaze defensively. 'There would have been no
point,' she said. 'What could you have done except watch my
belly grow? Besides, I did not know that I was carrying a child
at first. There had been no signs. In the early months my fluxes
had continued. And when I did find out, I had some thinking
to do.' She looked down at the baby and gently stroked his
cheek.

'You do not have to give him up,' Simon said. 'I would
furnish you a place to live, you know that.'

Sabina smiled sadly and shook her head. 'That would serve
for his early years,' she replied, 'but the time would soon come
for you to take him into your household and train him for
knighthood, and I would be left with naught to do but sit and
spin and brood. The parting will be better now than later. I
will have my devotions to keep me occupied, and the support
of Mother Abbess and the good sisters.' She raised her arm,
bringing the child closer to her gaze. 'I may be about to
renounce the world, but I want him to grasp it in both hands.
He is my healing,' she added, 'a gift from God. I did not think
to bear another child after I lost the others. Let him go out and
live his life.' Her voice had been steady and calm thus far, but
now it developed a wobble and her chin dimpled. 'Take him
. . . His name is Simon, for you.' She kissed the baby gently
on the brow, and gave him into his father's arms.

Simon looked down at the tiny swaddled scrap. Its eyes were
closed in slumber and the wisps of hair peeping from beneath
its linen bonnet were dark. Jesu God. He wanted to say that if
he had known this would be the result of that moment of lust
in Durazzo he would have abstained, but the words stuck in
his throat and then dissolved at the feel of the warm weight
and tiny skull. Sabina's son was indeed a gift – a wonderful and
very disturbing one.

'I have a carrying basket for him,' she said, 'and swaddling
bands that I stitched while awaiting my confinement.' She

spoke with a swift and almost desperate practicality. 'You will need to find him a wet nurse . . .'

'There are several at Gisors,' Simon said in a distracted voice. 'Some of the soldiers have wives with them, and the Earl of Chester has a woman with a babe in his household.'

'Sister Sabina will see you to the gate,' the Abbess said, granting them a leave of conversation alone.

Somehow Simon took a courteous farewell of the senior nun. He was still reeling, unable to comprehend that he had an almost newborn babe on his arm. Sabina walked at his side, carrying the basket and the swaddling.

'He's a good baby,' Sabina said as they walked. 'He should not trouble your journey . . .' At first glance she appeared composed, but there was no colour in her face and her lips were compressed. 'What will your wife do?' she asked.

Simon grimaced. The wind gusted about them and he carefully shielded the infant within a fold of his cloak. 'I will cross that bridge when I come to it,' he said. 'Hopefully her spirit will be generous enough to understand.'

'And if it is not?'

'I promise you that whatever she and I suffer, the child will not,' he said. 'The sin is yours and mine, not his.'

She nodded as if his words had eased a burden in her mind. 'It is hard to let him go,' she whispered. 'If I seem composed now, it is because I have given myself permission to grieve when you are gone . . .'

'Sabina . . .'

'Say nothing more. Just take him and go. All will be well . . . and better this way.'

At the gate they waited while the porteress again slid the bolt and unlocked the door. Sabina leaned over Simon's arm and placed a final, soft kiss on the baby's brow. 'Godspeed, little one,' she whispered.

For Simon himself there was no embrace, just a single, long look that said everything. Then she turned from him and went back to the abbey. The porteress let him out of the door with the basket and swaddling. 'You take care of that child,' she said sternly. 'God will know if you do not.' The heavy oak swung shut behind him and he heard the lock shoot back into place.

His men came to attention from their positions against the wall and looked at him askance.

'It's a baby!' Simon snapped. 'Haven't any of you seen one before? Here, strap this basket to the packhorse and cover it so that it doesn't get wet.' Handing his son briefly to Turstan he mounted his horse then leaned down to take the infant back in his arms and beneath the protection of his cloak.

No one asked questions, but everyone looked at each other and not at Simon.

Despite the inclement weather, Sabina retired to a corner of the cloisters to hug her grief instead of the warm body of her child. Softly she rocked back and forth, moaning to herself, the pain too deep for tears. It was thus that the Abbess found her and with infinite compassion brought her back within the abbey.

'A baby?' Hugh of Chester reddened alarmingly. Laughter brimmed in his eyes, and he was taken with a paroxysm of choking. Hastily he reached for the wine flagon, as usual close to hand, and took several gulps without recourse to a cup. 'Not even I have fornicated with a nun, and I'm reckoned without a shred of moral fibre!' he recovered enough to wheeze.

'She was not a nun at the time,' Simon said stiffly.

Flagon in hand, Chester leaned over the basket to regard the infant. It stared back at him out of the kitten-blue eyes of a newborn. 'You're sure it is yours? You don't think she's foisting a cuckoo on you?'

'No, it's mine,' Simon said, his eyelids tightening. He grabbed the flagon from Chester and took a long drink. 'I have to find a wet nurse among the women.'

'There's Alaise,' Chester said. 'She's weaning young Geoffrey, but she's still got enough milk to float a galley. She'll be glad to feed him. Means she'll not have to worry about conceiving another babe quite yet. Women don't grow big bellies while they're still giving suck.'

'Thank you.' Simon was irritated by his friend, but he was also immensely grateful for his practicality. Chester was a profligate lecher. Alaise was one of several mistresses, but he always returned to her and they had three sons, the most recent being a little over a year old.

'What will your wife say?' Laughter was still flushing Chester's face. His shoulders continued to twitch.

Simon did not want to think about that. 'I would hope that she would be generous,' he replied. 'The child is not to blame.'

'Aye,' Chester snorted. 'She'll take him in and throw you out.'

The baby opened its mouth and gave a small, experimental squeak. Chester snapped his fingers at a squire. 'Take this child to Mistress Alaise and tell her that Lord Hugh bids her tend it as one of her own.'

'Yes, my lord.' The youth picked up the basket as if it held a tangle of writhing snakes rather than a single whimpering baby, and made his way gingerly across the hall to the private apartments.

'It's good to know that you're capable of sinning as much as the rest of us!' Chester slapped Simon on the back. 'Don't you worry. Alaise is a good mother. She'll do for the nonce.' He dismissed the subject with a flick of one large, fleshy hand. 'I'm glad you are here. I sent a foraging party out towards Chaumont and they haven't returned. I thought that . . .'

'Who was leading?'

'Who do you think?' Chester said, and now there was no laughter in his eyes. 'Gerard de Serigny.'

Simon swore. De Bêlleme might have flayed De Serigny, figuratively if not literally, but that had been in public. In private Simon suspected that there was a different agenda. De Serigny was, after all, De Bêlleme's man and well placed to keep his master informed about everything that Simon and

Hugh Lupus did. Of course he was to be granted leeway. 'You want me to investigate?'

Chester spread his hands. 'You have the skills as a scout as well as a commander. Serigny is no loss if he has been captured by the French – De Bêlleme can pay the bastard's ransom, but he had a full conroi with him and I want to know what has happened. If they've raided a village and got drunk, I'll build a pyre for them myself.'

Simon nodded grim agreement. 'I'll go and arm up.' He was glad to have something to do. It meant he didn't have to think on matters complicated and domestic.

Before he left he paid a visit to the women's quarters. His son was drowsing on Alaise's ample white breast, his lips anchored to her nipple and his eyes closed in bliss. Now and again his small jaws would work, but more for security than sustenance.

'Must have been hard for his mother to give this one up,' Alaise said, her arm curving maternally around the small body. 'Is she truly a nun?'

Simon could see that this was a tale that was going to follow him the rest of his days, adding to his reputation in some quarters, destroying it in others. 'Not yet,' he said, 'And not as a penance for bearing him. And yes, it was hard for her to give him up.'

He left the chamber and went down to the courtyard where Turstan was holding the reins of his grey. Sabina had done what she thought best for the child. Now all he had to do was prove her right. He hoped that he was equal to the task.

CHAPTER 40

Northampton, March 1098

There was a robin on the sundial. Matilda watched it flirt its tail at her. Its breast feathers were the hue of hot embers against the soft brown wing. All around her the garden was showing the colours of spring. The apple tree even had a green suggestion of bud about the carefully pruned branches.

Its base was ringed with the glistening white milkflowers that Simon had brought her from Byzantium. To look at the small brown bulbs, she would not have guessed at the bravery and beauty of the blooms that had opened while the land was still in the grip of winter. They were past their best now, but the last ones to bud still carried their flowers. She wished wistfully that Simon could have been here to see them.

'Are you ready?' Jude asked.

She turned to her sister. Jude's arms were folded against her body and huddled under her cloak. She much preferred the warmth of a brazier and the cosiness of her embroidery to the outdoors – at least until true spring had put some warmth into the season. Her dark brows, brown eyes and warm complexion gave her a strong physical resemblance to their mother and sent a small pang through Matilda.

'Yes,' she said, 'I am.' A frown clouded her brow. 'Do you think I am doing the right thing in going to Simon?'

Jude contemplated, then nodded. 'Indeed I do. If our mother had followed her heart, she would have been the happier for it.'

Matilda managed a smile, but still felt a twinge of uncertainty. The need to go to Simon had had been born out of a gradual feeling of loneliness engendered by the act of clearing her mother's coffers and distributing her garments and effects to the poor. At the bottom of one of the coffers, amid scraps of dried rose petals and lavender stems, she had found a piece of embroidery depicting a copper-haired man on a chestnut stallion and riding beside him on a black mare a woman whose dark hair was shockingly bared to the world. The sight of the token had filled Matilda's eyes with tears. It had confirmed her mother's deathbed words. She had loved Waltheof. The tragedy was that she had never been able to show it, fettered as she was by her duty, by her Norman blood, and by the steep differences of nature that had separated her from her husband. The sight of that hidden length of embroidery had filled Matilda with an overwhelming need to go to Simon. To embrace their own differences of nature and negate them. She was afraid but steadfast. Jude would have custody of the children until her return.

'It is only fitting that you should see Normandy at least once,' Jude murmured as the sisters turned towards the garden gate. 'After all, we are half Norman, and I think it would have pleased our mother.' Jude had crossed the Narrow Sea on several occasions with Ranulf, and had been quite taken with the great stone abbeys and castles that populated the landscape.

Matilda wondered. For all that their mother was proud of her birth, she had chosen to live out her life in England and had shown no inclination to return to Normandy. However she said nothing to Jude, whom she sensed was only trying to offer her reassurance and comfort.

The children were waiting in the courtyard with Sybille to bid her farewell. Blinking back tears, Matilda embraced them both tenderly, and promised that she would be home soon. Waltheof patted her shoulder, offering her grave comfort, his manner more like that of an elderly man than a boy barely nine years old. His sister started to grizzle, but was easily persuaded out of her tears by the present of a sticky piece of honeycomb that Sybille had been keeping in reserve for just such an eventuality.

Matilda accepted a boost into the saddle from the waiting groom, and reined her horse to face the gates. It gave her a strange sense of freedom and fear to be the one riding away. Part of her wanted to turn back, but it was the lesser part, and she responded to it by nudging her mount to a trot.

The new castle of Gisors was a motley conglomeration of stone and wood rising out of a scarred landscape of felled trees and bare earth. A brown and grey wound on a land of bright spring green. Builders and masons toiled on the walls, each freshly mortared slab securing William Rufus' claim to the land.

Matilda drew rein and gazed upon the industry. Recent rain had turned the track to a churned brown glue, but not so wet that the wheels of the wains and ox carts became stuck in the mud. Soldiers were everywhere, some in mail, some in quilted linen gambesons, all of them watchful as cats and armed to the teeth.

A mile earlier, Matilda had dispatched a herald to give notice of her arrival. She narrowed her eyes upon the men at the gate, but could not see anyone that she recognised. No Turstan, no Toki . . . no distinctive blue and white cloak. She gnawed her underlip, caught herself in the mannerism and ceased with a small cluck that was half irritation, half nervousness.

Urging her mount, gesturing to the senior knights of her escort, she rode on to the outer gates of the half-grown castle. And saw that she was expected after all. Hugh Lupus, Earl of Chester, came forward to greet her, huge as a bear, light of tread, dark hair combed back from his broad forehead.

'Lady Matilda, be welcome,' he said and came to her saddle to lift her down.

Clad in mail, a fur-lined cloak clasped across his shoulders, he seemed more enormous than ever. His two chins had become three since last she had seen him and his paunch strained at the rivets of his hauberk.

'Lord Hugh,' she responded with a courteous smile. 'It is good to see you.' She was adept at the social niceties; greased wheels ran better than dry ones.

He drew her into the compound. Timber dwellings had been erected to house the population of the castle while the walls went up, and numerous tents dotted the sward like clusters of field mushrooms. She found herself anxiously scanning the banners flying from their posts to see if she could see any of Simon's, but, although there were a few she recognised, his was not among them.

As if reading her mind, Hugh Lupus touched her arm. 'Simon is out with a troop,' he said. 'We expect him back later today, or tomorrow.'

There was an odd expression in the Earl of Chester's eyes, a mingling of speculation, sympathy and grim amusement. Matilda's scalp prickled.

'There is more that you are not telling me, isn't there?'

Without reply, he led her to one of the timber buildings and waving the guard aside, pushed open the door. 'Your husband's chamber,' he said. 'We have not been dwelling in the most princely of circumstances, but I hope it will suffice.'

Matilda shrugged. 'I am not the kind to worry over lack of creature comforts,' she said. 'The peasants survive on far less.' She pinned him with her gaze. 'I hope you would tell me if there is anything amiss.'

He folded his arms across the wide bulk of his chest and looked over them to the layer of thick yellow straw covering the floor. 'It depends what you call amiss,' he said. 'As I told you, Simon is out with the troop.' He cleared his throat and rocked on his heels. 'I know your husband's abilities in the field and if I have no fears for him, neither should you.'

Matilda picked her way through what he had said. 'Then if there is no danger to my husband, why do you hesitate in your telling?' she asked.

Chester flicked her a look from beneath his brows. 'It is not every wife would follow her husband across the sea and to the edge of a battle field.' His tone was censorious rather than admiring.

Matilda lifted her chin. 'I am not every wife. I have scarcely seen my husband in two years. Even when he returned from the crusade we had no time together. My mother took ill and died, and he was called away to this war.' She flushed beneath Hugh Lupus' scrutiny. 'I have come to comfort him, and be comforted.'

The Earl's expression grew yet more wary. 'You may well achieve your goal,' he said. 'But I wonder how generous your nature is.'

It was clear from the way he spoke and his general stance that he was uncomfortable with her presence and viewed it as an irritation, like something full of little bones that had been added to his already piled trencher.

'I would appreciate it if you would tell me and be done,' she said with dignity.

Chester sighed. 'Come with me,' he said, and led her out of the building and across the sward to another, similar hall that housed his own retinue. Ducking through the doorway, he brought her to the central hearth and gestured to a woman sitting on a stool before the fire, tending a swaddled infant.

'This is Alaise, my mistress,' he said bluntly. 'Since she has milk in abundance, she has agreed to nurse your husband's child until other arrangements can be made.'

Matilda stared. 'My husband's child?' she said blankly.

'I am sorry that you should arrive to such tidings, but . . .' He made a shrug and a down-turned mouth serve for the rest.

'But wives who follow their husbands have to deal with the consequences,' she said in a hard voice that frighteningly reminded her of her mother.

'Yes, they do,' Chester answered, seemingly glad that she had articulated what he had not.

'How can this be his child?' she demanded with angry bewilderment. 'He has only been gone from me since the Christmas feast.'

Hugh Lupus nodded. 'And before that he was a crusader. Did you never wonder whether he took comfort along the way?'

Matilda swallowed. 'I . . .'

A young soldier approached the Earl and murmured that he was needed at one of the gates.

'You will excuse me,' Chester said. 'I will speak with you later. Whatever you need, just ask it of one of my attendants.' He left at a brisk walk for one so large, his relief obvious.

Matilda's body was rigid with the effort of maintaining her dignity. She looked down at the baby in the woman's arms. Its hair was jet-black, but otherwise it looked very similar to her own children when they had been newborn. Nine months ago, as Chester said, Simon had been returning from crusade. She remembered the way he had avoided her eye when he spoke of the laundress who had so neatly patched his chausses. A suspicion had crossed her mind then, but she had chosen to ignore, if not to forget it. It was in the past. But there was no ignoring this. For how long, she wondered, had this woman been his lover?

'Did you know the mother?' she demanded of Alaise. She made herself speak to the woman, even though she was the Earl of Chester's mistress and such knowledge was hard to swallow in the light of revelation.

'No, my lady. Earl Simon brought the babe here yesterday and I was asked to suckle him.' The woman's look was compassionate, but wary.

'Brought it back from where?'

'The nunnery at Evreux, my lady.'

'God's blood, his mistress is a nun?' Matilda's voice rose. She would kill him. She would take her knife and cut out his heart, but first she would slice off his balls and feed them to the hounds.

The baby gave a little start in response to the raised voice and began to wail. The woman unfastened the drawstring of her chemise to put him to her breast. 'I do not know, my lady. From the talk, I heard she hadn't taken her vows, but she wouldn't leave the nunnery.'

Matilda watched the infant nuzzle and take suck. Simon's

son by another woman – a nun. Had they talked tenderly as they lay together, or had it been a transaction of mere lust?

Stumbling from the dwelling, she leaned against the doorpost and drew deep gulps of the cold spring air. She had arrived in Gisors with visions of a tender reunion between herself and Simon. Instead she had been confronted by his betrayal. Suddenly she understood her mother's feelings all to well. The bitterness, the anger, the shame. All that remained in the end was duty, and its rigorous enforcing, because it was the only thing over which she had control.

Matilda lifted the cup to her lips and was surprised to find it already down to the lees. She fumbled for the pitcher only to discover that it too was empty.

'Go and fetch more wine,' she slurred at Helisende, who was watching her with a worried expression.

'My lady, the butlery will be closed now. They won't issue any more until the morrow.'

'They will for me . . . I'm a guest. I'm a countess . . .'

Helisende curled her hand around the pitcher's handle. 'Everyone is asleep,' she said. 'It is late in the night. I will have to rouse someone from their bed.'

'Then do it!' Matilda shouted. She rose from the low table where she had been drinking steadily for several hours, tripped on the hem of her gown and sprawled in the rushes. Helisende abandoned the pitcher and rushed to help her.

Matilda tried to bat the maid away but her arms felt as if they were lengths of wet rope. She hung her head, suddenly feeling very ill. Helisende smartly tipped some apples out of the wooden bowl on the table and just in time thrust it in front of Matilda's face.

Sobbing, heaving, Matilda was violently sick. She had never drunk even half a pitcher at once before and her body was rebelling in every fibre.

'That's it, my lady, better out than in,' Helisende crooned soothingly. 'You'll be all right presently.'

'I'll never be all right,' Matilda wept. 'Never again.'

Grimacing, Helisende went to dispose of the contents of the bowl down the latrine shaft, then she helped her mistress to bed.

Matilda resisted, hanging back. 'Not there,' she said, thrust-ing out her lower lip. 'Don't want to sleep in his bed.'

'It is better than the floor, my lady. Why should you punish yourself for his weakness?' Helisende demanded. 'He lay with another woman, she bore a child. Such matters are not the end of the world.'

'He betrayed me,' Matilda flung.

'Mayhap, but where you sleep will not alter things.' Helisende gave her a little shake, as if the gesture were capable of imparting reason. 'Besides, he could not have lain with her here. Three seasons ago Gisors was less than a stone in Robert de Bêlleme's eye. Come now.' As if dealing with one of Matilda's children, Helisende cajoled Matilda to lie down, removed her shoes and wimple, and drew the coverlet gently up to her shoulders. 'All will seem better in the morning,' she murmured.

'It won't,' Matilda declared mutinously. Through a wine haze she remembered Sybille leaning over her when she was a child, soothing her with promises that her father would be home soon. Promises that had lulled her to sleep only to prove how hollow they were in the cold light of day. Her lids felt as if they had been weighted with lead seals, her tongue seemed too large for her mouth, and her limbs belonged to someone else. Tomorrow. She would deal with it when it arrived, but she would not expect anything to be better.

Matilda awoke to a headache so huge that it seemed to fill the room and leave no space for anything but the appalling, drum-ming pain. Groaning, she pulled the coverlet over her head, but she could not settle back into the dark cocoon of oblivion. Her bladder was bursting and shifting position made no difference to the urgent demand.

Eyes half closed, she tottered from the bed to the waste shaft, somehow lifted her gown and chemise out of the way, and squatted. Outside she could hear the shouts of men at battle practice and the creak of cartwheels as supplies rolled into the compound. The day appeared to be well under way. Matilda decided she did not want to be a part of it and wandered blearily back towards the bed.

'My lady, you are awake?' Helisende appeared from the domestic end of the hall, a steaming cup of something herbal in her hand.

Matilda winced. 'If I am dreaming, it is a nightmare,' she said and taking the cup, inhaled the aroma of chamomile. She took a tentative sip and found the astringent taste had been made just about palatable with honey. Walking slowly, she returned to the bed and sat down on the coverlet.

Helisende went away but returned moments later with a ewer of scented water for washing. 'That woman of Chester's was asking me about the babe,' she said as she laid a folded linen towel on the bed.

'What babe?' Matilda asked, and then remembered. Her lips tightened and dark misery filled her mind. 'What of it?'

'She wanted to know if you were going to come and see him today.'

Matilda took another sip of the brew and rubbed her aching forehead. Last night she had told herself that only duty remained, and against that duty had drunk herself into the worst megrim of her entire life. 'I suppose if I must,' she snapped ungraciously and glared at the maid. 'I wonder what my lord would have said to me if he had returned from crusade and found me with another man's child in my arms? Would he have accepted it into his life as I am expected to accept this one?'

'Likely not, my lady,' said Helisende, 'but then men are simple creatures. Rope them by the loins and you may lead them anywhere . . . and they are always too willing to be thus captured.'

'And the women pay,' Matilda said bitterly. 'Either with their reputations or their lives.'

Helisende tilted her head to one side like an inquisitive bird. 'Will you forgive him, my lady?'

'I do not know yet,' Matilda said. 'You are asking me if I will recover from a wound that is still bleeding.'

When the potion had done its work and her head no longer felt as if it was being pounded from the inside by a spiked mace she pinned her cloak at her shoulders and crossed the path to Chester's dwelling. Helisende followed at her heels until Matilda turned.

'Go and find my groom and Sir Walter. Tell them to saddle the horses and have the men ready.'

'We are leaving, my lady?' Helisende looked at her askance. 'Is that wise?'

Matilda gave a bitter laugh. 'I do not know what is wise any more and what is not. What I do know is that I will have no peace until I have been to Evreux and seen for myself.'

'My lady I . . .'

'Do not argue – go!' Matilda's eyes flashed.

Helisende's lips tightened. 'Yes, my lady,' she said, 'and dipped her mistress a very proper curtsey to show her resentment.

Matilda responded with a glacial stare and the maid stalked off on her errand, head high and spine stiff with indignation.

Matilda closed her eyes, swallowed, and entered Chester's hall. There was no sign of the Earl, but Alaise was seated before the fire, the baby mewling in her lap as she changed his swaddling. Matilda made herself go and look at him, forced herself to pick him up and hold him along her arm. Whatever the circumstances of his begetting and birth, he was innocent. She had to accept him because he would be raised as part of Simon's household. It would be at least seven or eight years before he went away to be trained as a knight or a priest – perhaps not even then, if Simon chose to raise him at his side.

'Does he have a name?' she asked Hugh Lupus' mistress,

who was watching her with wary eyes as if she expected Matilda to dash the baby against the hearthstones.

'I believe he was christened for his sire, my lady.'

Simon. The name slashed Matilda like the whetted blade of a knife. What else had she expected? A mistress was bound to name her offspring after the father, to remind him of his obligation if naught else.

The baby's skin was as soft as the new petal of a rose. Although the tiny features were immature, she could see Simon in them clearly. His chin, the set of the lips. There was no doubting his paternity. Carefully, knowing that she dared make no sudden moves without snapping her precarious control, she returned the baby to the woman's arms.

'Do you ever think of Lord Hugh's wife when you bed with him and bear his bastards?' she demanded.

The woman shrugged. 'Why should I? As long as he don't bring me under the same roof as her, she's content. My lord is a man of strong appetite and she don't have much of one herself. They bide together out of duty.'

Duty, that word again. Matilda shrank from it. Was she more than a duty to Simon? 'And you bide with Lord Hugh out of love?' she scoffed.

Alaise gave a ripe snort of laughter. 'Oh aye,' she said forthrightly, 'I'm fond of the old fool, it is true, and he knows his way around the bedsheets for all his size, but I'd not be as fond if it weren't for this and this.' She plucked the rich red wool of her gown, and touched the gold brooch pinned high at her shoulder. 'We keep each other satisfied.'

Was that why she was looking at a baby and not at a mother and child? Matilda wondered. Was it lack of satisfaction that had driven Simon and his mistress apart?

The only way was to find out. 'Here,' she said to Alaise, and gave her a silver coin from the purse on her belt. 'Add this to your collection.'

CHAPTER 41

'Will you take wine, Countess? You must be thirsty after your journey.' The Abbess lifted a handsome silver flagon.

Matilda did not particularly want to drink wine with the Abbess, but she knew that the courtesies had to be observed before the meat of the matter could be discussed. 'Thank you,' she nodded. 'It is too early for the dust of the road to lodge in my throat, but I have travelled far.'

The Abbess poured the dark red wine into two exquisite goblets of carved rock crystal with silver bases. A wealthy convent, Evreux, not a place to take in common waifs and strays. But noble mistresses, perhaps.

Matilda took the solid weight of the goblet into her hands with a murmur. She sipped the wine and proclaimed agreeably on its excellence. They discussed the state of the roads and the dangers for travellers, and spoke of the turning season. Then the silence fell and the moment came. Matilda set her cup down on the trestle table at the side of her chair. 'You must have an inkling why I am here,' she said.

'The subject, perhaps, if not the reason.' The Abbess inclined her head. 'Indeed, Countess, when your husband visited us he did not mention that you were here in Normandy.'

'That is because he does not know.'

The Abbess' eyes widened briefly before she lowered them to contain and conceal her surprise. Her face remained smooth, expressionless. It was a skill of nuns, Matilda thought, and wondered if Simon's leman would have it.

'I intend to discuss the matter with him as soon as he returns from his duties in the field,' she said.

'I see,' the Abbess murmured.

Matilda had the uncomfortable notion that the woman did see – and all too well. 'I need to speak with the child's mother,' she said.

The Abbess started to shake her head.

'I will remain here until I do,' Matilda said determinedly. 'It goes without saying that I am prepared to be a generous benefactor for your support in this matter.' She lifted the travelling satchel she had brought with her onto the table and withdrew a fat leather pouch of silver coins.

The Abbess' nostrils flared. 'You need not resort to bribery, Countess,' she said coldly. 'Even were I to take it, I should tell you that Sister Sabina paid her dower in gold.' She rose to her feet. 'I will ask her if she wants to see you, but if she refuses I will not force her.'

Matilda wanted to withdraw the coin and crawl under a stone, but it was too late for either to be of much use. 'Then give this money to the needy,' she said. 'As alms without condition.'

The Abbess took the bag of coins and carried it to an aumbry set in the wall. She unlocked the triangular door using a key at her belt and placed the coins within the small cupboard. 'I will go and see if Sister Sabina will come to you,' she murmured. 'There is more wine in the flagon if you wish it.'

She left in a soft rustle of dark wool skirts. Matilda rose and wandered around the room. The walls, for all their limewashed spaciousness, felt as if they were pressing in upon her. Taking deep breaths, she went to the open shutters and looked out on a vista of trees, newly clothed in spring greenery. Sabina. Until the Abbess had spoken, Matilda had not known her name. It was of the nobility, or the merchant classes. And she had paid her dower to Christ in gold – her own, or Simon's? Throughout the journey from Gisors to Evreux, she had been pondering what to say, what to ask. How much could she bear to know? How much would she rather abjure? She had no answers, just more questions and uncertainty.

Behind her, the door quietly opened. She was aware of a cold draught on her spine, but she did not immediately look around. One more deep breath. One more moment to calm the thundering of her heart. Slowly, slowly she turned.

A young woman stood just over the threshold. Her dark gown was tidy, her rope girdle was neatly tied, and the knotted ends hung at precisely the same level. A string of polished amber prayer beads was looped through her belt, ending on a carved wooden cross. Her wimple framed a pale, oval face with delicate features and arresting, deep grey eyes with soot-black lashes. There were fine lines at her eye corners and the hint of others beginning between nose and mouth. Matilda had been prepared to face a simpering younger woman, all plump curves, and was thrown to discover that this Sabina was perhaps much closer to Simon's age than her own.

There was a tense moment that seemed to last for ever, stretching and stretching like a strand of raw fleece spun on the distaff, twirling, pulling out, preparing to snap.

'I wasn't going to come.' Sabina was the first to speak, her voice clear and steady, breaking the tension before it broke the thread. 'But then I thought that if you had come so far it would be discourteous and cowardly to refuse this interview . . . and in truth I was curious to see you.'

Her manner was stately and dignified. She neither curtseyed to Matilda nor yielded deference, but she was not insolent. Just supremely aware of her own worth.

'Curious?' Matilda smiled icily. She could feel all her Norman blood gathering and welling up in her, willing her to play the bitch. Her mother, her grandmother, Robert, Duke of Normandy, whom some had called Robert the Devil, and all held down hard by the generosity and strength that had been her father's mainstay and his failing. 'Well, perhaps no more curious than I have been to see you.'

'He told you about me then?'

Her composure was not as firm as it first appeared. Matilda saw the way the crucifix on her bosom shivered to the rapid beating of her heart.

'He told me nothing, nor does he know I am here. But your son and his lies in a basket in Gisors and I am expected to take him into my household.' A coal of anger burned in her voice. 'I came to see what manner of woman you were – pious nun, used innocent, or whylom whore.'

Sabina's eyes flashed and Matilda saw that she had drawn blood.

'I am no whore!' she said proudly. 'I have given myself to no man but my husband, God rest his soul . . .'

'And mine!' Matilda bit out.

Sabina gave her a look, which said she thought that Matilda was being unfair. 'And yours, my lady,' she concurred, 'but not for payment.'

'Then for what – love?' The word emerged raw with pain.

Sabina winced. 'By your mercy I would ask a cup of wine,' she said.

'Perhaps I do not feel merciful,' Matilda said coldly, but negated her words by stepping aside and gesturing to the trestle.

Sabina lifted the flagon and filled the rock crystal cup that the Abbess had been using. Then she took a long drink and Matilda saw that her hands were shaking. Compassion slipped past her guard, despite her determination to be ruthless.

'I knew Simon many years ago in the time of Rufus' father,' Sabina said as she lowered the cup. 'I was the daughter of one of the King's falconers and Simon was a royal squire. We were not lovers then, but we played at love for a summer.' She fixed her gaze firmly on Matilda. 'I came to my husband a maid, and never looked at another man for all the time we were wed.'

'Go on,' said Matilda harshly, refusing to give quarter.

Sabina bit her lip. 'Saer died on crusade – he drowned when our ship overturned in Brindisi harbour. I was witless with grief. Simon took me into his camp.'

'As a laundress,' Matilda said with a sarcastic nod.

A pink flush stained Sabina's cheeks. 'And nothing more, my lady,' she said in a voice that could have sharpened a knife. 'Not until he took sick of the evil humours in his leg and almost died. They fetched the priest to him twice.' She swallowed hard and her composure slipped another degree. 'I had lost my husband and my children. Should I have let the love of my youth die too? I fought for him tooth and nail. It was a bloody battle, but I won.' For a moment the memory of the triumph blazed out of her eyes, but as it faded she dropped her gaze and took another swallow of wine. 'Once he regained enough strength to appreciate his life, we celebrated our survival, and at the time it did not seem wrong. Home was so far away that it had almost no meaning. It was as if we were cast adrift. It was lust, I admit, but it was more than lust too.'

'And the child?'

Tears suddenly welled in Sabina's eyes. 'I had not reckoned on conceiving,' she said. 'But then I did ask God for one – it was the reason Saer and I went on crusade.'

'And yet you gave him up.'

'I had decided to take holy vows before I knew I was with child. I cannot keep him here for then he would be raised to become a monk. I wanted him to have more choice than that . . . and I thought it was fair that he should know his father and that his father should know him.'

Matilda considered Sabina through narrowed lids. 'But why settle for a nunnery?' she asked. 'Did you not want to remain as Simon's mistress? You could have kept your child then.'

The tears overflowed and spilled down Sabina's cheeks. 'Oh, I thought about it, my lady,' she said. 'But where would have been the peace in that? I would have wanted the whole, not the half – and it must be the same for you. It might have been different if Simon did not love you – but he does, deeply. I cannot compete with that.'

Matilda's brows rose. 'He has a strange way of showing it,'

she said. Her stomach churned. How did this woman know that Simon loved her when she did not?

A glimmer of impatience flickered in the tear-wet eyes. 'I make no excuses for either of us,' she said, 'save to say that given different circumstances it would never have happened. I know that he did not look at other women on our journey. There were brothels aplenty along the way and the only time he visited one was to drag Turstan out by the ears.' She sniffed and blotted her eyes on her sleeve. 'He bought you the bulbs of the milk-flower in the markets of Constantinople and he thought of you constantly. Are you going to crucify him for one frail slip?'

Matilda felt a burning begin behind her own eyes. She would not weep, she told herself furiously. 'I needed to know it was one frail slip,' she said, managing to keep her voice steady by keeping it hard. 'I needed to know why you chose the convent and gave up your child.'

Sabina nodded stiffly. 'I would have wanted to know the same,' she said.

Again a silence fell between the women, Matilda studying the smooth dignified features of the woman who had chosen the convent above the castle, and Sabina considering Matilda's statuesque Viking beauty and knowing that her choice was right.

'There is one boon I ask of you,' she said. 'From time to time, will you let me know how my son fares?'

Matilda inclined her head. 'Even had I hated you, I would have done my duty,' she said. 'Your son will be reared to fit whatever station he chooses, be it warrior or monk. And when the time is right, he will be told about his mother.'

'Thank you.' There was gratitude in Sabina's eyes. 'You do not hate me, then?' she said tentatively.

Matilda shrugged. 'I was prepared to,' she said. 'But I cannot. If I do not love you either, you will understand why.'

'And you do not hate Simon?'

An arid smile curved Matilda's lips. 'That remains to be seen,' she said.

CHAPTER 42

Simon laid his hand along the grey's arched neck in a soothing gesture, but the stallion still jibbed and sidled, showing the whites of its eyes.

They were entering territory that had been held by the French at the beginning of Rufus' campaign, and was still hotly disputed. He knew that De Serigny had come this way. A couple of villages had already attested to the passage of his troop: horses taken and not paid for, three suckling pigs lifted from a sty, a tavern relieved of a barrel of wine.

'Gently there, gently there,' he murmured, tugging the grey's ears and wondering what was disturbing the beast. To assuage the prickling of hair at his nape, he sent two soldiers forward to scout ahead. Slipping his shield from its long strap on his back, he brought it onto his left arm and thrust his hand through the two shorter leather grips. A gesture signalled his troop to do the same. At his shoulder, Toki ostentatiously unhooked his axe from his saddle and clutched the ash haft in his large, war-scarred fist.

Simon was beginning to wonder if his intuition had played him wrong when he inhaled the taint of smoke on the wind and suddenly the road ahead turned misty. The destrier's nostrils flared in alarm and its ears went back. His scouts reappeared at the gallop and drew rein before him in a shower of clods.

'My lord, De Serigny's men have fired a village!' one of the

soldiers panted, thumbing up his helm by the nasal bar. Foam
churned his mount's bridle-bit, and the animal was steaming
with sweat.

Cursing, Simon bellowed to his troop and spurred the grey.
The horse lunged into a gallop and he gasped as the high
pommel of the saddle butted his midriff. The smoke grew
thicker and more acrid and now they could hear the flames
roaring through the timber and thatch. The gleeful shouts of
men reached them too, and the wild squealing of a pig suddenly
cut short. Simon spurred around the last curve and entered
what looked like the mouth of hell.

Bodies strewed the village street, felled in the act of running
to judge from their sprawled positions. A man with a scythe,
his head almost cut through; an old woman, her corpse woven
with glistening bloody threads. A baby on a spear. Simon's
gorge rose. One of the younger men in his troop, green to the
atrocities of warfare, leaned over his saddle and was violently
sick.

A soldier ran out of one of the burning buildings, stuffing
a leather money pouch inside his gambeson. He turned on
seeing Simon's troop and his eyes widened in alarm until he
recognised Simon's banner. 'Come to join the entertainment,
my lord?' he said with a bow that bore as much mockery as
deference.

'Where's De Serigny?' Simon snapped.

'Further in.' He gave Simon a sidelong look. 'Their lord's
gone over to the French.' He bared his teeth. 'They deserve
what they get.'

A muscle bunched in Simon's jaw and he commanded his
men to disarm the soldier of his weapons and spoils. 'Take your
horse and go. Be thankful that I do not have the time to swing
you from the nearest tree.'

Still snarling, but knowing that escape was better than
choking on a rope, the soldier ran to his horse, vaulted into the
saddle and galloped off. Grimly, Simon spurred on.

The entire village was on fire. Choking gouts of smoke rose

from every dwelling. Not one had been spared. The church still stood, but the priest lay dead against the door, his skull crushed and his blood staining the stones. Half a dozen miserable survivors huddled in the square, roped to each other. Looking at them, Simon saw that they had only been allowed to live because they were useful. Four were young and reasonably attractive women. Two were strong men and would have crafts that could be utilised. Had Robert de Bêlleme himself been present, a few more might have been taken for later sport in the dungeons where the baron stored a terrifying array of instruments of torture.

De Serigny emerged on horseback from the church, his sword red-bladed in his fist and a grin dividing his dark moustache and beard. That grin vanished as he set eyes on Simon and his larger troop. Flourishing the sword, he spurred into the street. 'What's wrong, De Senlis? Don't you trust me to make a thorough job?' he sneered. A jewelled cross bulged from his saddle pack.

'You would desecrate a church?' Simon roared and his own blade flashed, the steel edge rippling with reflected fire and smoke. His rage was incandescent. 'Your soul will rot in hell!'

De Serigny snorted with contemptuous amusement. 'Hah! Perhaps marriage to an English wife has softened your brain as well as your sword!' he spat. 'The church holds no sanctuary for traitors! My Lord De Bêlleme would not be so squeamish!'

'I well know Lord De Bêlleme's attitude,' Simon growled, 'but he is not here, and you take your orders from me.'

'I think not,' De Serigny spat in the dust. 'Villages burn, peasants die. Wolves eat sheep – especially the lame weaklings.'

Simon's fury became a white wind, made all the more devastating because he so rarely lost his temper. He spurred the grey, and at the same time swung his sword.

De Serigny was ready and parried the blow, but there was a hint of surprise, almost fear in his eyes. Simon's control was legendary. He was known to be a good general and a fine reconnaissance soldier, but few had ever seen him in active engagement. It was assumed among the men that he avoided conflict because of the weakness in his leg.

Simon turned the grey and turned him again, always pressing the attack. His blows were not heavily landed, but each one was balanced and precise. De Serigny had no room for error, and when he opened up too far Simon struck with the speed of an adder. The sword slipped beneath the protection of hauberk and gambeson sleeve and gouged flesh from wrist to elbow. A rapid twist divided the forearm bones. De Serigny's voice rose and broke on a keening scream. He tried to retreat, but Simon withdrew his blade only to press the advantage – and did not stop until De Serigny fell from his horse and lay dead in the street among the bodies of the villagers. 'Never mistake a lion for a lamb!' he said contemptuously to the corpse.

There was an uneasy silence. Simon wiped his blade along his chausses several times and gazed around, hard-eyed, at De Serigny's shocked men. 'Does anyone else want to dispute from whom they take their orders?' he demanded. His heart was thudding furiously at the base of his throat and waves of nausea were beginning to surge from the hard ball in his stomach that had been the burning core of his rage. He had control of himself again and knew that he had to hold them with his words and the force of his stare. He was in no condition to take on more of their number.

'Good,' he said curtly. 'Then it is settled. Free those people and return to Gisors. I will have words to say later. And do not think to tell a tale of innocence to Hugh Lupus. He knows well enough De Serigny's reputation.'

Scowling, sullen, but not daring to disobey, De Serigny's men did as Simon bade. With bad grace, their second in command took his knife and slashed the rope binding the captives. De Serigny's corpse was slung across his horse like a giant bolster. Simon tugged the jewelled cross from the saddlebag, dismounted and limped into the desecrated church. The damage was superficial. The aumbry cupboards had been ripped open and candles crushed on the floor. A holy vestment coffer yawned open, its hasp hacked off and its contents rifled. A statue of the Virgin Mary had been decapitated and the head flung against the wall so that it had shattered in powdered fragments. There were signs of struggle, clots of blood and hair on the holy water stoup.

Simon returned the jewelled cross to the altar and genuflected. He bowed his head in swift reverence and prayer, then eased to his feet.

Outside, hooves thundered and someone shouted. Cursing his lameness, Simon hastened towards the door.

The soldier whom Simon had dismissed earlier was back, wild-eyed. Struggling to control his cavorting horse, he reined to face Simon.

'The French!' he bellowed. 'The French are here, my lord. I've just run into one of their patrols on the road!'

There was no time. Already the thunder of French hooves shook the ground, and Simon knew well how the French would react to this scene of carnage, and it wasn't with sweet forgiveness. 'Christ man, you're mounted up!' Simon snarled. 'Double round and get word to Gisors! The rest of you, to me, now!'

'I still say you should not have come,' said Hugh Lupus testily to Matilda. 'It is too dangerous for a woman.'

Matilda gave him a stubborn look that reminded him so much of her great uncle, the Conqueror, that despite his irritation and anxiety he was almost tripped into laughter.

'You have already made your opinion of the matter quite clear, my lord,' she said primly. 'Besides, you could have prevented me from riding with you had you truly desired. All you needed to do was put me under guard in the bower.'

Hugh Lupus did grin then. 'And have you escape by knotting the sheets together and climbing out of the window? No, my lady. I leave it to your husband to deal with you in a fit manner. I have no desire to handle such a termagant.' Actually he did. His wife was the model of what he expected a wife to be, dutiful, retiring, but capable of running a household. His mistresses were always attractive, flighty baggages with impudent tongues. Matilda of Northampton was an intriguing blend of both, and with more than a suggestion of temper at the moment. He had contemplated making overtures to her while she was reeling over her husband's infidelity. She might be persuaded that sauce for the gander was also sauce for the goose. However he valued Simon's friendship and prudence had tempered his intention. Also, he had not wanted the daggers in her eyes to become a dagger in her hand.

'I am no termagant,' she said.

Hugh Lupus snorted. 'That is what your grandmother Adelaide used to say,' he retorted, 'but I never believed her. The women of your house have always been formidable.' He looked at her. 'But I still do not see why you feel so strong a need to put yourself in danger, my lady. Your presence here will make no difference to the outcome – save that I must spare men to guard you.'

'It is my duty,' she said tightly.

He studied the firm line of her chin, the full lips now drawn in slightly and pursed, the determination in her eyes. 'Duty my arse,' he said. 'If you were a woman of duty, you would be at home minding your needle. If I did not know your mother better, I would say that she stinted on your training.'

She blazed him a glance that threatened to singe his eyebrows. 'My mother stinted not one whit on my upbringing,' she said in a voice that quivered. 'She stayed at home, minding her needle, and my father rode away to his death. I stayed at home, like a dutiful wife, while my husband rode away to the Holy Wars.' Her lips drew back, giving him a beneficial view of her strong, white teeth. 'I stayed at home nursing my children, tending our lands while he took up with another woman and got a bastard child on her. There is duty and there is duty, my lord. Do not seek to tell me which kind I should follow now for my own good.'

'I would also say that you are your mother's daughter,' Hugh

Lupus said wryly. 'A man would never tangle with her out of choice – excepting your father, and look what happened to him.'

Matilda whitened. For a moment he thought she might fall back on the feminine weapon of tears. Her throat worked, but she gained control of herself. 'That was unworthy, my lord,' she said.

Chester snorted. 'I am known for my plain speaking,' he retorted, 'not my chivalry.' Raising his head, he narrowed his eyes towards one of the scouts he had sent ahead of them. The man was returning at a gallop, lashing the reins down on his mount's neck.

'My lord, I pray you make haste!' he declared. 'Earl Simon is barricaded in the church and the French have broken through!'

'God's sweet bollocks!' Hugh Lupus swore. He turned to Matilda. 'I have no time to dally behind, nor to protect you,' he said curtly. Stay back with the baggage wain until told otherwise! You have no part to play in a battle, but you will be needed later to tend and succour the wounded!'

Mustering his troop, clapping spurs to his mount, he was gone in a shower of clods and stones.

'Best do as he says, my lady,' said the knight in command of the baggage wain, and grasped Matilda's bridle lest she harboured any different ideas. 'If there's hard fighting, no one wants a woman to hamper the swing of their sword.'

'No, but everyone will want one to tend their wounds and warm their beds in the aftermath!' she snapped at him. 'I may be a countess by birth, but I am no wilting flower.' She gave him a proud look. 'My grandfather was an axe-wielding Danish Viking who once fought a wild bear single-handed. I know my own worth.' She flicked her hand at him, commanding him to let go of her bridle.

He did so reluctantly, but rode his horse close, prepared to grab the rein at the first sign of skittishness on her behalf. Her stomach churned with anxiety, but she steadied herself. Even if she did charge after Hugh Lupus' knights and arrive in the thick of the fray, she could do nothing, and, as the young soldier said, she would only hamper their sword arms.

Ever since the news had been delivered, she had been vacillating between sick terror for Simon's safety and deep anger at him for the situation he had left her to discover at Gisors. Another woman. A newborn child. A side of his life he had concealed and she had not remotely guessed at. Her training ground had been a harsh one and she had maintained her external composure very well, but even like the best tempered steel she had a breaking point, and was close to it now. Catching her mood, her mount sidled and flickered its ears.

'How far to the fighting?' she demanded. Her hands twitched on the reins.

'About a mile, my lady,' the knight said, still eyeing her dubiously. 'Beyond that wooded hill.'

They followed the track around the foot of the slope, their horses trotting swiftly in the muddy scored hoofprints of Chester's main troop. There were heavy wheel ruts too, from laden carts. Rounding a curve, the smell of smoke hit them, and when Matilda gazed into the sky she saw the rising grey haze. Her heart began to pound. Her hands were suddenly slick on the bridle. Within a hundred yards the smoke had thickened and the smell had become a stench.

'My lady, perhaps you should stay back,' the knight cautioned, looking anxious.

A large part of Matilda agreed with him and wished that she had never left her garden in Northampton to follow her wayward husband. The larger part, however, was consumed by a desperate fear for Simon's safety and a need to be with him. 'No,' she said. 'I have to go on!' To give impetus to the bravado, she heeled her mare's flanks and sent her cantering into the village.

The sight that met her eyes was one of utter devastation. Heaps of charred wood marked the areas where dwellings had stood. Some still retained fragments of structure, twisted, black, skeletal. The corpses of pigs and dogs sprawled grotesquely among the debris. A scorched pail lay on its side next to a smashed well housing. Matilda swallowed the fluid that filled her mouth. 'Dear Jesu,' she whispered and crossed herself. There was a patch of garden neatly dug and tended. Herbs bordered the edge and new green shoots of onions, garlic and cabbage were growing strongly. Its owner lay in the middle, her kerchief torn off and her legs sprawled wide. A pitchfork pinned her body to the soil.

Matilda leaned over her horse's withers and retched. A garden was a place of nurture and sanctuary . . . not this vile destruction.

The knight grasped her mount's bridle and tried to lead the mare away, but Matilda struck his hand away.

'My lady, I beg you. It is not safe.'

'That I can see!' she sobbed, indicating the woman in the garden.

The village street was suddenly filled with soldiers on horseback. There was no time to move aside. Caught up in the flurry, Matilda's protectors drew their swords, but they were at a standstill and the oncoming men were at full gallop. Not Chester's, she had time to see, nor Simon's, and then they were too close and the battle closed over her head like a hungry open mouth.

There was a clash of blade on hauberk rivets, a whump of steel meeting flesh, and Matilda's guardian lost the hand that had been closed around her bridle. He screamed, the sound stopping short as a lance followed the work of the sword and ran him through. Matilda's mare reared and plunged in terror. Unable to hold her, scared witless herself, Matilda was thrown. She landed hard, struck her head and blackness hit her like a fist and left her sprawled in the road against the wrecked garden palisade.

Toki spared no time for dramatic gestures with his axe: up, round and down in a single blurred arc of steel to swipe aside the French soldier who had run at him down the nave. Beside him Simon used his shield to fend off another two, while he parried and thrust with his sword. They were holding the French, but only just, and for every one of the enemy downed there was a fresh man to take his place. There would be no ransoms taken this time. It was kill or be killed.

Simon's lungs were burning with effort. His shield felt as if it were made of lead, and he could feel the quiver of over-strained muscles in his weak left leg. Toki was tireless. He was even singing to himself as he swung and struck. Now Simon truly understood what his father and brother had faced on Hastings field.

Three more French soldiers came at them. Simon thrust his shield into the face of one, but the man was swift and strong. His sword found an opening and struck sidelong at Simon's ribs, raising blue sparks from the hauberk rivets. The air gasped from Simon's lungs and fiery pain streaked across his chest, but the heat of battle kept him upright and sheer desperation brought his own sword up to parry the next blow. Blade rasped on blade and slivers of metal flew from the Frenchman's, which was not as well tempered as Simon's. A shard lodged in the back of Simon's hand and the blood from the wound ran through the cracks in his clenched fist and fouled his grip on his sword. He used his shield to parry and was forced back-wards by the Frenchman's greater strength.

A horn sounded frantically somewhere. Simon was in too much extremity to do more than note the sound with a small corner of his mind, but that corner despaired, for it was the attack clarion and he was already overwhelmed. His left leg gave way and he went down, but as he fell he gave one last swipe with his sword. The blow connected with the Frenchman's knee and brought him down too. Lungs wheez-ing like worn-out bellows, Simon rolled over and with one last effort thrust his blade into his enemy's throat.

Stars burst before his eyes. The salty heat of blood sprayed him. On hands and knees he scrabbled for his shield, knowing that if he had to face anyone else he was finished. Pushing himself to his feet by will alone, he glanced around. A cursing Toki was wrenching his axe out of the second French soldier, who lay on top of the first. The church suddenly contained only Simon's gasping, exhausted men. Simon staggered to the door. There was fierce fighting in the street and he belatedly realised that the horn he had heard had meant salvation, not death – for some at least.

'If Hugh Lupus wasn't so fat, he might have got here sooner,' Toki panted, seeking to make light of the situation with sour jest. 'Any later and he would have been shovelling earth over our corpses as well as those of the French.'

'You have no gratitude,' Simon said and began to laugh, but as a release from tension rather than from genuine humour.

Toki snorted and clutched his shoulder. 'It is the English blood,' he retorted. 'We are ever ungrateful to our Norman masters.'

Simon sobered. 'It is I who should be grateful to you for saving my life a dozen times over,' he said. 'I can never repay the debt.'

'You could try,' Toki retorted with a grin. 'I would not object.' He pointed at the blood webbing Simon's hand. 'Better get yourself seen to, my lord.'

Simon nodded absently. The splinter of sword was still in his flesh. Raising his hand to his mouth, he gripped the sliver in his teeth and with a sharp tug pulled it out. Fresh blood gushed from the wound, but he bound it up tightly in a strip of linen purloined from the vestment coffer. The church was a total shambles, but the jewelled cross still gleamed softly over all, neither stolen nor dislodged during the intense fighting. That had to be a good omen.

Tottering outside, he became aware of his other aches and pains. Each breath drawn was a sawing ache. His legs felt like wet rope, but he managed to breathe and he managed to walk.

'God's arse but you get yourself into some situations!' Hugh Lupus declared striding up to him. His mail hauberk and the padding beneath made him look gargantuan. He had removed his helm and sweat was pouring down his face. Beads of it glistened in his saturated hair.

'Serigny burned the village, and a French patrol took exception,' Simon answered, grimacing through his teeth. 'I was in the wrong place at the wrong time.' He glanced around. 'And so were these poor people.' Suddenly he felt weary to death. All he wanted to do was lie down in a corner and close his eyes, but he was a commander and there was too much to be done.

Hugh Lupus' squire brought two cups of wine. Hugh seized one and drank it to the lees. 'Another,' he commanded the youth.

Simon swallowed his own and wiped his mouth on the back of his good hand.

'You might as well know, your wife is here,' Chester said with a certain relish. 'Arrived at the gates of Gisors as you left on patrol.'

'What?' Simon used the word as a flimsy handhold to grope for reason.

Chester repeated what he had said and drank his wine, pausing this time between swallows. 'Your wife knows about your mistress and to say that hell would seem cold by comparison is not an exaggeration. Countess Judith had a way of looking that could shrivel a man's cods in their sack, but her daughter's element is fire. Why any man should desire a mistress when he has such a woman for a wife is beyond me – unless you are a man who lusts after variety.'

'Sabina wasn't my mistress,' Simon said faintly, his wits further bludgeoned by the notion of Matilda's presence in all this.

'But the child is yours?'

'Christ yes, but . . .' Simon shook his head.' It is not what you think.' He hitched at his swordbelt. 'Where is Matilda now?'

'Back with my baggage wain.' Hugh said.

'What, you brought her here?' Simon was incredulous and horrified. 'Are you out of your wits?'

'I had no choice . . . short of binding her hand and foot and casting her in De Bêlleme's dungeon,' Hugh snapped. 'She wouldn't be stopped. It is all I could do to make her stay back. She said that it was her duty.'

Simon groaned and limped into the street. There was no sign of his wife. He wondered what had possessed her to travel from England, across Normandy to the dangerous war torn lands of the Vexin. She was too responsible to act on a whim . . . or was she? How much did he truly know about his wife? Perhaps as much as he had known about Sabina. Almost nothing.

Anger and anxiety surged through him, keeping the exhaustion at bay. He saw Chester's covered baggage wain lumbering into the bailey, drawn by two large black cobs. As it turned side on and drew to a halt, he also saw that there was a bay mare hitched to the back – a lady's mount, for no man rode a mare into battle unless he was a Saracen. But there was no sign of his wife.

He hastened towards the wain, uncaring that his limp was pronounced and for all to see. Uncaring that he stumbled. He reached the bay mare and, laying hands to the bridle, saw that it was Matilda's. The silver lozenges at browband and cheek-strap identified it beyond a doubt.

Then he looked in the wain and his heart froze.

'Matilda?' Abandoning the horse, he scrambled up into the covered cart. She lay on a makeshift bed of straw and sheep-skins amidst the various items of Hugh Lupus' travelling household, a cooking pot near her head, wooden tent struts at her feet. Her face was as pale as ice, and upon it the jagged cut and swollen blue bruise on her temple stood out in stark relief.

'Jesu God, Matilda?' He shook her shoulder but she was as limp and unresponsive as his daughter's cloth doll. Waves of fear rolled over him, making him cold and sick.

'She got tangled up with the French troops when they fled,' said the soldier who had been driving the wain. 'Got thrown by her horse.' He sleeved his nose and mouth. 'Can't see any other injuries on her, but she struck her head a heavy blow.'

He gave Simon a look in which there was speculation and sympathy. 'She hasn't moved since I picked her up.'

Simon swallowed. Tears prickled behind his lids and he blinked angrily. Long ago Waltheof had chastised him for self-pity and he had a morbid fear of becoming caught in its morass again. But if she died . . . He stroked one of her shining red-bronze braids. If she died, his life would not be worth the living.

CHAPTER 43

Matilda heard the low drone of a voice intoning in Latin and felt cool moisture on her brow as a gentle finger painted it with the shape of a cross. The click of prayerbeads joined the murmur. She wondered in confusion for whom everyone was praying. Perhaps she ought to join in . . . but she was very tired and her head ached so badly that even considering the notion made her feel sick. Perhaps if she slept first . . .

Simon had been watching Matilda's still face and thought he saw a ripple pass over it as the priest anointed her with the holy oil. But she did not move again, and no one else had seen a sign.

Three days she had lain in this cold trance. They had borne her back to Gisors on a litter and Simon had ridden alongside it, terrified that she was going to die. She hadn't, but he was aware of time trickling away and with it her chances of recovery. They had managed to dribble a small amount of milk down her throat, but she needed more sustenance than that. Already he fancied that the hollows beneath her cheekbones were cadaverous.

Chester gave Simon's shoulder a hearty slap. 'Come away,' he said. 'Leave her to the women. There is naught you can do here but get in their way.'

'I would rather stay,' Simon said and stiffened his spine, against the Earl's bonhomie. It was well intentioned, but it grated upon him like two ends of broken bone.

'Christ man, you're a soldier, not a wet nurse! She won't know if you stay or leave. Sink a few cups of wine. You'll feel the better for it.'

'She might not know, but I would,' he replied grimly. 'And sinking any more wine than I have done already will only give me a foul head.'

Chester grunted and spread his hands to show that he yielded. 'You are a couple well suited,' he declared. 'Both out of your wits.'

Chester left his irritation evident in the heaviness of his foot-steps, but Simon barely noticed except to be relieved that he had gone. He took Matilda's hand in his. The fingers were warm and relaxed. He rubbed the pad of his thumb over the carved stone of her wedding ring.

'Matilda . . .' he said softly and stroked her copper hair. 'Whatever I have done to you . . . I am sorry. If I have been faithless, it was out of my own lack . . . never yours. Why in God's name you wanted to follow me to Gisors, I do not know . . . surely there are more worthy causes to pursue than a wayward husband.' There was a tight lump in his throat. 'Unless you wake and tell me, I will never know . . .'

Her face remained smooth and slack, the lips slightly parted. The silence stretched out, broken only by the settling of the charcoal in the nearby brazier and the soft murmur of Helisende and the wet nurse beyond the bed curtains.

Simon bowed his head to pray, but the physical and mental exhaustion took its toll. He closed his eyes, intending to entreat God's aid for Matilda, and promptly fell asleep.

Matilda was woken by the sound of a baby crying and someone swiftly shushing it. Her vision blurred and sharpened by turns, making her feel queasy. A fat wax candle cast gold and shadows over the bed. She was aware of a splitting headache emanating from the region of her left temple. Memories swam across her mind like dark-coloured fish and vanished into the murk before she was able to net them. There had been shouting, and battle.

The glittering edge of a sword. Blood. Pain. Nothing.

Her mouth was dry, and she could not swallow because she was so parched. She tried to raise her right hand to summon aid and found that she could not, for there was a weight pressing it to the bed. Inching her head round with difficulty, pain stabbing in sharp flashes, she saw that Simon was kneeling at the bedside and that he had fallen asleep against her arm. His fingers were meshed through hers, binding her to him. There was a three-day growth of golden-brown beard outlining his mouth and the hair at his brow had grown overlong so that his fringe was almost in his eyes. A wave of tenderness engulfed her. And then she saw the bandage wound around his other hand and the brown stains where blood had soaked through and dried.

'Simon?' she mouthed. Her voice was a parched croak. He did not raise his head, but his hand tightened its grip on hers as if he feared that she might leave while he was unguarded. Making a huge effort, she nudged him and once more breathed his name. His head came up slowly like that of a man being roused from a drunken stupor and for a moment his eyes were fogged and unknowing.

'Simon, I need a drink,' she breathed, and began to cough.

His gaze sharpened and cleared. Reaching for the cup at the bedside, he held it to her lips.

She sipped the watered wine in the cup and the dark fish of memory swam closer to the surface. She had been riding from a convent where she had just confronted her husband's lover. From beyond the curtain, the baby wailed again and the focus of her mind sharpened a further degree.

'Thank Christ,' he said, in a voice that shook. 'I have never prayed so hard in my life as I have prayed these last days . . . When the priest came to shrive you, I thought I would go mad.'

'Then you know my condition,' she murmured. 'For I too have been mad . . . mayhap I still am.' She closed her eyes, feeling sick. Pain hammered through her skull. The world and its problems were too vast to take in. It was easier to shut them out and return to the darkness.

She slept again, and when she woke Simon was still there. Indeed, she did not think that he had moved from her side, for his stubble was now decidedly a beard and even if her eyes had remained closed, she would have detected his presence by pungent smell alone. The candle no longer burned at the bedside and the curtains had been pulled back, revealing that even if the morning was not well advanced, it was beyond dawn. There was no one else in the hall, even by the hearth in the centre of the room where the cooking tripod had been moved to one side away from the direct heat of the flames.

Her head still ached but her vision was clearer, and her stomach no longer made her feel as if she were on the heaving deck of a ship. She tried to sit up and Simon moved to help her, but immediately desisted with a gasp of pain. She managed to struggle upright on her own. Her skull thundered and she was dizzy for a moment, but she weathered the feelings and looked at him in concern. 'What's wrong?'

He sat back down on the bedside stool, his hand pressed to his side. 'My ribs,' he wheezed. 'I took a blade side on and I think I've cracked a couple at least.'

'You fool, why haven't you had the chirugeon tend you?' Matilda forgot her own discomforts in witnessing his. The bandage wrapped around his hand was as grubby as a beggar's toerag and, although he had removed his mail, his quilted gambeson was so marinated in the stink of sweat, smoke and blood that it could have stood up by itself and walked around.

He shrugged, then immediately winced. 'I had a vigil to keep.' He took her hand in his and stroked it. 'I realised what I stood in danger of losing.'

Matilda found a bleak smile. 'So did I,' she said.

With his free hand he poured her a cup of wine, took a drink himself and then put the cup to her lips. The gesture was almost like the ritual of the loving cup at a marriage where bride and groom would sip from the same place. This time the wine was not watered but contained a burn of usquebaugh that made her cough.

'Sorry,' he said. 'I had to have something to sustain me in the long watch of the night.'

She made a speechless gesture to show that she would be all right in a moment. The usquebaugh launched itself from gullet to belly and flashed like fire through her veins. Her throat opened again and she inhaled a fiery breath of air.

He studied at her sombrely. The shadows beneath his eyes were the colour of slate. 'Why did you follow me to Gisors?'

She looked at him then down at the coverlet. A loose thread poked out of the braid selvage and she plucked at it. 'I came to Gisors because of my mother. And in a way I went to Evreux because of her too.'

'Your mother?' he looked at her, nonplussed.

She pointed to the chest at the bedside. 'Open it,' she said, 'and take out the roll of linen on the top.'

Wincing at the pain from his ribs, he did as she requested. 'What is it?'

She gestured him to unfasten the braid binding and unroll it. 'An embroidery. I found it when I was clearing her coffer of clothing to give as alms to the poor. She kept it all those years.'

'She had many embroideries,' Simon said as he spread the canvas out on the bed.

'Not in the end. She gave them all away . . . save this one.'

Simon looked at it, following the pattern with his eyes. A young woman on a black horse, a red-haired man on a chestnut, the stitches so skilfully wrought that an observer could almost see the breeze in their garments and hear their laughter. He touched the figures with the fingertips of his good hand and raised his head to Matilda.

'My mother put all her love and longing into an embroidery and then confined it to the darkness of a chest,' Matilda said with a lump in her throat and tears in her eyes. 'I do not want to live my life like that.' She picked up the canvas and traced the lovingly worked red-haired man with her index finger. 'I have dwelt so long in the shadows my father left behind that I am in danger of becoming a shadow myself.' Drawing a deep breath, she raised her eyes to his. 'That is why I came to find you . . . as my mother never came to find her husband.'

Simon swore softly beneath his breath. 'As I remember, she felt he had betrayed her,' he said. 'Have I not betrayed you?'

Matilda's gaze remained steadfast. 'That was what I went to Evreux to find out.'

'You could have asked me.'

'Had you been in Gisors, I would have done – likely with a pair of sewing shears. As it was, I took my fury to Evreux.' At Simon's look of alarm, she smiled, although her eyes were narrow like a cat's. 'You need not fear. Sister Sabina is still in one piece. We might not have met and parted the best of friends, but we came to an understanding. She told me what was between you.'

His exhaustion-pale complexion showed a sudden flood of colour. 'I am not proud of what happened, but I will do my best to set it rights. The child is a blameless innocent.' He took her hands in his. 'It is my duty to take him into my household – and into my heart. I will understand if you cannot do the same, but I would ask you to try.'

'It is my duty too,' Matilda said, her laughter fading. 'Of course I will do my best.' She had been taught all about duty, and how there were times when the doing of it held the world together. 'Do you still want her?' she asked in a low voice. 'Is there no part of you that regrets she has taken holy vows?'

Simon shook his head. 'It was a fire lit at a single stopping place along the way and doused to mutual agreement. I want you.'

'Do you?' She searched his face.

He took hers between his hands, the good one and the bandaged. 'I wanted you when I saw you in the garden at Northampton, and that wanting has never gone away. Never,' he said. 'And I am not speaking as a courtier or someone trying to ingratiate himself.'

'Then as what?' she whispered. Their lips were almost touching. 'Tell me, Simon. I need to know.'

'As a man who loves his wife to distraction,' he said. 'For

her courage and her love and her forgiveness. For everything that she is.'

Matilda gave a small gasp and closed the infinitesimal space between their mouths. The kiss was tender and passionate, despairing and joyous, and when their lips parted they were both breathless.

'Close the bed curtains,' she panted, her eyes luminous.

He looked at her askance and shook his head. 'I don't think I can . . .'

'No, you fool.' She smiled at him through a shimmer of tears. 'Not for that reason! Neither of us is in a fit state. If you tried to stand up you would keel over, and my head is pounding fit to burst. I just want you beside me. Come to bed and sleep.' She flapped back the bedcovers.

He looked longingly at the space she made for him. 'I stink, I need to bathe,' he said with a grimace and a sniff of his armpit.

She shrugged. 'I have no complaint. The morrow will suffice. Come.'

He yielded to her insistence, and the fatigue rushed upon him like water through a burst dam. Somehow he managed to close the bed curtains and shut out the world. Somehow he stripped his gambeson and tunic, his leg bindings and hose. His hands fumbled, and his eyelids suddenly felt as if someone had weighed them down with death pennies. Still clad in braies and shirt, he tumbled into bed beside Matilda, pulled her close, and rested his chin against the top of her head. Within moments his breathing was slow and even.

Matilda nestled against him and heard the solid thud of his heart against her ear. She was not so naïve as to imagine that they had faced and defeated all their demons. There would be more quarrels, struggles and misunderstandings to strew their way with thorns. She knew that. But there was also the grace of reconciliation . . . and the light of love. The past was behind them; the future beckoned.

Thoroughly content, Matilda slipped her arm across Simon's waist and fell asleep with a smile.

AUTHOR'S NOTE

Now a note for those readers who are interested to know how much of the history in *The Winter Mantle* is true and how many liberties I've taken. This is quite a difficult question to answer, because some of the research has been contradictory and elusive, to say the least.

Waltheof of Huntingdon was beheaded for treason in 1076. From what the chroniclers of the time report, it would seem that he was foolish and easily led rather than filled with a wild rebellious zeal. He also had enemies at the Norman court who were only too willing to see him fall, and King William seems to have been swayed by their influence and perhaps by the thought that Waltheof had stepped over the line once too often. Judith is reported to have betrayed her husband to William, but after Waltheof's execution she was filled with remorse. Reading between the lines, I think that she expected her uncle to banish Waltheof as he had banished many other English lords who had rebelled against him, and she was shocked when he was beheaded.

Crowland Abbey still stands, partly in ruins, partly as a church in use, but there is little evidence of the abbey that stood on the site in Waltheof's time. It was seriously damaged by fire as mentioned in the novel and was rebuilt in the Norman style early in the twelfth century. Later on it was massively refurbished and it is these fourteenth-century remains that the visitor now sees when they visit Crowland. Despite the cult that was once attached to Waltheof, there is no mention of his tomb at Crowland, although the visitor can buy postcards of the skull of Abbot Theodore, who was murdered by raiding Danes in AD 850.

The tale of Judith rejecting Simon de Senlis because he was lame is reported in one chronicle, and I had to make use of it because it's just too good a story to pass up. Simon himself is something of an enigma. I found four dates for his birth, ranging from 1046 to 1068. Some sources say he was present at the battle of Hastings, others deny it emphatically. Being as this is a work of fiction, I chose the date that best suited me and that seems to tally with the other known information, and I went for 1058. I also found two different individuals cited as his father. I chose Richard de Rules because he was a royal chamberlain.

Simon was known to have gone on crusade, but he didn't reach Jerusalem because the chroniclers put him in the thick of William Rufus' war in the Vexin in 1098. With this detail in mind I felt free to invent a reason for his turning back. It is also known that he had an illegitimate son called Simon, but so far I've been able to turn up nothing else about the child. Again, I felt free to invent a background. Simon's legitimate children are given dates of birth that are all over the place, so I've gone with the story on this and kept them as close as possible to the probability. Amidst all this muddle and vague hints of facts, I came across the positive detail that Matilda's maid was called Helisende. Writing historical fiction can be as surprising and rewarding as it can be frustrating.

For those of you who are wondering about some of the other historical characters who also appear in the novel: Ralf de Gael did not reach Jerusalem but died at Antioch. Stephen of Aumale lived to return and continue with his life. Simon and Matilda had another son, named Simon, thus enabling young Waltheof to pursue a career in the church. He was later canonised as a saint in his own lifetime.

Simon died at the priory of Le Charite sur Loire in 1111 whilst attempting a second crusade. Matilda did not remain long a widow but married Prince David of Scotland, later to be King David, and in her forties bore him a son and two daughters.

I welcome responses from readers, and anyone who would like to get in touch with me can do so at *elizabeth.chadwick@bt internet.com*. I also have a website where you'll find more details about me and my work, including a glossary of medieval terms: *http://www.elizabethchadwick.com*